INTERNATIONAL LEGAL POSITIVISM IN A POST-MODERN WORLD

International Legal Positivism in a Post-Modern World provides fresh perspectives on one of the most important and most controversial families of theoretical approaches to the study and practice of international law. The contributors include leading experts on international legal theory who analyse and criticise positivism as a conceptual framework for international law, explore its relationships with other approaches and apply it to current problems of international law. Is legal positivism relevant to the theory and practice of international law today? Have other answers to the problems of international law and the critique of positivism undermined the positivist project and its narratives? Do modern forms of positivism, inspired largely by the theoretically sophisticated jurisprudential concepts associated with Hans Kelsen and HLA Hart, remain of any relevance for the international lawyer in this 'post-modern' age? The authors provide a wide variety of views and a stimulating debate about this family of approaches.

JÖRG KAMMERHOFER is a senior research fellow and senior lecturer at the Faculty of Law, University of Freiburg, Germany. He is also a visiting lecturer at the Vienna University of Economics and Business, Austria.

JEAN D'ASPREMONT holds the Chair of Public International Law at the University of Manchester. He is also Professor of International Legal Theory at the University of Amsterdam, the Netherlands.

INTERNATIONAL LEGAL POSITIVISM IN A POST-MODERN WORLD

Edited by

JÖRG KAMMERHOFER

JEAN D'ASPREMONT

Assistant editors

Kate Brookson-Morris

Brendon Plant

CAMBRIDGE
UNIVERSITY PRESS

CAMBRIDGE
UNIVERSITY PRESS

University Printing House, Cambridge CB2 8BS, United Kingdom

Cambridge University Press is part of the University of Cambridge.

It furthers the University's mission by disseminating knowledge in the pursuit of education, learning and research at the highest international levels of excellence.

www.cambridge.org
Information on this title: www.cambridge.org/9781107019263

First published 2014

A catalogue record for this publication is available from the British Library

ISBN 978-1-107-01926-3 Hardback

CONTENTS

CONTRIBUTORS

JEAN D'ASPREMONT is Chair of Public International Law at the University of Manchester, UK and Chair of International Legal Theory at the University of Amsterdam, the Netherlands.

JOCHEN VON BERNSTORFF is Professor of Public Law, International Law and Human Rights Law the University of Tübingen, Germany.

BEATRICE I. BONAFÉ is Associate Professor at the University of Rome 'La Sapienza', Italy.

PATRICK CAPPS is Professor of International Law at the University of Bristol, UK.

THÉODORE CHRISTAKIS is Professor of International Law at the University of Grenoble-Alpes, France.

RICHARD COLLINS is Lecturer in Law at the University of Sheffield, UK.

GLEIDER I. HERNÁNDEZ is Lecturer in Law at the University of Durham, UK.

FLORIAN HOFFMANN is Franz Haniel Chair for Public Policy at the University of Erfurt, Germany.

DOV JACOBS is Assistant Professor of International Law at the University of Leiden, the Netherlands.

JÖRG KAMMERHOFER is Senior Research Fellow and Senior Lecturer at the University of Freiburg, Germany and visiting lecturer of the Vienna University of Economics and Business.

JAN KLABBERS is Professor of International Organisations Law at the University of Helsinki, Finland.

DENNIS PATTERSON is Professor of Law and Chair in Legal Philosophy and Legal Theory at the European University Institute, Italy; Board of Governors Professor of Law and Philosophy, Rutgers University, United States; and Professor of Law and Chair in International Trade and Legal Philosophy, Swansea University, UK.

YAËL RONEN is Lecturer in Law at the Sha'arei Mishpat College, Israel.

SAHIB SINGH is a PhD candidate at the University of Cambridge, UK and Visiting Lecturer of International Law at the University of Vienna, Austria.

ALEXANDER SOMEK is Charles E. Floete Chair in Law at the University of Iowa, United States.

CHRISTIAN J. TAMS is Professor of International Law at the University of Glasgow, UK.

D. A. JEREMY TELMAN is Professor of Law at Valparaiso University, United States.

ANTONIOS TZANAKOPOULOS is Associate Professor of Public International Law at the University of Oxford, UK.

INGO VENZKE is Associate Professor at the University of Amsterdam, the Netherlands.

PREFACE

Legal theory is inherently comparative and polemical (in the word's original sense). Legal theories inevitably define themselves in relation to and in the struggle with other approaches. International legal theory is no different in this respect. As with any comparison, this is only possible to the extent that there is a common set of standards against which similarities and commonalities are measured. Yet, both in general jurisprudence and in international legal theory, it is positivism itself which has for a number of decades been the standard of reference against which theories are compared. In other words, legal positivism has long played a structural role in theoretical debates about law. Yet, surprisingly, this central standard of reference of contemporary legal theoretical debates has itself remained undefined and in constant flux. 'Positivism' has been ascribed so many different meanings that it has endangered the intelligibility of theoretical debates. The present volume was envisaged, written and edited against the backdrop of this dialectic tension between the near-definitional role of international legal positivism on the one hand, and the large measure of vagueness about what, exactly, 'positivism(s)' mean(s), on the other. The chapters of this book primarily reflect on the various possible meanings attributed to 'international legal positivism' and how all these variants of legal positivism have been related to other approaches, as well as applied to concrete legal problems.

This volume, the first study of the twenty-first century on the meanings and the cognitive, definitional and didactic roles of legal positivism in international law, is particularly unique, as all authors of this volume have been influenced (in very different ways) by the last two decades of critical thinking about international law. This is why the book should not be misunderstood as an attempt to proselytise for legal positivism. Rather, many of the arguments in this volume are perhaps better understood as a set of (sometimes self-)critical reflections about what we have made of the idea of legal positivism, i.e. how this idea has been used in arguing within, defining and structuring international legal theory. This reflexive framework explains why the views expressed in the following chapters are very diverse and occasional clashes occur. Critical engagement and debate within the book was encouraged as far as possible. This book can thus also be seen as an exhibition of the immense diversity of views about the meanings, relations and uses of international legal positivism in the twenty-first century.

It will not come as a surprise that organising a debate where people – each of them with a fundamentally different understanding of (international) law – are meant not to talk past one another, but engage in a common intelligible reflection, requires much effort. In these times, dominated as they are by economic considerations, it will surprise the reader even less to hear that material and financial support, both from within and outside the university, is a *conditio sine qua non* for such a project to succeed. This book and the organisation of an authors' workshop in Amsterdam in November 2011 would not have been possible without the tremendous investment of many people, as well the financial support of institutional partners. A preface always is also an opportunity for the editors to express their gratitude to those without which the project behind such a book would not have been possible.

Our first and foremost thanks go to all those who agreed to participate in this project in the capacity as authors of a chapter. Even where (for various reasons) a colleague did not participate to the end, their influence still made itself felt in more informal ways. A conversation among the contributors that proved most fruitful started even before the delivery of chapters. The editing process itself was a journey of discovery for everyone involved and the end product seems to provide sufficient evidence that both the editors and contributors were on this journey together. This project would not have been possible without the financial and organisational support of a number of institutions. Foremost among these is the Deutsche Forschungsgemeinschaft (German Research Council), which very generously and courageously invested in a project most unusual for German legal scholarship. The Koninklijke Nederlandse Akademie van Wetenschappen (Royal Dutch Academy of Sciences) supported the authors' workshop in November 2011.

Our home institutions, past and present – the Universiteit van Amsterdam, the Friedrich-Alexander-Univeristät Erlangen-Nürnberg, the Albert-Ludwigs-Universität Freiburg and the University of Manchester – all provided an optimal institutional setting for the preparation and execution of the project. A first series of thanks go to those who facilitated the project in Amsterdam, and especially to André Nollkaemper for his support, to the members of the Amsterdam Centre for International Law who, sometimes anonymously, contributed to the discussion, and to all those who made the Amsterdam workshop possible at that end. We would also like to thank Matthias Jestaedt for granting an unusually large measure of freedom and for turning the rigid German system into a strong system of support for all within the Lehrstuhlfamilie. We would also like to thank colleagues at the Hans-Kelsen-Forschungsstelle for their help and attention.

A large number of colleagues have supported this endeavour without being formally involved. There are too many to thank them all, but we would like to highlight the input by a few: Erik Breuker, Anne van Mulligen, Anne Peters, Rike Sinder and Martine van Trigt. Finally, two anonymous reviewers for Cambridge University Press provided valuable insight and guidance in their readers' reports. The very arduous task of editing this volume and running the project – including the tedious but incredibly important bits – would not have succeeded were it not for our very own editorial team: Kate Brookson-Morris, Malte Feldmann, Clarissa Henle, Vanessa Meißner, Brendan Plant and Camilla Schiefler. Their hard work, invaluable collaboration and patience in trying times made this project possible in the first place.

ABBREVIATIONS

ACHR	American Convention on Human Rights
AJIL	*American Journal of International Law*
ASIL	American Society of International Law
BYBIL	*British Yearbook of International Law*
CFI	Court of First Instance
CJEU	Court of Justice of the European Union
CLS	Critical Legal Studies
CWC	Chemical Weapons Convention
DPRK	Democratic People's Republic of Korea
EAL	economic analysis of law
ECHR	European Convention on Human Rights
ECtHR	European Court of Human Rights
ECJ	European Court of Justice
EEC	European Economic Community
EHRR	European Human Rights Reports
EJIL	*European Journal of International Law*
EU	European Union
FATU	*From Apology to Utopia*
GAL	global administrative law
HRC	Human Rights Committee
HRTB	human rights treaty body
ICC	International Criminal Court
ICCPR	International Covenant on Civil and Political Rights
IAComHR	Inter-American Commission on Human Rights
IACtHR	Inter-American Court of Human Rights
ICJ	International Court of Justice
ICL	international criminal law
ICLQ	*International and Comparative Law Quarterly*
ICRC	International Committee of the Red Cross
ICTR	International Criminal Tribunal for Rwanda
ICTY	International Criminal Tribunal for the former Yugoslavia
IDI	Institut de Droit International

IHL	international humanitarian law
ILA	International Law Association
ILC	International Law Commission
ILP	international legal positivism
ILR	*International Law Reports*
IMT	International Military Tribunal
IR	international relations
ISO	International Organization for Standardization
JCE	Joint Criminal Enterprise
LJIL	*Leiden Journal of International Law*
MN	Marginal Note
NAFTA	North-American Free Trade Agreement
NAIL	new approaches to international law
NGO	non-governmental organisation
NILP	new international legal positivism
NILR	new international legal realism
NLR	new legal realism
OAS	Organization of American States
PCIJ	Permanent Court of International Justice
PIL	public international law
SCSL	Special Court for Sierra Leone
STL	Special Tribunal for Lebanon
TEU	Treaty on European Union
TFEU	Treaty on the Functioning of the European Union
TWAIL	third world approaches to international law
UN	United Nations
UNIO	United Nations Conference on International Organization
US	United States
VCLT	Vienna Convention on the Law of Treaties
WTO	World Trade Organization

1

Introduction

The future of international legal positivism

JEAN D'ASPREMONT AND JÖRG KAMMERHOFER

1 Prolegomenon

Such a thing as post-modern*ist* international legal positivism cannot exist. Legal positivism – at least the modern variants discussed in this book – is inextricably linked to Modernism and cannot leave that basis, foundation and context without unravelling. This is a central premise of this book. Yet, and this is another cardinal assumption that informs the following pages, studies constructed around positivist methodological moves can benefit from those who question Enlightenment rationality and/or deconstruct orthodox understandings of international legal scholarship in a critical spirit. The claim is thus not that positivism is or should be based to any meaningful degree on the writings and ideas of those usually considered to be 'post-modernists' (or 'crits', even if not 'post-modernists' in a narrow sense). The ambition, as this introduction makes clear, lies elsewhere. For the sake of this book, the temporal dimension of the 'post-modern' (the post-modern *world*) and a particular approach (post-modern*ism*) must be distinguished; the former is partially an expression of the power-structures in our part of the scholarly sub-system; the latter is a particular world view, just as positivism or naturalism are.

2 Sociology: the Guild of International Lawyers

The concept of law is parochial.[1] Different communities, past and present, have different concepts of law without one having any ascendancy other

[1] Joseph Raz, 'Can There Be a Theory of Law?' in Martin P. Golding, William A. Edmundson (eds), *The Blackwell Guide to Philosophy of Law and Legal Theory* (Blackwell Publishing 2005) 324–342; Robert Alexy, 'On Two Juxtapositions: Concept and Nature, Law and Philosophy: Some Comments on Joseph Raz's "Can There Be a Theory of Law?"' 20 *Ratio Juris* (2007) 162–169 at 163; See also Brian H. Bix, 'Ideals, Practices, and Concepts in Legal

than social.[2] From such a sociological vantage point, legal scholarship is, as a result, a battleground where the legal scholar – even the nihilist – is necessarily an activist advocating a certain vision of the law and, hence, a given way to make sense of the world. Confrontation is the fate of the legal scholar.[3] In this adversarial mayhem, subtle argumentative engineering is being deployed through theories, doctrinal constructions, technicalities, ancestral names or traditions, aesthetics, or even intimidating tactics with a view to securing persuasion among peers as well as actors exercising law-based powers. The refinement of some of the argumentative ammunition used by the participants engaged in this pandemonium is particularly noteworthy, but certainly not surprising. Confrontation does not exclude finesse and delicacy. Rather, the former can constitute the driving force for the latter. As a result, it is tempting to simultaneously conceive the legal scholar not only as an activist, but also as a craftsman. What is more, craftsmen, like activists, generally coalesce in (what the former call) guilds designed around expertise, skills and political projects. Indeed, legal scholars – sometimes unconsciously – federate into groups designed along paradigmatic and methodological lines, political aspirations or, more simply, attitudes and mindsets.[4] In that sense, the binding agent among members of a guild of legal scholars is not necessarily faith or belief in a given paradigm or methodology; it can also be doubt and contestation, or, more modestly, a shared interest in a given *problematique*. This also explains why legal scholars potentially and subconsciously join multiple guilds

Theory' in Jordi Ferrer Beltrán, José Juan Moreso, Diego M. Papayannis (eds), *Neutrality and Theory of Law* (Springer 2013) 33–47 at 35.

2 Among others, see Liam B. Murphy, 'Better to See Law this Way' 83 *New York University Law Review* (2008) 1104–1108; Frederick Schauer, 'Positivism as Pariah' in Robert P. George (ed.), *The Autonomy of Law: Essays on Legal Positivism* (Clarendon Press 1996) 31–56 at 34; Jeremy Waldron, 'Normative (or Ethical) Positivism' in Jules L. Coleman (ed.), *Hart's Postscript: Essays on the Postscript to* The Concept of Law (Oxford University Press 2001) 411–433; Jason Beckett, 'Behind Relative Normativity: Rules and Process as Prerequisites of Law' 12 *EJIL* (2001) 627–650 at 648.

3 Jean d'Aspremont, 'Wording in International Law' 25 *LJIL* (2012) 575–602. See also Sahib Singh, 'International Law as a Technical Discipline: Critical Perspectives on the Narrative Structure of a Theory' in Jean d'Aspremont, *Formalism and the Sources of International Law: A Theory of the Ascertainment of Legal Rules* (2nd edn Oxford University Press 2013) 236–261 (also forthcoming, *BYBIL*).

4 David Feldman, 'The Nature of Legal Scholarship' 52 *Modern Law Review* (1989) 498–517 at 513.

at the same time. In this respect, international legal scholarship is no different.[5]

This volume takes a critical look at the shared paradigmatic, methodological and political choices as well as the common doubts, mindsets and attitudes of those international legal scholars whose education, geographical origin, affiliation, inheritance and training, as well as personal experience of scholarly confrontation and craftsmanship have stirred an interest in the possible value of international legal positivism. In their case, the interest in legal positivism does not necessarily involve fealty to a number of methodological and conceptual positions (and, perhaps, the political projects) that are commonly associated with legal positivism, such as formalism, autonomy or the separation of law and morals. Their intellectual appetite is whetted, rather, by the combination of two factors: sharing (to an extent) the common claim of a 'dead end' reached by 'classical' legal positivism, as well as the very radical and dismissive nature of most of the critiques of legal positivist approaches to law.[6] In that sense, what unites many of these scholars is both the rejection of the main tenets of classical legal positivism and a feeling of boredom with those objections against traditional legal positivism which either mechanically and uncritically repeat earlier critique, or are simply less than convincing in their argumentative capacity. It is obvious, however, that the guild into which they may have potentially coalesced is in constant flux.[7]

This volume gathers together the contributions of a wide range of scholars interested in debating the contemporary value of positivist approaches to international law. It rests on an endeavour to see where the positivist approach to international legal scholarship stands at the end of the first

[5] The way in which the confrontation of ideas unfolds and federations of participants emerge is similar for craftsmen and international legal scholars.

[6] Legal positivism has been the object of systematic condemnation in American jurisprudence, e.g. James Boyle, 'Ideals and Things: International Legal Scholarship and the Prison-House of Language' 26 *Harvard International Law Journal* (1985) 327–359. For the debate on positivism, see the remarks in Nicholas Onuf, 'Global Law-Making and Legal Thought' in Nicholas Onuf (ed.), *Law-Making in the Global Community* (Carolina Academic Press 1982) 1–81. On the negative implication of the use of the term 'positivism' in literature, see Georgio Gaja, 'Positivism and Dualism in Dionisio Anzilotti' 3 *EJIL* (1992) 123–138. For some exceptions in American international legal scholarship, see Alexander Somek, 'Kelsen Lives' 18 *EJIL* (2007) 409–451.

[7] In that sense, guilds bear great resemblance to communities of practice. See generally Emmanuel Adler, *Communitarian International Relations: The Epistemic Foundations of International Relations* (Routledge 2005) 14.

decade of the twenty-first century and what conceptual, methodological and epistemological value it has. This also means taking a hard look at whether positivism remains a cogent and useful approach for the future of international legal scholarship. The chapters in this book accordingly enquire whether the current state of international society and of international legal scholarship still calls for some form of positivist 'package', or whether it can be shown that abandoning any move that could be classified as 'positivist' is the only viable solution if one wants to make sense of international law today and in the future.

3 Moving away from 'classical' international legal positivism

It is important to repeat at this stage that the contributions in this volume do not seek to rehabilitate classical legal positivism.[8] 'Classical' variants of positivism in international legal scholarship are commonly said to be marked by a number of distinctive features. Most prominently, what we like to call 'old school' positivism is claimed to be focused nearly exclusively on the state. States, so the argument is reconstructed, are the exclusive makers of international law[9] and the only originary subjects of international law. Nineteenth-century positivists advocated, this narrative reports, that international law obliges and empowers only states and that individuals are mediated by the state. The most specific, powerful and controversial expression of this mentality can be found in the idea of consensualism: state consent is the (pre-legal) criterion giving law its binding force and legitimacy.[10] According to this construction, '[t]he rules of law binding upon States are said to emanate from their own free will'.[11] This famous passage from the judgment of the Permanent Court of International Justice in *Lotus* (1927) has been interpreted as supporting (and became the embodiment of) an extreme consensualism.[12] This

[8] Subject to Christakis, Chapter 16 at 423.

[9] E.g. Jochen von Bernstorff, *The Public International Law Theory of Hans Kelsen: Believing in Universal Law* (Cambridge University Press 2010) 28–30.

[10] *S.S. 'Lotus' (France v. Turkey)*, Judgment of 7 September 1927, PCIJ Series A No. 10 (1927) at 43–44 (Diss. Op. Weiss).

[11] *Lotus* (1927), n. 10 at 18.

[12] For some common criticisms of *Lotus*, see the individual opinions appended to *Nuclear Weapons* (*Legality of the Threat or Use of Nuclear Weapons*, Advisory Opinion of 8 July 1996, ICJ Reports (1996) 226, e.g. at 268–274 (Dec. Bedjaoui), 394–396 (Sep. Op. Shahabuddeen); Jörg Kammerhofer, 'Gaps, the *Nuclear Weapons* Advisory Opinion and the Structure of International Legal Argument between Theory and Practice' 80 *BYBIL* (2009) 333–360. More recently, see *Accordance with International Law of the Unilateral Declaration*

interpretation has survived throughout the twentieth century and into the twenty-first.[13] It is therefore no surprise that several of the authors of this volume pick up on the *Lotus* debate as central to our understanding and critique of (classical) international legal positivism.[14]

As the foregoing makes clear, this volume does not seek to resuscitate the classical versions of international legal positivism. The reasons for this are obvious. First, because, as some of the contributions in this volume will show,[15] the archetypical classical international legal positivist is – to an extent – a straw-man, a latter-day reconstruction of a historical fiction and its positions have never been advocated as such or as simplistically as claimed.[16] Indeed, it is not easy to find in scholarly writings those who actually espouse what James Leslie Brierly (discussing *Lotus*) has termed 'the extreme positivist school that the law emanates from the free will of sovereign independent states [only]'.[17] Second, classical legal positivism, irrespective of whether it has had any actual existence in scholarship, has been constructed on foundations – like apologetic consensualism/voluntarism – which cannot be reconciled with positivism's claim to fidelity to the law 'as it is', rather than as it should be. It is also often more indirectly in conflict with the philosophical and 'theory-of-science'

of Independence in Respect of Kosovo, Advisory Opinion of 22 July 2010, ICJ Reports (2010) 403 at 479 (Dec. Simma); Jörg Kammerhofer, 'Begging the Question? The Kosovo Opinion and the Reformulation of Advisory Requests' 58 *Netherlands International Law Review* (2011) 409–424; Alain Pellet, 'Lotus que de sottises on profère en ton nom! Remarques sur le concept de souveraineté dans la jurisprudence de la Cour mondiale' in Jean-Pierre Puissochet, Edwige Belliard (eds), *Mélanges en l'honneur de Jean-Pierre Puissochet: L'État souverain dans le monde d'aujourd'hui* (Pedone 2008) 215–230.

13 For criticisms of voluntarism, see Gerald G. Fitzmaurice, 'The General Principles of International Law Considered from the Standpoint of the Rule of Law' 92 *Receuil des Cours* (1957) 1–227 at 36; Alain Pellet, 'The Normative Dilemma: Will and Consent in International Law-Making' 12 *Australian Yearbook of International Law* (1989) 22–53 at 26; Bruno Simma and Andreas L. Paulus, 'The Responsibility of Individuals for Human Rights Abuses in Internal Conflicts: A Positivist View' 93 *AJIL* (1999) 302–316 at 304.

14 Collins, Chapter 2 at 26–27, 39–40; Klabbers, Chapter 10 at 286; Tams and Tzanakopoulos, Chapter 19 at 501.

15 Collins, Chapter 2 at 48.

16 Again, Théodore Christakis' contribution is perhaps best seen as an attempt to vindicate and modernise a *reconstructed* classical-consensualist position that historically might not have existed in this form: Christakis, Chapter 16.

17 James Leslie Brierly, 'The "Lotus" Case', reprinted in Hersch Lauterpacht, CHM Waldock (eds), *The Basis of Obligation in International Law and Other Papers by the Late James Leslie Brierly* (Clarendon Press 1958) 142–151 at 143–144. For a recent perpetuation of the straw-man of consensualism, see Ronald Dworkin, 'A New Philosophy for International Law' 41 *Philosophy and Public Affairs* (2013) 2–30 at 8.

foundations espoused by positivism (often implicitly). Very often, classical positivism is just as precipitate as naturalism and, in a way, is merely a statist variant of natural law doctrine.[18] It is therefore no surprise that many international lawyers have repudiated it in the second half of the twentieth century. 'If one does natural law', they could be said to be arguing, 'then why should one not proudly declare one's position; why hide behind a false fidelity to positive law?' Thus, those in this volume who do espouse non-classical forms of positivism have tried to refrain from this argumentative displacement of the 'political' by the allure of technocratic rationalities (à la 'governance'). These rationalities plant the idea in scholars' and decision-makers' minds that there is a 'technical' and 'scientific', a truly neutral and objective solution to political problems, empowering scholars and scientists and putting them in their 'right place' above mere politicians. This, however, is a chimera which leads to delusions of grandeur and orgies of essentialism.[19] Also, it cannot be said to promote hermeneutical necessity in law-ascertainment or content-determination processes. This is why many of the following chapters discuss the idea that legal interpretation can no longer be thought of as an act of cognition of a pre-existing truth, but is rather geared towards persuasion, whose validation hinges on the recipient epistemic community.[20] In that sense, this volume should not be seen as an attempt to salvage and renew the metanarrative of naive rationality associated with traditional positivism.[21] Modern forms of international legal positivism, instead, celebrate the role

[18] It may be helpful to remind ourselves of a rather forgotten fact: throughout history, natural law arguments have been used much more often to justify a state's powers (or the extant law) than to criticise them; one need only look to the decidedly natural law arguments to found the divine provenance of absolutist monarchs (Hans Kelsen, *General Theory of Law and State* (Harvard University Press 1945) 416–417).

[19] See generally Jörg Kammerhofer, 'Law-Making by Scholarship? The Dark Side of 21st Century International Legal "Methodology"' in James Crawford, Sarah Nouwen (eds), *Select Proceedings of the European Society of International Law: Third Volume: International Law 1989–2010: A Performance Appraisal. Cambridge, 2–4 September 2010* (Hart 2012) 115–126; Jörg Kammerhofer, 'Law-Making by Scholars' in Catherine Brölmann, Yannick Radi (eds), *Research Handbook on the Theory and Practice of International Law-Making* (forthcoming, Edward Elgar 2014); Gerald J. Postema, 'Law's Autonomy and Public Practical Reasoning' in Robert P. George (ed.), *The Autonomy of Law: Essays on Legal Positivism* (Oxford University Press 1996) 79–119.

[20] Stanley Fish, *Doing What Comes Naturally: Change, Rhetoric, and the Practice of Theory in Literary and Legal Studies* (Duke University Press 1989) 488–491; see also d'Aspremont, n. 3.

[21] Both Hart and Kelsen recognise that there is no meta- (or external) narrative against which the meaning of a rule can be determined; see Kammerhofer, Chapter 4 and d'Aspremont, Chapter 5.

of politics in international reality and, indeed, international legal practice even where they separate the realms of politics and scholarship.

We must also be clear in this introduction that, while not seeking to vindicate classical legal positivism, this book is not a project for the renewal, vindication or revolution of positivist thought, as attempted elsewhere.[22] *This book* does not contain an essentialist project to reconstruct a universal concept of international law[23] – the following chapters seek to evaluate, critique, contextualise and apply classical and non-classical forms of international legal positivism, not to push the agenda of one or the other approach. In the same vein, no one (the editors in their contributions included) seeks to offer a 'post-modern*ist*' or Critical Legal version of legal positivism – a concept rightly seen as a contradiction in terms.[24] Any 'ambition' this book has is far more modest: we seek to provide analysis and (self-)reflection by a group of scholars of a particular theoretical approach. Our aim as editors was to assemble contributions that go beyond uncritical espousal of traditional legal positivism, but also go beyond the all-too-common mechanical and unreflective rejection of positivism. This modesty is informed by the belief that legal positivism does not need to be rehabilitated or rejuvenated, but more simply needs to be aware of its own limitations and must continuously reflect on (the value of) its methodological and paradigmatic moves.[25]

4 A multitude of agendas

The self-reflection on which the contributors of this volume embark is not carried out agnostically and without prejudice. Even the doubts

22 E.g. Olivier Corten, *Le discours du droit international: Pour un positivisme critique* (Pedone 2008); Jörg Kammerhofer, *Uncertainty in International Law: A Kelsenian Perspective* (Routledge 2010); Jean d'Aspremont, *Formalism and the Sources of International Law: A Theory of the Ascertainment of Legal Rules* (Oxford University Press 2011).

23 On this debate, see Leslie Green, 'The Concept of Law Revisited' 95 *Michigan Law Review* (1996) 1687–1717; Frederick Schauer, 'Hart's Anti-Essentialism' in Luís Duarte d'Almeida, James Edwards, Andrea Dolcetti (eds), *Reading HLA Hart's 'The Concept of Law'* (Hart 2013) 237–246. Hart himself seems to have despised those engaged in the construction of the 'essential nature' of law (HLA Hart, *The Concept of Law* (Clarendon Press 1961) 1).

24 Singh, Chapter 11 at 297.

25 David Sugarman, 'Hart Interviewed: HLA Hart in Conversation with David Sugarman' 32 *Journal of Law and Society* (2005) 267–293 – Hart argues that the limits to analytical positivism is the beginning of the answer (290); see, however, the attempt to rehabilitate analytical jurisprudence by William Twining, 'Have Concepts, Will Travel: Analytical Jurisprudence in a Global Context' 1 *International Journal of Law in Context* (2005) 5–40.

about the value of legal positivism that are expressed in some of the following chapters are formulated within the remit of assumptions and with certain goals in mind. Although primarily of a self-reflective nature, the various pieces of this volume are thus functionally prejudiced. There necessarily remains an 'agenda'. More precisely, there is a vast multitude of agendas, ideologies and values at play in this introduction as well as all the other texts of this volume. These agendas sometimes collide and sometimes harmonise, but always influence the product. For the editors, it is clear that this introduction is the place to thematise some of these biases/prejudices (or, as Gadamer's improved understanding of the term *Vorurteil* very helpfully clarifies: the inevitable pre-judgments we all bring to any epistemic process)[26] or 'politics' that inform the contributions offered here. Despite significant divergences between the various agendas, there are a few common threads underlying many of the contributions in this book.

Among the several aspirations infusing this project, one could first mention a search for theoretical refinement. Such a move – which has been understood as a quest for aesthetics[27] – is certainly not uncommon, as one can say that international legal theory is entirely geared towards theoretical refinement. We think and would like to emphasise that we believe all of the contributors to this volume are very much aware that such theorising – and, for some, the construction of aesthetics that come with it – is also an exercise of power.[28] Even a self-reflecting exercise like the one initiated here inevitably contributes to a certain system of knowledge that is penetrated by power and leads to the creation of a given image of the world.[29] This insight, with all its inevitability, does not, in our view, attach a negative moral value to 'power',[30] nor does it invalidate scholarship per se – although some have inferred this consequence.

26 Hans-Georg Gadamer, *Wahrheit und Methode: Grundzüge einer philosophischen Hermeneutik* (6th edn J. C. B. Mohr (Paul Siebeck) 1990).

27 Singh, Chapter 11 at 293.

28 See in particular Michel Foucault, *Surveiller et punir* (Gallimard 1975); Michel Foucault, *Histoire de la sexualité I: La volonté de savoir* (Gallimard 1976); Venzke, Chapter 7 at 199–203; Singh, Chapter 11 at 291–294.

29 Venzke, Chapter 7 at 199–203.

30 'Il faut cesser de toujours décrire les effets de pouvoir en termes négatifs: il "exclut", il "réprime", il "refoule", il "censure", il "abstrait", il "masque", il "cache". En fait le pouvoir produit; il produit du réel; il produit des domaines d'objets et des rituels de vérité.' Foucault, *Surveiller et punir*, n. 28 at 227.

Another important aspect of the agenda shared by several of the following contributions pertains to the need felt by many authors to keep (particular forms of) inter-disciplinarity at bay.[31] Indeed, the preservation of law-ascertaining tools, which is one of the primary functions bestowed upon positivism, is vindicated by several authors. In so doing, they manifest some attachment to the necessity of drawing boundaries between disciplines. It is certainly not a rejection of all forms of inter-disciplinarity, but rather a repudiation both of over-inclusive approaches to law and of hegemonic moves of other scholarly enterprises on the scholarly cognition of law/rules/norms. It is an epistemological concern for distinction and autonomy. This undoubtedly can also be called a political – perhaps even protectionist – choice made by a group of professionals that assumes a politics of 'counter-disciplinarity'[32] and autonomy.[33]

While critiquing forms of inter-disciplinarity, some authors express sympathy for the idea that positivism can work in tandem with other approaches,[34] including Critical Legal Studies (CLS). This is especially so with regard to scholars like Martti Koskenniemi, whose plea for a 'culture of formalism'[35] – while not being grounded in a positivistic theoretical background itself[36] – has continued to carry out a project of universality

[31] Singh, n. 3.

[32] The expression is from: Martti Koskenniemi, 'Law, Teleology and International Relations: An Essay in Counterdisciplinarity' 26 *International Relations* (2012) 3–34; for a reaction, see Mark Pollack, 'Is International Relations Corrosive of International Law? A Reply to Martti Koskenniemi' 27 *Temple International and Comparative Law Journal* (2013) 339–375.

[33] Collins, Chapter 2 at 24.

[34] Klabbers, Chapter 10 at 269.

[35] The notion of a 'culture of formalism' has been spelled out by Martti Koskenniemi in several of his works; e.g. *The Gentle Civilizer of Nations: The Rise and Fall of International Law 1870–1960* (Cambridge University Press 2002) 502–509; 'What is International Law For?' in Malcolm Evans (ed.), *International Law* (3rd edn Oxford University Press 2010) 32–57 at 43–44. See also Martti Koskenniemi, 'Carl Schmitt, Morgenthau, and the Image of Law in International Relations' in Michael Byers (ed.), *The Role of Law in International Politics: Essays in International Relations and International Law* (Oxford University Press 2000) 17–34 at 32–33.

[36] For a tentative interpretation of Martti Koskenniemi's culture of formalism, see, among others: Emmanuelle Jouannet, 'Présentation critique' in Martti Koskenniemi (ed.), *La politique du droit international* (Pedone 2007) 7–48 at 32–33. Also Ignacio de la Rasilla del Moral, 'Martti Koskenniemi and the Spirit of the Beehive in International Law' 10 *Global Jurist* (2010) 1–42. See above all the insightful book review: Nicholas Tsagourias, '[Book Review:] Martti Koskenniemi, The Gentle Civilizer of Nations: The Rise and Fall of

of legal argumentation.[37] This belief in the possibility of ecumenical coexistence and cooperation between theories inevitably presupposes that the various approaches discussed here are *alia*, i.e. make arguments of a categorically different nature and do not neutralise one another.[38] It goes without saying that constructing such a relationship of theories is itself based, to an extent, on insularism that should not be obfuscated here.[39]

Finally, it should be acknowledged that many of the agendas found in the exercise carried out here have an epistemological dimension. Indeed, many of the contributions found in this book are also informed by a quest for 'maintain[ing] a structure within which meaningful discussion can occur'.[40] Albeit recognising the parochial character of law and the inherently pluralistic and non-essentialist nature of conceptual debates about international law, the self-reflection that unfolds in this volume does so against the backdrop of a concern for the possibility of communication within the epistemic community of international law.[41]

These considerations are just a few of the cross-cutting prejudices and aspirations shared by many of the contributors. It is needless to say that awareness thereof in itself neither dooms nor salvages[42] the theoretical foundations of the exercise. Yet, as indicated above, this book does not purport to cast a new positivist theory. In this volume we find, more simply, a group of scholars questioning the contemporary value of positivism in international legal scholarship without seeking to give self-sustaining and self-referential theoretical grounds to their scholarship (if only because such an enterprise is impossible).

International Law 1870–1960 (2002)' 16 *LJIL* (2003) 397–399, esp. 398–399; Hoffmann, Chapter 13 at 374–376.

37 For that reason, Martti Koskenniemi has been categorised as (only) a mild 'crit' for attempting to domesticate deconstruction. Such attempts to domesticate deconstruction have long been the object of criticism in general legal theory, e.g. Pierre Schlag, '"Le Hors de Texte, C'est Moi": The Politics of Form and the Domestication of Deconstruction' 11 *Cardozo Law Review* (1989–1990) 1631–1674.

38 Thomas S. Kuhn, *The Structure of Scientific Revolutions* (University of Chicago Press 1962).

39 Singh, Chapter 11 at 301–307.

40 Brian H. Bix, 'Conceptual Questions and Jurisprudence' 1 *Legal Theory* (1995) 465–479 at 469.

41 On this aspect, see Timothy Meyer, 'Review Essay: Towards a Communicative Theory of International Law: Jean d'Aspremont, Formalism and the Sources of International Law: A Theory of the Ascertainment of Legal Rules (2011)' 13 *Melbourne Journal of International Law* (2012) 921–939.

42 Singh, Chapter 11 at 291.

5 A project situated and contextualised

Although not seeking to rehabilitate or rejuvenate legal positivism, this volume remains premised on the fact that legal positivism and the images thereof that have travelled throughout the last century have, irrespective of their possible value, greatly shaped international legal scholars' understanding of the current international legal system. In that sense, the thoughts that constitute international legal positivism – advocated and fought over by several generations of scholars – cannot be un-thought.[43] Moreover, scholarly debate needs international legal positivism and other approaches as cannon fodder[44] and straw-men arguments,[45] because otherwise it would not and could not function as constitutive adversary.

It is because this volume also takes the idea of traditional legal positivism as a historical fact that cannot be unmade that this introduction must briefly situate the idea of legal positivism in the history of international legal scholarship. In the arena of scholarly debate, where legal scholars engage with one another to advocate a certain vision of the law and the way to make sense of the world, there have been variations in the influence and dominance that the guilds of international lawyers have managed to secure over time. These fluctuations in power and influence have even appeared circular to some.[46] It suffices to recall that natural law doctrine in its various forms had a firm grip on the early development of our discipline. Indeed, international law as a complete system of rules first emerged as a product of scholastic thought.[47] Emer de Vattel[48] was probably the first to make a significant step away from the dualism

43 Philip Allott, *Eunomia: New Order for a New World* (Oxford University Press 1990) 214, 288; earlier: Edward de Bono, *I am Right, You Are Wrong: From This to the New Renaissance, From Rock Logic to Water Logic* (Viking 1990) 288.

44 According to Richard Michael Fischl, 'Privileged Positions' 17 *Law and Social Inquiry* (1992) 831–838, once liberal legalism has been dismantled, the CLS movement would be debilitated.

45 Christopher Harding, 'Statist Assumptions, Normative Individualism and New Forms of Personality: Evolving a Philosophy of International Law for the Twenty First Century' 1 *Non-State Actors and International Law* (2001) 107–125 at 111.

46 David Kennedy, 'When Renewal Repeats: Thinking against the Box' 32 *New York University Journal of International Law and Politics* (2000) 335–500.

47 Anthony Pagden, Jeremy Lawrance (eds), *Vitoria: Political Writings* (Cambridge University Press 1991); Alberico Gentili, *De iure belli libri tres* (1612).

48 Emer de Vattel, *Le droit des gens ou principes de la loi naturelle* (1758); see Emmanuelle Jouannet, *Emer de Vattel et l'émergence doctrinale du droit international classique* (Pedone 1998); Nicholas Onuf, 'Civitas Maxima: Wolff, Vattel and the Fate of Republicanism' 88 *AJIL* (1994) 280–303.

of scholastic and early modern scholars.[49] Georg Friedrich de Martens departed more radically from the natural law tradition than Vattel[50] and strengthened a tradition of international law based on its systematic presentation in treaty and custom.[51] However, it took even longer for the move away from core naturalist beliefs (such as the primacy of extra-positive norms) to settle, and it was not until the early nineteenth century that the secularisation of our world-view had advanced enough in order for us to begin to question naturalism's inevitably theological-teleological theoretical basis. The assumption that values could be absolute or that 'human nature' or the existence of God was enough for norms to trump over the arbitrariness and vagaries of human law-creation was no longer universally accepted.

By the late nineteenth century, legal positivism in its 'classical' form – at least in the mainstream perception that we have of that period – came to outpace naturalism as the leading school of thought in international legal scholarship. The international legal scholars of the twentieth century, while recognising that natural law had 'supplied one of the necessary crutches with whose help mankind walked out of the institutions of the Middle Ages',[52] resolutely retreated from such dualism and endorsed a rule- or source-based approach to international law.[53] It must be pointed out, however, that the dominance of positivism in the international legal scholarship of the twentieth century was never as absolute as in many domestic legal traditions, and both positivism and naturalism continued to be influential. This 'reign' of classical positivism – in

[49] On the contribution of Grotius, see generally TMC Asser Instituut (ed.), *International Law and the Grotian Heritage: A Commemorative Colloquium Held at The Hague on 8 April 1983 on the Occasion of the Fourth Centenary of the Birth of Hugo Grotius* (TMC Asser Instituut 1985). See also Jouannet, n. 48 at 350–361.

[50] Georg Friedrich de Martens, *Primae lineae iuris gentium Europaearum practici in usum auditorum adumbratae* (Johann Christian Dieterich 1785).

[51] On the changes in the scholarship following Martens, see Edward Keene, 'The Age of Grotius' in David Armstrong (ed.), *Routledge Handbook of International Law* (Routledge 2009) 126–140 at 129.

[52] Lassa Oppenheim, 'The Science of International Law: Its Task and Method' 2 *AJIL* (1908) 313–356 at 329.

[53] Dioniso Anzilotti, *Il diritto internazionale nei giudizi interni* (Ditti N. Zanichelli 1905) 318; Thomas Joseph Lawrence, *The Principles of International Law* (7th edn D. C. Heath & Co. 1923) 1–14; Oppenheim, n. 52; Lassa Oppenheim, *International Law: A Treatise*, Vol. 1 (Longmans, Green and Co. 1905) 92; Georg Schwarzenberger, *International Law* (3rd edn Stevens & Sons 1957); Paul Guggenheim, 'What is Positive International Law?' in George Arthur Lipsky (ed.), *Law and Politics in the World Community: Essays on Hans Kelsen's Pure Theory and Related Problems of International Law* (University of California Press 1953) 15–30.

international law always tempered with a naturalist streak – was systematically weakened at the end of both world wars. Each of the two wars brought about a renewed strengthening of the naturalist approach and a feeling of a failure of the positivist project. In the second half of the twentieth century, classical international legal positivism was also confronted by powerful objections by realist, sociological and liberal schools of thought, as well as by various policy-oriented approaches such as the New Haven movement.

There is another very important development that has often been portrayed as the harbinger of death for classical positivism's hold over the minds of many international legal scholars. Although not specifically directed against any one legal theory, by the end of the twentieth century the CLS movement, or the emanation thereof in international legal scholarship,[54] showed how effective its fundamental critique of the orthodox ('mainstream') theoretical models of constructing law can be. Moreover, many streams of CLS introduced as-yet-not-received doubts about the nature of post-Enlightenment scholarship which, for example, the *Positivismusstreit* of the 1960s and 1970s[55] had engendered, to (international) legal scholarship. If anything, this decisively ended the dominance of classical international legal positivism and cast doubts on the Enlightenment project associated with it,[56] at least among many of those scholars interested in theory – although its influence was felt most in the Anglo-Saxon culture and least, perhaps, in parts of continental Europe. As a result of the change of leadership that was witnessed over fifty years in international legal scholarship, classical international legal positivism entered a new crisis of credibility.

Because classical international legal positivism arose, to some extent, out of artefacts made by its opponents, legal scholars – including legal positivists themselves – may have lost sense of what legal positivism really means.[57] As a result, much of the debate on legal positivism has become

[54] David Kennedy, *International Legal Structures* (Nomos 1987); Martti Koskenniemi, *From Apology to Utopia: The Structure of International Legal Argument* (Finnish Lawyers' Publishing Co., 1989, reissued Cambridge University Press 2005).

[55] Theodor Adorno *et al.*, *Der Positivismusstreit in der deutschen Soziologie* (Luchterhand 1969).

[56] On Kelsen and the Enlightement project, see Iain Stewart, 'Kelsen, the Enlightenment and Modern Premodernists' 37 *Australian Journal of Legal Philosophy* (2012) 251–278.

[57] Compare, e.g. the five meanings of positivism by HLA Hart, 'Positivism and the Separation of Law and Morals' 71 *Harvard Law Review* (1957–1958) 593–629 with the three meanings of positivism of Norberto Bobbio, 'Sur le positivism juridique' in Norberto Bobbio (ed.), *Essais de théorie du droit* (Michel Guéret (tr.), Bruylant LDGJ 1998) 23–38 at 24. See

unfathomable and unintelligible.[58] The same probably holds for post-modernism as well, the lines between CLS, post-structuralism, deconstruction and post-modernism being often unduly blurred in mainstream discourse.[59] 'International legal positivism' does not need to be defined in this volume. Although revolving around a few recurring 'theses' (for example, for Hartian positivism, the separation, autonomy and social or conventional theses) and paradigms (for example, the necessity for formal law-ascertainment, the political and creative character of interpretation, the idea of autonomy or the possibility of a critique of law),[60] the meaning of international legal positivism is not fixed and purposely left in flux for the sake of the reflexive exercise attempted here.

Yet, although left fluctuating, the idea of international legal positivism discussed here should certainly not be construed as being properly post-modernist. This would be a contradiction in terms. Post-modernism is used here in its historical dimension, that is to designate the disrepute into which mainstream approaches – and metanarratives – have started to fall in certain circles of international legal scholarship from the late 1980s; this was even more widespread in the late 1990s.[61] It is because it takes post-modernism in its historical dimension that the book explores the (im)possibility of a 'post-classical' phase in international legal positivism.[62]

6 The structure of this book

We felt very early in this project that the present volume should reflect different levels of engagement with international legal positivism. Three

Oppenheim's understanding of positivism in Oppenheim, n. 52 at 326, 333; Onuf, n. 6 at 1–13.

58 William Twining, *General Jurisprudence: Understanding Law from a Global Perspective* (Cambridge University Press 2009) 25; Giorgio Pino, 'The Place of Legal Positivism in Contemporary Constitutional States' 18 *Law and Philosophy* (1999) 513–536; See also Francois Chevrette and Hugo Cyr, 'De quel positivisme parlez-vous?' in Louise Rolland, Pierre Noreau (eds), *Mélanges Andrée Lajoie: Le droit, une variable dépendante* (Thémis 2008) 33–60; Koskenniemi, n. 54 at 131 (fn. 258).

59 On this point, see Singh, Chapter 11 at 301–304.

60 In that sense, many of the contributors to this volume would still qualify as 'sophisticated formalists', by opposition to 'vulgar formalists', as they recognise that legal reasoning is not mechanical; they still require identification of valid sources of law. On this distinction, see Brian Leiter, 'Legal Formalism and Legal Realism: What is the Issue?' 16 *Legal Theory* (2010) 111–133 at 112.

61 Venzke, Chapter 7.

62 Such studies have been common in connection with natural law. See Jonathan Crowe, 'Natural Law Beyond Finnis' 2 *Jurisprudence* (2011) 293–308.

avenues of research seemed to have the greatest potential for critical reflection. One, we wanted participants to reflect on the historical, logico-theoretical and philosophical foundations as well as the foundational theses at the heart of the positivist approaches to international law. Part I is entitled 'Theorising international legal positivism', although references to its 'foundational theses' should not be understood as necessarily implying that the authors share a specific set of foundational positivist theses or themselves seek to establish ('found') international legal positivism. Two, we felt very keenly that this family of approaches inevitably interacts with other approaches. Part II is entitled 'Relating international legal positivism' to express the idea that the contributions therein seek to relate classical and modern forms of positivism to other major ways of thinking about (international) law, including natural legal scholarship, legal realism and new approaches to international law (NAIL). Three, we felt that a number of contributions should shed light on the potential or actual uses made of positivist methodology/ies in scholarly writings on substantive topics of international law. This is why authors writing in Part III, 'Using international legal positivism', engage with positivist methodology/ies in constructing their topics, but also point out the challenges in applying positivist methodological moves. In doing so, the authors in this last part of the volume attempt a (self-)reflective understanding of international legal positivism, not one based on a uniform and homogenous understanding of its (criticisms of the) foundations, relations and practical uses.

The 'external' structure of a collection of essays can only partially reflect the views that actually emerge during writing and so it is here. A cross-cutting and prominent thread has emerged beyond the more formal structure. This is international legal positivism's 'frictions' with CLS (understood in a very broad sense), which constitutes a powerful attitude and mindset which many of the authors in this volume touch upon. We would like to foreground this issue, as manifested in the contributions in this book, in the remainder of this introduction. Post-modernism is a complex phenomenon which, as Singh argues, must be distinguished from Deconstruction and Critical Legal Studies. While, as highlighted above, post-modernity has primarily been construed as historical event, the following chapters show that NAIL/CLS, heavily influenced by post-modernist writers, can also operate as a form of catharsis for international lawyers. Indeed, there is a shared feeling among all contributors that NAIL/CLS helped international legal scholars to realise and identify a part of what was going wrong with traditional legal positivism. In particular, all authors but one (Christakis) embrace the rejection of voluntarism, for they all seek to come to terms with the ultimately irreconcilable tension between the quest for constructing a stable and objective international legal order and the subjective will of states. The compelling criticisms raised by NAIL/CLS thinkers against mainstream customary law theory and its presupposition of reading social realities in light of unstated and unexplained normative assumptions are reiterated in the chapters by Somek, Jacobs and Ronen and echo the rejection of a similar contradiction. This being said, shedding light on this fundamental tension is certainly not a legacy of theoretical traditions informed by the great post-modernist philosophers, as some of the following chapters argue. Such a tension was already at play, as explained by von Bernstorff, in nineteenth-century legal thinking. It was sometimes artificially created to support new reformist agendas, as explained by Collins in his study of twentieth-century inter-war international legal scholarship. As von Bernstorff, Telman, Hernández, Tams and Tzanakopoulos, d'Aspremont and Kammerhofer contend, twentieth-century positivist legal thinkers, irrespective of their successes or failures, sought to address the contradiction between objectivism and subjectivism. Some authors, like von Bernstorff, d'Aspremont and Kammerhofer, even go as far as to question the perpetuation of the search for the construction of international law as an objective community which in their view means that positivist approaches of the twentieth century are being paid insufficient heed. Post-modernism/NAIL/CLS does not have a monopoly on the discovery of the tension between objectivism and subjectivism in international legal studies. This leads Somek to recall the connection of positivist approaches to Skepsis, although he regrets how mediocre positivists have been in spelling their scepticism out. As illustrated by the generous references to Koskenniemi's work throughout this volume – irrespective of whether it is accurate to portray him as a 'true' post-modernist (Singh) – this tradition of legal thinking is perceived by most authors of this volume as that which allowed such an awareness to structurally gain ground in positivist international legal scholarship. In other words, it seems that it took the formidable, elegant and prolific post-modern blossoming as well as an additional half a century of scholarship to firmly anchor these realisations in the minds of contemporary international lawyers. This stream of the critique of traditional legal positivism is centre-stage in Ingo Venzke's chapter, where one finds the most differentiated critique of traditional legal positivism.

It is important to note that this cathartic effect, as embraced by the contributors of this volume, goes beyond a disavowal of the inextricable contradictions between objective order and subjective will. Other central theses of this stream of legal thinking are discussed extensively in the following chapters and will be mentioned briefly. Even though the question above is markedly present in the chapters by Venzke, Hernández, and Tams and Tzanakopoulos, the contributors to this volume are unanimous in their rejection of determinacy and objectivity in interpretation, as well as the idea that rules can be applied mechanically. Likewise, as illustrated by Somek and Jacobs, many of the following contributions relativise the quest for unity that is often part of positivist theories and the fragmentation of expertise, vocabularies and rationalities which nowadays tend to permeate the theory and practice of international law. The legacy of NAIL/CLS found in the chapters of this volume sometimes reveals itself in structures. For many contributors, indeterminacy is not only a phenomenon on the 'micro-level', affecting individual rules and institutions, but it also affects any kind of systemic construction – 'systematicity', as used, for example, in Somek's chapter – which, it is claimed, is inevitably loaded with ideological choices. This is probably where the legacy of NAIL/CLS has the greatest impact. There is also an awareness among many authors that positivism, even one not wedded to the doctrines of voluntarism, objectivity and determinacy, cannot, from a theoretical point of view, sustain itself on its own terms. As is explained by Venzke, Singh, Somek, Hernández, d'Aspremont and Kammerhofer, meaning cannot be internally generated and kept immune from normative choices and epistemic biases. The legal system cognised by positivism is itself bound to be generative and constitutive of the world according to certain frameworks determined by choices and biases. If this is assumed, international legal positivism has the potential, Telman argues, not to fetishise empiricism. Against this backdrop, many of the following chapters come to argue that positivist scholars can learn and/or have learned their 'lessons' from NAIL/CLS (respectively, from post-modernist thinking) – a claim disputed by Singh.

Whether the lessons have been learned 'correctly' is probably not the question which we can meaningfully discuss here, for it is far less interesting than that of the epistemological moves made by those who believe they *can* learn a lesson from NAIL/CLS. While there is a cross-cutting consensus among all contributors that it has left us with a rich legacy, authors are fundamentally divided as to how this legacy does and can (or should) interact with today's international legal positivism. More than the extent, meaning and effects of the main NAIL/CLS arguments, it is the relationship between them and the reflective exercise attempted in this book that witnesses the greatest discrepancy between chapters.

A first group of authors (Klabbers, Venzke, Hoffmann, Hernández, Bonafe, d'Aspremont and Kammerhofer) contend that international legal positivism, under certain conditions (foremost including a purge of certain methodological moves made by classical legal positivism) is not necessarily incompatible with certain arguments made by NAIL/CLS. It could even be said to show more affinity with positivism than with other schools of legal scholarship:[63] Klabbers argues, for example, that Koskiennemi's 'culture of formalism' shows that positivism and CLS need not be sworn enemies; for Hoffmann, positivism in the post-modern world could be the next step in achieving this culture of formalism. Klabbers, again, shows that the formalism found in positivism means that evaluation and hence critique of law is not excluded. The relationship between NAIL/CLS and international legal positivism is thus – to some degree – one of symbiosis and complementarity that does not need to make them necessarily incommensurable. For these scholars, those streams of positivism which do not seek to explain the law as totality and NAIL/CLS ask different questions and can work in tandem.

A second group of authors (Singh, Capps and Telman) is much more sceptical as to a possible symbiosis; these authors argue that the two traditions are unable to communicate with one another. They prove fundamentally foreign to one another and there are, in this sense, limited lessons that can be learned from the other approach. Modernism in positivism and the claim for a grand narrative that inevitably comes with it makes reconciliation impossible, as Singh (reacting to the first iteration of this introduction) argues. International legal positivism remains a fundamentally Modernist project, whether 'reformed' or 'rejuvenated'. Capps critiques the Hartian stream from a naturalist standpoint based on public practical reasonableness and the integration of law with morals. He claims that whatever reform of positivism is attempted, one cannot avoid the continuous resort to extra-legal normativity and isolation strategies. Thus, these authors do not believe that international legal positivism is able to assimilate the destabilising complexity either of post-modernist or of naturalist theory. For Singh and Telman, the argument made by the first group of authors is nothing less than a conflict-avoidance strategy. It amounts, in their view, to methodological reductionism that disables communication between theories in order to avoid (and deny) clashes.

[63] '[T]he main tenets of critical legal studies, including its emphasis on the emancipatory potential of international law, are quite possibly easier to reconcile with positivism than with naturalism' (Klabbers, Chapter 10 at 269).

Clearly, the above-mentioned epistemological dissonance between the chapters echoes the great theoretical pluralism at the heart of the reflection at issue in this volume. Finding that reformist moves attempted *with* and *within* positivist schools are possible or impossible is itself dependent on one's perspective. As Hoffmann argues, these divergences are themselves sometimes the manifestations of regional traditions. Such a pluralism explains why the sort of renewal of positivist approaches that the authors have variously called 'neo-ILP' (Singh), 'new ILP' (Telman) or 'neo-Formalism' (Hoffmann and Singh), 'naked positivism' (Hoffmann) or 'post-modern positivism' (Patterson) often remains unclear, hypothetical and speculative. This instability is exacerbated by the persistence of some of the – otherwise disavowed – argumentative moves found in traditional legal positivism like the search for certainty, clarity and a domestication of politics which sometimes comes to the fore in the chapters by Bonafé, Christakis, Ronen or Tams and Tzanakopoulos.

Such pluralism and perspectivism do not warrant the charge of 'irrelevance through relativism'. On the contrary, pluralism and perspectivism should be seen as constituting the very legacy of NAIL/CLS that is shared by most contributors. However modest and thin this may seem on the surface, this common denominator, irrespective of the great diversity of conceptual, methodological, theoretical and practical outcomes presented in these chapters, has the potential to sharpen positivist approaches to and thinking about international law and to liberate it from its (by default) static, dogmatic and under-theorised state in which it is too often found in contemporary 'black-letter' legal scholarship. Although, as Patterson argues, it remains too early to predict the final trajectory of the next decades of legal thinking on international law, paving the way for the possible emergence of a more fluid and dynamic type of international legal positivism, as contemplated by Tams and Tzanakopoulos as well as d'Aspremont and Kammerhofer, bears significant virtue.

PART I

Theorising international legal positivism

2

Classical legal positivism in international law revisited

RICHARD COLLINS

1 Introduction

In historical narratives on the development of modern international law, the nineteenth century is often portrayed in terms of a theoretical battle between naturalist and positivist schools, with international legal positivism winning out by the century's end.[1] The growing dominance of legal positivism during the century is, in turn, seen to buttress the sovereignty of states as a growing tide of nationalism eventually boils over into the outbreak of the First World War.[2] The emergence of 'modern' international law in the wake of the war – with its increasingly humanitarian agenda, diversification of legal actors and growing institutionalisation – sets itself up against this 'classical' legal positivism, which is dismissed as both theoretically untenable (falling foul of the so-called Austinian challenge)[3] and ideologically dangerous in sustaining the dominance of state sovereignty at the expense of international legal regulation.

In this chapter, I want to revisit this image of classical positivism in light of a recent resurgence of interest in the history of international law, with a number of authors beginning to challenge the accuracy of this portrayal of classical doctrine. I argue that this negative portrayal arose more as a result of the rhetoric of *inter-bellum* jurists themselves as they sought to explain why international law had failed, thus far, to operate as an autonomous restraint in international politics. In fact, I will argue that late-nineteenth-century jurists were well aware of the kind of theoretical problems which they were accused of perpetuating, and their positivist

[1] See e.g. Malcolm Shaw, *International Law* (6th edn Cambridge University Press 2008) 29–30.

[2] Stephen Neff, 'A Short History of International Law' in Malcolm Evans (ed.), *International Law* (3rd edn Oxford University Press 2010) 3–31 at 15–16.

[3] See Section 4.

method – to the extent that it (controversially) explained international law as grounded in state consent – reflected a desire to carve out a more legitimate, and in that sense persuasive, basis to enhance the authority of international law. Modern jurists' reaction to classical doctrine says less about the failings of nineteenth-century jurists and much more about the theoretical limitations of the assumption which they share with them: i.e. that international law can be explained as an autonomous legal order by reference to a domestic legal paradigm. I argue instead that it is the falsity of this assumption, an assumption equally shared by modern jurists, which explains the failure of classical doctrine, rather than the specific approach of late-nineteenth-century jurists, who themselves sought to formulate arguments to ground international law's autonomy. In this respect, it is this desire to explain the autonomy of international law which is the real legacy of classical legal positivism, demonstrating a greater amount of continuity between classical and modern doctrine than is often thought.

The chapter is structured as follows. In Section 2, I consider how a particularly negative view of classical legal positivism has come to prominence in the writings of many modern jurists, a perception which I reconsider in Section 3 in light of recent critical scholarship. While this scholarship has called into question the overly simplistic portrayal of the late nineteenth century as characterised solely by a voluntarist-positivist doctrine, I nonetheless acknowledge that a positivist understanding of international law came to dominate legal method by the early years of the twentieth century. However, in Section 4, I cast doubt on the claim that this commitment to legal positivism entailed a voluntarist legal method. I argue instead that the positivist method in international law can be seen as underpinned by both a social and a teleological assumption about the institutional structure of the international legal order. I observe that such assumptions were necessary to sustain the idea of international law as an autonomous legal order binding on states. Finally then, in Section 5, I argue that it is this claim to legal autonomy which is the main inheritance from nineteenth-century legal positivism, but it is the problem of sustaining such a claim in the decentralised international legal order which has caused jurists to take such a jaundiced view of the failure of nineteenth-century doctrine. I conclude that the failure of this claim to legal autonomy lies in the assumption that international law's conceptual autonomy can be theorised according to idealised conceptions of legality developed in a domestic legal context. It is this assumption which highlights greater continuity between classical and modern doctrines than is commonly acknowledged.

2 The birth of 'modern' international law and the rejection of classical legal positivism

'Modern'[4] international law was born in the wake of the First World War in a spirit of reformism and disciplinary renewal. The existential shock of the war had a profound effect on the development of twentieth-century international law. In particular, the idea that international law could, or should, have been able to prevent the war but had clearly failed in this respect was a recurring feature of *inter-bellum* debates, prompting jurists to stress the need for revisiting international law's theoretical bases and strengthening its institutional structures.[5] In this respect, for *inter-bellum* jurists the outbreak of the war was at least in part attributable to the failure of classical legal doctrine, which in both its naturalist and positivist forms was dismissed as either too fanciful and utopian to ground an autonomous legal order, or too deferential in being closely wedded to the sovereign rights of states.[6] As the American jurist, Manley O. Hudson, noted in 1923:

> As each belligerent nation sought in vain for a law which would restrain its enemies, as each neutral nation sought in vain for a law which would relieve it of the burdensome incidents of the struggle, the insufficiency of our pre-war law came to be felt in every part of the world. Its principles seemed inadequate, its limitations ineffective, and its bases insecure. In many quarters, belief in the utility of a law of nations was weakened, and faith in the efficacy of any effort to increase its authority was lost. Even

[4] My use of the term 'modern' and 'classical' as separating the pre- and post-First World War periods is used for illustrative purposes, rather than offering any definitive periodisation of international law's history. In fact, as my argument progresses, it will become clearer that there is greater continuity between pre- and post-war doctrines than many historical narratives suggest.

[5] See, inter alia, Martti Koskenniemi, *From Apology to Utopia: The Structure of International Legal Argument* (Finnish Lawyers' Publishing Co. 1989, reissued Cambridge University Press 2005) 159–162; Antony Anghie, *Imperialism, Sovereignty and the Making of International Law* (Cambridge University Press 2005) 124, 127–131; Thomas Skouteris, *The Notion of Progress in International Law Discourse* (T. M. C. Asser Press 2010) 103–120; Nathaniel Berman, '"But the Alternative Is Despair": European Nationalism and the Modernist Renewal of International Law' 106 *Harvard Law Review* (1993) 1792–1903 at 1800–1808. For a useful bibliographic summary of the reformist strand of *inter-bellum* international law, see Hersch Lauterpacht, 'The Definition and Nature of International Law and its Place in Jurisprudence' in Elihu Lauterpacht (ed.), *International Law Being the Collected Papers of Hersch Lauterpacht*, Vol. 1 (Cambridge University Press 1970) 9–50 at 10 (fn.1).

[6] As Koskenniemi notes, both types of criticisms can be levelled at naturalism and positivism: the former reduced either to unverifiable moral commands, or related too closely to the idea of natural rights of sovereigns; the latter either too analytical and abstract, or too closely related to state will. Koskenniemi, n. 5 at 164.

> our legal profession failed to withstand the effect of the general scepticism, and we allowed to be revived the futile discussions of the Austinian era as to the existence of a law of nations which might properly be called law.[7]

Hudson was no doubt influenced by the critical voice of the famous jurist Roscoe Pound, who expressed similar sentiments about the failure of classical international law:

> [I]t is not hard to see why the nineteenth-century achieved so little in international law. The jurists of the last century . . . did not seek to be active agents in legal development. *They expected legal development to operate itself from some international momentum.* The jurist was able to follow, arranging and ordering and systematizing or observing and verifying and thus discovering the foreordained lines of growth. Creative work in law, as in any other field, requires a plan, a design, a picture of what the worker seeks to make.[8]

Foremost among the targets of the *inter-bellum* jurists was the statist positivism which was seen to have prevailed over naturalist theories by the end of the nineteenth century.[9] It was this kind of positivist dogma which they associated with the Permanent Court of International Justice's (PCIJ) decision in the famous *Lotus* case, where the Court noted how '[t]he rules of law binding upon States . . . emanate from their own free will' and that '[r]estrictions upon the independence of States [could not] therefore be presumed'.[10] In a series of lectures on the 'new aspects of international law', delivered at Columbia University around the time of the Permanent Court's deliberation, the Greek jurist Nicolas Politis stressed the poverty of this kind of positivist reasoning:

> This explanation is hardly satisfactory, for if a rule of law is merely the product of free will it is not really binding, but remains at the discretion

[7] Manley O. Hudson, 'The Development of International Law since the War' 22 *AJIL* (1928) 330–350 at 330–331.

[8] Roscoe Pound, 'Philosophical Theory and International Law' 1 *Bibliotheca Visseriana* (1923) 1–90 at 88 (emphasis added).

[9] For perhaps the most critical attack on classical legal positivism, see Hans Morgenthau, 'Positivism, Functionalism, and International Law' 34 *AJIL* (1940) 260–284; although see also James Leslie Brierly, 'The Basis of Obligation in International Law' in Hersch Lauterpacht, CHM Waldock (eds), *The Basis of Obligation in International Law and Other Papers by the Late James Leslie Brierly* (Clarendon Press 1958) 1–67; and from the perspective of the emerging 'Vienna School' of modern positivism, Josef Kunz, 'On the Theoretical Basis of the Law of Nations' 10 *Transactions of the Grotius Society* (1924) 115–142.

[10] *S.S. 'Lotus' (France v. Turkey)*, Judgment of 7 September 1927, PCIJ Series A No. 10 (1927) at 18. For a typical criticism, see James Leslie Brierly, 'The "*Lotus*" Case' 174 *Law Quarterly Review* (1928) 154–163.

> of the States which created it, since by ceasing to will it to be binding they can disregard it. What will has done, will to the contrary may undo.[11]

Similarly, a couple of years prior to the Court's decision, writing in his first English language publication, Hersch Lauterpacht had decried the limits of legal positivism in even more forceful terms:

> [The positivist] method is fraught with danger. There is always the possibility that not only will the practice of states be taken as an unquestionable rule of law, but that the philosophy underlying this practice will be regarded as a true expression of the tendencies and the possibilities of the international society... Many a mischievous phrase derives its authority from well-meaning international lawyers.[12]

The reaction against classical doctrine, and legal positivism in particular, took many forms and was certainly not confined to international legal doctrine alone. The growth of legal realism and, more generally, the influence of the social sciences in American jurisprudence, particularly for jurists like Pound, led a number of international lawyers towards a more pragmatic, sociological approach.[13] In its most realist guise, this sociological turn would eventually lead to the establishment of a new discipline of International Relations, which was in many ways born of the rejection of the possibility of the kind of legal autonomy pursued by classical positivists.[14] In Europe, the discipline either retreated into a more scientific, normativist positivism,[15] or – with jurists like Lauterpacht or Brierly – embraced a 'mainstream' middle ground, re-engaging

[11] Nicolas Politis, *The New Aspects of International Law* (Carnegie Endowment for International Peace 1928) 5.

[12] Hersch Lauterpacht, 'Westlake and Present Day International Law' 5 *Economica* (1925) 307–325 at 323–324. Similar criticisms are developed in his first monograph on international law: Hersch Lauterpacht, *Private Law Sources and Analogies of International Law* (Longmans 1927) esp. 43–44.

[13] Compare, for instance, Samuel Astorino, 'The Impact of Sociological Jurisprudence on International Law in the Inter-War Period: The American Experience' 34 *Duquesne Law Review* (1996) 277–298 at 280, with Robert Kolb, 'Politis and Sociological Jurisprudence of Inter-War International Law' 23 *EJIL* (2012) 233–241. See also Carl Landauer, 'J. L. Brierly and the Modernization of International Law' 25 *Vanderbilt Journal of International Law* (1993) 881–917 at 884–899 in particular.

[14] See e.g. the critical remarks of one of the founding figures in International Relations, Hans Morgenthau, in Morgenthau, n. 9 at 263–273 in particular. On the birth of international relations as a rejection of legal autonomy, see Martti Koskenniemi, 'Carl Schmitt, Morgenthau, and the Image of Law in International Relations' in Michael Byers (ed.), *The Role of Law in International Politics: Essays in International Relations and International Law* (Oxford University Press 2000) 17–34.

[15] Particularly in the works of Hans Kelsen and the so-called 'Vienna School'. For an overview, see in particular Jochen von Bernstorff, *The Public International Law Theory of Hans*

with natural law traditions while grounding them in a more sociological empiricism.[16]

As such, while modern international law grew up to be defined in many ways by its theoretical heterogeneity, its unity lies in its rejection of the tenets of classical doctrine, which has become associated with the very problem to which modern approaches respond: how to create order in a world of sovereign states.[17] Two particular but related criticisms emerged from this time. First, classical legal positivism was critiqued as theoretically untenable, resulting either in the rejection of international law as law, or requiring a theory of auto-limitation, or voluntarism, which failed to provide an adequate foundation for an autonomous international legal order.[18] Second, because of this limitation, classical positivism is implicated ideologically as sustaining the dominance of state sovereignty at the expense of international legal regulation.[19]

I will return to consider the accuracy of the methodological critique in Section 4, but before doing so I want to revisit the period in question in light of recent literature which has sought to call into question, first, that pre-modern doctrine can be understood as dominated by legal positivism in this way, and second, to the extent that jurists did embrace a positivist method, that this shift can be seen as aimed at buttressing state sovereignty in the way that is often claimed.

3 Questioning the traditional narrative

This image of classical doctrine as theoretically impoverished and overly deferential to state sovereignty remains a popular characterisation of nineteenth-century international law, an era depicted often in terms of a move from an older tradition of enlightenment naturalism to a position

Kelsen: Believing in Universal Law (Cambridge University Press 2010) 44–118. See also Kammerhofer, Chapter 4.

16 E.g. Brierly, n. 9 at 64–67. Although as Lauterpacht noted, this natural law revival was not 'the old law of nature', but 'rather the modern "natural law with changing contents", "the sense of right", "the social solidarity", the "engineering" law in terms of promoting the ends of the international society'. Lauterpacht, 'Westlake', n. 12 at 315.

17 See in this respect, David Kennedy, 'International Law and the Nineteenth Century: History of an Illusion' 17 *Quinnipiac Law Review* (1997) 99–136 at 113–116 in particular.

18 E.g. James Leslie Brierly, *The Law of Nations: An Introduction to the International Law of Peace* (4th edn Oxford University Press 1949) 52–55; Brierly, n. 9 at 3–9; Lauterpacht, *Private Law Sources*, n. 12 at 43–50.

19 E.g. the criticisms contained in Alfred Verdross, 'Le fondement du droit International' 16 *Recueil des Cours* (1927) 247–324 at 262–286. See further Lauterpacht, *Private Law Sources*, n. 12 at 51–59.

of state-centric legal positivism. It is this transition, in turn, which is seen to have 'resulted in the glorification of the sovereign state',[20] or even as giving rise to the kinds of sovereigntist dogma which 'threatened to destroy international law'.[21] As Kennedy notes, this depiction of the nineteenth century seems ingrained in the consciousness of modern jurists as 'an image of the pre-modern, a baseline against which to measure the discipline's progress and [the twentieth century's] exceptionalism'.[22] However, as a number of critical voices have recently claimed,[23] this depiction is perhaps an overly simplistic representation of the disciplinary transition which occurred at this time; as Kennedy continues:

> This image, of a method before frustration with formalism, a doctrine before the erosion of sovereignty, and a legal philosophy before the pragmatic flight from theory, remains an active part of twentieth century disciplinary argument, although it reflects only dimly the actual doctrine, method or philosophy of the field before the First World War.[24]

Similarly, Koskenniemi has argued that the portrayal of the nineteenth century as an overtly positivist era tends to ignore 'persistent strands of "naturalism" in the century's legal doctrine, constantly referring back to the moral and civilizing forces of European law and practices'.[25] There is much in this critique. At times, this preservation of natural law argumentation was explicit, particularly for many English jurists like Robert

[20] Janne Elisabeth Nijman, *The Concept of International Legal Personality: An Inquiry into the History and Theory of International Law* (T. M. C. Asser Press 2004) 110. For a critical reflection on these kinds of narratives, see also Kennedy, n. 17, as well as Casper Sylvest, 'International Law in Nineteenth-Century Britain' 75 *BYBIL* (2005) 9–70 at 9–10 and generally.

[21] Peter Malanczuk, *Akehurst's Modern Introduction to International Law* (Routledge 1997) 18.

[22] Kennedy, n. 17 at 100.

[23] Of note includes: Kennedy, n. 17; Anghie, n. 5; Martti Koskenniemi, *The Gentle Civilizer of Nations: The Rise and Fall of International Law 1870–1960* (Cambridge University Press 2002); Martti Koskenniemi, 'The Legacy of the Nineteenth Century' in David Armstrong (ed.), *Routledge Handbook on International Law* (Routledge 2009) 141–153; as well as Koskenniemi, n. 5 at 71–157 (ch. 2); Sylvest, n. 20; Michael Lobban, 'English Approaches to International Law in the Nineteenth Century' in Matthew Craven, Malgosia Fitzmaurice, Maria Vogiatzi (eds), *Time, History and International Law* (Martinus Nijhoff 2007) 65–90; Amnon Lev, 'The Transformation of International Law in the 19th Century' in Alexander Orakhelashvili (ed.), *Research Handbook on the Theory and History of International Law* (Edward Elgar 2011) 111–142.

[24] Kennedy, n. 17 at 100. See further Skouteris, n. 5 at 117–120.

[25] Koskenniemi, 'Nineteenth Century', n. 23 at 14. Stephen Neff has made similar claims, even if overall he paints a picture of the century as dogmatically positivist: Neff, n. 2 at 18–19.

Phillimore (1818 to 1885),[26] or Travers Twiss (1809 to 1897),[27] or the more eccentric Scot, James Lorimer (1818 to 1890),[28] whose attachment to the natural law tradition lasted into the last decades of the nineteenth century. For others, natural law arguments were merely replaced by arguments from reason or moral conscience. For example, the English jurist Thomas Lawrence (1849 to 1919), though espousing a positivist method, retained a residual role for 'ethical considerations',[29] the preservation of which 'fulfilled the important function of offering arguments when positive ones were not available'.[30] Lawrence's writings show the influence of the historical school of jurisprudence,[31] particularly as championed by Henry Summer Maine (1822 to 1888), whose approach had done much to discredit Austinian positivism in English jurisprudence. Maine saw in international law the seeds of a juridical evolution similar to that which had come about in domestic legal orders, arguing that international law's historical grounding in natural law principles was common to most societies undergoing legal evolution[32] and had developed 'by help of fiction', only later embracing the 'scientific jurisprudence' of the study of positive law.[33]

Although there were (and remain) important differences in methodological approach between English jurists and their continental counterparts,[34] the influence of historical jurisprudence in some form was pervasive during this period. For instance, the Swiss jurist, Johann Caspar Bluntschli (1808 to 1881), influenced by the 'supranational

[26] E.g. Robert Phillimore, *Commentaries upon International Law* (3rd edn Butterworths 1879), particularly 14–29 on the sources of law, which Phillimore expounds according to Grotius' division between the natural law, divine law and positive law.

[27] Travers Twiss, *The Law of Nations Considered as Independent Political Communities* (Oxford University Press 1861), particularly 110–111, where he grounds his approach in the co-existence of the *ius naturale* and *ius positum*, propounded previously by Vattel.

[28] James Lorimer, *The Institutes of the Law of Nations: A Treatise on the Jural Relations of Separate Political Communities*, Vol. 2 (William Blackwood and Sons 1884).

[29] Thomas Joseph Lawrence, *A Handbook of Public International Law* (D. Bell & Co. 1898) 6–7; *The Principles of International Law* (7th edn MacMillan 1923) 12–13.

[30] Koskenniemi, n. 5 at 131.

[31] E.g. Lawrence, *Principles*, n. 29 at 10–12.

[32] Henry Sumner Maine, *Ancient Law: Its Connection with the Early History of Society, and its Relations to Modern Ideas* (John Murray 1861) 53. For a detailed exposition of Maine's theory in this respect, see the arguments of Sylvest, n. 20 at 42–43.

[33] The quotations are taken from Vinogradoff's summation of Maine's position: Paul Vinogradoff, *The Teaching of Sir Henry Maine: An Inaugural Lecture* (Henry Frowde 1904) 16–17.

[34] E.g. Lobban, n. 23 at 65–66.

historicism' of Friedrich Karl von Savigny (1779 to 1861),[35] saw the law's origins in the historical growth of society generally, a growth which was directed by a kind of cosmopolitan purpose. Thus, international law concerned the relations between states, but states embodied a collective will of their people, which in turn pointed with 'inner necessity to the higher unity of mankind of which the nations [were] only members'.[36]

This historical method and cosmopolitan ambition was shared by many of Bluntschli's contemporaries who sought to professionalise the discipline through the establishment of its first academic journals and professional associations, such as the *Institut de Droit International.* As Koskenniemi has described, although theoretically diverse in many ways, these men shared a liberal-internationalist sensibility which sought to derive the binding force of law from a kind of collective European moral consciousness aimed at the pacification of international relations.[37] A good example of this approach is contained in the work of the Swiss jurist, Alphonse Rivier (1835 to 1898), who described the ultimate source of the law's authority as the common juridical conscience ('la conscience juridique commune') which manifested itself through customary law and was given expression in multilateral treaties, or through 'les avis et les écrits des jurisconsultes'.[38] Similar positions were adopted by fellow members of the *Institut,* such as the Italian jurist Pasquale Fiore (1837 to 1914),[39] and the English liberal, John Westlake (1828 to 1913). For instance, Westlake argued that international law derived its binding force from the existence of the collective social will underpinning it,[40] and was defined, in extremely broad terms, as 'dealing with all human action not internal to a political body'.[41]

In all, much of the literature from the final third of the nineteenth century suggests that, far from being dogmatically positivist, many

[35] Koskenniemi, *Gentle Civilizer*, n. 23 at 45.

[36] Johann Caspar Bluntschli, *The Theory of the State*, English translation from the 6th German edn (Clarendon Press 1885) 25. And see further, Johann Caspar Bluntschli, *Le Droit International Codifié* (5th edn Guillaumin 1895) 1–2.

[37] Koskenniemi, *Gentle Civilizer*, n. 23 at 92–97.

[38] Alphonse Rivier, *Principes du Droit des Gens*, Tome I (Arthur Rousseau 1896) 27.

[39] Pasquale Fiore, *International Law Codified and Its Legal Sanction; or the Legal Organization of the Society of States* (Edwin M. Borchard (tr.), Baker, Voorhis & Co. 1918).

[40] E.g. John Westlake, *Chapters on the Principles of International Law* (Cambridge University Press 1894) 2–3.

[41] John Westlake, 'Introductory Lecture on International Law, 17 October 1888' in Lassa Oppenheim (ed.), *The Collected Papers of John Westlake on Public International Law* (Cambridge University Press 1914) 393–413 at 412.

international lawyers adopted much more eclectic theoretical positions. Still, in their efforts to professionalise the discipline, to codify and systematise the law, there is little doubt that they paved the way for the study of international law as a positivist science. Already by 1894, Westlake could confidently claim that it was with 'law as an institution or a fact that the legal student has to deal'.[42] Westlake's successor in the Whewell Chair at Cambridge, Lassa Oppenheim (1858 to 1919), only fourteen years later, was adamant in his assertion that it was now 'impossible to find a law which has its roots in human reason only and is above legislation and customary law'.[43] Oppenheim certainly was not alone in this respect; by the early years of the twentieth century few international lawyers thought of international law as anything other than an artificial law justified through some form of state consent,[44] and few considered the role of the international jurist as concerned with anything more than an 'analysis of the practice of the institutions of the State'.[45] While English jurists remained more pragmatic about the binding force of this positive law, a more analytical positivist method took hold in, inter alia, Germany[46] and Italy,[47] through the works of, for example, Georg Jellinek (1851 to 1911), Heinrich Triepel (1868 to 1946) and Dionisio Anzilotti (1869 to 1950), which aimed to find a consensual basis for the law's binding force.

Nevertheless, it is misleading to see this transformation as necessarily, or at least deliberately, buttressing state sovereignty. To ground the law in sovereignty reflected a procedural understanding of legal validity: a product of an emerging political and social context increasingly uneasy with a priori philosophical reasoning. The climate of political legitimacy

[42] Westlake, n. 40 at12.

[43] Lassa Oppenheim, 'The Science of International Law: Its Task and Method' 2 *AJIL* (1908) 313–356 at 329 (emphasis added).

[44] Anthony Carty, *The Decay of International Law: A Reappraisal of the Limits of Legal Imagination in International Affairs* (Manchester University Press 1986) 1–11 and generally. On this transition, generally, see Ronald Macdonald and Douglas M. Johnston, 'International Legal Theory: New Frontiers of the Discipline' in Ronald St John Macdonald, Douglas M. Johnston (eds), *The Structure and Process of International Law: Essays in Legal Philosophy, Doctrine, and Theory* (Martinus Nijhoff 1983) 1–14 at 6–7.

[45] Carty, n. 44 at 8. As he continues, '[i]n this context there is no significant difference between the common law and civil law jurisdictions in so far as concerns legal method. Study of the "practice" of judicial institutions follows the same analytical, i.e. above all logical, conceptual method, as study of the "emanations" of the will of the State'.

[46] On the positivist turn in German approaches, see Koskenniemi, *Gentle Civilizer*, n. 23 at 46, 186–188.

[47] E.g. Angelo Sereni, *The Italian Conception of International Law* (Columbia University Press 1943) 206 (ch. 12).

emerging by the late nineteenth century became increasingly dismissive of such philosophical argumentation, as that which remained of the classical natural law tradition was increasingly used to justify the *raison d'état*, than to oppose it.[48] Accordingly, late-nineteenth-century international lawyers sought new means for legitimising, and new ways of understanding, the legality of interstate relations. Arguments derived from natural law were derided not only as illegitimate and speculative, but were seen also as 'a set of excessively abstract (and in this sense arbitrary) maxims that could not form part of a practical *Jus publicum Europaeum*'.[49] For instance, Lawrence claimed that natural law 'was false historically, and untenable philosophically' for it 'confound[ed] together the actual and the ideal'. Furthermore, he asserted confidently that state officials no longer appealed publicly to 'innate principles and absolute rights, but to rules which can be proved to have been acted upon previously in similar circumstances by all or most civilised nations'.[50] This latter observation was in many respects true. One need only compare the reactionary and conservative legitimising principles and purposes underpinning the Vienna Settlement of 1814 to 1815 with the more liberal purposes and multilateral ordering principles of The Hague conferences at the turn of the next century to see the reality of this transition.[51]

What therefore united continental and Anglo-American jurists at this time was a professional ethos, or self-consciousness, to defend the coherence and efficacy of the law as a system of norms which could operate as an effective restraint in international politics.[52] To construct a more convincing vision of an international public order under law, international lawyers sought insights from domestic experience, where sovereignty was seen as having already been reconstructed in more relative terms, tamed and harnessed by principles such as the Rule of Law. This was not simply a matter of deriving law from the practices of states, but making sense of the

48 This was a common reflection among many European jurists writing towards the end of the nineteenth and in the early twentieth century: e.g. Gustave Rolin-Jaequemyns, 'De l'étude de la législation comparée et de droit international' 1 *Revue de Droit International et de Législation Comparée* (1869) 1–656 at 11, 256–267; Fiore, n. 39 at 8–9; Thomas Lawrence, *Essays on Some Disputed Questions in Modern International Law* (Deighton, Bell & Co. 1885) 236–237.

49 Koskenniemi, 'Nineteenth Century', n. 23 at 146.

50 Lawrence, *Handbook*, n. 29 at 6.

51 Christian Reus-Smit, *The Moral Purpose of the State: Culture, Social Identity, and Institutional Rationality in International Relations* (Princeton University Press 1999) 131–132, 153.

52 Koskenniemi, n. 5 at 122–123; Anghie, n. 5 at 48–52.

law by categorising it and – as Lawrence put this at the time – referring legal rules back to 'certain fundamental principles on which they are based'.[53] Accordingly, international lawyers gave shape to modern doctrines under the influence of principles such as juridical equality, non-discrimination and self-legislative justice, principles which they saw as delineating the allocation of political power within the state, as international law became increasingly perceived as an institutional practice structured on the basis of mutual consent and reciprocal equality (at least in a formal sense).[54] As Anghie notes, the late-nineteenth-century jurist saw the role of legal science as 'a struggle against chaos which could be won only by ensuring the autonomy of law, and establishing and maintaining the taxonomies and principles which existed in fixed relations to each other'.[55]

In this respect, the idea that the turn to positivism expressed an *amoral* view of the conduct of international relations downplays the motivations behind the emergence and eventual dominance of this methodological approach. Not only did classical positivists share in natural lawyers' ambition of enhancing the authority of international legal rules, but their efforts to build a complete system of law relied essentially on equally moralistic tenets, and, at times, aprioristic reasoning.[56] As such, if by the beginning of the twentieth century scholars like Oppenheim had come to espouse an avowedly positivist method, this has to be understood, at least in part, as a normative position[57] that such a view would better guarantee a condition of legality in the relations between sovereigns.[58] As Kingsbury notes:

> Oppenheim's commitment to a positivist approach to international law was not simply an assertion that a positivist concept of law was the only coherent one, but also embodied a normative or ethical view that a

[53] Lawrence, *Principles*, n. 29 at 1. See further Koskenniemi, *Gentle Civilizer*, n. 23 at 51–54.

[54] Reus-Smit, n. 51 at 129–131, 134–135. [55] Anghie, n. 5 at 51.

[56] Koskenniemi, n. 5 at 131–132.

[57] On positivism as a normative position, see further Jean d'Aspremont, *Formalism and the Sources of International Law: A Theory of the Ascertainment of Legal Rules* (Oxford University Press 2011) 142–146.

[58] On Oppenheim's positivism as normative, as opposed to merely methodological, see Benedict Kingsbury, 'Legal Positivism as Normative Politics: International Society, Balance of Power and Lassa Oppenheim's Positive International Law' 13 *EJIL* (2002) 401–436. On this distinction, generally, see Jeremy Waldron, 'Normative (or Ethical) Positivism' in Jules Coleman (ed.), *Hart's Postscript: Essays on the Postscript to* The Concept of Law (Oxford University Press 2001) 411–433; as applied to international law in particular, see Patrick Capps, *Human Dignity and the Foundations of International Law* (Hart 2009).

> positivist understanding of international law was best able to advance the realization in international society of a higher set of values to which Oppenheim adhered.[59]

Oppenheim was clear about these values in an important essay from 1908 in which he set out the 'task and method' of the international lawyer, which included not only the study of the existing law, but also its progressive development in line with values which he saw as intrinsic to international law, including, inter alia, 'peace among the nations and the governance of their intercourse by what makes for order and is right and just'.[60] In order to realise these ends, Oppenheim saw it as imperative to distinguish the legal from the non-legal, and only a positivist method would facilitate this. As he put this, the science of international law would not succeed 'unless all authors . . . ma[de] an effort to keep in the background their individual ideas concerning politics, morality, humanity, and justice'.[61]

As such, to the extent that many jurists founded the source of normativity on state sovereignty, this had little to do with state-centrism, and much more with making sense of international law as an autonomous order in an increasingly secular and pluralist era. A formalised idea of sovereignty as a delineated order of absolute competence provided an explanation for the possibility of autonomous law in the absence of an overarching moral theory or centralised sovereign authority – an idea no more clearly expressed than by the PCIJ in *Wimbledon* (four years before its *Lotus* decision).[62] As Koskenniemi observes:

> From the late nineteenth century onwards, international lawyers have been critics of 'sovereignty' as egoism, arbitrariness, and the absolutism of state power. The contrary to sovereignty was international law . . . The legacy of the nineteenth century was not excessive deference to sovereignty (arguments against such deference were common then as they are today) but rather the emergence of 'sovereignty' as the key *topos* of international law, leading the law into a formal and procedural direction, away from views about the substantive rightness or wrongness of particular types of behavior . . .[63]

59 Kingsbury, n. 58 at 431. 60 Oppenheim, n. 43 at 314 (emphasis added).

61 Oppenheim, n. 43 at 335.

62 Essentially, the court explained the ability to enter into international legal obligations (and thus be bound by international legal rules) as an attribute of a state's sovereignty. See *S.S. 'Wimbledon' (Great Britain, France, Italy, Japan, Poland (intervening) v. Germany)*, Judgment of 17 August 1923, PCIJ Series A No. 1 (1923) at 25.

63 Koskenniemi, 'Nineteenth Century', n. 23 at 150.

Kennedy has made a similar point:

> [F]rom the standpoint of international law, the sovereignty consolidated in the late nineteenth century was a very secular matter, a doctrinal project of practicality in a broader legal fabric whose existence, in turn, was simply obvious. *If nineteenth century international lawyers had a blind faith, it was in law, not sovereignty.* Sovereignty was their construct, their response, a project of earnest doctrinal elaboration, opening a space for a new form of statecraft in an ancient legal fabric.[64]

Bearing in mind the nature of this transition which the professionalisation of the discipline brought about, it is perhaps not unfair to conclude that positivism came to hold a dominant position in the practice of international law by the beginning of the twentieth century. Thus far, I have maintained that the reason for this transition itself cannot be seen as one of deference to the unrestrained sovereignty of states. Nonetheless, the question remains whether the classical positivist method resulted in justifying just such a sovereigntist doctrine; whether, in other words, the dominance of classical positivism resulted in the kind of voluntarist dogma later critiqued by modern jurists? It is to this question that I now turn my attention.

4 Classical legal positivism revisited[65]

While few works in international law have sought to give a detailed conceptualisation of classical legal positivism as a coherent approach or method in the study or practice of international law, Stephen Hall has recently provided a useful summation of what is commonly accepted as the classical position, which he claims can be defined by three core legal dogmas:[66]

- in contrast to the preceding natural law tradition, classical legal positivism did not merely make a claim to the validity of positive law as *one species of* international law, but asserted the necessary positivity of international law in its entirety;
- it claimed that for law to be valid it must have been laid down in some form of historical act by an authorised body, the 'sovereign'; and,
- it denied any *necessary* connection between the reasonableness or moral character of a legal norm and its legal validity as such.

[64] Kennedy, n. 17 at 121 (emphasis added). [65] Bernstorff, Chapter 3.

[66] Stephen Hall, 'The Persistent Spectre: Natural Law, International Order and the Limits of Legal Positivism' 12 *EJIL* (2001) 269–307 at 272.

How accurate are these criteria as a summation of those late-nineteenth- and early-twentieth-century jurists professing to adhere to a positivist method? In relation to Hall's first criterion, as we saw in the previous section, many of the jurists labelled as positivists in the nineteenth century actually retained a residual role for natural law in providing a basis for legal principles in the absence of positive codification, just as others maintained an important role for reason or juridical conscience in giving shape to the positive law. Nevertheless, as equally noted, argumentation from natural law began to lack legitimacy towards the end of the nineteenth century, ushering in a more exclusive positivist method (espoused in particular by Oppenheim). In this respect, Roberto Ago has similarly maintained that the defining feature of classical positivism was its disavowal of any other form of law other than positive law.[67] For Ago, this can be contrasted to an older tradition – running from Grotius through to Vattel – where the positive law (*ius positum*) and natural law (*ius naturale*) were seen to coexist as part of a total corpus of binding international legal principles.[68]

Insofar as one can therefore accept the assertion that classical positivism recognised only laws which have been in this sense posited, following Ago one can also see how Hall's second and third criteria follow naturally from the first:

> From the principle indicating that the distinctive character of law, of all law, is its historical derivation from certain pre-established 'formal sources,' there comes logically, as a corollary, the idea that legal science has no other means of knowing the legal force of a norm in any given system but to ascertain whether it was 'laid down' historically by a 'formal source' of that system. Thus the method of deducing the legal nature of the norms from their origin in given creative factors is considered to be the only one permissible in this science.[69]

Paulus and Simma, more recently, have developed a similar description of classical positivism, arguing that its distinctive feature was the recognition that the law must be laid down in the correct manner; that is, a norm's legal pedigree is determined by the concrete fact of its promulgation (by the sovereign), not its moral worth or political utility. They write:

67 Roberto Ago, 'Positive Law and International Law' 51 *AJIL* (1957) 691–733; and see also, more recently, Roberto Ago, 'Positivism' in Rudolf Bernhardt (ed.), *Encyclopaedia of Public International Law*, Vol. 3 (Elsevier 1997) 385–393.

68 Ago, 'Positive Law', n. 67 at 696–698; Ago, 'Positivism', n. 67 at 385–386.

69 Ago, 'Positive Law', n. 67 at 701.

> Law is regarded as a unified system of rules that . . . emanate from state will. This system of rules is an 'objective' reality and needs to be distinguished from law 'as it should be.' Classic positivism demands rigorous tests for legal validity. Extralegal arguments, e.g. arguments that have no textual, systemic or historical basis, are deemed irrelevant to legal analysis . . . For international law, this implies that all norms derive their pedigree from one of the traditional sources of international law, custom and treaty.[70]

Recognising that a norm's legal validity (in a narrow sense) derives from its source rather than its intrinsic moral worth or political utility is in itself a largely uncontroversial claim in modern jurisprudence,[71] and indeed is a view shared by self-describing (modern) positivists and many natural lawyers alike.[72] But note here how both Ago and Paulus and Simma do not just stress the idea of formal sources in an abstract sense, but locate the source of legal validity in the will of the state; that is, in the specific act of 'laying down' by the sovereign. Ago continues:

> Not only was it stated that law created by formal sources is the only true law, but all those acts which are not direct or indirect manifestations of the will of the state are excluded from the category of 'formal sources' of positive law, for only the state has the power to lay down legal norms.[73]

Ago traces this idea to the work of the English legal philosopher, John Austin (1790 to 1853), who essentially sought to outline a positivist jurisprudence based on a Hobbesian conception of sovereignty, whereby a law's binding force depended on its promulgation by a sovereign authority. International law being concerned with the 'conduct of sovereigns considered as related to one another',[74] Austin famously claimed that international law was (like municipal public law) not law as such, but at best 'positive morality',[75] for 'every positive law is set by a given sovereign

70 Bruno Simma and Andreas L. Paulus, 'The Responsibility of Individuals for Human Rights Abuses in Internal Conflicts: A Positivist View' 93 *AJIL* (1999) 302–316 at 304–305.

71 Positive law, as Ago observes, is not about consent as such, but just the need to demonstrate the positing of legal norms. It is scientific; it looks for a historical point of time when law was posited by agreed procedure. Ago, 'Positive Law', n. 67 at 698.

72 E.g. Gerald Postema, 'Law's Autonomy and Public Practical Reasoning' in Robert George (ed.), *The Autonomy of Law: Essays on Legal Positivism* (Clarendon Press 1996) 79–119 at 81–82. See also the preface to Robert George (ed.), *The Autonomy of Law: Essays on Legal Positivism* (Clarendon Press 1996) vii–viii, where he notes a certain accord between positivists and natural lawyers in this respect.

73 Ago, 'Positive Law', n. 67 at 698.

74 John Austin, *Lectures on Jurisprudence or the Philosophy of Positive Law* (Robert Campbell (ed.), 4th edn John Murray 1873) 231.

75 Austin, n. 74 at 188.

to a person or persons in a state of subjection to its author'.[76] As soon as this connection between formal source and sovereign will is made, one can better understand how the methodological critique arises. For Ago, two alternatives appear open to international lawyers: either to deny the ontological reality of international law, or to derive its binding force from the will of states through their own agreement. It is this latter alternative which is often associated with the kind of neo-Hegelian theory of *Selbstverpflichtungslehre* ('auto-limitation') propounded most famously by Jellinek,[77] which essentially results in a view of international law as 'external public law'.[78] As Ago notes, looked at from this perspective it is difficult to distinguish classical legal positivism from a theory of state voluntarism.[79] This view is echoed also by Paulus and Simma who expressly associate classical legal positivism with the kind of voluntarist rhetoric endorsed by the PCIJ in the *Lotus* case (above).[80] Reading classical positivism as a theory of state voluntarism, one can thus see how the criticism of amorality emerges, with positivism seen as buttressing a position where 'might makes right'.[81]

However, as a unifying claim, the idea of the nineteenth century as imbued with a voluntarist-positivist legal dogma has tended to both exaggerate and oversimplify the influence of (neo-)Hegelian ideas of sovereign freedom,[82] particularly as such views seem to underpin the kind of voluntarist dictum which was, in any event, *only later* espoused by the PCIJ in the *Lotus* case in 1927. Certainly, there was a distinctive stream of philosophically informed, continental (though largely Germanic) jurisprudence, which took its cue largely from Jellinek's formulation of the *Selbstverpflichtungslehre*,[83] but such theories were critically received by most, and were largely caricatured more than they were investigated in detail.[84] In fact, Jellinek's theory of auto-limitation is easily

[76] Austin, n. 74 at 188.

[77] Georg Jellinek, *Die rechtliche Natur der Staatenverträge* (A. Hölder 1880) 2, 42–49, 56–58.

[78] The term 'external public law' comes from Koskenniemi's reading of Jellinek: Koskenniemi, 'Nineteenth Century', n. 23 at 145. The idea of 'äußeres Staatsrecht' can be found much earlier in the work of Hegel himself: Georg Wilhelm Friedrich Hegel, *Grundlinien der Philosophie des Rechts* (1821) §§ 330–340.

[79] Ago, 'Positive Law', n. 67 at 699.

[80] Paulus and Simma, n. 70 at 303.

[81] Hall, n. 66 at 270.

[82] Shlomo Avineri, *Hegel's Theory of the Modern State* (Cambridge University Press 1972), particularly 200–205, where he deals with the implications of this theory for Hegel's view of international law.

[83] See discussion in Koskenniemi, *Gentle Civilizer*, n. 23 at 179–265.

[84] E.g. Koskenniemi, n. 5 at 128.

misunderstood as implying a view of 'might makes right' when, in fact, his position is underpinned by a much more objectivist account of state purpose, and the constraining influence of social interaction.[85] Nevertheless, Triepel and Anzilotti both rejected Jellinek's more philosophical account, for a more socio-empirical basis for international law's validity, which derived the binding force of the law from agreements between states (*Vereinbarung*),[86] although Anzilotti later moved to a more explicitly normativist framework influenced by the work of Hans Kelsen.[87] Underlying both, however, is an ethical precept, or an assumption of sociability on the part of states which sits outside the system of international law, which it precedes, and to which it gives force.[88]

Insofar as the idea of the *Selbstverpflichtungslehre* was influential for others, particularly for the German *émigré*, Oppenheim,[89] few jurists – Oppenheim included – developed this into the kind of sovereigntist dogma which we now associate with the *Lotus* case.[90] In fact, what became a more noticeable trend from this time was – as Triepel and Anzilotti's approach suggested – the need to ground the validity of rules in the consent of a community, or society of states, as distinct from its members (either individually or in aggregate). One can see this in Oppenheim's work, where he outlines three conditions for the objective existence of international law:

> There must, first, be a community. There must, secondly, be a body of rules for human conduct within that community. And there must, thirdly,

[85] Koskenniemi, *Gentle Civilizer*, n. 23 at 201, where he notes how criticisms of Jellinek's position 'fail . . . to address [his] move away from a pure voluntarism into a more genuinely sociological understanding of the law in terms of the structural constraints imposed on State will by the environment'.

[86] See generally Heinrich Triepel, *Völkerrecht und Landesrecht* (C. L. Hirschfeld 1899), and Heinrich Triepel, *Droit international et droit interne* (Pedone 1920) 27–61; Dionisio Anzilotti, *Corso di Diritto Internazionale* (4th edn CEDAM 1955) 82–85. See further Giorgio Gaja, 'Positivism and Dualism in Dionisio Anzilotti' 3 *EJIL* (1992) 123–138 at 127.

[87] See discussion in Gaja, n. 86.

[88] Dionisio Anzilotti, *Scritti di Diritto Internazionale* (CEDAM 1957), 57; and see remarks of Gaja, n. 86 at 127.

[89] However, Oppenheim expressly distanced his own approach from that of Triepel (as much as Jellinek and others). On both this influence and Oppenheim's distinctive approach, see Mathias Schmoeckel, 'The Internationalist as a Scientist and Herald: Lassa Oppenheim' 11 *EJIL* (2000) 699–712 at 701–702, 705–709.

[90] Schmoeckel, n. 89 at 707. Although, as a counterpoint, see the work of Alfred Lasson, *Princip und Zukunft des Völkerrechts* (Hertz 1871), discussed in detail in Koskenniemi, *Gentle Civilizer*, n. 23 at 32–33.

> be a common consent of that community that these rules shall be enforced by external power. *It is not an essential condition either that such rules of conduct should be written rules, or that there should be a law-making authority or a law-administering court within the community concerned.*[91]

What was therefore at the base of international law's binding force for Oppenheim, ultimately, was what he referred to as the 'family of nations'; a concept that was not merely an aggregation of the particular interests of states, but an a priori assumption about their inherent sociability.[92] As Schmoeckel claims:

> [Oppenheim] did not have to adopt Jellinek's theory of self-restraint as the foundation of law... Law was not forced on states because they live in a society, but living in society causes the will to consent. Both seem very close in theory and may have been influenced by the same sources, yet they formed distinct approaches.[93]

It was only by differentiating the whole from its constituent parts in this way that international lawyers felt that they were able to sustain the idea of international law as an autonomous order, binding upon states.[94] This presumption of sociability, or idea of a society or community of states, is the analytical framework upon which classical positivism proceeds.[95] As Anghie asserts:

> [S]ociety, rather than sovereignty, is the central concept used to construct the system of international law... Despite the positivist claims that the sovereign was the exclusive basis for the international system, *it was only if society was introduced into the system that positivists could approximate the idea of 'law' to which they urged adherence.* Society, then, provides the matrix of ideas, the analytical resources which allied with sovereignty, could establish a positivist international legal order.[96]

International law was legitimate as based in state consent, but this was a broader, community will, not necessarily the same as the aggregated interests of each state in isolation.[97] One can see this quite explicitly –

91 Lassa Oppenheim, *International Law: A Treatise*, Vol. 1 (Ronald F. Roxburgh (ed.), 3rd edn Longmans, Green and Co. 1920) 7 (emphasis added).

92 Kingsbury, n. 58 at 409.

93 Schmoeckel, n. 89 at 707; see also Anthony Carty, 'Why Theory? – The Implications for International Law Teaching' in Philip Allott *et al.*, *Theory and International Law: An Introduction* (British Institute of International and Comparative Law 1991) 73–104 at 81.

94 Anghie, n. 5 at 47. 95 Anghie, n. 5 at 48.

96 Anghie, n. 5 at 48 (emphasis added).

97 Triepel makes this point explicitly: Triepel, *Völkerrecht*, n. 86 at 56.

and perhaps much more pragmatically – in the approach of many of the English jurists who sought to demonstrate the limitations of Austin's conception of legal positivism. Westlake, for instance, claimed that Austin had not exactly erred, jurisprudentially speaking, but had narrowed down his enquiry too far by ignoring the fact that the ultimate binding force of law depended on the willingness of any society to ensure its enforcement.[98] Westlake described the normative autonomy of the law as related to an underlying social interest or a collective will opposable to that of the individual state;[99] or as he put this himself, law could be found and enforced through the 'general *consensus* of opinion within the limits of European civilisation'.[100]

The stress on the close connection between law and society – *ubi societas ibi ius est* – was a recurring rhetoric from this time, each concept mutually supporting the other. For instance, although a more state-centric concept of community than that applied by Westlake, Oppenheim's idea of a 'family of nations' fulfilled a similar function, as we saw above, ultimately securing the binding force of law through the 'common consent' of the community as a whole.[101] For an avowed positivist, such as Oppenheim, Austin was clearly mistaken in missing the social aspect of legal enforcement:

> [M]unicipal law, constitutional law, ecclesiastical law, and international law are all branches of the same tree of law in general as a body of rules for the conduct of the members of a community, which rules shall by common consent of the community be *eventually* enforced by external power, in contradistinction to rules of morality which by common consent of a community concerned are to be enforced by conscience only.[102]

Oppenheim accepted a central tenet of Austin's theory – i.e. the need for material sanction in the law – but claimed that Austin had simply confused the nature of sanction in international law, which relied on mechanisms of self-help rather than centralised authority.[103] Others, however, played down the differences between national and international law. For instance, Lawrence claimed that even at the domestic level the 'command theory' had been discredited, with the recognition that public

98 Westlake, n. 40 at 11–15; John Westlake, *International Law: Part I, Peace* (Cambridge University Press 1904) 7–8.

99 Westlake, n. 40 at 16.

100 Westlake, n. 40 at 78.

101 Oppenheim, n. 43 at 317, 331; see also Oppenheim, n. 91 at 3–7.

102 Oppenheim, n. 43 at 331 (emphasis added).

103 Oppenheim, n. 91 at 11.

opinion had replaced the need for physical force as the core of juridical sanction.[104] Similarly, perhaps the archetypal legal positivist, W. E. Hall (1835 to 1894), argued that the sanction of international law lay in international public opinion rather than organised force.[105] International law was thus clearly less perfectly formed than domestic law, but this difference did not denigrate the former's categorisation as law per se.

In all, there was widespread acknowledgement that, lacking centralised organs to embody this societal or community will, the international system was less well developed than domestic legal orders. But while this might have detracted from the material completeness of international law, it did not undermine its conceptual autonomy as such.[106] There was still a sufficient similarity between domestic and international legal orders in order to make the comparison; as Westlake noted:

> [S]tates live together in the civilised world substantially as men live together in a state, *the difference being one of machinery*, and we are entitled to say that there is a society of states and a law of that society, without going beyond reasonable limits in assimilating variant cases to the typical case.[107]

However, this observation is revealing of a second idea crucial in sustaining this vision for legal autonomy: the idea of international law's development possessing a clear teleology. By claiming that international law's structural dissimilarities compared to domestic law related to its material or institutional underdevelopment, this provided a 'scientific' means for predicting the future evolution of international law. Although many international lawyers had answers to how international law could be enforced in a material way in a decentralised legal order – for example, Oppenheim's reliance on self-help – most drew also on historical and teleological argument in order to demonstrate how international law would develop a more centralised architecture in future.[108] By claiming that international law's structural dissimilarities compared to domestic law related to its material or institutional underdevelopment, this provided a means by which to account for the dissimilarity between international

104 Lawrence, n. 48 at 20–23.

105 William Edward Hall, *A Treatise on International Law* (2nd edn Clarendon Press 1884) 14–15. See also a similar view espoused by the American jurist, Elihu Root: 'The Sanction of International Law' 2 *AJIL* (1908) 451–457. See also Koskenniemi, *Gentle Civilizer*, n. 23 at 82–83, on the presumption of an inherent sociability underlying Hall's position.

106 Westlake, n. 40 at 12.

107 Westlake, n. 40 at 7 (emphasis added).

108 Oppenheim, n. 43 at 317–318.

and domestic legal orders while at the same time strengthening the basis of the comparison itself.

This teleological argument underpins the sociological claim. The two rely on each other: it was only by acknowledging international society as similar to domestic states that late-nineteenth and early-twentieth-century jurists could sustain the idea that it was binding as positive law in the same way; but it was only in assuming that international law would necessarily develop in the future to more fully approximate this domestic paradigm that they could sustain the basis of the comparison in the first place. By introducing teleology into the argument, Austin's criticism can be turned on its head as a means of response; international law's weaknesses help prove its similarity to the 'typical case'.

One can clearly see here the influence of the historical jurisprudence developed by Maine, the predecessor of Oppenheim and Westlake in the Whewell Chair at Cambridge.[109] The use of such evolutionary argument allowed lawyers to dismiss Austin, without undermining the basis of the comparison between international and domestic legal orders. Simply by placing his command theory on a linear historical trajectory, they were able to account for positive international law, like the 'law of nations' tradition before it, as an earlier (and imperfect) stage of societal development.[110] As Maine was forced to conclude:

> The want of coercive power is, in fact, the one important drawback which attends all attempts to improve International Law by contrivances imitated from the internal economy of states, by something like legislation, and by something like the administration of law by organised tribunals.[111]

5 Straw men, scapegoats and the claim to legal autonomy

This attempt to correct Austin's mistakes, just as Triepel and Anzilotti attempted to correct Jellinek's, nevertheless comes at something of a high price. However crude Austin's command theory might have been, in their attempts to refute him many late-nineteenth-century jurists also,

[109] As Berman notes, this historicist approach seemed primarily to be aimed at tempering the more nihilistic implications of Austin's claims, but without 'recourse to the more murky [sic] (and less legitimate) forms of natural law thinking'. Harold Berman, 'World Law Transcendent' 54 *Emory Law Journal* (2005) 53–77 at 55.

[110] Maine, n. 32 at 53. For a detailed exposition of Maine's theory in this respect, see the arguments of Sylvest, n. 20 at 42–43.

[111] Henry Sumner Maine, *International Law: A Series of Lectures Delivered Before the University of Cambridge 1887* (John Murray 1888), 213.

at least in part, subtly buttress his main argument. In making the comparison between international and domestic legal orders and accounting for the difference between them, these jurists set international law up against a command-based ideal. They might have argued that Austin had misunderstood the basis of sanction in international law (for example, Hall, Lawrence, Oppenheim), confused a condition of the possibility of international law with the current state of international organisation (for example, Westlake), or just thought him overly pedantic in what could constitute law in the first place (for example, Lawrence). But for all concerned, a collective anxiety remained as to the fragility of the edifice of international law as a fledgling order of positive law. The lack of organised and centralised mechanisms for enforcing, adjudicating upon or developing the law appeared – whatever way they could justify it – as international law's distinct institutional weakness or imperfection.[112]

To be clear, my point is not to endorse an Austinian understanding of international law. Rather, I seek to show how its main flaw has been overlooked. By accepting a concept of law (however modified or qualified) based on domestic experience, most late-nineteenth-century jurists dealt mostly with the empirical observations underpinning Austin's theory, often over-simplifying its central point;[113] but also missing its overall conceptual weakness. It is true that Austin saw the study of jurisprudence as concerned solely with the study of positive law, and that, for him, positive law could only be derived from the will of the sovereign. However, at no point did Austin deny that what he classified as positive morality was any less binding than positive law (nor in fact did Austin deny that there was such a thing as natural law). However, he thought that legal science should be concerned to study only those laws which actually pertained in any given society in an observable sense – otherwise, one risked substituting one's own moral sensibilities for rules actually in force. As he noted:

> Grotius, Puffendorf, and the other writers on the so called law of nations, have fallen into a . . . confusion of ideas: they have confounded positive international morality, *or the rules which actually obtain among civilised nations in their mutual intercourse*, with their own vague conceptions of international morality as it *ought to be*, with that indeterminate something which they conceive it would be, if it conformed to that indeterminate something which they call the law of nature.[114]

[112] Lawrence, n. 48 at 252 and generally. [113] Lobban, n. 23 at 80.
[114] Austin, n. 74 at 222 (emphasis added).

As is clear from this paragraph, Austin clearly saw international law as consisting of rules of conduct applicable to states, but saw a danger of distortion if one were to theorise it on the same basis as either natural law or positive law. Austin's purpose was one of classification, believing that a better understanding of different forms of law would lead to their improvement – he, like his mentor, Bentham, having a clear preference for the certainty and efficacy of positive law.[115] In that respect, his classification of international law (and domestic constitutional law) as positive morality was not to suggest that the sovereign was free from any limitations, nor to deny that international law (even if he believed it should be referred to as positive morality) did not bind sovereign states.[116]

My point here is not that Austin's conceptualisation of domestic law's binding force was correct – the deficiencies of his approach as a conceptualisation of legal normativity generally have been set out convincingly by HLA Hart, among others[117] – but rather that if one sets out to demonstrate that international law can be theorised as a coercive system by reference to a paradigm of legality developed in a domestic context, then something like the Austinian challenge will arise as a challenge to the cogency of the comparison. As Anghie notes, Austin had already anticipated, for example, Oppenheim's argument of the common basis of custom in all forms of law; his point was merely that it would remain (for him) a form of positive morality, rather than law, until it had been recognised in common law (by a court) or statute (by a legislature).[118] That it would be

[115] Jeremy Bentham, *An Introduction to the Principles of Morals and Legislation* (J. H. Burns, HLA Hart (eds), Athlone Press 1970). In fact, Bentham had made similarly critical remarks about the weakness of international law conceived not as a positive law. See remarks quoted in Mark W. Janis, 'Jeremy Bentham and the Fashioning of "International Law"' 74 *AJIL* (1984) 405–423 at 411–412. There are important differences in their respective approaches, however. On this point, see further d'Aspremont, n. 57 at 47–48.

[116] See, in particular, Thomas Broden Jr, 'The Straw Man of Legal Positivism' 34 *Notre Dame Law Review* (1958–1959) 530–555 at 531–535. That an adoption of Austin's jurisprudential frame need not necessarily lead to a denial of the existence of international law is no more evident than in the work of Thomas Holland, who not only wrote an influential text on the study of jurisprudence (*Elements of Jurisprudence* (12th edn Oxford University Press 1916) which adopted Austin's central claim that international law had only moral force, but he was also a celebrated international lawyer of his time (occupying the Chichele Chair at Oxford for thirty-six years, from 1874–1910) and a leading member of the *Institut*. While he saw international law as law by analogy only, Holland differed from Austin only in his classification of international law as 'private law writ large' (at 134–135, 394).

[117] E.g. HLA Hart, *The Concept of Law* (2nd edn Oxford University Press 1994) 18–25.

[118] Anghie, n. 5 at 46.

better if international law evolved to introduce central organs designed to enhance this element of legal certainty was rarely contested by international lawyers at the time, or by many since.

Ultimately, by trying to account for international law's source and authority using concepts derived from domestic legal experience, the late-nineteenth-century professionals erected a view of positive international law as a fragile edifice, craving the legal certainty of autonomous law-giving, adjudicating and enforcing institutions evident in the paradigmatic legal archetype drawn from domestic experience.[119] And by arguing that nineteenth-century jurists had failed to find a convincing ground for international law's autonomy (rather than questioning the basis on which this autonomy was theorised), the exact same problem faced the *interbellum* jurists and explains why the discipline fractured in the way that it did. For sceptics like Morgenthau, the answer was to deny the possibility of autonomy in international law; for a progressive mainstream, following in the footsteps of, for example, Lauterpacht, the desire for legal autonomy has become a postponed goal, requiring the building of institutional structures capable of functionally compensating for international law's formal constitutional weakness. As Lauterpacht was to put this:

> International law can form part of jurisprudence only when its present imperfections are regarded as transient. These imperfections are fundamental, and it is only because they are deemed to be provisional that it is possible to treat international law as part of jurisprudence. Once they are regarded as permanent, international law vanishes completely from the horizon of jurisprudence.[120]

Such a conclusion seems inevitable if one attempts, as many modern international lawyers do, to follow in the footsteps of an analytical jurisprudence tradition which itself has sought to explain international law's reality according to an ideal of legality developed with reference to domestic

[119] It was the troubling nature of this paradox which pushed Holland to describe international law as the 'vanishing point of jurisprudence' – the point being that a command-led view of the law seemed to simply make international law vanish into (super-)state law. Holland, n. 116 at 369.

[120] Hersch Lauterpacht, 'The Place of International Law in Jurisprudence' in Elihu Lauterpacht (ed.), *International Law: Being the Collected Papers of Hersch Lauterpacht*, Vol. 1 (Cambridge University Press 1970) 193–215 at 208 (paper originally published in French as Hersch Lauterpacht, 'Règles générales du droit de la paix' 62 *Recueil des Cours* (1937) 95–422). Lauterpacht was making reference here to Holland's assertion that international law was the 'vanishing point of jurisprudence'. Holland, n. 116 at 369.

legal orders.[121] To explain international law as an ordered, hierarchical legal order in this way seems to highlight its weaknesses and primitiveness at the institutional level – as both Kelsen and Hart were both later forced to admit.[122] International law's apparent 'immaturity', particularly its failings when compared to national legal systems, has remained a source of constant apologia in international legal scholarship. Such anxieties seem ingrained into the very substance of international law as a professional discipline and academic practice, which has to constantly reassert its relevance as a controlling force in international affairs. However, that international law should act as a controlling force in this way is an assumption which has undergone little scrutiny within the terms of the inherited theoretical frame which has been bestowed from classical to modern international law.

6 Conclusion

That modern international law moves within this inherited frame is difficult to deny. Rather than revisit the assumptions upon which modern international law has been erected, the modern discipline exists responding to a challenge of the denial of its autonomy according to a concept of legality ill-suited to ground any such claim. Classical jurists' attempts to account for international law against this paradigm had built a 'straw-man' figure of Austin's theory as a denial of the law's autonomy, without seeing its conceptual weakness as a tool by which to explain such autonomy in international law. *Inter-bellum* jurists distanced their own approaches from a 'straw-man' figure of classical legal positivism, without seeing how their own approaches adopted the same assumptions which had failed pre-war jurists. And it is of little surprise that the 'modern positivism' which characterises much of today's mainstream scholarship has

[121] I reflect on this more in Richard Collins, 'Modernist-Positivism and the Problem of Institutional Autonomy in International Law' in Richard Collins, Nigel White (eds), *International Organizations and the Idea of Autonomy: Institutional Independence in the International Legal Order* (Routledge 2011) 22–47.

[122] For Kelsen's views on the primitiveness of international law, see Hans Kelsen, 'Théorie du droit international public' 84 *Recueil des Cours* (1953) 1–201 at 31–34, 131. He expressed this view most explicitly, perhaps, in his political writings: e.g. Hans Kelsen, *Law and Peace in International Relations, The Oliver Wendell Holmes Lectures* (Harvard University Press 1942) esp. 51–55. See Hart's discussion of international law in Hart, n. 117 at 213–237. The perception of international law as a primitive or otherwise deficient legal order has been a recurring theme in international law scholarship. E.g. Angus Campbell, 'International Law and Primitive Law' 8 *Oxford Journal of Legal Studies* (1988) 169–196.

become vulnerable to a further, post-modern attack. As Koskenniemi has argued, burying the knowledge of this theoretical incongruence behind a veil of institutional pragmatism, many modern jurists have assumed 'that frustration about theory can be overcome by becoming technical, or doctrinal'.[123] In that sense, the scapegoat of a demonised classical legal positivism lives on in the modern psyche as the embodiment of the problem to which modern jurists are themselves unable to convincingly respond: the problem of legal autonomy in a world of sovereign states.

123 Koskenniemi, n. 5 at 687.

3

German intellectual historical origins of international legal positivism

JOCHEN VON BERNSTORFF*

> Subjective and objective notions of law are locked in a struggle over contemporary jurisprudence. The theory of international law, in particular, vacillates back and forth uncertainly between the antipodes of a state-individualistic and a human-universalistic perspective, between the subjectivism of the primacy of the legal order of the state and the objectivism of the primacy of international law . . . [1]

1 Introduction

The German nineteenth-century international law discourse is profoundly shaped by the concept of freedom in the tradition of German idealism and by the notion of the 'state' as a personified organism. It reflected within the field of international law the deeper philosophical debate over how order can be conceptualised on the basis of a strong notion of individual autonomy. How can an objective order above the state emerge out of pure subjectivity, the latter consisting of volatile individual preferences of free sovereigns? Those German-speaking writers who thought of themselves as 'positivists' used different methodological conceptions in their search for an 'objective' principle of international law. Their aim was to contribute to a theoretical harmonisation of the presumed binding nature of international law, on the one hand, with the Hegelian assumption that the free sovereign will of the state formed

* This is a revised version of: Jochen von Bernstorff, *The Public International Law Theory of Hans Kelsen: Believing in Universal Law* (Cambridge University Press 2010) 15–43.

1 Hans Kelsen, *Das Problem der Souveränität und die Theorie des Völkerrechts: Beitrag zu einer reinen Rechtslehre* (2nd edn J. C. B. Mohr 1928) 319–320.

the basis of the validity of international law, on the other. Such a construct posed considerable problems for those who wrote about international law, because in contrast to state law, there was no central authority that stood above the states and was charged with enacting norms and enforcing the law. Those who created the law and those to whom it was addressed were one and the same.

Moreover, German international legal discourse was shaped by various methodological reorientations in general nineteenth-century jurisprudence,[2] out of which decidedly anti-naturalist approaches increasingly dominated the German scholarly scene over the course of the century. The search for an objective principle of international law assumed central importance in the second half of the nineteenth century precisely because a simple identification of international legal norms with rules of morality and reason seemed increasingly untenable under the reign of 'positivist' sensibilities in general German jurisprudence and German public law. In this peculiar German nineteenth-century intellectual landscape, international law became engraved with the semantic imprint of German *Staatswillenspositivismus.* In what follows, I will engage with the works of some of the most influential German nineteenth-century international law scholars in an attempt to trace an intellectual tradition, which became foundational for international legal positivism all over Europe in the early twentieth century.

2 Kaltenborn and the 'objective principle' of international law

In 1847, Carl Kaltenborn, in his *Kritik des Völkerrechts* (*A Critique of the Law of Nations*), had undertaken a comprehensive analysis of the textbooks on international law that had appeared in Germany in the first half of the century.[3] On the basis of this critical examination, he went on to develop his own positivistic approach to international law, which would substantially shape Kelsen's theory of international law that emerged sixty years later. Kaltenborn had published his *Kritik des Völkerrechts* at a time that was particularly fruitful for the German field of international jurisprudence. The work of the same title published by Heinrich von

[2] On the contemporary public law landscape comprehensively: Michael Stolleis, *Public Law in Germany, 1800–1914* (Pamela Biel (tr.), Berghahn Books 2001) 313.

[3] Carl Kaltenborn von Stachau, *Kritik des Völkerechts: Nach dem jetzigen Stand der Wissenschaft* (Gustav Mayer 1847) 266, on the 'common international existence' (*internationale Gemeinexistenz*) as the first principle of the law of nations.

Gagern as early as 1840 had ended what Kaltenborn called a time of 'lazy stagnation', and it had sparked a series of fundamental monographs on international law over the next seven years.[4] As Kaltenborn noted in his introduction:

> Added to this is the fact that precisely the abundant recent literature has laid an important groundwork for criticism, and because of the strictly scientific character of the post-Gagern achievements, especially for learned criticism. The splendid studies of the likes of Heffter, Pütter, Oppenheim, Wheaton, Cussy, and Stein have made a scientific critique of international law easier, though they have inevitably also raised the bar for such a critique.[5]

His critique of the literature on international law, which took Grotius as its starting point, was based on a concept of modernisation. For Kaltenborn, a modern 'science' of international law had to proceed first of all from the positive law of nations of the European states. To that extent, Georg Friedrich von Martens had laid a foundation stone for a 'further elevation of the positive science of international law' through his '*Primae lineae juris gentium Europaearum practici*' from 1785. His grasp of the genuinely positive material had made him the father of the nineteenth-century science of international law.[6]

Since that time, however, the field had not moved beyond the collection and arbitrary systematisation of the positive material.[7] Still missing was a philosophical permeation of the positive material, in the sense of an identification of the highest objective principles.[8] Although various attempts at a philosophical interpretation of positive international law had been undertaken in recent times, these had not led to the establishment of an objective principle of international law:

> Fully in the spirit of this general subjective direction of philosophy, the more recent conception and account of the philosophy of law, and especially of the philosophy of international law, is encumbered with a subjective type. All the numerous treatments of the law from a philosophical point of view, especially those of Kant, Fichte, and Hegel, more or less carry the stamp of subjectivity within themselves.[9]

[4] Heinrich von Gagern, *Critik des Völkerrechts: Mit praktischer Anwendung auf unsere Zeit* (F. A. Brockhaus 1840).

[5] Kaltenborn, n. 3 at 9–10. [6] Kaltenborn, n. 3 at 101. [7] Kaltenborn, n. 3 at 103.

[8] Kaltenborn, n. 3 at 128. [9] Kaltenborn, n. 3 at 129–130.

Kaltenborn was referring to the reception of Kantian or Hegelian philosophy in the science of international law, which had supposedly led to international law being given a state-focused, subjectivist foundation.

A closer look at Kaltenborn's critique of the 'subjective principle' in international jurisprudence in the first half of the century must be preceded by an explanation of how this term was used in Hegel and Kant.

2.1 The 'subjective principle' in Kant and Hegel

For Kant, 'a state, as a moral person, is considered as living in relation to another state in the condition of natural freedom and therefore in a condition of constant war'.[10] This tenet, which goes back to Hobbes and which Kant took from Pufendorf,[11] applied the state of nature between humans to relations between states. For Kant, however, the goal of international law in the sense of an a priori postulate of reason was the gradual overcoming of the subjective will of the states by creating universal peace as a legal state of affairs (*Rechtszustand*). Although 'perpetual peace' remained for Kant an 'unachievable idea', the constant approximation to this condition through a permanent league or congress of states was a task for humans and states.[12]

Hegel, by contrast, described international law as 'external state law' (*äußeres Staatsrecht*). The foundation of this law was the 'autonomy' of nations, which, and here he agreed with Kant, were in a state of nature in their relationships to one another.[13] The law between states rested merely on its recognition, interpretation and application by the individual states.[14] Because of the principle of autonomy, the rights of states

[10] Immanuel Kant, *The Metaphysics of Morals* (Mary Gregor (tr., ed.), Cambridge University Press 1996) 114 (§ 53).

[11] Thomas Hobbes, *Leviathan* (1651) 92–96; on the history of the reception of Hobbes, see Heinhard Steiger, 'Völkerrecht' in Otto Brunner, Werner Conze, Reinhart Koselleck (eds), *Geschichtliche Grundbegriffe: Historisches Lexikon zur politisch-sozialen Sprache in Deutschland*, Vol. 7 (Klett-Cotta 1992) 97–140 at 115.

[12] Kant, n. 10 at 119 (§ 61); this was not a world republic or world state, which Kant regarded as impossible because of the fear of despotism by a supreme ruler; see Heinhard Steiger, 'Völkerrecht und Naturrecht zwischen Christian Wolff und Adolf Lasson' in Diethelm Klippel (ed.), *Naturrecht im 19. Jahrhundert: Kontinuität, Inhalt, Funktion, Wirkung* (Keip 1997) 45–74 at 54–56.

[13] Georg Wilhelm Friedrich Hegel, *Die Philosophie des Rechts: die Mitschriften Wannemann (Heidelberg 1817/18) und Homeyer (Berlin 1818/19)* (Karl-Heinz Ilting (ed.), Klett-Cotta 1983) 159 (§ 159).

[14] Hegel, n. 13 at 193 (§ 161), and Ilting's commentary at 348.

towards each other had their reality only in a special, and not in a constitutionalised, general will.[15] Given that treaties of international law in the Hegelian system had no reality within the 'general will', their observance should, in the final analysis, also be left to the discretion of the states: '[a] mere ought-to-hold (*Haltensollen*) of the tractates takes effect. This ought is a coincidence.'[16]

Thus, in Hegel, in contrast to Kant, a continuous approximation to a 'perpetual peace' through the gradual overcoming of the subjective principle in the sense of an a priori postulate of reason is not possible. Rather, in Hegel, the place of the Kantian league of peace is taken by the historical-philosophical assumption of 'world history as world judgment', in which competing 'national spirits' struggle for hegemony.[17] According to the Hegelian approach of 'external state law', later adopted by Karl Theodor Pütter,[18] international law thus has its reality only in the sovereign will of individual states. For Pütter, the 'peculiar nature of international law lies in the fact that the will of the state, in its conduct toward other nations, is self-determined with absolute freedom'.[19]

2.2 Humanity as a 'community of law' in Kaltenborn

In his quest for an objective philosophical principle of international law, Kaltenborn subjected especially the Hegelian construct of international law to a sharp critique. He described the sole recourse to the 'subjective principle' of the sovereign will of the state in Pütter as too one-sided a construct. Such an idolisation of the state excluded a priori the notion of a higher order – in the sense of an international community – above the states.[20]

This critique of the Hegelian doctrines of international law already adumbrated Kaltenborn's own conception. To him, the state is not the highest and absolute institution of the law. There is still a higher community, one that makes the state appear as a subordinate branch of a higher

[15] Hegel, n. 13 at 193 (§ 162). [16] Hegel, n. 13 at 193 (§ 162).

[17] Georg Wilhelm Friedrich Hegel, *Grundlinien der Philosophie des Rechts* (Eva Moldenhauer, Karl Markus Michel (eds), Suhrkamp 1970) 503–512 (§§ 341–360).

[18] Karl Theodor Pütter, 'Die Staatsehre oder -Souveränetät als Princip des practischen Europäischen Völkerrechts', 6 *Zeitschrift für gesammte Staatswissenschaft* (1850) 299–384 at 304–305 (§ 14); at 307, Pütter himself points to Hegel's philosophy of law as the theoretical foundation of his own scientific elaborations.

[19] Karl Theodor Pütter, *Beiträge zur Völkerrechts-Geschichte und -Wissenschaft* (A. Weinbrack 1843), quoted in Kaltenborn, n. 3 at 163.

[20] Pütter, quoted in Kaltenborn, n. 3 at 163.

legal entity: 'In this way, the legal life of the state, which is inherently only national, is elevated into a general human community of law that goes beyond the nation, into an international order of law.'[21] For Kaltenborn, we are dealing here with the 'objective principle' of international law, which did not, however, rule out the recognition of states as subjects of the international community. Rather, it was not possible for the international community to rise to a height that would completely undermine the 'subjective principle' in the sense of a legitimate autonomy of the individual state.[22]

In Kaltenborn, international law over and above the state thus results from the assumption of an international community that emerges organically from the coexistence of the nations.[23] However, this supreme principle of international law cannot be deduced from the tenets of natural law or reason, but follows from the profound realisation of the historically evolved culture of the European-Christian community of nations.[24] Here, we see Kaltenborn's methodological closeness – demonstrated by Anthony Carty through Kaltenborn's doctrine of sources – to the historical school of law.[25] This methodological orientation also prompted Kaltenborn's critique of Christian Wolff's conception of international law, formulated 100 years earlier. Wolff's work on international law, which Kelsen himself tells us was the inspiration, along with Kaltenborn, for his own theory of international law developed in *Problem der Souveränität*, had declared that the community of international law, as an abstract system, was situated

[21] Here is the full quote: 'But just as the nation is thus merely a part, a branch of humanity, and as a branch of a whole has its wholeness in humanity, the state, as the expression of the legal community of a nation, must recognize in the legal community of states as the political unity of humanity a higher power than himself, and to act as a branch of this higher legal community... In this way, the legal life of the state, which is inherently only national, is elevated into a general human community of law that goes beyond the nation, into an international order of law. If, then, the law is the norm and order for the human community in all its dimensions and gradations, that community of state must be described as the highest and final community of the law. The law here is what one usually calls the law of nations.' Kaltenborn, n. 3 at 260–261.

[22] Kaltenborn, n. 3 at 262.

[23] Kaltenborn, n. 3 at 260.

[24] In this way, the international law that arose in Europe is identified with the international law of all of humanity and in this sense seems indissolubly linked with Christian culture; on this see Steiger, n. 11 at 133.

[25] Anthony Carty, *The Decay of International Law* (Manchester University Press 1986) 30–35; on the legal source doctrine in Kaltenborn, see Ludwik Ehrlich, 'The Development of International Law as a Science' 105 *Recueil des Cours* (1962) 173–265 at 246–247; on the methodological orientation of his work on state law, see Stolleis, n. 2 at 313.

above the state as a '*civitas maxima*'.[26] The idea of the '*civitas maxima*', which originated in Stoicism, was understood by Wolff as a politically organised entity that stood above the state and had a comprehensive legislative authority.[27]

Kaltenborn's critique of Wolff maintained that his construction had been developed purely deductively as an analogy to the natural law conception of international law, and not out of the specific nature of the conditions of the law of nations:[28] 'This deduction seems to us to be completely inadequate, and were it truly possible, it would destroy international law and turn it into state law.'[29] For Kaltenborn, the 'universal state' is an exaggeration of the objective principle of international law. By positing it, Wolff failed to recognise that a certain autonomy of the individual states was justified.[30] Wolff's '*civitas maxima*' was, as Heinhard Steiger has pointed out, the object of criticism early on.[31] Wolff's contemporaries and students already feared that the individual states could be entirely stripped of their sovereignty in a despotic *über*-state.[32]

Despite this criticism, the proximity of Kaltenborn's conception to Wolff's approach on the question of the objectification of international law remains striking. Kaltenborn also rejected the doubts – put forth by the so-called deniers of international law – that international law had the quality of law because it lacked enforceability by referring back to Wolff's notion.[33] The enforcement of international law takes place either through voluntary behaviour on the part of states, through mediation, or – as a final resort – through physical force. The latter option leads to war, which should thus be seen as the implementation of the legal claims of the community:

> War differs only in degree from the other means of enforcing the law. A criminal judge, in the worst case, has an individual beheaded and broken on the wheel. War, in the worst case, destroys the existence of this or that

[26] Christian Freiherr von Wolff, *Jus gentium* (1749), 5–17 (§§ 7–23); on this see Steiger, n. 11 at 114–115; on the reception of Wolff's 'civitas maxima' in Emer de Vattel, see Steiger, n. 12 at 46–53.

[27] Wolff, n. 26 at 9 (§ 11). [28] Kaltenborn, n. 3 at 72. [29] Kaltenborn, n. 3 at 72.

[30] Kaltenborn, n. 3 at 73. [31] Steiger, n. 11 at 115.

[32] Dietrich Heinrich Ludwig von Ompteda, *Litteratur des gesammten sowohl natürlichen als positiven Völkerrechts*, Vol. 1 (1785) 324 (§ 94); however, what was preserved was, e.g., the 'société universelle' in Emer de Vattel, *Das Völkerrecht oder Grundsätze des Naturrechts: angewandt auf das Verhalten und die Angelegenheiten der Staaten und Staatsoberhäupter* (Wilhelm von Euler (tr.), J. C. B. Mohr 1959) 21 (§ 11); instructive: see Steiger, n. 11 at 115.

[33] Kaltenborn, n. 3 at 75.

> criminal state. The fact that at times innocent people are beheaded and that innocent states are defeated or even subjugated in war in spite of their good law negates neither state law nor the international legal order.[34]

That the international community of states possessed a monopoly of force that was implemented in a decentralised fashion by way of lawful wars was something that Wolff had already spelled out 100 years earlier to defend the coercive character of international law.[35]

Both Wolff and later Kaltenborn thus saw international law as an objective law above the state with coercive character. Moreover, in Kaltenborn, this universalistic view of the law of nations, which originated in the natural law concept of the Spanish late scholastics, had found in the nineteenth century a proponent who regarded himself as a positivist. The scientific contradiction between the grounding of international law on a voluntaristic basis of individual states and a view of that law as standing above the state – and thus universalistic – remained alive also in the second half of the nineteenth century. Under changing methodological premises, the discourse on the theory of international law continued to oscillate between the 'subjective' and the 'objective' principle. Within the German-language theory of international law in the second half of the nineteenth century, which was moving increasingly away from the basic assumptions of the historical school of law, the question as to the relationship between the subjective and the objective principle now arose against the backdrop of a specifically juridical construct of international law.

3 Bergbohm and Fricker: 'the problem of international law revisited'

This debate found new nourishment immediately after the founding of the Reich. In 1871, Adolf Lasson had picked up again on the Hegelian approach centred on the individual state. But in his conclusions, he went far beyond Pütter: 'The state can therefore never submit to a legal order, nor, in fact, to any will outside of itself. The state that prevails between states is therefore a completely lawless one.'[36] But this assumption did not prevent Lasson from drawing up a system of prudent rules to which

34 Kaltenborn, n. 3 at 312.

35 'Paradoxum, hoc videbitur iis, qui nexum veritatum non prospiciunt et ex factis jura aestimant . . . Et in genere notandum est, nobis jam quaestionem esse de jure, cujus capaces sunt homines pro conditione praesenti, minime vero de factis, quibus jus vel contemnitur, vel violatur.' Wolff, n. 26 at 11 (§ 13); this passage is invoked by Kaltenborn, n. 3 at 75.

36 Adolf Lasson, *Princip und Zukunft des Völkerrechts* (Wilhelm Hertz 1871) 22.

states should voluntarily adhere. However, given the lack of a supra-state authority endowed with coercive power, for him it was not possible to speak in this context of law.[37]

In a work published six years later, *Staatsverträge und Gesetze als Quellen des Völkerrechts* (*State Treaties and Laws as Sources of International Law*),[38] Carl Bergbohm, a professor from Dorpat, affirmed, on the basis of similar theoretical premises, the legal character of the law of nations. Bergbohm had likewise set international law on the sole foundation of the will of the sovereign state. For Bergbohm, however, international law was not merely 'external state law' in the Hegelian sense, but objective law resting on the will of the state. That was expressed most clearly in the positive treaties of international law.[39] Over the course of history, Bergbohm argued, international law had freed itself increasingly from being intermingled with related matters, such as politics and morality, and was slowly evolving from mere custom and habit to written law:[40] 'The legal norm, which destroys the rule of feeling, wrests itself away from the mere feeling of right (*Rechtsgefühl*), which is subject to every change in sentiment; the subjective-internal conviction becomes the objective-external norm.'[41] Custom appears in Bergbohm as an obsolete, pre-positive source of law, which had to gradually yield to written law as a higher stage of legal development.

Bergbohm criticised the repeated theoretical attempts to devise closed systems or codifications of international law.[42] It was unavoidable in such attempts that gaps would be filled with recourse to the law of reason or politics, which had nothing to do with the positive law of nations.[43] Bergbohm's was a reductionist approach to international law, which sought to explain the existence of objective international law solely from positive 'general state treaties', as, for example, the Act of the Congress of Vienna (1815), the Paris Declaration of Maritime Law of 1856 and the Geneva Convention of 1864. For Bergbohm, law was not, as it still was with

[37] On Lasson, see Klaus Lüderssen, *Genesis und Geltung in der Jurisprudenz* (Suhrkamp 1996) 223–250.

[38] Carl Bergbohm, *Staatsverträge und Gesetze als Quellen des Völkerrechts* (C. Mattiesen 1877).

[39] Bergbohm, n. 38 at 81–101. [40] Bergbohm, n. 38 at 3. [41] Bergbohm, n. 38 at 3–4.

[42] The best-known attempt was that of Bluntschli, who had drawn up a law book built on individual paragraphs, in the sense of a comprehensive codification of the law of nations: Johann Caspar Bluntschli, *Das moderne Völkerrecht der civilisirten Staaten als Rechtsbuch dargestellt* (3rd edn C. H. Beck 1878).

[43] Bergbohm, n. 38 at 8.

Kaltenborn, a historical product of the Christian-European community of states, but a secularised, universally valid expression of the positive will of all 'civilised states' (*Culturstaaten*).[44]

For Bergbohm, the validity of this objective law depended always on the consent of all recognised 'civilised states' as the law-creating 'total authority':

> For this final authority is never a single one, is not a legal unity, but remains always merely an aggregate of sovereign, individual wills, each of which, independent of all others, maintains his territory subject to his law.[45]

Bergbohm's objective law thus consisted of what was in the 1870s still a very fragmentary body of general multilateral treaties, which, moreover, would cease to belong to this body of objective law if merely a single state withdrew from a treaty.[46] As a result of the disregard of a historically evolved body of customary legal norms that was relatively immune to expressions of individual will, the 'subjective principle' had a particularly strong effect in Bergbohm's theory. Because both the genesis as well as the validity of international law was consistently linked to the will of the state as manifested in written law, his objective law remained utterly dependent on the individual expressions of will by the states.

From the perspective of the objective principle, this conception of international law left itself vulnerable by invoking the subjective will of the state as the formal basis of the law. The most pointed critique is found in Karl Viktor Fricker's 1878 essay 'Noch einmal das Problem des Völkerrechts' ('The Problem of International Law Revisited').[47] This was the reincarnation of the quarrel between an 'objective' and a 'subjective' grounding of international law against the backdrop of a changed methodological orientation in public law and an increasingly universalised practice of international law in the last decades of the century. Fricker analysed Bergbohm's voluntaristic foundation from the perspective of the question of whether it was indeed possible to construct an objective law of nations in this way. Forty years later, Kelsen made Fricker's argument the basis of

[44] On the dissolution of the distinction between the law of nations of Europe and of other legal communities outside of Europe into a universal international law, David Kennedy has remarked: 'By the end of the nineteenth century, there was but one sovereignty and one international law.' David Kennedy, 'International Law and the Nineteenth Century: History of an Illusion' 65 *Nordic Journal of International Law* (1996) 385–420 at 411.

[45] Bergbohm, n. 38 at 89.

[46] Bergbohm, n. 38 at 90.

[47] Karl Viktor Fricker, 'Noch einmal das Problem des Völkerrechts' 34 *Zeitschrift für die gesamte Staatswissenschaft* (1878) 368–405.

his critical analysis of the voluntaristic theory that he developed in *Das Problem der Souveränität und die Theorie des Völkerrechts*.[48]

As Fricker saw it, Bergbohm's attempt – using the sovereign will of the state as his basis and simultaneously rejecting a law of nations that stood above the states – to arrive at an 'objective international law' between states in the form of general treaties was doomed to failure from the outset:[49]

> I believe that this attempt has not succeeded and cannot succeed. I do not think it possible to escape the following dilemma: either the wills of the individual states stand above the common will, that is, the latter is in no way detached as a special, objective will from the individual wills – in which case an objective law of nations is unattainable; or the common will, once it has taken shape, stands above the wills of the individual states with its own objective authority – in which case one does arrive at an international law, but the latter is a special will that is distinct from the will of the state.[50]

Nowhere, either before or after Fricker, was the dilemma of the voluntaristic model in the theory of international law spelled out more incisively than in this brief passage. To Fricker, the 'power of the objective law', regardless of whether one described it as between or above the states, lay in the fact that the individual state, once the law has been created with its participation, can no longer unilaterally escape its authority.[51] But it was precisely this construct of a united legal authority in the form of the Kaltenbornian community of states that Bergbohm had replaced with an 'aggregate of sovereign wills of individual states'. By allowing the state to withhold its consent at its own discretion, Bergbohm had relinquished the common objective law of nations he was seeking.[52]

By contrast, Fricker regarded the prerequisite of a higher authority as indispensable for positing an objective law that could claim to have binding force. The lack of a power organised above the states had to be recognised – in agreement with those who denied international law – as a weakness of the international legal order. To that extent, international law was still an incomplete law.[53] A certain degree of organisation had already been achieved in that the state was acting as the organ of international law and thereby endowing the legal order with power.[54] In Fricker's own conception, which he merely adumbrated, the state, following Kaltenborn, became an organ of a community of law that stood above the state. Fricker

[48] Kelsen, n. 1 at 183. [49] Fricker, n. 47 at 368. [50] Fricker, n. 47 at 377.
[51] Fricker, n. 47 at 382. [52] Fricker, n. 47 at 382. [53] Fricker, n. 47 at 395.
[54] Fricker, n. 47 at 398.

thus followed the Wolffian-Kaltenbornian notion of a higher community of states and conceived of international law as the legal order of that community. For him, this legal order was fundamentally capable of developing a stronger, centralised overall authority, even if it should still be seen as incomplete in this regard.[55]

In spite of his fundamental critique of placing international law on a voluntaristic foundation, Fricker sought to end his article, if not on a harmonising, then at least a conciliatory note:

> Bergbohm's notion and the notion of international law as an incomplete law are much closer than Bergbohm believes. They both spring from a critical stance, they both still want to conceive of international law as law, and they both recognize that it cannot be conceived of as a formally structured law above the states. Because B. regards as law only the law in its most developed form, as the will of the state, he has to dissolve the law into a multitude of laws belonging to the individual states and valid for each only as its own will, while the other view, invoking the concept of development, regards the same thing as an attempt to place the actions of states under the rule of law... Bergbohm cannot forego the notion of communality for his law of nations, without, however, being able to conceive of it as something legal; but he does recognize it as a necessary effect of a cultural development. The other view understands this notion itself already as a manifestation of a legal development.[56]

Fricker's view of international law as 'incomplete law' is a conception open to development, one that contains an evolutionary-dynamic component in the direction of a progressive degree of organisation of the community of states, reminiscent of the Kantian *telos* of progressive legal institutionalisation. To that end – and this was going beyond Kant's continuous commitment to state sovereignty – the sovereign will of the state must be transcended in favour of an international community of states pervaded by law. Kelsen would consistently advance this view of international law with the help of his own, new theoretical approach. He received the crucial methodological impulses from his critical engagement with Georg Jellinek's notion of international law.

4 Jellinek as synthesis

In 1880, the Viennese docent Georg Jellinek inserted himself into the 'Bergbohm–Fricker controversy' about the foundation of international law. With the goal of continuing to develop Bergbohm's doctrines

[55] Fricker, n. 47 at 399. [56] Fricker, n. 47 at 399–400.

methodologically, and as an answer, as it were, to Fricker's contribution, Jellinek articulated his own theoretical approach, one that sought to take into account both the objective and the subjective principle of international law. The impact of Jellinek's doctrine of international law was considerable. All large theoretical constructs of international law before the First World War and during the Weimar period entered into an extensive dialogue with Jellinek's conception. In part they did so by adopting his theoretical approach or developing it further, in part, as with the Vienna School, by turning ostentatiously away from it.

Both in his first monograph on international law, *Die rechtliche Natur der Staatenverträge* (*The Legal Nature of State Treaties*, 1880), and in his *Lehre von den Staatenverbindungen* (*Theory of International Federations*, 1882), Jellinek considered it advisable to 'cast a searching look at the foundations and the method of state and international law'.[57] Jellinek claimed to be introducing a new, 'more secure method'[58] for the study of the basic concepts of international law. The law of nations, he argued, should catch up with the 'formal development' of the general notion of law that had been achieved in the previous decades through systematic works.[59] Evidently, Jellinek was referring here to the accomplishments of positivism in German legal scholarship. His intent was to apply a strict, positivist methodology also in the field of international law.[60] In spite of the triumph of state law positivism in Germany, natural law approaches and principles – which Kaltenborn had already criticised – still played a considerable role in the leading textbooks on international law in the middle of the nineteenth century. To be sure, the complete identification of natural law, divine law and international morality was hardly found any longer in the continental discipline of international law in the second half of the century. Still, frequent recourses to 'philosophical' or 'natural' international law can still be found in the important monographs of the nineteenth century.[61]

57 Georg Jellinek, *Die Lehre von den Staatenverbindungen* (Alfred Hölder 1882) 4.

58 Jellinek, n. 57 at 10. 59 Jellinek, n. 57 at 2.

60 On the early Jellinek, who was close to Laband, see Christoph Schönberger, 'Ein Liberaler zwischen Staatswille und Volkswille: Georg Jellinek und die Krise des staatsrechtlichen Positivismus um die Jahrhundertwende' in Stanley L. Paulson, Martin Schulte (eds), *Georg Jellinek: Beiträge zu Leben und Werk* (Mohr Siebeck 2000) 4–9; on state law positivism in the 1890s, see the important study by Christoph Schönberger, *Das Parlament im Anstaltsstaat: Zur Theorie parlamentarischer Repräsentation in der Staatsrechtslehre des Kaiserreichs (1871–1918)* (Vittorio Klostermann 1997).

61 E.g. August Wilhelm Heffter, *Le Droit International de l'Europe* (E. H. Schröder and Cotillon et fils 1873) 5; Heinrich Bernhard Oppenheim, *System des Völkerrechts* (A. Kröner

The high phase of international law positivism in Germany thus coincided with the time of Bergbohm and Jellinek.[62] All subsequent important German textbooks on international law[63] dispensed entirely with a philosophical-natural law basis until the mid 1920s. Jellinek argued that only a positivistic method that did without material ideas of law and was in line with the rest of public law could, once and for all, allay the frequent doubts that international law was genuine law and lead the discipline of international law towards the 'scientific' level of a modern public law. What Jellinek was after was a theoretical construct of international law that was to be erected without recourse to the principles of natural law.[64] Jellinek sought to arrive at an objective principle by proceeding in a strictly positivistic manner and thus positing a sovereign will of the state as the basis from which the law of nations drew its validity. The middle way taken by Jellinek was an attempt to synthesise the two opposing constructs of international law, that is, the individualistic one based on the state, and the universalistic one. And Jellinek did not wish to dispense with either the free will of the state as the basis of the validity of all law, or with the assumption of an objective law of nations. The formal stringency of the Hegelian notion of will was to be reconciled with the liberal notion of a binding obligatory international law of a universal community of states, which was close to Jellinek's own liberal world-view. What Jellinek believed to be merely an apparent contradiction between the freedom of the sovereign state and a legally ordered community of states became the crucial theoretical question of his theory of international law.

1866) 2–4; Johann Ludwig Klüber, *Droit des gens moderne de l'Europe* (J. G. Cotta 1819) 15–16; on philosophical natural law in the discipline of international law in the nineteenth century, see Steiger, n. 12 at 64–74.

62 For the assessment by a contemporary, see August Michael von Bulmerincq, '[Book Review:] Georg Jellinek, Die rechtliche Natur der Staatenverträge. Wien 1880' 4 *Jahrbuch für Gesetzgebung, Verwaltung und Volkswirthschaft im Deutschen Reich* (1880) 606–609.

63 Franz von Liszt, *Völkerrecht* (11th edn Julius Springer 1918); Emanuel von Ullmann, *Völkerrecht* (J. C. B. Mohr 1908); Paul Heilborn, 'Grundbegriffe des Völkerrechts' in Fritz Stier-Somlò (ed.), *Handbuch des Völkerrechts*, Vol. 1.1 (W. Kohlhammer 1912); Julius Hatschek, *Völkerrecht als System rechtlich bedeutsamer Staatsakte* (Deichert 1923).

64 On this, Jellinek unambiguously remarked, in line with the positivistic tradition of Kaltenborn and Bergbohm: 'While all other areas of the law have long since recognized the untenability of a doctrine that creates both legal subjects and rights and duties on the basis of a legal order that precedes positive law and commands it, the old natural law is still celebrating its well-known orgies in the systems of international law, which are only now and then rudely interrupted by a "denier of international law" and then soon begin again.' Georg Jellinek, *System der subjektiven öffentlichen Rechte* (2nd edn Mohr 1905) 311.

4.1 *The free will of the state as the formal ground of all law*

Jellinek's intent was to show that 'the same notion of law that underlies the unquestioned parts of the law also forms the essence of the provisions that are valid for international relations'.[65] With this, Jellinek was turning away from the assumption of a special substantive source for the law of nations, as, for example, the legal consciousness of the nations (Carl Friedrich von Savigny, Hugo Hälschner),[66] or the idea of a reasonable order of the international community (Kaltenborn, Robert von Mohl).[67] Instead, Jellinek, following Bergbohm, insisted that the same formal foundation had to be demonstrated for international law as for the other sub-fields of law.[68]

It was this quest for a monistic conception of law that led Jellinek to the nation (*Volk*) as an organised entity and thus to the state as a basis of his conception. For from a strictly positivist perspective, one could recognise the legal character only of those propositions that could be traced back to a verifiable act of establishment. However, only the state – which established law as the 'sovereign will of all'[69] – was a candidate as a law-creating organ.

Here, Jellinek also explicitly invoked Hegel, who had demonstrated that as long as there was no power that was superimposed upon the states, the rights and duties of the states could find their origins only in their particular will.[70] Consequently, only propositions that were demonstrable as the will of the state could be regarded as law. In this way, the legal quality of international law was directly linked to the empirically verifiable process of creation. The attempt at a theoretical separation of

65 Georg Jellinek, *Die rechtliche Natur der Staatenverträge* (Alfred Hölder 1880) 1.

66 Hugo Hälschner, 'Zur wissenschaftlichen Begründung des Völkerrechts' 1 *Zeitschrift für volkstümliches Recht und nationale Gesetzgebung* (1844) 26–66, where he adopted Savigny's conception.

67 Robert von Mohl, 'Die Pflege der internationalen Gemeinschaft als Aufgabe des Völkerrechts' in Robert von Mohl, *Staatsrecht, Völkerrecht und Politik*, Vol. 1: Staatsrecht und Völkerrecht (Akademische Druck- u. Verlagsanstalt, 1962), 584; for another, later example, see Friedrich von Martens, *Das internationale Recht der civilisierten Nationen*, Vol. 1 (Carl Bergbohm (tr.), Weidmann 1883) 200.

68 Jellinek, n. 65 at 2; the critical review of this work by Bulmerincq opposed this approach: 'Every legal discipline is sovereign as a science and will not tolerate mediatization by other legal disciplines . . . The law of nations, however, remains a legal discipline also with a different legal principle and a different legal systematics.' Quoted from: Bulmerincq, n. 62 at 257; for Bulmerincq, the international belief in the law was the source of the law of nations (256).

69 Jellinek, n. 65 at 2.

70 Jellinek, n. 65 at 2; Hegel, n. 17 at 499–500 (§ 333).

the question of legal character (*Rechtsqualität*) from the norm-creating entity (states) by invoking the notion of the 'idea of law' (*Rechtsidee*) was dismissed, in classic positivist fashion, as 'speculation' from the realm of formal jurisprudence. Although Jellinek did not go so far as to describe the free will of the state as the final philosophical basis of the law, which he, too, believed could be found only in an 'objective-metajuridical' principle, the jurist could not and should not recognise any formal ground of the law other than the free will of the community of nations and states.[71] Otherwise, he would relinquish the boundaries he had so laboriously drawn around his subject, and that could very likely cast the legal scholar 'into the confusion and lack of clarity that is to him the real chaos'.[72]

Therefore, the legal character of international law – and for Jellinek there was no getting around this if one took a strict positivist approach – had to be grounded in the sovereign will of the state:

> The sharp formal development that the concept of law has undergone through the systematic work of the last decades, causes all demands that flow solely from the idea of law, for all the other value they may possess, to appear no longer as a law that can assert its existence alongside, above, or even against positive law . . . With this, the only possible path for a legal grounding of international law is indicated. It must be shown to be grounded in the free will of states or nations.[73]

The criticism that Kaltenborn, Fricker, as well as Bluntschli and von Mohl directed against Pütter's incorporation of the Hegelian concept of will into international law[74] was rejected by Jellinek, who argued that it negated the applicability of the general concept of law to the law of nations and in so doing prevented that area of the law from becoming more deeply pervaded by legal scholarship.[75]

In grounding international law theoretically in the sovereign will of the state, Jellinek was drawing directly on Carl Bergbohm's monograph mentioned previously, which had appeared three years earlier and which

[71] Jellinek, n. 65 at 3 (fn. 3). [72] Jellinek, n. 65 at 3, n. 3. [73] Jellinek, n. 65 at 2.

[74] Robert von Mohl, *Die Geschichte und Literatur der Staatswissenschaften*, Vol. 1 (Ferdinand Enke 1855) 382; Bluntschli, n. 42 at 60.

[75] Jellinek, n. 65 at 3 (fn. 3). Bluntschli, in his review of this work, criticised precisely this starting point of the destructive Hegelian 'juristic construct' and pointed instead to the 'originary natural law' as the foundation of every legal statute; see Johann Caspar Bluntschli, '[Book Review:] Georg Jellinek, Die rechtliche Natur der Staatenverträge. Wien, A. Hölder, 1880' 22 *Kritische Vierteljahresschrift für Gesetzgebung und Rechtswissenschaft* (1880) 579–581.

he described as an 'excellent work'.[76] But Jellinek wanted to go beyond Bergbohm and construct a truly binding law of nations on the shared voluntaristic premise.[77] With this endeavour, Jellinek was turning against the theory of the 'external state law', which had denied that international law possessed its own quality as objective law.

How, then, did Jellinek attempt to escape the dilemma of the voluntaristic foundation of international law that Fricker had spelled out? Jellinek's answer was two-tiered. First, by way of an abstract, preliminary examination, Jellinek discussed the question of how the free will of the state can be thought of as law in the first place. Here, he introduced the figure of the self-obligating will. It was only in the second step that Jellinek raised the question of whether the law created by the free will of the state could be objectified.

4.2 The concept of 'self-obligation' and the obligatory nature of public law

It is the idea of law's binding nature that Jellinek linked with the free will of the state when he wrote:

> It does not exhaust the nature of law that it is the will of the state, for it is not the will of the state as such that is law, but the binding will of the state.[78]

Because Jellinek sought to construct international law on the basis of the autonomy of the individual state, proof of the juridical existence of international law depended in his view on the question of whether the state could bind itself through its own norms. For without a supraordinated, law-creating power, a relationship of obligation could be conceived of only as the identity between the party imposing the obligation and the party being obligated.[79]

The theoretical justification of the concept of self-obligation or 'auto-limitation' provides a deeper insight into Jellinek's methodological approach. In a first step, the goal was to furnish the abstract proof of the

[76] Jellinek, n. 65 at 5.

[77] Cf. on Jellinek's strategy to reconcile the free will of the state with a binding international law compared to John Austin's theory, Martti Koskenniemi, *From Apology to Utopia: The Structure of International Legal Argument* (Finnish Lawyers' Publishing Co. 1989) 128–130.

[78] Jellinek, n. 65 at 6. [79] Jellinek, n. 65 at 7.

possibility and necessity of creating law through self-obligation. In a second step, Jellinek then examined the deduced category of self-obligation against the practice of state law.[80]

This methodological approach proves to be characteristic for Jellinek's theory of international law. Deductively derived, clearly delimited concepts are inductively established – as simultaneous proof of their high potential for systematisation – through the praxis of the state. First, the logical possibility of self-obligating one's own will is demonstrated through the insights of modern ethics and with examples from everyday life.[81] The plane of comparison here is the human will as the object of psychological understanding.[82] The verifiable act of will was merely the formal legal basis of the obligation. The final, psychological basis of every legal obligation, however, lay in the fact that the will regarded itself as bound by its expression.[83] Jellinek thus ascribed the idea of the binding nature of the law not to a normative-theoretical manifestation, but to the psychological manifestation of 'the feeling to have obliged oneself'.

Jellinek carried out the subsequent, inductive demonstration of the concept of self-obligation by way of state or constitutional law (*Staatsrecht*):

> It must be shown that a reflexive element exists within internal state law, that there are legal propositions – whose juristic quality is evident – that emanate from the state and bind the state. Should this demonstration succeed, the legal basis of international law will have been found.[84]

In order to prove that the power of the state can be limited, he pursued a dialogue with the classic (Bodin, Hobbes, Rousseau) and contemporary (Stahl and Ihering) proponents of a theory of unlimitable state power, ultimately by using the practice of state law itself. In the realm of state law, he concluded, we are dealing with norms by which the state limited

[80] 'Deduction shall be followed by induction, to confirm as real, through the analysis of the concrete manifestations, what presented itself to us as necessary a priori.' Jellinek, n. 65 at 18.

[81] Jellinek, n. 65 at 15.

[82] 'Once the logical thinkability of self-obligation has been derived in this way, it is, on the other hand, ethically and legally necessary, legally in the sense of the idea of law, because it is the indispensable precondition of an ordered life within a community.' Jellinek, n. 65 at 16.

[83] Jellinek, n. 65 at 17.

[84] Jellinek, n. 65 at 6–7.

itself. Every law was, in the final analysis, a self-limitation of the will of the state.[85]

4.3 The theory of the guaranteed norm

For Jellinek, the law was a psychological phenomenon inherent in human beings:[86] 'This is the necessary consequence of the realization that the law is within us, that it is a function of the human community and must therefore rest on purely psychological elements.'[87] Because Jellinek thus saw the law as merely a part of human intellectual constructs, the question of validity could also be disconnected from the prerequisite of an authority endowed with coercive power. Instead, the validity of the law rested on the belief in its validity among those to whom a legal norm was addressed.[88] Still, Jellinek, too, proceeded from the assumption that this psychological validity had to be 'guaranteed'. Such a guarantee existed if 'socio-psychological forces' reinforced the motivating power of the prescriptions, thereby endowing them with a general ability to assert themselves against countervailing, individual motivations of the addressees of the norms.[89]

Jellinek thus gave preference to the broader notion of 'guarantee' over that of 'coercion'. As guarantees of state law Jellinek pointed to the organisation of the state, and for international law to the conditions of international relations and other shared interests of the community of states.[90] On the basis of this psychological approach, international law was placed on an equal footing with state law, and via the 'theory of the guaranteed norm' it acquired, for Jellinek, the quality of law in spite of the absence of a supraordinated coercive power.

4.4 Jellinek's 'objective international law'

4.4.1 The 'nature of the thing' as a principle of objectification

Jellinek conceptualised the sovereign will of the state as the final formal ground and the 'feeling of self-obligation' as the final psychological ground of the law. But how was it possible, on this basis, for norms to emerge that could bind the state to the self-obligation it had entered into, independent of individual changes in will? In answering this question,

[85] Jellinek, n. 65 at 27.
[86] Georg Jellinek, *Allgemeine Staatslehre* (2nd edn Häring 1905) 324.
[87] Jellinek, n. 86 at 326. [88] Jellinek, n. 86 at 326. [89] Jellinek, n. 86 at 326.
[90] Jellinek, n. 86 at 328.

Jellinek's interest was directed above all at those legal rules that dealt with the creation, duration and termination of treaties in international law: 'Treaties between states can have the character of law only when there exist norms that stand above the treaties, and from which the treaties receive their legal validity.'[91] These norms created a standard against which individual treaties between states had to measure themselves, and they were to that extent 'objective in nature'.[92] With this, Jellinek had arrived at the central question, namely, how such general norms that are the equivalent of law can be conceived between sovereign actors on the level of international law. To answer that question, Jellinek searched for a principle of objectification that could hold up to the arguments that the idea of self-obligation always implied simultaneously the possibility that the state could also free itself again from any possible content of will. Fricker articulated this critique of the voluntaristic theoretical approach this way: 'What is valid only for me because I will it cannot create law between me and someone else who is my equal.'[93]

The possibility, inherent in free will, of self-liberation through a change of will had to be limited in Jellinek's construct through an objective principle. And here the recourse to natural law principles, which could still be encountered frequently in Germany, especially at the beginning of the century, was ruled out by Jellinek from the outset. Nor, according to Jellinek, was it possible to see the more frequently advocated analogies to private law as a sustainable construct on such a vital question.[94] Jellinek was clearly searching for a meta-juristic principle, since he also did not embark on the conceivable path of a positivistic derivation of a system of norms of customary international law with a relatively inherent stability vis-à-vis the changing will of the individual state.

Instead, Jellinek at this point revealed to his curious readers the – long withheld – final *philosophical* ground of law, which could be found only in an 'objective principle':

> This principle, which we must now name, is the nature of the conditions of life that require legal normativization. This nature is as untouchable by the will of the state as nature is by the will as such . . . Here, then, we have an objective barrier to the will that is beyond any question.[95]

91 Jellinek, n. 65 at 5. 92 Jellinek, n. 65 at 4. 93 Fricker, n. 47 at 394.

94 'There must first be an objective international law, before analogy can begin its supplementary function.' Jellinek, n. 65 at 51.

95 Jellinek, n. 65 at 43; on the 'nature of the thing' as an instrument for objectifying legal argumentation and for an overview of the relevant legal-theoretical literature, see Theo Mayer-Maly, 'Die Natur der Sache und die österreichische Rechtspraxis' in Werner Krawietz, Theo

According to Jellinek, the objective nature of the state and of relations between states thus entailed a logically inherent limitation on the individual will of the state. It was among the elementary purposes of a state to engage in relations with other states, and to that extent it was also a demand of the nature of the state to create norms by which the relations to other states were regulated.[96]

Jellinek further attempted to identify a connecting link between the self-obligating will of the state and the 'objective' law of nations that arose from the nature of the relations between states. To that end, he turned to the concept of 'recognition'. The moment a treaty was entered into, the contracting states, according to Jellinek, recognised the 'objective elements' of the treaty. Through this 'recognition',[97] the subjective will admitted into itself the 'objective elements', that is to say, the binding rules underlying the conclusion of the treaty and its termination.[98] Recognition is thus drawn from the subjective will and is regarded as confirmation on the part of the individual state of the objective nature of international relations. Objective law arises by way of this objective-legal enrichment of the element of the subjective will through the vehicle of recognition.

The circularity of this argument becomes especially obvious in Jellinek's answer to Fricker's question of what would happen should the state refuse recognition. According to Jellinek, that should not be possible in the sense that recognition itself was, in turn, not within the discretion of the states, but followed inevitably from the objective nature of the relations between states.[99] It is at this methodological point of fracture between a legal construction of international law based on the formally verifiable will of the state, and the sociological assumption of the state's communal constraint (*Gemeinschaftsgebundenheit*) as a necessity that precedes the will of the state that Jellinek's conception of himself as a jurist becomes clear: beyond

Mayer-Maly, Ota Weinberger (eds), *Objektivierung des Rechtsdenkens: Gedächtnisschrift für Ilmar Tammelo* (Duncker & Humblot 1984) 273–289.

96 Jellinek, n. 65 at 45; here, the connection to Jellinek's doctrine of the purposes of the state becomes apparent, although it is striking that Jellinek rejected the existence of objective state purposes in the general theory of the state. For Jellinek, this must therefore be a subjective purpose of state, though one that is inherent in all states because of objective nature. On the doctrine of the purpose of the state, see Jellinek, n. 86 at 223–258.

97 'Recognition' (*Anerkennung*) thus means for Jellinek not merely recognising another state as a legal subject; it has the additional function of the 'acceptance' (*Übernahme*) of the objective law of the community of states into the own will. On recognition see Jellinek, n. 64 at 320.

98 Jellinek, n. 65 at 51.

99 Jellinek, n. 65 at 48.

formal positivism, the legal scholars should or must incorporate psychological and sociological perspectives into the understanding of the law. Kelsen would later criticise this approach as 'methodological syncretism' and contrast it with his own 'pure' method of legal scholarship.

4.4.2 'Shared interests' and 'purpose of the state' as the final sociological foundation

Behind the objective nature of international relations as a barrier to the sovereign will of the state stood Jellinek's own conception of an international 'community of states'. For him, however, this community of states was not an idea of natural law, but the sociological product of the growing international intertwinement of state interests, of the kind that had become especially apparent in the nineteenth century.[100] To that extent, the cooperation of the individual state with other states was in accord with the purpose of the state.[101] From Jellinek's perspective, the state could no longer be described abstractly as an entity that was autarkic and could not be placed under obligation, since the assumptions derived from such a premise utterly failed to reflect the real conditions.[102] Instead, the state was contingent on the totality of the states in all aspects of its existence and actions. The 'community of states' was a fact, and ignoring it made any deeper comprehension of the problems related to the state impossible.[103] This was especially true in the realm of the 'civilised' European nations, which was, in Jellinek's words, wrapped in a 'web of international legal norms'.[104]

Ten years after his monograph on international treaty law, Jellinek continued to develop the relationship between 'state community and the 'objective law of nations' in his work *System der subjectiven öffentlichen Rechte* (*The System of Individual Rights*). Through membership[105] in the 'community of states', the state was bound to 'objective international law'. From the perspective of the individual state, this resulted in claims upon the various members that they respect the state's personhood, extend the right of legation, and fulfil their obligations arising from treaties.[106]

100 Jellinek, n. 97 at 320.
101 Jellinek, n. 65 at 41; on Jellinek's strategy to reconcile the free will of the state with a binding international law through references to the purpose of the state, see Koskenniemi, n. 77 at 129–130.
102 Jellinek, n. 57 at 92. 103 Jellinek, n. 57 at 92–93. 104 Jellinek, n. 57 at 96.
105 A state acquired membership in turn through the instrument of recognition under international law: Jellinek, n. 97 at 320.
106 Jellinek, n. 97 at 321.

However, because of the specific architecture of his theory of international law, Jellinek could count not only the rule '*pacta sunt servanda*', but also the '*clausula rebus sic stantibus*' as part of the objective law of nations.[107] The coexistence of the '*clausula rebus sic stantibus*' as a doctrinal emanation of state sovereignty and '*pacta sunt servanda*' as the basic precondition of a binding international law reflects Jellinek's attempt to bring together contrary constructs of international law.

For Jellinek, the derived 'objective' norms of international law give rise to claims with a public law character, which were admitted as rights of states (*Staatenrechte*) into his system of public law. However, this objective international law, which arises from the nature of the relations between states, constituted only about one-tenth of the tenets of international law.[108] The other nine-tenths were subjective treaties involving legal transactions, in which the states behaved like parties to a contract.[109] In that sense, the objectification of international law comprised for Jellinek only the sphere of an elementary constitution, which was in the final analysis deduced from an 'objective nature' of the community of states that was presupposed a priori. However, in contrast to the principles of natural law, it was more like a procedural order of relations between states than a substantive constitution.[110]

The international law derived in this way carried the dual aspect of a universalistic construction of international law, on the one hand, and a construct based on the individual state, on the other: it was objective and thus binding law, but because of the absence of a superimposed authority, it remained for Jellinek an 'anarchic law'.[111] In Jellinek, the sought-after

[107] 'The state's self-obligation cannot be an absolute one either in duration or in terms of the sphere to which it applies. Since every state obligation, with respect to its substantive side, is a fulfillment of the purpose of state, it exists only as long as it satisfies that purpose. That is why every act of will by the state carries within itself the clause: *rebus sic stantibus*. The self-obligation of the state has absolute binding force only for the time during which the objective conditions, for the normativization of which the law is intended, have remained the same unchanged.' Jellinek, n. 65 at 40–41.

[108] Jellinek, n. 97 at 321. [109] Jellinek, n. 97 at 321.

[110] It is also in this context that one should place Jellinek's critique of the construction of so-called 'basic rights' of states. These were nothing other than a description of the '*status libertatis*' under international law, although it could never be unequivocally laid down in legal terms. However, claims were being arbitrarily deduced from the basic rights derived from natural law. Instead of describing what was permitted to the state, the point was to examine the limitations on the state's freedom through the objective law of nations. On the basic rights, see Jellinek, n. 97 at 316–320.

[111] Jellinek, n. 86 at 368.

synthesis between the perspective of international law based on the individual state and the universalistic perspective was accomplished through a sociological approach that reckoned relations with other states among the most elementary or inherently necessary purposes of the state. For him, the legal community of states was not, as in Kaltenborn or Wolff, the starting point for the construction of international law; instead, the 'objective law of nations' of this community of states[112] was the sociologically necessary, final limitation on the state's presupposed freedom of will. In that sense, the emphasis on the sociological dimension of international law was certainly congruent with Jellinek's two-sided theory of the state, according to which the state should be seen and analysed on the one side as a sociological and on the other side as a legal phenomenon.[113] In addition, he sought to defend the legal character of international law against those who denied its very existence with the help of the concepts of 'self-obligation' and 'guarantee', which he introduced via a psychological perspective on the law.

With this, Jellinek had methodically expanded Bergbohm's strictly voluntaristic international law positivism through his own multidimensional approach. As he saw it, this allowed him to dissolve the antagonism between the view of international law as based on the concrete will of individual states, and the universalistic view of international law as a legal order binding upon states.[114] In fact, however, Jellinek had not dissolved the oscillating movement between the subjective and the objective principle, but had instead integrated it into his own theory as an inherent tension.

112 Jellinek had already tried in his *Habilitation* thesis on criminal law to reconcile the premise of the free individual with the conception of a community of individuals. In his construct, the community took precedence, 'because we stand from the first to the last breath under the rule of large, social laws, in accordance with which we must all complete the cycles of existence'. Quoted from Georg Jellinek, 'Moralstatistik und Todesstrafe' in *Ausgewählte Schriften und Reden von Georg Jellinek*, Vol. 1 (Häring 1911) 69–75 at 69. The construct state/community of states from *Die rechtliche Natur der Staatenverträge* published a year later followed the same structural principle. The freedom of the state encounters its limits only in its reasonable nature as a state, which is shaped by the necessary co-existence with other states. The objective law of nations thus appears as the 'ethical minimum' in the co-existence of the states. In connection with criminal law, Reinhard Moos spoke of an 'objective social ethics' in Jellinek: Reinhard Moos, *Der Verbrechensbegriff in Österreich im 18. und 19. Jahrhundert: Sinn und Strukturwandel* (L. Röhrscheid 1968) 489–493 at 493.

113 Jellinek, n. 86 at 9–13.

114 Martti Koskenniemi interprets this argumentative strategy as 'a standard form of reconciling an ascending and a descending argument' (Koskenniemi, n. 77 at 129).

5 The resilience of German *Staatswillenspositivismus* in the twentieth century

The positivist explanatory model for a binding law of nations à la Jellinek initially found numerous adherents in Germany, but also in other European countries. The main German-language textbooks on international law at the time,[115] by Ullmann,[116] Heilborn[117] and Liszt,[118] referred directly to Jellinek when explaining the basis of obligation of international law. Although French international lawyers mostly drew upon the doctrine of the basic rights of states (*droits fondamentaux des états*), criticised by Jellinek as a kind of clandestine natural law, Carré de Malberg,[119] under the influence of Jellinek, also traced international law back to the self-obligating will of the state.[120]

The foundation offered by Jellinek, by bridging the premise of the free will of the state and the idea of a binding order of international law, had an unusual ability to connect with other theories. Precisely because this approach did not rely exclusively on the idea of the sovereign will of the state, it set itself apart from the conservative 'Bonn School' and its revival of the Hegelian theory of 'external state law'.[121] It could even be used

115 Karl Strupp prefaces his own principles of international law with an overview of the most important textbooks: Karl Strupp, *Grundzüge des positiven Völkerrechts* (5th edn L. Röhrscheid 1932) vii.

116 Ullmann, n. 63 at 250. 117 Heilborn, n. 63 at 29–31. 118 Liszt, n. 63 at 2.

119 Raymond Carré de Malberg, *Contribution à la théorie génerale de l'état, spécialment d'après les donnés fournis par le droit constitutionnel français* (Recueil Sirey 1920) 234.

120 On the French development at the *fin de siècle* and the prevailing doctrine of the basic rights of states, see Léon Duguit, *Souveraineté et Liberté: Leçons faites à l'Université Columbia (New York) 1920–1921* (Alcan 1922) 105–110. In his lectures, Duguit compared the German doctrine, influenced by Jellinek, to the French doctrine of the basic rights of states: '[l]a doctrine allemande était plus brutale. J'en trouve surtout l'expression dans les ouvrages d'un juriste allemand éminent, dont on ne saurait méconnaître le role et l'influence, le professeur d'Heidelberg, aujourd'hui décédé, Jellinek' (107–108).

121 The so-called Bonn School revived the subjective principle of international law in strict adherence to Hegel. On the members of the Bonn School, see Strupp, n. 115 at 9–10. Rejecting the attempts at objectivisation undertaken by Jellinek and Triepel, this school drew again directly on the Hegelian construct of international law. The sovereign state was the centre of law, and international law was merely 'external state law'. According to Philipp Zorn – the founder of the school and adviser on international law to Emperor Wilhelm II – and his son, Albert Zorn, an agreement among states should 'occur only by way of self-obligation after a preceding agreement about the shared interests to be regulated, and the legal nature of international law thus rests on this obligation of the individual state through its will and thus on its right vis-à-vis the other states' (Albert Zorn, *Grundzüge des Völkerrechts* (2nd edn J. J. Weber 1903) 7–8).

by progressive international lawyers with a pacifist background like the Swiss Nippold, who, within the milieu of the Hague Movement, was one of the most ardent champions of the idea of international arbitration and a general juridification of international relations.[122]

Heinrich Triepel's doctrine of agreement (*Vereinbahrungslehre*) can also be seen as a critique and simultaneously as an adaptation of Jellinek's ideas. Triepel, among Germany's most renowned scholars of international law until the 1930s, likewise sought to construct the law of nations as an objective legal order without having to give up the subjective principle. However, he rejected the recourse solely to the self-obligating individual state as inadequate:

> That the will is capable of subordinating itself to its own commandments is certainly correct for the realm of ethics. But that a legal obligation for a subject toward other subjects can come only from its own commandment to itself, is something I regard as a logical absurdity.[123]

According to Triepel, state law and international law must be traceable to different sources because of their invariably different objects of regulation.[124] Triepel further maintained that only a will that was superior to those to whom the law was addressed was capable of creating objective law. This consideration led him to posit the existence of a 'common will' (*Gemeinwille*) of the states that was independent of the will of the individual state.[125] This common will did not arise from treaties of a contractual nature, which represented only the respective wills of the individual states, but only from 'agreements' (*Vereinbarungen*) that carried objective obligations.[126] According to Triepel, such agreements arose when states, through an agreement of wills, not only established subjective rights and obligations through a legal transaction, but also

[122] Otfried Nippold, *Die Fortbildung des Verfahrens in völkerrechtlichen Streitigkeiten* (Duncker & Humblot 1907) 46; however, Nippold described 'international solidarity' as the source of objective international law.

[123] Heinrich Triepel, *Völkerrecht und Landesrecht* (C. L. Hirschfeld 1899) 77.

[124] Triepel, n. 123 at 18–20.

[125] The same argument was put forth by Anzilotti with the 'voluntà collettiva': Dionisio Anzilotti, *Corso di diritto internazionale*, (2nd edn Athenaeum 1912) 26; later, Anzilotti would resort to Kelsen's concept of the basic norm; see Dionisio Anzillotti, *Lehrbuch des Völkerrechts* (Walter de Gruyter 1929) 33.

[126] Triepel, n. 123 at 63–74.

sought to create objective, lasting law.[127] In this way, Jellinek's 'objective international law', which was tied back to state recognition and derived from the objective nature of the community of states, was thus replaced with the concept of 'agreement' adopted from Binding.[128] For Triepel, the question from where the agreement acquired its binding force was a meta-legal one: 'I believe one can be content with the assurance that the state feels obligated by it.'[129]

One year after the first Hague Conference, Triepel, relying heavily on the building blocks of German *Staatswillenspositivismus* à la Jellinek, had conceived a model to explain the binding effect of inter-state regulations that were spreading in various sectorial areas, without having to engage in an open conflict with the prevailing notion of sovereignty. Introducing the notion of 'agreement' or 'common will' as the source of international law had allowed Triepel to cloak the dilemma of the voluntaristic basis through the concept of agreement. For while the agreement arose from the sovereign will of the state, it simultaneously transformed the sum of individual wills into the 'common will' as a source of international law that was different and autonomous from state law.

Völkerrecht und Landesrecht became the most successful German-language monograph on international law at the dawn of the twentieth century. The influence of Triepel, who still upheld the fundamentals of his theory in the 1920s,[130] on the international legal literature especially in Germany and Italy was multifarious. Alexander von Hold-Ferneck declared the 'agreeing will' of the states[131] to be the foundation of the law of nations, Theodor Niemeyer said it was the 'consensus of states',[132] and Julius Hatschek adopted the separation between agreements and contractual treaties in his textbook on international law.[133] The common will appeared as 'common consent' also in Lassa Oppenheim.[134] Moreover,

[127] 'The states can create objective law if they agree on a rule by which their future behaviour shall be permanently determined' (Triepel, n. 123 at 70).

[128] Karl Binding, 'Die Gründung des norddeutschen Bundes' in *Festgabe der Leipziger Juristenfakultät für Dr. Bernhard Windscheid zum 22. Dezember 1888* (Duncker & Humblot 1888) 1–72 at 69–72.

[129] Triepel, n. 123 at 82.

[130] Heinrich Triepel, 'Les rapports entre le droit interne et le droit international' 1 *Recueil des Cours* (1923) 77–121.

[131] Alexander von Hold-Ferneck, *Lehrbuch des Völkerrechts* (Meiner 1930) 110.

[132] Theodor Niemeyer, *Völkerrecht* (Walter de Gruyter 1923) 12.

[133] Hatschek, n. 63 at 8–10.

[134] Lassa Oppenheim, *International Law: A Treatise*, Vol. 1 (Longmans, Green and Co. 1905) 15.

this dualistic approach was widely adopted not only in Germany,[135] but also in Italy.[136]

6 Conclusion

German international law theory in the nineteenth century follows, beyond its close link to the theory and method of general public law, a particular discursive logic. The explanation for this lies in the central question underlying every quest for a theoretical foundation of international law: namely, the relationship between the German public law notion of the 'state' and the norms of international law. It is the problem of whether – and if so, how – international law can be theoretically construed as an objective law of an international community of states that confronts the individual states with a claim to be binding upon them. Such a construal posed specific difficulties for scholars, because in contrast to state law, international law lacked a central institutionalised authority that stood above the states and was charged with enacting norms and implementing the law. Those who created the law and those to whom the law was addressed were identical.

As a result, two contrary constructs of international law emerged in the debate over a positivistic foundation within German-language international legal scholarship: according to the 'objective principle' that Kaltenborn introduced into the positivist discourse, the 'community of states' represented a higher legal community in which the states functioned as organs of this legal order. By contrast, the move to place international law on a voluntaristic foundation, which went back to Hegel, regarded the sovereign will of the state – in the sense of a subjective-individualistic understanding – as the fundamental principle of the law of nations.[137] Throughout the nineteenth century, these two positions were

[135] Explicitly in Gustav Adolf Walz, *Völkerrecht und Staatliches Recht: Untersuchungen über die Einwirkungen des Völkerrechts auf das innerstaatliche Recht* (Kohlhammer 1933), 11–40, although he regards the term 'dualism' as linguistically incorrect and speaks instead of a 'pluralistic' theory. After the Nazis came to power, Walz readily placed his creative academic energy in the service of Nazi ideology; see Michael Stolleis, *A History of Public Law in Germany, 1914–1945* (Thomas Dunlap (tr.), Oxford University Press 2004) 412–413.

[136] E.g. Anzilotti, *Lehrbuch des Völkerrechts*, n. 125 at 36–47.

[137] Jochen von Bernstorff, 'Georg Jellinek – Völkerrecht als modernes öffentliches Recht im fin de siècle' in Stanley L. Paulson, Martin Schulte (eds), *Georg Jellinek: Beiträge zu Leben und Werk* (Mohr Siebeck 2000) 185–186.

repeatedly revived – under the influence of methodological revisions – in German and Austrian jurisprudence.

I have tried to show that the objective and the subjective approaches in nineteenth-century German legal discourse, by each neglecting the other principle, opened themselves up – or became invariably vulnerable – to attack. As Martti Koskenniemi has demonstrated for various fields of international legal doctrine, any objective grounding of international law, which dispenses with the concretely demonstrable will of the individual state, can be criticised as mere deduction or blatant natural law. Conversely, critics of constructs that base themselves on the vacillating will of individual states can charge that they are unable to establish the objectively binding nature of international law.[138]

At the end of the nineteenth century, Jellinek and Triepel (building on Jellinek) sought to synthesise the subjective and the objective principle in their theories. The 'common will' (Triepel) and the sociologically grounded 'objective nature' of relations between states (Jellinek) were set up as objectifying principles that constrained the subjective will of the state. However, the two antagonistic positions were not really synthesised in this way; rather, they were incorporated into the theoretical approaches as an unresolved tension.

It was Hans Kelsen in the 1920s who was the first author who attempted to break with this tradition of German *Staatswillenspositivismus* in international law on explicit 'positivist' premises. He developed the first in-depth structural critique of the semantic cage, which this tradition had erected:

> The theory of international law, in particular, vacillates back and forth uncertainly between the antipodes of a state-individualistic and a human-universalistic perspective, between the subjectivism of the primacy of the legal order of the state and the objectivism of the primacy of international law.[139]

The crux of the Kelsenian critique was the elimination of the prevailing notion of the personified state capable of will. From the perspective of a 'pure' jurisprudence, the state is for Kelsen identical with the state's legal system. This so-called 'identity thesis' draws on the Neo-Kantian separation of Is- and Ought-systems and on Vaihinger's *The Philosophy of*

[138] For a comprehensive post-modern account of this inner movement ('ascending' and 'descending' arguments) of international legal doctrine, see Koskenniemi, n. 77.

[139] Kelsen, n. 1 at 319–320.

'As If'. Kelsen argued that in the misguided juristic thinking, the proper function of the legal person as the unity-creating point of attribution of norms was turned into a living, human-like figure, a state organism. This critical assumption was a rupture with Jellinek's voluntaristic foundation of international law. With the identity thesis, international law was supposed to be disconnected from the notion of the state as a 'person' capable of will.

In a radicalised neo-Kantian version of positivism, international law is valid because international lawyers assume it to be valid. This hypothesis underlying international legal discourse is embodied in Kelsen's notion of the hypothetical *Grundnorm*, replacing the circular move between the sovereign will and the objective and binding law above the state. Very much in the spirit of the inter-war movement to modernise international law, the monumental 'dogma' of the sovereign will of the individual state was emphatically knocked off its pedestal by Kelsen and his students. Its foundational role is being rejected. But this was far too radical for international legal scholarship to swallow. Jellinek and his followers continued to dominate international legal discourse of the first half of the twentieth century. German *Staatswillenspositivismus* was here to stay.

But is this tradition still with us in the twenty-first century? Considering the central role 'consensus' continues to play in modern international law and considering how international lawyers time and again rediscovered the alleged 'objective grounding' immune to the subjective will of the state, it in fact seems as if nothing much has changed since the heydays of German *Staatswillenspositivismus*. Granted, since the 1950s, international lawyers have become ever-more sentimental about the 'foundation' of the international legal order. Universal values were being added to Jellinek's pragmatic 'common interests' of European nations as a presumed new humanitarian substratum or 'constitution' of that order. But all of these conceptual moves have continued to take place in the semantic cage of German *Staatswillenspositivismus*. Even when prominent scholars like Christian Tomuschat insist on the emergence of new value-based obligations beyond the will of individual states, they methodologically do so only on the basis of the notion of a 'consensus-based structure of international law'.[140] *Ius cogens* norms, for instance, are generally being considered binding even against the contravening individual will of the

[140] Christian Tomuschat, 'International Law: Ensuring the Survival of Mankind on the Eve of a New Century: General Course on Public International Law' 281 *Recueil des Cours* (1999) 9–438 at 28–29.

state because a great majority of states have consented to them in the first place. And whenever consent alone does not seem to suffice to fully justify the assumed obligation so close to the heart of a particular author, he or she might refer to universal values allegedly lying behind this order.

The legacy of German *Staatswillenspositivismus* combined with Western humanitarianism seems to force authors to express their personal utopias in the foundational semantics of 'constitutionalism', 'common interests' or 'universal values' as being validated by an objective 'consensus' among states. One of the problems of this 'genetic code' is that it is incapable of addressing the role of international legal norms in perpetuating violence and exploitation in a conflictual and antagonistic world. For, as long as the international legal order is the embodiment of universal values and common interests based on consent, how could individual norms belonging to that order possibly be seen to entrench injustice?[141] Blending German *Staatswillenspositivismus* with Western humanitarianism in constitutionalist semantics is therefore likely to repress the best elements of both classical naturalism and positivism. It fails to encapsulate the critical bite of revolutionary natural law by its focus on inter-state consent and it equally fails to keep the reflexive distance of radical positivism vis-à-vis the contingent content of the legal order in the Kelsenian tradition. Constitutionalism as sentimental *Staatswillenspositivismus* thus combines the least desirable ingredients of both the positivist and the naturalist tradition: shallow Western humanitarianism and affirmative idealisations of the current content of the international legal order.

[141] More generally on moral foundationalism in international law, see Jochen von Bernstorff, Ingo Venzke, 'Ethos, Ethics and Morality in International Relations' in Rüdiger Wolfrum (ed.), *Max Planck Encyclopedia of Public International Law*, Vol. 3 (Oxford University Press 2012) 709–718; see on international humanitarianism, David Kennedy, *The Dark Side of Virtue: Reassessing International Humanitarianism* (Princeton University Press 2008).

4

Hans Kelsen in today's international legal scholarship

JÖRG KAMMERHOFER

> Our view is directed exclusively towards the law that is presented to us by cognition; we attack current forms of positivism not because we ourselves are not focussing on the law presented by experience, but because we believe that this is the mistake of current forms of positivism. They are characterised by their exclusive reliance on 'state will', which they see as a somehow sociological or psychological, but, at any rate, as a meta-legal fact.
>
> Alfred Verdross (1923)[1]

1 Introduction

Can we call Hans Kelsen's Pure Theory of Law an example – or even the epitome – of post-modern international legal positivism when his theory is so very clearly not post-modern? The arguments Kelsen or, rather, the Pure Theory of Law advances[2] are a product of the early twentieth

[1] '[U]nser Augenmerk ist vielmehr ausschließlich auf Recht gerichtet, das Erfahrung darbietet; wenn wir dennoch dem herrschenden Positivismus Kampf ansagen, so nicht deshalb, weil wir die Erfahrung des Rechts verlassen, sondern weil wir meinen, daß er diesen Fehler begeht. Der herrschende Positivismus charakterisiert sich dadurch, daß er das Recht auf den "Staatswillen" aufbaut, den er irgendwie als soziologisches oder psychologisches, jedenfalls aber als metarechtliches Faktum denkt.' Alfred Verdross, *Die Einheit des rechtlichen Weltbildes auf Grundlage der Völkerrechtsverfassung* (J. C. B. Mohr 1923) viii (all translations are the author's own).

[2] This chapter is not primarily concerned with an intellectual-historical retracing of Kelsen's theory of law or doctrine of international law. Others have done so in near-encyclopaedic form, e.g. Alfred Rub, *Hans Kelsens Völkerrechtslehre: Versuch einer Würdigung* (Verlag Österreich 1995). Since the present chapter focuses on the use we can make of a specific approach – the Pure Theory of Law which was pioneered by Kelsen – it will seek to portray the relevance of this particular approach, not the state of Kelsen's thought in general. At certain points, the chapter may therefore claim that in order to be consistent with the Pure Theory's aims, it may be necessary to contradict Kelsen's writings.

century and they are certainly not post-modern*ist*. However, its radical programme rivals that of many other critical scholarly projects en vogue today. As a 'down-to-earth' critical enterprise, its deconstructive arguments hit orthodox doctrine harder than those of most post-modernists. Moreover, it also contains a constructive side whose structural-analytic and nomo-epistemic orientation is superior to other theories of law, and to rival positivist theories in particular.

This chapter first and foremost aims to show that the Pure Theory can be an attractive approach for international legal scholars, but it does not assert its inevitability. After all, there is a reason why the name 'Kelsen' receives such varied treatment: it is often mentioned, less often quoted with approval, and seldom understood in international legal scholarship. Why, one might ask, is Kelsen so unpopular with international lawyers, particularly those hailing from the Anglo-American legal tradition? Why is Hart, by comparison, such a success story among the world's (international) legal positivists?[3] Is the stringency required of the legal scholar by Kelsen truly odious to the modern international lawyer? Are the sometimes unwelcome consequences of the consistent application of Kelsen's positivism so unpalatable in our post-modern world, full as it is of complexities and fragmentation? Is it perhaps all a matter of 'legal culture' – can the continental European, the 'system-building' Kelsen simply not communicate with the Anglo-American pragmatist? Exploring these questions is a second, minor, aim of this chapter.

The chapter's main line of argument is developed through four topics, grouped in pairs. In the first set of topics, two key features of the Pure Theory of Law are introduced, developed and discussed. Section 2 outlines the Pure Theory's radical programme for a science of law. Its dramatic departure from the orthodox opinions of the day – through the purification of legal scholarship – is still with us today. One of the key dualities of the Pure Theory's approach is explored in Section 3. The two conceptual poles of 'normativism' and 'positivism' may look like thesis and antithesis, but they are united in synthesis in the legal theory of Kelsen and his followers; they do not constitute two extremes on an oscillating – and irreconcilable – pendulum.[4] The second set of topics map the

[3] D'Aspremont, Chapter 5 at 114.

[4] Martti Koskenniemi, *From Apology to Utopia: The Structure of International Legal Argument* (Finnish Lawyers' Publishing Co. 1989, reissued Cambridge University Press 2005) 59.

structural analysis provided by the Pure Theory of Law onto the sources of international law. Section 4 discusses the Kelsenian *Grundnorm* and contrasts it with Hart's Rule of Recognition, before assessing this debate in connection with the origins and foundations of the formal sources of international law. Finally Section 5 focuses attention on one of the least 'positivist' sources: the 'general principles of law recognized by civilized nations' (Article 38(1)(c) of the ICJ Statute).

2 Kelsen's radical programme of a true legal science

Hans Kelsen was not a professional philosopher, nor was he a scholar of our 'post-modern' times. Therefore, he did not seek to explain the philosophical foundations of his theories nor expand upon his theory of science. At least, he did not do so in the way we would today. Yet, it is abundantly clear that the Pure Theory of Law is based on a radical programme of re-imagining the theoretical and epistemological basis of legal scholarship to the point of forming a true *science of law*.[5] This section will briefly highlight the two most important elements of this approach – the Pure Theory's largely implicit theory of science and the fundamental and foundational Is–Ought duality – before moving on to more specific questions.

Hans Kelsen set out to found a science of law; he wanted to purify the scholarly enterprise, keeping it free from all those 'elements foreign to the specific methods of a science whose only purpose is the cognition of law'.[6] The Vienna School of Jurisprudence (another of the early twentieth-century *Wiener Schulen*)[7] was a Modernist enterprise just like the Vienna Circle in philosophy. However, Kelsen never claimed to be a 'modernist' and the Pure Theory does not espouse the logical (or empirical)

5 Hans Kelsen, *General Theory of Law and State* (Harvard University Press 1945) xiv. The use of the German word 'Wissenschaft', denoting both 'science' and 'scholarship', as used also in 'Rechtswissenschaft' ('legal science' or 'legal scholarship'), does not distinguish between natural sciences and other scholarly enterprises. When Kelsen writes in English, or his work is translated into English, the word 'legal science' is used in order to express Kelsen's intention to found a true 'science of law'.

6 Kelsen, n. 5 at xiv.

7 Stanley L. Paulson, 'Zwei Wiener Welten und ein Anknüpfungspunkt: Carnaps *Aufbau*, Kelsens Reine Rechtslehre und das Streben nach Objektivität' in Clemens Jabloner, Friedrich Stadler (eds), *Logischer Empirismus und Reine Rechtslehre: Beziehungen zwischen dem Wiener Kreis und der Hans Kelsen-Schule* (Springer 2001) 137–190.

positivism of the Vienna Circle,[8] even though they share some common ground.[9] Moreover, Kelsen himself did not discuss the theory-of-science aspects of the Pure Theory in a sustained fashion, mainly because his 'late-Enlightenment' understanding of scholarship was not much in doubt in the early twentieth century. In seeking to understand Kelsen's science-of-law project, we can only draw on his own sparse comments, mainly in introductions and prefaces, and extrapolate certain axioms from the totality of Kelsen's writings and his contemporary and present-day followers. In the preface to *General Theory of Law and State* (1945), he writes:

> When this doctrine is called the 'pure theory of law', it is meant that it is being kept free from all the elements foreign to the specific method of a science whose only purpose is the cognition of law, not its formation. A science has to describe its object as it actually is, not to prescribe how it should be or should not be from the point of view of some specific value judgments.... The reality... at which a science of law is directed, is not the reality of nature which constitutes the object of natural science... Legal reality, the specific existence of the law, manifests itself in... the positiveness of law.[10]

Some of the central, but only half-acknowledged, axioms of Kelsen's 'theory of (legal) science' are:[11]

[8] Hans Kelsen, 'Was ist juristischer Positivismus?' 20 *Juristen-Zeitung* (1965) 465–469, reprinted in Hans Klecatsky, René Marcic, Herbert Schambeck (eds), *Die Wiener rechtstheoretische Schule: Ausgewählte Schriften von Hans Kelsen, Adolf Julius Merkl, Alfred Verdross* (Europa 1968) 941–953 at 941; Clemens Jabloner, 'Kelsen and his Circle: The Viennese Years' 9 *EJIL* (1998) 368–385 at 379; Robert Walter, 'Der Positivismus der Reinen Rechtslehre' in Clemens Jabloner, Friedrich Stadler (eds), *Logischer Empirismus und Reine Rechtslehre: Beziehungen zwischen dem Wiener Kreis und der Hans Kelsen-Schule* (Springer 2001) 1–17 at 1–2.

[9] Clemens Jabloner, 'Beiträge zu einer Sozialgeschichte der Denkformen: Kelsen und die Einheitswissenschaft' in Clemens Jabloner, Friedrich Stadler (eds), *Logischer Empirismus und Reine Rechtslehre: Beziehungen zwischen dem Wiener Kreis und der Hans Kelsen-Schule* (Springer 2001) 19–43 at 19. On the question of the Pure Theory's Modernist connections, see Jörg Kammerhofer, 'Hans Kelsen as the Epitome of Legal Modernism', working paper (2007), available at http://ssrn.com/abstract=1566432.

[10] Kelsen, n. 5 at xiv. Note that the last statement (existence equals positiveness) is probably not Kelsen's considered position.

[11] These are adapted from an earlier publication: Jörg Kammerhofer, 'Hans Kelsen's Place in the Theory of International Law' in Alexander Orakhelashvili (ed.), *Research Handbook on the Theory and History of International Law* (Edward Elgar 2011) 143–167 at 147–148.

- Science means finding 'the truth'.[12] 'Truth' in the legal sense means the correspondence of the valid legal norm with legal cognition without the validity of a norm (its existence) becoming a 'truth'.[13]
- Even if 'truth' is a problematic concept or if reality is difficult or even impossible to cognise, we must strive for its cognition. Kelsen does not abandon the quest for truth just because it turns out to be problematic. A modernist does not abandon the search for objectivity in cognition just because we have realised that scientific cognition may be influenced or biased.[14]
- The goal of legal science is to apprehend or cognise the law.[15] Scholars choose their own object of cognition; hence the choice of cognising law is arbitrary. The consequences for the method of cognition begin with the notion that law is comprised of norms, i.e. of 'ought'.[16] For Kelsen, the possibility of norms is expressed in the Is–Ought dichotomy.
- Norms are a distinct concept, a specific form of existence and can be cognised. From a general philosophical point of view, to be able to conceptualise 'ought' requires a modicum of idealism.[17] Only if we believe that an ideal can form a 'reality' in some sense, rather than trying to reduce 'the world' to brute reality, can we conduct a legal *science*.

Next to its concept and claim of 'scientificality' in legal scholarship, the Pure Theory of Law's other fundamental axiom is that of a categorical distinction between the realms of Is and Ought. This does not mean

[12] Horst Dreier, 'Hans Kelsens Wissenschaftsprogramm' in Helmuth Schulze-Fielitz (ed.), *Staatsrechtslehre als Wissenschaft* (Duncker & Humblot 2007) 81–114; Franz W. Jerusalem, *Kritik der Rechtswissenschaft* (Knecht 1948) 59.

[13] Hans Kelsen, *Allgemeine Theorie der Normen* (Manz 1979) 143–144, 287.

[14] Compare Max Weber's parallel modernist programme where he develops similar thoughts: Max Weber, 'Die "Objektivität" sozialwissenschaftlicher und sozialpolitischer Erkenntnis' 19 *Archiv für Sozialwissenschaft und Sozialpolitik* (1904) 22–87 at 27; Max Weber, 'Der Sinn der "Wertfreiheit" der soziologischen und ökonomischen Wissenschaften' 7 *Logos* (1918) 40–88; Max Weber, 'Wissenschaft als Beruf' (unpublished, 1919) in Johannes Winckelmann (ed.), *Gesammelte Aufsätze zur Wissenschaftslehre von Max Weber* (3rd edn Mohr Siebeck 1968) 582–613 at 600–603.

[15] Julius Binder, 'Der Wissenschaftscharakter der Rechtswissenschaft' 25 *Kant-Studien* (1920) 321–365 at 340; Hans Kelsen, *Das Problem der Souveränität und die Theorie des Völkerrechts: Beitrag zu einer reinen Rechtslehre* (Mohr 1920), iv; Hans Kelsen, *Reine Rechtslehre* (2nd edn Franz Deuticke 1960) iii–iv, 72–78; Franz Weyr, 'Rechtsphilosophie und Rechtswissenschaft' 2 *Zeitschrift für öffentliches Recht* (1922) 671–682 at 672, 678.

[16] Kelsen, *Rechtslehre*, n. 15 at iii.

[17] Hans Kelsen, *Hauptprobleme der Staatsrechtslehre entwickelt aus der Lehre vom Rechtssatze* (Mohr 1911) vi.

that the theory of legal science and the dichotomy are not connected: for Kelsen's 'pure science of law', this ideal requires that we distinguish between Is and Ought.[18] In a passage in the posthumous *Allgemeine Theorie der Normen* (1979), Kelsen explains the dichotomy in terms which cannot be read as postulating a merely linguistic duality:[19]

> The dualism of Is and Ought is [viz. coincides with] the duality of reality and value. Therefore, we cannot deduce values from reality or reality from values . . . It is the case that something can actually exist where no norm says it *ought to* exist; also, a norm can stipulate that something ought to exist which does not – in fact – *exist*. Thus, it does not follow from the fact that something *is* that it *ought to be* and – vice versa – because something *ought to be* that it *is*. The relationship of Ought to Is is that of an insoluble *dualism*.[20]

In order for us to be able to cognise or 'perceive' norms, it is necessary to distinguish categorically Is from Ought. (Kelsen had indeed at one point identified Ought as a transcendental Category in a Kantian sense[21] and, in the 1979 book, still speaks of Is and Ought as 'basic categories'.)[22] Ideals have the form of Ought, of norms, i.e. are mostly a prescription for human behaviour. Without the possibility of the Ought form, we could not possibly see the point of an imperative. 'Sit down!' or 'Don't kill that man!' or 'Men ought to take off their hat when entering a church' would not be intelligible.[23] Hence, humans, as soon as they perceive 'you ought to do x' as something different from 'you are doing x', have already made the categorical distinction between 'the ideal' and 'the real'. Oughts are norms; norms are a 'claim to be observed', i.e. mostly a claim that

18 Hans Kelsen, 'Was ist die Reine Rechtslehre?' in *Demokratie und Rechtsstaat: Festgabe zum 60: Geburtstag von Zaccaria Giacometti* (Polygraphischer Verlag 1953) 143–161, reprinted in Hans Klecatsky, René Marcic, Herbert Schambeck (eds), *Die Wiener rechtstheoretische Schule: Ausgewählte Schriften von Hans Kelsen, Adolf Julius Merkl, Alfred Verdross* (Europa 1968) 611–629 at 614.

19 Such a reading is possible for other passages in the book: Kelsen, n. 13 e.g. at 44, 48–49.

20 'Der Dualismus von Sein und Sollen fällt mit dem Dualismus von *Wirklichkeit* und *Wert* zusammen. Daher läßt sich aus der Wirklichkeit kein Wert und aus dem Wert keine Wirklichkeit ableiten . . . Da etwas sein kann, das nicht in einer Norm *gesollt* ist, und etwas in einer Norm gesollt sein kann, das nicht – in Wirklichkeit – *ist*, kann daraus, daß etwas *ist*, nicht folgen, daß etwas sein *soll*, und daraus, daß etwas sein *soll*, nicht folgen, daß etwas *ist*. Sollen und Sein stehen im Verhältnis eines nicht auflösbaren *Dualismus*.' Kelsen, n. 13 at 47, 49.

21 Hans Kelsen, *Reine Rechtslehre. Einleitung in die rechtswissenschaftliche Problematik* (Franz Deuticke 1934) 21–24.

22 'Ursprüngliche Kategorie' – Kelsen, n. 13 at 2.

23 Again, this statement should not be interpreted in linguistic(-philosophical) terms only. Kelsen was not an analytic philosopher like Hart.

the behaviour of one or more individuals accords with the prescription.[24] They are no more than a claim – they do not change reality on their own – but are also no less than a claim – all norms are claims, none is a priori better than another. Since the norm is a claim, the form alone defines its very 'existence' in the realm of ideals, i.e. its validity. There are no non-valid norms: Ought ≡ bindingness ≡ validity ≡ 'existence'. For a norm – legal or otherwise – to be valid (to 'exist'),[25] it does not require further validation as 'legitimate' or as partaking of a 'moral obligation to obey'.[26]

3 The positivism-normativism dialectic in the Pure Theory of Law

The Pure Theory of Law can be described as a positivist-normativist approach to legal scholarship. On a first and untechnical approximation, 'positiveness' is the 'real' quality of law, its connection to reality, whereas 'normativeness' is its 'standard-setting' element, the factor that commands obedience. This well-established duality in legal philosophy was brought to the fore once more in what is now one of the standard works on international legal theory: Martti Koskenniemi's *From Apology to Utopia* (1989). Although focusing on the argumentative practice of international lawyers, rather than on the law itself (the distinction between the two is in itself extremely important), his duality of Apology and Utopia, of ascending and descending patterns, has made palpable that there seems to be an inherent tension in the combination of 'positive' and 'law'. Koskenniemi writes (again referring to discursive practices):

> There are two ways of arguing about order and obligation . . . One argument traces them down to justice, common interest . . . [which] are anterior, or superior, to State behaviour, will or interest . . . Another argument bases order and obligation on State behaviour, will or interest. It . . . attempts to construct a normative order on the basis of the 'factual' State behaviour . . . The two patterns are both exhaustive and mutually exclusive.[27]

24 Kelsen identifies four norm-functions: (i) obligation/prohibition; (ii) permission; (iii) empowerment (to create norms); and (iv) derogation (Kelsen, n. 13 at 76–92). Only the first two refer to human behaviour with a 'claim to be observed'.

25 On the notion that validity is the specific form of existence of norms, see Kelsen, n. 13 at 22–23.

26 HLA Hart, 'Positivism and the Separation of Law and Morals' 71 *Harvard Law Review* (1957–1958) 593–629 at 622.

27 Koskenniemi, n. 4 at 59.

Because of the irreconcilable nature of the two patterns and their interdependence, international legal discourse is inevitably locked in an oscillation or a pendulum between the two patterns.[28] Put thus, the choice seems stark, the pendulum inescapable and discourse doomed. Against Koskenniemi's structural analysis, Kelsen would probably first point out that the analysis of lawyers' arguments is not a proper function of legal scholarship, but perhaps a task for linguists, sociologists or anthropologists. But we will not focus on this point in this chapter. Rather, the place that 'positiveness', represented by 'apology' in Koskenniemi's system, and 'normativeness', represented by 'utopia', is accorded in the Pure Theory of Law will be discussed. In a second step, it will be shown that the duality is a contradiction only in limited ways and, within Kelsen's oeuvre, forms a dialectic in which one element is dependent on the other. Both elements together, understood correctly, form a synthesis which – if the predatory use of Hegel can be excused – results in an *Aufhebung*.

Kelsen's positivism criterion accords with the Latin origin of the word. Law is positive if it has been *positus*, i.e. set/put into the world, as the sense of an act of will (*Willensakt*).

> A norm which was created [set] by [or: through the use of] an act of will taking place in reality is a *positive* norm. For a moral or legal positivism, only positive norms, i.e. such norms as are created by human acts of will, are considered as possible objects of cognition. Norms which were created [set] by human acts of will are 'arbitrary' in the original sense of the word.[29]

Thus, Kelsen holds that 'the positivity of morals and law lies . . . in this act of creation by human acts . . . the Is-Fact . . . of Being-Enacted [is a] condition . . . for the validity of a norm, but not validity itself.'[30] In his

[28] Koskenniemi, n. 4 at 64, 565.

[29] 'Eine durch einen in der Seinswirklichkeit stattfindenden Willensakt gesetzte Norm ist eine *positive* Norm. Vom Standpunkt eines Moral- oder Rechtspositivismus kommen als Gegenstand der Erkenntnis nur positive, d.h. durch Willensakte, und zwar durch menschliche Willensakte, gesetzte Normen in Betracht. Normen, die durch menschliche Willensakte gesetzt werden, haben – in des Wortes eigentlicher Bedeutung – einen willkürlichen Charakter.' Kelsen, n. 13 at 4. The etymology of the German word 'willkürlich' points to its original meaning, as 'Kür' is an act of choice or decision (or creation), whereas 'Wille' is will, i.e. creation by act of will. The English word 'arbitrary' has similar origins: an arbiter is the arbitrator or judge, one whose will is decisive; the Latin *arbitrium* is the judgment or decision more generally.

[30] 'In diesem – durch menschliche Akte – Gesetzt-Sein . . . liegt die *Positivität der Moral und des Rechts* . . . die Seins-Tatsache . . . des Gesetzt-Werdens [ist eine] Bedingung . . . der Geltung einer Norm, aber nicht diese Geltung selbst.' Kelsen, n. 13 at 114.

late writings, he uses a pointed phrase to express this aspect of positivism: 'No imperative without an emperor, no norm without a norm-creating authority, i.e. no norm without an act of will whose sense it is.'[31] While there is some intramural discussion among Kelsen scholars about the development of Kelsen's thought on this over the years and attendant critique of, inter alia, the Kantian *Sinn*-element and the 'psychologisation' of the act of will,[32] the above seems a good indication of the core of Kelsen's conception of positivism in the late phase. The act-of-will theory is susceptible to three avenues of critique.

(i) An act of will is not required for the creation of law under all sources of international law, particularly for the creation of customary international law and general principles of law. This argument is largely based on a *petitio principii*, as many writers argue that we can tell how law is created by looking at how law has 'actually' been created in the past.[33] However, we cannot know how law is created if we do not know the rules of law-creation; law is not a butterfly whose coming-about is 'certain' if we can observe it living. In other words: norms are not corporeal objects whose existence we can verify simply by way of an act of observation. Also, Kelsen did acknowledge the problem of customary law in his writings and claimed that the *opinio necessitatis* at least fulfils the will-criterion.[34] There are doubts about his solution.[35] While there is insufficient space here to discuss these doubts in general, we will deal with the particular problem of the 'positivity' of general principles of law in Section 5.

[31] 'Kein Imperativ ohne Imperator, keine Norm ohne eine normsetzende Autorität, d.h. keine Norm ohne einen Willensakt, dessen Sinn sie ist.' Kelsen, n. 13 at 187.

[32] E.g. Clemens Jabloner, 'Kein Imperativ ohne Imperator. Anmerkungen zu einer Theorie Kelsens' in Robert Walter (ed.), *Untersuchungen zur Reinen Rechtslehre II: Ergebnisse eines Wiener Rechtstheoretischen Seminars 1988* (Manz 1988) 75–95; Kazimierz Opałek, *Überlegungen zu Hans Kelsens 'Allgemeiner Theorie der Normen'* (Manz 1980); Ota Weinberger, 'Der normenlogische Skeptizismus' 17 *Rechtstheorie* (1986) 12–81 at 25–45.

[33] E.g. Johan G. Lammers, 'General Principles of Law Recognized by Civilized Nations' in Frits Kalshoven, Pieter Jan Kuyper, Johan G. Lammers (eds), *Essays on the Development of the International Legal Order* (Sijthoff and Noordhoff 1980) 53–75 at 56. He argues that the question of whether general principles of law 'do exist or not, must be ascertained on the basis of empirical research'. This 'empirical research' can only cover the discovery of specific principles, not of general principles as source of international law (see Section 5), as the scholar conducting such 'research' already presupposes what she or he sets out to find.

[34] E.g. Kelsen, *Rechtslehre*, n. 15 at 9, 234; Kelsen, n. 8 at 944; Kelsen, n. 13 at 2, 113.

[35] Jabloner, n. 32 at 84–87; Weinberger, n. 32 at 43; Jörg Kammerhofer, *Uncertainty in International Law: A Kelsenian Perspective* (Routledge 2010) 82–85.

(ii) Another critique is that, in his late phase, Kelsen had become an Austinian and is therefore subject to the criticisms levelled against that theory. The slogan 'no imperative without emperor' is indeed reminiscent of Austin's definition of positive law as 'set, directly or circuitously, by a sovereign individual or body, to a member or members of the independent political society wherein its author is supreme'.[36] Kelsen's 'emperor theory' could be called closer to Austin than his earlier writings. Even on a superficial view, however, this analogy does not ring true. Kelsen himself dealt with Austin's command theory and distanced himself from it: 'Thus binding law cannot be the psychological will of the lawmakers even though a real act of will is necessary to make the law.'[37]

(iii) The third avenue of criticism holds that Kelsen, if not a neo-Austinian, is nonetheless a 'voluntarist'[38] positivist and subject to the critique that is applied to traditional forms of positivist approaches to international law. One of the central tenets of this chapter is that the Pure Theory of Law is not a traditional positivist approach to international law. Indeed, the present volume is premised on the assumption that there are positivist approaches that do not share traditionalist views. Hence, before we can explore the normativism–positivism dynamic further, we will have to distinguish the Pure Theory from previous positivist approaches.

The late nineteenth and early twentieth centuries indeed saw a focus on the role of state consent or state will as the law-creating fact in international law.[39] Whether international law is viewed as being formulated as a result of 'self-obligation' (*Selbstverpflichtung*),[40] common will (*Gemeinwille*)[41] or simply 'state consent',[42] the structure of the argument in classical voluntarism is the same. 'State will', 'the state', 'power' and 'sovereignty'

[36] John Austin, *The Province of Jurisprudence Determined* (John Murray 1832) 378.

[37] Hans Kelsen, 'The Pure Theory of Law and Analytical Jurisprudence' 55 *Harvard Law Review* (1941) 44–70 at 55.

[38] At one point, Kelsen, perhaps flippantly and only in a very specific sense, even calls himself a 'voluntarist': Kelsen, n. 8 at 944.

[39] This is not the place for a detailed discussion of these views; see instead Collins, Chapter 2 and von Bernstorff, Chapter 3.

[40] E.g. Georg Jellinek, *Die rechtliche Natur der Staatenverträge: Ein Beitrag zur juristischen Konstruktion des Völkerrechts* (Alfred Hölder 1880) 7.

[41] E.g. Heinrich Triepel, *Völkerrecht und Landesrecht* (C. L. Hirschfeld 1899) 27–32; Karl Bergbohm, *Jurisprudenz und Rechtsphilosophie*, Vol. 1 (Duncker & Humblot 1892) 18–21.

[42] E.g. Percy E. Corbett, 'The Consent of States and the Sources of the Law of Nations' 6 *BYBIL* (1925) 20–30 at 23, 30.

are all pre-legal entities; the necessary basis and originary source of all international law is presupposed as a matter of speculative introspection, rather than as an analysis of the law on law-making. Heinrich Triepel, one of the most important German voluntarists of the late nineteenth century, uses language that seems to come close to Kelsen in the following passage:

> The will whose content will form the legal rule, the will from which the legal rule flows, we call source of law . . . What kind of will is able to create international law with binding force? . . . This will can only be the will of states . . . Only the common will of many states, joined as a unity of will through a unification of will, can be the source of international law.[43]

Only on a prohibitively loose reading, however, can Kelsen and Triepel be called close. The origin of the notion of 'will', for example, or the role it plays within the legal system is crucially different. For Triepel, will is not a necessary but a sufficient condition for law. The relevance of will is not determined by further law (although he is aware of that problem);[44] the common will is a priori – necessarily – law-creating. This is a presupposition of a different kind, but of the same *type* of absolute and external standard as natural law. The method for justifying law is essentially the same and is open to the same critique.

Nor should we forget that it was Kelsen who, in a new era of (international) legal positivism, was the first to criticise traditional positivism just as fiercely as natural legal doctrine. His was, to use Horst Dreier's formulation, a 'two-front-war'[45] against the 'syncretism of method'[46] in legal scholarship. The role played by positivity in the Pure Theory of Law is entirely different. As detailed above, for the Pure Theory, the positivity of a norm is merely one of its properties, while validity is its form of 'existence'.[47] Valid non-positive norms are possible in specific

[43] 'Den Willen nun, dessen Inhalt der Rechtssatz bildet, den Willen aus dem er fliesst, nennen wir Rechtsquelle . . . Welcher Wille . . . ist im Stande mit verbindlicher Kraft [Völkerrecht] zu erlassen . . . ? . . . [D]ieser Wille [kann] hier nur ein . . . Wille von Staaten sein . . . Nur ein zu einer Willenseinheit durch Willenseinigung zusammengeflossener Gemeinwille mehrerer oder vieler Staaten kann die Quelle von Völkerrecht sein.' Triepel, n. 41 at 30–32 (emphasis removed; some gaps closed in the English translation).

[44] Triepel, n. 41 at 81–82.

[45] Horst Dreier, *Rechtslehre, Staatssoziologie und Demokratietheorie bei Hans Kelsen* (Nomos 1990); Horst Dreier, 'Rechtsdeutung zwischen Normativierung der Natur und Naturalisierung des Normativen am Beispiel von Kelsens Rechtsbegriff' in Clemens Jabloner, Friedrich Stadler (eds), *Logischer Empirismus und Reine Rechtslehre: Beziehungen zwischen dem Wiener Kreis und der Hans Kelsen-Schule* (Springer 2001) 291–305 at 298.

[46] Kelsen, n. 21 at 2.

[47] Kelsen, *Rechtslehre*, n. 15 at 10.

normative orders; what is more, in positive normative orders, the act of will is not sufficient to create a norm of that order (though see Section 4.1 for the roles of the *Grundnorm*). In positive/dynamic as opposed to fictional/static normative orders, the successful creation of a 'lower' norm requires two elements: first, the 'existence' (validity) and the fulfilment of the conditions of a 'higher' empowerment norm, a norm authorising the creation of further norms (for example, a constitution authorising and regulating the creation of statutory law); second, the act of will by a person or persons directed towards the creation of that norm, as specified in the empowerment norm.[48] The first element ensures its validity as a norm of that normative order; the second ensures its membership *qua* positivity.[49] Law-making within a normative order is itself positivised; the positivity element is not an a priori meta-legal construct, but a feature of positive law and determined by it. For Kelsen, then, the two elements of 'positivity' and 'normativity' are inevitably interlinked in positive normative orders and, since legal orders are always positive orders,[50] we can see the synthesis of this dialectic at work. The Is–Ought dichotomy, as the basic axiom for the possibility of norms via the hierarchy of norms, provides the validity ('existence') of the norm, whereas the act of will provides the positivity. At least for positive normative orders, the two are combined and no norm can exist without the two elements coming together.

At two points, however, we can see the synthesis being put to the test. One is the question of how positivity can exist without further normative validation at the apex of a normative order. Kelsen developed the *Grundnorm* to answer this question; despite exhaustive debate in scholarly literature, this construct is not the problem it is sometimes held up to be. The other point comes to the fore when we discuss the problem of 'erroneous decisions' of organs against which no legal redress is possible, which is particularly relevant in highly developed legal orders with court hierarchies. 'Erroneous decisions', i.e. norms not fulfilling all

[48] Kelsen, n. 13 at 238.

[49] Moreover, a fictional norm cannot be part of a positive normative order, just as little as a positive norm can be created from a fictional normative order. On this point, see Kammerhofer, n. 35 at 222–223.

[50] This writer believes that the Pure Theory of Law as a scholarly approach should tackle the question of the definition of law as seeking to find the *differentia specifica* vis-à-vis other normative orders on a quasi-empirical level. This he does in light of Kelsen's ambiguity on this issue, where the elements of 'effectiveness' or 'coerciveness' could in some formulations of some writings be said to constitute an a priori element. On this point, see e.g. Jörg Kammerhofer, 'Kelsen – Which Kelsen? A Reapplication of the Pure Theory to International Law' 22 *LJIL* (2009) 225–249 at 236–240.

the legal rules for the creation of norms (*Rechtserzeugungsregel*),[51] are a particularly puzzling case. They raise the question of how to determine the location of the *Grundnorm* and the possibility of the relativity of such a construct with the attendant consequences for the conceptual fragmentation of legal orders.[52] This section is limited in what it can say on this complex topic, but it can at least point out the consequences for the normativism–positivism duality.

On the one hand, a norm of a legal order, for example, a Supreme Court judgment, is only validly created when it meets all the necessary conditions of the law for its creation. The normativity element, springing from the duality of Is and Ought, requires that the validity of norms is only founded in further norms. Without such a basis, alleged norms cannot be norms – it would simply be impossible to cognise this 'something' as norm. *The normativity of normative systems demands a strict foundation in norms.*

On the other hand, the act of will to create a positive norm is clearly present even in an 'erroneous' decision. The empowerment norm does not 'contain' the norms that can potentially be created under it; as detailed above, a real act of will is necessary to create a positive norm. In positive legal orders, law-making is 'autonomous': in case a decision does not conform to the conditions of the original legal order, the act of will by the organ is constitutive of a new legal order, consisting of the *Grundnorm* and the 'erroneous decision' – if we presuppose a *Grundnorm* at that point. *The positivity of norms gives positive acts of will creative powers.*

Under this analysis, the two elements of the Pure Theory of Law, positivity and normativity, seem to collide. The paradox of positive normative orders is that a truly superior norm endangers positivity, while a truly positive norm endangers the unity of the normative order. The central

[51] Fritz Sander, 'Das Faktum der Revolution und die Kontinuität der Rechtsordnung' 1 *Zeitschrift für öffentliches Recht* (1919–1920) 132–164 at 150; Kelsen, *Souveränität*, n. 15 at 97, 232 (as 'Erzeugungsregel'); Adolf Julius Merkl, 'Prolegomena einer Theorie des rechtlichen Stufenbaues' in Alfred Verdross (ed.), *Gesellschaft, Staat und Recht: Untersuchungen zur Reinen Rechtslehre* (Julius Springer 1931) 252–294, reprinted in Hans Klecatsky, René Marcic, Herbert Schambeck (eds), *Die Wiener rechtstheoretische Schule: Ausgewählte Schriften von Hans Kelsen, Adolf Julius Merkl, Alfred Verdross* (Europa 1968) 1311–1361 at 1319, 1345–1346 (as 'Rechtserzeugungsregel'); Robert Walter, *Der Aufbau der Rechtsordnung: Eine rechtstheoretische Untersuchung auf Grundlage der Reinen Rechtslehre* (Leykam 1964) 55, 61.

[52] While this problem may converge with recent discussions concerning the issue of 'fragmentation', a different aspect of the problem will be discussed here. For a more expansive discussion of this point, see Kammerhofer, n. 35 at 187–193.

question seems indeed to be where the observer (as a cognising agent) imagines the *Grundnorm* to be.

4 The *Grundnorm* and the foundation for international law's sources

With the Is–Ought dichotomy as the basis of the possibility of norms or values, Kelsen was also equipped with a method for avoiding that perennial question in legal philosophy: the question of the ultimate basis of law's validity. The *Grundnorm* is the answer, but only for a specific normative (legal) order and only one that is relative and epistemic, not absolute and metaphysical. The *Grundnorm* is much discussed, both in primary texts[53] and in secondary literature.[54] But since the *Grundnorm*, despite its central place in the Pure Theory, is not central to this chapter, Section 4.1 will offer only a brief sketch. Instead, this chapter will focus, in Section 4.2, on the far more interesting parallels between the *Grundnorm* and Hart's Rule of Recognition, or more specifically, the relationship between the present 'neo-Kelsenian' positivist project[55] and Jean d'Aspremont's neo-Hartian theory of law-ascertainment. The most interesting and testing questions arise not so much from the abstract concepts of the *Grundnorm* (or Rule of Recognition), but from their application to a specific legal order and their sources.

4.1 The Grundnorm as nomo-epistemic tool[56]

At first blush, it would seem that the *Grundnorm* is Kelsen's answer to the question of the fount of validity, but on closer inspection it becomes clear that the Pure Theory does not wish to provide an 'ultimate' or 'absolute' foundation for the validity of norms. The validity-founding exercise is in a certain sense an epistemic tool, and the basic norm is self-referential and does not anchor the law in 'the cosmos of values'.[57] The Pure Theory's

53 E.g. Kelsen, n. 21 at 62–73; Kelsen, n. 5 at 110–122; Kelsen, *Rechtslehre*, n. 15 at 196–227; Kelsen, n. 13 at 203–208.

54 See by way of example the contributions by Raz, Honoré, Edel and Luf in the influential edited volume: Stanley L. Paulson, Bonnie Litschewski Paulson (eds), *Normativity and Norms: Critical Perspectives on Kelsenian Themes* (Oxford University Press 1998).

55 Kammerhofer, n. 11.

56 For a detailed discussion of the concept of the *Grundnorm*, as applied to international law, see Kammerhofer, n. 35 at 241–259.

57 Alfred Verdross, *Die Verfassung der Völkerrechtsgemeinschaft* (Springer 1926) 24.

radical claim is that while the term '*Grundnorm*' may have been coined by Kelsen, it is not dependent on this particular theoretical approach. All human beings necessarily presuppose a *Grundnorm* when they perceive norms as norms; it is the only way in which humans can conceive of norms. This necessity springs from the Is–Ought dichotomy and is in turn the dichotomy as concretised for a specific normative order. This explains also why the *Grundnorm* can be said to be analogous to Kant's Categories. The *Grundnorm* has four functions.[58]

(i) It is the expression of the dichotomy of Is and Ought. As mentioned above, the dichotomy enables cognition of norms as norms; it is an epistemic tool to help us perceive the difference between reality and another realm which posits some status or behaviour as ideal. The *Grundnorm* is the concrete expression of the dichotomy for a specific normative order.[59] It is thus self-referential, yet hardly trivial. The idea of the ideal[60] (the Ought) is contained in a purported 'norm' only if one presupposes the *Grundnorm* to be above each normative order. The source of the normativity of law and the *Grundnorm* are one and the same.[61]

(ii) It is the highest basis of validity (*Geltungsgrund*) of a normative order. The validity regress is a standard ploy in legal philosophy and is often cast as a series of questions along the lines of: 'Why is a norm valid, what is its basis of validity?'[62] For the Pure Theory, the basis of a norm's validity can only be the empowerment norm which authorises the creation of that norm (Section 3).[63] This understanding of validity founds the membership of norms in a normative order, but it ends at the highest

[58] Others have identified a larger number of functions, see: Stanley L. Paulson, 'Die unterschiedlichen Formulierungen der "Grundnorm"' in Aulis Aarnio *et al.* (eds), *Rechtsnorm und Rechtswirklichkeit: Festschrift für Werner Krawietz zum 60. Geburtstag* (Duncker & Humblot 1993) 53–74 at 58–63; Jens-Michael Priester, 'Die Grundnorm – eine Chimäre' in Werner Krawietz, Helmut Schelsky (eds), *Rechtssystem und gesellschaftliche Basis bei Hans Kelsen* (Duncker & Humblot 1984) 211–244 at 211–232.

[59] Robert Walter, 'Die Grundnorm im System der Reinen Rechtslehre' in Aulis Aarnio *et al.* (eds), *Rechtsnorm und Rechtswirklichkeit: Festschrift für Werner Krawietz zum 60. Geburtstag* (Duncker & Humblot 1993) 85–99 at 85.

[60] This is a phrase borrowed from Philip Allott, see e.g.: Philip Allott, *Eunomia: New Order for a New World* (Oxford University Press 1990, 2001) xxii (preface to the paperback edition); Philip Allott, *The Health of Nations: Society and Law beyond the State* (Cambridge University Press 2002) 33.

[61] Paulson, n. 58 at 57; Joseph Raz, 'Legal Positivism and the Sources of Law' in Joseph Raz, *The Authority of Law: Essays on Law and Morality* (Oxford University Press 1979) 37–52 at 48.

[62] 'Warum gilt eine Norm, was ist ihr Geltungsgrund?' Kelsen, *Rechtslehre*, n. 15 at 196.

[63] Kelsen, *Rechtslehre*, n. 15 at 196.

positive norm which was created without positive-legal authorisation.[64] How can the first positive norm be created without transcending the Is–Ought divide?[65] Only a capstone – an expression of the very idea of the ideal – will avoid the infinite regress without resorting to natural law doctrine and thus transcending the dichotomy. The *Grundnorm* founds the validity of the whole normative order[66] without itself needing any such foundation. Kelsen's *Grundnorm* is self-referential;[67] it answers by reference to itself by assuming validity:[68] we act *as if* the normative order were valid. 'On the precondition [assumption] that it is valid, the whole legal order under it is valid.'[69] This is a merely hypothetical and relative foundation of a legal order, but under the dichotomy of Is and Ought, it is the only possible one.

(iii) It constitutes the unity and identity of a normative order. The connection between norms is not absolute, but contingent; in establishing the validity-relationship, the *Grundnorm* also unites the normative order[70] 'by being the basis for the validity of all norms belonging to this order'.[71] However, we can presuppose a *Grundnorm* at any point in the normative order and thus declare any norm to be the highest positive norm. (See Section 4.2.)

64 Geert Edel, 'The Hypothesis of the Basic Norm: Hans Kelsen and Hermann Cohen' in Stanley L. Paulson, Bonnie Litschewski Paulson (eds), *Normativity and Norms: Critical Perspectives on Kelsenian Themes* (Oxford University Press 1998) 195–219 at 213.

65 Kelsen, *Rechtslehre*, n. 15 at 197; Jürgen Behrend, *Untersuchungen zur Stufenbaulehre Adolf Merkls und Hans Kelsens* (Duncker & Humblot 1977) 64.

66 Robert Alexy, 'Hans Kelsens Begriff des relativen Apriori' in Robert Alexy *et al.* (eds), *Neukantianismus und Rechtsphilosophie* (Nomos 2002) 179–202; Edel, n. 64 at 213.

67 Stig Jørgensen calls it 'tautological' in Stig Jørgensen 'Grundnorm und Paradox' in Werner Krawietz, Helmut Schelsky (eds), *Rechtssystem und gesellschaftliche Basis bei Hans Kelsen* (Duncker & Humblot 1984) 179–191 at 187–188.

68 Alfred Verdross, 'Zum Problem der völkerrechtlichen Grundnorm' in Walter Schätzel, Hans-Jürgen Schlochauer (eds), *Rechtsfragen der internationalen Organisation: Festschrift für Hans Wehberg zu seinem 70. Geburtstag* (Klostermann 1956) 385–394, reprinted in Hans Klecatsky, René Marcic, Herbert Schambeck (eds), *Die Wiener rechtstheoretische Schule: Ausgewählte Schriften von Hans Kelsen, Adolf Julius Merkl, Alfred Verdross* (Europa 1968) 2203–2212 at 2203.

69 'Unter der Voraussetzung, daß sie gilt, gilt auch die Rechtsordnung, die auf ihr beruht.' Kelsen, n. 21 at 66; Kelsen, n. 5 at 111; Kelsen, *Rechtslehre*, n. 15 at 201; Kelsen, n. 13 at 206–207.

70 Behrend, n. 65 at 68–69; Uta U. Bindreiter, 'Presupposing the Basic Norm' 14 *Ratio Juris* (2001) 143–175 at 147; Raz, n. 61 at 48; Robert Walter, 'Entstehung und Entwicklung des Gedankens der Grundnorm' in Robert Walter (ed.), *Schwerpunkte der Reinen Rechtslehre* (Manz 1992) 47–59 at 47; Walter, n. 59 at 92–93.

71 '. . . indem sie den Grund für die Geltung aller zu dieser Ordnung gehörigen Normen darstellt', Kelsen, *Rechtslehre*, n. 15 at 197.

(iv) In positive orders, the *Grundnorm* identifies the individual who is authorised to create the highest norm. Following from its nature as a special kind of empowerment norm,[72] an ancillary function of the *Grundnorm* in positive normative orders is to identify which individuals are authorised to create the highest positive norm of that order.[73] However, the identification is not the same as with other empowering norms (i.e. the positive empowering norms), because the *Grundnorm* always identifies an already created 'something' as norm. Its content is determined by the last positive norm, not vice versa. In effect, it seems that Hart's social thesis serves the same function and could therefore mean that a *Grundnorm* is superfluous.[74] This leads us to the question of whether the Rule of Recognition is significantly different from the *Grundnorm*, a question to be addressed in the next section.

4.2 The Rule of Recognition and formalist international law-ascertainment

Two main streams of post-modern positivism are active in legal theory: Hartianism and Kelsenianism.[75] Neither of these streams are classically positivist; both share certain superficial traits, but their meta-jurisprudential foundations – and the philosophical socialisation of their founders – are very different. This is not the place for a comparison of the origins, causes and manifestations of the different jurisprudential cultures of Kelsenianism and Hartianism,[76] but since these are the two main streams of 'non-classical' positivism (notwithstanding streams that go 'beyond' Kelsen and Hart)[77] and since they offer the best chance of a theoretically sustained non-trivial account of positivist international legal scholarship, a brief exploration of a particular parallel in Hart's and Kelsen's structural analysis of legal orders will be attempted here. If we

[72] Kelsen, n. 21 at 64, 66; Kelsen, *Rechtslehre*, n. 15 at 197, 199; Edel, n. 64 at 218; Paulson, n. 58 at 57; Priester, n. 58 at 223–225.

[73] Kelsen, n. 21 at 65; Sylvie Delacroix, 'Hart's and Kelsen's Concepts of Normativity contrasted' 17 *Ratio Juris* (2004) 501–520 at 508.

[74] This is, indeed, claimed by some Anglo-American legal philosophers, foremost Herbert Hart himself: see HLA Hart, *The Concept of Law* (Oxford University Press 1961) 246.

[75] Jörg Kammerhofer, 'Positivism' in Anthony Carty (ed.), *Oxford Bibliographies Online: International Law* (2012), available at www.oxfordbibliographiesonline.com.

[76] The present writer has changed his views on the comparability of these two approaches since this chapter was concluded, e.g. Jörg Kammerhofer, 'Positivistische Normbegründung' in Eric Hilgendorg, Jan C. Joerden (eds), *Handbuch Rechtsphilosophie* (forthcoming, Metzler 2015), available at http://ssrn.com/abstract=2296874.

[77] Somek, Chapter 6.

refrain from comparing the Rule of Recognition with the *Grundnorm* – as is usually done – but instead compare it with the highest positive norms of a given normative order, what Kelsen called the 'historically first constitution' (*historisch erste Verfassung*), the models merge somewhat. The parallel is interesting inter alia, because both Hart and Raz variously claim that the *Grundnorm* (as an element that goes beyond even the highest positive norm) is redundant, a 'needless reduplication'.[78]

What, then, is this mythical 'first constitution'[79] and what role does it have in international law? For the Pure Theory, the key question concerns the sources of international law, specifically: 'where do the sources of law come from?' A source of law is a meta-law on law-creation,[80] the norm-function 'authorisation' (i.e. norms empowering the creation of other norms). This holds true even where authorising norms hold a subordinate position within a normative order as a source of law, such as the authorisation to create Security Council resolutions *qua* norms by the combined force of Articles 25, 39 and 41 of the UN Charter. The 'sources of law' are not an absolute, found by way of extra-legal considerations, and are not necessarily on one and the same hierarchical level, but merely a convenient description of a specific norm-function. The Kelsenian approach can also be distinguished with regard to the Hartian view of this as a 'source thesis'[81] or theory of sources. Far more than with the Rule of Recognition and other secondary rules in the Hartian mould, for Kelsen, sources are *part of the legal order*, positive norms within a legal order. They can be found at nearly all levels of the legal order[82] (from constitutions to statutes to administrative orders). They are no more than norms fulfilling the function of 'empowerment'. Like substantive rules, therefore, the sources of law do not exist by virtue of scholarly

[78] Hart, n. 74 at 246; Joseph Raz, *The Concept of a Legal System: An Introduction to the Theory of Legal System* (2nd edn Oxford University Press 1980) 100–109; thus also d'Aspremont, Chapter 5 at 139.

[79] E.g. Hans Kelsen, *Principles of International Law* (Rinehart and Co. 1952) 411.

[80] Kelsen, n. 79 at 303; Kelsen, *Rechtslehre*, n. 15 at 238–239; Valentin Petev, 'Rechtsquellenlehre und Reine Rechtslehre' in Werner Krawietz, Helmut Schelsky (eds), *Rechtssystem und gesellschaftliche Basis bei Hans Kelsen* (Duncker & Humblot 1984) 273–287 at 273.

[81] Raz, n. 61 at 47.

[82] On this, see Adolf Merkl's Janus-faced character of the law in complex legal orders, except for the *Grundnorm* and the last act of enforcement, as simultaneously law-applying and law-creating. Adolf Julius Merkl, 'Das doppelte Rechtsantlitz: Eine Betrachtung aus der Erkenntnistheorie des Rechtes' 47 *Juristische Blätter* (1918) 425–427, 444–447, 463–465, reprinted in Hans Klecatsky, René Marcic, Herbert Schambeck (eds), *Die Wiener rechtstheoretische Schule: Ausgewählte Schriften von Hans Kelsen, Adolf Julius Merkl, Alfred Verdross* (Europa 1968) 1091–1113 at 1095–1097.

theorisation.[83] Contrary to Jean d'Aspremont's argument,[84] sources (*tout court*) in the Kelsenian realm are not the closest equivalent to Hart's Rule of Recognition.

The answer to the question of where sources come from is clear. We have to look for those norms which authorise the creation of the norms that, in turn, authorise the creation of customary international law or international treaty law.[85] The Pure Theory of Law enjoins us to ask for and find positive norms of international law that create source-law. The norm (or the norms) of international law which authorises the creation of the sources of international law can probably be considered to be international law's historically first constitution. These norms are both chronologically and logically prior in the hierarchy of validity. Kelsen writes:

> If one asks why norms which regulate the creation of general norms are valid, one may find a yet older constitution, i.e. the validity of the present constitution is based in its being created according to the provisions of a previously valid constitution by way of an amendment of the constitution. Thus at the end one comes to the historically first constitution, which cannot be founded in a positive norm, a constitution which came into validity through a revolutionary process. If one asks why the historically first constitution is valid the answer can only be that the validity of this constitution, the assumption that it is a binding norm must be *presumed*.[86]

The historically first constitution is the highest positive norm of a positive normative order. It is not derived from a higher *positive* norm. The Austrian post-1945 constitutional 'reinstatement' is a perfect example. In 1945, Austria's main political parties declared that the 1920 constitution

[83] Despite some vagueness, this seems to be the argument in d'Aspremont, Chapter 5 at 136–138.

[84] D'Aspremont, Chapter 5; Jean d'Aspremont, *Formalism and the Sources of International Law: A Theory of the Ascertainment of Legal Rules* (Oxford University Press 2011).

[85] Rub, n. 2 at 312–313.

[86] '[F]ragt man nach dem Geltungsgrund der Normen, die die Erzeugung der generellen Normen regeln ... so gerät man vielleicht auf eine ältere Staatsverfassung; das heißt: man begründet die Geltung der bestehenden Staatsverfassung damit, daß sie gemäß den Bestimmungen einer vorangegangenen Staatsverfassung im Wege einer verfassungsmäßigen Verfassungsänderung ... zustande gekommen ist; und so [gerät man] schließlich auf eine historisch erste Staatsverfassung, die nicht mehr auf eine [positive] Norm zurückgeführt werden kann, eine Staatsverfassung, die revolutionär ... in Geltung getreten ist ... [F]ragt man nach dem Grund der Geltung der historisch ersten Staatsverfassung ... dann kann die Antwort ... nur sein, daß die Geltung dieser Verfassung, die Annahme, daß sie eine verbindliche Norm sei, *vorausgesetzt* werden muß ...' Kelsen, *Rechtslehre*, n. 15 at 203.

was reinstated.[87] This declaration did not conform to the provisions of the 1920 constitution and the validity of Austria's constitution is now based on the 1945 norm, not on the original 1920 constitution. This is the highest positive norm of the Austrian legal order, its historically first constitution.[88]

Since the *Grundnorm*'s content is not imposed on a normative order, but moulds itself to the highest positive norm, Hart is correct in his observation that, for Kelsen, the validity of that positive norm is not derived from further positive norms. Equally, in international law, does it not make sense to identify the three Article 38 sources by way of Hart's socio-empirical Rule of Recognition and then ascribe Hart's quasi-empirical validity to them? In doing so, could we thus avoid the awkward question of the inter-relationship of the three classical sources? Could we also avoid the thorny matter of possible new sources of international law, such as 'global administrative law'?

At first blush, Hart's more flexible approach seems attractive. It is modelled on the seemingly value-neutral sociological criteria of acknowledgement and acceptance *in fact*; the dynamic duo of Rule of Recognition and Rule of Change require much less and can accommodate much more. Hart's self-description of the *Concept of Law* as an 'essay in descriptive sociology'[89] has been criticised, but it can be argued that he is given too little credit for it: that is exactly what he was doing. In other words, the difficulty lies not in distinguishing Hart from other positivists such as Kelsen, but distinguishing his approach from that of Legal Realism. Hart writes that '[w]henever such a rule of recognition is accepted, both private persons and officials are provided with *authoritative criteria for identifying* primary rules of obligation'.[90] He continues in the endnotes to say that '[t]he question whether a rule of recognition exists . . . is regarded . . . as an empirical . . . question of fact'.[91] It is clear that for him, this feature of his theory is a procedure for identifying an obedience habit among certain classes of people. With the Rule of Recognition, Hart describes a socio-empirical method – a tool of a special kind of sociology – which is

[87] Art I, III Unabhängigkeitserklärung, in: Proklamation [über die Selbständigkeit Österreichs], StGBl 1945/1 read in conjunction with Art 1 Verfassungsgesetz vom 1. Mai 1945 über das neuerliche Wirksamwerden des Bundes-Verfassungsgesetzes in der Fassung von 1929 (Verfassungs-Überleitungsgesetz – V-ÜG), StGBl 1945/4.

[88] For ease of argument, the preceding sentence ignores the possibility that the Austrian legal order (or any other municipal legal order for that matter) is merely a sub-order of international law.

[89] Hart, n. 74 at vii.

[90] Hart, n. 74 at 97 (emphasis added).

[91] Hart, n. 74 at 245.

able to detect, by way of specific criteria, what is law in a certain society and what is not.

But does not Kelsen also take the factually most effective authority – a matter of fact, indeed, of the authority recognised as such – and simply graft the elusive *Grundnorm* onto it in order to perform the transfiguration of that authority into a legal order? Yes and no. There are several crucial differences between them: for one, Kelsen's value relativism operates differently from Hart's. Kelsen simply accords the name 'law' to the most effective normative order[92] as a matter of normative epistemology. Less effective or ineffective normative orders can still be perceived. Thus, in Austria in 1945, both the new democratic legal order and the National Socialist regime can be understood as legal orders: both presented claims to be observed – both stipulated 'oughts' – but it just so happened that the *debellatio* of the latter made it ineffective. The *Grundnorm* is not a touchstone to transform something into law, it is the as-if assumption which all people – even non-Kelsenians – make every time they perceive something as a norm, as an Ought. As a positivist theory, the Pure Theory operates with facts (in Kelsen's case, acts of will) that are relevant in making a norm positive (see Section 3). However, this is a necessary condition for validity and not, as Hart argues, a sufficient one.[93]

The problems with Hartian theory are linked to the idea that a sociological enquiry,[94] an empirical identification mechanism, is the true way to cognise law, and that such an enquiry can *somehow* determine, or constitute, the *validity* of the law. This means one of two things. On one hand, it could mean that Hart is a legal realist, a radical non-cognitivist who reduces all law to a prediction of future behaviour, a charge which Hart specifically sought to avoid. The argument against this viewpoint

92 This, admittedly, is a re-reading or re-construction of Kelsen and is arguably closer to the theoretical foundations of the Pure Theory of Law (see Section 2) than to the historical Kelsen. The argument can, however, indirectly be seen in Kelsen's writings, e.g. Kelsen, *Rechtslehre*, n. 15 at 72 (the object of a legal science is the cognition of legal orders) read in conjunction with 31–59, especially 48 (legal orders are empirically defined as coercive social orders with a minimum degree of effectiveness). On the view of the Pure Theory presented here, Kelsen was being particularly unhelpful in his formulations – arguably writing contrary to the spirit of the Pure Theory of Law – when at points he defined the (overall) efficacy of a legal order as a condition for its continued validity, e.g. Kelsen, n. 5 at 41–42 or Kelsen, *Rechtslehre*, n. 15 at 10–11.

93 Hart, n. 74 at 246: 'The distinction between the historical cause and the reason for the validity of a given rule of law can be drawn only where the system contains a rule of recognition, under which certain things . . . are accepted as identifying marks of valid law.'

94 D'Aspremont, Chapter 5 at 135.

remains cogent: a factual enquiry cannot 'decipher' the proposition that 'you *ought* to do this' – it can only yield a result along the lines that 'if you don't do this, there is a 0.934 likelihood that something else is going to happen'. That is not a normativist science and thus Hart's enquiry is reduced to a particularly unsophisticated form of sociology.

On the other hand – and this is the way d'Aspremont's formalism of law-ascertainment seems to be leaning – Hart could be said to accept the 'transformation' from social fact to legal value. In d'Aspremont's 'reductionist' reading of Hart, however, legal scholarship takes on an unexpectedly important role, mandated in part by the crucial notion of the 'internal point of view' *qua* social practice or acceptance by 'law-applying authorities',[95] but problematic nonetheless. D'Aspremont describes this role as follows: 'Hart's positivism . . . confines legal positivism to a theory about the determination of the existence of law by virtue of a theory of sources, i.e. a theory of the *ascertainment of rules*.'[96] This equivocation of ascertainment with law-making[97] continues throughout his chapter, for example, in the phrase 'grounding the ultimate law-ascertaining rule in a social practice'.[98] Both for Hart and d'Aspremont, the Rule of Recognition is a cognitive tool of a descriptive sociology, yet it turns out to also be something that creates norms from facts. In the specific application to international law espoused by d'Aspremont in Chapter 5, it is clearest when he denies that Hart's theory provides a basis for the validity of law,[99] while at the same time explicitly affirming that 'from a Hartian perspective, international legal positivism . . . should be confined to a thesis about the *validity-condition of legal norms*'.[100] Concomitantly, this dual and syncretic argument is clear when he both implicitly denies[101] and explicitly affirms[102] that validity is the specific form of 'existence' for legal rules/norms. Let us take as an example the possibility for a Hartian theory of international law to accommodate new sources of international law. D'Aspremont argues that 'source theory' – not the law, but legal scholarship – may be able 'to accommodate . . . new pluralised forms

[95] D'Aspremont, Chapter 5 at 121.
[96] D'Aspremont, Chapter 5 at 115 (emphasis added).
[97] Also in his earlier monograph, see d'Aspremont, n. 84 at 50, 53.
[98] D'Aspremont, Chapter 5 at 121.
[99] D'Aspremont, Chapter 5 at 139 ('It is argued here, however, that, *as far as the ascertainment of international legal rules is concerned*, the social thesis makes the question of the validity of the international legal order as a whole utterly vain') and 140.
[100] D'Aspremont, Chapter 5 at 115 (emphasis added).
[101] D'Aspremont, Chapter 5 at 140.
[102] D'Aspremont, Chapter 5 at 123.

of exercises of public authority'. The method to be employed is to devise '[n]ew formal international law-ascertainment criteria . . . as to elevate the norms . . . into rules of international law'. This elevation is to be achieved, as the footnote tells us, as an exercise of 'scholarly reflection'.[103] In effect, therefore, new formal sources of international law are created by scholars apprehending this; is this not taking the Kantian insight into the 'creative' effect of apperception[104] one step too far?

Against the argument that Hartian theory is in danger of confounding Is and Ought (and is thus unable to even conceive of the 'you *ought* to do this' at all) when it accords sociology this foundational character, d'Aspremont argues:

> [T]his objection does not really undermine the theory of ascertainment presented here . . . This is a fundamentally different debate from that of law-ascertainment . . . even if the social thesis, by bypassing the question of the validity of the international legal system as a whole and grounding law-ascertainment in facts, were to lead legal science to encapsulate sociological analysis, such an enlargement of scope of the science of law . . . would then be the necessary condition for a lasting and solid theory of ascertainment of international legal rules.[105]

To even begin to ascertain law as rules, as Ought, rather than as mere behavioural pattern, we have to presuppose validity *qua* existence *qua* Ought and that is what the *Grundnorm* is about, rather than some absolute foundation of hierarchy of value. As far as it looks at law as Ought, even a 'descriptive sociology' of law such as Hart's also *implicitly* presupposes a specific normativistic viewpoint as part of its calculus. The critique formulated by Kelsen in an important, if overlooked, 1914 article entitled *Eine Grundlegung der Rechtssoziologie* (basically a polemic against Eugen

103 D'Aspremont, Chapter 5 at 138.

104 Immanuel Kant, *Kritik der reinen Vernunft* (Johann Friedrich Hartknoch 1781, 1787) B 137–138; see, however, Kelsen, *Rechtslehre*, n. 15 at 74–75: 'Es ist auch richtig, daß, im Sinne der Kantschen Erkenntnistheorie, die Rechtswissenschaft als Erkenntnis des Rechts, so wie alle Erkenntnis, konstitutiven Charakter hat und daher ihren Gegenstand insofern "erzeugt", als sie ihn als ein sinnvolles Ganzes begreift . . . Aber diese "Erzeugung" hat einen rein erkenntnistheoretischen Charakter. Sie ist etwas völlig anderes als . . . die Erzeugung des Rechts durch die Rechtsautorität.' ('It is also true that, according to Kant's epistemology, legal science as cognition of law – like all cognition – has a constitutive character and "creates" its object insofar as it comprehends the object as a meaningful whole . . . This "creation", however, has a purely epistemological character. It is fundamentally different than . . . the creation of law by the legal authority.')

105 D'Aspremont, Chapter 5 at 141.

Ehrlich's expansionist notions of legal sociology), can be taken to apply here as well. In it he writes:

> Legal sociology is not an autonomous science; from the point of view of general sociology, it is an arbitrary section of a science that cognises and explains societal life as a whole. This is because the separation of this *legal* sociology can only be achieved by using a concept which originates in a categorically different viewpoint than that of an explicative sociology, i.e. in normativist scholarship's concept of law. Legal sociology cannot determine . . . what law is, as it has to presuppose normativist scholarship's concept of law.[106]

As detailed above, this is Hart's major failing: in trying to construct a sociological account while not degenerating into legal realism (which denies the oughtness of rules), he has to implicitly acknowledge the dichotomy of Is and Ought. In attempting to avoid both the reduction of law to a prediction of future behaviour and the radical denial of Ought, he has to provide for a 'transformation' of facts into law. He finds himself in exactly the same predicament as Kelsen, but he seems not to have fully grasped the depth of the problem. His solution – the conjunction of the source thesis with the social thesis – therefore fails to provide an account that separates Is and Ought and can thus, from the perspective of the Pure Theory of Law, rightly be called a variant of natural law.[107] Again, *Eine Grundlegung der Rechtssoziologie* provides cogent arguments *avant la lettre* against the Hartian social thesis and it seems apt to quote Kelsen here again:

> How humans regularly behave in specific instances is a categorically different matter from what they ought to do according to the law even if the content of the norms regulating their behaviour is conterminous with the

[106] 'Rechtssoziologie ist im Grunde genommen gar keine eigene Wissenschaft; es ist ein vom Standpunkte soziologischer Erkenntnis durchaus willkürlicher Ausschnitt aus einer allgemeinen, das soziale Leben betrachtenden und erklärenden Wissenschaft. Denn die Abgrenzung dieser *Rechts*soziologie muß durch einen Begriff vollzogen werden, dessen Bestimmung von einem ganz anderen Standpunkte aus erfolgt, als der einer explikativen Soziologie ist, nämlich durch den normativen Rechtsbegriff. Was Recht ist . . . das kann die Rechtssoziologie nicht bestimmen; sie muß den normativen Rechtsbegriff voraussetzen.' Hans Kelsen, 'Eine Grundlegung der Rechtssoziologie' 39 *Archiv für Sozialwissenschaft und Sozialpolitik* (1914–1915) 839–876 at 875 (3 *HKW* 357) (original emphasis removed).

[107] Kammerhofer, n. 35 at 224–230.

> content of the propositions describing actual behaviour, in other words: if there were none bar customary law.[108]

One is tempted to add that this applies with particular force to a theory for which the sources of a legal order are established by a scholarly-sociological description of how a subset of individuals in a given society (Hart's 'officials') behave, i.e. through a quasi-sociological and quasi-psychological description of the state of mind of law-appliers.

5 General principles of law and Kelsenian positivism

5.1 The problems of orthodoxy – a problem for the Pure Theory?

Section 3 sought to demonstrate that for Kelsen's brand of positivism – or, rather, for his concept of positivity – the existence of a real act of will is at the very least a necessary condition for the positivity of norms. What, then, of the 'general principles of law recognized by civilised nations' as codified in Article 38(1)(c) of the ICJ Statute? By common consent, they are a source of international law, yet (so it is claimed) they obviously are not created by an act of will. The majority of writers argue that, at least in part, '[t]hey are principles arrived at by way of a comparison, generalisation and synthesis of rules of law . . . common to various systems of national law'.[109] It is, in effect, a variant of 'law-making by analogy', a technique

108 'Dasjenige, was die Menschen in irgend einer Beziehung regelmäßig tun, und dasjenige, was sie von Rechts wegen tun sollen, muß selbst dann noch als etwas formal gänzlich Verschiedenes gelten, wenn der Inhalt der Normen, die bestimmen, was geschehen soll, mit dem Inhalt jener Regeln zusammenfällt, die aussagen, was tatsächlich geschieht; m.a.W., wenn es kein anderes als ein Gewohnheitsrecht gäbe.' Kelsen, n. 106 at 841 (3 *HKW* 321).

109 Hersch Lauterpacht, 'International Law – the General Part' (unpublished) in Elihu Lauterpacht (ed.), *International Law: Being the Collected Papers of Hersch Lauterpacht*, Vol. 1 (Cambridge University Press 1970) 1–178 at 74. See also M. Cherif Bassiouni, 'A Functional Approach to "General Principles of International Law"' 11 *Michigan Journal of International Law* (1989–1990) 768–818 at 768–769; Frances T. Freeman Jalet, 'The Quest for the General Principles of Law Recognized by Civilized Nations – A Study' 10 *UCLA Law Review* (1963) 1041–1086 at 1056; Robert Kolb, 'Principles as Sources of International Law (with Special Reference to Good Faith)' 53 *Netherlands International Law Review* (2006) 2–36 at 3–4; Hersch Lauterpacht, *Private Law Sources and Analogies of International Law (with Special Reference to International Arbitration)* (Longmans 1927) 69; Alain Pellet, 'Article 38' in Andreas Zimmermann, Christian Tomuschat, Karin Oellers-Frahm (eds), *The Statute of the International Court of Justice: A Commentary* (Oxford University Press 2006) 677–792 at 766–767, 772; Advisory Committee of Jurists, *Procés-Verbaux of the Proceedings of the Committee June 16th–July 24th 1920, with Annexes* (Van Langenhuysen Bros 1920) 335 (Phillimore; Lapradelle); Rudolf Berthold

that today's international constitutionalist[110] or global administrative law scholars also employ. This method is one where 'the processes of comparison of the law of various countries [are combined with a] deduction from such comparison'.[111] Among the writers surveyed, Robert Kolb is perhaps clearest in describing what this entails: 'you may have rules which are not created by a process of legislation, but which simply exist: e.g. general principles of law'.[112] 'Rules which are not created but simply exist' is a concept which, while apparently solving one problem, at the same time poses another problem in respect of a theory of norms (and, incidentally, exposes the natural law origins of the idea of 'general principles of law').

The problem is twofold: it is positivism's problem with general principles just as much as it shows orthodox international legal scholarship's problem with consistent positivism. Not surprisingly, some scholars who see general principles as a crucial part of international law have attempted to show that their existence among the canon of sources proves that positivism is not the right or only approach to international law. For Shabtai Rosenne, the inclusion of subparagraph (c) in the Statute means that general principles are now 'on a footing of formal equality with the two *positivist* elements of custom and treaty'[113] – positiv*ist*, not positive. Kelsen's conception of positivism as a scholarly approach as described in Section 2 could not even begin to conceive of a source of law as 'positivist' or 'naturalist', as these adjectives pertain to a scholarly approach, and do not apply to a source, to law-cognition, nor to law-creation. True, much of the problem that these scholars have with general principles under the positivist family of approaches is due to the straw-man of voluntarism[114] that they confound with positivism.[115] Bassiouni, for example, argues that 'a basic question arises under a strict positivist approach, which would see

Schlesinger, 'Research on the General Principles of Law Recognized by Civilized Nations: Outline of a New Project' 51 *AJIL* (1957) 734–753 at 735; Georges Vallindas, 'General Principles of Law and the Hierarchy of the Sources of International Law' in Dimitrios Constantopoulos, Konstantinos Efstathiadis, Charalambos Fragistas (eds), *Grundprobleme des Internationalen Rechts: Festschrift für Jean Spiropoulos* (Schimmelbusch 1957) 425–431 at 427–428.

110 For a critique of this stream along similar lines, see Jörg Kammerhofer, 'Constitutionalism and the Myth of Practical Reason: Kelsenian Responses to Methodological Confusion' 23 *LJIL* (2010) 723–740.

111 Lauterpacht, 'International Law', n. 109 at 71.

112 Kolb, n. 109 at 4 (fn. 8).

113 Shabtai Rosenne, *The Law and Practice of the International Court 1920–2005*, Vol. 4 (4th edn Martinus Nijhoff 2006) 1549 (emphasis added).

114 Collins, Chapter 2.

115 Freeman Jalet, n. 109 at 1053.

"General Principles" as . . . source of law which would have the capacity of binding States to that to which they have not specifically consented'.[116] This is based on a fallacious equivocation of positivism and voluntarism. The result for Bassiouni – predictably less positivist in his approach – is that general principles cannot be part of positive law:

> Positivists espouse the view that . . . the only international law that exists is that which has been stated in positive terms. That which has not been established in positive terms is outside the scope of the law. Consequently, there is no need for 'General Principles.' To take this position, however, is to deny reality and the needs of the international legal system. That which is not covered by positive international law exists . . . [117]

While Bassiouni's specific argument fails on other grounds – how can general principles, for example, be 'beyond accepted normative positive law because they too derive from positive law'[118] – the root of the problem identified by these scholars holds true even for Kelsen's non-voluntarist conception of positivity. While Kelsen (very occasionally) argues that customary modes of law-creation are not will-based, yet still result in positive law,[119] this view is not entirely compatible with the Pure Theory of Law's positivist elements as detailed in Section 3. An act of will – even if masquerading as *opinio iuris* – is necessary. The general principles of law must thus be considered a test case for Kelsen's positivism. What, then, is his position?

5.2 The historical Kelsen and the ICJ's lex arbitri

Kelsen sets out to shock orthodox sensibilities; for him, '[i]t is more than doubtful whether such rules, if they exist, are part of international law'.[120] At this point, we have to be careful not to muddle the many strands of argument and – most importantly – not to muddle Kelsen's own arguments with those that can be made from the perspective of the Pure Theory of Law. These are linked, but in his writings, Kelsen highlighted only one important aspect: the function of Article 38 of the ICJ Statute as

[116] Bassiouni, n. 109 at 785. [117] Bassiouni, n. 109 at 792.

[118] Bassiouni, n. 109 at 786; similarly: Bin Cheng, *General Principles of Law as Applied by International Courts and Tribunals* (Stevens & Sons 1953) 22–23.

[119] Kelsen, n. 13 at 2; the role of acts of will in customary international law is further discussed in Kammerhofer, n. 35 at 82–85.

[120] Hans Kelsen, *The Law of the United Nations: A Critical Analysis of its Fundamental Problems* (Stevens & Sons 1950) 533.

lex arbitri. Kelsen distinguished Article 38 of the Statute from the question of the existence of 'general principles of law' as a source, arguing that Article 38 gives the *lex arbitri* for one specific tribunal and that role is fundamentally different from that of a source. The Article only provides rules on how the tribunal shall decide and does not determine the formal sources of international law in its entirety. One could argue that the difference is crucial, but is a distinction that has been taken much too lightly in scholarship. Indeed, ever since the *Procès-Verbaux* of the Committee of Jurists that first drafted the provision in 1920, scholars continue to conflate four questions: (i) what are the sources of international law? (ii) what norms should a given tribunal be tasked with applying? (iii) are there gaps in the law and how should these be filled? and (iv) how do we – or, indeed, do we need to – avoid a finding of *non liquet* by this tribunal?[121]

These questions have confused many scholars. A court established by international law proper can also be tasked, for example, with applying a normative order outside (or non-identical with) international law. Private arbitration frequently allows for the parties to decide upon – and even modify – the *lex arbitri.* The codification of 'general principles' in Article 38 – whether or not its *chapeau* is right in stipulating that the Court decides 'in accordance with international law'[122] – is not determinative of their status as a source of international law, only of their status as *lex arbitri.* (Also, but equally non-determinative, a court can be asked to fill gaps and avoid a *non liquet* whether or not, theoretically speaking, gaps can exist.) Kelsen writes that 'they are norms which become international law applicable before the International Court of Justice, [*only*] because Article 38(1)(c) authorises the International Court of Justice to apply them'.[123] If general principles were not to be found to be a source of international law – as Kelsen thinks – the Statute has authorised the Court to decide on the basis of 'a norm which the Court considers to be a "general principle of law

[121] E.g. Lauterpacht, 'International Law', n. 109 at 75; Advisory Committee of Jurists, *Procès-Verbaux*, n. 109 at 293–346; Alfred Verdross and Bruno Simma, *Universelles Völkerrecht: Theorie und Praxis* (3rd edn Duncker & Humblot 1984) 382–389; the distinction is made more sharply in Freeman Jalet, n. 109 at 1044; Pellet, n. 109 at 772; Schlesinger, n. 109 at 738. With regard to the last two issues, the present author has tried to distinguish them elsewhere – see Jörg Kammerhofer, 'Gaps, the *Nuclear Weapons* Advisory Opinion and the Structure of International Legal Argument between Theory and Practice' 80 *BYBIL* (2010) 333–360.

[122] Kelsen, n. 79 at 394.

[123] '... daß es sich um Normen handelt, die [nur] dadurch von dem Internationalen Gerichtshof anzuwendendes Völkerrecht werden, daß Art. 38 § 1 c den Internationalen Gerichtshof ermächtigt, sie anzuwenden.' Kelsen, n. 13 at 99 (emphasis added).

recognized by civilised nations," if the Court deems this principle more satisfactory than the existing customary and contractual international law'.[124] It would be like allowing the Court to apply 'Oompa-Loompa law' and would simply mean that the Court can decide freely. Kelsen's own solution means denying the positivity of general principles of law beyond the *lex arbitri*.

5.3 General principles as formal source of law

But what of the role of 'general principles of law' outside the purview of the Court's applicable law provisions, i.e. as a source of international law *tout court*? Inclusion in Article 38 – while certainly an indication of the drafters' and state parties' belief that they are somehow part of international law – does not legally make Article 38(1)(a) to (c) the highest sources of international law.[125] Article 38's status as the sole indicator of the sources is often taken a little too seriously. Equally unhelpful is the distinction drawn by some authors between general principles *of law* and general principles of *international law*.[126] This argument is based on the fundamental misconception that general principles, even if they are 'legally relevant' to international law, are still not principles *of* international law. Another variant of this misconception is Bin Cheng's assertion that 'it is precisely of the nature of these principles that they belong to no particular system of law, but are common to them all'.[127] If these principles are norms, then they of necessity belong to a normative order: in order even to be able to conceive of a norm as norm (as Ought), a norm belongs to a normative order (at a minimum consisting of the norm itself and the *Grundnorm* which enables perception of that norm).[128]

If general principles of law are, as the majority claims, made a source of international law through a sort of analogical law-making procedure, international law incorporates national law. In legal theory, incorporation does not establish a connection between the referring norm/normative order and the norm/normative order referred to. It does not, strictly speaking, make an alien norm part of the order in question, but is instead a normative 'short cut'. Through this process of incorporation, a norm

[124] Kelsen, n. 120 at 534. See also Kelsen, n. 79 at 393; Kelsen, n. 13 at 266 (fn. 80).

[125] Kammerhofer, n. 35 at 208–210.

[126] E.g. Lammers, n. 33 at 59, 74; Pellet, n. 109 at 768; Vallindas, n. 109 at 427–428; Alfred Verdross, *Die Quellen des universellen Völkerrechts: Eine Einführung* (Rombach 1973) 128–129; Verdross and Simma, n. 121 at 386.

[127] Cheng, n. 118 at 390.

[128] Kammerhofer, n. 35 at 191.

with the same content as (but different from) the norm referred to is created. In our case – and assuming that the orthodoxy is correct – international law now actually includes a number of 'general principles' *qua* norms of international law with the same content as (generalised) municipal norms, although it only says so in shorthand form. The King Midas principle applies: 'In this respect law resembles King Midas. Just as everything he touched turned into gold, everything the law refers to turns into law.'[129]

But part of the confusion about the precise nature of the general principles of law in international law is the result of confusion in general jurisprudence. Principles can be, and generally are, seen in one of two ways. (i) Principles are norms with a very general material scope and as such it is perfectly possible for them to be part of international law, but it requires an act of will to make them into positive law. (ii) Principles are a scholarly generalisation of a number of norms either from different normative orders or from one and the same order. As such, they do not need an act of will and can be analogised to municipal law, but as scholarly generalisations or analogies they cannot be part of the legal order. As H. C. Gutteridge puts it:

> There is, of course, no such thing as 'comparative' law... The stages of analysis and synthesis of the rules of two or more systems of law which constitute the comparative process cannot and do not result in the formulation of any independent body of law.[130]

On a legal-theoretical view, the problem arises when scholars confuse the two functions[131] and seek to create norms out of their own statements – yet another example of 'law-making by scholarship',[132] which is as impotent an attempt to create law as it is an impudent imposition of power.

[129] 'In dieser Hinsicht gleicht das Recht dem König Midas. So wie alles, was dieser berührte, sich in Gold verwandelte, so nimmt alles, worauf sich das Recht bezieht, Rechtscharakter an.' Kelsen, *Rechtslehre*, n. 15 at 282.

[130] Harold Cooke Gutteridge, 'Comparative Law and the Law of Nations' 21 *BYBIL* (1944) 1–10 at 1.

[131] E.g. Lammers, n. 33 at 74.

[132] E.g. Jörg Kammerhofer, 'Law-Making by Scholarship? The Dark Side of 21st Century International Legal "Methodology"' in James Crawford, Sarah Nouwen (eds), *Select Proceedings of the European Society of International Law: Third Volume: International Law 1989–2010: A Performance Appraisal: Cambridge, 2–4 September 2010* (Hart 2012) 115–126.

5.4 *An alternative solution?*

A classic attempt to solve the problem of the positivity of general principles is to argue that their 'authority... as a source of international law is grounded in international custom itself'[133] or, in Verdross' slightly more precise words: 'The validity of the third source of international law is based in customary international law. While *individual norms*... are not created by a customary process, this third source was received into international law *in toto* by concordant state practice.'[134] Apart from doubts about the possibility of a customary empowerment norm – customary international law is incapable of empowering the creation of further norms (creating a subordinate source), because norm-creation is not based on a factual pattern (state practice), but refers to an 'ought'[135] – this argument cannot alleviate or counter positivists' problems with the non-willed creation of general principles. Even if the meta-law of general principle-creation is part of customary international law, this does not mean that these customary norms prescribe a customary form of creation (state practice plus *opinio iuris*) for general principles. Indeed, that is the very point of general principles: they are not created by custom (or treaty) – otherwise, they would not be a third source of law, but part of customary international law.[136]

There is another solution to the problem of positivity of general principles which is consistent with the Pure Theory's basic commitments. The key to this solution is the word 'recognized' in Article 38(1)(c). As some authors have pointed out,[137] this could be understood to mean a specific recognition that principles common to the legal systems of the 'civilized nations' are explicitly recognised *as international law* and thus created as international legal norms and not merely recognised as principle in domestic law. Gaja argues: 'Art. 38(1)(c) ICJ Statute requires a

[133] Lauterpacht, 'International Law', n. 109 at 76. See also Vallindas, n. 109 at 426–428.

[134] 'Die Geltung der dritten Völkerrechtsquellen gründet sich zunächst auf das völkerrechtliche Gewohnheitsrecht. Zwar werden die *einzelnen Normen* der in Rede stehenden allgemeinen Rechtsgrundsätze nicht in diesem Verfahren erzeugt, wohl aber erfolgte die Rezeption dieser dritten Quellengruppe *in toto* durch die übereinstimmende... Staatenpraxis', Verdross, n. 57 at 59.

[135] Kammerhofer, n. 35 at 74. [136] Kelsen, n. 79 at 394; Vallindas, n. 109 at 428.

[137] Giorgio Gaja, 'General Principles of Law' in Rüdiger Wolfrum (ed.), *Max Planck Encyclopedia of Public International Law*, Vol. 4 (Oxford University Press 2012) 370–378 at 374 (MN 19); Lammers, n. 33 at 74; unclear: Bassiouni, n. 109 at 768–769; Gutteridge, n. 130 at 2; limited support: Kelsen, n. 13 at 266 (fn. 80).

general principle of law to be "recognized by civilized nations" . . . for a principle to exist it would be necessary that States acknowledge . . . that this principle applies to their international relations.'[138] Here, we *would* have acts of will creating positive international law; principles would thus be a sort of customary international law without the custom. The only drawback is that 'recognized' in Article 38(1)(c) probably means recognised in municipal law, rather than in international law,[139] but outside the ICJ Statute's remit, we are not bound by its wording, only by the way in which the meta-law on source-creation (Section 4.2) is shaped. And that is the crux: we probably cannot know how the sources of international law come about and there is even the possibility that such an overarching law was not created.[140]

But does this help us in 'proving' that the Pure Theory of Law – this most uncompromisingly modernist form of international legal positivism – can solve a specific problem like the positivity of the general principles of law? Yes and no. It is not helpful, because if general principles cannot be proven to be based on acts of will, then these principles cannot exist as a formal source of law. The Pure Theory is not an instrumentalist approach, helping us to best shape the law for our policy goals. It is useful, on the other hand, because Kelsen's reflection on what legal scholars can validly do without distorting their findings can help us to find the proper role and limits of our craft. The best and the worst we can say about Kelsen's Pure Theory of Law is that it is an expression of legal common sense: we expect to talk about the law when we set out to talk about the law.[141]

6 Conclusion

At first glance it is perhaps ironic that a quotation from Alfred Verdross,[142] that giant of modern natural legal scholarship, should be the motto for this chapter. This is due as much to Verdross' genius as to his being a student of Kelsen. Unreflective positivism is the true enemy of natural law – as it is of the Pure Theory of Law – a 'positivism' in which state consent becomes an

138 Gaja, n. 137 at 374 (MN 19).

139 Vallindas, n. 109 at 427–428; Freeman Jalet, n. 109 at 1045; Advisory Committee of Jurists, *Procés-Verbaux*, n. 109 at 335.

140 Kammerhofer, n. 35 at 235–240.

141 Kammerhofer, n. 132 at 125–126; Jörg Kammerhofer, 'Orthodox Generalists and Political Activists in International Legal Scholarship' in Matthew Happold (ed.), *International Law in a Multipolar World* (Routledge 2011) 138–157 at 154–157.

142 Verdross, n. 1 at viii.

absolute, necessary basis of all international law. This, as the foregoing has tried to show, is not Kelsen's positivism. True, Kelsen does not construct a law out of the absolute 'cosmos of values',[143] as Verdross puts it. True, he requires – for the positivity, not the normativity/validity/'existence', of law – a real act of will by real people. But the requirements and procedures are formulated by, and dependent upon, the positive empowerment norm; they are contingent on regulation, not necessarily 'state will', i.e. human will ascribed by the law to international law's juristic person 'state'. It just so happens to be the case that, at the moment, treaty law and customary international law require state will; it might and can be different. True positivism – one that takes the word *positus* seriously – cannot hide behind 'necessary contents of the law' when the law should prescribe something that may be antithetical to the positivist scholar's personal ideology. We have opened with a quotation from Verdross and will close with another: 'Each positive legal order is valid only in relation to the factual acts of a legal community, because its positivity consists precisely of its hierarchically ordered concretisation by way of legal acts which were actually laid down.'[144]

143 Verdross, n. 57 at 24.

144 '[J]ede positive Rechtsordnung gilt nur unter Beziehung auf den tatsächlichen Handlungszusammenhang einer Rechtsgemeinschaft, da ihre Positivität gerade in ihrer stufenförmigen Erfüllung durch tatsächlich gesetzte Rechtsakte besteht', Verdross, n. 57 at 6 (emphasis removed).

5

Herbert Hart in today's international legal scholarship

JEAN D'ASPREMONT

1 Introduction

In all areas of the humanities, there are authors of whom any member of the epistemic community concerned assumes a good knowledge. Herbert Hart is certainly among these authors who, in international legal scholarship, have become a vernacular reference.[1] That Hart, despite his famous disdain for international law,[2] is now a standard reference in international legal scholarship is not surprising. Hart's social fact-based positivism is far more accessible than many of his peers' intricate constructions. His approach – at least on the surface – is simple, as it rests on a few, seemingly uncomplicated, conceptual dichotomies. It is this simplicity which makes Hart's insights universally appealing, but which also makes them an obvious target for critique among scholars of international law. This chapter draws on the quasi-universal familiarity with the tenets of Hart's theory and, after highlighting the shortcomings of the Hartian perspective for the study of international law, seeks to bring to the fore those of Hart's insights that can advance our understanding of the subject, especially with regard to an epistemic community that now claims to have moved beyond modernity.

[1] On the various wording tactics of international legal scholars, see generally Jean d'Aspremont, 'Wording in International Law' 25 *LJIL* (2012) 575–602.

[2] HLA Hart, *The Concept of Law* (2nd edn Oxford University Press 1994) 212–237. For a rejection of Hart's understanding of international law, see e.g. Ian Brownlie, 'International Law at the Fiftieth Anniversary of the United Nations: General Course on Public International Law' 255 *Recueil des Cours* (1995) 9–228 at 25; Anthony D'Amato, 'What "Counts" as Law?' in Nicholas Onuf (ed.), *Law-Making in the Global Community* (Carolina Academic Press 1982) 83–107 at 106; see also Thomas Franck, 'The Legitimacy of the International Legal System' 82 *AJIL* (1988) 705–759 at 751–759.

This chapter argues that the most relevant of Hart's insights for contemporary international legal scholarship are to be found in his reductionism.[3] Indeed, I contend that the Hartian concept of law is germane to the extent that it helps international legal scholars to restrict international legal positivism to a mechanism for determining the mode of existence of norms; that is, their validity.[4] I contend that Hart's positivism is reductionist in that it confines legal positivism to a theory about the determination of the existence of law by virtue of a theory of sources, i.e. a theory of the ascertainment of rules. In that sense, Hart's theory renders legal positivism a tool of limited scope which does not lay down a grand theory of law, and which is certainly not a content-determining mechanism. According to this view, Hart's *Concept of Law* is alien to the search for legal certainty and immanent truth as regards the content of law. This is why it is argued here that, from a Hartian perspective, international legal positivism is not about determining the right content of norms and the right adjudicative truth.[5] Instead, international legal positivism should be confined to a thesis about the validity-condition of legal norms. The Hart-inspired international legal positivism which is put forward here is premised on the idea that international legal positivism is deficient when it comes to deciphering and unravelling the other dimensions of international law such as the creation of subjects, the description of the multi-dimensional phenomenon of law-making or the compliance pull of international legal rules to name only a few. This understanding of international legal positivism simultaneously brings with it a division of tasks among various approaches to international law within international legal scholarship, each of them recognised as having distinct merits that can be mutually reinforcing.

This chapter starts by sketching Hart's reductionism in Section 2. The familiar charges against Hart's reductionism are briefly recalled in Section 3 with a view to shedding some light on the limitations of Hart which one needs to be aware when making use of a Hartian approach to law. Taking into account these challenges of Hartian reductionism, Section 4 then seeks to emphasise those aspects of Hart's reductionism

[3] In the same vein, see Andrei Marmor, 'Farewell to Conceptual Analysis (in Jurisprudence)' in Wil Waluchow, Stefan Sciaraffa (eds), *Philosophical Foundations of the Nature of Law* (Oxford University Press 2013) 209–229.

[4] For a similar conception of international legal positivism, see John Gardner, 'Legal Positivism: 5½ Myths' 46 *American Journal of Jurisprudence* (2001) 199–227 at 227.

[5] Christoph Kletzer, 'Kelsen, Sander, and the *Gegenstandsproblem* of Legal Science' 12 *German Law Journal* (2011) 785–810 at 786.

that are particularly relevant to international legal scholarship at a time of growing pluralisation and complexity in the international legal order. Section 4 shows that reductionism can give rise to some form of cognitive positivism[6] which can prove to be useful for the production of knowledge about international law in the twenty-first century.

2 Hartian reductionism

As an introductory caveat, it is important to recall that Hart's social fact-based positivism did not seek to offer a general theory of law. His 'Rule of Recognition' is not meant to constitute a logically necessary part of a normative system, nor does his approach claim to be a complete, holistic, transcendentalist or Kantian theory. It does not purport to provide legal certainty, nor does it offer any immanent truth regarding the content of law. For that reason, Hart's *Concept of Law* cannot be put in the same league as Kelsen,[7] whose approach to validity is meant to be more complete and sophisticated.[8] In that sense, Hart's theory is minimalistic.[9] Likewise, it has limited descriptive virtue with regard to the very phenomenon of law. Thus, it should only be construed as a modest theory which provides conceptual tools to decipher only one limited dimension of law: law-identification.[10]

Before proceeding to sketch Hart's understanding of a source-based conception of law, it is necessary to point out that Hart's focus on the constituent elements of a legal system, and hence on law-ascertainment, was not entirely unprecedented. Hart's reductionism is in some ways a successor to the work of John William Salmond, even though Hart never fully acknowledged Salmond's legacy. Although Hart's reductionism came to depart from Kelsen's Kantian ambitions, the latter deeply informed the former and must thus be mentioned. Section 2.1 will consider briefly the work of those two predecessors.

6 On the notion of cognitive positivism, see Owen Fiss, 'The Varieties of Positivism' 90 *Yale Law Journal* (1981) 1007–1016.

7 See Kammerhofer, Chapter 4.

8 It has been argued that, to some extent, they talk past each other. See Matthew H. Kramer, 'The Rule of Misrecognition in the Hart of Jurisprudence' 8 *Oxford Journal of Legal Studies* (1988) 401–433 at 425.

9 Nigel Simmonds, 'Bringing the Outside In' 13 *Oxford Journal of Legal Studies* (1993) 147–165 at 154.

10 Kramer, n. 8 at 407.

2.1 Reductionism before Hart: from John William Salmond to Hans Kelsen

More than Bentham,[11] the thinker to which Hart's debt is most obvious is the New Zealander legal theorist, John William Salmond. Long before Hart derailed Austin for good, Salmond had already proposed a theory moving away from Austinian methodology. Indeed, he refused to identify law with the exercise of state coercive power, on which view law is confused with imperative law.[12] According to him, a principle of law 'is a principle of law, not because it is true, but because it is accepted and acted upon by the State as true ... for the purposes of action'.[13] Prefiguring Hart, he contended that the validity of law is strictly a function of judicial recognition and this recognition is a matter of social fact. The ultimate rule of validation is not derived or postulated, but lies in the facts of the unified recognitional practice of courts.[14] As will be seen below, the kinship of Hart's theory with Salmond's is undeniable. The most glaring difference between the two is probably that, for Salmond, courts have a moral obligation to recognise these principles in virtue of their oath of office, but there is no legal obligation to do so.[15]

It is certainly intriguing that the legacy of Salmond on British analytical jurisprudence is generally neglected. Indeed, Salmond is barely referred to in the work of Hart, who barely acknowledges his debt to him.[16] However, core elements of Hart's social thesis were already to be found in Salmond's approach to law. It is this paradox that led Postema to observe that 'Hart rescued from obscurity an idea first announced by Salmond and made it a pivot of his theory of law, but he did not rescue Salmond's work itself'.[17] This is certainly not the place to revisit the reasons why the legacy of

[11] While Bentham espouses Hobbes' source thesis, he dismisses Hobbes' social contract theory and hails Hume's for having, before him, shown its weaknesses. See Jeremy Bentham, *A Fragment on Government* (Cambridge University Press 1988) 51. See the comments of Hart: HLA Hart, 'Sovereignty and Legally Limited Government' in HLA Hart, *Essays on Bentham: Studies in Jurisprudence and Political Theory* (Clarendon Press 1982) 220–242 at 221.

[12] John W. Salmond, *Jurisprudence: Or the Theory of the Law* (7th edn Sweet & Maxwell 1924) 49–54.

[13] John W. Salmond, *First Principles of Jurisprudence* (Stevens and Haynes 1893) 83.

[14] Salmond, n. 12 at 57. [15] Salmond, n. 12 at 56.

[16] HLA Hart, 'Positivism and the Separation of Law and Morals' in HLA Hart, *Essays in Jurisprudence and Philosophy* (Clarendon Press 1983) 49–87 at 61.

[17] Gerald J. Postema, *Legal Philosophy in the Twentieth Century: The Common Law World* (Springer 2011) 24.

Salmond and his invention of the social thesis are so often overlooked.[18] It suffices here to highlight that the rise of Hans Kelsen as one of the central legal theorists of the first half of the twentieth century probably contributed to the fact that Salmond's work fell out of prominence.

Although he is an anti-reductionist figure, Kelsen ought to be mentioned here because his influence on Hart is indisputable. Like his predecessors, Kelsen supported the separation thesis – the idea that the identification of law is solely based on its source and is distinct from its moral value[19] – as a necessary consequence of the source thesis. He even pushed the argument further by inferring from the separation thesis an unprecedented restrictive understanding of the appropriate tasks of legal scholarship. Indeed, he argued that, while law itself cannot be 'pure' because it is the product of political activity, legal scholarship can only be a pure theory – and allow for critiques of law[20] – if it zeroes in on the description of law and strips away from the objects of its investigation anything that is not law. The Pure Theory of Law thus eliminates moral judgments from any legal science properly so called.[21]

[18] Postema, n. 17 at 24.

[19] On Kelsen's separation thesis, see Jochen von Bernstorff, *The Public International Law Theory of Hans Kelsen: Believing in Universal Law* (Cambridge University Press 2010) 250–255.

[20] Kelsen's argument that the source thesis allows for criticism of law is similar to that of Bentham. See Hans Kelsen, 'Law, State and Justice in the Pure Theory of Law' 57 *Yale Law Journal* (1948) 377–390 at 377, 383–384: 'The real effect of the terminological identification of law and justice is an illicit justification of any positive law.'

[21] The implicit agenda behind some aspects of Kelsen's Pure Theory has been the object of much discussion. See, for instance, Simma, according to whom Kelsen was intent on countering Hegel who had been 'translated' into legal theory by Jellinek and thus aimed at strengthening the idea of an international rule of law: Bruno Simma, 'The Contribution of Alfred Verdross to the Theory of International Law' 6 *EJIL* (1995) 33–54 at 41. Some similar arguments are made by Rigaux, who argues that Kelsen opposed not only Hegel, but also Triepel's dualism: François Rigaux, 'Hans Kelsen on International Law' 9 *EJIL* (1998) 325–343 at 326. See the criticism of Hegel by Kelsen: Hans Kelsen, 'Les rapports de système entre le droit interne et le droit international public' 14 *Recueil des Cours* (1926) 227–331 at 324. The Kantian dimension of Kelsen's agenda and his ambition to devise a theory of law directed at the pacification of inter-state relations have also attracted much attention. See Danilo Zolo, 'Hans Kelsen: International Peace through International Law' 9 *EJIL* (1998) 306–324. See also Charles Leben, *Hans Kelsen: Ecrits français de droit international* (Presses Universitaires de France 2001) 19; Charles Leben, 'Avant-propos' in Hans Kelsen, *Controverses sur la théorie pure du droit: remarques critiques sur Georges Scelle et Michel Virally* (Charles Leben, Robert Kolb (eds), Panthéon-Assas/LGDJ 2005) 9–32 at 11. See also Janne Elisabeth Nijman, *The Concept of International Legal Personality: An Enquiry Into the History and Theory of International Law* (T. M. C. Asser Press 2004) 176–177; David Dyzenhaus, *Legality and Legitimacy: Carl Schmitt, Hans Kelsen and Hermann*

Kelsen's theory has captivated international lawyers, for Kelsen devoted much work to the study of international law which, contrary to Austin, he considered to be a legal system. For the sake of our study, of greater importance is the revolution brought about by Kelsen's theory in placing formal law-ascertainment at the centre of his concept of law. Indeed, Kelsen adroitly brought formal law-ascertainment into the centre of the picture, as he reasoned that the validity of law cannot be conceived without the *Grundnorm*. In this sense, one can only determine what law is on the basis of such a *Grundnorm*. Because law is identified in accordance with the rules about how law is made, or in other words because law regulates its own creation, a formal test becomes necessary to identify the law. Law is law because it can be certified that it has been created in accordance with the rules regulating the creation of law. As a result, *the existence of law becomes a question of validity*, validity being the specific form of existence of rules.[22] It can be said that Kelsen gave consistency to the idea that validity and the existence of rules about rules are two sides of the same coin. On the one hand, a rule needs to be validated according to the law-ascertaining rules in order to exist. On the other hand, law cannot exist without law-ascertaining rules. Transforming the law-identification process into a formal pedigree test is probably Kelsen's most important contribution to the theory of ascertainment. Indeed, Hart and his followers adopted Kelsen's approach in this respect. As a result of Kelsen's work, identifying law became a strictly formal test based on its conformity with the law-ascertaining rules of the system.

As was said above, Kelsen aimed at providing a general theory of law and did not limit it to ascertainment. It is not necessary here to discuss the other main tenets of Kelsen's theory, such as the hypothetical *Grundnorm* or the equation between the law and the state,[23] both of which are inherent in Kelsen's attempt to maintain the categorical separation of Is and Ought. Yet, a few words must still be said about the foundation of the *Grundnorm* as it inevitably bears upon the foundations of formal law-ascertainment discussed here. As is well known, Kelsen grounded the ultimate regulation

Heller in Weimar (Clarendon Press 1997) 157–158, cited by Frank Haldemann, 'Gustav Radbruch vs. Hans Kelsen: A Debate on Nazi Law' 18 *Ratio Juris* (2005) 162–178 at 174.

22 On the extent of this conceptual revolution, see Norberto Bobbio, 'Kelsen et les sources du droit' in Norberto Bobbio, *Essais de théorie du droit* (Michel Guéret (tr.), Bruylant/LGDJ 1998) 227–236.

23 On Kelsen's conception of law as a coercive order, see Hans Kelsen, 'Theorie du droit international public' 84 *Recueil des Cours* (1953) 1–203 at 28. On this particular aspect of Kelsen's theory, see Jörg Kammerhofer, 'Kelsen – Which Kelsen? A Reapplication of the Pure Theory to International Law' 22 *LJIL* (2009) 225–249 at 227–233, 236–240.

of law's creation in the *Grundnorm*. Although the argument can be made that he subsequently changed his mind on this point[24] and came close to construing the *Grundnorm* as a fiction,[25] Kelsen argued that this ultimate law-ascertaining rule is hypothetical – a position which is not devoid of Kantian overtones.[26] This position has been much criticised in the literature.[27] While this is not the place to discuss this aspect of Kelsen's theory, it suffices to note that Hart – and his followers – departed from this aspect of Kelsen's theory. Such a move was made possible by the invention of the so-called 'social thesis' (or 'conventionality thesis'). The social thesis constitutes the linchpin of Hart's reductionism and ought to be recalled here.

2.2 Hart's social thesis in a nutshell

As indicated in the introduction, Hart's theory – as well as his life[28] – is well known to most international legal scholars and it would be of no avail to repeat or summarise his general concept of law. In particular, it is not necessary to revert to the oft-discussed dichotomy between primary and secondary rules. Nor is it necessary to expound here upon the *soft* or *inclusive positivism* endorsed by Hart at the end of his life, according to which nothing prevents the emergence of rules of recognition that identify the law by reference to moral criteria (the so-called 'incorporation thesis'). This modest concession to natural lawyers that morality can be a law-ascertaining criterion has provoked a significant amount of literature[29] and has even been challenged by some of Hart's

24 See Paulson's controversial contention that Kelsen eventually reverted to classical voluntary positivism: Stanley L. Paulson, 'Toward Periodization of the Pure Theory of Law' in Letizia Gianformaggio (ed.), *Hans Kelsen's Legal Theory: A Diachronic Point of View* (Giappichelli 1990) 11–47.

25 I owe this point to interesting exchanges with Séverine Helbert.

26 On the neo-Kantian character of the *Grundnorm*, see Stanley L. Paulson, 'The Neo-Kantian Dimension of Kelsen's Pure Theory of Law' 12 *Oxford Journal of Legal Studies* (1992) 311–332. See also Jörg Kammerhofer, *Uncertainty in International Law: A Kelsenian Perspective* (Routledge 2010) 250–253.

27 For an attempt to rebut this criticism of Kelsen, see Kammerhofer, n. 26 at 197.

28 See Nicola Lacey, *A Life of HLA Hart: The Nightmare and the Noble Dream* (Oxford University Press 2004).

29 See, for instance, the contributions compiled in the book edited by Jules Coleman: Jules L. Coleman (ed.), *Hart's Postscript: Essays on the Postscript to* The Concept of Law (Oxford University Press 2001). See also Matthew H. Kramer, *In Defense of Legal Positivism: Law without Trimmings* (Oxford University Press 1999) 199; Robin Bradley Kar, 'Hart's Response to Exclusive Legal Positivism' 95 *Georgetown Law Journal* (2007) 393–461.

followers.[30] These aspects will not, however, be discussed. Only the main tenets of Hart's reductionism are recalled.

As a preliminary reminder, it is interesting to note that Hart refined the idea that membership of the legal system is a matter of pedigree by backing away from the command-based concept of law of his predecessors. He followed Kelsen in putting the legal system (instead of the law-making Sovereign) at the centre of his concept of law and subjecting the identification of law to law-ascertaining rules.[31] In doing so, he reinforced the reversal of the dichotomy between law and authority undertaken by Kelsen. However, he stopped short of making these law-ascertaining rules depend on a hypothetical ultimate norm. While strictly abiding by the proposition that the identification of law requires a formal test on the basis of law-ascertaining rules, Hart replaced the hypothetical rule of Kelsen by a social fact, i.e. the practice of law-applying authorities. This *tour de force* has been called the *social thesis* (or the *conventionality thesis*).[32] It is argued here that grounding the ultimate law-ascertaining rule in a social practice – the social thesis – constitutes Hart's most important contribution to the theory of law as well as to the theory of sources in international law.[33]

Before outlining the main features of the social thesis, it is necessary to highlight that Hart considered that the legal system precedes the law-making authority. In so doing, Hart followed Kelsen and not Hobbes, Bentham and Austin. As a consequence, law is inevitably the result of a law-making process defined by law itself. It is thus the system that ascertains law and not the authority. To identify law, therefore, one

30 Joseph Raz and Scott Shapiro opposed Hart's inclusive legal positivism. See e.g. Scott J. Shapiro, 'On Hart's Way Out' in Jules L. Coleman (ed.), *Hart's Postscript: Essays on the Postscript to* The Concept of Law (Oxford University Press 2001) 149–191 at 191. For another criticism of inclusive legal positivism, see Joshua P. Davis, 'Jurisprudential Jujutsu', University of San Francisco Law Research Paper No. 2012–01. It is well known that Waluchow and Coleman sided with Hart by pursuing his inclusive legal positivist approach. See Wilfrid J. Waluchow, *Inclusive Legal Positivism* (Clarendon Press 1994) 80–164; Jules L. Coleman, 'Incorporationism, Conventionality and the Practical Difference Thesis' in Jules L. Coleman (ed.), *Hart's Postscript: Essays on the Postscript to* The Concept of Law (Oxford University Press 2001) n. 29, 99–148. See McCormick's attempt to reconcile exclusive and inclusive legal positivism in Neil McCormick, *Institutions of Law* (Oxford University Press 2009) 263–279.

31 On this abiding conceptual question, see Shapiro, n. 30 at 152–153.

32 According to Raz, of all these theses, the social thesis is the most fundamental. It is also the one that gave its name to 'positivism', which indicates that the law is 'posited', i.e. that law is made by the activities of human beings. Joseph Raz, 'Legal Positivism and the Sources of Law' in Joseph Raz, *The Authority of Law: Essays on Law and Morality* (Clarendon Press 1983) 37–52 at 38.

33 This is what I have argued elsewhere. See Jean d'Aspremont, 'Hart et le positivisme postmoderne' 3 *Revue générale de droit international public* (2009) 635–654.

needs to look at the law-ascertaining rules (what he calls 'rules of recognition'). Again, as in Kelsen's theory, these law-ascertaining rules must themselves be ascertained as rules of the legal system. There is, however, one important distinction between the theories of Kelsen and Hart on the nature of these law-ascertaining rules from which all secondary rules are derived. While Kelsen sees all secondary rules as having been ultimately validated as rules of the system by a hypothetical *Grundnorm*, Hart construes the ultimate Rule of Recognition from which all secondary rules are derived as being grounded in the social practice of the law-applying authorities, who must feel an internal sense of obligation to obey the rules that is quite separate from the threats or rewards they associate with compliance (the 'internal point of view'). In that sense, law exists when there is a community of officials who perceive the law as having a distinctive authority and when a sufficient number of citizens conform to the primary rules, regardless of their reasons for conforming. For Hart, the reasons why officials abide by the Rule of Recognition does not matter and is beside the point, providing the officials engage in the sort of conduct that bespeaks commitment or supportiveness, which sustains the functioning of the legal system. As a result, the ultimate Rule of Recognition from which all the rules of the system are derived is neither valid nor invalid. It simply exists (or does not exist) as a matter of social fact.[34]

As the foregoing shows, the so-called 'internal point of view' is what allows Hart to ground the law-ascertaining rules in social conventions. It is thus the central tenet of his social thesis.[35] It means that law-applying officials uphold the rules not simply as commonly accepted standards, but as common standards for themselves and others. The internal point of view – which was probably not invented by Hart[36] – is another major difference between Kelsen and Hart.[37] Even though both Hart and Kelsen placed validity at the centre of their understandings of law, the test of validity in Kelsen's theory remains carried out from an external point of view, for the *Grundnorm*, being hypothetical, is not grounded in the

[34] In particular, Hart, n. 2 at 116–117.

[35] For further discussion on the internal point of view, see McCormick, cited in John Finnis, 'On Hart's Ways: Law as Reason and as Fact' in Matthew H. Kramer *et al.* (eds), *The Legacy of HLA Hart: Legal, Political and Moral Philosophy* (Oxford University Press 2008) 3–28 at 12. For criticisms of the internal perspective, see 3–25. See also Robin Kar, who argued that Hart's theory must be refined by adding the reference to the second-person standpoint in order to reconcile Hart, Shapiro and Dworkin. Kar, n. 29.

[36] Uberto Scarpelli, *Qu'est-ce que le positivisme juridique* (Bruylant/LGDJ 1996) 38.

[37] Marmor, n. 3.

system itself, but outside it. For Hart, testing validity – and thus the existence of rules – can only be done from an internal perspective, because the law-ascertaining criteria necessarily originate in a practice within the legal system.[38]

The internal social practice on which Hart's concept of law rests is what makes the emergence of a language of law possible despite law's inevitable indeterminacy. Hart acknowledges that law, because its commands are conveyed through words, is fundamentally indeterminate.[39] So too are the rules of recognition.[40] Hart, in that sense, follows Bentham, for he rejects any Aristotelian proposition of the existence of an inner meaning of words, including the standardisation of rules of recognition. For Hart, the meaning of words is thus not already given, but is found in internal social practice. He contends that, to know the meaning of words, we must look at concepts when they are at work. Social practice thus provides the meaning of the words upon which the language of law is based. This manifestation of the social thesis has been called the *semantic thesis*.[41] Rules are thus ascertained by a practice conceived in terms of convergent behaviours and agreements in judgments among law-applying authorities.[42]

It is important to note that Hart does not claim that his social thesis completely eliminates the indeterminacy of law. Social practice itself is beset by ambiguities and will not always substantiate the meaning of rules.[43] However, for Hart, what is required is not that law be fully

[38] This is the interpretation of Scarpelli, n. 36 at 35–45.

[39] It has been argued that HLA Hart only restricted indeterminacy to problems of vagueness and ignored problems of ambiguity. On this point, as well as the work of Michael Thaler on the distinction between vagueness (denotation) and ambiguity (connotation), see Kammerhofer, n. 26 at 118.

[40] Hart, n. 2 at 144–150.

[41] Raz, n. 32 at 37.

[42] HLA Hart, 'Jhering's Heaven of Concepts and Modern Analytical Jurisprudence' in HLA Hart, *Essays in Jurisprudence and Philosophy*, n. 16, 265–277 at 277.

[43] Hart, n. 2 at 144–150. This 'concession' by Hart is not, however, as groundbreaking as it is sometimes portrayed in general legal theory. Indeed, the rejection of the idea of an intrinsic meaning of words was already found in Bentham's work. Bentham was opposed to the expert language deployed by lawyers, as he considered its use to be a tactic of intimidation. Bemoaning the fact that such technical language has so often been used as an instrument of mystification and oppression to deceive men, Bentham – probably influenced by Hobbes – dismissed the Aristotelian idea that words have meaning of their own. In doing so, he came to be one of the first thinkers to contend that sentences, not words, are the unit of meaning and that the meaning of sentences is thus informed by practice. Bentham, although his accounts of legal statements remained reductive, thus opened the door for a conceptualisation of the formal identification of rules based on social practice. In that sense, by breaking with the Aristotelian tradition, he prefigured the idea that the meaning of law-ascertainment criteria is based on communitarian semantics. See Jeremy Bentham,

determinate; Hart's social thesis accommodates some unavoidable uncertainty. Instead, according to Hart, a legal system simply needs sufficiently clear formal law-ascertainment standards. The internal social practice usually provides such elementary yardsticks to make law normative.[44]

It is no secret that this aspect of Hart's social thesis – and the proposition that the meaning of words, and hence the meaning of rules, must be acquired by looking at how words are ordinarily used – is claimed to be derived from the philosophy of language, and especially that of Wittgenstein.[45] According to that communitarian conceptualisation of the meaning of rules which is found in the philosophy of language, the meaning of formal law-ascertainment criteria arises out of their *convergence in use*. That means that it is law-ascertainment 'at work' that informs the meaning of the formal criteria of law-identification. That also indicates that the meaning of law-ascertainment criteria originates in the convergences of the practice of law-applying authorities. It is this concept of the meaning of rules that influenced Hart and informed his social thesis.[46] This in turn was instrumental in the development of his famous 'internal point of view'.

The extent of Wittgenstein's actual influence on Hart has been subject to some controversy.[47] It has even been contended that Hart's foray into

An Introduction to the Principles of Morals and Legislation (first published 1781, Kessinger Publishing 2005 edn), 332–333. On this particular point of Bentham's theory, see the remarks of Hart in 'The Demystification of the Law' in HLA Hart, *Essays on Bentham: Studies in Jurisprudence and Political Theory* (Clarendon Press 1982) 21–39 at 29–30.

44 '[Dworkin's] criticism of soft positivism seems to . . . exaggerate both the degree of certainty which a consistent positivist must attribute to a body of legal standards and the uncertainty that will result if the criteria of legal validity include conformity with specific moral principles or values . . . [T]he exclusion of all uncertainty at whatever costs in other values is not a goal which I have ever envisaged for the rule of recognition.' Hart, n. 2 at 251.

45 E.g. Hart, n. 42 at 271. On Wittgenstein's influence on Hart, see generally Nicos Stavropoulos, 'Hart's Semantics' in Jules L. Coleman (ed.), *Hart's Postscript: Essays on the Postscript to* The Concept of Law (Oxford University Press 2001) n. 29, 59–98 at 59 and 86. The influence of Wittgenstein on Hart has been qualified by Lacey, n. 28 at 218–221.

46 HLA Hart, 'Introduction' in HLA Hart, *Essays on Bentham: Studies in Jurisprudence and Political Theory* (Clarendon Press 1982) 1–20 at 10. See also Hart's essay: Hart, n. 42 at 277. See the remarks by Stavropoulos, who argues that such a concept of meaning can only come from Wittgenstein: Stavropoulos, n. 45 at 86.

47 Timothy Endicott, 'Herbert Hart and the Semantic Sting' in Jules L. Coleman (ed.), *Hart's Postscript: Essays on the Postscript to* The Concept of Law (Oxford University Press 2001) n. 29, 39–58 at 41. Lacey also argues that 'one can speculate with more confidence about the intellectual basis for Herbert's engagement with the linguistic philosophy school'. Lacey, n. 28 at 142. She also submits that at a later stage, Hart 'came to regard the illuminating power of linguistic philosophy as more limited than he had in the 1940s and 1950s'. Lacey, n. 28 at 143, see also her comments at 218–219. Cf. Stavropoulos, n. 45 at 59.

Wittgenstein's philosophy was unproductive, because Hart actually failed to make full use of Wittgenstein's insights.[48] I do not need to discuss that question here. Whether the idea of communitarian semantics comes from Wittgenstein or not is of little importance. It suffices to recall that Wittgenstein denied the possibility of private language and thus participated in the demise of philosophical foundationalism.[49] Wittgenstein arguably[50] rejected the idea that language has a structure and a meaning that can be revealed through analysis.[51] Yet, as is well known, Wittgenstein did not stand by utter scepticism as he came to envisage a communitarian foundation for the meaning of rules.[52] To Wittgenstein, clarification of the meaning of words – a task which he assigns to Philosophy[53] – is all about

48 Joseph Raz, 'Two Views of the Nature of the Theory of Law: A Partial Comparison' in Jules L. Coleman (ed.), *Hart's Postscript: Essays on the Postscript to* The Concept of Law (Oxford University Press 2001) n. 29, 1–38 at 6, see also Endicott, n. 47 at 41.

49 The abandonment of the varieties of philosophical foundationalism is described in Richard Rorty's famous book: *Philosophy and the Mirror of Nature* (30th anniversary edn Princeton University Press 2009).

50 There are scholars who contend that Wittgenstein did not intend to convey that meaning is derived from the practice of rule-followers, but rather that only the rule itself can be the source of its meaning. They argue that Wittgenstein requires an 'internal relation' between a rule and a practice and that the practice only shows that people are actually complying with the rule. For a classical example of that approach, see e.g. Gordon P. Baker, Peter Hacker, *Scepticism, Rules and Language* (Blackwell 1984). Departing from that first interpretation, there are other scholars who understand Wittgenstein as constructing the determination of meaning as an entirely social question. According to that interpretation, meaning is not found in the rule itself, but lies in the temporary consensus of the society. It is grounded in a 'bedrock of practice' by the community of rule-followers: see Brian Langille, 'Revolution Without Foundations' 33 *McGill Law Journal* (1988) 451–505 at 498. It is thus the conduct of the social group that determines the meaning of the rule – at least what constitutes acting in accordance with the rule: see Norman Malcolm, *Nothing is Hidden* (Blackwell 1986). This interpretation is the so-called 'community consensus': see Dennis M. Patterson, 'Law's Pragmatism: Law as Practice and Narrative' in Dennis M. Patterson (ed.), *Wittgenstein and Legal Theory* (Westview Press 1992) 85–90 at 86. It corresponds with the 'private language argument' as interpreted by Saul A. Kripke, *Wittgenstein: On Rules and Private Language* (Harvard University Press 1982). Kripke's interpretation of Wittgenstein has been much discussed. For a criticism, see Brian Bix, 'The Application (and Mis-Application) of Wittgenstein's Rule-Following Considerations to Legal Theory' in Dennis M. Patterson (ed.), *Wittgenstein and Legal Theory* (Westview Press 1992) 209–223 at 210.

51 On David Hume's scepticism towards private causation, see David Hume, *A Treatise of Human Nature* (Dover Publications 2003) 50. On the differences between Hume and Wittgenstein, see Kripke, n. 50 at 62.

52 'And hence also "obeying a rule" is a practice. And to *think* one is obeying a rule is not to obey a rule. Hence it is not possible to obey a rule "privately"; otherwise thinking one was obeying a rule would be the same thing as obeying it.' Ludwig Wittgenstein, *Philosophical Investigations* (G. E. M. Anscombe (tr.), Blackwell 1953) 81e (§ 202).

53 Ludwig Wittgenstein, *Tractacus Logico-Philosophicus* (Dover Publications 1999, first published 1922) para. 4.112.

how the participants in human activities conduct such a clarification.[54] The meaning of words thus stems from the agreement in action.

Whatever the paternity of the social thesis, one of Dworkin's criticisms against Hart's social thesis must be mentioned already.[55] To the former, it may well be a fruitless exercise to seek unanimity among all law-applying authorities of a legal system as to the criteria for identifying law. According to this argument, there will never be total agreement among law-applying authorities. Moreover, even when the law-applying authorities may on the surface yield the impression that they are applying the same law-ascertainment criteria, their readings of the meaning of these criteria may not be the same.[56] Indeed, there is always a risk that law-applying authorities are not talking about the same thing. Yet, according to Wittgenstein, and subsequently Hart, the social foundation of formal ascertainment of international legal rules does not call for actual, total and absolute agreement among law-applying authorities. It essentially requires a shared *feeling* for applying the same criteria. Moderate misunderstandings that can beset the use of words – and hence the use of law-ascertainment criteria – do not constitute an insurmountable obstacle to the emergence of communitarian semantics. What is simply needed is the *feeling* of using the same criteria and the possibility of communication.[57] It is not necessary to say that such a feeling will necessarily hinge on their respective understandings of formal law-ascertainment criteria *dovetailing to a reasonable extent*. Short of any minimal correspondence in meaning, law-applying authorities will never come to share the feeling that they speak the same language and, hence, their practice will not generate any communitarian semantics.

According to Wittgenstein, at least as he has been interpreted by Kripke,[58] the reasons underlying such a feeling of a common language are irrelevant. What matters is simply that law-applying authorities do in fact share such a feeling. This similarly corresponds with what Hart defended when he submitted that the reason why law-applying authorities abide by

[54] See the famous example by Wittgenstein, n. 52 at § 1.

[55] Section 3 of this chapter. See also Jean d'Aspremont, *Formalism and the Sources of International Law: A Theory of the Ascertainment of Legal Rules* (Oxford University Press 2011) 88–90.

[56] Walter B. Gallie, 'Essentially Contested Concepts' 56 *Proceedings of the Aristotelian Society* (1955) 167–198, cited by Bix, n. 50 at 220.

[57] See the remarks of Raz, n. 48 at 19. Cf. Brian Z. Tamanaha, *A General Jurisprudence of Law and Society* (Oxford University Press 2001) 153–154.

[58] Kripke, n. 50 at 96.

the Rule of Recognition does not need to be answered and that the meaning of the Rule of Recognition is independent from the motives behind any such converging attitude of law-applying authorities.[59]

3 Hartian reductionism challenged

The social thesis at the centre of Hart's reductionism has provoked a number of important objections. These criticisms, without bringing reductionism as a whole into question, confirm that Hartian reductionism needs to be refreshed in order for it to be able to provide useful insights for an international legal scholarship confronted with an increasingly pluralised and complex international legal order.

3.1 Hartian reductionism's deficiencies

There is abundant literature on the deficiencies of Hart's social positivism. Only the key objections need to be mentioned here, specifically those which pertain to: its cursoriness; limited exportability; false agnosticism; naivety; sociologism; the semantic sting; as well as a few others.

3.1.1 Cursoriness

A traditional criticism of Hart's reductionism is that it is partly half-baked and that it is not fully developed or thought through. In particular, it is said that Hart failed to elaborate on the *amount* and the *type* of practice which is necessary for it to crystallise into a social law-ascertaining convention.[60] This explains why Hart's *Concept of Law* has been deemed to contain 'much unfinished business'.[61] The cursoriness of Hart's *Concept of Law* is probably the reason why Hart has proved both very accessible but also much criticised. While being instrumental in his popularity among international legal scholars, the laconism of Hart and his tendency not to explore all the dimensions of his thoughts have allowed adverse positions

[59] Hart, n. 2 at 115–116. This part of Hart's argument has not always been construed like this. For a different interpretation of Hart on this point, see Gerald J. Postema, 'Coordination and Convention at the Foundations of Law' 11 *Journal of Legal Studies* (1982) 165–203.

[60] Such a criticism was made by Joseph Raz, 'The Identity of Legal Systems' in Joseph Raz, *The Authority of Law: Essays on Law and Morality*, n. 32, 78–102 at 92, as well as by Stavropoulos, n. 45 at 72.

[61] Neil MacCormick, 'The Concept of Law and "The Concept of Law"' in Robert P. George (ed.), *The Autonomy of Law: Essays of Legal Positivism* (Oxford University Press 1996) 163–194 at 191.

to flourish. More precisely, his laconism has allowed others to overstate his position and make him a convenient straw-man against whom one's position could more easily be articulated. This is not surprising and Hart must have been aware of it.[62]

3.1.2 Limited exportability

Besides the sense of 'unfinished business', a strong substantive objection levelled against Hartian positivism relates to its presupposition of an institutional framework or a pre-existing Rule of Recognition.[63] If the law-applying authorities are the source of the semantics for law-ascertainment criteria, it is necessary to identify these authorities. In other words, Hart's theory presupposes an already existing system. In the same vein, it has been objected that Hart's presupposed authorities are endowed with competences which are often elusive in a legal order in its infancy.[64] In that sense, Hart's theory has been described as circular and only capable of application to an already existing system.[65] By the same token, it has been argued that Hart's approach, because it was devised with reference to the model of domestic law, does not capture all the contemporary complexities of other legal systems.[66]

3.1.3 False agnosticism

It has been contended that Hart did not identify the political foundations of reductionist positivism. He made a subtle and convincing plea for formal law-ascertainment, but failed to spell out why such a blueprint should be preferred to any other. In that sense, it is as though Hart did not deem it necessary to defend the cogency of his understanding of formal law-ascertainment. It could be extrapolated from this that Hart probably thought that utilitarian philosophy provided sufficient explanation as to the desirability of his conceptualisation.[67]

[62] On defensive use of laconism in the international legal scholarship, see d'Aspremont, n. 1.

[63] Kramer, n. 8 at 407; Jason Beckett, 'The Hartian Tradition in International Law' 1 *The Journal Jurisprudence* (2008) 51–83 at 58.

[64] Marmor, n. 3 at 24.

[65] On this point, see MacCormick's defence of Hart (Neil MacCormick, *Legal Reasoning and Legal Theory* (Clarendon Press 1978); see also discussion in Kramer, n. 8 at 413). On MacCormick's post-positivism, see Karen Petroski, 'Is Post-Positivism Possible?' 12 *German Law Journal* (2011) 663–692 at 665.

[66] William Twining, *General Jurisprudence: Understanding Law from a Global Perspective* (Cambridge University Press 2009) 12.

[67] In his 1957 article, Hart simply referred to utilitarian theories of ethics developed by utilitarians like Bentham. See HLA Hart, 'Positivism and the Separation of Law and

3.1.4 Objective naivety

Another common criticism is that Hart's work rests on a type of empiricism that boils down to naive objectivism,[68] a trap which Kelsen is said to have avoided by relying on Kantian conceptualism.[69] Indeed, it can be argued that Hart did not define how the communitarian practice is captured and then imported into the law, whereas, like the cognition of any practice, the observation of the practice of law requires that the empirical framework be preliminarily defined. This is the idea that 'the bearing of nonlegal content on the content of the law is not mechanical'[70] and calls for 'value facts . . . to make it intelligible that law practices support certain legal propositions over others'.[71]

3.1.5 Sociologism and naturalism

Authors embracing a Kelsenian understanding of law commonly argue that removing the question of the validity of a legal system by grounding law-ascertainment in social practice demotes legal science to legal sociology. Such a conception of law-ascertainment includes the study of 'Is' in the scope of a science which should only be concerned with the study of 'Ought'.[72] It is noteworthy that this charge has always been expressly conceded and even assumed by Hart himself.[73] In the same vein, Kelsenian scholars argue that the extra-systemic social foundation of Hart's theory of law is nothing more than a new naturalism.[74]

3.1.6 Semantic sting

It is well known that Dworkin discredits the *social thesis*, for, according to Dworkin, the criteria that make the Rule of Recognition must be accepted not only by officials, but also by citizens.[75] More fundamentally, Dworkin rejects Hart's social thesis because it suffers from what has been called

Morals' 71 *Harvard Law Review* (1958) 593–629. I have further elaborated on that point in d'Aspremont, n. 33.

68 See generally Beckett, n. 63 at 51–83.

69 Kletzer, n. 5 at 787.

70 Mark Greenberg, 'How Facts Make Law' 10 *Legal Theory* (2004) 157–198 at 177.

71 Greenberg, n. 70 at 173 (emphasis omitted).

72 Kammerhofer, n. 26 at 227.

73 Hart, n. 2 at 5.

74 E.g. Kammerhofer, n. 26 at 226. See also Kammerhofer, Chapter 4.

75 As is well known, Hart denies that possibility. For Hart, it is implausible that most members of the public in a complex society will grasp and accept the criteria of recognition. It suffices that citizens display obedience. For Hart, the reasons why officials abide by the rule of recognition does not matter and are beside the point, provided the officials engage in the sort of conduct that attests to the commitment which sustains the functioning of the legal system: Hart, n. 2 at 110–111.

the *semantic sting*, that is, 'the argument that unless lawyers and judges share factual criteria about the grounds of law there can be no significant thought or debate about what the law is'.[76] As has been explained above, for Hart, the language of law can be meaningful only if lawyers share the same tests – that is, if they abide by the same law-ascertaining criteria. If they disagree about these criteria, law ceases to be meaningful. For Dworkin, this makes Hart's theory unable to explain disagreements among lawyers. Lawyers disagree, according to Dworkin, because they have competing conceptions of some concepts. They rely upon substantively different understandings of the relevant concept, and they exchange arguments in support of one understanding or the other. Hart's idea that lawyers must share the same law-ascertainment tests makes such disagreement impossible because, according to Dworkin, an agreement about the law-ascertainment tests involves agreement about their correct application. As a consequence, the social thesis cannot explain how law accomplishes what Hart considered to be its basic function, that is, to provide standards that guide behaviour.[77]

3.2 The need to refresh Hartian reductionism: a possible agenda for a new international legal positivism

The above-mentioned objections against the Hartian social thesis are well known and have been the subject of much discussion in the scholarly literature. While a few of these criticisms seem slightly excessive, others are compelling and must be taken into account when attempting to make sense of Hartian reductionism for international legal scholarship.

3.2.1 Downplaying the challenge

While these varied objections point to apparent weaknesses in Hart's reductionist theory, it is possible to query the significance of at least three of these critiques. First, it is argued here that the social thesis at the heart of Hartian reductionism, despite having an inevitable normative dimension, should not be conflated with naive objectivism. Indeed, being entirely dependent on contingent communitarian semantics and making the quest for validity of international law as a whole utterly moot (at least

[76] Ronald Dworkin, *Law's Empire* (Hart 1986) 44–45.

[77] Dworkin, n. 76 at 32. On this point of disagreement, see the remarks of Endicott, n. 47 at 40–41.

for the sake of law-ascertainment),[78] reductionist positivism does not presuppose any objectivism or naturalism[79] and so does not constantly oscillate between the two contradictory positions of apology and utopia.[80] There is no such thing as an objective agreement among law-applying authorities as to the criteria for distinguishing between law and non-law. There is only a shared feeling that they use the same criteria to ascertain international legal rules, a feeling which is reconstructed by virtue of some methodological and cognitive choices.

Second, it is not entirely clear if Dworkin's semantic sting argument necessarily frustrates the social thesis at the heart of Hart's reductionism. Indeed, Dworkin infers from the existence of an agreement on law-ascertaining criteria an agreement on their application. It is not clear that Hart held such a position, nor that he went so far as to claim that the social thesis implies an agreement about the application of secondary rules. One can bemoan the fact that Hart, in his postscript to the *Concept of Law*, flatly denied that his theory suffers from the so-called semantic sting, and that he made little effort to reply directly to Dworkin's argument on this point.[81] His postscript is mostly directed at Dworkin's criticism of his source thesis. That being said, Dworkin's attack on the social thesis remains highly speculative, for Hart did not specify that an agreement on how to apply law-ascertaining criteria is inherent in the social thesis.[82] Moreover, it must be acknowledged that Dworkin's argument was premised on his ambition to construct a theory of adjudication[83] which, if correctly followed, only yields answers

[78] D'Aspremont, n. 55 at 203–213, 215–217.

[79] It will be recalled that the scholars who espouse a Kelsenian understanding of law argue, however, that the social thesis presupposes the same type of absolute and external standard as natural law does. See e.g. Kammerhofer, n. 26 at 226.

[80] This contradiction is described in Martti Koskenniemi, *From Apology to Utopia: The Structure of International Legal Argument* (Finnish Lawyers' Publishing Co. 1989, reissued Cambridge University Press 2005) 303.

[81] Hart, n. 2 at 246. See the remarks of Endicott, who argues that Hart, in the postscript, seems 'mystified' by Dworkin's allegation: Endicott, n. 47 at 40.

[82] See also Raz's criticisms of Dworkin's semantic sting argument. According to Raz, Dworkin is wrong to think that Hart and others were concerned with the meaning of the word 'law'. Dworkin's semantic sting argument is meant to show that certain concepts cannot be given a semantic account. For Raz, Dworkin's conclusion that certain concepts, the concept of law among them, cannot be explained rests on the claim that the application of concepts based on criteria cannot be subject to dispute, especially with regard to what he calls 'pivotal cases'. Raz, n. 48, esp. at 3 and 13.

[83] Jules L. Coleman, Brian Leiter, 'Legal Positivism' in Dennis Patterson (ed.), *A Companion to Philosophy of Law and Legal Theory* (Blackwell 1999) 241–242 at 242. In the same vein,

to questions of American law.[84] Hart's social thesis, for its part, was not aimed at establishing a convincing theory of adjudication. It was simply meant to supplement the source thesis, which allows for the formal ascertainment of rules.[85] This does not mean, however, that Dworkin's and Hart's theories can be reconciled.[86] Rather, it signifies that 'the debates between Dworkin and his opponents create the impression of being missed connections more often than responsive encounters'.[87]

Third, the explanatory value of Hart's theory for emerging or immature legal systems is extremely limited. This may be true; however, it is not necessarily problematic, for two reasons. First, precisely because Hartian legal positivism is reductionist, it is not intended to provide a Kantian theory that can explain the whole phenomenon of law, including membership of all rules to all legal systems. Although Hartian reductionism is unable to provide the key for understanding the emergence of legal systems, it can still prove decisive to understand law-ascertainment in international law. Second, as far as international law is concerned, the legal system already seems to have reached – contrary to what Hart contended[88] – a certain level of maturity, especially in terms of density and sophistication of the secondary rules. Given that the international legal system is no longer in its infancy, it seems of little use to devise an approach which seeks to analyse and explain its emergence. If it were necessary to explain the emergence and consolidation of that system, it would be possible to resort to other theories. The international legal positivism envisaged here is not meant to explain all dimensions of international law.[89]

see Jason Beckett, 'Behind Relative Normativity: Rules and Process as Prerequisites of Law' 12 *EJIL* (2001) 627–650, especially at 629.

84 Raz, n. 48 at 27–28. 85 D'Aspremont, n. 55 at 48–56.

86 Raz, n. 48 at 36–37. For a tentative attempt to reconcile Hart's rule of recognition with Dworkin's semantic sting, see Scott J. Shapiro, 'What is the Rule of Recognition (and Does it Exist)?' in Matthew Adler, Kenneth Einar Himma (eds), *The Rule of Recognition and the US Constitution* (Oxford University Press 2009) 235–268.

87 Kramer, n. 29 at 128. See also Coleman, according to whom much of the debate between positivists and Dworkin 'appears rather foolish unless there is a version of positivism that makes Dworkin's criticisms, if not compelling, at least relevant'. Jules L. Coleman, 'Negative and Positive Positivism' in Dennis Patterson (ed.), *An Anthology of Philosophy of Law and Legal Theory* (Blackwell 2003) 116–133 at 119.

88 Hart, n. 2 at 213–237. For a criticism of that view, see n. 1.

89 For a similar conception of international legal positivism, see Gardner, n. 4 at 227.

3.2.2 Assuming the challenge

While it is possible to downplay some of the objections discussed above, others remain compelling, with the result that Hartian reductionism is in clear need of refinement, especially in connection to international law. The three areas for refining reductionism outlined here correspond to three questions where international legal theory could bring useful insights. These three questions constitute a research agenda for positivist international legal theory. They pertain to the cognition of the social practice that generates the necessary semantics for the Rule of Recognition; the identification of the law-applying authorities in the international legal order; the political motives behind a choice for reductionism; and, finally, the sociology and naturalism inherent in the social thesis.

3.2.2.1 Cognising the social practice It cannot be denied that Hart fell short of providing the tools (and disclosing the choices) required to apprehend the social practice which generates the communitarian semantics that in turn determine the meaning of the Rule of Recognition. So did his followers.[90] From this shortcoming stems the question of which behaviour structures the Rule of Recognition: what can be considered as law-ascertainment practice for the sake of the social practice? This is a normative choice[91] about the kind of value fact[92] that allows the capture of the social practice. In the context of international law, this means determining which acts or behaviours constitute a law-ascertainment practice, besides judicial pronouncements containing a law-identification component. The conceptual tools – i.e. the value facts – devised to capture the social practice will fundamentally impinge on how international lawyers decipher that practice. In particular, they will inform their perception of the legitimacy of the process by which social practice is produced.

3.2.2.2 Broadening the concept of law-making authority The second issue – closely intertwined with the first one – where Hartian reductionism requires refinement concerns the determination of which actors structure the Rule of Recognition.[93] Indeed, Hart espoused a very strict

[90] D'Aspremont, n. 55 at 57–62.

[91] Liam B. Murphy, 'Better to See Law This Way' 83 *New York University Law Review* (2008) 1104–1108.

[92] Greenberg, n. 70 at 177.

[93] Kramer, n. 8 at 406.

conception of law-applying authority which he equated to judicial domestic authorities. It is argued here that, in the context of international law, such a restrictive notion surely is deficient. International legal theory would benefit from revisiting the concept of law-applying authority and adjusting it to the specificities of the international legal sphere. It is well known that a refinement of the concept of law-applying authorities has been offered by Brian Tamanaha. According to the – controversial – modernisation proposed by Tamanaha, a law-applying authority is 'whomever, as a matter of social practice, members of the group (including legal officials themselves) identify and treat as "legal" officials'.[94] Accordingly, the social practice on which the Rule of Recognition is based must not be restricted to strictly-defined law-applying officials, but must include all social actors.[95] This expansion of the concept of law-applying authority is undoubtedly of great relevance in a legal order, like the international legal order, which lacks any vertical and institutional hierarchy. Tamanaha's definition, although somewhat all-embracing, can help provide a better grasp as to who actually engages in the ascertainment of international legal rules and generates the social practice of law-ascertainment. This definition surely points to the insufficiency of a narrow construction of the concept of law-applying authority, as well as to the necessity of not restricting the production of communitarian semantics to the practice of judicial authorities only. In international law, it can hardly be contested that other 'social actors' participate in the practice of law-ascertainment and should be taken into account in determining the communitarian semantics which constitute the law-ascertainment criteria. The question especially arises in connection to the law-ascertainment activities of codifying bodies like the International Law Commission, the *Institut de Droit international* or the International Committee of the Red Cross.

3.2.2.3 Disclosing the politics of reductionism It is true that Hart did not identify the political foundations of his reductionist positivism, maybe because he thought that utilitarian philosophy provided a sufficient explanation for the desirability of that conceptualisation.[96] Certainly, reductionism rests on a political choice which must be assumed. (International)

[94] Tamanaha, n. 57 at 142. For a similar pluralised account, see Keith C. Culver and Michael Guidice, *Legality's Borders: An Essay in General Jurisprudence* (Oxford University Press 2010).

[95] Tamanaha, n. 57 at 159–166.

[96] As was indicated above, in his 1957 *Harvard Law Review* article (Hart, n. 67), Hart simply referred to utilitarian theories of ethics developed by utilitarians like Bentham. I have further elaborated on that point in d'Aspremont, n. 33.

law's indeterminacy inevitably condemns (international) lawyers to making choices. Indeed, if law is indeterminate because its commands are conveyed through a language which is itself indeterminate, (international) lawyers invariably face the question of what they ought to do with such indeterminacy.[97] Each mode of disambiguation will itself boil down to a political decision, for there are political stakes associated with each mode of disambiguation,[98] especially when no authority can decisively clinch the issue for practical purposes.[99] In that sense, reductionism only constitutes one of the several political options available to (international) lawyers – and particularly legal scholars – who decide to assume the indeterminacy of law. There may be a string of different reasons motivating the political choice of reductionism. For present purposes, it is only necessary to highlight that such choice should be made in full awareness of its underlying agenda and entirely assumed.[100]

3.2.2.4 Expanding the role of the international legal scholars and assuming naturalism It has been said that reductionism in the sense of espousing the social thesis condemns international legal scholars to engage with sociological enquiries for which they may not be well equipped. This is undeniable. Hart himself expressly conceded the sociological prejudice to which the social thesis condemns legal scholars.[101] Such a charge originates, however, in a very orthodox understanding of what constitutes the 'science' of international law and, correspondingly, the role of international legal scholars. In other words, this objection is chiefly informed by how one construes the profession. Certainly, this author is sympathetic to the idea that international legal scholarship is primarily grammarian.[102]

[97] Susan Marks, *The Riddle of All Constitutions: International Law, Democracy, and the Critique of Ideology* (Oxford University Press 2003) 144.

[98] Murphy, n. 91 at 1104; Liam Murphy, 'The Political Question of the Concept of Law' in Jules L. Coleman (ed.), *Hart's Postscript: Essays on the Postscript to* The Concept of Law (Oxford University Press 2001) n. 29, 371–409 at 371. See also Liam Murphy, 'Concepts of Law' 30 *Australian Journal of Legal Philosophy* (2005) 1–19. See Scarpelli, n. 36 at 57; Frederick Schauer, 'Positivism as Pariah' in Robert P. George (ed.), *The Autonomy of Law: Essays of Legal Positivism* (Oxford University Press 1996) 31–56 at 34; John Waldron, 'Normative (or Ethical) Positivism' in Jules L. Coleman (ed.), *Hart's Postscript: Essays on the Postscript to* The Concept of Law (Oxford University Press 2001) n. 29, 411–434 at 411–433; Beckett, n. 83 at 648; Jason Beckett, 'Countering Uncertainty and Ending Up/Down Arguments: Prolegomena to a Response to NAIL' 16 *EJIL* 213 (2005) 213–238 at 214–219.

[99] Benedict Kingsbury, 'The Concept of Law in Global Administrative Law' 20 *EJIL* (2009) 23–57 at 26.

[100] In the same vein, see Beckett, n. 63 at 64. [101] Hart, n. 2 at 5.

[102] On the traditional role of the scholar, see the illuminating account given by Virally in Michel Virally, *La penseé juridique* (LGDJ 1960) xxii, 93. See also the enlightening

However, the argument can be made that being a grammarian does not necessarily entail that one's role be restricted to intra-systemic enquiries. It is true that extra-systemic enquiries of international legal scholars may be reminiscent of naturalist methodology. This is precisely the gist of the second objection of Kelsenian scholars who contend that the extra-systemic foundation of law is nothing more than a new naturalism. If seeking extra-systemic foundations for international law leads international legal positivism to suffer the same fate as the naturalists, so be it. Why would our understanding of international law necessarily need to rest on self-sustaining soil?[103] Indeed, it is argued here that international law does not need to enshrine all the mechanisms for sustaining its boundaries. Such mechanisms do not need to be internal. International law can remain a self-sufficient system and be the object of an autonomous cognition even though it may have external foundations.

4 Hartian reductionism beyond the challenge: cognitive international legal positivism

If grounded in the above-mentioned *reformed* Hartian reductionism, international legal positivism remains of particular relevance for international legal scholars, even though it is not able to explain the whole phenomenon of law. The following section outlines five particular aspects where a reformed reductionist international legal positivism can provide most insights. Reference is made to the dynamic theory of sources; the question of the validity of international law; content-determining techniques; voluntarism and state-centricism; as well as ecumenism and the division of tasks in the international legal scholarship.

and famous interpretation of the role of scholars by Paul Reuter, 'Principes de droit international public' 103 *Recueil des Cours* (1961) 425–656 at 459: 'Le droit n'est pas seulement un produit de la vie sociale, il est également le fruit d'un effort de pensée, s'efforçant d'agencer les données ainsi recueillies dans un ensemble cohérent et aussi logique que possible. C'est l'aspect systématique du droit international, il est à la fois plus important et plus délicat que celui des droits nationaux. Il est plus important parce que les sociétés nationales, du fait qu'elles sont profondément centralisées par l'autorité étatique, engendrent un droit déjà systématisé par ses conditions d'élaboration. Au contraire, la "décentralisation du pouvoir politique" qui règne dans la société internationale rejette sur le juriste un fardeau plus lourd. Il est plus délicat parce que le désordre de la société internationale n'est pas tant désordre de la pensée que désordre du pouvoir; certes le juriste peut se laisser aller à la systématisation, mais s'agit-il de systématiser seulement ses pensées ou de systématiser aussi la réalité? Certes, de par sa nature même, le droit est avide d'ordre mais à quoi servirait-il, par excès de rigueur dans la pensée, de poursuivre une systématisation en dehors du cadre des solutions admises.'

[103] The expression is borrowed from Kramer, n. 8 at 428.

4.1 *A dynamic theory of the sources of international law*

It is argued here that Hartian positivism, because it is reductionist in the sense mentioned above, can be very conducive to ensuring the sustainability and dynamism of a source-based account of validity. In particular, it helps show that cognising international law necessitates a theory of sources that is not static, but can rather evolve together with the social practice of law-applying authorities.

First, the reductionism presented here helps preserve the centrality of the theory of sources as a cognising tool. Indeed, from the reductionist perspective defended here, international law can be identified through formal criteria enshrined in the rules on law-making (the 'sources of law'), albeit in a different way from the current model offered by the mainstream theory of sources.[104] In particular, according to the reading of Hart advocated here, the theory of sources remains at the centre of scholars' modes of cognising the law in that the rules of the international legal system can be ascertained via the formal pedigree defined by a theory of sources. In doing so, such reductionism can help contain the deformalisation of law-ascertainment observed in the contemporary international legal scholarship which I have described elsewhere.[105]

Second, the theory of sources preserved by such a Hartian reductionism is dynamic. In that sense, reductionism does not rehabilitate the highly deficient mainstream theory of sources. Rather, it fosters a dynamic conception of the sources of international law which can accommodate the changes in contemporary international rule-making and evolve together with the practice of international law-applying authorities. This point needs to be explained further. By definition, law-ascertainment produces a static snapshot of rules existing at the moment cognition of rules is sought. The static character of this mapping of rules on a given topic at a given moment of time is precisely why one carries out the operation of law-ascertainment. The static character of the operation of law-ascertainment is precisely what allows law-ascertainment to fulfil its functions, for example, indicating the applicable law in a contentious case before an international tribunal. While the product of ascertainment is by definition static, the rules of recognition need not be so and can evolve with the social

[104] D'Aspremont, n. 55.

[105] For an outline of the different dimensions of this deformalisation, see Jean d'Aspremont, 'The Politics of Deformalization in International Law' 3 *Göttingen Journal of International Law* (2011) 503–550.

practice. In other words, although geared towards a static result, i.e. a snapshot of existing rules at a given time, the reductionism depicted above is in itself dynamic as it fluctuates and changes along with the practice of law-ascertainment by international law-applying authorities. This means that if today social practice still involves adherence to the mainstream concept of sources generally conveyed under the banner of Article 38 of the Statute of the International Court of Justice, reductionism allows social practice to produce law-ascertainment criteria beyond that model. In that sense, reductionism makes it possible for the source theory to accommodate some day within international law the new pluralised forms of public authority which currently cannot be apprehended by the mainstream doctrine of sources. Indeed, from the reductionist perspective presented here, it is – at least theoretically – conceivable that the mainstream model of ascertainment of international legal rules can be reconstructed in a way that allows the normative products thereof to fall within the scope of international law. New formal international law-ascertainment criteria could accordingly be devised in a way which elevates the norms originating in these pluralised exercises of public authority at the international level into rules of international law.[106]

4.2 Extra-systematicity and the vainness of the question of the validity of international law

As has been recalled above, Hartian reductionism is made possible by resort to an extra-systemic foundation of law, i.e. the social practice. It makes the cognition of the international legal system possible even if that

[106] It is not the ambition of this chapter to prejudge the outcome of this scholarly reflection. Yet, it must be acknowledged that such attempts inevitably stumble upon a paradox. Indeed, it can hardly be contested that the products of such normative activities have been consciously and purposely used and designed by international actors to remain outside the traditional channels of international and domestic law-making. If encapsulated in international law by virtue of newly designed law-ascertainment criteria, any inclusive theory of the sources of international law would most likely prod international actors to reinvent again other forms of norm-making processes to escape such an ever-expanding international law. In that sense, any new expansion of international law towards a more inclusive conceptualisation of the sources of international law could arouse a new move by international actors towards even more deformalised forms of norm-making. Such a paradox certainly does not mean that attempts to revamp the ascertainment of international legal rules with a view to embracing pluralised forms of exercise of public authority ought to be abandoned. This simply calls for a greater awareness of the risk that international legal scholars and international actors end up in a perpetual circular move that can exacerbate the misunderstanding between them.

system does not rest on self-sustaining soil. It is argued here that such a move allows international legal scholars to circumvent, for the sake of law-ascertainment, some of the abiding theoretical difficulties inherent in the question of the overall validity of international law.[107] In particular, explaining the overall validity of the international legal system has been one of the abiding difficulties confounding the theory of international law.[108]

It is well known that Kelsen – who, on this point, was partly followed by some important international legal scholars such as Anzilotti[109] and Guggenheim[110] – argued that the whole system necessarily rests on a *Grundnorm* which itself must be presupposed.[111] This aspect of Kelsen's theory is not discussed here.[112] Kelsen's ambition to design a general theory of law may well have required such a construction.[113] It is argued here, however, that, *as far as the ascertainment of international legal rules is concerned*, the social thesis makes the question of the validity of the international legal order as a whole utterly vain. Ascertaining legal rules only necessitates a sufficiently clear and consistent social practice able to produce enough communitarian semantics. This social practice does not need to unfold under the umbrella of a *Grundnorm* that guarantees the validity of the international legal system and ought not to be subject to a judgment of validity to produce the communitarian semantics necessary for law-ascertainment.[114] The social practice of law-ascertainment is not

107 I have further elaborated on that point in d'Aspremont, n. 33.

108 On positivism in international law, see d'Aspremont, n. 55 at 18–29.

109 Anzilotti adopted Kelsen's understanding of validity as resting on a hypothetical norm. Dionisio Anzilotti, *Scritti di diritto internazionale pubblico* (CEDAM 1956–1957) 57.

110 Georg Schwarzenberger, *International Law* (3rd edn Stevens 1957); Paul Guggenheim, 'What Is Positive International Law?' in George A. Lipsky (ed.), *Law and Politics in the World Community, Essays on Hans Kelsen's Pure Theory and Related Problems of International Law* (University of California Press 1953) 15–30.

111 Hans Kelsen, 'Théorie générale de droit international public: problèmes choisis' 42 *Recueil des Cours* (1932) 117–352 at 124–137.

112 It is well known that some scholars have construed that aspect of Kelsen's theory as a 'closure of convenience'. See e.g. Norberto Bobbio, Danilo Zolo, 'Hans Kelsen, the Theory of Law and the International Legal System: A Talk' 9 *EJIL* (1998) 355–367 at 355. For an attempt to rebut that point, see Kammerhofer, n. 26 at 197 and 231. See also Kammerhofer, Chapter 4.

113 On Kelsen, see d'Aspremont, n. 55 at 48–56.

114 As Kelsen himself would argue, there cannot be contradiction between an 'ought' proposition and an 'is' proposition, that is between a rule and a fact. See Hans Kelsen, *Introduction to the Problems of Legal Theory* (Bonnie Litschewski Paulson, Stanley L. Paulson (trs), Clarendon 1992) 30.

valid or invalid, it is simply a fact. In other words, if the criteria for formal ascertainment of international legal rules are solely a question of social practice by law-applying authorities and a few non-state actors as has been argued,[115] it is not necessary to seek the validation of that practice. What matters is simply that law-applying authorities, sharing some sufficient social consciousness and making use of similar law-ascertainment language, do actually recognise some norms as constituting international legal rules.

It is true that the existence of the legal system is to some extent dependent on there being valid legal rules within that system. Indeed, if a legal system does not recognise any single rule as valid, it can hardly exist as a legal system. Yet, this does not mean that, from the standpoint of law-ascertainment, the existence of a legal system boils down to a question of validity similar to that of individual rules[116] – and this is the reason why validity is not necessarily tautological and circular as it has sometimes been contended.[117] If we can say of the system itself that it is valid, this is only in the sense that its rules are valid.[118] Seen through the lens of law-ascertainment, the existence of a legal system – and the same is true with regard to the international legal system – is not a question of validity.[119] While the validity of a given norm must be appraised in the light of the norm from which it is derived, it makes no sense, from the standpoint

[115] D'Aspremont, n. 55 at 203–213.

[116] It is commonly accepted that a rule which is not valid within that system is not a legal rule within that system. See Joseph Raz, 'Legal Validity' in Joseph Raz, *The Authority of Law: Essays on Law and Morality*, n. 32, 146–159 at 146; Kelsen, for his part, famously argued that validity is the specific form of existence of legal rules in a given system, such contention applying to all norms. See Hans Kelsen, *General Theory of Law and State* (Harvard University Press 1945) 175–177. But see the critique by Scandinavian realists, who see a contradiction between the existence of the rule and its reality. See Alf Ross, *Introduction à l'empirisme juridique: Textes théoriques* (Éric Millard and Elsa Matzner (trs), LGDJ 2004) 25–26.

[117] This argument has been made by Martti Koskenniemi, 'Hierarchy in International Law: A Sketch' 8 *EJIL* (1997) 566–582 at 578.

[118] Raz, n. 116 at 148.

[119] Hart, n. 2 at 100, in particular 108–109: 'We only need the word "validity" and commonly only use it to answer questions which arise within a system of rules where the status of a rule as a member of the system depends on its satisfying certain criteria provided by the rule of recognition. No such question can arise as to the validity of the very rule of recognition which provides the criteria; it can neither be valid nor invalid, but simply accepted as appropriate for use in this way.' In the same vein, see Joseph Raz, 'Legal Reasons, Sources, and Gaps' in Joseph Raz, *The Authority of Law: Essays on Law and Morality*, n. 32, 53–77 at 69; see also Virally, n. 102 at 140.

of law-ascertainment, to gauge the legal system as a whole in the same manner.[120] The existence of the (international) legal system boils down to a *mere question of fact.*

As mentioned above, authors embracing a Kelsenian understanding of law will commonly argue that side-stepping the question of the validity of the international legal system by grounding law-ascertainment in social practice demotes what is rightly legal science to legal sociology.[121] Whether true or not, this objection does not really undermine the theory of ascertainment presented here, for it only pertains to a question of how one construes the mission(s) of (international) legal scholarship and the scope of the 'science' of law. This is a fundamentally different debate from that of law-ascertainment which is at the heart of this chapter. Ultimately, even if the social thesis, by bypassing the question of the validity of the international legal system as a whole and grounding law-ascertainment in facts, were to lead legal 'science' to encapsulate sociological analysis, such an enlargement of scope of the 'science' of law – far from being unprecedented[122] – would then be the necessary condition for a lasting and solid theory of ascertainment of international legal rules.

Certainly, if applied to international law, the contention that the existence of the legal system is a question of fact is not entirely unheard of. Some international legal scholars, while refraining from grounding their contention in a strong theory of law-ascertainment,[123] have occasionally claimed that the question of the validity of international law as a whole is vain and that questions of validity ought to be restricted to problems

[120] It would be misleading to conceal that such a 'retreat' in the direction of empirical sources has remained – although unconvincingly – immune from controversy. See Sean Coyle, 'Hart, Raz and the Concept of Legal System' 21 *Law and Philosophy* (2002) 275–304 at 288–289.

[121] Kammerhofer, Chapter 4. See also Kammerhofer, n. 26 at 227.

[122] It probably is a lesson learned from legal realism as well as policy-oriented jurisprudence. See d'Aspremont, n. 55 at 85–88, 105–110. For a contemporary attempt to ground the study of international law in its social context, see Moshe Hirsch, 'The Sociology of International Law: Invitation to Study International Rules and Their Social Context' 55 *University of Toronto Law Journal* (2005) 891–939. On the possible roles for sociology in the study of international law, see also Anthony Carty, 'Sociological Theories of International Law' in Rüdiger Wolfrum (ed.), *Max Planck Encyclopaedia of Public International Law*, Vol. 9 (Oxford University Press 2012) 252–265 at 263–264 (MN 42–46).

[123] On the anti-theoretical attitude of the international legal scholarship, see d'Aspremont, n. 55 at 66–77.

of existence of individual rules.[124] A Hartian reductionist positivism can provide additional underpinnings to their discerning intuitions.

4.3 Abandoning content-determining techniques

The reductionist positivism sketched here allows international legal scholars to forsake their adherence to theories of adjudicative neutrality and immanent intelligibility of legal arguments, which is probably the dominant understanding of legal positivism in general legal theory. In that sense, reductionism contributes to the estrangement of legal positivism from formal content-determination techniques. This position corresponds to the rejection by Hart of 'formalism' construed as an approach aimed, mistakenly, at minimising uncertainty in law-application and maximising legal certainty and predictability.[125] Indeed, in Hart's view, formalism was the antithesis of rule-scepticism or legal realism, which construes law-application as totally indeterminate and which equates law with law-application. Hart uncompromisingly rejected formalism as a theory of adjudicative neutrality and immanent intelligibility of legal arguments, characterising it as just as misleading and inaccurate as rule-scepticism. In his view, formalism and rule-scepticism are the 'Scylla and Charybdis of justice theory'.[126] It is noteworthy that Hart himself praised some aspects of the legacy of legal realism: 'its main effect was to convince many judges, lawyers, practical and academic, of two things: first, that they should always suspect, although not always in the end reject, any claim that existing legal rules or precedents are constraints strong and complete enough to determine what a court's decision should be without other extra-legal considerations; secondly, that judges should not seek to bootleg silently into the law their own conceptions of the law's aims or justice or social policy or other extra-legal element required for decision but should openly identify and discuss them'.[127]

[124] E.g. Brownlie, n. 2 at 30–31. In the same sense, see Gerald G. Fitzmaurice, 'The General Principles of International Law Considered from the Standpoint of the Rule of Law' 92 *Recueil des Cours* (1957) 1–227; Luigi Condorelli, 'Custom' in Mohammed Bedjaoui (ed.), *International Law: Achievements and Prospects* (Martinus Nijhoff 1991) 179–211 at 180.

[125] See generally Hart, n. 2 at 124–154. On that particular aspect of *The Concept of Law*, see Roger A Shiner, 'Hart on Judicial Discretion' 5 *Problema* (2011) 341–362.

[126] Hart, n. 2 at 124–154.

[127] HLA Hart, 'American Jurisprudence through English Eyes: The Nightmare and the Noble Dream' 11 *Georgia Law Review* (1976–1977) 969–990 at 978.

Paradoxically, formal content-determination of law is how legal positivism is most commonly understood.[128] This type of formalism has, in the history of most legal systems, been subject to oscillations, with periods when formal legal argumentation has been dominant followed by dramatic movements towards deformalisation of legal argumentation.[129] Much of the criticism of formalism in legal scholarship – and thus of the type of international legal positivism with which it is associated – has been directed at an understanding of formalism reminiscent of a Kantian conception of universal reason. This is particularly true with regard to the realist objections against the 'abuse of logic',[130] the 'abuse of deduction'[131] and the 'mechanical jurisprudence'[132] that are supposedly brought about by this type of international legal positivism.[133] Again, all these critiques are premised on the idea that formalism is first and foremost a theory of adjudication[134] and constitutes some form of dispute-management technique which allows for the identification of the specific rules meant to settle legal disputes.[135] Although its theory about making social choices also includes a law-ascertainment dimension, the process-based approach of the New Haven School primarily construes formalism as a theory of adjudication and legal argumentation for the promotion of reform.[136]

[128] E.g. Charles C. Goetsch, 'The Future of Legal Formalism' 24 *American Journal of Legal History* (1980) 221–256. See also Ernest J. Weinrib, 'Legal Formalism' in Dennis Patterson (ed.), *A Companion to Philosophy of Law and Legal Theory* (Blackwell 1996) 332–342. See also the remarks of Olivier Corten, *Méthodologie du droit international public* (Editions de l'Université de Bruxelles 2009) 57.

[129] This has been insightfully described by David Kennedy, 'When Renewal Repeats: Thinking against the Box' 32 *New York University Journal of International Law and Politics* (1999–2000) 335–500 at 335. It is interesting to note that such a finding had already been made by Hart. Hart, n. 2 at 130.

[130] Anthony J. Sebok, 'Misunderstanding Positivism' 93 *Michigan Law Review* (1994–1995) 2054–2132 at 2093.

[131] David Kennedy, *The Rise and Fall of Classical Legal Thoughts* (Beard Books 2006) xviii.

[132] This is the famous expression of Roscoe Pound, 'Mechanical Jurisprudence' 8 *Columbia Law Review* (1908) 605–623.

[133] See also the criticisms of Richard H. Pildes, 'The Dark Side of Legalism' 44 *Virginia Journal of International Law* 145 (2003–2004) 145–167.

[134] On the realist criticisms of formalism as a theory of legal reasoning in adjudication, see generally Sebok, n. 130 at 2071. See also d'Aspremont, n. 55 at 85–88.

[135] This understanding permeates the critique of positivism by Benedict Kingsbury, 'The International Legal Order' NYU Law School Public Law & Legal Theory Research Paper No. 01–04 (2003) and Institute for International Law and Justice, History and Theory of International Law Series, Working Paper No. 2003/1.

[136] E.g. Rosalyn Higgins, 'Policy Considerations and the International Judicial Process' 17 *ICLQ* (1968) 58–84; Michael Reisman, 'The View from the New Haven School of

Many scholars affiliated with Critical Legal Studies (CLS) also understand formalism from the vantage point of legal argumentation.[137]

As the foregoing has demonstrated, the reductionist positivism defended here is, by definition, exclusive of formal content-determination methods. It is only meant to provide one part of the answer to the fundamental questions raised by the cognition of international law and does not seek to explain the whole phenomenon of law, and certainly not its content nor adjudicative truth.[138] In that sense, reductionist positivism does not include theories of interpretation, as it does not consider them to be a constitutive component of international legal positivism. In other words, international legal positivism is not about providing means to establish authoritative interpretation. The complex theories of interpretation that have been established to provide rationality (and hence authority) to argumentative reasoning do not belong to the knowledge of international law. They are, more simply, theories of argumentation.

4.4 Moving away from voluntarism and state-centricism

Commentators often equate positivism with a conception of sources of law that is exclusively based on state consent.[139] Construed in this way, legal

International Law' 86 *ASIL Proceedings* (1992) 118–125; Lung-chu Chen, 'Perspectives from the New Haven School' 87 *ASIL Proceedings* (1993) 407–411 at 408.

137 E.g. David Kennedy, 'The Disciplines of International Law and Policy' 12 *LJIL* (1999) 83–101; Kennedy, n. 129; Martti Koskenniemi, *The Gentle Civilizer of Nations: The Rise and Fall of International Law 1870-1960* (Cambridge University Press 2002) 502; Koskenniemi, n. 80 at 306; Nigel Purvis, 'Critical Legal Studies in Public International Law' 32 *Harvard Journal of International Law* (1991) 81–127 at 81; Thomas Skouteris, 'Fin de NAIL: New Approaches to International Law and its Impact on Contemporary International Legal Scholarship' 10 *LJIL* (1997) 415–420; Thomas Skouteris, *The Notion of Progress in International Law Discourse* (T. M. C. Asser Press 2010) 93–157. For a similar interpretation of formalism from the vantage point of critical legal studies, see Iain Scobbie, 'Towards the Elimination of International Law: Some Radical Scepticism about Sceptical Radicalism' 61 *BYBIL* (1990) 339–362 at 345.

138 Gardner, n. 4 at 227.

139 This perception permeates different strands of contemporary legal scholarship. See e.g. Anthony Carty, 'Conservative and Progressive Visions in French International Legal Doctrine' 16 *EJIL* (2005) 525–537; David Kennedy, 'The Sources of International Law' 2 *American University Journal of International Law and Policy* (1987) 1–96 at 20; Kennedy, n. 129 at 355, 366; Jutta Brunnée and Stephen J. Toope, 'An Interactional Theory of International Legal Obligation' University of Toronto Legal Studies Research Series, No. 08–16, 12 July 2008, 31–33, available at http://ssrn.com/abstract=1162882. On this association, see the remarks of Owen Elias, Chin L. Lim, *The Paradox of Consensualism in International Law* (Kluwer Law International 1998) 193; or the remarks by Corten, n. 128 at 53–54 and 58.

positivism has been lampooned for assuring the continued authority of the state.[140] The international legal scholarship of the nineteenth century is often portrayed as promoting such a conception of positivism, which ultimately became an acclamation of state 'sovereignty'. There is no doubt that, if conflated with voluntarism, legal positivism remains inextricably plagued by contradictions and fails to offer a satisfying theory to explain the binding character of international law.[141]

According to the argument made here, however, voluntarism is primarily an approach to authority and legitimacy of international law and is a different issue from that of the ascertainment of rules.[142] Reductionism, and the cognitive positivism for which it paves the way, do not ignore the impact of formal law-ascertainment on the authority and legitimacy of international law, but nor do they seek to explain why international law is binding or why subjects abide by its rules.[143]

It is true that, on the basis of the current law-ascertainment practice of international law-applying authorities, scholars approach the creation of international law from a primarily state-centric perspective. This is due to the fact that mainstream conceptions of the sources of international law remain largely informed by state consent. Yet the current state-centric character of the mainstream theory of sources in international law does not require that, as a matter of principle, international legal positivism be assimilated with state intent,[144] as was claimed in the work of

[140] Carty, n. 139 at 525–537.

[141] E.g. Koskenniemi, n. 80 at 303–387; Carty, n. 139 at 534.

[142] Using the distinction between the question of the *sources* of law and the question of the *foundations* of law, Kolb makes the same argument. See Robert Kolb, *Réflexions de philosophie du droit international: Problèmes fondamentaux du droit international public: Théorie et Philosophie du droit international* (Bruylant 2003), 51; see also Samantha Besson, 'Theorizing the Sources of International Law' in Samantha Besson, John Tasioulas (eds), *The Philosophy of International Law* (Oxford University Press 2010) 163–185 at 166; for Besson, however, consent is insufficient to ensure the authority and legitimacy of international legal rules, see 166 and 175. In the same vein, see Nico Krisch, *Beyond Constitutionalism: The Pluralist Structure of Postnational Law* (Oxford University Press 2010) 3. Cf. David Lefkowitz, 'The Sources of International Law: Some Philosophical Reflections' in Samantha Besson, John Tasioulas (eds), *The Philosophy of International Law*, 187–206 at 192–194.

[143] The conflation between formalism and consensualism has long been rejected by normativist approaches to international law, as is illustrated by Kelsen. In the same vein, see also Besson, n. 142 at 166. See generally, d'Aspremont, n. 55 at 48–56.

[144] For similar criticisms of the association of the source doctrine and consensualism, see G. J. H. van Hoof, *Rethinking the Sources of International Law* (Kluwer Law 1983) 289. See also Mehrdad Payandeh, 'The Concept of International Law in the Jurisprudence of HLA Hart' 21 *EJIL* (2010) 967–995 at 970–971.

pre-modern international legal scholars and classicists.[145] International legal positivism does not mean that law exclusively emanates from the state: reductionism – as described here – is indifferent to the actual *material source*[146] of law. The possible mechanisms of law-ascertainment which reductionist positivism advocates here might well lead to the identification of certain norms as legal rules despite the fact that they do not originate in the will of states. For instance, in the pluralised contemporary international legal system, it would be entirely conceivable for law to emanate from non-state entities.[147] The reductionism identified in this chapter is thus not averse to the theoretical possibility of international legal rules made by non-state entities or through pluralised processes.

4.5 Ecumenism and division of tasks in twenty-first-century international legal scholarship

Finally, it is worth noting that the reductionist positivism advocated in the previous paragraphs – i.e. positivism limited to law-ascertainment grounded in social practice – comes with some doctrinal conciliatory and ecumenical virtues. As it does not seek to explain the whole phenomenon of law and because its descriptive benefit remains limited, the reductionist positivism presented here necessarily needs to be complemented by other approaches to international law. It could even be argued

145 D'Aspremont, n. 55 at 63–66.

146 On the distinction between material and formal sources, see generally, Lassa Oppenheim, *International Law: A Treatise*, Vol. 1 (Hersch Lauterpacht (ed.), 8th edn Longmans, Green and Co. 1955) 24. See the remarks of Percy E. Corbett, 'The Consent of States and the Sources of the Law of Nations' 5 *BYBIL* (1925) 20–30; Charles Rousseau, *Principes généraux du droit international public*, Vol. 1 (Pedone 1944) 106–108; Gerald G. Fitzmaurice, 'Some Problems Regarding the Formal Sources of International Law' in Frederik M. van Asbeck (ed.), *Symbolae Verzijl* (Martinus Nijhoff 1958) 153–176; Georges Abi-Saab, 'Les sources du droit international. Essai de déconstruction' in *Le Droit international dans un monde en mutation: liber amicorum en hommage au Professeur Eduardo Jimenez de Arechaga* (Fundación de Cultura Universitaria 1994) 29–49 at 30. See also the controversial account of this distinction made by Georges Scelle, 'Essai sur les sources formelles du droit international' in *Recueil sur les sources en l'honneur de Francois Gény*, Vol. 3 (Sirey 1935) 400–430; Quôc Dinh Nguyên, Patrick Dailler, Alain Pellet, *Droit international public* (6th edn LGDJ 1999) 111–112; Alain Pellet, 'Article 38' in Andreas Zimmermann, Christian Tomuschat, Karin Oellers-Frahm (eds), *The Statute of the International Court of Justice: A Commentary* (Oxford University Press 2002) 677–792 at 714–716.

147 On this aspect of the pluralisation of international law and the role of non-state actors, see Jean d'Aspremont (ed.), *Participants in the International Legal System: Multiple Perspectives on Non-State Actors in International Law* (Routledge 2011).

that the extra-systemic foundation of law inherent in reductionist legal positivism inevitably stimulates ecumenist overture to other approaches to international law.

First, reductionist legal positivism does not mean that the only criticisms of law should be source-based.[148] On the contrary, it is argued that source-based validity reinforces the possibility of a moral, political and economic critique of law. Indeed, the argument can be made that the possibility of an ascertainment of international legal rules is also a necessary condition for the critique itself. Any critique of law – whether moral, economic, political, etc. – presupposes that international rules can be preliminarily ascertained. Short of any ascertainment, there simply is no critique possible for lack of an object.[149] It should nonetheless be made clear that, while being a necessary condition for the critique of law, the reductionist positivism advocated here does not provide for the standard of evaluation for that critique.

Second, as has been emphasised, reductionist legal positivism is not meant to describe the entire phenomenon of law and in particular the dynamics at the heart of the creation and operation of international law.[150] The social thesis, as presented here, only informs the meaning of the formal indicators which allow a distinction between law and non-law. In that sense, the social thesis is not necessarily incompatible with some of the descriptive theories of international law, even if they are inspired by modern natural law theories.[151] Likewise, the social thesis allows for a reduced emphasis on words, together with an ever-increasing emphasis on behaviour (as was advocated by the legal realists). In that sense, it can be contended that Hart's approach can accommodate, and is usefully complemented by, the empirical turn witnessed in international legal scholarship nowadays.[152] Furthermore, the social thesis that is outlined here helps to alleviate some of the concerns that have inspired the sociological approaches to international law, as international law cannot

[148] For a criticism of this confusion, see Gardner, n. 4 at 209.

[149] Twining, n. 66 at 27; Joseph S. Boyle, 'Positivism, Natural Law and Disestablishment: Some Questions Raised by MacCormick's Moralistic Amoralism' 20 *Valparaíso University Law Review* (1985–1986) 55–60; Allen Buchanan, *Justice, Legitimacy and Self-Determination: Moral Foundations for International Law* (Oxford University Press 2007) 21.

[150] D'Aspremont, n. 55 at 12–29.

[151] D'Aspremont, n. 55 at 96–100, 119–127.

[152] Gregory Shaffer and Tom Ginsburg, 'The Empirical Turn in International Legal Scholarship' 106 *AJIL* (2012) 1–46.

be severed from the context of its making or that of its application.[153] Hopefully, it is also apparent from the preceding discussion that the reductionist, international legal positivism presented here comes with some cosmopolitan virtues,[154] for it has been suggested that the concept of law-applying authorities generating social practice ought to be revamped as to include a wide variety of actors in order to better reflect the current move away from a state-centrist to a more cosmopolitan international society.[155]

Attention is also drawn to the fact that the conceptualisation presented here underpins the mutually enriching character of the multiple strands of contemporary international legal scholarship. For instance, the current configuration of the processes of production of communitarian semantics in the international legal order makes the call for 'a culture of formalism' developed by Martti Koskenniemi[156] even more relevant.[157] Likewise, the social thesis leaves intact some of the objections of the critique made by CLS and deconstructivism. In particular, the social thesis relocates the indeterminacy of the source thesis and does not purport to allay the contradictions of international legal argumentation.[158] In the same vein, because the production of the communitarian semantics necessary to ensure an elementary meaning of the formal yardstick of law-ascertainment still suffers from gender, cultural and geographical biases, the conceptualisation of the foundations of reductionism adopted here can still benefit from the insights of feminist[159] and TWAIL[160] approaches

[153] D'Aspremont, n. 55 at 96–100.

[154] On the various conceptions of cosmopolitanism in international legal studies, see H. Patrick Glenn, 'Cosmopolitan Legal Orders' in Andrew Halpin, Volker Roeben (eds), *Theorising the Global Legal Order* (Hart 2009) 25–37. See also the various contributions found in Roland Pierik, Wouter Werner (eds), *Cosmopolitanism in Context: Perspectives from International Law and Political Theory* (Cambridge University Press 2010).

[155] D'Aspremont, n. 55 at 203–213.

[156] D'Aspremont, n. 55 at 18–29.

[157] D'Aspremont, n. 55 at 213–215.

[158] D'Aspremont, n. 55 at 12–37, 138–142.

[159] D'Aspremont, n. 55 at 111.

[160] These are the so-called TWAIL (Third World Approaches to International Law). See generally Makau Mutua, 'What is TWAIL?' 94 *ASIL Proceedings* (2000) 31–38. See Antony Anghie and B. S. Chimni, 'Third World Approaches to International Law and Individual Responsibility in International Conflicts' 2 *Chinese Journal of International Law* (2003) 77–103; Karin Mickelson, 'Taking Stock of TWAIL Histories' 10 *International Community Law Review* (2008) 355–362. See also Martin Gallié, 'Les théories tiers-mondistes du droit international (TWAIL): Un renouveau?' 39 *Etudes Internationales* (2008) 17–38; Hilary Charlesworth, 'Feminist Ambivalence about International Law' 11 *International Legal Theory* (2005) 1–8; Karin Mickelson, 'Rhetoric and Rage: Third World Voices in International Legal Discourse' 16 *Wisconsin International Law Journal* (1998) 353–419; Upendra Baxi, 'What May the Third World Expect from International

to international law and not exclude them at all. In addition, the necessity to ensure a social consciousness among the actors contributing to the emergence of a social practice for the sake of the ascertainment of international legal rules bolsters the need to continue researching the channels of dialogue among law-applying authorities, as has been pursued by scholars affiliated with the so-called liberal school of international law.[161]

Despite the non-exclusive, non-confrontational and conciliatory character of the international legal positivism defended here, it is less certain that it can be reconciled with legal pluralism.[162] Indeed, if legal pluralism is understood as eschewing legal unity and a common framework of identification,[163] the preservation of formal indicators for international law-ascertainment purposes may well come at the expense of legal pluralism, although it cannot be excluded that the social practice gives rise to several rules of recognition.[164]

By the same token, I acknowledge that reductionist international legal positivism remains at odds with theories of the sources of international law based on substantive validity.[165] This being said, it is of the utmost importance to indicate that the possibility cannot be excluded that the social practice generating the communitarian semantics for the sake of law-ascertainment might itself be inspired by normative

Law' 27 *Third World Quarterly* (2006) 713–725; Antony Anghie, *Imperialism, Sovereignty and the Making of International Law* (Cambridge University Press 2004); David P. Fidler, 'Revolt against or from within the West: TWAIL, the Developing World, and the Future Direction of International Law' 2 *Chinese Journal of International Law* (2003) 29–76; Madhav Khosla, 'The TWAIL Discourse: The Emergence of a New Phase' 9 *International Community Law Review* (2007) 291–304; Obiora C. Okafor, 'Newness, Imperialism, and International Legal Reform in Our Time: A TWAIL Perspective' 43 *Osgoode Hall Law Journal* (2005) 171–191.

161 See generally Anne-Marie Slaughter, 'A Global Community of Courts' 44 *Harvard International Law Journal* (2003) 191–219.

162 Krisch, n. 142 at 11–12, 69–105.

163 On the multiple meanings of legal pluralism, see Krisch, n. 142 at 71–78.

164 See, however, on the possibility of withholding a rule of recognition and safeguarding pluralism, Besson, n. 142 at 184; William Twining, 'Implications of "Globalisation" for Law as a Discipline' in Andrew Halpin, Volker Roeben (eds), *Theorising the Global Legal Order* (Hart 2009) 39–60 at 44–45. On the specific question of whether Hart's theory can sustain legal pluralism, see John Waldron, 'Legal Pluralism and the Contrast between Hart's Jurisprudence and Fuller's' in Peter Cane (ed.), *The Hart–Fuller Debate in the Twenty-First Century* (Hart 2010) 135–155; Margaret Davies, 'The Politics of Defining Law' in Peter Cane (ed.), *The Hart–Fuller Debate in the Twenty-First Century* (Hart 2010) 157–167.

165 D'Aspremont, n. 55 at 96–100, 119–127.

considerations.[166] In that sense, the theory of law-ascertainment presented here could be usefully complemented by research on the normative driving forces of the practice of law-ascertainment. However, the inspiration that law-applying authorities could draw from normative principles does not in itself elevate such principles into law-ascertaining criteria: law-identification operates solely on the basis of the linguistic indicators generated by that practice.

A final remark must be put forward on the normative character of the choice in favour of the reductionist international legal positivism that has been advocated in this chapter. Certainly, the above-mentioned observations provide numerous indications as to the underlying normative motives that can guide the choice for the reductionism embraced here. Whatever these motives may actually be, it remains that jurisprudential choices are informed by one's research interest. Indeed, it can hardly be denied that one necessarily embraces an approach or a method that fits with the type of research which one is interested in carrying out. Reductionist international legal positivism is no different in this respect. In particular, it should not come as a surprise that reductionist legal positivism reflects an interest in the cognition of the formal limits of international law. More specifically, the choice for reductionism boils down to an expression of preference for studies in international law based on the identification of rules rather than the determination of their content or the evaluation of their moral value. In that sense, reductionist legal positivism stems from a preference for a cognitive type of positivism.[167]

[166] In the same vein, see Benedict Kingsbury, Megan Donaldson, 'From Bilateralism to Publicness in International Law' in Ulrich Fastenrath *et al.* (eds), *From Bilateralism to Community Interest: Essays in Honour of Judge Bruno Simma* (Oxford University Press 2011) 79–89 at 89.

[167] On the notion of cognitive positivism, see Fiss, n. 6 at 1008: 'Cognitive positivism establishes a priority for a type of study or inquiry, at times more grandly referred to as "scholarship" which is distinguished by two criteria, one going to object, the other to method. Cognitive positivism claims that the proper object of study is the actual behaviour of people and institutions. It places a premium on knowledge of what is rather than what out to be . . . A positive study of law describes how the legal system works.'

6

Beyond Kelsen and Hart

ALEXANDER SOMEK*

1 Introduction: legal positivism and the loathed question

If one were to ask scholars of public international law whether they can think of the one question that is the most uninspiring to ask about their discipline, their primary candidate might be the foundational question of whether public international law *really* is law. Well-versed experts in, say, international investment law or the law of armed conflict would consider even raising this question uncouth. In the face of the evident effectiveness of the contemporary international legal system,[1] indeed, it is simply preposterous to repeat tirelessly the Austinian allegation[2] that public international law is not law since it lacks centralised enforcement.[3] Public international law is widely adhered to, in particular within functionally specific regimes. Even where breaches occur, these do not invalidate the law in question; they even give rise to the production of more law.[4] Finally, most prominent instances of non-compliance – i.e. acts by the United States of America – are notoriously accompanied by rationalisations saying that what happens as a matter of might also happens as a matter of right. Rationalisations reconfirm validity, just as feelings of

* I would like to thank Eric Andersen, Jonathan Carlson, Jean d'Aspremont, Kate Brookson-Morris, Marcella David, Paul Gowder, Herbert Hovenkamp, Nicholas Johnson, Jörg Kammerhofer, Todd Pettys, Brendan Plant, Margaret Raymond, John Reitz, Caroline Sheerin and my wife Sabine for helpful comments on earlier drafts.

1 The effectiveness needs to be qualified, however, for it is, at its core, the effectiveness mediated by various functionally differentiated regimes. See Martti Koskenniemi, 'The Fate of Public International Law: Between Technique and Politics' 70 *Modern Law Review* (2007) 1–30 at 7.

2 John Austin, *The Province of Jurisprudence Determined* (Prometheus Books, 2000) 142.

3 See merely Mary Ellen O'Connell, *The Power and Purpose of International Law: Insights from the Theory & Practice of Enforcement* (Oxford University Press 2008).

4 Hans Kelsen, *Introduction to the Problems of Legal Theory* (Bonnie Litschewski Paulson, Stanley L. Paulson (trs), Clarendon Press 1992) 28, for the perennial insight that acts contrary to law do not really 'break' the law. They trigger the production of even more law.

guilt reveal the superego. As a discourse explaining and justifying state action, public international law is undoubtedly universally relevant.

Nonetheless, both classical and post-classical authors of legal positivism have made it difficult for public international law to pass as a legal system. While Austin was struck by the absence of sovereignty, Hart denied public international law the status of a legal system owing to the lack of secondary rules for the creation of primary rules of obligation.[5] Kelsen alone had no qualms about admitting the legality of international law because, in his view, what had been considered by Austin and Hart as disqualifying factors should rather be understood as ordinary features of legal systems in general. Public international law is marked by decentralised enforcement[6] (i.e. the absence of Austin's sovereign) and indeterminate rules of rule-creation (i.e. what Hart considered to be lacking, because alleged rules would merely defer to what states observe in fact). The centralisation of enforcement and the determinacy of secondary rules, however, are not questions of 'either/or' with regard to the existence of a particular legal system, but rather questions of 'more or less' *within* it. In other words, centralised enforcement or determinate secondary rules cannot be criteria for the identification of legal systems because for any such system matters of centralisation and determinacy can merely be a matter of degree. Legal systems exist with a higher or lower degree of decentralisation and indeterminacy, and it would be wrong to draw an arbitrary line within this continuum.[7] At the same time, however, Kelsen recognised that, owing to its decentralised method of enforcement, public international law is a 'primitive' legal system. He thereby used a distinction that cannot be properly understood unless one perceives it as preparing the ground for an evaluation.

A sceptical attitude towards the exuberant self-characterisation of social practices as 'law'[8] is one of legal positivism's enduring virtues.[9] At the same time, positivists have not been terribly sophisticated at spelling this

[5] HLA Hart, *The Concept of Law* (Clarendon Press 1961) 228–231. Hart considered it pointless, in particular, to repeat on the level of the Rule of Recognition the fact that states observe certain standards as binding rules (at 230).

[6] Hans Kelsen, *Pure Theory of Law* (Max Knight (tr.), University of California Press 1967) 323.

[7] In other words, the continuum is marked by what Hegel would have called 'intensive quanta', that is, matters of mere degree. Georg Wilhelm Friedrich Hegel, 'Wissenschaft der Logik I' in *Werke in zwanzig Bänden*, Vol. 5 (Suhrkamp 1986) 250–252.

[8] On the self-identification of social facts *qua* legal phenomena, see Kelsen, n. 4 at 9.

[9] This is what I have argued before. See Alexander Somek, 'The Spirit of Legal Positivism' 12 *German Law Journal* (2011) 729–756.

scepticism out. Quite possibly, the ethos of descriptive accuracy ('value-free legal science' and 'the separation of law and morals', respectively) has posed a major obstacle. The positivists' understanding of law renders law as an object that is essentially someone's product.[10] Owing to this basic understanding of what law is, positivists have to presuppose institutions whose relevance to the legal system is only accounted for inasmuch as they are perceived to be necessary to producing the object form. The world of legal positivism is always already inhabited by either the coercive apparatus of the state or adjudicating bodies. What is thereby eclipsed, however, is the 'relational' aspect of law, in other words, the fact that law is not merely a product ('norms') backed up by coercion, but constitutive of a specific form of relation among actors. It has escaped the attention of legal positivists, therefore, that self-characterisations of social practices as 'law' may be wrong or ideologically distorted not only because of a lack of centralised coercion or unclear secondary rules, but because the underlying relation does not pass muster as 'legal'. In order to explore this issue with regard to public international law, one needs to move beyond Kelsen and Hart. This is what this chapter proposes to do. What it seeks to retain, nonetheless, is the critical spirit of legal positivism.[11]

By shifting the perspective from the legal positivist's understanding of law *qua* special type of product to law *qua* special type of relationship, the foundational challenge can be formulated in a manner that is perhaps less prominent, but also more profound. The question is then whether public international law, at least certain of its parts, really partakes of legal *form*.[12] This form is tied to, but not exhausted in, the core promise of legality according to which rights and obligations are to be knowable in advance of action or an imposition of sanctions.[13]

With this in mind it may, at least in certain instances, be open to debate whether we are dealing with a legal system where claims of right are based on surprisingly novel understandings of sources or else unconcerned

[10] On the underlying ontological issue, see generally Martin Heidegger, 'Die Grundprobleme der Phänomenologie' in Friedrich-Wilhelm von Herrmann (ed.), *Martin Heidegger Gesamtausgabe*, Vol. 2.24 (Vittorio Klostermann 1975) 1–469 at 130.

[11] Somek, n. 9.

[12] A recent and most comprehensive exploration of law's form and legal formality is offered by Robert S. Summers, *Form and Function in a Legal System: A General Study* (Cambridge University Press 2006).

[13] Ronald Dworkin, *Justice in Robes* (Harvard University Press 2006) 169: 'Legality insists that [state] power be exercised only in accordance with standards established in the right way before that exercise.' See also Lon L. Fuller, *The Morality of Law* (2nd edn Yale University Press 1969) 48, 53, 157.

about legal 'pedigree'.[14] Should public international law lack the relevant rigour[15] and be divined in a more or less ad hoc manner, the relation between and among states would no longer be of a *legal* but of a *different* kind.[16] Depending on the circumstances, it might be a relation of domination, administrative comradeship, teamwork, a rite of passage or a structure of social interaction that creates opportunities to guide dumbfounded folk. Since the self-presentation of relationships as 'law' has in one way or another legitimising effects, the critical perspective developed here invites attention to encounters with the 'ideology of law',[17] that is, the interpretative use of legal vocabulary and legal ideas in order to cover up what may turn out to be, upon closer inspection, essentially non-legal phenomena.[18]

Attaining a critical perspective on the self-interpretation of social acts is in and of itself intriguing.[19] But the chapter sweeps even more broadly. Shifting the focus from enforcement to form sheds new light on the most loathed question. This is the case for two reasons.

First, once the foundational question ('Is it *really* law?') is asked not about a potential *product* of human interaction ('Is *this* a legal system?') but about a *relationship*, it becomes broader in scope. Indeed, it turns out that the object-question is also implicitly about a relation, merely viewed from a certain angle. The Austinian enforcement challenge is a component of the question of form. Legal relations typically involve a modicum of reciprocity of control.[20] Not only is there no legal relation where the subjects are unable to make out what the commander wants them to do, a legal relation also does not obtain where the commander lacks the wherewithal to motivate compliance through the threat of sanctions or

[14] See, most recently, Roozbeh (Rudy) B. Baker, 'Customary International Law in the 21st Century: Old Challenges and New Debates' 21 *EJIL* (2010) 173–204. See also the discussion of effect-based and process-based accounts of public international law in Jean d'Aspremont, *Formalism and the Sources of International Law: A Theory of the Ascertainment of Legal Rules* (Oxford University Press 2011) 122–127.

[15] As is well known, this has been the fear most forcefully expressed by Prosper Weil, 'Towards Relative Normativity in International Law?' 77 *AJIL* (1983) 413–442 at 417.

[16] For a similar observation, see Martti Koskenniemi, 'Constitutionalism as Mindset: Reflections on Kantian Themes about International Law and Globalization' 8 *Theoretical Inquiries in Law* (2007) 9–36 at 13, 23.

[17] This is, of course, an old slogan of the critical legal studies movement.

[18] D'Aspremont, n. 14 at 122 (discussing deference to the mindset of the norm-user as a trend in current scholarship).

[19] For a similar ambition, see Jeremy Waldron, 'The Concept and the Rule of Law' 43 *Georgia Law Review* (2008) 1–61 at 13.

[20] See, quite perceptively, Fuller, n. 13 at 39, 66.

other symbolic means apt to signal the counterfactual stubbornness of validity. Just as there is no law, but perhaps terror, where subjects are left clueless, legality disappears when these subjects realise that they are free to disregard legal obligations with impunity. Hence, the challenge that is posed in an object-form ('This is not law!') can be reformulated as a relationship challenge without thereby losing its force.

Second, and even more intriguingly, ideological self-obfuscation appears to be inherent in the culture of public international law. In fact, it springs from what Kelsen recognised to be its primitive nature,[21] which is manifest in a relatively high degree of decentralisation in both the creation and enforcement of norms. Along with international agreements, custom is still an important source of public international law.[22] But not only is custom one source of law among others, it is also a fairly unreliable guide of legal obligation.[23] The reason is that it rests on gross idealisations of criteria of norm creation, for example, the criterion of 'general' and 'consistent' practice. The application of these criteria presupposes reading social realities in light of unstated normative assumptions with regard to how many instances of practice, and enacted by whom, are sufficient to constitute the type of practice that is both general and consistent.

A legal system that does not equip itself with reliable procedures for the creation of general norms is deficient from a constitutional point of view.[24] If anything, the most elementary point of having a constitution is that it creates as much clarity as possible about who gets to lay down the law and in which manner.[25] Constitutional deficiency, however, is a matter that affects the relation between and among agents of the system and its subjects. If there is no reliable legal way of guiding conduct, the relation that obtains between the guides and the guided becomes one of

21 Kelsen, n. 6. I shall return to this characterisation below and also try to explain that public international law attempts to overcome this primitiveness.

22 Of course, it is a source of law that is troublesome. See Andrew T. Guzman, 'Saving Customary International Law' 27 *Michigan Journal of International Law* (2005) 116–176.

23 For a particularly helpful discussion, see Jörg Kammerhofer, 'Uncertainty in the Formal Sources of International Law: Customary International Law and Some of Its Problems' 15 *EJIL* (2004) 523–553.

24 As is well known, HLA Hart concluded for that reason that public international law is not a legal system: see n. 5. I think that Hart's observation is better described as an observation regarding the constitutional deficiency of public international law. Alexander Somek, 'Kelsen Lives' 18 *EJIL* (2007) 409–451 at 433. See also the very perceptive observations by Kammerhofer, n. 23 at 536, 550.

25 This premise is not accepted by those who are currently observing a 'constitutionalisation' of public international law. See, most recently, Jan Klabbers, Anne Peters, Geir Ulfstein, *The Constitutionalization of International Law* (Oxford University Press 2009).

more or less haphazard interventions, on the one hand, and more or less educated guesses about their occurrence, on the other.

This chapter defends the change of perspective involved in conceiving of law as a particular type of relation rather than as a special object. Lest the overall argument be misunderstood, it is submitted that it is *not* an attempt to disparage international law or to present it as a second-rate legal system. It is merely an attempt to arrive at a clearer perspective on it.

Developing an understanding of law in terms of a type of relation is, nonetheless, confronted with a major intellectual obstacle. This obstacle has to be removed before the analysis can return to public international law. It concerns the ordinary approach to the rule of law, which is essentially about the interaction between the public authority and its subjects. It is argued below that the adjuration of 'the rule of law' is a highly unfortunate manner of reconstructing what accounts for a legal relationship. A brief discussion of Hayek aims to elucidate this point. It will be seen that adjurations of the rule of law ignore that the systematic elaboration of normative meanings is intrinsic to a legal relation. In other words, doctrine and scholarship, far from *referring* to the law as an object, are essential to *constituting* its full social significance.

This realisation opens the door to an understanding of sources that goes beyond post-classical legal positivism – indeed, it faithfully returns to the constructivist approach that historically preceded positivist doctrine. According to this understanding, all legal knowledge is self-knowledge. That is, it is not only knowledge *of* the law, but also knowledge *by* the law. Sources of law are social media for knowing the law. They are not merely social facts to which legal norms attribute normative significance; they are authoritative ways of knowing what the law is. In this respect, they appear to be internally related. Any later source in the historical sequence is best understood as an attempt to cure the deficiencies of the former. Public international law provides straightforward examples for this: the 'codification' of customary law, for example, clarifies. The same is true, ideally, of exposition of public international law in a treatise of a recognised publicist. The knowledge produced by the source is accurate as long as it allows constructing legal relations.

The chapter therefore turns to sources doctrine, where public international law is perennially confronted with the perplexity of customary law. It tries to explain how doctrine, in an effort to resolve it, is subject to capture by a project-driven and hence defective conception of legality. As the legal relationship becomes colonised by another type of relation, the attempt to arrive at an improved understanding of custom creates a hybrid version of this source, which combines isolated instances of state practice with doctrinal *opinio iuris.* In developing such a muddled form of recognising itself, public international law remains in a state in which it expects validation by legislation, which is, however, never going to come to pass. In order to prepare the relation perspective, Section 2 offers a brief critique of the ordinary conception of the rule of law. This is followed, in Section 3, by a defence of the 'relational' approach to law. Sections 4 and 5 conjecture that progressive public international law doctrine has over-determined the legal relation with a project-driven vision of the international system. Section 7 attempts to explain how this move beyond law is reflected in a sources discourse that creates a hybrid of state practice and doctrinal *opinio iuris.* Since this hybrid has only little support in social practice, doctrine develops imaginary forms of legislation in order to avail itself of validation. It is at this point that the sources doctrine betrays the absence of the legal relation. More precisely put, it turns into the symptom of this absence.

The chapter offers a different way of stating the deficiency of international law. According to this view, the problem is neither the lack of centralised enforcement nor the mere indeterminacy of secondary rules of law-creation. The problem is that doctrine wishes to use public international law as a means of making progress in spite of the absence of sufficient political support. The result is an ideology of law, that is, an image of law concealing its own disintegration.

2 Celebrating the epiphenomenal, or, Hayek's flaws

The rule of law is an important ideal. When it is adhered to one does not have to worry about Danegeld payments to the police in order to avert sudden abduction and indefinite detention. Where an administration that works poorly cannot be lubricated even through substantial bribes, the rule of law is held in high regard. Incompetence which is impervious to corruption retains the impersonality that we associate with government that is good.

Given that the rule of law is so highly conducive to the quality of life, it is perhaps puzzling that it is a rather tiresome subject. Most often, its meaning has been explained in the manner exemplified by Dicey's classical statement.[26] A number of elements are identified that are supposed to

26 A. V. Dicey, *Introduction to the Law of the Constitution* (Roger E. Michener (ed.), Liberty Fund 1982) 110, 115.

make the rule of law *intelligible*. We are told, for example, that authority ought to be exercised on the basis of public norms rather than personal whim; that standards governing conduct are to be laid down in advance; that laws ought to be general in their application and that disputes over what is lawful are to be adjudicated by independent tribunals. When the question is asked what it is that lends coherence to these elements – thereby making *intelligible* elements also *reasonably* coherent – they are often brought in a causal nexus with values such as liberty, dignity and equality.[27] Laws ought to be general, for this is part of what it takes to treat people as equals. Laws ought to be clear so that ordinary folk are capable of planning their conduct accordingly. Any indeterminacy of obligation is likely to have a chilling effect on liberty, for it gives rise to the fear that its exercise might be met with sanctions.[28]

Through the lens of such an instrumental relationship, the rule of law no longer appears to be a self-standing ideal, but rather an interface for the realisation of others.[29] If Rawlsian parlance were the canonical language of legal philosophy, one would have to characterise the rule of law as a second-order primary good.[30] Like other primary goods, such as liberties and material resources, the rule of law is something that everyone has general reason to want regardless of what one happens to want in particular; it is a primary good of a second order, however, inasmuch as it is instrumental not for the pursuit of a life-plan directly, but rather for the enjoyment of other primary goods, notably liberties. Thus understood, the rule of law is the epiphenomenal overlap of strategies to bring about other goods.

By contrast, ordinary instrumental accounts of the rule of law gravitate towards a lowest common denominator, which can be called the 'formal' concept of the rule of law.[31] It is reflected in how Friedrich August von

[27] For a more sophisticated account of the rule of law *qua* 'justice as regularity', which is essential for the realisation of a system of equal liberty, see John Rawls, *A Theory of Justice* (Harvard University Press 1971) 235–243.

[28] Rawls, n. 27 at 239.

[29] Very much like federalism, the rule of law appears to be not an independent political idea, but rather a method of realising others.

[30] Puzzlingly, Rawls did not venture to do so himself. See the absence in Rawls, n. 27 at 240, but see at 62 his notion of primary goods as all-purpose means.

[31] For an extremely useful analysis of different conceptions of the rule of law, see Brian Z. Tamanaha, *On the Rule of Law: History, Politics, Theory* (Cambridge University Press 2004) 91–113.

Hayek took the rule of law to be necessary for what he considered to be liberty,[32] namely, freedom from incalculable state interference:

> While every law restricts individual freedom to some extent by altering the means which people may use in the pursuit of their aims, under the Rule of Law the government is prevented from stultifying individual efforts by ad hoc action. Within the known rules of the game the individual is free to pursue his personal ends and desires, certain that the powers of government will not be used deliberately to frustrate his efforts.[33]

The connection thereby established is remarkably implausible. If it were indeed the case that liberty is the offspring of calculability, then the rule of law would not necessarily be the only means to attain it. Assuming that *imperatrix* accorded to each and every individual special treatment by looking into the hearts of her subjects, her conduct would be calculable for at least those among them who are capable of reading her mind and to see what she sees when exploring other souls. Calculability does not necessarily presuppose guidance by rules on the part of the actor. Whether it obtains or not depends on the subject's judgment. If anything, this is what the experience with intimate relationships teaches. Hayek's conception of what lends unity to the rule of law presupposes, therefore, what it wishes to demonstrate. It is interested in calculability that is derivative of, and constrained by, treating like situations alike on the basis of the general rules. But this calculability, certainly, is already a secondary effect of the abstract personhood[34] of all that is given recognition through the use of *general* rules. It has nothing to do, principally, with freedom as envisaged by Hayek.

If freedom that depends on calculability is not what lends unity to the rule of law, then something else might. Indeed, Hayek himself hinted at it when he said under the rule of law 'we are not subject to another man's will' because the law is not made by someone for us at the moment

[32] Those who are not initiated in the German legal tradition would have to understand, of course, that freedom in a Hayekian sense is freedom from unlawful interference as envisaged by Georg Jellinek. See Georg Jellinek, *System der subjektiven öffentlichen Rechte* (2nd edn J. C. B. Mohr 1905) 103.

[33] Friedrich August von Hayek, *The Road to Serfdom* (Routledge and K. Paul 1962) 54.

[34] I am convinced that Hayek would have been extremely pleased about seeing his ideas expounded in Hegelian language. See Georg Wilhelm Friedrich Hegel, *Elements of the Philosophy of Right* (Allen W. Wood (ed.), H. B. Nisbet (tr.), Cambridge University Press 1991) 69 (§ 36).

of its application.[35] Again, the claim is not terribly well founded, for it is perfectly consistent with freedom, as envisaged by Hayek, that one is subject to laws of which one has no authorship whatsoever. The point of freedom à la Hayek must be different from not being subject to the will of another person. What matters, rather, is the *manner* of subjection.

One merely needs to move beyond the narrow intellectual confines of neoliberal ideology in order to discover an undercurrent legacy in rule of law orthodoxy whose intellectual origins may even extend back to Roman law. It is reminiscent of the type of freedom that Skinner deemed to have been the mark of liberty *before* liberalism.[36] Whereas the liberty of liberalism is freedom *from* obstacles and *of* choice, pre-liberal liberty is what makes a person or a polity *sui iuris*. What matters, in this regard, is independence from having to follow capricious directions given by others. The antithesis to liberty is not being subject to constraints, but being vulnerable to whim. It is servants, serfs and, worse still, slaves who are paradigmatically exposed to the sudden and unpredictable orders of whoever happens to be their master.

3 The legal relation

So-called 'formal' conceptions of the rule of law emphasise that general rules guiding conduct in advance are, regardless of their substance,[37] conducive to liberty. Freedom of choice would be undermined if someone were in a position to penalise its exercise or to frustrate plans.[38] But this connection between rules and predictability is not necessary. Conceivably, a perfect servant is always in the position to please the master since a servant of this kind is capable of divining the master's caprice. In a sense, a servant of this type is the external deposit of the master's will, for

[35] Friedrich August von Hayek, *The Constitution of Liberty* (Chicago University Press 1960) 153.

[36] See the excellent study by Quentin Skinner, *Liberty before Liberalism* (Cambridge University Press 1997); see also Quentin Skinner, *Hobbes and Republican Liberty* (Cambridge University Press 2008).

[37] In its formal understanding, the rule of law is capable of accommodating various obnoxious things, as has been pointed out by Raz and Tamanaha. Joseph Raz, 'The Rule of Law and its Virtue' in Joseph Raz, *The Authority of Law: Essays on Law and Morality* (Clarendon Press 1979) 201–229 at 211; Tamanaha, n. 31 at 93.

[38] Rawls, n. 27 at 239.

he is making himself into a means to the master's ends.[39] The servant's personality is possessed by the master.

By juxtaposing rules and calculability, expositions of the rule of law, at least of a formal variety, ignore what is truly at stake.[40] The point is not that law protects against caprice owing to calculability; it rather protects against calculability that presupposes identification, empathy or some other insider access. The law makes it possible for the ruled to remain uninvolved in the ratiocinations and projects of their rulers. Not only does one not have to speculate about what the boss would want to happen in this or that situation, appeals to what would please the boss are excluded from the legal domain proper.[41] This is what it means to stand in a legal relation. This explains also why having a boss, no matter how kind that person may be, threatens to interfere with our liberty beyond the mere subjection to commands. One is always in danger of becoming entangled in a far too close relationship where one has to conduct oneself on the basis of guesses about what might please one's superior.

Adjurations of the rule of law never arrive at this analytical point. This explains why, as indicated above, the rule of law is a lacklustre topic. The matter is exacerbated by the notorious sloppiness with which the correlations between situation-independent generality and predictability are said to obtain only 'ideally' and to be realised only 'in approximation'.[42] Why should one be excited about an ideal without knowing how much approximation is enough in order to render it *not* delusional? Rule of law advocacy shies away from taking on this challenge; indeed, it is constituted by its reluctance. It produces commonsensical assurances about how the law is in 'most cases' predictable. But these assurances are difficult to reconcile with the experience that owing to the increasing reflectivity

39 By analogy, legal scholarship can be said to remain in a slavish state when it studies the ideological, political and religious predilections of judges in order to make out how one might please judges when an argument is supposed to please the court. Against this background, the core maxim that is buried underneath the superficial designator of the rule of law is the idea that people are free when they are in a legal relation. Others have only power over you, but no superior reason.

40 Exempted from this charge is in particular: Tamanaha, n. 31.

41 I do not mean to deny that the law makes it possible to create a relation of this type, however, only on the basis of a legal relation, which demands that the subjected person remains free to end the relation at any time.

42 See, for statements to this effect, Jeremy Waldron, 'Are Sovereigns Entitled to the Benefits of the Rule of Law?' 22 *EJIL* (2011) 315–343 at 326, 335–336.

of legal reasoning, the predictability of law can no longer be taken for granted.[43]

The formal conception of the rule of law trivialises a much richer concept, namely, the concept of legality. It denotes not merely an instrumental but an intrinsic relation between the law and a certain type of freedom among equals.[44] The latter is manifest in most elementary form in what Kant described as external compliance with norms.[45] It means the legitimate abstention on the part of the addressees from immersing themselves in the plans or the mind of the law-giver.[46] This can be achieved, as will be argued below, by paying attention to the language of authoritative enactments, to powers limiting the exercise discretion and by reading norms against their overall systematic context. How one draws out the meaning of legal norms is decisive for giving legality effect.[47] The formal conception of the rule of law is just a narrower way of addressing legality. The narrowness is owing to an overlay of legality with economic rationality. Predictability is legality perceived from the perspective of calculability.

A legal relationship is 'external'. This is signalled, not least, through the presence of coercive threats. Yielding to threats is the antithesis to making the law-giver's way of thinking or plans one's own. More precisely, a legal relationship is external inasmuch as it comprises *two* forms of distance. First, it does not ask more of people than to adopt the perspective of the 'bad man' who wishes to avoid adverse reactions by the state apparatus.[48] Second, beyond the bad man's *distance in compliance* the anticipation of these potential reactions must not require understanding or sharing the projects of the law-giver. The latter aspect of the external character can be called *distance in engagement.* The generality of rules is one way of

[43] A great virtue of Tamanaha's work on the rule of law is that it confronts this predicament head-on.

[44] The concept of the legal relation can be linked to what Oakeshott described as civic association. It is an association with no final or ulterior purpose. It begins and ends in the recognition of rules. Michael Oakeshott, *On Human Conduct* (Clarendon Press 1975) 128–129.

[45] Immanuel Kant, *The Metaphysics of Morals* (Mary Gregor (tr.), Cambridge University Press 1991) 20.

[46] It is quite surprising that a recent book entitled 'Legality' does not at all reflect this traditional understanding of the term and rather assimilates law to the implementation of large scale plans. See Scott Shapiro, *Legality* (Harvard University Press 2010) 195–200.

[47] This was, indeed, one of the insights of Max Weber. Max Weber, *Economy and Society*, Vol. 2 (Guenther Roth, Claus Wittich (eds), Ephraim Fischoff *et al.* (trs), University of California Press 1978) 775–776.

[48] See, famously, Oliver Wendell Holmes, 'The Path of the Law' 110 *Harvard Law Review* (1996–1997) 991–1009 (reprinted; first published in 1897).

establishing this distance. In order to avoid sanctions, one merely needs to find out whether one belongs to the set of addressees comprised by the rule.

Legality is fully constituted only if distance in compliance is mediated by distance in engagement. If a legal relation lacks the mediation of the former by the latter, it becomes defective. Since distance in engagement[49] is a sufficient condition for distance in compliance, the manner in which legal doctrine ascribes meanings to legal rules is essential to sustaining legality. Distance in engagement has to match the defiant attitude of external compliance, which may legitimately amount to the mere yielding to coercive threats. This can be effected by, first, limiting attention to the meaning of words, second, the absorption of vagueness through the construction of limited legal powers to lay down the law, and, third, the determination of the scope of application of legal norms against a larger systematic context.

First, law-applying officials who honour legality do not contact the law-givers in order to find out what they are supposed to do in this or that case. They could not care less. They apply rules. Should the law-givers, hypothetically, reproach them for having taken their orders too literally, they would reply that the law-givers should have chosen their words more carefully. Rules matter. They do not implement plans that happen to be expressed in rules. Second, the vagueness of legal language can be resolved by constructing limited legal powers to state authoritatively what the law means. The meaning of the norm is what the legally empowered law-applying official says it is.

Third, the most important way of constituting distance in engagement consists in treating norms as elements of a legal system and to construe their meaning accordingly. The meaning of these norms is thus determined not in light of the law-giver's plan, but by the place that they have within a system. The system provides the unifying perspective, which is articulated in various principles guiding the application of norms. This is consistent with what the norm-addressees have in common. It is their subjection to the same set of norms. They are addressees of the same coercive legal order. The systematic determination of their meaning makes this purely external relation to norms consistent with equal treatment.

49 Fuller, n. 13 at 92, was aware of the distanced character of the relation when he noticed that less internal morality of law is necessary the more the law conforms to external conventional morality. Fuller thereby captured that the law governs a relation among strangers.

As stated above, law becomes defective if distance of compliance cannot be mediated by distance of engagement, that is, when the very determination of the legal position of the addressee, who *appears* to be externally bound, actually presupposes internal engagement with a project that goes beyond distinguishing the scope of application of rules.[50] Such engagement is called for wherever people are expected either to adapt flexibly or to commit themselves actively to one or the other cause. In both cases, innovation and originality are either passively accepted or actively pursued out of personal identification with a faith, a calling, a mission or a project. Whoever identifies with a cause can easily see herself in the role of a leader or a follower or, in a more egalitarian vein, a comrade or a team-player. By contrast, one can only observe externally what one is bound to do when one does not have to surrender to the divinations of prophets or inventors. Where the genius of innovation is deemed to be a major legitimating factor of adjudication and doctrine, legality is skidding into a defective mode.[51]

4 A reply to objections

Stated in such a brief form, the characterisation of defective law has to invite objections. In the understanding presented above, the existence of a legal relationship seems to preclude legal subjects from embarking on common projects, also on common legislative projects, for their success would require taking political objectives into account in the course of implementation and adjudication. If, however, legal relationships were to exclude common efforts, it would be impermissible to use law as a medium for the realisation of justice, which presupposes, according to Rawlsians, conceiving of society as a system of cooperation. Finally, it is rather bizarre to suppose that the evolution and refinement of the systematic dimension of the legal system should not be a common venture, in particular, if it is believed to be 'interpretative' and therefore to require reading legal evolution in light of a purpose.

The first two objections can be addressed by clarifying the normative role of the legal relationship vis-à-vis other forms of human interaction.

50 According to Fuller, one would have to describe such incongruence as a conflict between the internal and the external morality of law. Fuller, n. 13 at 44.

51 Tamanaha and I appear to agree on this point, even if in different vocabulary. Brian Tamanaha, *Law as a Means to an End: Threat to the Rule of Law* (Cambridge University Press 2008) 236, 244; Alexander Somek, 'The Emancipation of Legal Dissonance' in Henning Koch *et al.* (eds), *Europe: The New Legal Realism* (DJØF Publishing 2011) 679–713.

Law is an enabling condition for sustaining relationships in which people relinquish control and make themselves vulnerable to others. Indeed, if it were not for legally specified conditions, entertaining other relationships would scarcely be acceptable. One could not reasonably succumb, in the context of organisations, to voracious expectations concerning the dedication to one's job if it were not for the limits set by rights (for example, working-time regulations). If those rights were determined by the functional necessities of organisations, they would likely turn out to be nugatory. The employment relation would encroach upon the legal relation. Similarly, it is noble to allow oneself to be taken up in a political movement, but one would be unreasonably exalted if one agreed to have one's political rights defined by the exigencies of the political struggle. Generally, the legal relation erodes if the functional requirements of other forms of human dealing, which may legitimately coexist with the legal relation, define rights and obligations.

By contrast, invoking the legal background from within their midst of other relationships invests these with a chilling strangeness. Familiarity, trust and intimacy are suddenly suspended. The terms of the relationship are seen from the vantage point of someone who could be anyone. It is as though a stranger had entered the room. The situation becomes abstract in that it ignores the moral complexity that is due to the influences of courtesy and routine. The abstraction creates an intellectual space where reasons are no longer linked to the richer textures of working or living together, but rather based on recognising a mutual disagreement on how and where to live. Not by accident, contract is the core legal form of being with others, for it constitutes concern without loyalty, a mere matter of honouring promises under conditions that are believed to be beneficial for oneself.

Conceiving of the legal relation in this manner is entirely consistent with an understanding of justice that takes society to be a system of cooperation. The conditions outlined by such a theory prescribe the limits of what the social world has to respect in order to be just. Establishing legal relations is essential to realising a system of justice. Arguably, the distinction between principles and policies, which was very much in the foreground of Dworkin's earliest legal theory,[52] offers merely a different perspective on the same point. Arguments from principle were supposed to establish a right and, in that capacity, to be more reasonable than mere public policy considerations. This was another way of stating that the pursuit of common projects must not invade the determination of legal

[52] Ronald Dworkin, *Taking Rights Seriously* (2nd edn Harvard University Press 1978) 90.

rights and obligations. Rights are essential to the legal relation, for they help to preserve distance.

The third objection says that the systematic exposition of law is, if anything, also a project. It would be erroneous, therefore, to dissociate legality from the collective pursuit of social ambitions. In reply, it has to be conceded that while the addressees of legal rules remain uninvolved with regard to their obligations, they have to be involved, even if only hypothetically, in the systematic reasoning process leading up to the perennial differentiation of various types of case. Legality is minted in the terms of this reasoning process. But for this reason alone it is not on a plane with the various other engagements. The pursuit of legality requires sticking to sources, for these are the reasons that can be shared among strangers, and being heeded of exit options. This is different from playing with sources in order to foreclose the exit for those who would find interpretive tinkering unacceptable.

The third objection is a salutary reminder that the law is always in danger of being perturbed by what it is supposed to contain. Obviously, a perturbation of this kind can be observed whenever new sources are invented in the interpretative pursuit of some noble idea. Moreover, what has been observed above for relationships between and among addressees also holds true for the relationship between legal subjects and the process of adjudication. If the process of legal interpretation takes a surprising turn, then the legal relation requires an exit option. In the case of the legal system, any 'exit' from the evolution of case law involves 'voice'.[53] In other words, a legislature is needed, acting on behalf of people who want to sustain their legal relation.

We shall see below how the modern doctrine of customary international law not only transformed one source of law into another, it also created, in order to justify this bold step, imaginary equivalents of legislation. It will be argued that the legality of international law has been thereby rendered defective.

5 From detached obedience to engaged participation

But why should states not merely act as team players on the international plane and faithfully commit themselves to projects?[54] Many

[53] On the concepts of 'exit' and 'voice', see Albert O. Hirschman, *Exit, Voice, and Loyalty: Responses to Decline in Firms, Organizations, and States* (Harvard University Press 1970).

[54] For an intriguing exploration of this possibility, see Waldron, n. 42.

transnational interactions are established in order to facilitate cooperation among national and international administrators even under only a very loosely defined legal framework.[55] This is particularly true of more experimental administrative arrangements where states explore various strategies in order to find out what, if anything, they really want.[56] In important areas of public policy, the relation between national administrations and international institutions has taken on this shape. More generally, there is a strong tendency among states, even when using multilateral treaties, to provide merely a basic framework for situation-sensitive and expertise-dependent processes of balancing in individual cases.[57]

Beyond the segment of public international law which can rightly be described as 'administrative' and which has been the subject, in particular, of the global administrative law project,[58] for quite some time the role of states in the international community has been viewed differently. At any rate, those scholars who accord to the international community normative priority vis-à-vis the state perceive the latter as a mere agent of the international system.[59] As will be explained below, this shift of perspective has a profound influence on the conception of international legality. Its significance can best be explained by analogy to individual dealings.

Modern economic life is dominated by bureaucratic organisations. In order to achieve their mission, these organisations expect their members to participate intelligently and to show a certain measure of dedication by demonstrating their skill and ingenuity. It is not surprising that a quite substantial part of modern management busies itself with pedagogical concerns, such as motivating and invigorating employees. The latter need to be sufficiently stimulated in order to perform at their peak level and, most importantly, drilled into playing well with equally stimulated others.

55 For a case study of the coordination of border control in the EU, which actually raises a number of rule of law concerns, see Johannes Pollak, Peter Slominski, 'Experimentalist But Not Accountable Governance? The Role of Frontex in Managing the EU's External Borders' 32 *West European Politics* (2009) 904–924 at 907–908, 921.

56 Pollack and Slominski, n. 55 at 905–906.

57 For a description of this trend, see Koskenniemi, n. 1 at 9–15.

58 For a programmatic statement, see Benedict Kingsbury, Nico Krisch, Richard B. Stewart, 'The Emergence of Global Administrative Law' 68 *Law and Contemporary Problems* (2005) 15–61.

59 Christian Tomuschat, 'International Law: Ensuring the Survival of Mankind on the Eve of a New Century' 281 *Recueil des Cours* (1999) 9–438 at 161: 'states are no more than instruments whose inherent function is to serve the interests of their citizens as legally expressed in human rights'.

Employees are not only expected to align their conduct in light of the organisation's point of view, but also expected to take steps towards improvement. Under highly competitive conditions, businesses would be doomed to extinction if they did not continually move ahead. Playing by the rules is not enough, for this would tie the organisation to the past rather than drive it towards the future. In a sense, therefore, being a good employee requires an attitude of (feigned) identification. Or, put in other words, external compliance with directives is inexorably blended with the requirement to excel, which could not be met without a modicum of dedication and individual initiative.

Membership in the international system is, of course, unlike employment in a business bureaucracy. But the analogy is nonetheless sound when participants in the international system are not just regarded as addressees of norms with which they have to comply *externally*, but as comrades who participate in a common enterprise. The teleology of the pursuit of goals affects the nature of obligations.[60] Compliance is done well only if it is ideally also a step towards further development.[61] The rationality of the *system* to sustain itself through its own optimisation feeds back into the rationality of *action*. Respecting norms is not enough. Rather, concerns with flexibility, adaptability, or improving one's understanding and the use of 'rolling rules'[62] supplant the perspective of playing by the rules. Borrowing an old Habermasian analogy, it can be said that normative orientations become 'colonised' by the rationality of *social systems*.[63]

6 Competitive progressivism

If membership in the international community involves, in acts of *compliance*, working towards *improving* public international law, then, as Koskenniemi reminds us, participation in one of the highly specialised discourses comprising this system means committing oneself to one or

[60] In Kantian terms, one might have to conclude that one is dealing with duties of virtue and not with legal duties, since the duties have to do with an end. Kant, n. 45 at 64.

[61] See the characterisation of this spirit in d'Aspremont, n. 14 at 119.

[62] William H. Simon, 'Toyota Jurisprudence: Legal Theory and Rolling Rule Regimes' in Grainne de Búrca, Joanne Scott (eds), *Law and New Governance in the EU and the US* (Hart 2006) 37–64 at 58.

[63] Jürgen Habermas, *Theorie des kommunikativen Handelns*, Vol. 2: *Zur Kritik der funktionalistischen Vernunft* (Suhrkamp 1981) 522.

the other project of 'progress'.[64] If states perceive that their obligations are not circumscribed clearly or applied to them in unanticipated ways they may rightly be told, for example by Tomuschat,[65] that this is what one gets when one is aligned to the cause of improving human well-being. Unlike individuals, participants in such a system are not entitled to benefit from legal certainty or any other value associated with the rule of law.[66] Far from being expected to dispose of obligations with an attitude of disengagement, they are called upon to build actively a better international community. Arguably, then, an international organisation, such as the European Union, which has been given the power of rule-making, may legitimately exercise its powers very broadly even if this gives rise to concern on the part of the participating states that this is not what they had originally bargained for; they may have to learn that provided the broad and unpredictable use of powers satisfactorily resolves collective action problems and removes externalities in the interest of the peoples affected, then states must not complain that the rule of law has been impaired since this principle is inapposite here.

The situation is, in fact, more complicated, but the complexity makes the analogy to business bureaucracies even more accurate. As Koskenniemi[67] has also reminded us, the international community is increasingly fragmented into functionally specified regimes. Each harbours its very own structural bias in favour of core values, such as the environment, human rights, international trade or bringing wrongdoers to justice. The regimes come with their vocabularies and selective schedules of relevance. Within each of these regimes the world is given a specific outlook.[68] Indeed, effecting problem-solving in a manner that confirms

[64] Martti Koskenniemi, 'The Politics of International Law – 20 Years Later' 20 *EJIL* (2009) 7–19 at 12. See also Susan Marks, *The Riddle of All Constitutions: International Law, Democracy, and the Critique of Ideology* (Oxford University Press 2000) 32.

[65] Tomuschat, n. 59. [66] Waldron, n. 42.

[67] On the following, see in particular Martti Koskenniemi, 'International Law: Constitutionalism, Managerialism and the Ethos of Legal Education' 1 *European Journal of Legal Studies* (2007) 1–18.

[68] According to Koskenniemi, n. 64 at 13, regimes are characterised by: 'solipsism and imperialism, both self-absorption and the urge to translate everything on sight into their own preferred idiom'. There is, however, a managerial mindset common to all regimes that is revealed at the level of language through various substitutions (from 'rules' to 'regulations', from 'government' to 'governance', from 'responsibility' to 'compliance', from 'international law' to 'international relations'), at 12.

regime bias asserts the regime's presence and relevance.[69] Legal judgment becomes subservient to the regime's system rationality.[70] Hence, as the regimes and their respective languages struggle to take the lead,[71] a *competitive* element is introduced into the realisation of the values of the international community.

When the focus of international law comes to rest on optimising *competing* regimes, a relationship that used to be based on compliance with rules becomes inhabited by a non-legal form of human dealing. One encounters the rationality of bureaucratic organisations wherever one looks.[72] The analogy to the individual level may, again, turn out to be helpful. Throughout our lives, we are immersed in non-legal relationships. We cherish them and permit invasions of our liberty since they are prerequisites for self-transcendence. However, we let this happen because we trust that when things go sour we still retain our rights, which, at the minimal level, protect our choice to exit such a relationship at will. At the end of the day, we can return to the level where we no longer are partners in the same enterprise, but merely strangers to one another. Such a fall-back position is unavailable to states when their legal relationship is *replaced* by a relationship of mutually engaged participation in one or the other competing project of international integration (trade, environment, human rights or criminal justice). Necessarily, then, acts of law-application must be perceived as occasions to set off, to continue or to reinvigorate a movement towards . . .[73] I will sketch below how such a transformation of the legal relationship into a complex tangle of more or less well-performing teammates emerges from a struggle with sources of law.

[69] Koskenniemi refers to this attitude in one context as 'managerialism'. That is, the performance of a regime devoted to a certain task is enhanced through some innovation when a legal technique is used to attain certain ends (as in the *Tadić* case, the shift from the effective to the overall control standard). Managerialism, thus understood, means taking legal expertise as a means to achieve what one fancies to be good ends. In another context, however, 'managerialism' is identified by Koskenniemi with rational choice approaches to international law and their assimilation to international relations. These approaches are dismissed by him as empirically delusional. Koskenniemi, n. 64 at 15.

[70] Koskenniemi, n. 67 at 14.

[71] On the clash of idioms, see Koskenniemi, n. 64 at 11.

[72] See also Koskenniemi, n. 67 at 12: 'law is finally drained out of international law, conceived as a professional technique for the management of values, purposes, ideals'.

[73] See, generally, Martti Koskenniemi, *From Apology to Utopia: The Structure of International Legal Argument* (Finnish Lawyers' Publishing Co. 1989, reissued Cambridge University Press 2005).

7 Customary international law

7.1 The core difficulty

Customary law is a legal system in a nutshell.[74] It combines reference to what is lawful – in this case, an observable general and consistent pattern of practice – along with its self-knowledge *as* law (*opinio iuris*).[75] This self-knowledge is mediated by the participants in that practice. They are, severally, capable of knowing the law. Whoever is considered to have authority to say what the law is, is also a source of law. Knowing is mediated by being the law.

The persistent relevance of custom to international law is one of the factors that illustrates its constitutional deficiency.[76] Not only is it unclear what grounds the authority of customary law,[77] the determination of what constitutes norm-creating behaviour is not governed by *formal* procedures.[78] A constitutionally deficient legal system is nonetheless composed of norms. Their normatively binding force is socially manifest in what Hart famously called the internal aspect of rules, that is, a critical reflective attitude towards instances of compliance or application.[79] From within this attitude *opinio iuris* reveals itself, for example, in statements that such and such is wrong because of this or that norm.[80]

[74] I am aware that with this statement I gloss over tremendous complexities that the concept of customary international law gives rise to. They are examined by Jörg Kammerhofer, *Uncertainty in International Law: A Kelsenian Perspective* (Routledge 2011) 59–86. I am also aware that hardcore Hartians would voice an objection regarding the absence of secondary rules complementing primary rules of obligation.

[75] Not by accident, *opinio iuris* is most clearly revealed in statements. See Anthony D'Amato, *The Concept of Custom in International Law* (Cornell University Press 1971) 89–90, 160. The interpretation of *opinio iuris* in these terms avoids the difficulty of whether *opinio iuris* denotes a belief that something is or that something ought to be law. In both cases, the belief is manifest in the critical reflexive attitude. But see the discussion in Kammerhofer, n. 74 at 83.

[76] Kelsen, n. 6. I should add, as a cautionary remark, that had the UN Charter been successfully established as the constitution of the international community, the matter would indeed look differently. For that perspective, see Bardo Fassbender, 'United Nations Charter as a Constitution of the International Community' 36 *Columbia Journal of Transnational Law* (1998) 529–620.

[77] Kammerhofer, n. 23 at 550.

[78] See Fastenrath, who explains that formulations of customary international law are *ab ovo* contested. Also, the qualitative and quantitative conditions for the generation of custom are not clear. Ulrich Fastenrath, 'Relative Normativity in International Law' 4 *EJIL* (1993) 305–340 at 316, 321–322; see also d'Aspremont, n. 14 at 162.

[79] Hart, n. 5 at 86.

[80] Obviously, in order to resolve the 'paradox' of custom mentioned below, one needs to distinguish between *opinio iuris de lege lata* and *de lege ferenda*. See John Tasioulas,

In the context of a purely customary system, the critical reflexive attitude can only draw on consistent practice in order to avail itself of a standard. It will then say: This is what we have done before and that this is our law.[81] Using the voice of mute participants as *la bouche de la loi*, it states that what has happened de facto before has happened as a matter of right.[82] In this archaic form, normativity has tremendous force over us.[83] The paradox involved therein is well known; for the present purposes it is given an additional twist.[84] *Opinio iuris* asserts that something has already become law without its own contribution even though something can only become law by virtue of being endorsed by it. *Opinio iuris* is hence mistaken not only about what the law is, but also about its own constitutive role.[85] It is perplexingly self-effacing.[86]

Not surprisingly, older sources discourse clung to state practice[87] and inferred the normative intent of practice from its generality and consistency.[88] This comes perilously close to surrendering the

'Customary International Law and the Quest for Global Justice' in Amanda Perreau-Saussine, James B. Murphy (eds), *The Nature of Customary Law* (Cambridge University Press 2007) 307–335 at 323.

81 *North Sea Continental Shelf (Federal Republic of Germany/Denmark, Federal Republic of Germany/Netherlands)*, Judgment of 20 February 1969, ICJ Reports (1969) 3 at 47.

82 I am aware of simply glossing over a number of puzzles that have fascinated the discipline, such as the question of whether *opinio iuris* is an act of will that expresses consent or the manifestation of a belief in bindingness. For an illuminating discussion, see Kammerhofer, n. 23 at 533–535. I shall also ignore the difficulty that *opinio iuris* could also be understood in a constative mood and hence as a *proposition* made by states about what states perceive to be law. Such a view gives rise to a series of difficulties, chief among them the difficulty that if erroneous statements about general and consistent state practice can give rise to law, then the state practice requirement might be dispensed with altogether. For an illuminating and nuanced discussion, see Kammerhofer, n. 74 at 80–85.

83 Christoph Menke, *Die Gegenwart der Tragödie: Versuch über Urteil und Spiel* (Suhrkamp 2001) 75–78.

84 Ordinarily, the paradox is characterised by saying that owing to *opinio iuris* a customary norm can only come into existence by virtue of an erroneous belief over its existence. See Brian D. Lepard, *Customary International Law: A New Theory with Practical Applications* (Cambridge University Press 2010) 22.

85 Throughout the nineteenth century, customary law was taken to be a manifestation of pre-existing law; see Kammerhofer, n. 23 at 534.

86 The paradox disappears, however, when it is understood as an act of reflective endorsement: '[t]his is what we have done before and, guess what, we like it that way.' It is immaterial whether the 'liking' has just started.

87 Of course, what belongs to the set of 'state practice' is also anything but clear. Kammerhofer, n. 74 at 62–68.

88 Baker, n. 14 at 176. For a certain period of his theorising, Kelsen believed that there was nothing but state practice when it came to customary international law; see Kammerhofer, n. 74 at 79.

normativity of norms to the facticity of facts.[89] However, any generalisation of practice needs to be guided by something beyond practice serving as a standard with regard to the instances of practice that *count*. This something, which is not nothing, is left indeterminate in blind assertions of customary law. What lends guidance to *opinio iuris* remains mysterious (which explains why some understand it to be a 'mere' act of will). Likewise, there is no hope of establishing clear criteria for the quality and quantity of practice that is necessary to constitute custom.[90] Not only would it be unclear if they had binding authority were they to emerge from state practice, they could also be abrogated, at any time, by any substantive rule of customary law, for any such rule could implicitly claim to *exemplify* a revised understanding of what and how much practice it takes to create customary law. Customary law, most elementarily understood, is a *formally irrational* form of law. The assertability conditions for custom are not governed by any clearly discernible criteria.[91] As a consequence, the assertion of customary law will tacitly looks out for the practice of the 'relevant' or 'grand' powers. In this respect, it begins to transform custom into an (oligarchic) form of legislation.

7.2 Project-driven legality: from custom to doctrine

It cannot come as a surprise, therefore, that the abundant and meritorious attempts to address the perplexities of customary law-making necessarily and inadvertently alter the nature of this source itself. More precisely, they are tacitly pushing it towards both systematic doctrine and legislation.[92]

This can be observed, in particular, when public international law is given a programmatic twist. The legitimacy of international law may then be seen, for example, as:

89 On the problem that statements about norms might be counted as state practice, see Kammerhofer, n. 23 at 525.

90 D'Aspremont, n. 14 at 168.

91 Max Weber, *Economy and Society*, Vol. 2 (Guenther Roth, Claus Wittich (eds), University of California Press 1978) 656. On the absence of formal criteria, see d'Aspremont, n. 14 at 152–153.

92 Of course, the law needs to be known. Hence, a customary system of law can transcend the implicit knowledge inherent in practice once there is a legal science ascertaining which parts of practice are to be counted as compliance with a legal rule. Since this determination is made by legal science *qua* organ of legal self-knowledge, it is the articulation of *opinio iuris*.

> [D]ependent on its furtherance of certain values, e.g. human rights, peaceful co-existence, environmental protection, etc. as tempered by the requirements of the rule of law (predictability, liberty, etc.) and the values of political participation (including the political self-determination of states).[93]

From such an exalted point of view, traditional sources are necessarily perceived as vehicles for the practical realisation and articulation of a pre-given normative substance. It is conceivable, then, to obtain guidance from values for the attribution of good *opinio iuris*, which, owing to its goodness, is allegedly capable of generating customary law even if it has been manifested so far only in the conclusion of (or accession to) treaties.[94] Moreover, once *opinio iuris* is supposed to express commitments to values, it can be severed from the lowly details of state practice[95] and deemed to be discernible also in more explicit pronouncements such as resolutions by the General Assembly or other more informal statements.[96] One might even go so far as to defuse the emphasis on the sovereign state and include non-state actors, such as international organisations or non-governmental organisation, into relevant 'voices' of the international community.[97] Not by accident, then, the centre of gravity for the determination of custom's substance migrates from elusive state practice[98] to whatever is believed to exhibit a commitment to the progressive realisation of an improved international value order.[99] Custom may then be even asserted with an emphasis on documented *opinio iuris* alone[100] in the face of inconsistent practice (see the *Nicaragua* case).[101]

93 Tasioulas, n. 80 at 329.

94 Lepard, n. 84 at 146–147.

95 On the problem, see Kammerhofer, n. 23 at 525.

96 The *Nicaragua* case appears to be an epitome for such a transformation. See John Tasioulas, 'In Defence of Relative Normativity: Communitarian Values and the *Nicaragua* Case' 16 *Oxford Journal of Legal Studies* (1996) 85–128 at 98, 100.

97 Tasioulas, n. 80 at 328.

98 Of course, state practice cannot denote anything that would not be already the result of a reflective generalisation.

99 For a brief reconstruction of the difference between traditional and modern approaches to custom, which does not, however, refer to the background of values, see Anthea Elizabeth Roberts, 'Traditional and Modern Approaches to Customary International Law' 95 *AJIL* (2001) 757–791 at 758–760. On *opinio iuris* as 'shared understandings', see Michael Byers, *Custom, Power, and the Power of Rules: International Relations and Customary International Law* (Cambridge University Press 1999) 148–149.

100 Tasioulas, n. 80 at 331.

101 *Military and Paramilitary Activities in and against Nicaragua* (*Nicaragua v. United States of America*), Merits, Judgment of 27 June 1986, ICJ Reports (1986) 14 at 186.

As is well known, the relevant major shift in sources discourse has emerged in scholarship since the 1960s[102] and in ICJ opinions such as *Barcelona Traction*,[103] *North Sea Continental Shelf*[104] and *Nicaragua*.[105] This development has been portrayed – not exclusively, but definitely most pointedly – as a gestalt shift that alters the imagery of public international law from a law of nations, which coordinates and constrains the conduct of heterogeneous sovereigns on the basis of their unanimous consent,[106] to a system that is *programmed* to realise a number of core world order values,[107] chief among them essential human rights and the prohibition of the use of violence in international affairs.[108] The imprint that this transformation has arguably left on the international legal system has given rise to increasing vertical stratification (for example, *ius cogens*) and the gradual demise of voluntarism (evident in the rise of *obligationes omnium* binding states even against their declared will).[109]

The teleological pull of core values becomes expressed in the grammatical forms of sources doctrine, in particular custom. These forms obscure

[102] On scholarship, see the useful summary in Baker, n. 14 at 180–183.

[103] *Barcelona Traction, Light and Power Company, Ltd (New Application: 1962) (Belgium v. Spain)*, Second Phase, Judgment of 5 February 1970, ICJ Reports (1970) 3 at 33–34 (on basic rights of human persons as being so foundational to the international system such as to give rise to *erga omnes* obligations).

[104] *North Sea Continental Shelf*, n. 81 at 42–43 (on widespread and representative participation of states in a convention and passage of only a short period of time as sufficient to transform a conventional rule of international law into a rule of customary international law).

[105] *Nicaragua*, n. 101 at 188 (severing indications of *opinio iuris* from their manifestation in widespread state practice).

[106] Weil, n. 15 at 418–419. 'The international normative system has traditionally been characterized by its unity: whatever their formal origins (custom or conventions, for example), whatever their object or importance, all norms are placed on the same plane, their interrelations ungoverned by any hierarchy, their breach giving rise to an international responsibility subject to one uniform regime' (Weil, n. 15 at 423).

[107] For a formulation that locates values in the unwritten constitution of the international community, see Christian Tomuschat, 'Obligations Arising for States Without or against Their Will' 241 *Recueil des Cours* (1993) 195–374 at 303.

[108] For a perceptive account, see Tasioulas, n. 96 at 88, 95, 109, 117. Of course, constitutionalisation discourse is the most recent exemplification of this transformation. For a critical introduction, see Alexander Somek, 'From the Rule of Law to the Constitutionalist Make-Over: Changing European Perceptions of Public International Law' 18 *Constellations* (2011) 567–588.

[109] For a critical commentary, see Weil, n. 15 at 437; see also Tasioulas, n. 96 at 102–103. For a dissident voice, see Jan Klabbers, 'Law-making and Constitutionalism' in Jan Klabbers, Anne Peters and Geir Ulfstein, *The Constitutionalization of International Law* (Oxford University Press 2009) 81–125 at 122.

the reality. What happens in fact is the sublation of custom into different sources of law. Tasioulas' otherwise admirably lucid defence of an altered understanding of custom unwittingly falls victim to this.[110] From his new perspective on customary law, both state practice and state *opinio iuris* are transformed into the 'raw materials' that have to be taken into account by any interpretative reconstruction of international law in order to satisfy the requirement of 'fit', while, at the same time, keeping an eye on fundamental values in order to possess moral appeal. Obviously, the respect that is owed to manifestations of the will of states is itself linked to morally significant values, such as predictability and democratic legitimacy. Tasioulas does not make explicit, however, that according to the new perspective the self-knowledge of the law is no longer mediated by state *opinio iuris*, but rather by the *opinio iuris* of doctrine. Law's self-knowledge is no longer constituted by what states believe, if states believe anything at all, but rather by how doctrine fits manifestations of state behaviour (or the views of states) into a 'best possible' justification of international law.

Opinio iuris is originally taken to be manifest in the conduct of some states doing or saying what the law is, while other states are either nodding or ducking as bystanders. Doing, saying, ducking or nodding is what mediates the self-knowledge of law. The task of doctrine is to recognise this. It does not strive to make any progress on the basis of such a recognition. From the new perspective, by contrast, the *opinio iuris* of states finds itself on a plane with state practice. It is 'raw material', which is potentially subject to reflective endorsement by the best possible justification of public international law. Now *both* state practice and state *opinio iuris* stand in the same relation to doctrinal *opinio iuris* in which state practice used to stand vis-à-vis state *opinio iuris*. As 'raw materials', they are candidates for 'reflective endorsement',[111] depending on how well they cohere with values. Now doctrine is what mediates the self-knowledge of law. Knowing what the law is by virtue of insight into what is supposed to be good law is what makes it into its source.

Tasioulas' theory is not an account of customary law. Rather, it is a disguised defence of doctrine *qua* source of law inasmuch as it is composed of an elaborate critical reflective attitude ('interpretation') which endorses certain social facts, such as practice and various statements about what

[110] Tasioulas, n. 80 at 325–326.

[111] On the notion, see Christine M. Korsgaard, *The Sources of Normativity* (Cambridge University Press 1996) 50.

ought to be law. The set of these facts is broader than in the case of custom, for it now includes expressions of *opinio iuris* by states or even 'civil society' actors.[112] In the case of customary law, the state *opinio iuris* is nothing but the endorsement of practice, which is believed to occur either implicitly or explicitly. It now itself becomes the subject of reflective endorsement by doctrine. It is 'decoupled'[113] from state practice and offers, in this form, a broader range of options for doctrine to find support, at the level of social facts, for advancing international law as a project of progress.

7.3 From doctrine to imagined legislation

As long as it remains encased in customary law, *opinio iuris* may not amount to more than an inchoate sense of right and wrong. Doctrine is a more refined and self-reflective version of it. Above, it was claimed that the constructive work of doctrine is essential to constituting the full social significance of the legal relation. In order to accomplish this task, it has to perceive a totality of relevant norms as elements of one system and concern itself with the question of which norm is appropriately applied in what type of situation. The emphasis rests on the equality of application across a number of norms and not on improving the norms themselves. Whatever legitimacy can be obtained from adjudication, it derives from treating norms as elements of a system and not from the quality of the elements or the legitimacy of the system itself.

Thus understood, the normative premises of doctrine require, lest they claim to represent natural law, social validation. Without such validation, doctrine is likely to behave in the manner reminiscent of the demeanour that Machiavelli observed in oligarchs vis-à-vis the lesser sort.[114] It becomes insolent and boisterous. When unleashed from political authority, doctrine runs a high risk of becoming indistinguishable from exuberant prophesies and divinations of supreme principles. Doctrine without practice is fanciful; it begins to design projects of legal reform, for it is always inclined to purify the system of those principles that threaten to render it murky. Doctrine must protect itself against its own insolence vis-à-vis politics.[115] Therefore, as soon as it expresses *opinio iuris*, it needs

112 Tasioulas, n. 80 at 328.
113 Tasioulas, n. 80 at 328.

114 Niccolò Machiavelli, *Discorsi sopra la prima deca di Tito Livio* (1531) ch. 4.

115 D'Aspremont, n. 14 at 169.

to limit itself through the recognition of legislation.[116] The predicament confronting general public international law is, of course, that a legislative body does not exist. It can only be imagined. This is what happens in the context of the new theories of customary law. Imagined legislatures serve as the vehicles for advancing a project of progress. Wearing the vestiges of customary law, they are presented as socially validated manifestations of state *opinio iuris*, such as 'instant custom'[117] or 'legislative treaties'. Conventions of the latter type are believed not merely to codify existing custom, but to formulate customary law by virtue of their conclusion.[118] The idea is that widespread and representative participation in a convention might suffice to transform a purely conventional rule into a rule of customary law.[119] Alternatively, custom is also said to change overnight as long as there is *some* trace of states' belief in its desirability.[120] These are all informal ways of transmuting the remains of custom into legislation, for legislation is nothing but the socially manifest will to adopt something as a binding norm regardless of pre-existing common practice.

The result of this transformation is inaccurately presented as a 'sliding scale' approach to customary international law, for it lumps together two different sources. It says, roughly stated, that the closer an issue is to core values, the less state practice is needed to prove customary law, while more evidence is to be adduced when it comes to technical matters.[121] At one end of the spectrum arise issues of high moral salience for which 'custom' is already deemed to be established on the basis of some express commitments to core values; at the other end one finds consistent and general practice for which there is no explicit endorsement. The image is well crafted. Nonetheless, it is misleading, for it presents two different layers of international law as if they were one. The first layer suggests the imagination of an equivalent of legislation by doctrine and the second

116 Which explains why the concept of custom is more generally moved towards legislation. See Baker, n. 14 at 179.

117 Bin Cheng, 'The Future of General State Practice in a Divided World' in Ronald St John Macdonald, Douglas M. Johnston (eds), *The Structure and Process of International Law: Essays in Legal Philosophy, Doctrine, Theory* (Martinus Nijhoff 1983) 513–554 at 531–532.

118 Anthony D'Amato, 'The Concept of Human Rights in International Law' 82 *Columbia Law Review* (1982) 1110–1159 at 1129.

119 *North Sea Continental Shelf*, n. 81 at 42.

120 *North Sea Continental Shelf*, n. 81 at 117.

121 Tasioulas, n. 96 at 109–110; Tasioulas, n. 80 at 325, in both instances referring to Frederic L. Kirgis, 'Custom on a Sliding Scale' 81 *AJIL* (1987) 146–150. A similar approach is also favoured by Roberts, n. 191 at 760, 788–791 and Fastenrath, n. 78 at 338. See also Lepard, n. 84 at 124.

the old conception of customary international law. These layers represent two different ages of international law.

Nevertheless, it cannot be denied that the substitution of state *opinio iuris* with its more elaborate counterpart, doctrinal *opinio iuris*, and the replacement of the elusive requirement of general and consistent practice with equivalents to legislation are markers of a process of rationalisation. The reasons underpinning international law become much more fully revealed. Unfortunately, however, the self-transcendence of custom remains incomplete. The constitutional deficiency of the international system persists owing to the absence of a common legislative body. Public international law suffers from existing in more consolidated form only in 'teachings of the most highly qualified publicists of the various nations'.[122] Jurists cannot supersede custom as a source. As a result, the self-transforming moment of custom is diverted into a strange channel where the upgrading of the doctrinal *opinio iuris* is only abetted by what doctrine fancies to be equivalents of legislation in the name of 'custom'.

Public international law tries to overcome its very primitiveness by outgrowing custom into doctrine and legislation. But it does not advance very far. It remains stuck half way, as it were, since it is not supported by political developments. The self-transcendence of primitiveness, which is a permanent feature of the system, is not accompanied by a *true* constitutionalisation. This explains why public international law, even though undoubtedly noble in its ambition, remains defective. At any rate, in its more exuberant renderings, distance of compliance cannot be mediated by distance of engagement. It is addressed to participants of a common enterprise, who believe in progress through law and are therefore ready to aggregate traces of socially manifest *opinio iuris* into equivalences of legislation.

8 Conclusion

In the case of domestic legal systems, at least of the continental variety, the terms of the post-customary synthesis appear to be clear. Whatever wisdom doctrine may possess as the ultimate source of law, in order for it to be valid it requires endorsement by legislation. Systematic legal reasoning has to be underpinned by methods linking juristic ingenuity with written communications of the legislature through some canon of interpretation. Once a legal system has outgrown its customary character,

[122] Art. 38(1)(d) Statute of the International Court of Justice.

legal doctrine and legislation keep each other mutually in check. The same observation might be made with regard to international agreements – unless, of course, one is confronted with the European Union.[123] The evolution of doctrine that identifies social markers of *opinio iuris* in official statements wherever doctrinal inference is poised to lend its stamp of approval leads to a subtle reformation of the international system along several channels.

First, one encounters observations pointing to substantive changes, such as a finding of a customary prohibition on the use of violence or, perhaps more surprisingly, the discovery of a fundamental principle of civic inviolability.[124]

Second, one is confronted with recalibrations of the *formal* qualities of norms, such as their force or scope of application. Such alterations are sometimes rationalised by appeal to quasi-legislative consideration, for example, the existence of majority support.[125]

Both developments involve a profound reversal of the relevance of state practice and state *opinio iuris.* They try to compensate for the missing authority of doctrine (and the absence of legislation) through tinkering with elements of custom.[126] But this is not the end of the story.

Third, doctrine implicitly begins to take for granted amendments of the elements constituting custom on the basis of expert *opinio iuris* alone as soon as it has left its trace in adjudication. If Baker is right, this development can be observed by how doctrine has reacted to the jurisprudence of special tribunals, such as the ICTY and ICTR, whose jurisdiction rests on an executive mandate by the Security Council.[127] While one would have ordinarily treated the substantive and personal scope of unprecedented – and troubling[128] – developments in the case law of these tribunals as a *leges speciales,* they have come to be regarded by some as new customary international law or at least as evidence of law that has come to be

[123] For an attempt to come up with an account, see n. 51.

[124] Anne-Marie Slaughter, William Burke-White, 'An International Constitutional Moment' 43 *Harvard International Law Journal* (2002) 1–21.

[125] *Ius cogens* is the case in point, even though not only the substantive scope but also the factors constituting *ius cogens* are subject to dispute. See Baker, n. 14 at 177.

[126] According to Baker, n. 14 at 184, elevation of an *opinio iuris* that vies for support in more informal and aspirational declarations vis-à-vis state practice has not been adopted as standard within the field.

[127] See references in Baker, n. 14 at 185 (fn. 76).

[128] Particularly troubling is the deeply reactionary use of an objective *mens rea* standard by the ICTY. See Baker, n. 14 at 197.

'in flux'.[129] The purportedly new international law is then faithfully given effect in certain domestic jurisdictions for the reason of being 'higher law'. This would, indeed, relegate the authorship of public international law to a one-two pass game between legal experts serving on these tribunals and their peers who comment on their work.[130]

If public international law is basically understood to be the project of reshaping the received legal practice among nations in light of some imagined blueprint, it may be possible to anticipate certain developments by putting oneself, potentially, into the shoes of an enthusiast engaged in building the system. Enthusiasm, however, is not a substitute for compelling reasons. System-building involves ideologically charged choices. Not everyone will agree, for example, that aggravating criminal responsibility or licensing violence are unequivocal marks of progress. Unaided by legislation, it is impossible from the perspective of a disengaged addressee to make out the direction into which some specialised legal expertise will push the international system. From the perspective of such an observer, it would be desirable to receive from public international law what it cannot deliver as long as it remains in the hands of publicists, namely, a political choice that would ratify certain particular emanations of scholarly insight while rejecting others.

A constitutionally deficient system of public international law looks, from that perspective, like a system of legal claims that originate from one or the other reform project pursued by self-appointed reformists who have made it their task to improve the world. This is defective legality, for it puts addressees in the position of disciples who find themselves challenged to execute tasks whose definition is beyond their control.

129 For references, see Baker, n. 14 at 188 (fn. 90), 189 (fn. 104).

130 George P. Fletcher, *The Grammar of Criminal Law: American, Comparative, and International*, Vol 1: *Foundations* (Oxford University Press 2007).

7

Post-modern perspectives on orthodox positivism

INGO VENZKE*

1 Introduction

This contribution explains the travails of international legal positivism (ILP) from post-modern perspectives. It identifies conventional precepts of orthodox ILP and shows how variants of post-modern thinking unravel them. It thereby provides part of the background against which current ILP needs to argue. The focus rests on three main such precepts and their critique: first, orthodox ILP works against the backdrop of a given language that stands stable and unsoiled from the operation of the law. Second, it embraces a political philosophy that gives the legal subject – traditionally the sovereign state – a foundational role. Third, orthodox ILP sees but a small space for politics in international law that is confined to law's creation through legal sources. These three basic precepts relate to *linguistics* (the location and generation of meaning), to *subjectivity* (the place of state consent) and to *politics* (here understood as the struggle for power and its exercise).

I will present key concepts of post-modern thinking to question each of these precepts. The vivacious concept of *performativity* embodies lessons of the linguistic turn. It lets go of the idea that language operates as a scheme that exists independent of its operation and instead appreciates how social practices create the language they use. Performativity internalises the generation of meaning into communicative practice and reveals that legal interpretation is a creative activity that contributes to the making of what it purports to find. *Deconstruction* suggests unveiling conflicting diversity underneath harmony and unity not only within legal and social order, but also within any subject. It disassembles state consent as a foundational anchor and further lays bare how consent can be an expression of power structures. *Governmentality*, finally, exposes the

* Parts of this chapter draw on Ingo Venzke, *How Interpretation Makes International Law: On Semantic Change and Normative Twists* (Oxford University Press 2012).

many faces of power that not only work through hard law and variants of visible coercion, but also in much more penetrating ways. Law and politics are much more entangled than ILP would traditionally have it.

The primary concern, which I understand to lie at the heart of legal positivism and its specifically international variant, is the autonomy of law in relation to other normative orders.[1] On a positivist account, law gains and maintains its autonomy above all through a distinct modus of law-creation and law-application. Law enters the world in a way that separates it from everything else. From the view of positivism, (international) law is artificial. It is a product of human action rather than natural design. Law is positive because man has made it, and man has made it as law.[2] The underlying political philosophy that typically comes with legal positivism teaches that law is authoritative because its subjects have accepted it as binding against themselves. As such, positivism ties law to human action. How can ILP meet this main concern?

Sure enough, it faces a number of perennial problems in this regard that have been fought out with some wins and many draws where judgment calls hinge on yet grander normative vantage points.[3] In this chapter I will concentrate on how ILP has traditionally tried to meet its main concern, what basic claims it had to make along the line, and what happens to its line of argument when viewed from post-modern perspectives. This, I hope, clarifies at least in part the travails that contemporary ILP encounters.

I ultimately argue that strands of post-modern thinking – revolving around performativity, subjectivity and governmentality – set out significant challenges to orthodox ILP that its contemporary variants struggle to wring down. As a project, however, positivism is not necessarily defeated and anxieties about its arguably indefensible bases seem to be exaggerated. In spite of all challenges, legal practice reproduces itself as a distinct enterprise. Post-modern thinking typically wants to disrupt and unnerve in a struggle against submission to metanarratives, to apparently preordained decisions, and to new and still masked forms of power. It also pursues many quintessentially modern themes by other means and does not necessarily stand in poisonous opposition to positivism. ILP will do best to confront post-modern challenges head-on and to then pursue its

[1] HLA Hart, 'Positivism and the Separation of Law and Morals' 71 *Harvard Law Review* (1957–1958) 593–629.

[2] Georg Wilhelm Friedrich Hegel, *Grundlinien der Philosophie des Rechts* (Suhrkamp 1986) 34 (§ 3); d'Aspremont and Kammerhofer, Chapter 1.

[3] Liam Murphy, 'Better to See Law This Way' 83 *New York University Law Review* (2008) 1088–1108.

normative ambitions more compellingly. Clarifying the travails of positivism thus responds not only to theoretical but also to practical concerns of a normative agenda.

In summary, I provide the background of three basic precepts that sustain orthodox ILP (Section 2), then unravel them in post-modern perspectives by focusing on assumptions pertaining to linguistics (Section 3.1), subjectivity (Section 3.2) and governmentality (Section 3.3). I will conclude by sketching how ILP may respond and which dead-ends it had better avoid (Section 4).

2 Orthodox precepts of international legal positivism

2.1 The externalisation of meaning

ILP traditionally runs on the background assumption of a given language that the law can use, but that is not itself affected or shaped by the operation of the law. Like other basic precepts, this first core assumption can well be gleaned from the way in which orthodox ILP constructs the making of law in terms of sources and from its take on the nature of legal interpretation.

Positivism understands legal sources as norms that set out the criteria in accordance with which actors can create law. Those norms also spell out for everyone engaged in the legal enterprise where to look if they want to know what counts as law. Something is law when 'it crystallises through the relevant sources of law'.[4] Once it has thus entered the world, it can be used and applied. Alexander Orakhelashvili opines that use of the law merely 'deduce[s] the meaning exactly of what has been consented to and agreed'.[5] Interpretation is understood as something categorically different from law-making. The latter is a matter of sources alone.

Further examples abound in this regard. In their contribution on Article 31 in the recent commentary on the Vienna Convention on the Law of Treaties (VCLT), Jean-Marc Sorel and Valérie Boré Eveno for instance contend that interpretation is of fundamental importance because it results in 'releasing [*dégager*] the exact meaning and the content of the rule of

[4] Alexander Orakhelashvili, *The Interpretation of Acts and Rules in Public International Law* (Oxford University Press 2008) 55.

[5] Orakhelashvili, n. 4 at 286; see also, critically, Michael Waibel, '[Review Essay]: Demystifying the Art of Interpretation' 22 *EJIL* (2011) 571–588 at 583.

law that is applicable to a given situation'.[6] From this perspective, interpretation could concretise the law, perhaps, but surely does not make it.

The categorical distinction between making law by way of sources and interpretation that deduces meaning is sustained by the assumption that the meaning of legal texts lies outside the interpretative process. Law uses language, but does not contribute to its making. It is thus never the use of language that leads to semantic change – a change of law's content – but typically a change in environmental circumstances or in normative convictions.[7] Interpretation, that is the bottom line, is not a creative activity, but an act of discovery. Law is only created through legal sources. Were this otherwise, law's autonomy would arguably be under siege.[8]

When it comes to customary international law, positivist legal doctrine more readily shows an inkling that the distinction between applying the law and making it is indeed a difficult one.[9] It is precisely the interpretative practice of some (state) authorities that is recognised as contributing to the creation of custom.[10] The most promising avenue to sustain a distinction would be to assimilate custom to treaty law, not in the quaint fashion of 'tacit consent', but in the sense that also customary norms take the form of rules that are interpreted and applied.[11] It may also help that customary norms often have quasi-authoritative textual formulations, for instance by virtue of the International Law Commission's codification projects.[12] But any distinction between applying and making customary law is

[6] Jean-Marc Sorel and Valérie Boré Eveno, 'Article 31' in Olivier Corten, Pierre Klein (eds), *The Vienna Conventions on the Law of Treaties: A Commentary* (Oxford University Press 2011) 804–837 at 806.

[7] Sabine Müller-Mall, *Performative Rechtserzeugung: Eine theoretische Annäherung* (Velbrück 2012) 24.

[8] Stanley Fish, 'The Law Wishes to Have a Formal Existence' in Stanley Fish, *There's No Such Thing as Free Speech and It Is a Good Thing Too* (Oxford University Press 1991) 141–179 at 142.

[9] Albert Bleckmann, 'Zur Feststellung und Auslegung von Völkergewohnheitsrecht' 37 *Zeitschrift für ausländisches öffentliches Recht und Völkerrecht* (1977) 504–529 at 520–521 (trying to distinguish the identification and application of customary international law from its making).

[10] Maurice Mendelson, 'The Formation of Customary International Law' 272 *Recueil des Cours* (1998) 155–410 at 174–175.

[11] On the central role of textuality in legal positivism, see Dennis M. Patterson, *Law and Truth* (Oxford University Press 1999) 96.

[12] Hersch Lauterpacht, 'Codification and Development of International Law' 49 *AJIL* (1955) 16–43; Julius Stone, 'On the Vocation of the International Law Commission' 57 *Columbia Law Review* (1957) 16–51.

troubled by methodical uncertainty.[13] Positivist international legal doctrine certainly struggles in this regard.[14] Here, I only take these struggles to be indicative of the more general difficulty of constructing an account of norms that exist independently of their application.

2.2 The foundational role of subjectivity

Next to locating meaning outside the operation of the law, orthodox ILP places the sovereign state as the foundational legal subject at the heart of legitimate order. Positivist accounts of international law notably developed and grew in finesse with the diminishing universal appeal of other normative substructures of religious and natural law types. In the heyday of classic liberalism, domestic contractual theories were projected onto the international level so that states assumed internationally the place that individuals enjoyed domestically.[15] Classic liberalism in international law provides the backdrop for seeing law almost exclusively the positivist way. It offers a first grasp at traditional ILP's political-philosophical inspiration.[16]

In blunt analogies, it projected fundamental individual rights carved out in the French Revolution onto states in their international affairs.[17] This is evident, for instance, in Immanuel Kant's projection of Hobbesian

[13] Martti Koskenniemi, *From Apology to Utopia: The Structure of International Legal Argument* (Finnish Lawyers' Publishing Co. 1989, reissued Cambridge University Press 2005) 397–473.

[14] Robert Kolb, 'Selected Problems in the Theory of Customary International Law' 50 *Netherlands International Law Review* (2003) 119–150; see already Michael Akehurst, 'Custom as a Source of International Law' 47 *BYBIL* (1976) 1–53.

[15] Gerry Simpson, 'Imagined Consent: Democratic Liberalism in International Legal Theory' 15 *Australian Yearbook of International Law* (1994) 103–128; Julius Goebel, *The Equality of States: A Study in the History of Law* (Cambridge University Press 1925) 34. See also Paul Guggenheim, 'Contribution à l'histoire des sources du droit des gens' 4 *Recueil des Cours* (1958) 1–84 at 20–35. Sources doctrine was used before this move to voluntarism, to be sure, but in this new context it grew in importance: see Jean d'Aspremont, *Formalism and the Sources of International Law: A Theory of the Ascertainment of Legal Rules* (Oxford University Press 2011) 63–66.

[16] Collins, Chapter 2 (likewise arguing that ILP, at this nineteenth-century outset, had been a normatively driven perspective); Murphy, n. 3 (arguing that the choice of how to see law is a normative one).

[17] E.g. the Déclaration du droit des gens (1795) treats states and peoples like individuals – the people has many of the relevant attributes of individuals and forms part of the human family. See Wilhelm G. Grewe, *The Epochs of International Law* (Michael Byers (tr.), Walter de Gruyter 2000) 415.

contractual theory onto the international level in his *Metaphysik* (1797)[18] as well as in the classic liberal conception of international law that Jeremy Bentham developed a year later in his influential *Principles of International Law* (1798).[19] The long-lasting repercussions of this move are inter alia reflected in the famous first article of the Montevideo Convention on the Rights and Duties of States, which defines '[t]he state as a *person* of international law'.[20] Constructing the state as the subject of international law brought with it a host of related tropes.[21] In particular, states could express a will, give their consent and create international law as an instrument of auto-determination. International law and legal thinking have certainly developed significantly since those formative times. Yet the conception of anthropomorphic states as foundational subjects remains omnipresent in scholarly and practical discourses.[22]

In order to ensure that international law is nothing else than what sovereign states have consented to, it is necessary to set out the modus in which law is created – this, once again, is what the doctrine of sources does. While dissatisfaction with Article 38 of the ICJ Statute (following verbatim Article 38 of the PCIJ Statute) is legion, it has continuously been the dear focal point of ILP.[23] According to Orakhelashvili: '[i]t follows from the basic concept of the sources of international law, as specified in Article 38 of the ICJ Statute, that the validity of legal rules derives from the agreement and acceptance of States'.[24] The word 'States' is notably capitalised. In the traditional positivist reading, each of the elements of Article 38 aspires to

18 Immanuel Kant, *Die Metaphysik der Sitten* (Suhrkamp 1977) 466–467 (§ 53).

19 Jeremy Bentham, 'Principles of International Law' in John Bowring (ed.), *The Works of Jeremy Bentham*, Vol. 2 (William Tait 1843) 535–571.

20 Convention on the Rights and Duties of States ('Montevideo Convention'), 26 December 1933, 165 LNTS 19 (emphasis added).

21 Janne Elisabeth Nijman, *The Concept of International Legal Personality: An Inquiry Into the History and Theory of International Law* (Asser Press 2004). How deeply thinking about the state as a person is seated is reflected in many metaphors such as 'head of state' or 'state organ', see Reinhart Koselleck, 'Staat und Souveränität III' in Otto Brunner, Werner Conze, Reinhart Kosseleck (eds), *Geschichtliche Grundbegriffe: Historisches Lexikon zur politisch-sozialen Sprache in Deutschland*, Vol. 6 (Klett-Cotta 1990) 25–64.

22 Armin von Bogdandy, Sergio Dellavalle, 'Ad hostes docere: Zu den Ursprüngen und zur Präsenz partikularistisch-holistischen Denkens' in Andreas Fischer-Lescano *et al.* (eds), *Frieden in Freiheit – Peace in Liberty – Paix en liberté: Festschrift für Michael Bothe zum 70. Geburtstag* (Nomos 2008) 847–863.

23 Thomas Skouteris, 'The Force of a Doctrine: Art. 38 of the PCIJ Statute and the Sources of International Law' in Fleur Johns, Richard Joyce, Sundhya Pahuja (eds), *Events: The Force of International Law* (Routledge 2011) 69–80.

24 Orakhelashvili, n. 4 at 112.

translate consent to be bound into law.[25] ILP traditionally places states as foundational subjects at the core of the international legal order.

2.3 *The small space of politics*

It has for a long time been a core proposition of legal positivism that law is an artefact and is subject to politics. In fact, ILP generally seeks to ensure that international law is *nothing but* a product of political struggle.[26] But politics can only make law in ways that are recognised to meet the demands of sources doctrine. Otherwise it could not be ensured that states are only bound by what they have consented to.[27] At the moment of its source, law meets politics and politics becomes law. What happens before is a matter of politics. What happens after is a matter of operating the law, not a matter of politics.

It is a third precept of orthodox ILP that what is important comes as hard law, identified as such by the sources of law. The argument is compellingly circular: international law obligates and constrains its subjects and therefore it must be based on their consent. Sources tell how consent can be turned into law. Nothing else could create legal obligation because law would then loose its consensual basis.

In turn, orthodox ILP tends to know only one kind of legal normativity: hard law.[28] It also approaches other legally relevant phenomena such as 'soft law' through the lens of hard law. Resolutions of the General Assembly – the focal point of many of the debates – could help interpret treaties or assist in finding customary international law.[29] But ultimately something is either law because it was created in ways recognised by the

[25] Maarten Bos, 'Recognized Manifestations of International Law: A New Theory of Sources' 19 *German Yearbook of International Law* (1977) 9–76; Godefridus J. H. van Hoof, *Rethinking the Sources of International Law* (Kluwer 1983).

[26] Ulrich Fastenrath, 'A Political Theory of Law: Escaping the Aporia of the Debate on the Validity of Legal Argument in Public International Law' in Ulrich Fastenrath *et al.* (eds), *From Bilateralism to Community Interest: Essays in Honour of Bruno Simma* (Oxford University Press 2011) 58–78.

[27] Orakhelashvili, n. 4 at 30.

[28] The possibilities and limits of seeing 'soft law' from the perspective of traditional and modern legal positivism are discussed in further detail in Matthias Goldmann, *Handlungsformen internationaler öffentlicher Gewalt: Zur Dogmatik von Soft Law und Informationsakten im Recht der internationalen Institutionen* (doctoral thesis, University of Heidelberg, 2013) 130–154. Relevant parts have been published in English as Matthias Goldmann, 'We Need to Cut Off the Head of the King: Past, Present, and Future Approaches to International Soft Law' 25 *LJIL* (2012) 335–368.

[29] Goldmann, *Handlungsformen*, n. 28 at 140–148.

sources of law, or it is not law and can thus neither create legal obligations. 'Soft law' is thus often presented as an oxymoron. 'Softness' may relate to the vagueness of law's contents, but not to its degree of obligation, which is binary: law ('on') or not ('off').[30] In the orthodox positivists' mind, soft law is not legally binding because it typically lacks the prerequisite formal pedigree. For many authors, soft law is a 'convenient description for a variety of non-legally binding instruments used in contemporary international relations by States and international organisations'.[31] The way it matters, if at all, is through its interplay with hard law.

3 Post-modern perspectives

Having carved out three main precepts of conventional ILP, this section now unsettles each from post-modern perspectives. *Performativity* unravels the externalisation of meaning (Section 3.1), *deconstruction* undercuts the foundational role of the subject (Section 3.2), and *governmentality* significantly expands the space of politics (Section 3.3).

3.1 Performativity: semantic change and creative interpretations

3.1.1 The linguistic turn

Scholarship in the wake of the 'linguistic turn' has refined the idea that meaning is generated in social practices and internal to interpretative processes. It suggests that neither language nor law exist as schemes independent from their use. It thereby disturbs orthodox ILP's background assumption of a given and rather static language, which ensured that law can be created at one point in time to then be used in interpretation. Two strands of theoretical developments shake this first core assumption.

The first sets out with the work of Ferdinand de Saussure whose *Course on General Linguistics* successfully defeated the long-held view that the meanings of words are revealed through the connection with something they represent. He rejected this basis of stability and instead argued that linguistic signs only gain their meaning through their difference from

[30] Prosper Weil, 'Towards Relative Normativity in International Law?' 77 *AJIL* (1983) 413–442.

[31] Alan Boyle, 'Soft Law in International Law-Making' in Malcom D. Evans (ed.), *International Law* (2nd edn Oxford University Press 2006) 141–157 at 142.

other linguistic signs.[32] Not representation but difference constitutes meaning. Only the tradition of language usage can to some extent stabilise fluctuating distinctions.[33]

Another line of thinking takes off with Wittgenstein's piercing view that words do not have a meaning other than that attributed to them by their use.[34] In his solemn observation, the best that can be done is to observe and to find rules that describe the use of an expression. In attempting to find the meaning of a rule, it is necessary to find the rule that explains the use of that rule.[35] The meaning of the explanatory rule is of course subject to the same fate so that one is caught in an infinite regress: 'any interpretation . . . hangs in the air along with what it interprets, and cannot give it any support'.[36] In the notes *On Certainty*, Wittgenstein summed up his insights: '[y]ou must look at the practice of language, then you will see it'.[37] That also holds true for international law. It is necessary to look at its practice in order to see it.[38]

In this line of thought, the challenge for traditional ILP is further polished by John Austin, the twentieth-century philosopher of language, not the nineteenth-century founding father of analytical jurisprudence. Austin coins the concept of performative speech, which refers to communicative utterances that change the world.[39] The worn example is the utterance of the words 'I do' that can create the bond of marriage if

[32] Ferdinand de Saussure, *Course in General Linguistics* (Open Court 1983) 65, 106. See Sybille Krämer, *Sprache, Sprechakt, Kommunikation: Sprachtheoretische Positionen des 20. Jahrhunderts* (Suhrkamp 2001) 19–36.

[33] De Saussure, n. 32 at 67–69.

[34] Such semantic pragmatism in the wake of Wittgenstein can find considerable common ground. For a concise and accessible account, see Dennis M. Patterson, 'Dworkin on the Semantics of Legal and Political Concepts' 26 *Oxford Journal of Legal Studies* (2006) 545–557 (inter alia specifying semantic pragmatism's main contentions and excluding a range of alleged implications that do not follow); Damiano Canale, Giovanni Tuzet, 'On Legal Inferentialism: Toward a Pragmatics of Semantic Content in Legal Interpretation?' 20 *Ratio Juris* (2007) 32–44; Markus Winkler, 'Die Normativität des Praktischen' 64 *JuristenZeitung* (2009) 821–829.

[35] Ludwig Wittgenstein, *Philosophical Investigations* (Blackwell 1958) para. 43. See also Krämer, n. 32 at 128.

[36] Wittgenstein, n. 35 at para. 198.

[37] Ludwig Wittgenstein, *On Certainty* (Blackwell 1969) para. 501.

[38] In detail, see Ingo Venzke, *How Interpretation Makes International Law: On Semantic Change and Normative Twists* (Oxford University Press 2012).

[39] John L. Austin, *How to Do Things with Words* (Oxford University Press 1979) 138–139. Further expanded in John L. Austin, 'Performative Utterances' in James O. Urmson, Geoffrey James Warnock (eds), *Philosophical Papers* (Oxford University Press 1979) 233–253.

performed in the right context. In a clever move, Austin tries to come up with distinctions that separate creative *performative* speech acts from simple *constative* speech acts such as 'this is an apple'.[40] If an interpreter only engaged in constative acts of the kind 'this is what the law is', then she could possibly withdraw from any charge of actually making law rather than applying it. Austin suggests, however, that this is simply impossible.[41] It is impossible to use legal norms without interpretation and without performing an act.[42] He ultimately comes to the conclusion that every attempt at distinguishing performative from constative acts fails because it is unfeasible to withhold from interpreting even simple objects such as apples, let alone complex phenomena such as the law.[43] Judicial interpretations present themselves as declaring what the law 'really is' and contribute to the law's creation.

The linguistic turn is multifaceted and extends to a broader reconsideration of the relationship between language and the world.[44] For the present discussion of ILP's travails, its central emphasis on *performativity* is of main importance. It highlights the inevitable creativity, roughly, that is nested in any reiteration of a rule.[45] The concept of performativity builds on the idea that the use of words generates their meaning and captures the simultaneous presence in any linguistic utterance of a transformation of the past as well as the placing of something new into the world.[46]

Jean-François Lyotard placed performativity centre stage in his epochal treatise *The Postmodern Condition: A Report on Knowledge*.[47] He uses the notion slightly differently. In Lyotard's work, performativity draws

[40] Austin, *Words*, n. 39 at 140–141. [41] Austin, *Words*, n. 39 at 141.

[42] Cf. Niklas Luhmann, *Das Recht der Gesellschaft* (Suhrkamp 1993) 256 (agreeing that it is impossible not to interpret and to thus contribute to the construction of the law).

[43] Austin, *Words*, n. 39 at 142–143; Krämer, n. 32 at 135–153; Stanley Fish, *Doing What Comes Naturally: Change, Rhetoric, and the Practice of Theory in Literary and Legal Studies* (Duke University Press 1989) 488–491.

[44] Richard Rorty (ed.), *The Linguistic Turn: Essays in Philosophical Method* (Chicago University Press 1992).

[45] For an introduction to the concept in legal theory, see Ralph Christensen, Kent D. Lerch, 'Performanz: Die Kunst, Recht geschehen zu lassen' in Kent D. Lerch (ed.), *Die Sprache des Rechts*, Vol. 3 (Walter de Gruyter 2006) 55–132; Müller-Mall, n. 7.

[46] The concept has been refined in the works of Jacques Derrida and Judith Butler especially. See Jacques Derrida, *Of Grammatology* (Gayatri Chakravorty Spivak (tr.), Johns Hopkins University Press 1997); Judith Butler, *Excitable Speech: A Politics of the Performative* (Routledge 1997).

[47] Jean-François Lyotard, *The Postmodern Condition: A Report on Knowledge* (University of Minnesota Press 1984).

together factors that channel knowledge and that sustain the success of inevitably creative statements about the world.[48] What I take from the concept is the inescapable creativity of using a language. Turning to law and ILP, with baggage and nuance lost, performativity places the construction of meaning into the operation of the law and thus unravels orthodox ILP's first basic precept. Performativity internalises meaning.

3.1.2 Sources and semantic change

Performativity suggests that the law placed into the world through the channels of sources is subject to a process of continuous creation simply by being interpreted and applied. A quintessentially modern anecdote clarifies the point: already at the time of the French Revolution, it was argued perceptively that change should be induced by conceptual anticipation, that is, through the use of arguments in speech and writing.[49] First among others, Denis Diderot designed the *Encyclopédie* to fix then the spirit of the revolution and carry it henceforth.[50] But when he recognised the power of words to reach into the future, he immediately saw words' double-edged quality: if *he* was in a position to shape words to meet the ends of the revolution, so could others.[51] In an attempt to tie the meanings of words to revolutionary ideals, he therefore advocated that 'les paroles nationales seront souverains de tous les souverains'.[52] The sovereign as a source of legitimacy should decide about the meaning of words. At the same time, words should be sovereign; they should have the ultimate authority. There is a readily visible and intricate tension between the fact that the words are *souverains* (noun, not adjective) and the fact that revolutionary thinkers tried to shape those same words to advance their own ideas. Words should be the ultimate authority, but they should mean what the authors of the *Encyclopédie* intended them to mean.

The same tension troubles ILP. Legal subjects enter into legal commitments, reach into the future, carefully formulate the words with which

[48] Lyotard, n. 47.

[49] Reinhart Koselleck, *Begriffsgeschichten: Studien zur Semantik und Pragmatik der politischen und sozialen Sprache* (Suhrkamp 2006) 298, referring to Brigitte Schleiben-Lange, 'Die Französische Revolution und die Sprache' 41 *Zeitschrift für Literaturwissenschaft und Linguistik* (1981) 90–123.

[50] See Koselleck, n. 49 at 299.

[51] Reinhart Koselleck, 'Begriffsgeschichte and Social History' in Reinhart Koselleck, *Futures Past: On the Semantics of Historical Time* (Keith Tribe (tr.), Columbia University Press 1979) 75–93 at 80.

[52] '[N]ational words will be sovereign of all the sovereigns': 'Abondance' in *Nouveau Dictionnaire Historique* (1791), quoted from Koselleck, n. 49 at 300 (author's translation).

they do so, and then submit those words to processes of interpretation that escape their control. If international norms change in the process of interpretation after they are placed into the world, then this process distances the law from its source and, possibly, from the consent of its foundational subjects.

The anecdote features three key insights for the fate of traditional ILP. First, the authors of the *Enyclopédie* recognised how words are powerful in the sense that they can constrain others in what they can say or do. That is a thought which positivism certainly cheers, but perhaps just a bit too much because words are not so powerful as to *determine* their future use. Revolutionary thinkers understood, second, that actors fight about semantic content in pursuit of their interests and convictions. They saw and expected meanings to shift over time in such semantic struggles. While they tried to coin *paroles nationales* when writing the *Encyclopédie*, they realised that these words would take on a life of their own and would possibly escape their control. For ILP, such semantic change is problematic because it effectively shifts the law in a way that escapes the reach of legal sources. The authors of the *Encyclopédie* saw the answer in arguing, third, that the meaning of words be tied back to the legitimating subject, the people. But that was surely a highly aspirational and ultimately impossible argument. Once the *Encyclopédie* was published, its meaning would change in semantic struggles and control over its life would escape its creators.

In short, when traditional ILP and its classic liberal impetus suggest in a crudely simplified fashion that unitary states are sovereign and that they make the law that constrains them, the underlying confidence in the stability of semantic content is at least shaky. Certainly, recognising the creativity of the interpretative process renders the distinction between making law through sources and law-making by way of interpretation neither impossible nor superfluous.[53] But the distinction needs to be re-articulated by placing emphasis on distinct argumentative demands that characterise each modus of law-making. Both forms of law-making also work differently. Law-making by way of interpretation, for instance, hinges more on persuasion and on other actors' acceptance. But how creative or constrained then is the semantic struggle that changes the law? In other words, how is legal interpretation constrained by international law if it is that same interpretative practice that creates the law?

[53] Armin von Bogdandy, Ingo Venzke, 'On the Democratic Justification of International Judicial Lawmaking' 12 *German Law Journal* (2011) 1341–1370 at 1344–1349.

3.1.3 Rule-following, creative and constrained interpretations

Traditional legal positivism would find the answer in limits set by the law itself. The limits stem from the terms of the treaty, which must be interpreted according to its 'ordinary meaning . . . in their context and in the light of [the treaty's] object and purpose'.[54] Seeing that these limits are themselves produced in the practice of interpretation questions these constraints. Scholarship connecting to notions of performativity then suggests that the law itself does not give away the limits to its interpretation. What is limiting is the need of an interpreter to find acceptance for its interpretations within a community of interpreters.[55]

Philosopher Robert Brandom explains further that when an actor has consented to a rule – has acted in a way that creates law – she has committed herself in relation to others to using certain expressions. The actual content of those commitments, the meaning of expressions, then results from a process of 'negotiation' with others:

> [T]he boundaries around what one has and has not committed oneself to by using a particular concept (and what is and is not a correct application of it) are determined by a process of *negotiation* among actual attitudes of application and assessments of application.[56]

This brief summary of his refined argument for now leaves a number of open questions. But it does offer an alternative ground for assessing whether the interpretation of a norm was (in)correct. Brandom rightly submits that this assessment can only be part of the communicative practice itself. In this practice, applications of a concept in the present have to connect to the past in a way that convinces future applications: '[t]he current judge is held accountable to the tradition she inherits by the judges yet to come'.[57] Contents of commitments gain shape and develop in the practice of demanding and giving reasons for or against a particular application of a concept (a particular interpretation of an international norm).

[54] Art. 31 VCLT. [55] Fish, n. 43 at 488–491.

[56] Robert Brandom, 'Some Pragmatist Themes in Hegel's Idealism: Negotiation and Administration in Hegel's Account of the Structure and Content of Conceptual Norms' 7 *European Journal of Philosophy* (1999) 164–189 at 173.

[57] Brandom, n. 56 at 181. For a concise introduction and summary, see Jasper Liptow, *Regel und Interpretation: Eine Untersuchung zur sozialen Struktur sprachlicher Praxis* (Velbrück 2004) 220–226; Ralph Christensen, 'Neo-Pragmatismus: Brandom' in Sonja Buckel, Ralph Christensen, Andreas Fischer-Lescano (eds), *Neue Theorien des Rechts* (Lucius und Lucius 2009) 239–262; Winkler, n. 34.

Brandom follows in the footsteps of semantic pragmatism that has learned the lessons of the linguistic turn. But he is hardly a post-modern thinker. In particular, he leaves another fundamental category intact that would typically be attacked in post-modern scholarship: subjectivity.

3.2 Deconstruction: consent and agreement

3.2.1 Unity and diversity in conflict

It is a basic suggestion in post-modern thinking to uncover conflict and diversity underneath harmony and unity. This impetus is directed against metanarratives that operate at a high level of abstraction and create mythical images of reality. Lyotard sees working against such abstraction to be the defining feature of post-modernity: '[s]implifying to the extreme', he writes, 'I define *postmodern* as incredulity toward metanarratives'.[58] The narrative of classic liberalism, reciting that international law is what sovereign states have wanted it to be, would be a prime example of such a metanarrative.[59] The work of Lyotard's *confrère*, Jacque Derrida, on deconstruction as a style of enquiry pursues a very similar quest and is designed to help uncover suppressed antagonisms.[60]

Deconstruction could take a genealogical style by retracting the history of a concept or idea. It could thereby show how contested as well as contingent its development has in fact been.[61] Deconstruction would rediscover rivalling understandings and destabilise the winning side of history.[62] Another, less historical style would concentrate on identifying paradoxes in seemingly stable conceptual relationships. A prime example, which Derrida plays out in detail in his *Force of Law: The 'Mystical Foundation of Legal Authority'*, is the relationship between law and justice. He uncovers three *aporiae* – moments of undecidability – in this relationship.[63] If legitimate power is to be distinguished from ordinary violence, it is because it follows rules that authorise it. But what

[58] Lyotard, n. 47 at xxiv.

[59] Jean-François Lyotard, 'Memorandum über die Legitimität' in Peter Engelmann (ed.), *Postmoderne und Dekonstruktion: Texte französicher Philosophen der Gegenwart* (Reclam 2004) 54–75.

[60] Jacques Derrida, 'Force of Law: The "Mystical Foundation of Authority"' 11 *Cardozo Law Review* (1990) 920–1045.

[61] Derrida, n. 46; such deconstructive genealogy was foreshadowed prominently by Nietzsche and also practised by Michel Foucault, 'Nietzsche, Genealogy, History' in Donald F. Bouchart (ed.), *Language, Counter-Memory, Practice: Selected Essays and Interviews* (Cornell University Press 1977) 139–164.

[62] Derrida, n. 60. [63] Derrida, n. 46.

authorises the creation of those rules? Further, rules do not determine their own application. How then can the exercise of legitimate power be rule-bound? Finally, how can justice be achieved if it continues to escape the reach of rules? Derrida's answer to these questions, all of this 'simplifying to the extreme', points to deconstruction itself as a technique to show the possibility of deciding differently. On this note, deconstruction is justice. It struggles with every trick in the book against the reification of law and justice and seeks to prevent the violent submission of one alternative to the benefit of another. It upholds contingency.

The subject is no longer the rock-solid building block of legitimate order. The subject is the construction of metanarratives that overshadow diversity. If anything, it is the meeting-point of competing factors that stand in unresolvable tension. The post-modern pop-slogan, which announces the 'death of the subject', brings this to the point.[64]

3.2.2 Disaggregating the subject

Part of the legacy of classic liberalism's projection of domestic contractual theories onto the international level is the picture of the sovereign state as a person of international law. The anthropomorphic state makes the law that constrains it. And if it is not the state that acts as a person, then it is its head or its organs.[65] The post-modern critique of abstract unities challenges this metanarrative on different levels: on a fundamental and far-reaching note, it questions any and all ideas about autonomous will formation. It suggests that one should better look at the social structures that form will, generate preferences, and constitute the subject. On a slightly less penetrating level that leaves parts of the state intact, it highlights that actions of specific state organs may only be linked back to 'the state' at a tenuous stretch. In fact, institutions and individuals forming part of all branches of government can and do engage as independent actors in the interpretation of international law.

[64] This pop slogan was originally part of an argument directed *against* the dissection of the subject through market forces. See Theodor W. Adorno, *Minima Moralia: Reflections from Damaged Life* (E. F. N. Jephcott (tr.), Verso 1978); likewise Herbert Marcuse, *One-Dimensional Man: Studies in the Ideology of Advanced Industrial Society* (Beacon Press 1964). It then resurfaced in Michael Foucault's emphasis on pervasive power/knowledge structures, which undermine conditions of human agency, to which I return in Section 3.1. See Michel Foucault, 'Two Lectures' in Colin Gordon (ed.), *Power/Knowledge: Selected Interviews and other Writings 1972–1977* (Alessandro Fontana, Pasquale Pasquino (trs), Pantheon Books 1980) 78–108; Amy Allen, 'The Anti-Subjective Hypothesis: Michel Foucault and the Death of the Subject' 31 *Philosophical Forum* (2000) 113–130 (showing the ambivalence of Foucault's position towards the possibility of human agency).

[65] Koselleck, n. 21 at 26.

The state falls into distinct parts, each acting autonomously, often contravening the action of the executive to which ILP has traditionally granted prime place. Domestic courts in particular have become increasingly significant and confident in the making of international law.[66] In some fields, they might even form a 'united, coordinated judicial front'.[67] Of course, legal doctrine has ways of capturing and absorbing domestic courts' actions into its framework, for instance by recognising their practice in the formation of customary international law.[68] But the state as the main subject of international law does not have a will. It falls apart into competing actors. As Eyal Benvenisti notes, the phenomenon of transnational judicial cooperation 'demonstrates yet again the consequences of the "disaggregated state" as both the national government and the national court seek foreign allies in their quest to balance each other out'.[69] Often, domestic courts do not say what the head of state thinks.

Network theory and scholarship inspired by systems theory further contend that the societal action falls along sectoral lines and is driven by particular rationalities such as those of the market, human rights or security. Such views let go of the belief in *one* rationality that traverses all human action. Instead, they see a plurality of functional rationalities.[70] State consent can hardly play a foundational role from this perspective. There is no aspiration to construct international law as a coherent system that could be held together by conflict rules of treaty law or by harmonious interpretation. The search for legal unity in the fragmentation of global law is simply vain.[71] The disaggregation of the subject into its parts and the operation of competing rationalities not only touch on ideas of state consent in making law by way of sources, but also on ideas of

66 André Nollkaemper, *National Courts and the International Rule of Law* (Oxford University Press 2011) 6–10; August Reinisch, 'The International Relations of National Courts: A Discourse on International Law Norms on Jurisdictional and Enforcement Immunity' in August Reinisch, Ursula Kriebaum (eds), *The Law of International Relations: Liber Amicorum Hanspeter Neuhold* (Eleven 2007) 289–309 at 309 (concluding that 'in the long run, national courts will increasingly shape international law through their transnational exchanges').

67 Eyal Benvenisti, 'Reclaiming Democracy: The Strategic Uses of Foreign and International Law by National Courts' 102 *AJIL* (2008) 241–274 at 249.

68 See already Hersch Lauterpacht, 'Decisions of Municipal Courts as a Source of International Law' 10 *BYBIL* (1929) 65–95 at 92.

69 Benvenisti, n. 67 at 244.

70 Gunther Teubner, *Constitutional Fragments: Societal Constitutionalism and Globalization* (Oxford University Press 2012).

71 Andreas Fischer-Lescano and Gunther Teubner, 'Regime-Collisions: The Vain Search for Legal Unity in the Fragmentation of Global Law' 25 *Michigan Journal of International Law* (2004) 999–1045.

interpretation. What does it mean that an actor needs to find acceptance for her interpretative claims? More specifically, what could possibly be the nature of such acceptance?

3.2.3 Hegemonic contestation and the nature of agreement

One central and all too obvious strategy for interpreters to find acceptance is that they simply present their claims as the 'right' interpretation in all the ways in which an interpretation could possibly be considered right. Embracing once again the idea that unity should arguably be unravelled to expose conflicting diversity, it would be a small further step to think of all legal interpretations as hegemonic:

> International actors routinely challenge each other by invoking legal rules and principles on which they have projected meanings that support their preferences and counteract those of their opponents . . . To think of this struggle as *hegemonic* is to understand that the objective of the contestants is to make their partial view of that meaning appear as the total view, their preference seem like the *universal preference.*[72]

Interpretation does not uncover the law that is laid down in legal sources, nor could capable legal scholars recognise the outer limits that separate permissible from impermissible interpretations. No stable ground appears to be available from which to judge. Any interpretation would be hegemonic due to its attempt at making inevitably particular claims prevail in the cloak of universal rightness.[73]

On the premise that there is indeed no external yardstick against which disputes about the meaning of (legal) expressions could be assessed, any meaning would be a function of power relations. Chantal Mouffe made the point clear when she wrote that 'power is constitutive of the social because the social could not exist without the power relations through which it is given shape'.[74] And 'since power relations are constitutive of the social, every order is by necessity a hegemonic order'.[75] On her

[72] Martti Koskenniemi, 'International Law and Hegemony: A Reconfiguration' 17 *Cambridge Review of International Affairs* (2004) 197–218 at 199.

[73] With regard to the specific example of international trade law, see Jason Beckett, 'Fragmentation, Openness and Hegemony: Adjudication and the WTO' in Meredith Kolsky Lewis, Susy Frankel (eds), *International Economic Law and National Autonomy* (Cambridge University Press 2010) 44–70.

[74] Chantal Mouffe, *On the Political: Thinking in Action* (Routledge 2005) 18.

[75] Mouffe, n. 74 at 106.

account, only power is left as a constitutive building block for social order.[76]

Strikingly, such a spirited critique of metaphysics rests on the equally metaphysical and therefore equally unsupported assumption that there are no such things as moral values or – turned into inter-subjective relationships – of a rationality that allows for something like genuine agreement. Metaphysical claims need to be avoided on both sides. Beyond doubt, however, interpretation is a site of politics, to which I now turn with the help of a third core concept: governmentality.

3.3 Governmentality: politics and what matters

3.3.1 The many faces of power

Orthodox ILP's third basic precept, which pertains to the space of politics, crumbles in light of post-modern reassessments of how power is exercised. The concept of governmentality highlights the larger space of politics in legal interpretation and in the generation of legal normativity through soft law instruments. Michel Foucault coined the enigmatic concept of governmentality (*gouvernementalité*) to refer to the ways through which power is exercised over a population, to the growth of government in exercising such power, and to the historical transformation of the state into the administrative state.[77] One of Foucault's decisive contributions to social theory has been his nuanced understanding of how power does not only come in forms of coercion and constraints. Power is also at work in the production of reality. It permeates systems of knowledge and, fundamentally, shapes subjects – their identity, cognitive frames and preferences. Power, Foucault suggests, not only takes the shape of law that commands and constrains, but also the penetrating form of being productive in the sense of constituting subjects and the world that surrounds them.

[76] From the wealth of literature on this issue, see in particular Michel Foucault, 'Afterword: The Subject and Power' in Hubert L. Dreyfus, Paul Rabinow (eds), *Michel Foucault: Beyond Structualism and Hermeneutics* (University of Chicago Press 1983) 208–226; Lyotard, n. 47. Cf. Maurice Merleau-Ponty, 'Everywhere and Nowhere' in Maurice Merleau-Ponty, *Signs* (Richard C. McCleary (tr.), Northwestern University Press 1964) 126–158 at 153 ('Subjectivity was not waiting for philosophers . . . They constructed, created it . . . And what they have done must perhaps be undone.').

[77] Michel Foucault, 'Governmentality' (Rosi Braidotti and Colin Gordon (trs)) in Graham Burchell, Colin Gordon, Peter Miller (eds), *The Foucault Effect: Studies in Governmentality* (University of Chicago Press 1991) 87–104 at 102–103.

His treatment of law is as sparse as it is ambivalent. But unmistakably he rejects the idea that the only thing that matters is hard law: 'We shall try to rid ourselves of a juridical and negative representation of power, and cease to conceive of it in terms of law, prohibition, liberty, and sovereignty.'[78] Juridical power, Foucault argues, has in fact been on the decline for quite some time. It is overtaken by other forms of governmentality that lean on no less intense and influential mechanisms of 'disciplining' the subject.[79]

Foucault argued with domestic political systems in mind, but his work has been taken up in research on global governance just as well.[80] It highlights the 'constitution of all social subjects with various social powers through systems of knowledge and discursive practice of broad and general social scope'.[81] Fixing the meaning of core legal terms is a prime expression of productive power. Cases in point include prevailing understandings of 'civilian' and 'combatant' in the laws of war as well as the definition of 'refugee'.[82] Foucault generally inspires an investigation of semantic struggles over what the law means as a prime site for the exercise and manifestation of power.

At the same time, his concept of governmentality draws attention to early transformations in the modes of governing and to dissonances between traditional understandings of (juridical) power and largely neglected workings of power.[83] Likewise, the exercise of power on the international level and its relationship with law has developed to now include a multitude of alternative soft law instruments.[84] While Foucault

[78] Michel Foucault, *History of Sexuality*, Vol. 1 (Robert Hurley (tr.), Vintage Books 1990) 90; quoted in Tanja E. Aalberts, Ben Golder, 'On the Uses of Foucault for International Law' 25 *LJIL* (2012) 603–608; Thomas Biebricher, 'Macht und Recht: Foucault' in Sonja Buckel, Ralph Christensen, Andreas Fischer-Lescano (eds), *Neue Theorien des Rechts* (Lucius und Lucius 2009) 139–162.

[79] Foucault later described these mechanisms piercingly as 'biopolitics'; for the international context see Michael Hardt, Antonio Negri, *Empire* (Harvard University Press 2002).

[80] See on 'sovereignty as subjectivity', inspired by Foucault, Tanja E. Aalberts, *Constructing Sovereignty between Politics and Law* (Routledge 2012) 125–142.

[81] Michael Barnett, Raymond Duvall, 'Power in Global Governance' in Michael Barnett, Raymond Duvall (eds), *Power in Global Governance* (Cambridge University Press 2005) 1–32 at 20.

[82] Ingo Venzke, 'Legal Contestation about "Enemy Combatants": On the Exercise of Power in Legal Interpretation' 5 *Journal of International Law & International Relations* (2009) 155–184; Helen M. Kinsella, 'Securing the Civilian: Sex and Gender in the Laws of War' in Michael Barnett, Raymond Duvall (eds), *Power in Global Governance* (Cambridge University Press 2005) 249–272; Bhupinder S. Chimni, 'The Meaning of Words and the Role of UNHCR in Voluntary Repatriation' 5 *International Journal of Refugee Law* (1993) 442–460; Venzke, n. 38 at 72–134.

[83] Fleur Johns, *Non-Legality in International Law: Unruly Law* (Cambridge University Press 2013).

[84] Goldmann, *Handlungsformen*, n. 28 at 6.

rejects the narrow focus on law as a site of power due to the usually narrow conception of what law is, he in effect offers inspiration and tools for expanding what matters 'legally'.

3.3.2 Politics in legal interpretation

The central place of performativity in post-modern thinking flares up again in seeing a wider space for politics in international law that is not confined to law-making by way of sources. Instead it also extends to processes of interpretation. Interpretations produce law and as such they are as much an exercise of power or authority. Understanding successful interpretations as acts of power usefully highlights how actors seek to tap law's force to their advantage. If an interpretation becomes an accepted statement about what the law is, others have to struggle against it.[85]

The picture of legal interpretation that arises from this perspective is certainly not one of uncovering the law in an apolitical exercise of archaeology, but one of a political struggle in which actors interpret in an attempt to implement meanings that are aligned with their interests or convictions.[86] Success in interpretation translates into 'winning' a semantic struggle in a particular instance by finding acceptance for a certain legal claim. Dietrich Busse suitably notes that '[t]he "winner" of a semantic struggle has succeeded in establishing his or her own rule-of-use as the linguistic norm for the linguistic community'.[87]

Participants in legal discourse craft claims about (il)legality, seek to bend the pay-offs distributed by international law and try to tap law's symbolic power.[88] Power as a vector of sovereignty thus extends to the ability to shape meanings. Carl Schmitt – the arch theorist of the political – enigmatically noted that 'whoever has true power is able to determine the content of concepts and words. *Caesar dominus et supra grammaticam.* (Caesar is also lord over grammar).'[89] The notion of semantic struggle captures precisely this thought. Writing on 'semantic strategies as a means of politics', Busse found that:

85 Venzke, n. 82.

86 On the concept of semantic struggle in a historical as well as linguistic perspective, see Koselleck, n. 51 at 80; Dietrich Busse, 'Semantic Strategies as a Means of Politics: Linguistic Approaches to the Analysis of "Semantic Stuggles"' in Pertti Ahonen (ed.), *Tracing the Semiotic Boundaries of Politics* (Walter de Gruyter 1993) 121–128.

87 Busse, n. 86 at 122–123.

88 Pierre Bourdieu, 'The Force of Law: Toward a Sociology of the Juridical Field' 38 *Hastings Law Journal* (1987) 814–853 at 838. See also Matthew Eagleton-Pierce, *Symbolic Power in the World Trade Organization* (Oxford University Press 2013).

89 Quoted in Mouffe, n. 74 at 87.

> [T]he semantic possibilities of linguistic signs correspond to the form of reality, or the view towards reality, admitted by society. Politicians and political agencies that desire to influence the publicly accepted view of political reality will try to dominate the linguistic possibilities within the discourse of politics. Thus language (especially the semantics of political terminology) becomes a means of political action: the so called 'semantic struggles' arise.[90]

This observation holds true all the same for legal terminology. As of late, legal scholars of different *couleur* agree that legal interpretations depend on a political choice. In light of theoretical or practical indeterminacy of the law, unavoidable choices have pervasively but evasively been termed 'political'.[91] At times it seems as though saying that something is political is the post-modern way of ending an argument. Other times, and that is the more productive take, saying so starts an enquiry into the (societal/structural) factors that lead to one decision rather than another.

3.3.3 On what matters

If Article 38 of the ICJ Statue was taken as a formulation of international law's sources,[92] then soft law typically refers to those instruments that do not fit its framework and are thus not considered legally binding even if they show certain legal effects. ILP has tried to accommodate this tension within its framework but, overall, continues to embrace a binary conception according to which something is either law (tested by formal pedigree) or it is not.[93] The concept of governmentality draws together ideas appreciating Foucault's call that we should in fact 'rid ourselves of a juridical and negative representation of power'.[94] Sticking to a narrow conception of law, he argues, neglects all the other ways in which government works and disciplines. Upscaling Foucault's insight onto the international level, work in the exercise of international public authority has highlighted the variety of legal instruments that create legal

90 Busse, n. 86 at 121.

91 Martti Koskenniemi, 'The Politics of International Law' 1 *EJIL* (1990) 4–32.

92 That Art. 38 is hardly the whole story can even be seen from the practice of the ICJ, whose jurisdiction Art. 38 in fact regulates. A prominent example is the binding effect of unilateral declarations, see *Nuclear Tests (Australia v. France)*, Judgment of 20 December 1974, ICJ Reports (1974) 253 at 267 (para. 43); *Nuclear Tests (New Zealand v. France)*, Judgment of 20 December 1974, ICJ Reports (1974) 475 at 472 (para. 46).

93 Weil, n. 30. 94 Foucault, n. 78 at 90.

normativity, that do not fit sources doctrine and that all the same do matter.[95]

What can be witnessed on the international plane at the moment is indeed an increasing dissonance between acts that generate legal normativity and acts that traditionally qualify as a source of law.[96] Drawing a compelling parallel to Foucault's study of governmentality, Matthias Goldmann argues that the exercise of international public authority has undergone a process of transformation that legal scholarship still struggles to conceptualise adequately. On his account the difficulty stems largely from continuing to try to channel all legal normativity through the bottleneck of sources and, in tandem, from continuing to adhere to a binary concept of law. Such a narrow conception, he argues, should be abandoned in favour of a continuum of legal normativity that connects to standard instruments in global governance and that choses the concept of public authority, rather than law, as the focal point for considering what matters.[97]

4 Prognosis: the travails of international legal positivism

What happens to (international) legal positivism's main concerns against the background of post-modern perspectives? How can international law be tied to human action and uphold its claim to autonomy in relation to other kinds of normative orders? Those concerns, to be sure, continue to be salient ones. As Brandom puts it:

> Commitments and responsibilities are seen as coming into a disenchanted natural world hitherto void of them, as products of human attitudes of acknowledging, endorsing, undertaking, or attributing them... [R]ules get their normative force, come to govern our doings, only in virtue of our own attitudes.[98]

Legal positivism pursues its main concerns through claims about the creation of law and its interpretation. It presents both as a formal,

[95] Armin von Bogdandy *et al.* (eds), *The Exercise of Public Authority by International Institutions: Advancing International Institutional Law* (Springer 2010); Nico Krisch, 'Global Governance as Public Authority: An Introduction' 10 *International Journal of Constitutional Law* (2012) 976–987; Neil Walker, 'Postnational Constitutionalism and Postnational Public Law: A Tale of Two Neologisms' 3 *Transnational Legal Theory* (2012) 61–85.

[96] Venzke, n. 38 at 223–245; see further David Kennedy, 'The Mystery of Global Governance' 1 *Ohio Northern University Law Review* (2008) 827–860.

[97] Goldmann, 'Head of the King', n. 28.

[98] Brandom, n. 56 at 170–171.

rule-guided activity. In its orthodoxy, I have argued, ILP has furthermore relied above all on three specific precepts: the externalisation of meaning, the role of states as foundational subjects, and the small space for politics. Performativity unsettles the first precept and undercuts a distinction between making law by way of sources and finding it at a later stage. Second, post-modern views deconstruct subjectivity to unveil conflicting diversity underneath masquerading unity. The notion of governmentality, finally, highlights transformations in the way in which power is exercised at the international level. It destabilises the traditionally narrow boundaries of the political space. How do these challenges bear on the possibilities of a positivist account of international law?

The following chapters in the present volume, even if they might not in detail share my description of the travails, respond to that question. Other scholars have certainly done so as well.[99] In these prognostic paragraphs, I only wish to convey two arguments about what follows in my outlook for the future programme of positivist international legal thinking. The first pertains to sources doctrine and the other to interpretation.

4.1 The fate of the sources doctrine

It is necessary to free thinking about law-making in terms of sources from its metaphorically hazy overtones. Hans Kelsen has already done so in his writings when he offers the appealing view that sources are simply norms that authorise actors to create other norms. They empower actors to make law on the conditions and within the confines that they spell out.[100] Such authorising norms provide the basis of validity for the norms created according to their instructions. They also separate law from non-law. A norm only belongs to the law – is a *legal* norm – when it is based on another norm that vouches for its validity.[101] In short, according to Kelsenian positivism, it is possible to tell whether a norm is a valid legal

[99] Within the context of international law, see among others Beckett, n. 73; Fastenrath, n. 26.

[100] Hans Kelsen, *Principles of International Law* (Rinehart 1952) 303; Adolf Merkl, 'Prolegomena einer Theorie des rechtlichen Stufenbaus' in Alfred Verdross (ed.), *Gesellschaft, Staat und Recht: Festschrift Hans Kelsen zum 50. Geburtstag gewidmet* (Springer 1931) 252–294; Bettina Stoitzner, 'Der Stufenbau der Rechtsordnung' in Stanley L. Paulson, Robert Walter (eds), *Untersuchungen zur Reinen Rechtslehre* (Manz 1986) 51–90; Jörg Kammerhofer, *Uncertainty in International Law: A Kelsenian Perspective* (Routledge 2011) 197–199.

[101] The 'first' norm, the *Grundnorm*, can therefore only be presumed, according to Kelsen.

norm – and this is a core proposition of legal positivism across the board – by investigating its formal pedigree. In a similar fashion, Herbert Hart understands sources as rules of recognition, that is, as rules identifying the practice that creates the law and that distinguish law from other things.[102] Both Kelsen and Hart maintain that law-making is a matter of legal sources alone in a way that embraces much more dynamism and that is not equally subject to post-modern critiques.

Herbert Hart has rescued, with some inspiration from Wittgenstein, the thesis that law is created through formal sources from the whirl of the linguistic turn. The sources thesis, Jean d'Aspremont argues, can be rooted in the social thesis, which means that in order to know what counts as a source of law, we need to look at the social practice of official law-applying authorities.[103] For Hart, writing with the British legal system in mind, those 'law officials' were judges. For the international context, the spectrum of law-applying authorities would most likely be wider.[104] Either way, looking at the practice of 'law officials' responds to the paradox of rule-following that also befalls sources doctrine, which, after all, spells out another kind of rules, 'rules of recognition': how is it possible to follow/apply a rule if following/applying that rule makes that rule?

I have argued in Section 2.1 that an answer threatens to be trapped in an infinite regress. When rules do not have a meaning other than that attributed to them by their use, then the best that can be done is to observe and find rules that describe the use of an expression. In attempting to find the meaning of a rule, it is necessary to find the rule that explains the use of that rule, and so on.[105] In response, only practice

102 HLA Hart, *The Concept of Law* (Clarendon Press 1961) 92; d'Aspremont, Chapter 5.

103 D'Aspremont, n. 15.

104 D'Aspremont, n. 15 at 203, with reference to Brian Z. Tamanaha, *A General Jurisprudence of Law and Society* (Oxford University Press 2001) 142.

105 Wittgenstein, n. 35 at para. 43. Kant's work already offers an early account of infinite regress when it comes to applying a general norm to concrete facts. See Immanuel Kant, *Critique of Pure Reason* (Paul Guyer, Allen W. Wood (trs), Cambridge University Press 1998) 268 ('Now if [general logic] wanted to show generally how one ought to subsume under . . . rules, i.e., distinguish whether something stands under them or not, this could not happen except once again through a rule. But just because this is a rule, it would demand another instruction for the power of judgment, and so it becomes clear that . . . the power of judgment is a special talent that cannot be taught but only practiced.'). For a discussion of different strands pertaining to the issue of rule-following, see Dennis M. Patterson, 'Law's Pragmatism: Law as Practice and Narrative' 76 *Virginia Law Review* (1990) 937–996.

can help.[106] For Wittgenstein, practice is akin to habit or custom. It is a cultural phenomenon of almost natural quality. Actors acquire the ability to follow a rule in processes of socialisation, of training and teaching.[107] An actor must have learned in practice what a rule means. She must have internalised the practice so as not to be in doubt about its meaning: 'I obey the rule blindly', Wittgenstein writes.[108]

Hart's social thesis vindicates the sources thesis by looking at the practice of law-applying authorities. This might hold some sway for some domestic contexts where the 'law officials' whose practice matters form a close community of members that have undergone similar drilling exercises. Placing emphasis on the practice thesis to vindicate the sources thesis might run into more profound difficulties on the fragmented international level.[109] To be clear, the sources do not hold the parts together, but it is precisely the parts that are supposed to say what the sources are. What is more, among the dissonant and fragmented voices of international law, it would be difficult to see not only whose claims matter and should count, but also what it is that law-applying authorities are saying. Such a look on practice seems to require *normative* re-construction. The history of ILP has testified to its strong political-philosophy underpinnings that used to point towards state consent as precisely such a vantage point. This now also needs updating.

In any event, under the conditions of the linguistic turn, it is no longer possible to claim that law-making is a matter of sources alone. Conversely, it is simply unconvincing to term everything that matters legally a source of law (a distinction between 'formal' and 'material' sources does not help either). That would spell apology. Sources are part of a normative reconstruction of legal practice. In the meantime, it might be more promising

[106] Wittgenstein, n. 35 at para. 202; cf. Charles Taylor, 'To Follow a Rule . . . ' in Craig Calhoun, Edward LiPuma, Moishe Postone (eds), *Bourdieu: Critical Perspectives* (University of Chicago Press 1993) 45–60; Brian Bix, *Law, Language and Legal Determinacy* (Clarendon Press 1993) 38–45.

[107] Wittgenstein, n. 35 at para. 206–208. Cf. Martti Koskenniemi, 'International Law: Constitutionalism, Managerialism and the Ethos of Legal Education' 1 *European Journal of Legal Studies* (2007) 1–18 at 15–16 ('[legal training] would have law as a mindset with which the law-applier approaches the task of judgment within the narrow space between fixed textual understandings (positivism) on the one hand, and predetermined functional objectives (naturalism) on the other, without endorsing the proposition that the decisions emerge from a "legal nothing" (decisionism). I think about this in terms of the spirit of the legal profession, and the aim of legal training.').

[108] Wittgenstein, n. 35 at para. 219.

[109] Against those difficulties stands the plea of a 'communitarian semantics', see d'Aspremont, n. 15 at 213–15.

to react to transformations of governmentality by focusing on the exercise of public authority rather than the concept of law and its sources in an effort to rectify the dissonance between what matters and what comes within the purview of formal international law-making.[110]

What could possibly be a vantage point for normative reconstruction? Deconstructing the subject and transformations of governmentality has profoundly shaken ILP's orthodox political philosophy. The challenge is not only that semantic change distances the law from its presumed foundation, but that this foundation itself falls apart. Deconstruction strikes at both the state and the individual as legitimating subjects. As regards the state as an aggregate actor, further normative inspiration may be sought from considering which of its particular institutions are likely to express 'good' legal claims. The benchmarks could vary from how prone an institution is to interest capture or to what extent it realises inclusive decision-making. The deconstruction of the individual would strike a more fatal blow to almost all kinds of legitimacy considerations. What remains in most post-modern writings is the struggle against power to liberate (parts of) any subject. It seems that ultimately the main critique *against* some overreaching post-modern arguments has some bite: they cannot do without subjectivity.[111]

4.2 *The fate of interpretation*

The second main concluding point, which pertains to interpretation, is much more simple. ILP can live, flourish and maintain its quest for the autonomy of international law without postulating the determinacy of legal concepts. Hans Kelsen already went a long way in this regard when he powerfully critiqued orthodox judicial methodology for wanting to make believe that the act of interpretation is nothing but an act of understanding and clarification. The general and abstract norm, he argued, cannot serve as a basis for recognising what the concrete norm in the individual case must be. The norm for any specific case (the *Fallnorm*) cannot be discovered, but only created.[112] Applying a norm creates a new

[110] Goldmann, 'Head of the King', n. 28.

[111] Jürgen Habermas, *Der Philosophische Diskurs der Moderne: Zwölf Vorlesungen* (Suhrkamp 1988).

[112] Hans Kelsen, *Reine Rechtslehre: Einleitung in die rechtswissenschaftliche Problematik* (Deuticke 1934) 74, 95.

norm for which the norm to be applied serves as a basis of validity – or, simply, as a source.[113]

But Kelsen did not consider the impact that applying a norm has on the norm to be applied. That norm remains untouched and unchanged by its application. It exists in the abstract and separately from the concrete operations of the legal system. Such a view was only stringent. Otherwise the chain of legal validity would collapse. If a norm authorises the creation of another norm and vouches for that norm's validity, then it could not be that the latter norm in effect changes the former.[114] Applying the law makes new law, but it does not change the law that already exists. That law could only change by virtue of the higher norm on which it is based (and so on).

The travails of ILP are thus at least twofold when it wants to offer an account of interpretation on the heels of Kelsen. First, it has to let go of any argument suggesting that applying the law is an act of deduction or discovery. Such ideas place too much faith in the capacity of the cognising subject. Legal interpretation can no longer be thought of as an act of cognition. Likewise, it will probably have to develop a more solid argument on how to distinguish, as Hart put it, between core meaning and its penumbra.[115] ILP has to sever all essentialist ties that connect expressions with something outside, behind or beyond language itself. It must let go of any suggestion that there is 'some way of breaking out of language to compare it with something else'.[116] If there is a stable core, it is typically due to the absence of dispute and not the other way round. Convention stabilises the core.

Second, ILP needs to refine how it is possible to distinguish a right from a wrong interpretation *according to the law*. This was Kelsen's quest, precisely not to seek stability or foundation for the practice of the law outside that same practice. Keep the law free from all subjective leanings

[113] Kelsen, n. 112 at 82–83, 95. On this point, Kelsen draws heavily on Adolf Merkl, 'Das Doppelte Rechtsantlitz: Eine Betrachtung aus der Erkenntnistheorie des Rechtes' 47 *Juristische Blätter* (1918) 425–427, 444–447, 463–465.

[114] This is why he had such troubles in coming to terms with wrong but effective decisions. Cf. András Jakab, 'Probleme der Stufenbaulehre: Das Scheitern des Ableitungsgedankens und die Aussichten der Reinen Rechtslehre' 91 *Archiv für Rechts- und Sozialphilosophie* (2005) 333–365.

[115] Hart, n. 1 at 607.

[116] Richard Rorty, 'Introduction: Pragmatism and Philosophy' in Richard Rorty, *The Consequences of Pragmatism: Essays 1972–1980* (University of Minnesota Press 1982) xiii–xlvii at xix; see also Stanley Fish, *Is There a Text in This Class? The Authority of Interpretive Communitites* (Harvard University Press 1980).

of morality and politics – keep it *empty*.[117] But how can interpretation be judged against an essentially empty form? The challenge here comes in terms of singularity and temporality. In Lyotard's piercing view, every instant of acting 'formulates the rules that will have been done'. 'Work and text', he writes, 'have the characters of an *event*... they always come too late for their author, or what amounts to the same thing, their being put into work, their realisation (*mise en oeuvre*) always begin too soon. *Post modern* would have to be understood according to the paradox of the future (*post*) anterior (*modo*).'[118] Each interpretative event falls back onto itself, a singular event in an ever-moving present.

ILP will have to develop an account of how to speak of correct interpretations according to the law without reaching out to false beliefs about the ability of interpreters to deduce true meanings from the text, from the context, from the text's true purpose or from the parties' real intentions. The stability of legal interpretation does not flow from any foundation in the law itself. And yet, interpretative communities still have the capacity to scrutinise interpretations and they tie the interpreter to the law. The paradox of judging interpretations against rules that such interpretations themselves produce resolves in practice.[119] In this sense, positivism needs to shift from a vertical understanding of interpretation, i.e. one that is tied to deep-structures underlying the surface of the law, to a horizontal understanding focused on the semantic struggle for the law on the terrain of the law.[120]

It matters what interpreters 'can get away with' within the community of interpreters. The question could thus be rephrased: 'what makes an interpretation acceptable?'[121] On such an account, the struggle for the law is also a political struggle where actors seek to exercise semantic authority by establishing their own statements about the law as reference points for later legal discourse.[122] The answer to the question of what amounts to a right interpretation will have to be gleaned from the interpretative

[117] Jochen von Bernstorff, *The Public International Law Theory of Hans Kelsen: Believing in Universal Law* (Cambridge University Press 2010) 271.

[118] Lyotard, n. 47 at 81; cf. Fleur Johns, Richard Joyce, Sundhya Pahuja (eds), *Events: The Force of International Law* (Routledge 2011).

[119] Systems theory has made that argument powerfully for some time, Niklas Luhmann, *Law as a Social System* (Oxford University Press 2004) 125–128.

[120] Ralph Christensen, Hans Kudlich, *Gesetzesbindung: Vom vertikalen zum horizontalen Verständnis* (Duncker & Humblot 2008).

[121] See Fish, n. 116 at 338–355.

[122] Venzke, n. 38 at 62–64 and 221 (on the concept of semantic authority).

practice itself. Without speculating about the motives or mindsets of any interpreter who makes legal claims, it is safe to assume that they are overall manifold and often of an instrumental kind. Does that threaten the autonomy of the law? It does not seem to do so as long as making legal arguments that testify to the autonomy of the law counts as the main asset contributing to an actor's semantic authority.

PART II

Relating international legal positivism

8

International legal positivism and modern natural law

PATRICK CAPPS*

1 Introduction

Hart writes in *The Concept of Law* that:

> The absence of ... institutions [such as a legislature, court 'with compulsory jurisdiction', and 'a system of centrally organized sanctions'] means that the rules for states resemble that simple form of social structure, consisting only of primary rules of obligation, which, when we find it among societies of individuals, we are accustomed to contrast with a developed legal system.[1]

International law is, then, a primitive order – a 'simple regime ... of customary law' – which lacks secondary rules of change, adjudication and recognition.[2] The lack of a Rule of Recognition indicates that there is no systematic way to specify 'the "sources" of law'[3] that would, in turn, allow the identification of international legal rules by relevant officials (for example, international lawyers) and subjects (for example, state officials) alike. However, international law is not 'positive international morality', as Austin puts it, but instead is similar to the 'central case' of legality.[4]

For Hart, this similarity is best understood as indicating that international law is a 'peripheral' case of law, in that it contains some characteristics of the 'central case' of legality, but not others, such as a secondary

* Thanks to the editors of this volume as well as Stuart Toddington and Julian Rivers for comments on earlier drafts of this chapter.

[1] HLA Hart, *The Concept of Law* (2nd edn Oxford University Press 1994) 214.

[2] Hart, n. 1 at 214. [3] Hart, n. 1 at 214.

[4] HLA Hart, 'Problems of the Philosophy of Law' in HLA Hart, *Essays in Jurisprudence and Philosophy* (Oxford University Press 1983) 88–119 at 89; Hart, n. 1 at 79; John M. Finnis, 'Grounds of Law and Legal Theory: A Response' 13 *Legal Theory* (2007) 315–344 at 316; Ronald Dworkin, 'A New Philosophy for International Law' 41 *Philosophy and Public Affairs* (2013) 2–30 at 2.

Rule of Recognition. To put it in Finnis' language, it is a 'watered down' case of legality.[5] Even for international lawyers inspired by Hart, this view is largely discredited empirically.[6] Thus, (the practice we familiarly refer to as) international law now exhibits a fairly clear Rule of Recognition. On this account, international lawyers and state officials have a *duty* to use this Rule of Recognition to distinguish and apply legal rules, and not to apply other social rules operating on the international plane in normal circumstances.

As a matter of legal philosophy, there are some interesting debates to be had about Hart's claims concerning putative 'peripheral cases' of law, such as international law or unjust laws, and what they tell us about the epistemic status of the union of primary and secondary rules. A detailed discussion of this issue is best reserved for another work, but a short summary of my general point about Hart's claim is necessary to proceed. Hart regards his central case as a tracing of the analogies between familiar, or paradigm, cases of law. Hart's concept of law is drawn from paradigm cases of law as understood by ordinary language users.[7] As Stavropoulos states, the resulting concept of law 'cannot transcend actual usage',[8] but it is an attempt to discover the 'rationale behind a word's extension'.[9] His project is to establish '*those* features of law [that] are . . . simply the least controversial sorts of statement that can be made about paradigm legal systems'.[10]

Hart's central case is to be understood as being both looser and more malleable than a strict definition such as that found in Austin's 'criterial semantics'. Thus, 'the diverse range of cases of which the word "law" is used are not linked by . . . simple uniformity, but by less direct relations – often of analogy of either form or content – to a central case'.[11] So, when Hart refers to the union of primary and secondary rules as the *necessary*

[5] John M. Finnis, *Natural Law and Natural Rights* (Oxford University Press 1980) 11. The phrase 'peripheral case' is used in distinction to 'central case' in the Aristotelian scholarship upon which this jurisprudential debate is rooted. For a discussion, see William Fortenbaugh, 'Aristotle's Analysis of Friendship: Function and Analogy, Resemblance, and Focal Meaning' 20 *Phronesis* (1974) 51–62.

[6] Even in Hart's time, his understanding of international law was crude. See Benedict Kingsbury, 'The Concept of "Law" in Global Administrative Law' 20 *EJIL* (2009) 23–57 at 28 (fn. 15).

[7] Timothy Endicott, 'Herbert Hart and the Semantic Sting' in Jules Coleman (ed.), *Hart's Postscript: Essays on the Postscript to* The Concept of Law (Oxford University Press 2001) 39–58 at 41–47.

[8] Nicos Stavropoulos, 'Hart's Semantics' in Jules L. Coleman (ed.), *Hart's Postscript: Essays on the Postscript to* The Concept of Law (Oxford University Press 2001) 59–98 at 80.

[9] Stavropoulos, n. 8 at 81. [10] Endicott, n. 7 at 47. [11] Hart, n. 1 at 81.

and *sufficient* conditions for the existence of a legal order, this is a clarification, simplification or rationalisation of the conceptual distinctions that are implied by, and underpin, ordinary language usage.[12] Hart's claims are both *drawn from*, and *defeasible* against, ordinary language-use and the conceptual distinctions found within it. Therefore, his central case is insecure on account of the malleability of language, the existence of peripheral cases of law and the 'complex and multiple relations among instances of law'.[13]

The problem Hart must face is that if his central case of law is as epistemically mundane as he claims it to be, then it must be questionable or revisable given the existence of cases of law that do not conform to his central case. Indeed, sociological jurisprudence has shown us that there are, in fact, many rule systems which perform functions generally associated with law, but which do not straightforwardly or obviously conform to Hart's central case. International law is often considered to be the leading example. Hart's position is that to say that international law is a form of law is to commit a linguistic error. A linguistic error arises when the word 'law' is used to refer to social practices that do not fall, or do not fall fully, within the extension of his central case of law. But if Hart's central case is defeasible against ordinary usage, as was suggested above, then surely it is *as appropriate* to modify the central case of law as it is to declare unorthodox usage as linguistic error. Why should Hart not conclude that in fact a secondary Rule of Recognition is not required for the existence of legality given cases of law such as international law?

The answer to this question is that Hart's conceptual analysis must be more ambitious than has just been described with regard to the epistemic significance of his central case. Uncontroversially, Stavropoulos claims that, for Hart, there are a set of judgments and claims about law 'on which most agree' and that these are 'the applications [of the word law] most are disposed to make'.[14] Hart's central case is not defeasible against ordinary language. Rather, it is based upon paradigm cases which are 'secure from discounting' and linguistic or conceptual errors are determined with reference to it. But Hart is not now just tidying up language. Rather, he is introducing a central case of law by which we *judge* familiar cases *qua* cases of legality. He concludes, as has been just set out, that it is correct to refer to unjust laws as laws, but it is an error to refer to international

[12] Stavropoulos, n. 8 at 66.
[13] Stavropoulos, n. 8 at 66.
[14] Stavropoulos, n. 8 at 75.

law as law. However, in Hart's own words, 'no other social rules are so close to municipal law as those of international law'.[15]

Once this step is made, though, Hart's concept of law becomes disconnected from ordinary usage and paradigm cases. Instead, he is making a judgment about our usage and cases. For his position not to merely be a subjective one which is vulnerable to the criticisms of critical legal scholarship, he must offer an explanation, or a *rationale*, as to why sometimes our intuitions about law are correct, and when they are false, about when we get it right about the nature of legality, and when we get it wrong. Put the other way around, he cannot now revert to ordinary language to vindicate his central case because he is selecting from those usages and cases those that are important, and distinguishing them from those that are peripheral.

Hart perhaps recognises this point when he changes methodological tack in Chapter 5 of *The Concept of Law*. Here, he refers to the inefficiencies of a system of primary rules. For those subject to a system of primary rules alone, the content of the body of primary legal rules is up for grabs, and it is unclear what the law requires of them. Thus, the Rule of Recognition is able to specify clearly to officials and subjects alike the body of rules which are to be regarded as having the character of law, and this permits or enhances social coordination. If a legal order's function is to effectively or efficiently coordinate human conduct, then we can explain how a secondary Rule of Recognition, specifying the sources of law, is prima facie instrumentally rational. Hart offers a *reason* why legal subjects and officials *value* a Rule of Recognition, and this reason is that the rule efficiently serves the *value* of legality. That is, the Rule of Recognition is not merely significant because it somehow resonates with our intuitions, but rather because it performs an important function within any legal order. That is, it allows the distinction to be made between those social rules that are law, and those that are not. Thus, citizens *qua* practical reasoners are able to cognise the obligations which are placed on them as a matter of law, and they are given a prima facie reason for compliance (that is, law serves an important social goal: coordinating human activity). Thus, Hart provides a rationale for his central case of legality. If international law lacks a Rule of Recognition, then it is *defective* as a system of law given its function. Unjust legal orders, which have a Rule of Recognition, are not defective, even though they may be deplorable in other ways, and this is why, for Hart, they fall within the central case of legality.

15 Hart, n. 1 at 237.

Hart, in his Postscript to *The Concept of Law*, has argued that this is not an appropriate way to see his legal theory,[16] even though it seems difficult to substantiate Hart's more ambitious epistemology without taking his claims about the value or function of law very seriously. And if this is the case, we might remark that Hart looks like a modern version of earlier (substantive, political or normative) legal positivists[17] (such as Hobbes, Bentham[18] and arguably Kant[19]). This tradition of legal positivism is given expression by several influential and important versions of international legal positivism. These normative forms of international legal positivism are considered in this chapter, and I do not consider neo-Kelsenian forms of international legal positivism here.[20] My aim is to show that normative international legal positivism is unsustainable on its own terms and must collapse into a form of natural law theory.

2 Legal autonomy and international legal positivism

Jörg Kammerhofer and Jean d'Aspremont explain in the introduction to this book that there are classical and post-modern variants of international legal positivism. The classical variant, adopted by Lassa Oppenheim and Prosper Weil among others, will be familiar: states, through their consent, create valid international legal norms. The post-modern variant does not prejudge the structure and form of international legality in the way the classical variant does. Instead, it offers a more sophisticated and nuanced account of legal validity that can incorporate non-consensual and even constitutional norms. They partially reject the substantive institutional core – rooted in consent – that lies at the heart of the classical variant on the grounds that it is too blunt and empirically insensitive. Post-modern international lawyers influenced by Hart, such as d'Aspremont and Kingsbury, argue that international law is identified by reference to

16 Hart, n. 1 at 250.

17 Jeremy Waldron, 'Normative (or Ethical) Positivism' in Jules L. Coleman (ed.), *Hart's Postscript: Essays on the Postscript to* The Concept of Law (Oxford University Press 2001) 411–433.

18 Gerald J. Postema, *Bentham and the Common Law Tradition* (Clarendon Press 1989).

19 Jeremy Waldron, 'Kant's Legal Positivism' 109 *Harvard Law Review* (1996) 1535–1566; Thomas Pogge, 'Is Kant's *Rechtslehre* a "Comprehensive Liberalism"' in Mark Timmons (ed.), *Kant's* Metaphysics of Morals: *Interpretative Essays* (Oxford University Press 2002) 133–158.

20 See Jörg Kammerhofer, *Uncertainty in International Law: A Kelsenian Perspective* (Routledge 2011).

an underlying Rule of Recognition that may incorporate, in part, state consent as a source of international legality.

Post-modern international legal positivism shares at least four similarities with its predecessor. First, both regard international law as being 'posited by human creation' such as the consent of states, or official actions in accordance with a Rule of Recognition. Second, they both accept that law need not be just in order to be law. This is the separation thesis. Third, they often accept moral relativism or pluralism. Put negatively, they are sceptical of the natural lawyers' claim that international law should be 'informed by immutable and absolute global values'[21] or a 'primal commitment to equal concern and respect in relation to every human individual'.[22]

The fourth similarity, which concerns the claims of both forms of international legal positivism regarding function and legitimacy, often arises from their moral relativism or pluralism. One version of this argument is that there is moral diversity as a matter of fact. This fact is part of an argument which leads to the conclusion that international law should provide a system of regulation which *functions* to allow states, groups, ethnicities or regions, which hold different moral positions, to peacefully inter-relate, cooperate and coexist.

If this is the function of international law, then it makes sense for international legal rules to be easily identified through state consent in the classical variant of international legal positivism. This is because an isolated domain of legal norms, each of which is valid due to state consent, helps to establish the conditions by which states can cooperate and coexist and through which peace is maintained.[23] The same argument about function appears in the post-modern variant in that the Rule of Recognition is argued to provide a degree of stability in international relations by allowing states to distinguish law from non-legal standards.

Both variants of international legal positivism also share an account of the legitimacy of international law. Legitimacy is attached to international legal norms because they are settlements over contested issues

[21] Kingsbury, n. 6 at 28. [22] Kingsbury, n. 6 at 28.

[23] Dworkin, n. 4 at 10 writes: '[the consent based theory of international law] also resonates with a very popular conception of political legitimacy: that coercive dominion can be justified only by the unanimous consent of those subject to that dominion'. The obvious problem here is that the state is seen as a monadic agent – and this legitimacy claim does not take into account the grounds upon which state decision-making takes place – and whether this, in itself, passes tests of legitimacy (against, e.g. human rights or democratic standards).

between a set of morally diverse states (as well as other international actors). By resolving these points of contestation and establishing the conditions by which cooperation is possible, important normative goals are realised. In fact, these goals are held to be so important that states will treat international legal norms as being legitimate and pre-emptive, thus precluding action on conflicting non-legal norms which have a different substantive content. For classical international legal positivism, a further claim to legitimacy is that by rooting international law in state consent, the *moral autonomy* of states is respected given the diverse interests expressed through their governments. For post-modern international legal positivism, fidelity to the Rule of Recognition by legal officials is the basis (in part, at least) of international law's legitimacy claim: that is, international lawyers *normally only* apply international legal norms, and do not do so vis-à-vis extraneous (for example, moral) norms.

2.1 Legal autonomy

These ideas of function and legitimacy within international legal positivism map directly onto a set of claims that have been called the 'Autonomy Thesis' by Gerald Postema.[24] The core idea here is that it is only if law is isolated from other forms of practical reasoning (for example, morality) can it achieve 'its proximate aim and defining task [which] is to supply a framework of practical reasoning designed to unify public political judgment and co-ordinate social interaction'.[25] In doing so, it achieves its 'focal purpose'[26] that is 'to help us solve problems of social co-operation'.[27] By '[s]implifying and focusing our practical reasoning, law mediates between our conflicting interests and our ultimate, often contested, values and principles, on the one hand, and our concrete decisions and actions, on the other'.[28] Instrumentally, this is achieved by '*displacing* or focussing practical reasoning onto a limited domain

[24] Gerald J. Postema, 'Law's Autonomy and Public Practical Reason' in Robert George (ed.), *The Autonomy of Law: Essays on Legal Positivism* (Clarendon Press 1996) 79–118. By advocating a rationale for function and legitimacy, both classical and post-modern variants of international legal positivism appear to be distinguishable from legal positivism in general jurisprudence. However, this conclusion is premature. First, both variants have strong connections to normative (substantive, ethical or political) legal positivists such as Hobbes and Bentham (Postema, n. 18; David Dyzenhaus, Thomas Poole (eds), *Hobbes and the Law* (Cambridge University Press 2012) 186–209). Second, it was argued above that Hart must provide a rationale for his analytical legal positivism, and claims on the basis of function and legitimacy are perhaps the strongest candidates for it.

[25] Postema, n. 24 at 80.

[26] Finnis, n. 5 at 3–19 (ch. 1).

[27] Postema, n. 24 at 91.

[28] Postema, n. 24 at 91.

of publicly accessible norms, and *isolating* that reasoning from the conflicting interests, principles, and values that stand as obstacles to social co-operation'.[29] Here, then, is the isolation strategy which lies at the heart of the Autonomy Thesis which requires a *separation* of legal norms from the moral (and other) judgments each of us makes about how we are to act. By doing so, law allows us to cooperate effectively. For Postema, there are three interlocking and essential features that describe aspects of this isolation strategy at the heart of the Autonomy Thesis:

- *Limited domain thesis.* For the Autonomy Thesis, law 'defines a limited domain of practical reasons or norms for use by officials and citizens alike'.[30] There is a set of norms or reasons that are distinctively legal in distinction to other sorts of reasons or norms.
- *Pre-emption thesis.* This thesis 'offers an account of how the introduction of law into the practical reasoning of individual agents *alters* it'.[31] By claiming that law is pre-emptive, Postema means the following: '[l]egal norms not only provide rational agents with positive (first-order) reasons to act in certain ways, but they also provide them with second-order reasons for *not acting* on certain *other* reasons',[32] where these other reasons are ones which fall outside the limited domain of law. These second-order reasons do not outweigh those reasons outside the limited domain. Rather, they 'preclude acting for other reasons'.[33] The pre-emptive reasons offered by law, then, 'provide grounds for vindication or legitimation (to some degree) of actions taken in accord with them . . . it *alters* our framework of practical reasoning in a material way'.[34]
- *Sources thesis.* This means that the norms located within law's limited domain are ascertainable only by reference to social fact (primarily, enactment by a competent legal actor in accordance with conventional norms) and not with regard to moral argument. So, the boundaries of the limited domain are not 'defined substantively – that is, in terms of the content or importance or soundness of norms or reasons – but rather by "content independent" criteria'.[35] For legal positivists, this is traditionally the will of a sovereign, or a formal rule such as the Rule of Recognition.

[29] Postema, n. 24 at 91. [30] Postema, n. 24 at 82. [31] Postema, n. 24 at 83.
[32] Postema, n. 24 at 85. [33] Postema, n. 24 at 82. [34] Postema, n. 24 at 83.
[35] Postema, n. 24 at 83.

For the Autonomy Thesis, law must be modelled on these three theses if it is to be able to achieve its function, which is variously understood in terms of conflict resolution, the stabilisation of social relations or expectations and the achievement of social order. This means–ends relationship follows for a number of reasons. One is that if the austerity of the limited domain thesis or sources thesis is violated, the content of law would become ambiguous. It does not provide clear standards which can guide an individual's actions. Similarly, if law did not attain a pre-emptive status, individuals might act on their subjective reasons rather than specifically legal reasons. As a result, those regarding the law as pre-emptive could not predict how others would act. It would not then serve its purpose of stabilising people's expectations as to how others will probably act. Therefore, it is plausible to hold that if these three features of the Autonomy Thesis are not adopted, the end to which a legal order is committed would be frustrated. Here are four classical and post-modern international legal positivists who have adopted a version of the Autonomy Thesis.

2.2 Lassa Oppenheim

Kingsbury, in the leading analysis of his work, tells us that Oppenheim's 'legal positivism was normatively justified as being the best conception of law for the realization of higher normative goals relating to peace, order, certain forms of justice, and the legal control of violence'.[36] So, to serve these 'certain ends outside itself',[37] international law should adopt certain positivist institutional characteristics. These characteristics constitute 'a minimal architecture necessary to an international order'[38] which fleshes out into (i) the principle of sovereign equality and (ii) consent as the source of international legal obligation. Oppenheim considers that international law must adopt positivism in order to achieve the ends of global order.

The specific features of the Autonomy Thesis can be found in Oppenheim's position. That Oppenheim adopts the limited domain thesis is made clear by Kingsbury when he writes that for Oppenheim, the 'need for authoritative articulation of international legal rules necessitated building

36 Benedict Kingsbury, 'Legal Positivism as Normative Politics: International Society, Balance of Power and Lassa Oppenheim's Positive International Law' 13 *EJIL* (2002) 401–436 at 402–403.

37 Lassa Oppenheim, 'The Science of International Law: Its Task and Method' 2 *AJIL* (1908) 313–356 at 314.

38 Kingsbury, n. 36 at 407.

institutions capable of determining a legal rule even where there existed disagreement about the relevant principles of justice'.[39] This requires a prototype pre-emptive thesis; Kingsbury argues that for Oppenheim 'judges must decide according to the law, not on extraneous moral or political grounds'.[40] This is well put by Oppenheim when he writes 'our science will not succeed . . . unless all authors . . . make an effort to keep in the background their individual ideas concerning politics, morality, humanity and justice'.[41] It also requires the sources thesis:

> [I]f Rule X met a relatively stringent sources test – it satisfied the requirements for custom binding the states concerned, or was embodied in a binding and applicable treaty – it was a rule of international law, and if it did not meet these requirements, it was not.[42]

Without this separation, the function of international law will be frustrated:

> How is it possible to offer a body of firm, distinct, and clear-cut rules of law, if rules of morality and of religion, if political aspirations and chimerical schemes for a better future, are constantly mixed up with what is really law?[43]

The attention to factual and non-evaluative criteria for determining legal validity is clear. Therefore, international law is law not because it passes a test of reasonableness or rationality, rather it has a social source that is found in the consent of states.

2.3 Prosper Weil

Prosper Weil claims that international law is a system of norms that is functionally orientated towards the twin ends of cooperation and coexistence.[44] Weil's classical positivistic conception of international law centres on three features: voluntarism or consent, moral and political neutrality, and positivism (which for him means *lex lata* rather than *lex*

[39] Kingsbury, n. 36 at 424. [40] Kingsbury, n. 36 at 426.

[41] Kingsbury, n. 36 at 427. See also Oppenheim, n. 37 at 355.

[42] Kingsbury, n. 36 at 433. See also Oppenheim, n. 37 at 334.

[43] Oppenheim, n. 37 at 327.

[44] Prosper Weil, 'Towards Relative Normativity in International Law?' 77 *AJIL* (1983) 413–442; John Tasioulas, 'In Defence of Relative Normativity: Communitarian Values and the Nicaragua Case' 16 *Oxford Journal of Legal Studies* (1996) 85–128; Ulrich Fastenrath, 'Relative Normativity in International Law' 4 *EJIL* (1993) 305–340; Jason Beckett, 'Behind Relative Normativity: Rules and Process as Prerequisites of Law' 12 *EJIL* (2001) 627–650.

ferenda). By adopting these features, it is able to achieve the ends or function of international law. These three features reflect the Autonomy Thesis. So, it can be said that international law should be based upon a limited domain of legal rules that are generated via state consent. This is a non-evaluative, 'content-independent' and social source of law. It also requires the exclusion of substantive moral tests and *lex ferenda*. Moreover, the advent of norms of *ius cogens* and obligations *erga omnes* undermines the efficiency of international law because it blurs the 'normativity threshold'.[45] This means that it introduces a substantive moral test of legal validity that can 'destabilize the whole international normative system and turn it into an instrument that can no longer serve its purpose'.[46] This implies that states should not act upon such norms when they conflict with those legal obligations which are generated by state consent. This can be interpreted as a version of the pre-emptive thesis. By adopting this concept of international law, state X is unable to claim that a norm that it had consented to is not authoritative because it considers the norm substantively unjust. State Y, then, can have a plausible expectation that state X will comply with its obligations, thus rendering international relations relatively stable. In this sense, both state consent, and the rational interests states have in a shared system of coordination, ground the legitimacy, and pre-emptive status, of the international legal order.

2.4 Jean d'Aspremont

Jean d'Aspremont defends a Hartian concept of international law, but rejects the claims about international law made by Hart which were considered in the introduction to this chapter. To explain, Hart claims that when faced with questions about whether international law is a form of law, they should be answered, in part, by considering whether it serves 'any practical . . . aim' to do so.[47] A concept of law serves a practical aim if it operates in 'the instruction or assistance of lawyers concerned primarily with the outcome of litigation or court proceedings'.[48] By implication, legal officials should not straightforwardly treat international legal norms as law because the international legal order lacks a Rule of Recognition which can be accepted by such international lawyers and state officials. It is not straightforwardly law in this practical sense.

[45] Weil, n. 44 at 415. [46] Weil, n. 44 at 423.
[47] Hart, n. 1 at 214. [48] Hart, n. 4 at 90.

Hart's claim, about which we ought rightly to be sceptical, is rejected by Jean d'Aspremont. For d'Aspremont, there are sources of law in the international legal order which are considerably more complex than those supposed by classical international legal positivism. If there are such rules (which jointly form a rule (or rules) of recognition), then the demarcation between international law and other international rules (international morality, soft law) becomes a relevant practical issue for international lawyers and state officials. That is, the Rule of Recognition assists these groups of lawyers and officials when determining the legal rules that apply and are legally obligatory when a dispute arises under international law.

D'Aspremont wants to defend a normative understanding of the *value* of the Rule of Recognition. It is in this specific sense that his approach is similar to that of Weil and Oppenheim and post-modern international legal positivists in that all defend the *virtues* of the isolation of international law within a limited domain of norms. Reminiscent of the tone, if not the substance, of Weil's work, d'Aspremont defends the formalisation of law, and criticises the deformalising tendencies in both international legal scholarship and practice. Formalism is understood to refer to the idea that a rule that corresponds to predefined formal standards of legality – that is a Rule of Recognition – is a legal rule. His formalism, then, is closer to normative legal positivism, and does not hark back to the delusions of scientific juridical method defended by, for example, Langdell.[49]

In Postema's language, d'Aspremont is making a case for the virtues of a limited domain of international legal norms with clear sources of law. There are three virtues: (i) put negatively, if international law becomes less formal, it becomes less capable of subjecting human conduct to the governance of rules. He writes:

> [I]n the absence of . . . elementary formal standards of identification . . . actors are not able to anticipate – and thus adapt to – the effects (or lack thereof) produced by the rule in question [where] the rule that cannot be clearly ascertained will fall short of generating any change in the behaviour of its addressees.[50]

There is a sense here that legal subjects should be treated by international law as agents who are capable of orientating the action to legal

[49] Neil Duxbury, *Patterns of American Jurisprudence* (Oxford University Press 1997) 9–64 (ch. 1).

[50] Jean d'Aspremont, *Formalism and the Sources of International Law: A Theory of the Ascertainment of Legal Rules* (Oxford University Press 2011) 30.

norms rather than objects to which power is exerted over.[51] However, his point is also a logical one: if a legal subject is not clear what the law is or requires, then it simply cannot act in accordance with it. (ii) The Rule of Recognition promotes, inter alia, the goals of 'predictability in judicial decisions',[52] 'legal certainty',[53] 'order and peace'[54] and 'self-government and individual freedom'.[55] Functionally, in a way that is identical to the Autonomy Thesis, international law is concerned with settling disputes over what states, and other international actors, should do, by making concrete judgments over matters that are generally contested. (iii) D'Aspremont argues that without formalism, 'international law would fail to realize most of the possible goals ascribed to it and would be stripped of authority, legitimacy and efficacy.'[56] He seems to be arguing here that formalism is instrumentally valuable because it is a means to a range of plausible ends to which international law is oriented. It is on this ground that international law has legitimacy, and is thus able effectively to coordinate international relations. This may be his position when he writes that unless international law rests 'on a minimum consensus over some elementary formal standardization', its rules cannot 'remain normative.'[57] The claim is that formalisation of international law contributes to claims that it is pre-emptive in the sense that this characteristic allows international legal norms to offer exclusionary reasons for action. The isolation strategy and its component parts, which jointly form the Autonomy Thesis, are present in d'Aspremont's work.

2.5 Benedict Kingsbury

Kingsbury argues that the classical vision of international law – rooted in states and their consent – no longer reflects the realities of regulation beyond the state. Instead, we see a constellation of institutions that

[51] On this, see Lon L. Fuller, *The Morality of Law* (Yale University Press 1964) 162–163.

[52] D'Aspremont, n. 50 at 143. [53] D'Aspremont, n. 50 at 143.

[54] D'Aspremont, n. 50 at 143–144. [55] D'Aspremont, n. 50 at 144.

[56] D'Aspremont, n. 50 at 145.

[57] D'Aspremont, n. 50 at 30. These claims about the value of formalism do not sit easily with d'Aspremont's later claim that the identification of international law is a purely factual matter (d'Aspremont, n. 50 at 216). I will make no comment on this here, because I want to attack those international legal positivists who adopt the Autonomy Thesis, except to remark that a similar point has been made about Hart's apparent confusion about the character of the Rule of Recognition as a valid norm. See Deryck Beyleveld and Roger Brownsword, 'Normative Positivism: The Mirage of the Middle-Way' 9 *Oxford Journal of Legal Studies* (1989) 463–512.

collectively form a decentralised and unsystematic form of global governance called global administrative law. These institutions (ranging from international organisations, such as the United Nations and its agencies, to transnational institutions such as the International Organization for Standardization and private standard-setting agencies, such as GlobalGAP,[58] to agencies and courts within states) form a somewhat unsystematic, 'decentralised' and 'variegated'[59] network of institutions that have juridical and quasi-juridical status and roles, and which have between them complex formal and informal inter-relations. Each institution has varying levels of integration within global administrative law, and makes different sorts of claims to authority (for example, some claim political or legal authority, others epistemic authority). There is empirical evidence to suggest that shared 'administrative law-type principles and practices' are emerging between these institutions.[60]

Kingsbury adopts a version of Hart's concept of law to interpret the variegated network of institutions that comprise global administrative law in both a conceptual and normative sense. It is the case that many of the institutions that comprise global administrative law do not intuitively seem like legal institutions. Conceptually, then, Kingsbury's concept of law requires a judgment to be made about the legal character of these institutions. That is, legal science is able to apprehend its object of enquiry (that is, global administrative *law*) by adopting his Hartian concept of law. His focus, however, is on a normative claim as to why global administrative law should generally take a particular *form* so as to ensure the proper 'channeling, managing, shaping and constraining of public power'[61] and thus distinguished from the exercise of bare power.

The institutional form that Kingsbury considers to be central to legality is a form of 'extended positivism'. At first, he adopts Hart's concept of law. Thus, relevant officials accept as a guide to their conduct a Rule of Recognition that determines for them a limited domain of legal norms. For global administrative law there is no one Rule of Recognition, but a multitude for individual or groups of institutions. There may be 'different rules of recognition within different social-institutional-sectoral groupings in specific practice areas of global administrative law', and

[58] GlobalGAP is a private sector body that sets voluntary standards for the safety certification of agricultural production processes. Its membership is dominated by large supermarket chains. It is intended to improve standards for consumers. However, such standards are *adopted* by retailers, and *demanded* of suppliers as they have some important reputational, legal, technical and financial advantages for the former.

[59] Kingsbury, n. 6 at 25. [60] Kingsbury, n. 6 at 25. [61] Kingsbury, n. 6 at 32.

global administrative law is 'shaped by treaties and fundamental customary international law rules'.[62] Global administrative law cannot then be said to be a single legal order and it is not unified. One of the conditions by which legitimate authority may emerge in global administrative law is if those legal officials *only* apply those norms found in the limited domain. That is, there is a sense that those officials are playing by the rules, and as a result those subject to those rules may be expected to do the same. This is a very thin conception of procedural fairness in law-creation and application, but it is from this basis that Kingsbury argues that there are some good reasons for treating global administrative laws as legitimate and thus able to pre-empt other non-legal norms. In summary, if global administrative law is to be treated as pre-emptive by those subject to it, it must clearly distinguish itself from other sorts of norms and establish a limited domain governed by a Rule of Recognition. This is another version of the Autonomy Thesis.

To this version of the Autonomy Thesis, Kingsbury adds a series of principles of 'publicness'.[63] Publicness comprises five principles familiar to administrative lawyers: (i) the principle of legality (he writes: '[o]ne major function of public law is the channelling and organizing of power . . . which can mean actors within the power system are constrained to act in accordance with the rules of the system');[64] (ii) the principle of rationality; (iii) the principle of proportionality; (iv) rule of law; and (v) human rights. These principles operate with regard to constitutive administrative law (i.e. setting out legal powers), substantive administrative law (i.e. setting of the content of norms that will be enforced) and procedural administrative law (i.e. setting out ways in which legal powers can be lawfully exercised and including arrangements for review, transparency or reason-giving).[65]

Kingsbury's step here seems to take him very close to, and perhaps even beyond, Fuller's 'procedural' natural law theory,[66] and Brunnée's and Toope's application of it to international law.[67] However, Kingsbury

[62] Kingsbury, n. 6 at 30 and 29, respectively.

[63] Kingsbury, n. 6 at 29. [64] Kingsbury, n. 6 at 32.

[65] Kingsbury, n. 22 at 34; David Dyzenhaus, 'Accountability and the Concept of (Global) Administrative Law' in Hugh Corder (ed.), *Global Administrative Law: Innovation and Development* (Clarendon Press 2009) 3–31.

[66] Fuller, n. 51.

[67] Jutta Brunnée, Steven Toope, *Legitimacy and Legality in International Law: An Interactional Account* (Cambridge University Press 2010).

does not consider that he has made this step towards a natural law. He recognises the objection just stated, but then rejects it, arguing:

> [T]he potential alignment with the above-mentioned elements of Hart's concept of law is much closer, if the rule of recognition is understood as including a stipulation that only rules and institutions meeting these publicness requirements immanent in public law (and evidenced through comparative materials) can be regarded as law.[68]

This claim needs further discussion and it is, in itself, insufficient to convince those who are sceptical of Kingsbury's positivist credentials. Below, I suggest that Kingsbury regards the principles of publicness as being *conventional* shared values adopted by modern administrative lawyers, and this is how he attempts to distance his work from natural law theory and its moral foundationalism. This said, the principles of publicness developed by Kingsbury do offer an intriguing solution to a problem with the Autonomy Thesis that I will now set out. For this reason, I will reserve further consideration of these principles until this problem has been made clear.

3 Legal autonomy and public practical reasonableness

While there are important formal differences between the normative international legal positivists just considered, they all accept the Autonomy Thesis. In this section, I offer a *reductio ad absurdum* of the isolation strategy at the heart of the Autonomy Thesis. The claim is that effective coordination of states or other international actors cannot be achieved successfully unless those interpreting and applying global and international laws take sufficient account of principles of practical reasonableness. The principles of practical reasonableness are fundamental and deeply embedded principles of *civil association*, which are given *authentic* expression through legal procedures and rules. They place a duty on each of us to respect the most important interests of those we interact with and as such are moral principles.[69] If this argument follows, the forms of international legal positivism just discussed must either reject their account of

[68] Kingsbury, n. 6 at 30.

[69] There are many attempts to defend and articulate this position. See e.g. Alan Gewirth, *Reason and Morality* (University of Chicago Press 1978); Deryck Beyleveld, *The Dialectical Necessity of Morality: An Analysis and Defense of Alan Gewirth's Argument to the Principle of Generic Consistency* (University of Chicago Press 1991); James Griffin, *On Human Rights* (Oxford University Press 2008).

the function of international law *or* reject the isolation strategy. On the assumption that the functional aspirations of international law are genuinely valuable, and the isolation strategy is only of instrumental value, the isolation strategy should be rejected. Natural law should be rationally preferred to international legal positivism, *given* positivism's account of function, because it rejects the isolation of law, and defends the integration of legal norms with principles of practical reasonableness.[70]

3.1 Institutionalised autonomy

The features of law for the Autonomy Thesis are valuable or justified to the extent that they assist in the resolution of international disputes over contested values, stabilise interactions between states or achieve peace between subjects (states and other global institutions and entities). But this argument proves problematic once it is recognised – which it surely must be – that international legal norms often require interpretation. Once the Autonomy Thesis is considered in its institutional setting, and where international, transnational and state institutions are tasked with working through disagreements over the content of international legal norms, certain difficulties emerge. First, international legal norms underspecify what is to be done in a particular circumstance.[71] The norm cannot be a true algorithm of how legal subjects ought to act in all circumstances to which the norm is connected. If there is more than one possible meaning of a legal norm in a particular circumstance, an interpretation must be made which will specify what we ought to do. This will alter the meaning of the legal norm under consideration. Second, two or more international legal norms may require the subject to undertake different actions in the same circumstances. Canonical formulations of the norm cannot solve these norm-collisions unless a normative hierarchy is specifically written into its formulation. Without this stated normative hierarchy, which we cannot assume exists in relation to all relevant norms, an authoritative interpretation must be made about which norm is to apply. Third, when there is no source-based norm to determine the outcome of a dispute

70 On the main claims of natural law, see Mark Murphy, *Natural Law in Jurisprudence and Politics* (Cambridge University Press 2006) 8–60 (ch. 1); Deryck Beyleveld, Roger Brownsword, *Law as a Moral Judgment* (Sweet & Maxwell 1986) 1–82 (chs 1–2).

71 Amanda Perreau-Saussine, James Bernard Murphy, 'The Character of Customary Law: An Introduction' in Amanda Perreau-Saussine, James Bernard Murphy (eds), *The Nature of Customary Law: Legal, Historical and Philosophical Perspectives* (Cambridge University Press 2007) 1–10 at 5 (discussing an unpublished paper by Onora O'Neill). See also Dworkin, n. 4 at 7.

(i.e. there is a *lacuna*), there is a need to fill in gaps in the limited domain of legal norms.

Each of these three difficulties points towards a system of norm-interpretation as a functionally necessary characteristic of law for the Autonomy Thesis. In the international legal order, this function is (unsystematically) performed by international organisations and courts and through the operation of the law of state responsibility. Within this system of norm interpretation, officials charged with interpreting and applying international law cannot conclusively settle questions concerning its content simply by resorting to the limited domain of norms. Pointing to non-justiciable or political issues cannot rebut this argument. True, there may be some issues over which relevant international legal norms afford discretion to states and other international legal actors (and thus are not strictly speaking *lacunae*). But this use of discretion does not coincide with the three examples given above where there are, in each case, relevant legal norms which may apply to the conduct in question.

3.2 Function

Within general jurisprudence, Postema and Simmonds have separately identified a problem with the Autonomy Thesis once its necessary institutional character is recognised. In support of the Autonomy Thesis, Simmonds writes of the virtue of 'predictability and the requirement that judges should be bound by rules published and ascertainable in advance'[72] that comes from law being isolated from other forms of practical reasoning. It is 'the judge's apparent freedom to tinker with [i.e. interpret] the rules on each occasion that they are applied'[73] which is a problem. This is because:

> [T]he positivist is forced to treat much that would ordinarily be seen as interpretation and application of rules as being an instance of rule-modification . . . the rules seem increasingly loosely related to the occasions when we might seek to rely upon them.[74]

Legal officials, then, have a simple choice: they must remain silent when legal norms are silent, or they must engage in rule-modification and rule-creation through the process of interpretation, gap-filling and balancing

[72] Nigel Simmonds, 'Between Positivism and Idealism' 50 *Cambridge Law Journal* (1991) 308–329 at 310.

[73] Simmonds, n. 72 at 310. [74] Simmonds, n. 72 at 318–319.

the normative requirements of conflicting norms. To do the former means that disputes over controversial matters will not be able to be resolved. This merely replicates the problems which law, for the Autonomy Thesis, is functionally designed to solve. To do the latter means that judges must resort to reasons outside of the limited domain of law when making judgments as to what the law requires. However, if this is the case, then legal norms are not wholly determinative of a dispute, and consequently, law becomes less predictable as soon as it is applied.[75] But the whole point of having a limited domain of law is so that subjects know what the law requires of them. If reasons or norms outside the limited domain are being employed to determine cases, individuals cannot entirely have recourse to the limited domain to ascertain what they are required to do, or the standards of conduct that they might expect from others. That is, they fail as a settlement in matters of disagreement and conflict. Of course, it is likely that over time some convergence in meaning of legal norms, as well as practices to deal with the hierarchy and gaps between norms, will emerge between officials. However, it will still be the case that this process that refined the content of international law relied upon norms outside the limited domain, and these external norms are still required as novel disputes arise moving forwards. Thus, the functional problem remains. D'Aspremont may well dismiss this problem as a 'moderate misunderstanding' in legal word-use.[76] But whether 'moderate' or not, some means is required for resolving these disagreements over what international law requires from its subjects in a way that is principled, for without this, legal subjects will be unsure about what the law requires. The resources for this must be extra-legal normative because if they came from within the limited domain, the problems described above would not have arisen: that is, we are faced with situations where the law has no conclusive answer, and we need the resources to deal with this. This argument applies equally to accounts of international law modelled on the Autonomy Thesis, as it does in general jurisprudence.

[75] Postema argues 'it rests on the recognition that we seek both to *settle* matters that are in dispute and threaten to disable necessary social co-operation and to *settle them justly*, and on the recognition that these aspirations cannot be radically separated' (Postema, n. 24 at 112). Simmonds says: '[m]y object is simply to suggest that, in a chaos of subjectivity, a shared body of rules . . . require shared interpretations, but shared interpretations could not emerge in a chaos of subjectivity. When the legal positivist solution to the problem of co-existence in a world of disagreement seems most *necessary*, it turns out to be *impossible*' (Simmonds, n. 72 at 314).

[76] D'Aspremont, n. 50 at 201.

3.3 Legitimacy

The Autonomy Thesis also fails if legal norms are not just, in the sense that that they do not provide a conclusive practical reason for compliance. Postema tells us that '[t]he isolation strategy seeks to overcome obstacles to social co-operation by influencing *the practical reasoning* and deliberation of people through issuing authoritative directives with pre-emptive force'.[77] But crucially '[t]hose directives give pre-emptive practical guidance only when people to whom they are addressed *regard* them as pre-emptive and so *accord* them that force in their practical reasoning'.[78] Therefore, in order for law to function according to the rationale of the Autonomy Thesis, it is not simply enough for the law to purport, or for legal officials to claim, that it has legitimate authority. Rather, it must actually be considered legitimate authority from the point of view of legal subjects if it is to regulate their behaviour. Therefore, 'the isolation strategy can work only if legal directives are *widely regarded* as pre-emptive'[79] in the sense of offering second-order reasons for not acting on non-legal reasons which require actions contrary to the content of law.

What reasons might rational agents have for considering the law pre-emptive? For those positivists who support the Autonomy Thesis, the reason accords with their view of the function of law. Postema puts this reason this way: 'it is clear to most people that it is more important that they co-ordinate their interaction around a common scheme . . . even if people are not indifferent among the available arrangements'.[80] So, whatever their subjective view might be about the particular institutional arrangements offered by a legal order, legal subjects realise that it is rationally preferable to have law, and to follow it, than otherwise. The isolation strategy carries with it a claim to legitimacy. This claim, roughly, is that it provides a valuable system by which legal subjects can coordinate, it gives fair warning to subjects of those rules that will be enforced against them, together with an assurance that the officials will 'play by the rules'.

The problem with this claim is that 'it is not clear that according law pre-emptive status is *necessary* in such cases'.[81] Law purports to *offer* persuasive reasons for it being a legitimate authority, but do these reasons necessarily follow for every individual subject to it? Postema thinks that these reasons do not *necessarily* secure the pre-emptive force of law. This is because the reasons offered by the Autonomy Thesis, which are

[77] Postema, n. 24 at 104. [78] Postema, n. 24 at 104. [79] Postema, n. 24 at 104.
[80] Postema, n. 24 at 105. [81] Postema, n. 24 at 105.

ultimately based upon the value to all of a stable system of coordination, are 'hostages to contingent fortune'.[82] That is, if the law is to work, it must be pre-emptive vis-à-vis other reasons for acting. Therefore, the reasons for compliance offered by the Autonomy Thesis must, in principle, require that in some circumstances legal subjects follow what, in a subjective, societal or transcendental sense, might be considered immoral or imprudent rules. This places a serious burden on legal officials offering reasons for compliance based upon the legitimacy-claim at the heart of the isolation strategy. After all, it certainly is prima facie reasonable for a legal subject to do what is morally or prudentially rational rather than comply with bigoted, partial or unjust laws. But the Autonomy Thesis holds that, however much an individual suffers because of bigoted norms, the need to coordinate is a sufficient reason to comply with their immoral or imprudent dictates. If this is not the case, then law cannot be pre-emptive, and thus law functionally fails to coordinate.

If there are losers who suffer systematic prejudice through the enforcement of the norms of a legal order which is formally structured according to the Autonomy Thesis, we may ask whether the value attached to a system of stable cooperation provided by law is sufficient to ground the pre-emptive thesis in all circumstances. Postema argues that there are three reasons why the unjust law is insufficient to ground law's pre-emptive status: first, 'the implementation and enforcement of the law's solutions may appear worse than having no solution at all' for those who suffer unjust norms.[83] This may or may not be the case, but it cannot be ruled out as a rational response to injustice. Second, it becomes increasingly difficult to realise that reasons of coordination are pre-emptive reasons for either the losers or for others: '[t]he moral or political conflict may blind them to opportunities for co-operation still open to them'.[84] Third, others who see the injustice will presume that the law will not be pre-emptive for those who suffer it and may suspect that losers will not follow unjust norms. If others think that the losers will not treat the law as pre-emptive, the reasons for others to follow the law are weakened as they cannot rationally suppose that others will do the same. These are the 'costs' of adopting the isolation strategy.[85]

These costs can be illustrated with reference to a familiar example from international investment law. As has already been stated, the heart of classical international legal positivism is the claim that consent by a

[82] Postema, n. 24 at 105.
[83] Postema, n. 24 at 106.
[84] Postema, n. 24 at 106.
[85] D'Aspremont, n. 50 at 5.

state is a sufficient condition for international law to be valid, for it to possess legitimate authority, and for it to fall within the limited domain of the international legal order. However, it is well known that foreign investment and trade between poor but resource-rich states and foreign companies has been conducted on the basis of grossly unjust treaty agreements. This injustice arises primarily because these treaties do not serve the interests of the local population and the price at which the resources which are the subject of the treaty are sold does not reflect the value of the resources on the open market. These treaty obligations can be distinguished from similar treaties between states where both have more legitimate, and more stable, forms of government, and where the states are less economically or politically unequal. The reason why poor states enter into such treaties is often because of the high levels of corruption of the regime that claims to be competent to enter into bilateral investment treaties on behalf of the poor state. International law regarding foreign investment has traditionally been that when a less corrupt regime follows the corrupt regime, the extant, and often unfair and onerous, treaty obligations remain binding on the state.[86]

Returning to the general argument just made, relatively frequently a state suffering under a bilateral investment treaty may choose to continue to comply with unjust treaties because to do otherwise incurs serious reputational costs and undermines the valuable system of coordination provided by international law. However, history tells us that states do not always accept this reason for compliance with international law: changes of government in the Middle East and Africa provide ample examples of situations where developing states have acted on other, non-legal, reasons, simply because international law which governs them is perceived to be, and is, unjust.[87] Postema's view that 'the implementation and enforcement of the law's solutions may appear worse than having no solution at all' seems an appropriate description of the attitudes of newly formed governments towards extant legal norms, when they attempt to use the natural resources they control for the benefit of the people they govern. This perception of the injustice of these international laws may lead developing states to become wary of these laws as a solution to their disputes and problems, and thus it fails to be a source by which

[86] *Aguilar-Amory and Royal Bank of Canada Claims [Tinoco Arbitration] (Great Britain v. Costa Rica)*, Award of 18 October 1923, 1 RIAA 369.

[87] See e.g. Iran–USCT, *Amoco International Finance Corp. v. Government of the Islamic Republic of Iran et al.*, Award 310–56–3 of 14 July 1987, 15 Iran–USCTR 189.

cooperation between states can be secured. Moreover, if developed states value the stable system of coordination provided by international law, such states also must have a rational interest in fair or just agreements because they are more likely to be complied with. In sum, the injustice of international legal norms threatens the capacity of the international legal order to achieve its purpose of maintaining the conditions by which states can cooperate and coexist peacefully.

3.4 Public practical reasonableness

The function and legitimacy problems just described can be solved by the integration, rather than isolation, of law with a broader set of norms shared by legal subjects that lie beyond the limited domain of international legality. And these norms, let us assume, are *principles of practical reasonableness*: that is, they concern those interests of others of which states should take account when acting. Such principles are moral because they have this other-regarding character.[88] Furthermore, such principles of practical reasonableness are *public* in the sense that they are known to, and shared by, those subject to them.

These principles, the content of which is outlined below, help to solve the function and legitimacy problems just outlined. They ensure that legal subjects know the sorts of reasons those applying international law will resort to when making decisions beyond the limited domain. That is, officials do not apply their own, subjective, moral beliefs when going beyond international law (which are likely to be variable). Instead, they resort to public and shared reasons and norms.[89] States, as well as other subjects of international law, can be aware of the principles interpreters of international law will use when offering reasons for their judgments. Furthermore, these principles legitimise decisions that apply legal norms within, and non-legal norms beyond, the limited domain of international law. By being responsive to, incorporating or integrating such principles, the function of international law can be fulfilled, and the problems just set out avoided. Put another way, if international law is reasonably just, it is more likely to engender compliance and, at least, the presumption that states will consider international legal norms as legitimate and thus pre-emptive, will arise. A stable international legal

[88] Gewirth, n. 69 at 1–21.

[89] This is similar to the argument in: Ronald Dworkin, *Law's Empire* (Harvard University Press 1986) 87–113 (ch. 3).

order is achieved by a strategy of *integration* with wider principles of practical reasonableness rather than a strategy of isolation. How this integration should occur is an important issue for natural lawyers. For present purposes, an example of a solution to this issue will suffice. Alexy argues that these principles are employed by law interpreters to offer reasons to invalidate grossly unjust putative legal norms, and as a general interpretative tool. His approach probably also implies that law-creating systems are procedurally and substantively just.[90] In summary, though, while a clear and publicly ascertainable set of international legal norms is a virtue, this is not sufficient for international law to fulfil its function. International law must also adopt a strategy of integration with principles of practical reasonableness.

The idea of principles of public practical reasonableness needs to be refined, if not specifically defended. Such principles are public (i.e. known and shared) and not private, and they are practically reasonable (i.e. they concern how we should relate to each other morally and how we should be governed by law). At this general level, this idea does not seem dissimilar from Kingsbury's 'enhanced positivism' in which a Rule of Recognition, which incorporates principles of publicness (for example, principles of administrative law and fundamental human rights), is the basis upon which a claim to legitimacy of global institutions is to be defended. These principles may well fill exactly the space left by the criticism of the Autonomy Thesis set out above. However, it is doubtful whether his proposal is best understood as a form of international legal positivism.

It is unambiguous that, by introducing publicness, Kingsbury is making the claim that international or global administrative law cannot exist within a limited domain if it is to achieve the function of 'channelling, managing, shaping and constraining of public power'.[91] To be distinguished from bare power, and to be legitimate, global or international law must incorporate principles of publicity in the constitutive, substantive and procedural aspects of its form. As already suggested, this does not appear to be very different from various natural law accounts of international law (for example, Brunnée and Toope). Kingsbury, however, is convinced that his concept of law remains positivist as set out above. Here are two arguments he appears to use to defend his claim.

90 Robert Alexy, *The Argument from Injustice: A Reply to Legal Positivism* (Oxford University Press 2010).

91 Kingsbury, n. 6 at 32.

The first argument is that there is a distinction to be drawn between the Rule of Recognition (by which global or international law is identified *qua* law) and principles of publicness (which affords legitimacy or 'weight'[92] to those legal norms). Although Kingsbury is not entirely clear at this point, it seems to me that this distinction should be rejected. To do otherwise would be to afford legal validity and pre-emptive status (because they provide a system of coordination) to laws that fail against standards of publicity. Thus, he appears to afford legal validity to putatively *unjust* or *defective* laws. For legal officials within an institution, such norms might have the character of law inter se. But, given the account of the function of law Kingsbury seems to endorse, they can at best be considered *defective* laws in that they do not offer a decisive, pre-emptive reason for compliance.[93] If the arguments advanced in this chapter concerning legitimacy and function follow, it seems that there are strong reasons for restricting our account of global or international law to those norms or institutions that exhibit principles of publicness. That the solution to this functional problem is for international law to be reasonably just implies natural law theory.

The better argument suggested by Kingsbury to support positivism is that principles of publicness are expressions of ideas of what is to count as good administration within a 'common normative practice'.[94] I would suggest here that such principles are *conventional* and rooted in *shared beliefs* rather than 'primal' commitments to universal human values as the natural lawyers would have it. This is entirely consistent with Hart's view of the nature of the Rule of Recognition as a fundamental convention within each legal order. Kingsbury's principles of publicness describe a set of shared beliefs about good administration held by a range of institutions within the global administrative landscape.

Both positivists and natural lawyers may well share the principles of publicness. But the grounds upon which they are considered part of the law are different. For the positivist, such as Kingsbury, such principles are conventional and based upon shared values. For the natural lawyer, principles of publicness are fundamental and deeply embedded principles of *civil association*, which are given *authentic* expression through legal procedures and rules. Put another way, they are rational practical principles that secure for human beings freedom from the physical and ideological domination of powerful groups, and ensure that law remains committed to this end. They cash out into various principles associated

[92] Kingsbury, n. 6 at 31. [93] Murphy, n. 70 at 1. [94] Kingsbury, n. 6 at 30.

with the rule of law and civil rights.[95] That such principles are public, rather than private, points to the idea that they should stand a test of publicity. Kant, Rousseau and Fuller,[96] among others, have argued that if principles are public, they must be able to be accepted as practically reasonable by those subject to them. Private reasons are ones that cannot survive this test because they may only be reasonable for certain individuals (often those seeking to gain from them). Injustice, unfairness and forms of maladministration are often the product of a lack of publicity.

Often, whether one is a positivist or natural lawyer does not matter. The problem emerges for the positivist when there is disagreement or contestation over the validity of the principles of publicness.[97] Hart's apparent claim that legal conventions are incontestable does not seem plausible.[98] If they are not, then the natural lawyer is able to offer a rational defence of such principles. The positivist seems to fall back on a folk theory that is adopted by relevant actors: these principles are generally held to be good ones.[99] The positivist response does not seem to me to offer any convincing reasons for their acceptance at all, but the natural law account may do.

A positivist can reply using the same sort of arguments as the natural lawyer. Thus, the positivist may claim that the generally held principles that most people believe are good can be rationally defended. I am not sure how this differs from the natural law position. A distinction re-emerges

[95] Frederick Neuhouser, 'Freedom, Dependence and the General Will' 102 *Philosophical Review* (1993) 363–395; Patrick Capps, *Human Dignity and the Foundations of International Law* (Hart 2009) 215–242 (ch. 9).

[96] Immanuel Kant, *The Metaphysics of Morals* (Mary Gregor (tr.), Cambridge University Press 1996) 123–140; Amanda Perreau-Saussine, 'Immanuel Kant on International Law' in Samantha Besson, John Tasioulas (eds), *The Philosophy of International Law* (Oxford University Press 2009) 53–78; Patrick Capps, Julian Rivers, 'Kant's Concept of International Law' 16 *Legal Theory* (2010) 229–257; Marcus Willaschek, 'Which Imperatives for Right? On the Non-Prescriptive Character of Juridicial Laws in Kant's Metaphysics of Morals' in Mark Timmons (ed.), *Kant's* Metaphysics of Morals*: Interpretative Essays* (Oxford University Press 2002) 65–87; Jean-Jacques Rousseau, *The Social Contract and Discourses* (G. D. H. Cole (tr.), Dent 1979) 191–193; Kingsbury, n. 6 at 48–50; Lon L. Fuller, 'The Case Against Freedom' in Kenneth Winston (ed.), *The Principles of Social Order: Selected Essays of Lon Fuller* (Hart 2001) 315–330.

[97] See Alexy, n. 90 at 5–8 for a discussion of the points where natural law and legal positivism diverge in judicial practice.

[98] Ronald Dworkin, *Taking Rights Seriously* (Harvard University Press 1978); Jules L. Coleman (ed.), *Hart's Postscript: Essays on the Postscript to* The Concept of Law (Oxford University Press 2001); Ronald Dworkin, 'Hart's Postscript and the Character of Political Philosophy' 24 *Oxford Journal of Legal Studies* (2004) 1–37; and see d'Aspremont, n. 50 at 89.

[99] Stavropoulos, n. 8 at 75.

if the positivist argues that it is possible for global or international law to adopt conventions by which law can be identified as valid, but for which there are no strong reasons for compliance. At this point, we are straight back to the argument made above: this allows the term 'law' to describe norms that are defective in achieving the function of law accepted by normative international legal positivists. Once again, this points to the plausibility of the natural lawyer's argument, even though this begs a defence of the claim that principles of practical reasonableness (which may be captured more or less by Kingsbury's principles of publicness) are fundamental and universal principles of civil association and governance by law.[100]

Some proponents of international legal positivism, and the Autonomy Thesis, seek to defend their position by resorting to the moral relativist's claim that such principles of practical reasonableness do not exist or cannot be morally justified in the way in which natural law thinks they can. This is, in fact, at the heart of the legitimacy claim adopted by Weil and Oppenheim. Thus, the best international lawyers can hope for is to ground international law on the basis of the thin legitimacy claim such as that embedded in the Autonomy Thesis and the isolation strategy. However, this is the wrong conclusion to draw for the following reason. If the moral relativists and pluralists are right, and my arguments about function and legitimacy are correct, the conclusion must be that international law suffers from a 'legitimation crisis'.[101] Principles of public practical reasonableness are *necessary* for international law to be legitimate and thus function, but these are not forthcoming. In a sense, the legitimacy claims of international legal positivism, which are very thin, are being asked to do too much work.

4 Conclusion

The various forms of classical and post-modern international legal positivism set out in this chapter cohere around the Autonomy Thesis. For these positivists, international law is a form of law to the extent that it

[100] This brings into focus a different picture of international legality. For natural lawyers, it is inaccurate to say that international laws are binding because they have been formally validated by a substantive Rule of Recognition as Kingsbury suggests. Instead, they are binding by virtue of a duty for states (or other international law-making institutions, agencies or actors) to come to general agreements on matters of disagreement and moral concern, and which generally inhibit the global maintenance of universal values. For Dworkin, this is alluded to in his 'principle of salience', although we see a similar point made by Hersch Lauterpacht in his 'progressive interpretation' set out in various works in the first half of the twentieth century. See Dworkin, n. 4; Patrick Capps, 'Lauterpacht's Method' 82 *BYBIL* (2011) 248–280.

[101] Jürgen Habermas, *Legitimation Crisis* (Thomas Mccarthy (tr.), Beacon Press 1975).

adopts the isolation strategy, by which the function of law, described by the Autonomy Thesis, can be fulfilled. It was then argued that the isolation strategy, which is at the heart of the Autonomy Thesis, must be rejected if international law is to fulfil its coordinatory role successfully. Instead, we should adopt an integrated version of the Autonomy Thesis, which means that the international legal order should be consistent with underlying principles of public practical reasonableness in its constitutive, substantive and procedural form. These principles are the fundamental moral principles by which human beings can flourish, have independence, and not be dominated by others or by the state institutions that govern them. Working out the full consequences of this position is not for this chapter. Rather, the aim was to show why the good sense – the *rationale* or *value* – of positivism implies the *integration* of international law with what are broader moral concerns, and this is a natural lawyer's position. If one is sympathetic to this argument, one should be sympathetic with Kingsbury's claims about the value of publicness too. Although he might not see it as his position, it is an example of exactly the sort of integration between law and morality which lies at the heart of a natural law account of international legality.

9

International legal positivism and legal realism

D. A. JEREMY TELMAN

1 Introduction

The initial encounter between legal realism and legal positivism in the United States did not go well.[1] During the first half of the twentieth century, legal realism came to dominate the legal academy in the United States. Although they shared many assumptions with legal positivism, legal realists utterly ignored Kelsenian legal positivism, seeing it as a version of the various formalisms that legal realism had rejected. HLA Hart's positivism was largely quarantined in jurisprudence courses far from the core of professional training that is the main mission of law schools in the United States.

But twentieth-century legal realism has itself come to seem rather quaint. Its early practitioners aspired to a social scientific approach, but they lacked the requisite empirical and methodological tools. In the past decade, a new legal realism has emerged, and its practitioners are as a group more philosophically sophisticated and more familiar with empirical social scientific methods than were the original legal realists. Perhaps as an inevitable by-product of globalisation, some US academics have attempted to apply the new legal realism to international law, and since positivism is a far greater force in the academic discourse relating to international law than it is in the domestic context, international law becomes the realm in which a dialogue between the new legal realism and legal positivism becomes both inevitable and necessary.

This chapter is a contribution to that dialogue. It begins with two background sections that describe the initial encounter between legal realism and legal positivism in the US academy and the elements of the new legal realism, including examples of new legal realist approaches to international law. In a third section, this chapter notes that the new

[1] Anthony J. Sebok, *Legal Positivism in American Jurisprudence* (Cambridge University Press 1998) 1–2 (fn. 6).

international legal positivism (NILP) holds out great promise for specifying the nature of international legal norms and the potential limitations on the efficacy of such norms. With its forthright embrace of the inescapability of uncertainty in law, NILP adopts a sceptical position very similar to that of legal realism. However, NILP still requires a New International Legal Realist supplement in order to provide a fuller understanding of the way in which legal norms interact with non-legal factors and to help us describe, predict and analyse the behaviour of actors in international affairs. At the same time, New International Legal Realists can learn from the sceptical attitude towards sources of law developed by the new international legal positivists. The two movements can be symbiotic if brought into closer dialogue. Nonetheless, this section concludes with a dose of pessimism about the capacity of any of the currently available theories of international law to fully assimilate the complexities of both post-modern theory and post-modern global society into a comprehensive theory of international law in the post-modern world.

2 Legal realism and positivism

In the United States, the home of legal realism, the positivist tradition is largely represented through the work of HLA Hart and various responses thereto.[2] The vast majority of American academics, to say nothing of law students and practising attorneys, are unfamiliar with the work of Hans Kelsen, and most of those familiar with it have little good to say about it. This section proceeds in three parts. After a quick review of the basic themes of legal realism, the section addresses the reasons why Hans Kelsen's legal theory found no footing on American soil. Finally, the section will briefly address the very different reception that HLA Hart's positivist legal theory received in the world of legal realism.

2.1 Elements of legal realism

As Brian Leiter has noted, many who write about legal realism reject the notion that there is any core coherence to the movement.[3] The

[2] Sebok treats the legal process school, especially as represented by Herbert Wechsler's 'neutral principles' approach and the originalist movement that followed from it, as a variant of legal positivism. Sebok, n. 1 at 113–216.

[3] Brian Leiter, *Naturalizing Jurisprudence: Essays on American Legal Realism and Naturalism in Legal Philosophy* (Oxford University Press 2007) 16.

movement, if it can be so called, consisted of a diverse group of legal scholars[4] committed to the view that legal decision-making turned on 'something other than, or at least much more than, positive law, legal rules, legal doctrine and legal reasoning as traditionally conceived'. However, there was no consensus as to what that 'something' was.[5]

Nevertheless, intrepid scholars, including Leiter, claim to identify as the twin hallmarks of realism two forms of rule-scepticism: the view that legal rules are a myth because law consists only of the decisions of courts, and the view that statutes and other legislative creations are too indeterminate to constrain judges or govern their decisions.[6] This may be so because individual rules are indeterminate or because multiple rules are available and legal decision-makers are unconstrained in choosing among them.[7] Brian Tamanaha has summarised realist perspectives as committed to the views that: (i) the law is filled with gaps and contradictions and thus is indeterminate; (ii) every legal rule or principle has exceptions and thus precedents can support different results; and (iii) judges decide cases based on their personal preferences and then 'construct the legal analysis to justify the desired outcome'.[8] Brian Leiter reduces realism still further to a 'core claim' about judicial decision-making: 'judges respond primarily to the stimulus of facts'.[9]

2.2 Legal realism and Kelsen's US reception

The US legal academy's rejection of Kelsen's Pure Theory of Law was over-determined. Kelsen's lack of influence in the United States is best understood as a product of four phenomena that relate only tenuously to the substance of Kelsen's theories. They are: (i) legal realism's hostility to anything smacking of formalism; (ii) the general view that positivism was too politically anaemic to stand up to the challenges to the rule of law in the twentieth century; (iii) the incompatibility of Kelsenian and common law approaches to adjudication; and (iv) the nature of US law schools

4 Michael Steven Green, 'Legal Realism as a Theory of Law' 46 *William and Mary Law Review* (2005) 1915–2000 at 1919.

5 Frederick Schauer, 'Legal Realism Untamed' 91 *Texas Law Review* (2013) 749–780 at 756.

6 Green, n. 4 at 1917–1918.

7 Schauer, n. 5 at 750 (fn. 2).

8 Brian Z. Tamanaha, *Beyond the Formalist-Realist Divide: The Role of Politics in Judging* (Princeton University Press 2010) 1.

9 Leiter, n. 3 at 21.

as relatively a-theoretical training grounds for professionals rather than scholars.

First, before realism arrived on the scene, US legal scholarship had been dominated by a formalist concept of law, which stressed 'the purported autonomy and closure of the legal world and the predominance of formal logic within this autonomous universe'.[10] Realism defined itself in opposition to this idea of law,[11] and Kelsen's approach must have appeared to the realists to be a version of the formalism that they had just energetically rejected and were in the process of eliminating from legal pedagogy and legal doctrine.

Second, Kelsen's theory failed political litmus tests because, although Kelsen personally supported parliamentary democracy, his desire to produce a pure theory of law required him to avoid connecting the system of law to any substantive political theory.[12] As early as 1946, Gustav Radbruch declared that positivism had rendered the German legal profession defenceless against laws with arbitrary or even criminal content.[13] Lon Fuller, one of the most influential philosophers of law in the United States during Kelsen's lifetime, concluded that legal positivism had helped pave the way for the Nazi seizure of power. In a 1954 essay, Fuller wrote that the Nazis 'would never have achieved their control over the German people had there not been waiting to be bent to their sinister ends attitudes towards law and government that had been centuries in the building'. These attitudes included being 'notoriously deferential to authority' and having 'faith in certain fundamental processes of government'.[14] In a 1958 exchange with HLA Hart, Fuller declared positivistic philosophy incompatible with the ideal of fidelity to law.[15] At a time when fascism and totalitarianism posed genuine threats to the ascendancy of democracy as the global model for governance, Kelsen's theory did not seem to US academics to provide a sufficiently robust defence of democracy or for

[10] Hanoch Dagan, 'The Realist Conception of Law' 57 *Toronto Law Journal* (2007) 607–660 at 611.

[11] Dagan, n. 10 at 612.

[12] Hans Kelsen, *Introduction to the Problems of Legal Theory* (Bonnie Litschewski Paulson, Stanley L. Paulson (trs), Clarendon Press 2002) 3.

[13] Gustav Radbruch, 'Gesetzliches Unrecht und übergesetzliches Recht' 1 *Süddeutsche Juristen-Zeitung* (1946) 105–108 at 107.

[14] Lon L. Fuller, 'American Legal Philosophy at Mid-Century' 6 *Journal of Legal Education* (1954) 457–485 at 466–485.

[15] Lon L. Fuller, 'Positivism and Fidelity to Law – A Reply to Professor Hart' 71 *Harvard Law Review* (1958) 630–672 at 646.

sufficient safeguards against abuses of the law by fascist or totalitarian governments.

Kelsen faced and continues to face two additional problems in the US legal academy relating to issues of pedagogy and the nature of legal education. The first problem is that legal education in the United States is a form of professional training. Students did not – and still often do not – come to law school in search of enlightenment. They come in order to get the skills, the professional credentials and the contacts that will enable them to succeed in their chosen profession. Theorising about the nature of the law occurs at the margins of the law school experience, with most students taking only one or two classes during the course of their legal educations that focus on jurisprudence. In addition, common law legal education is a very practical affair, in which the students engage intensively with the case law. Kelsen's highly abstract and theoretical approach to the law could not have been more alien to the way in which US students are inculcated into legal doctrine. Untethered as the Pure Theory of Law is to any concrete examples drawn from familiar cases or even statutes, it had almost no chance of appealing to students in US law schools.

Given the development of legal education in the United States as a form of professional training, with jurisprudence sequestered in a tiny corner of the curriculum, Kelsen's approach was unlikely to have much appeal for US lawyers-in-training. Although the recent Carnegie report on legal education faults law schools for focusing on teaching doctrine at the expense of ethical formation,[16] students actively resist the latter and crave the former. Even if students were inclined towards theory, most do not arrive at law school with the sort of analytical skills that would enable them to understand, much less appreciate, Kelsen's Pure Theory of Law.

2.3 Legal realism and Hartian legal positivism

Until relatively recently, legal realism and legal positivism were routinely viewed in the American academy as incompatible.[17] Brian Leiter has argued otherwise.[18] It may be that the two jurisprudential approaches, while perhaps not incompatible, are concerned at their core with different questions. Legal positivism attempts to explain what law is, and legal realism attempts to understand how judges decide cases – in particular

[16] William M. Sullivan *et al.*, *Educating Lawyers: Preparation for the Profession of Law* (Jossey-Bass 2007) 144.

[17] Leiter, n. 3 at 59. [18] Leiter, n. 3 at 80.

how they decide the relatively rare 'hard case'.[19] If that is so, then legal realism exists as a supplement to legal positivism, illustrating how law works at the margins (or penumbra) of clear legal rules whose 'core' meaning is routinely enforced and adhered to.[20] However, some defenders of legal realism argue that the effect of its insights into the nature of law and legal processes cannot be so constrained. As Frederick Schauer has recently observed, '[d]etermining whether and when [Legal Realism's] genuinely non-traditional and destabilizing version of law's operation is true is an empirical question, the pursuit of which is an important part of future research in the Realist spirit'.[21]

3 Elements of the new legal realism

In an American legal academy in which it has long been a cliché to observe that 'we are all Realists now',[22] one might wonder why there would be a need for a revival of legal realism. In fact, the label new legal realism (NLR) seems to refer to two distinct movements, one of which might be a subset of the other. One branch of NLR takes up the legal realist project, narrowly defined, as one concerned with what judges do, but the new legal realists are far more proficient in empirical research methods and thus can far better assess the interplay of law, politics and judicial personality. More broadly understood, NLR is the methodological successor to legal realism: it applies social scientific and empirical methods to all of the subject matters with which legal academics concern themselves and offers solutions with an eye to promoting progressive social change.

3.1 Inheritance from (old) legal realism

Both variants of NLR see themselves as building on original legal realism by using social science to advance legal knowledge. Thomas Miles and Cass Sunstein describe NLR as 'an effort to understand the sources of judicial decisions on the basis of testable hypotheses and large data sets'.

19 HLA Hart, *The Concept of Law* (Oxford University Press 1961) 136–147; Karl Llewellyn, 'Some Realism about Realism' 44 *Harvard Law Review* (1931) 1222–1264 at 1239.

20 HLA Hart, 'Positivism and the Separation of Law and Morals' 71 *Harvard Law Review* (1958) 593–629 at 607–608.

21 Schauer, n. 5 at 780.

22 Laura Kalman, *Legal Realism at Yale: 1927–1960* (University of North Carolina Press 1986) 229; Green, n. 4 at 1917.

They view this project as a realisation of Karl Llewellyn's goals for legal realism.[23] In particular, Miles and Sunstein discuss a body of work that attempts, through empirical, quantitative investigation, to specify the effect of judicial 'personality' on legal outcomes, as well as the institutional contexts that encourage or constrain the effects of judicial temperament on legal outcomes.[24] While the research is not yet advanced enough to establish robust conclusions, this scholarship indicates that, for the most part, judicial 'personality' comes into play only in the 'hard cases', either because judges are constrained by law in most cases to rule in certain ways regardless of their political or ideological orientations, or because the members of the judiciary are so similar to one another in outlook, training and core values that they tend to all exercise their discretion in the same way, while a body more representative of the general population might produce a greater variety in outcomes.[25] The former explanation tames realism; the latter leaves it untamed.[26]

More broadly understood, NLR employs both legal theory and empirical approaches in order to both explain doctrine and promote legal solutions to public policy dilemmas.[27] Thus, in a volume of essays on behavioural law and economics, which Daniel Farber termed a new form of legal realism,[28] Cass Sunstein collects some essays on the effects of heuristics and biases in legal decision-making,[29] but most of the contributions take on legal problems beyond judicial decision-making, such as contract formation, stock market analysis, vaccination decisions, jury awards, redistributive effects of legal rights, nuisance law, risk regulation, legal bargaining dynamics and tax.[30] As Farber notes, like the legal

[23] Thomas Miles, Cass Sunstein, 'The New Legal Realism' 75 *University of Chicago Law Review* (2008) 831–854 at 831.

[24] Miles and Sunstein, n. 23 at 834.

[25] Miles and Sunstein, n. 23 at 845.

[26] 'Tamed' and 'untamed' are Frederick Schauer's terms for a realism that only affects outlier (hard) cases and a realism that goes to the core of all legal decision-making processes. Frederick Schauer, n. 5 at 749.

[27] Howard Erlanger *et al.*, 'Foreword: Is it Time for a New Legal Realism?' *Wisconsin Law Review* (2005) 335–363 at 337.

[28] Daniel Farber, 'Toward a New Legal Realism' 68 *University of Chicago Law Review* (2001) 279–303.

[29] Mark Kelman, Yuval Rottenstreich, Amos Tversky, 'Context-Dependence in Legal Decision Making' in Cass R. Sunstein (ed.), *Behavioral Law and Economics* (Cambridge University Press 2000) 61–95; Jeffrey J. Rachlinski, 'A Positive Psychological Theory of Judging in Hindsight' in Cass R. Sunstein (ed.), *Behavioral Law and Economics* (Cambridge University Press 2000) 96–116.

[30] See range of essays in Cass R. Sunstein (ed.), *Behavioral Law and Economics* (Cambridge University Press 2000) 116–186, 211–421.

realists, the behavioural law and economics approach seeks 'to use the social sciences to understand the behaviour of legal decision-makers and the effects of legal rules'.[31]

While Brian Leiter has called into question claims that legal realism actually engaged in empirical research drawing on the social sciences,[32] NLR insists on doing legal scholarship from the bottom up and from the top down simultaneously by making use of empirical research as well as qualitative methods and theoretical insights developed in the social sciences.[33] If nothing else, it seems that NLR is grappling with the challenges of introducing specialised knowledge and methodology into legal discourse in a more systematic way than old legal realism did.[34]

NLR also associates itself with a progressive politics, based on the naive hypothesis that social scientific enquiry into the efficacy of political structures would yield a progressive critique of those structures.[35] With its combination of empiricism, a call for the incorporation of social scientific methods into legal scholarship, and its progressive politics, NLR seems at times like a rebranding of the Law and Society movement, as both NLR and Law and Society have been associated with the University of Wisconsin,[36] and NLR invokes both pragmatism and the Law in Action approach, which is also related to Law and Society.[37]

3.2 The new international legal realism

Just as NLR can be divided into a narrow and a broad version, the new international legal realism (NILR) comes in two very different strains. The first is rationalism, which ranges from a law and economics to a behavioural economics of international law. But various

[31] Farber, n. 28 at 303.

[32] Brian Leiter, 'Legal Realisms Old, and New' 47 *Valparaiso University Law Review* (2012–2013) 949–963 at 955.

[33] Erlanger, n. 27 at 339–340.

[34] Erlanger, n. 27 at 341–342; Miles and Sunstein, n. 23 at 831.

[35] Erlanger, n. 7 at 344.

[36] Four of the six co-authors and co-organisers of the *Wisconsin Law Review*'s special issue on NLR were professors of the University of Wisconsin at the time.

[37] Erlanger, n. 7 at 356–357. Two of the three editors of a large anthology of Law in Action articles, Stewart Macauley and Elizabeth Mertz, are also University of Wisconsin law professors and key players in NLR. Stewart Macauley *et al.*, *Law in Action: A Socio-Legal Reader* (Foundation Press 2007).

normative theories associated with international relations – liberalism[38] and constructivism[39] – as well as international legal theories ranging from Harold Koh's Transnational Legal Process[40] to Paul Schiff Berman's Global Legal Pluralism,[41] could also be viewed as qualifying as variants of legal realism in international legal theory.[42]

3.2.1 Rationalist international legal theory

While NLR draws broadly on social scientific methodologies derived from fields like history, anthropology, sociology and psychology, rationalist international legal theory, developed by scholars like Eric Posner, Jack Goldsmith, Oona Hathaway and Andrew Guzman, supplements Chicago-school law and economics with behavioural law and economics while retaining assumptions associated with traditional international relations realism.[43] While rationalism has its roots in NLR, there are subtle differences in the methodological recipe that lead NILR to have dramatically different political valences from NLR.

While NLR is clearly a progressive movement, NILR is politically diverse, and given the left-wing tilt of the legal academy generally and of international legal scholarship in particular, this diversity puts NILR on the conservative end of the scholarly spectrum. For example, Eric Posner and Miguel F. P. de Figueiredo used classic NLR methods to demonstrate that justices of the International Court of Justice (ICJ) exhibit bias

38 Anne-Marie Slaughter, *A New World Order* (Princeton University Press 2004); Andrew Moravcsik, 'Taking Preferences Seriously: A Liberal Theory of International Politics' 51 *International Organization* (1997) 513–553.

39 Nicholas Onuf, *Making Sense, Making Worlds: Constructivism in Social Theory and International Relations* (Routledge 2013); Alexander Wendt, *Social Theory of International Politics* (Cambridge University Press 1999); Friedrich V. Kratochwil, *Rules, Norms and Decisions: On the Conditions of Practical and Legal Reasoning in International Relations and Domestic Affairs* (Cambridge University Press 1989).

40 Harold Hongju Koh, 'Transnational Legal Process after September 11' 22 *Berkeley Journal of International Law* (2004) 337–354; Harold Hongju Koh, 'Transnational Legal Process' 75 *Nebraska Law Review* (1996) 181–207.

41 Paul Schiff Berman, *Global Legal Pluralism: A Jurisprudence of Law beyond Borders* (Cambridge University Press 2012).

42 Terminological confusion seems unavoidable. The international law and international relations theories that I am discussing here as a variant of legal realism are all clearly distinguishable from and in many cases a reaction against the international relations realism that has dominated the field in the United States since the middle of the twentieth century.

43 Andrew T. Guzman, *How International Law Works: A Rational Choice Theory* (Oxford University Press 2008); Jack L. Goldsmith, Eric A. Posner, *The Limits of International Law* (Oxford University Press 2005).

towards their own countries, their countries' allies and to countries that are, in some respect, similar to their own countries.[44] Posner then follows up with an argument that, as a result of this exhibited bias, the ICJ has experienced a decline in its institutional legitimacy, resulting in a smaller docket consisting of less momentous cases.[45] Posner applies classic legal realist methods in service of a revisionist scholarship at odds with the progressive agenda of both classic legal realism and NLR.[46]

Rationalist international legal theory focuses on states as the relevant actors,[47] and assumes that states are unitary actors[48] and that states for the most part pursue their self-interest in the conduct of their international relations.[49] This new rationalism benefits from the long-delayed[50] dialogue between international legal theorists and international relations theorists within the US academy.[51]

The great advantage of the rationalist approach to international law is its parsimony.[52] The rationalist model has very few working parts; it takes into account only a few variables and thus seeks to transform international legal theory from a descriptive into an explanatory and predictive model.[53] While rationalists acknowledge that non-state actors play a role in international affairs, they do not consider the role of non-state actors to be so significant that rationalist theory needs to take non-state actors into account in order to explain and predict the course of international law.[54] Rationalist models thus do not account for sub-state units, multinational corporations and transnational NGOs.[55]

44 Eric A. Posner, Miguel de Figueiredo, 'Is the International Court of Justice Biased?' 34 *Journal of Legal Studies* (2005) 599–630.

45 Eric A. Posner, *The Perils of Global Legalism* (University of Chicago Press 2009) 144–145.

46 Oona Hathaway, Ariel Lavinbuk, 'Book Review: Rationalism and Revisionism in International Law: Jack L. Goldsmith, Eric A. Posner, The Limits of International Law (2005)' 119 *Harvard Law Review* (2006) 1404–1443 at 1406–1407.

47 Goldsmith and Posner, n. 43 at 3; Guzman, n. 43 at 17.

48 Guzman, n. 43 at 19; Hathaway and Lavinbuk, n. 46 at 1432.

49 Guzman, n. 43 at 17; Goldsmith and Posner, n. 43 at 13.

50 Oona Hathaway, Harold Hongju Koh, *Foundations of International Law and Politics* (Foundation Press 2005); Stephen Krasner, 'International Law and International Relations: Together, Apart, Together?' 1 *Chicago Journal of International Law* (2000) 93–99 at 93.

51 Emilie M. Hafner-Burton, David G. Victor, Yonatan Lupu, 'Political Science Research on International Law: The State of the Field' 106 *AJIL* (2012) 47–97 at 48.

52 Guzman, n. 43 at 21.

53 Hathaway and Lavinbuk, n. 46 at 1424.

54 Guzman, n. 43 at 8–9; Goldsmith and Posner, n. 43 at 4–5.

55 Goldsmith and Posner, n. 43 at 5; Guzman, n. 43 at 21.

Rationalists are generally committed to treating states as unitary actors.[56] Rationalist theory associates the preferences of states with states' 'leadership',[57] which usually means the leaders of the states' executive branch of government, since that branch has the dominant role in formulating foreign policy. Rationalist theory thus downplays the importance of competing factions within the executive branch, nor does it devote much attention to legislative input into international law-making or foreign policy decision-making. Some rationalists assume that domestic courts can and should play no role in shaping international legal rules or compliance with such rules.[58] Finally and not surprisingly, rationalism assumes rationality. 'Rationality' here means that states are guided by their perceived self-interest and not by legal norms, which rationalists treat as a product of state interests.[59]

Rationalists set out to improve the discipline of international legal scholarship by establishing standards of methodological and empirical care. Thus, like NLR, rationalism seeks to improve on the methodological rigour with which legal realism is practised. Rationalism has clear scientific – or at least scientistic – ambitions. It aspires to 'frame claims as testable hypotheses'.[60] In order to do so, it self-consciously simplifies the world of international relations of international law.[61] It sweeps aside suggestions that states might be motivated by considerations other than self-interest, as well as the perhaps more significant challenges associated with the maddeningly complex processes whereby states identify and pursue their interests.

3.2.2 Normative realist theory

In this short chapter, it is impossible to do justice to the wealth of fresh theoretical approaches that have recently emerged in international legal scholarship. What unites the approaches addressed here under the rubric of normative NILR is a twofold rejection of rationalism. First, normative NILR rejects the assumptions that states are unified, rational actors and that one can either describe international relations or predict behaviour

56 Guzman, n. 43 at 19.

57 Goldsmith and Posner, n. 43 at 6; Jack L. Goldsmith, Eric A. Posner, 'The New International Law Scholarship' 34 *Georgia Journal of International and Comparative Law* (2006) 463–484 at 472.

58 Posner, n. 45 at 207–225.

59 Goldsmith and Posner, n. 43 at 13.

60 Goldsmith and Posner, n. 57 at 466.

61 Robert Hockett, 'The Limits of Their World' 90 *Minnesota Law Review* (2006) 1720–1790 at 1724.

by focusing exclusively on state action. Second, normative NILR theorists view legal norms as having an independent valence that affects the choices of legal decision-makers. In short, normative NILR looks beyond the maximisation of self-interest in order to explain how various actors behave on the international stage. As we shall see in the discussion below, while NILR is in some ways compatible with positivism, most NILR theorists are traditional legal realists who believe that non-legal factors play a very large role in the formation, interpretation and (selective) enforcement of international legal rules. Normative NILR also provides useful insights into the limits of rationalist NILR.

As its normative NILR critics note, rationalists generally promote the advantages of their understanding of international law vis-à-vis other theoretical models based on their model's superior ability to predict state behaviour with regard to international law.[62] In practice, however, rationalism has not established itself as a useful predictive tool, in part because the rationalist model often simply assumes rather than establishes that states are self-interested, rational actors.[63] Rationalists renounce all assumptions as to the interests that drive state conduct and acknowledge that generalisation is hazardous.[64] Sometimes states are driven by pursuit of security; sometimes by pursuit of prosperity. Rationalist theory cannot tell us when one interest will prevail over another or if we can even know what interest is driving foreign policy.[65] As a result, rationalists run into difficulties because they are no better at identifying states' interests than are international legal scholars who adopt normative theories. Even when rationalists focus on particular case studies, they can offer only 'reasonable conjectures' about state interests.[66]

In addition, NILR scholarship rebuts the rationalist assumption that states are the only relevant actors in international affairs by detailing the range of international agreements and both international and domestic adjudications to which entities other than states have been parties,[67] while also noting that customary international law, including customary human rights and humanitarian law, can bind private actors, such as

[62] Hathaway and Lavinbuk, n. 46 at 1424; Goldsmith and Posner, n. 57 at 473.

[63] Paul Schiff Berman, 'Book Review Essay: Seeing Beyond the Limits of International Law: Jack L. Goldsmith, Eric A. Posner, The Limits of International Law (2005)' 84 *Texas Law Review* (2006) 1265–1306 at 1271.

[64] Goldsmith and Posner, n. 57 at 474.

[65] Hockett, n. 61 at 1729–1730.

[66] Goldsmith and Posner, n. 57 at 475.

[67] Jordan J. Paust, 'Nonstate Actor Participation in International Law and the Pretense of Exclusion' 51 *Virginia Journal of International Law* (2011) 977–1004 at 978–985.

corporations.[68] More generally, much of NILR theory recognises that individuals, acting singly or in association with others, play a role in the 'formation, reaffirmation, and termination of international law'.[69]

In its quest for parsimony, rationalism can simplify the world of international relations and international law beyond recognition.[70] Robert Hockett characterises the dangers of rationalism as leaving us with:

> [A] world of fetishized, black-boxy Scrooge-states, incomprehensibly seeking in large part to eat one another, calculating and gaming with those and with cognate objectives in view, constrained by no more than the weapons that others possess all while 'empt[il]y, happ[il]y' or mendaciously speaking as if the routines and mere memoranda of understanding that emerge from this contest were law.[71]

Rationalists justify their focus on states as the relevant actors in international law on the ground that doing so in no way hinders them from developing testable theses that can help predict conduct in the realm of international affairs. However, rationalism has yet to make any testable predictions, and its critics maintain that it is incapable of doing so in its present form.[72] On the other hand, while critics of rationalism point out the dangers of a predictive model that derives from assumptions that may not completely reflect the complexities and subtleties of international relations, those same critics acknowledge that their own more complex models do not so readily generate testable hypotheses and lack predictive force.[73]

As a result, NILR, in its two variants, is an incomplete theory of international law. Rationalism purports to create working models that can both explain and predict state behaviour, but its models are so fundamentally flawed as to be of limited value. Moreover, as normative NILR recognises, by focusing exclusively on states, rationalism tells only part of the story of international law's development and impact. Normative NILR provides a far richer descriptive model of the interaction of the various actors relevant to an understanding of the workings of international law,

[68] Paust, n. 67 at 987. [69] Paust, n. 67 at 1001.

[70] Kal Raustiala, 'Refining the Limits of International Law' 34 *Georgia Journal of International and Comparative Law* (2006) 423–444 at 424.

[71] Hockett, n. 61 at 1722 (quoting Goldsmith and Posner, n. 43 at 267).

[72] Hathaway and Lavinbuk, n. 46 at 1425.

[73] John Gerard Ruggie, 'What Makes the World Hang Together? Neo-Utilitarianism and the Social Constructivist Challenge' 52 *International Organization* (1988) 855–885 at 885.

but that very richness prevents normative NILR theorists from articulating a coherent approach. Focused like rationalists on the extent to which international law is an efficacious force in the world, their models for identifying the mechanisms through which laws are made and distinguished from non-legal rationales for behaviour remain underdeveloped.

4 Overlap and divergence in international legal realism and international legal positivism

On the surface, NILR and NILP seem like irreconcilable movements. To the extent that NILP is committed to the Kelsenian project of a Pure Theory of Law, its project is unsullied by the political, contextual, sociological, psychological, economic and ethical considerations that go to the heart of NILR. And yet, there are ways to put the two approaches to international law into conversation with one another. Just as legal realism adopted positivist assumptions regarding the nature of law and of legal authority, the assumptions informing NILR put it far closer to positivism than to natural law theory. Where the two approaches diverge, that divergence is best understood as a product of the very different questions that they pose. NILP, like classical international legal positivism and legal positivism more generally, attempts to ascertain what law is and whence legal norms derive their authority. NILR, while informed by positivist notions about the derivation of legal norms, is far more dedicated to the question of, to borrow a title from a leading NILR practitioner, how international law works.[74]

4.1 Elements of the new international legal positivism

One hesitates to even acknowledge NILP's existence, as it is difficult to identify the adherents of the movement. In promoting formalism in law-ascertainment, Jean d'Aspremont does not offer a defence of legal positivism as a whole. D'Aspremont gives two main reasons for resisting the conflation of positivism and formalism. First, formalism is but one of many tenets of positivism, not all of which he is willing to embrace. More importantly, even among themselves, positivists cannot agree on how to define and delimit their approach to the law.[75] For the purposes of the

[74] Guzman, n. 43.

[75] Jean d'Aspremont, *Formalism and the Sources of International Law: A Theory of the Ascertainment of Legal Rules* (Oxford University Press 2011) 25–27.

discussion to follow, we will treat formalism as to law-ascertainment as a component of NILP, while acknowledging that the approaches are related but distinct.

NILP differentiates itself from classical international legal positivism for two reasons: new theoretical challenges arose; and the world changed. Classical international legal positivism developed at a time when it did not have to respond to legal realism or critical legal studies (CLS), as these movements focused their energies primarily on national legal systems. In the past forty years or so, as Jörg Kammerhofer and Jean d'Aspremont have noted, critical approaches found their way into the literature on the nature of international law.[76] At the same time, international relations theory and some international legal theory began to take note of the significance of non-state actors in world affairs and began to conceptualise international law in ways that did not treat states as the sole or even the main relevant actors. These new conceptions of international law and international relations began to call the assumptions of classical international legal positivism into question.

In articulating the characteristics of NILP, Kammerhofer and d'Aspremont accept *arguendo* a narrative, according to which classical international legal positivism was done in by its own limitations – its focus on states and on the need for state consent to create binding rules of international law.[77] NILP thus adapts the fundamental positivist doctrine – that law is a human creation to be evaluated based on its pedigree rather than in respect of moral or ethical values – to a world in which law-creating authorities and processes can be diverse, overlapping and contested. This complicates the positivist project, but also adds to its potential as a descriptive and predictive theoretical model.

NILP is also distinguished from its classical predecessors in its forthright acknowledgement that the battle against uncertainty is unwinnable, and in so doing, it adopts sceptical attitudes towards legal rules that are very similar to those that inform legal realism, although NILP focuses on a narrower set of sources of uncertainty in law. NILP poses problems for which it can provide no solutions in its own terms. NILP elaborates on mechanisms for determining what the law is, but determining how legal norms and non-legal norms interact to shape the behaviour of actors in international affairs is beyond the scope of the NILP project.[78] For example, Jean d'Aspremont acknowledges that his formalist

[76] D'Aspremont and Kammerhofer, Chapter 1.

[77] D'Aspremont and Kammerhofer, Chapter 1 at 4–5.

[78] D'Aspremont, n. 75 at 10–11.

approach to the ascertainment of law does not reach issues of interpretation. Moreover, even with regard to law-ascertainment, d'Aspremont acknowledges that, because of the indeterminacy of language, 'formalism inevitably brings about some indeterminacy'.[79] Jörg Kammerhofer's approach helps us to understand the various types of uncertainty that bedevil our attempts to identify legal norms, but even if we try to address such uncertainty through a 'utopian' act of will and adopt the Kelsenian *Grundnorm* theory, ontological uncertainty will persist.[80]

As a result of these insights, NILP confronts a familiar, post-modern world. It does so with a sophisticated version of philosophical scepticism while working within a tradition that is for the most part simply modern, as opposed to post-modern. In some ways, NILP's inheritance from classical legal positivism creates tensions with versions of NILR that have their own inheritance of legal realism's hostility to anything that smacks of formalism and to any approach to legal theory that attempts to bracket out legal from non-legal reasoning. There is nonetheless a great deal of overlap in the world views of NILP and NILR writers.

4.2 Divergence: rationalism and the limits of international law

To the extent that variants of rationalism deny law any independent valence and insist that states comply with international law only when doing so accords with the states' perception of their self-interest, NILR and NILP cannot be reconciled.[81] Similarly, to the extent that NILP dismisses arguments sounding in pragmatism, political expediency, effectiveness or *Realpolitik* as not legal in nature,[82] even if NILP recognises that non-legal arguments may be relevant to legal outcomes, it rules out any possible dialogue between the two approaches, unless the parties agree that NILR is a sort of extra-legal supplement to NILP approaches.

But NILP also highlights the weakness of rationalism to the extent that rationalism treats law not only as largely irrelevant, but also as largely fixed. Jean d'Aspremont correctly notes that rationalism has not had much success in the realm of international legal theory, even if it is accorded a more respectful audience in international relations theory.[83]

79 D'Aspremont, n. 75 at 15, 139.

80 Jörg Kammerhofer, *Uncertainty in International Law: A Kelsenian Approach* (Routledge 2010) 240.

81 Jack Goldsmith and Eric A. Posner embody this variant of NILR. Goldsmith and Posner, n. 43.

82 Kammerhofer, n. 80 at 26, 28, 34.

83 D'Aspremont, n. 75 at 103.

Rationalism asks what motivates states to comply or to fail to comply with legal obligations, but it rarely takes into consideration the complexities involved in determining what those legal obligations are. In some ways, NILP takes the lessons of the 'untamed realism' of the CLS movement to heart far more than NILR does. NILP more thoroughly acknowledges the epistemological and ontological uncertainties that confound our attempts to identify legal norms.[84]

4.3 Overlap: normative theory and the future of international law

NILR and NILP may be most united in a question that seemed to divide traditional legal realism from earlier variants of legal positivism. Both are interested in the problem of uncertainty in international law. NILR looks beyond the law to economic theory, politics, history and culture in order to explain the ways in which legal norms arise, develop and harden into rules or lapse into something akin to positive morality. NILP seeks to identify the sources of uncertainty and through both theoretical and legal mechanisms, reduce uncertainty in the law wherever possible.

A formalist approach seems to limit the possibility that uncertainties might arise by disfavouring certain types of authority on which parties might seek to rely in order to create uncertainty where formal rules are otherwise clear. However, d'Aspremont defines the concept of 'law applying authorities' broadly to include 'who[]ever, as a matter of social practice, members of the group . . . identify and treat as "legal" officials'.[85] While d'Aspremont gives priority to written instruments in the ascertainment of legal rules,[86] those written instruments must be understood in light of actual practice.[87] But d'Aspremont seeks to bring the potential cacophony to order with the aid of his version of Hart's 'social thesis', which is informed by the philosophy of language.[88] Ultimately, criteria of law-ascertainment are to be looked for in the 'converging practice of law-applying authorities'.[89] In short, the existence of legal rules requires both formal (preferably written) evidence and some regularity of observation. D'Aspremont avoids specifying the required degree of regularity, beyond the statement that a *feeling* among law-applying authorities that they are

[84] D'Aspremont, n. 75 at 3–4.

[85] D'Aspremont, n. 75 at 203, citing Brian Z. Tamanaha, *A General Jurisprudence of Law and Society* (Oxford University Press 2001) 142.

[86] D'Aspremont, n. 75 at 12. [87] D'Aspremont, n. 75 at 13.

[88] D'Aspremont, n. 75 at 200. [89] D'Aspremont, n. 75 at 201.

applying the same criteria is required.[90] Here, the distance between NILP and NILR seems to be little more than a matter of where one places the emphasis in the interplay between words and deeds in the creation of legally binding obligations.

Timothy Meyer provides a sort of soft rationalist NILR perspective (he calls his approach 'institutionalist') on d'Aspremont's work.[91] Much of Meyer's review is appreciative of d'Aspremont's contributions to our understanding of law-ascertainment, but Meyer rejects d'Aspremont's distinction between law and non-law based on formal indicators and argues that informal signalling mechanisms grant states flexibility and enhance opportunities for international cooperation.[92] Where NILP attempts to identify and categorise ambiguity in legal rules, Meyer's NILR recognises that ambiguity has its uses. Relying on behavioural studies, Meyer contends that parties inclined to be law-abiding and risk averse are more likely to comply with fuzzy rules than with strict ones, as they go out of their way to avoid even the appearance of non-compliance.[93] In addition, Meyer expresses concern that legal formalism can inhibit dynamism in international law, and without such dynamism, international law would remain powerless over non-state actors and over realms of law (such as international criminal law and international humanitarian law) where law's efficacy is greatly reduced if it cannot regulate the conduct of non-state actors.[94] But here, too, the difference might just amount to a matter of emphasis. As Meyer acknowledges,[95] d'Aspremont's social thesis incorporates the sort of dynamism that his formalism seemingly undercuts.

Indeed, Meyer brings NILP and institutionalism together through the shift from traditional legal positivism's focus on the intent on the part of states that were bound by international law to a focus on the *expectations* of what d'Aspremont calls law-applying authorities.[96] Meyer restates d'Aspremont's thesis in institutionalist terms:

> [I]nternational law is most likely to be effective in generating behavioral change, not when states act out of a sense of legal obligation, but rather

90 D'Aspremont, n. 75 at 201.

91 Timothy Meyer, 'Review Essay: Towards a Communicative Theory of International Law: Jean d'Aspremont, Formalism and the Sources of International Law: A Theory of the Ascertainment of Legal Rules (2011)' 13 *Melbourne Journal of International Law* (2012) 921–939.

92 Meyer, n. 91 at 933.

93 Meyer, n. 91 at 933.

94 Meyer, n. 91 at 933–934.

95 Meyer, n. 91 at 934.

96 Meyer, n. 91 at 936.

when there are shared expectations about the kinds of obligations created by an instrument and what the instrument requires of states.[97]

NILP may distinguish itself from classical international legal positivism by the extent to which it acknowledges the limitations of what can be accomplished through an analysis of law as such. NILP practitioners are constantly reminding their audience that their subject matter is law and legal analysis alone. Kammerhofer repeatedly advises against methodological syncretism in legal analysis, which he believes would hinder scholarly cognition.[98] This is not to discount the importance of other factors that might affect the behaviour of legal decision-makers, but NILP insists on drawing clear lines between legal and non-legal analysis.

In fact, NILP requires assistance from non-legal analysis because it concludes that legal analysis alone cannot resolve legal issues. For example, Jörg Kammerhofer concedes at the conclusion of his monograph on *Uncertainty in International Law* that there is no possible way of remedying uncertainty through the mechanisms of legal positivism.[99] If the goal is to create a world in which the application and enforcement of legal norms is stable and predictable, NILP requires a supplement, but that supplement is not legal analysis. NILR can provide the necessary supplement, but in order to do so, it needs to develop a more robust appreciation for the uncertainty in legal norms that NILP identifies, rather than treating legal norms as established facts from which international legal actors depart because they value non-legal considerations over adherence to legal norms. Just as NILP is in need of a realist supplement, NILR needs NILP, as Jean d'Aspremont puts it, 'for the sake of the ascertainment of international legal rules and the necessity to draw a line between law and non-law'.[100]

Still, one might wonder, if NILP cannot provide any sort of legal certainty with regard to the specification of legal rules, how its project could be of use. NILP has the great advantage of bringing seriousness and rigour to the analysis of how we ascertain legal rules and identify legal norms. But a rigorous enquiry into these questions yields only uncertainty, meaning that ultimately the question of how norms are to be interpreted, what norms are applicable to a specific legal question, or how to adjudicate differences in cases of overlapping and seemingly contradictory norms

[97] Meyer, n. 91 at 936–937.
[98] Kammerhofer, n. 80 at 201, 210.
[99] Kammerhofer, n. 80 at 240.
[100] D'Aspremont, n. 75 at 5.

cannot be answered exclusively with the tools for legal analysis provided by NILP. Nevertheless, legal questions are decided, and legal realism suggests that such decisions have more to do with extra-legal factors than with legal positivism's ultimately futile attempts to reconstruct legal norms through recourse to legal analysis alone.

The answer might depend on the pervasiveness of legal uncertainty. There may be no ultimate answer to the question of how legal norms are to be recognised, interpreted or reconciled, but there may be an answer *for us*. That is, given an actual dispute and a set of possible outcomes, we may be able to reach a consensus in many cases, purely on the basis of proper legal analysis, as to the proper outcome. NILP is extremely useful in these cases, and then the challenge is to specify the extent of the world of easy cases. Jean d'Aspremont defends the usefulness of establishing 'elementary indicators as to what is law and what is non-law'. He also notes that indeterminacy is reined in through the social practice of law-applying authorities.[101] Nonetheless, for 'untamed' versions of NILR, which would treat all controversies as 'hard cases', whether or not legal analysis leads to clarity or ambiguity is irrelevant, as cases are ultimately decided on non-legal grounds.

4.4 International law and the challenge of post-modernism

While both NILR and NILP pride themselves on their cognisance of certain developments in post-modern theory, it is not clear that international law as a field has really come to terms with the challenges of the post-modern world. It may well be that the consequences of post-modernism are simply too destabilising to incorporate into an approach to law. There is nothing new under the sun. Post-modern insights were anticipated in earlier thinkers, going back at least to Heraclitus. As one theory of post-modern theory is a radical form of scepticism that arises in response to a post-modern world, one can say that Hans Kelsen's positivist theory at least anticipates post-modern international legal positivism.[102] But there are aspects of post-modernism that are far more threatening to the NILP (and NILR) project.

To the extent that one can generalise about 'post-modern theory', it is safe to say that post-modernism is a response to both the intellectual tradition of structuralism and to the influence of technology on historical

[101] D'Aspremont, n. 75 at 141. [102] Kammerhofer, Chapter 4 at 81.

consciousness and self-conceptualisation.[103] Post-modernism is generally suspicious of master historical narratives and grand theories of the human sciences. This scepticism is an abreaction against the teleology and optimism that came to be associated with Enlightenment rationality, especially as forms of rationality also became associated with twentieth-century crimes against humanity.[104]

While structuralism in linguistics and anthropology claimed to have uncovered the systems of binary oppositions that underlie all manners of communication, deconstruction is a form of ideology-criticism that focuses both on the distortions created by our mental habit of thinking in binaries and on the hierarchical and discriminatory nature of binary oppositions. Deconstruction challenges legal theory especially forcefully, because binary oppositions (legal–illegal, guilty–innocent, binding–non-binding, written–oral, timely–late, substantive–procedural) are the very stuff of legal systems. Law students are taught to diagram doctrinal areas through decision trees, each branch of which is a binary opposition. Still, while a systematic deconstruction of international law and the international legal system has not been attempted, critical approaches to international law do incorporate the scepticism attendant to deconstruction to challenge both binary oppositions and the hierarchies that are dependent on the binary oppositions on which the international legal order rests. To the extent that NILP insists on the usefulness of strict oppositions between the legal and the non-legal, between writings and conduct, and between formal and informal processes, it swims against a post-modern tide. What does international legal positivism look like in a world where *il n'y a pas de hors-texte*?[105]

Post-structuralism also challenges the opposition of structure and agency. Poststructuralist New Historicists, for example, speak not of relationships of power and domination, but of 'the circulation of social energy'.[106] This post-modern perspective is a product of our awareness

[103] Jean-Francois Lyotard, *The Postmodern Condition: A Report on Knowledge* (University of Minnesota Press 1984) 3.

[104] Ernst Breisach, *On the Future of History: The Postmodernist Challenge and Its Aftermath* (University of Chicago Press 2003) 16–17; Joyce O. Appleby, Lynn A. Hunt, Margaret Jacob, *Telling the Truth about History* (Norton 1994) 205–206.

[105] Jacques Derrida, *Of Grammatology* (Gayatri Spivak (tr.), Johns Hopkins University Press 1976) 158.

[106] Stephen Greenblatt, 'The Circulation of Social Energy' in Stephen Greenblatt, *Shakespearean Negotiations: The Circulation of Social Energy in Renaissance England* (University of California Press 1988) 1–20 at 6.

that we, as human actors, are buffeted by natural forces that we do not completely understand and cannot control and by technological forces that we have created and yet also cannot control. Technological forces are products of human agency, yet they can become far more powerful than any individual will. Certain institutionalist forms of NILR have come to recognise that institutions develop a dynamic of their own, becoming what Pierre Bourdieu called both 'structured structures' and 'structuring structures'.[107] For the most part, however, while normative NILR expands the players who may interact in international legal processes and develops complicated models for their interactions, NILR has not worked out a post-structural theory of the dialectic of structure and agency in international affairs. NILP, with its focus on generation of norms, often brackets questions of structure and agency, as well as the crucial issue of power, which is at the centre of Foucaultian post-structuralism.

It is therefore unclear that either NILP or NILR truly grapple with the theoretical and real-world challenges of the post-modern world. Post-modernism is not a theoretical construct foisted upon an unsuspecting world; it responds to real-world stimuli. In the case of international law, those stimuli include the proliferation of international actors, international law's pluralist nature and the advent of technologies, ranging from cyber-attacks to bitcoins, which blur, or in some instances, erase distinctions between virtual and actual phenomena. But post-modernism also challenges us to interrogate and ultimately move beyond the binary oppositions that are the building blocks of the ways in which we construct our understandings of legal systems. It challenges us to think in new ways about what we might call the circulation of legal energies through overlapping systems and connections and also to think about resistances, which may be structural or volitional, to the flow of legal energies through the network of connections.

5 Conclusion

One can easily imagine a new generation of international legal scholarship in which the distinctions between realism and positivism become unimportant compared to the enormous overlap in perspective among scholars who see themselves as working in the two supposedly divergent traditions. Both NILR and NILP have abandoned the exclusive, and in

[107] Pierre Bourdieu, *Outline of a Theory of Practice* (Richard Nice (tr.), Cambridge University Press 1977) 72.

some cases even the primary, focus on states as the relevant actors in international legal affairs. While NILP continues to favour some version of formalism, in which the focus of scholarship is on relatively traditional, hard-law sources, those sources are understood in a sophisticated manner that accounts for law generation processes that encompass the entire realm of social interactions that informs norm creation domestically and internationally. Most forms of NILR recognise the importance of formal legal rules, but NILR approaches can help positivists add new nuance to their understanding of the social processes underlying the creation of legal norms. While NILR's indebtedness to legal realism's enthusiasm for social scientific and empirical approaches can only help it to enrich the methodology of international legal scholarship, NILP provides a philosophical rigor that will protect the field from a form of empirical fetishism. In any case, increased cross-disciplinary interaction can only enhance our understanding both of international law and of the role international legal scholarship in not only explaining but also in helping to shape international legal rules and rule-making processes.

10

International legal positivism and constitutionalism

JAN KLABBERS

1 Introduction

Much has been written recently, and in manifold ways, about the putative constitutionalisation of international law. Sometimes this has been done in direct and rather unapologetic fashion. Thus, international lawyers have proclaimed the emergence of an international constitutional order;[1] they have sought to suggest that the UN Charter might be akin to a constitution for the international community;[2] and they have held that the WTO might represent something like a world trade constitution.[3] Many have also written on what might be called aspects of constitutionalisation: judicial review by the ICJ of decisions of international organs,[4] or the prevalence of human rights as a superior normative baseline. In the aftermath of the ground-breaking *Kadi* decision of the ECJ (nowadays CJEU),[5] it has even been held that domestic courts would be allowed to ignore binding decisions of international organs which are difficult to reconcile with this superior base of human rights norms.[6]

[1] Erika de Wet, 'The International Constitutional Order' 55 *ICLQ* (2006) 51–76.

[2] Bardo Fassbender, *The United Nations Charter as the Constitution of the International Community* (Martinus Nijhoff 2009).

[3] John O. McGinnis, Mark L. Movsesian, 'The World Trade Constitution' 114 *Harvard Law Review* (2000) 511–605; see also Deborah Cass, 'The Constitutionalization of International Trade Law: Judicial Norm-Generation as the Engine of Constitutionalization' 12 *EJIL* (2001) 39–77.

[4] E.g. Erika de Wet, *The Chapter VII Powers of the United Nations Security Council* (Hart 2004).

[5] ECJ, *Yassin Abdullah Kadi and Al-Barakaat International Foundation v. Council of the European Union and Commission of the European Communities*, Joined Cases C-402/05 P and C-415/05 P, Judgment (Grand Chamber) of 3 September 2008, [2008] ECR I-6351.

[6] Antonios Tzanakopoulos, *Disobeying the Security Council: Countermeasures against Wrongful Sanctions* (Oxford University Press 2011).

Others simply skip a step and sketch the possible contours of a new, constitutional relationship between the international order and domestic orders, proposing general notions of subsidiarity[7] or a generalised margin of appreciation doctrine to apply to international law.[8] Even without the self-description as constitutional, nonetheless these presuppose a constitutionalist global order: in the classic Westphalian order, there is no room for subsidiarity or a margin of appreciation, as these are built-in, so to speak. It is only in a system characterised by normative hierarchy, with international law being deemed superior, that those notions can meaningfully find a place.

Generally speaking, the tone of these constitutionalist writings[9] has been hopeful and endorsing: the underlying thought seems to be one of almost inevitable, and highly desirable, progress.[10] Friedmann already suggested half a century ago that international law was moving from a law of coexistence to a law of cooperation;[11] constitutionalisation would simply be the next and final step, in much the same way in which classic Marxism predicted the inevitability of the worker's paradise, following some dialectic moves and perhaps with some collateral damage.

This constitutionalist drive is inspired by a number of factors. First, it is possibly no coincidence that it coincides with the emergence of a serious wave of globalisation: against the growing interconnectedness of global culture, society and economy, the state-oriented Westphalian order looks hopelessly inadequate. Surely, the challenges posited by a unified world must be met by a unified legal order, and one way to overcome the

7 Paolo G. Carozza, 'Subsidiarity as a Structural Principle of Human Rights Law' 97 *AJIL* (2003) 38–79.

8 Yuval Shany, 'Toward a General Margin of Appreciation Doctrine in International Law?' 16 *EJIL* (2005) 907–940.

9 To be sure, some scepticism has been recorded as well. See, for instance, Jeffrey L. Dunoff, Joel P. Trachtman (eds), *Ruling the World: Constitutionalism, International Law, and Global Governance* (Cambridge University Press 2009); Jan Klabbers, 'Setting the Scene' in Jan Klabbers, Anne Peters, Geir Ulfstein, *The Constitutionalization of International Law* (Oxford University Press 2009) 1–44; earlier, Jan Klabbers, 'Constitutionalism Lite' 1 *International Organizations Law Review* (2004) 31–58.

10 A striking example of such a progress narrative, complete with dialectic setbacks, is the brief editorial introduction to Ronald St John MacDonald, Douglas M. Johnston, *Towards World Constitutionalism: Issues in the Legal Ordering of the World Community* (Martinus Nijhoff 2005) xiii–xviii.

11 Wolfgang Friedmann, *The Changing Structure of International Law* (Columbia University Press 1964).

scattered nature of a system based on agreement between independent and sovereign actors is to proclaim the order to be constitutional.[12]

Second, constitutionalisation aims to provide an answer to the fragmentation of international law resulting from increased specialisation: if trade lawyers only communicate with trade lawyers, and security specialists only with security specialists, then the system requires some glue to hold it together. The putative constitutionalisation of international law then provides the glue, suggesting that after all there is some system to what appears to be chaos.

Third, the vocabulary of constitutionalisation suggests a vision of unity that the earlier international law vocabulary, with its insistence on sovereignty and independence, could never provide. While earlier generations of international lawyers hoped to remedy this by invoking notions of *ius cogens* or *erga omnes* obligations, these never really took off. Hence, the turn to constitutionalisation represents, to some extent, a semantic turn, recording the *ennui* of international lawyers with the vocabulary traditionally at their disposal.

And fourth, there is room for the suggestion that constitutionalisation functions as ideology, in order to complement the ideology of globalisation. After all, as has been suggested, globalisation comes with winners and losers, and is much more fun for the jet-setting elite of businessmen, highly educated professionals and academics than it is for the poor and dispossessed. The latter might need employment, job security and basic goods (from safe drinking water to a minimum level of nutrition) more than they need the values often associated with constitutionalisation. Yet, to endorse liberal values tends to result in undermining the position of those for whom globalisation only adds to their daily struggle, and therewith requires an ideological justification.[13]

All this results in the circumstance that international lawyers use the term 'constitutionalisation' in a specific sense: constitutionalisation signifies the creation, emergence or existence of a unified system and, what is more, a system that boasts considerable political legitimacy because it is based on widely shared liberal values. The term is not used in a purely

[12] One variation on this theme is 'compensatory constitutionalism': since domestic constitutional orders are rendered relatively powerless in the face of globalisation, this must be compensated for at the international level. Anne Peters, 'Compensatory Constitutionalism: The Function and Potential of Fundamental International Norms and Structures' 19 *LJIL* (2006) 579–610.

[13] Jonathan Friedman, 'Globalization' in David Nugent, Joan Vincent (eds), *A Companion to the Anthropology of Politics* (Blackwell 2004) 179–197.

descriptive sense, as in 'the global order is constituted upon independent states'; if that were the case, then the Westphalian order too could be considered constitutional.[14] Hence, there is something specific about the way in which the term is used: the putative constitutional order is seen as a legitimate political order; if it would not be coupled with legitimacy, it would not be worth striving for.[15]

In doing so, global constitutionalism taps into naturalist legal thought, and arguably is forced to do so, in the absence of a written global constitution or other positive sources of constitutionalism. Yet, it steers clear from all too naturalist approaches and also taps into positivist thought. Many of the constitutionalist writings make a point of empirically validating their approaches. They can do so by referring to the case law of human rights tribunals, to recommendations and declarations emanating from the UN General Assembly and other international organs, statements of political leaders, etc. Much of this is, obviously, in the eye of the beholder, and is self-constructed to a large degree: the same evidence can be used, often enough, to deny that constitutionalisation is taking place.

This chapter will proceed as follows. In the next section (Section 2), I will discuss the possibilities for positivism after the critical revolution, and will conclude that positivism and critical approaches may well work in tandem, if only because they are informed by some of the same concerns. I will then move on to constitutionalism, and argue that constitutionalism, at least in the liberal version that is so much in vogue, tends to depend on the interplay between positivism and naturalism (Section 3). As a result, it is fundamentally unstable, at least when it comes to ascertainment of the law. It should come as no surprise then, that in order to do justice to constitutionalist sentiments, international law is increasingly losing sight of what used to be called 'sources doctrine' and substituting accountability for sources. In other words – and it is not immediately self-evident whether this is a felicitous move – instead of asking whether international law has come into being in some recognisable manner, its existence is often very loosely assumed, with actors being held accountable against standards which may or may not be part of the *corpus iuris* of international law (Section 4). Instead of focusing on jointly formulating desirable rules for living together, the focus rests increasingly on applying whatever the

[14] Hints to this effect can be found in Hedley Bull, *The Anarchical Society: A Study of Order in World Politics* (MacMillan 1977).

[15] See similarly Nico Krisch, *Beyond Constitutionalism: The Pluralist Structure of Postnational Law* (Oxford University Press 2010).

applier holds to be desirable rules; as if time's arrow moves backwards. Doing so is difficult to reconcile with positivist givens, not only the requirement of consent, but also the distinction between *lex lata* and *lex ferenda* or the separation of law and morals. History rarely being unilinear, however, countermoves can be observed, such as the attempt to ground the validity of international rules in their legitimacy (Section 5).[16] In response, this chapter suggests in Section 6 that perhaps a more persuasive view may be to adopt what can be called a 'presumptive positivism', and provides an outline of some of its main features when it comes to separating law from non-law.

2 Post-revolutionary positivism

As a starting point, this chapter embraces the working definition of positivism adopted for this volume and assumes that positivism somehow relates to formal criteria for the identification of law and the legal order itself, with the task of scholarship limited to a cognitive one (as opposed to a law-generating task) and trying not to conflate the law as it stands and the law as it ought to be.[17] In other words, it will be assumed that positivism relates to the idea that 'what counts as law . . . is fundamentally a matter of social fact or convention'; that law and morality are not necessarily connected; and that law must be somehow cognisable or, as Coleman and Leiter put it, 'accessible to the human mind'.[18]

That is no easy task for positivism, and perhaps two issues need to be discussed in light of the late 1980s 'critical revolution' in international law.[19] In particular, the distinction between *lex lata* and *lex ferenda* is difficult to maintain in light of the forceful critique stemming from the Critical Legal Studies (CLS) movement to the effect that legal rules are essentially indeterminate: if that is the case (and many would accept this, regardless of their theoretical persuasion),[20] then it becomes difficult

16 This needs to be sharply distinguished from the legitimacy of institutions, individual political leaders, states, regimes or the global order at large, as briefly intimated in Section 5 of this chapter.

17 See d'Aspremont and Kammerhofer, Chapter 1.

18 Jules L. Coleman, Brian Leiter, 'Legal Positivism' in Dennis Patterson (ed.), *A Companion to Philosophy of Law and Legal Theory* (Blackwell 1996) 241–260 at 241.

19 The seminal work is Martti Koskenniemi, *From Apology to Utopia: The Structure of International Legal Argument* (Finnish Lawyers' Publishing Co. 1989, reissued Cambridge University Press 2005).

20 See already Hart's famous statement that 'all rules have a penumbra of uncertainty where the judge must choose between alternatives'. HLA Hart, *The Concept of Law* (Clarendon Press 1961) 12.

to delineate the *lex lata* with any degree of precision, and thus also to maintain a strict separation between *lex lata* and *lex ferenda.*

Second, positivism is right to insist on formal criteria for the identification of law and legal order; otherwise law collapses into descriptive or prescriptive sociology and loses its 'relative autonomy'.[21] Still, such entails a discussion as to what these formal criteria might be. Leading critical legal scholarship has perhaps not been very outspoken on the need to keep law and non-law separate, but does contain hints to this effect. Moreover, in the nature of things, it would seem that critical legal scholarship shows more affinities with positivism than with its counterpart.

While critical legal scholarship has not been very outspoken on the need to keep law separate from non-law and may prefer to think of the basis of obligation in law as a 'mystery',[22] nonetheless Martti Koskenniemi in particular has warned about the risk of colonising the law by means of power,[23] and has unequivocally pointed out that the adoption of legitimacy as somehow being of relevance carries much more political bias than is often realised.[24] For Koskenniemi, the good life would seem to involve the possibility of being able to participate in politics and decision-making, probably on the basis of equality, and all this presupposes a legal order whose norms are cognisable.[25] In the same vein, he has advocated the embrace of a 'culture of formalism' in an attempt to safeguard the possibility of a democratic politics,[26] and it is difficult to see how this might work in a naturalist legal order. This suggests, as a minimum, that positivism and CLS need not be sworn enemies: the main tenets of critical legal studies, including its emphasis on the emancipatory potential of international law, are quite possibly easier to reconcile with positivism than with naturalism.[27]

[21] The same risk attaches to inter-disciplinary scholarship. Jan Klabbers, 'The Relative Autonomy of International Law or the Forgotten Politics of Interdisciplinarity' 1 *Journal of International Law and International Relations* (2004–2005) 35–48.

[22] Martti Koskenniemi, 'The Mystery of Legal Obligation' 3 *International Theory* (2011) 319–325.

[23] Martti Koskenniemi, 'International Law and Hegemony: A Reconfiguration' 17 *Cambridge Review of International Affairs* (2004) 197–218.

[24] Martti Koskenniemi, 'Legitimacy, Rights, and Ideology: Notes towards a Critique of the New Moral Internationalism' 7 *Associations* (2003) 349–373.

[25] Martti Koskenniemi, 'What Use for Sovereignty Today?' 1 *Asian Journal of International Law* (2011) 61–70.

[26] Martti Koskenniemi, *The Gentle Civilizer of Nations: The Rise and Fall of International Law 1870–1960* (Cambridge University Press 2002). See also Martti Koskenniemi, 'Constitutionalism as Mindset: Reflections on Kantian Themes about International Law and Globalization' 8 *Theoretical Inquiries in Law* (2007) 9–36.

[27] See already, Jan Klabbers, *The Concept of Treaty in International Law* (Kluwer 1996).

The same point can be made in a different, and perhaps more appropriate, manner. If one of the central propositions of CLS holds that legal rules are indeterminate and dependent on ad hoc and contextual political agreement to fill them with contents, then it follows that CLS alone does not allow for judgments as to whether behaviour is illegal or legal or, more accurately perhaps, justifiable or not.[28] In order to make such evaluations, the critical legal scholar too must resort to something additional to the indeterminate rule; hence, critical legal scholarship inevitably ends up in tandem with either positivism or (less likely) naturalism, unless the critical legal scholar concerned refuses to come down from Mount Olympus and refuses to ever express a reasoned evaluation of actual state behaviour. Yet it may well be supposed that in coffee shops all over the world, whether in Cambridge, Massachusetts or Cairo, Egypt, critical legal scholars do voice their approval or disapproval with policy, and do so in a recognisably legal vocabulary.

A concrete example may perhaps clarify the point. Our critical legal scholar[29] cannot condemn the US invasion in Iraq without having some idea as to what the legal rules on the use of force and invasion say. If she is right that those rules themselves do not say much, she must base her judgment on something else, and it is most likely that she does so on the basis of written rules (Article 51 of the UN Charter, for example, however indeterminate), generally accepted precedent (think of the *Caroline* incident), the opinions of respected colleagues, etc. Policy arguments may also play a role here, although the critical legal scholar, if sincere (as we must assume) will realise that her policy preferences are no substitute for the law – again, however indeterminate. In other words, the critical legal scholar is almost inevitably driven to some kind of positivism; a drive towards naturalism is less likely, precisely because the distinction between legal arguments and policy preferences is less rigid in naturalism. In addition, moreover, the typical foil of the critical legal scholar is liberalism, and liberalism – simplistic as this may sound – is more closely aligned with naturalism than with positivism. The liberal might feel that the invasion in Iraq was justified in order to make the world safe for democracy, but this is something our critical legal scholar would have a hard time

[28] See similarly Philip Liste, *Völkerrecht-Sprechen* (Nomos 2012).

[29] I refer to 'scholar' here because any other construction is awkward: 'critical legal student' is ugly; 'crit' is too colloquial and perhaps too much in line with the self-identification of this group of scholars and therewith reifying, while 'critical lawyer' would seem to encompass a broader group than adherents to critical legal studies. I do not, however, wish to imply that no critical voices can be heard outside academia.

accepting in the absence of some evidence of there being a rule which could possibly be interpreted as allowing for democratic intervention.

The only way out, for our critical legal scholar, would be never to present an evaluation of any policy, actual or proposed, and there are probably examples of critical legal scholars who come close to such aloofness. Generally, though, this would be difficult to reconcile with the political instincts of the critical legal scholar – one becomes a critical legal scholar, it may be presumed, precisely because of an overwhelming interest in the political side of the law[30] or, in case of critical international lawyers, an abiding interest in the political side of international affairs.[31]

There is yet a third way leading to the same point, and that is this. CLS is very good at dissecting the structure of international law and the way in which the international legal order functions. It is capable of generating insightful hypotheses[32] and has great explanatory potential – as a heuristic device, the critical approach can be of great value.[33] By its own admission, however, it is not good at stating the contents of the law, partly because this is not its object of research. The critical scholar will rarely, if ever, engage in a quest for the proper meaning of Article 6 of the European Convention on Human Rights, or what it means to ensure 'prompt, adequate and effective' compensation in the law on the protection of investments. These questions fall outside the critical agenda and, what is more, cannot take a place there without betraying the core proposition that such rules have no 'proper' meaning. If the critical legal scholar looks at these at all, it is with a view to determining (perhaps with some *ennui*,

30 Possibly the best example is Duncan Kennedy, *A Critique of Adjudication (Fin de Siècle)* (Harvard University Press 1997). Many critical legal scholars place themselves on some point on the left of the political spectrum and would probably agree that a positivist conception of law is of more use to the poor and dispossessed than a naturalist conception, at least to the extent that the latter often masks hegemonic uses.

31 I put it this way for ease of expression, and by no means aim to suggest or imply that law and politics are separate spheres.

32 Here it should be pointed out that critical scholarship is often uncritically accepted as the new orthodoxy: a generally accepted hypothesis that never gets investigated. For a subtle comment along these lines, see David Kennedy, 'The Last Treatise: Project and Person (Reflections on Martti Koskenniemi's *From Apology to Utopia*)' 7 *German Law Journal* (2006) 982–992.

33 On a personal note, the way in which I discuss the main features of the law of international organisations and of international law in general owes much to critical legal studies without, arguably, forming a recognised or recognisable manifestation of critical legal scholarship. Jan Klabbers, *An Introduction to International Institutional Law* (2nd edn Cambridge University Press 2009); Jan Klabbers, *International Law* (Cambridge University Press 2013).

by now) that these rules too lack a fixed content. And yet, in legal practice, such rules are invoked and relied upon by individuals or companies as well as by states; they are applied by judges and arbiters and will, consequently, be given some meaning, however incidental and however contextual. In other words: the critical scholar asks different questions than does the positivist or the naturalist, and at least to some extent those different questions may be complementary rather than contradictory. And there is quite obviously no problem with the critical legal scholar recognising that a rule laid down in a treaty can function as a powerful argument in political debate.

To cut a long story short: there is something of a symbiosis (or at least possible symbiosis) between positivism and critical scholarship, and it is surely no coincidence that critical legal scholars have insisted on the separation of law and non-law. Here, then, critical legal scholarship and positivist scholarship can operate in tandem. The question remains, of course, what the ideal or most workable criterion can be. Some, having taken the critical lessons to heart, have advocated an increased resort to linguistic indicators and the practice of law-applying authorities, predominantly so as to overcome an undue reliance on the subjective intentions of actors.[34] Others may still feel that consent (note: not intent) plays a relevant role, if only because the governments of powerful states tend to think in terms of sovereignty and consent. If positivism, post-modern or otherwise, comprises a willingness to separate the desirable from the existing (this would, I guess, be a defendable position, while acknowledging that 'the existing' is in itself difficult to delineate), then the possible role of consent as part of a positivist attitude to international law cannot be dismissed without losing empirical traction.[35]

3 Between positivism and naturalism: from *ius cogens* to *erga omnes*

Ever since the critical revolution took international law by storm in the late 1980s, it is almost a truism to suggest that international law oscillates,

[34] Jean d'Aspremont, *Formalism and the Sources of International Law: A Theory of the Ascertainment of Legal Rules* (Oxford University Press 2011). While I would agree with d'Aspremont that the intent of parties alone cannot and should not be decisive, I would maintain that there is a difference between intent and consent, a difference that seems to be downplayed by d'Aspremont.

[35] Note that this is not saying that the validity of positivism as such depends on empirical plausibility. On this, see Jörg Kammerhofer, *Uncertainty in International Law: A Kelsenian Perspective* (Routledge 2011) in particular at 259–261.

and always has oscillated, between naturalism and positivism. In order to be convincing, so the main critical claim holds, any legal argument must tap into considerations of both state consent and normativity, for a positivist, consent-based claim is always vulnerable to naturalist critique, whereas an overtly normative argument is always open to the criticism that it is not based on what states or others actually do.

The constitutionalism debate and its antecedents have not been able to escape these trappings either. Perhaps the best example is the way in which Article 53 of the Vienna Convention on the Law of Treaties formulates what it takes to identify a *ius cogens* norm. Such norms, as is well known, are norms from which no derogation is permitted: this testifies to its naturalist orientation. Yet, in order to become effective, such norms must be 'accepted and recognised' as *ius cogens* norms 'by the international community of States as a whole'.

In other words, it does not suffice for a norm to be universally accepted. Such universal norms do exist: think, for instance, of the sanctity of the diplomatic bag, or the right of innocent passage. These are universally (or near-universally) accepted, but they are not accepted as norms from which no derogation is permitted. Hence, no matter the degree of acceptance (and acceptance or consent are often, rightly or wrongly, seen as positivist features), they fail to qualify as *ius cogens* norms, in that the naturalist element is lacking.

Conversely, norms of great moral fibre may not qualify either, unless they are accepted and recognised by the international community of states as a whole. Obnoxious as the death penalty may be, its prohibition will not qualify as a *ius cogens* norm as long as powerful states continue to endorse it. *Mutatis mutandis*, the same applies to child labour, or the use of individuals below the age of 18 in the armed forces. As a result, there are few norms that unambiguously qualify as *ius cogens*: perhaps the most convincing candidate is the prohibition of genocide, and it is perhaps no surprise that, to date, this is the only norm that has been considered part of *ius cogens* by the International Court of Justice.[36]

Much the same applies to the *erga omnes* concept, famously launched by the ICJ in its 1970 *Barcelona Traction* decision,[37] and after application

[36] In its 2012 state immunity judgment, the ICJ merely assumed, for argument's sake, that certain rules had the status of *ius cogens*, without actually saying that they did. See *Jurisdictional Immunities of the State (Germany v. Italy: Greece intervening)*, Judgment of 3 February 2012, ICJ Reports (2012) 99 at 140 (para. 93).

[37] *Barcelona Traction, Light and Power Co., Ltd (New Application: 1962) (Belgium v. Spain)*, Second Phase, Judgment of 5 February 1970, ICJ Reports (1970) 3 at 32 (para. 34).

a year later, in *Namibia*,[38] proved awkward,[39] effectively ignored ever since. As is well known, the Court designated the prohibitions of aggression and genocide, as well as slavery and racial discrimination, as obligations *erga omnes*. Again, then, these are norms of high moral fibre, suggesting a naturalist inspiration. Still, the Court could not help but use positive verbs to describe how these norms had come to be *erga omnes* obligations: this had resulted from the 'outlawing' of acts of aggression and genocide, and some of the corresponding rights of protection had been 'conferred' by international instruments or entered into, more amorphously, the corpus of general international law.[40]

The latter scenario may be seen as a nod to naturalism, in particular also in light of the single reference provided by the Court. It referred to its Advisory Opinion on *Reservations to the Genocide Convention*[41] and, without spelling it out, probably meant to refer to its oft-quoted statement that the principles underlying the Convention are binding on states 'even without any conventional obligation'. Even here there is room for doubt, however: the finding about the absence of conventional obligation was preceded by the claim that this idea was 'recognised' by civilised nations as binding them, and this points to recognition of a moral obligation strictly speaking, rather than to a moral obligation turned law. Moreover, and not less importantly, the Court stressed the 'common will' of the parties repeatedly. In other words, the opinion on *Reservations to the Genocide Convention* can be read as acceptance by the Court (and states generally) of the existence of a moral obligation, which many states had seen fit to turn into a legal obligation as well by concluding a treaty to that effect.

Again, then, positivist and naturalist thought intersect, and do so in particular by the Court insisting that a naturalist sentiment can only become of legal relevance through the regular consent-based procedure. Otherwise, it remains a moral obligation.[42] As with the formulation of *ius cogens* norms contained in Article 53 of the Vienna Convention on the

[38] *Legal Consequences for States of the Continued Presence of South Africa in Namibia (South West Africa) notwithstanding Security Council Resolution 276 (1970)*, Advisory Opinion of 21 June 1971, ICJ Reports (1971) 16.

[39] See the discussion in Jan Klabbers, 'The Scope of International Law: *Erga Omnes* Obligations and the Turn to Morality' in Matti Tupamäki (ed.), *Liber Amicorum Bengt Broms* (Finnish ILA Branch 1999) 149–179.

[40] *Barcelona Traction*, n. 37, at 32 (para. 34).

[41] *Reservations to the Convention on the Prevention and Punishment of the Crime of Genocide*, Advisory Opinion of 28 May 1951, ICJ Reports (1951) 15.

[42] *Reservations*, n. 41, at 23.

Law of Treaties, the naturalist sentiment, valuable as it is, is deemed unable to stand on its own: it needs to be supported by a positivist methodology.

Arguably, the main exception in the case law of the International Court concerning the strict separation of law and morality is to be found in one of its earliest post-war decisions. In *Corfu Channel*,[43] the Court held that Albania could be held responsible for the presence of mines in the Corfu Channel, partly because of 'elementary considerations of humanity'. Here, then, an argument can be made that since the Court had a hard time identifying an applicable legal norm, it fell back on morality as a guiding device.

Even this is not free from ambiguities, however. First, the Court made clear that the 'elementary considerations of humanity' were not the sole reason for finding Albania responsible. Other reasons included more robustly legal norms: the freedom of maritime communication, and the obligation not to allow one's territory to be used for acts contrary to the rights of others.[44] Second, it is not implausible to suggest that the Court, while technically barred from applying the UN Charter (Albania was not a UN member at the time), nonetheless found inspiration in the prohibition of the use of force laid down in the Charter and, given the language used by the Court, it may equally have been inspired by the gateway provision of the famous Martens clause, a generally accepted part of international humanitarian law.

What *Corfu Channel* suggests then is still a fairly strict separation between law and morality: it was the combination of the two which impelled the Court to hold Albania responsible; at no point did the court suggest that the 'elementary considerations of humanity'[45] were anything other than a moral command, and while the Court attached legal responsibility to the breach of a moral command, it is not self-evident that it would have done so without the additional considerations it cited, as mentioned above.

But even if the reference to 'elementary considerations of humanity' is taken in isolation, all *Corfu Channel* suggests is a liberal attitude to accountability: responsibility need not per se involve the breach of international legal obligations alone. This may be difficult to reconcile with the principle of legality ('*nulla crimen sine lege*'), but it is arguable that

[43] *Corfu Channel (United Kingdom v. Albania)*, Merits, Judgment of 9 April 1949, ICJ Reports (1949) 4.

[44] *Corfu Channel*, n. 43, at 22.

[45] *Corfu Channel*, n. 43, at 22.

in international relations, and in particular between states, this principle used to play a less pronounced role than it has in liberal domestic societies.

Either way, the bigger picture that presents itself is that of mutual dependence of positivist and naturalist considerations, at least where law-making is concerned. The *Corfu Channel* court refrained from framing 'elementary considerations of humanity' in terms of a strict legal obligation; yet its willingness to hold Albania responsible for violating 'elementary considerations of humanity' cast a shadow of the future.

4 Towards accountability

It has been noted that identifying rules of international law has become increasingly difficult in recent decades.[46] Legally relevant instruments are produced by states meeting through the regular diplomatic channels in the form of treaties, but it is well documented that legally relevant materials are also produced elsewhere: in networks of civil servants or governors, by ministry representatives meeting outside diplomatic channels, by international institutions, etc.[47] Much of this has proved difficult to capture in terms of the traditional sources of international law,[48] and much of this is caused by the impossibility of making naturalism and positivism work in tandem.

Early attempts to capture these modes of possible law-making would do so under the label soft law, thereby infelicitously suggesting that law can come, like politics or morality, in varying degrees of bindingness and, what is more, can do so as a formal matter.[49] These attempts have failed to convince, however, and the international judiciary was never persuaded to begin with.[50] Hence, the vocabulary of soft law has slowly receded, and is being replaced by a new, equally problematic vocabulary:

[46] Indeed, it has been noted that there are several layers of uncertainty. Kammerhofer, n. 35.

[47] Anne-Marie Slaughter, *A New World Order* (Princeton University Press 2004).

[48] Alan Boyle, Christine Chinkin, *The Making of International Law* (Oxford University Press 2007).

[49] To say that rules can have different degrees of binding force because they contain different words would hardly be controversial: a promise 'never under any circumstances' to engage in behaviour X is a lot harder than a promise to 'endeavour to refrain' from engaging in behaviour X. Jan Klabbers, 'The Redundancy of Soft Law' 65 *Nordic Journal of International Law* (1996) 167–182.

[50] Jan Klabbers, 'International Courts and Informal International Law' in Joost Pauwelyn, Ramses Wessel, Jan Wouters (eds), *Informal International Lawmaking* (Oxford University Press 2012) 219–240.

that of 'transnational law'.[51] The notion of 'transnational law' currently in vogue aims to capture normatively relevant utterances made by those not formally empowered, by actors other than states or their representatives, etc.[52] This too is bound to remain unsuccessful, if only because it reproduces the same questions and same open-ended answers as the soft law discussion did. And the reason why the 'transnational law' conception cannot rise beyond reproducing the earlier discussion is because there is fundamental disagreement as to how to tell law from non-law.

Possibly as a result, the discipline has started to look elsewhere, and has started to look in particular at accountability, thus turning the traditional scheme of things on its head. Whereas the classic position, solidified in the Articles on State Responsibility, held that responsibility could only be attached to an internationally wrongful act, and therewith presupposed the existence and identification of a valid rule or principle of international law, the current trend works the other way around. Recent discussions of accountability in international law start from the position that wherever public authority is exercised on the international level, there must be the possibility to hold those who exercise it responsible for doing so, regardless of whether their behaviour actually violates any recognised rule or principle of international law. In doing so, the spirit of the *Corfu Channel* judgment is upheld, however unwittingly, perhaps.

This move from 'sources' to 'accountability' is perhaps most clearly visible in the work of the International Law Association on the accountability of international organisations. The ILA Committee wrote that international organisations could be held accountable for not living up to a set of 'recommended rules and practices'. This label, so it suggested, was explicitly chosen 'so as not to prejudice whether any [of these recommended rules and practices] should be seen as a recommendation for sound internal practice or whether it was operative on a legal level, and in the latter case whether it was de lege lata or de lege ferenda'.[53] Sir Frank Berman, Chair of the Committee, put it even more clearly: the term 'was a deliberate choice to avoid pre-judging whether the reference was

[51] For an early formulation of this move, see Jan Klabbers, 'Reflections on Soft International Law in a Privatized World' 16 *Finnish Yearbook of International Law* (2005) 313–328.

[52] A useful recent contribution is Paulius Jurcys, Poul Kjaer, Ren Yatsunami (eds), *Regulatory Hybridization in the Transnational Sphere* (Martinus Nijhoff 2013).

[53] International Law Association, Committee on Accountability of International Organisations, 'Final Report' in ILA, *Report of the Seventy-First Conference Berlin 2004* (ILA 2004) 164–241 at 170–171.

to an existing rule of law, to a rule in course of development or to good practice'.[54] Sir Frank also made clear what inspired this breaking of new ground, as he called it: 'The question of the law applicable to International Organisations was a surprisingly difficult one to answer.'[55]

Indeed, the Committee was perfectly clear that at least some of its proposed recommended rules and practices did 'not necessarily' reflect existing legal rules, and held that these were 'derived from common principles, objectives and notions' and 'reflect considerable practice'.[56] In short, the ILA Committee on the Accountability of International Organisations in essence gave up on trying to identify rules of international law binding on international organisations, and strongly suggested that what matters is not so much whether organisations respect international law, but whether they behave properly, thus substituting a vague ethical standard for hard law. Improper behaviour would lead to accountability, regardless of whether or not the improper behaviour would involve any breach of an international legal obligation.[57]

Something similar applies to the well-known global administrative law (GAL) project, pioneered at New York University and Rome's La Sapienza University. Here, the underlying idea is that much of legally relevant activity takes place in a 'global administrative space', by states as well as other entities, and that somehow it stands to reason to hold the actors operating in that space accountable for improper behaviour, in particular relating to transparency and participation in decision-making, reasoned decision-making and the notion of legality. In what is arguably GAL's manifesto, the authors recognise that it may be difficult to locate the precise sources of global administrative law, although they are attracted by 'a revived version of *ius gentium* that could encompass norms emerging among a wide variety of actors and in very diverse settings'.[58] Yet, they acknowledge that such a conceptualised *ius gentium* is not unproblematic: it leaves open whose acts count as relevant for the creation of rules, and how much consistent practice is needed. Tellingly perhaps,

[54] ILA, n. 53, at 236. [55] ILA, n. 53, at 238. [56] ILA, n. 53, at 172.

[57] The same applies to testing whether or not actors violate the 'interim obligation' of Art. 18 of the Vienna Convention on the Law of Treaties 1969: here too what often matters is the propriety of behaviour, rather than its strict legality. Jan Klabbers, 'How to Defeat a Treaty's Object and Purpose Pending Entry into Force: Towards Manifest Intent' 34 *Vanderbilt Journal of Transnational Law* (2001) 283–331.

[58] Benedict Kingsbury, Nico Krisch, Richard B. Stewart, 'The Emergence of Global Administrative Law' 68 *Law and Contemporary Problems* (2005) 15–61 at 29.

the legal force of rules is expressed, at times, in terms of a legitimacy discourse: what matters is not so much whether a rule is formally accepted or recognised as such, but rather whether it is able 'to generate a strong pull for adhesion'.[59] Surely, it is no coincidence, then, that its spiritual fathers attach the emerging global administrative law to three functional concerns: administrative accountability, protection of rights and promotion of democracy.[60] Global administrative law exists to serve these aims; on this conception, the existence of clear legal standards as traditionally conceived by the discipline of international law is of secondary relevance only.

That is not to say that proponents of global administrative law are blind to issues relating to the basis of legal obligation. A group of scholars working at the Max Planck Institute for Comparative Public Law and International Law in Heidelberg has aspired to connect global administrative accountability to the notion of general principles of law,[61] and Benedict Kingsbury has attempted to infuse a Hartian Rule of Recognition (or several rules of recognition, in fact, for distinct governance regimes) into global administrative law.[62] Still, this stops short, for the time being, of developing clear criteria for the identification of rules of law, and again, it is telling perhaps that Kingsbury feels compelled to refer to a legitimacy discourse when talking about the 'normative pull' of putative principles of global administrative law.[63]

In short, the traditional focus on 'sources' is in the process of being replaced by a focus on 'accountability'. It is no longer considered all that relevant to be able to point to a precise legal obligation, in large measure because the very concept of legal obligation has become obfuscated: all the talk about soft law, symptomatic of a managerial approach to global governance,[64] has created the illusion that law comes in varying shades of grey, from the very soft to the extremely hard and, accordingly, that it actually does not really matter all that much whether a putative rule can be

[59] Kingsbury, Krisch and Stewart, n. 58, at 31.

[60] Kingsbury, Krisch and Stewart, n. 58, at 43.

[61] Armin von Bogdandy *et al.* (eds), *The Exercise of Public Authority by International Institutions: Advancing International Institutional Law* (Springer 2010).

[62] Benedict Kingsbury, 'The Concept of "Law" in Global Administrative Law' 20 *EJIL* (2009) 23–57.

[63] Kingsbury, n. 62, at 57.

[64] See also Martti Koskenniemi, 'The Fate of Public International Law: Between Technique and Politics' 70 *Modern Law Review* (2007) 1–30.

classified as 'legal'. Instead, there appears to be a widespread approach to the effect that if public power is exercised improperly, those who exercise it ought to be held accountable. While impropriety is still cast in terms of rules or standards, it is abundantly clear that traditional tests concerning the basis of obligation have lost much of their relevance. Few wonder whether the World Bank, if and when accused of violating human rights, is actually under a legal obligation to respect the human right in question, let alone where the Bank's obligation would stem from.

In the process, it would also seem that the underlying concept of accountability itself is subtly undergoing change. When lawyers talk of accountability, they can no longer be taken simply to refer to being held responsible *ex post facto* for wrongful behaviour and a liability to make good or compensate. Instead, accountability is in the process of being re-worked as a relational concept. On the theory that relations between entities and their stakeholders are reiterative, it makes little sense to think of accountability as merely a liability to make good without also addressing the root causes of wrongful behaviour. This is visible, to a considerable extent, in the practice under multilateral environmental agreements, where dispute settlement takes the form of compliance procedures, concentrating not on compensation or restoration, but on offering assistance so as to create lasting norm-conforming behaviour.[65] Likewise, the emergence of international criminal law has also seen an increase of attention for alternative methods, in particular truth and reconciliation commissions.[66]

This is not to say that more traditional notions of responsibility and what it entails have been thrown out of the window. But it is to say that a subtle shift is taking place, advocated by some as a move towards 'intelligent accountability',[67] and theorised by others as a move towards a more relational notion, 'oriented to learning and through learning to trust and civic virtue'.[68]

[65] See for a critical discussion, see Jan Klabbers, 'Compliance Procedures' in Daniel Bodansky, Jutta Brunnée, Ellen Hey (eds), *The Oxford Handbook of International Environmental Law* (Oxford University Press 2007) 995–1009.

[66] For a balanced assessment, see Mark A. Drumbl, *Atrocity, Punishment, and International Law* (Cambridge University Press 2007).

[67] Onora O'Neill, *A Question of Trust* (Cambridge University Press 2002).

[68] Edward Weisband, 'Conclusion: Prolegomena to a Postmodern Public Ethics: Images of Accountability in Global Frames' in Alnoor Ebrahim, Edward Weisband (eds), *Global Accountabilities: Participation, Pluralism, and Public Ethics* (Cambridge University Press 2007) 307–339 at 336–337.

5 Franck's legitimacy approach

When Benedict Kingsbury appeals to the 'compliance pull' of rules (as noted above), he seems to refer to the concept of legitimacy developed by Thomas M. Franck which, for a while, appeared to offer a serious alternative to traditional sources doctrine. For Franck, recognising the poverty of traditional sources doctrine in international law and the awkward way in which sources doctrine would be able to handle recent developments, what mattered was not so much whether rules would be formally binding, or 'legal', but rather whether they would exercise a compliance pull, and they would do so if regarded as legitimate. Legitimacy then was a function of the rule's determinacy, its symbolic validation, whether it would coherently fit with other rules, and what Franck called 'adherence': the extent to which they conform to an ultimate Rule of Recognition.[69]

In practice, this would mean that norms could emerge without going through the traditional sources tests. Thus, in a wonderful illustration, Franck suggested in the early 1990s that international law was starting to recognise an 'emerging right to democratic governance', and did so by carefully avoiding any language reminiscent of classic traditional sources doctrine, in particular (given the absence of a clear treaty norm on democratic entitlement) of customary international law. His analysis was not based on state practice and *opinio iuris*, but, instead, on whether international actors would support the underlying right of self-determination (he answered in the affirmative), whether the international community has been active in monitoring democracy and elections (again affirmative) and whether the right to free expression had met with widespread recognition (yet again, affirmative). To drive the point home, finally, Franck wondered whether the right to peace, linked in Kantian manner to democracy, had met with general recognition, and once again answered in the affirmative.[70] This allowed him to conclude that '[b]oth textually and in practice, the international system is moving toward a clearly designated democratic entitlement, with national governance validated by international standards and systematic monitoring of compliance'.[71]

In other words, the ultimate validity requirement for international law, according to Franck, was to be legitimacy, rather than such notions

[69] Franck set this out with his usual clarity in Thomas M. Franck, *The Power of Legitimacy among Nations* (Oxford University Press 1990).

[70] Thomas M. Franck, 'The Emerging Right to Democratic Governance' 86 *AJIL* (1992) 46–91.

[71] Franck, n. 70, at 91.

as state consent or, as he famously wrote, justice. To Franck, legitimacy enjoys 'lexical priority... over justice',[72] meaning that it is easier to find global concord over what constitutes legitimacy than what constitutes justice; considerations of justice therefore must be left to another day.

Yet, legitimacy as the ultimate criterion of the validity of international law is problematic. For one thing, legitimacy comes in so many guises and can relate to so many different things that at the very least conceptual clarity would be required. Legitimacy can attach to states and their governments.[73] It can attach to international institutions. It can attach to the activities of those states, governments and institutions. It can attach to the legal instruments produced by those states, governments and institutions. It can even attach to the global order at large.[74] At the very least, then, an appeal to legitimacy should spell out what exactly is deemed to be legitimate, mindful of the consideration that however conceptualised, it will be perfectly possible for a legitimate institution to engage in illegitimate acts or adopt illegitimate laws, whereas it cannot readily be excluded that illegitimate entities nonetheless produce laws that can be considered legitimate.[75]

The bigger problem though – and the one Franck aimed to tackle by conceptualising legitimacy in the way he did – is that legitimacy as such is very much in the eye of the beholder. This works in at least two different ways. First, and rather obviously, people of different political orientations may reach different conclusions about the legitimacy of a state, an institution or a piece of legislation. Hence the need, recognised by Franck, to develop further criteria. Second, and more problematically for present purposes, different stakeholders may also reach different conclusions regarding the legitimacy of an entity or an instrument. To adapt an example borrowed from Grant and Keohane, a project sponsored by the World Bank may be considered legitimate by the US Treasury (presumably, it displays sound financial management), yet be illegitimate in the eyes of the poor and dispossessed whom it affects.[76] In other words,

72 Franck, n. 69, at 236.

73 E.g. Allen Buchanan, *Justice, Legitimacy, and Self-Determination: Moral Foundations for International Law* (Oxford University Press 2004).

74 Hilary Charlesworth, Jean-Marc Coicaud (eds), *Fault Lines of International Legitimacy* (Cambridge University Press 2010).

75 For further discussion, see Jan Klabbers, Touko Piiparinen, 'Normative Pluralism: An Exploration' in Jan Klabbers, Touko Piiparinen (eds), *Normative Pluralism in International Law: Exploring Global Governance* (Cambridge University Press 2013) 13–34.

76 Ruth W. Grant, Robert O. Keohane, 'Accountability and Abuses of Power in World Politics' 99 *American Political Science Review* (2005) 29–43 at 33.

different stakeholders will operate on different conceptions of legitimacy, even regardless of political cleavages, and as long as that is the case, legitimacy is not particularly suitable as a criterion for the validity of rules.

The point is not merely to stipulate that different actors may invoke different normative orders in support of their positions (such would be a trivial claim), the point is that even within the same normative order – international law – such conflicting views on legitimacy can hardly be avoided in the absence of a recognised hierarchy between norms. The US Treasury, to resort to the above-mentioned example, will be able to enlist the World Bank's Articles of Agreement in support of its construction of legitimacy; the poor and dispossessed will be able to invoke human rights law in support of their construction of legitimacy – or illegitimacy, as the case may be. The vocabulary of legitimacy not only obscures matters by suggesting that it is non-legalistic and more in tune with both the real and the desirable than law can ever be, but is singularly suspect as a criterion for the validity of both norms and action.

6 Presumptive international law

As noted above, sources doctrine is in the process of being displaced by a focus on accountability, but this development must be deemed less than fully satisfactory, in particular in light of the discussion on constitutionalism in international law. After all, in a liberal constitutional order,[77] there must be some minimum idea as to what the law says, and this minimum must be cognisable before actors engage in their activities, rather than afterwards. Hence, while the reconfiguration of accountability is possibly a felicitous development, it does not displace the need for a reliable indicator telling people whether behaviour is legally ordained or permitted.

This holds true all the more so in a constitutional order, at least as that term is commonly understood in liberal international legal discourse. Such a constitutional order is generally supposed to be more or less democratic, and is supposed to guarantee some respect for fundamental rights of its constituent elements, individuals as well as states. It is difficult to see how such a constitutional order can be non-positive: appeals to faith, *recta ratio*, the actual compliance with norms or legitimacy are too open-ended to serve, and holding actors accountable *ex post facto* without there being clarity as to what is expected of them seems difficult

77 Since the constitutionalisation of international law is invariably discussed in liberal terms, I will limit myself here to discussing such a liberal vision; see also Section 1.

to reconcile with the principle of legality, which must be considered one of the core notions of any constitutional order. Hence, constitutionalism and positivism need to go hand in hand.[78]

This implies that the constitutionalising international legal order requires a validity criterion so as to separate law from non-law. Traditionally, international law found this, for better or for worse, in the notion of state consent: treaties could only bind those states that had expressed their consent to be bound. And while consent could be expressed in manifold and highly informal ways, nonetheless it was required. Exceptions were (and are) few and far between: some might suggest that so-called objective regimes can come to bind third parties without their consent (although this has proven to be difficult to sustain),[79] and it has been argued that perhaps the UN Charter is an exception.[80] By and large, though, treaties require consent, as reflected in the Vienna Convention on the Law of Treaties.

Likewise, at least in theory, customary international law requires consent (more on this below), either in the form of affirmative state practice and expressions of *opinio iuris* or, more problematically still, in tacit form.[81] The recognition of the institution of the 'persistent objector' indicates that there is a theoretical possibility not to become bound by emerging rules of customary international law, and that this is a function of the absence of consent. Circular as this may be (the absence of consent testifies to the relevance of consent), that does not mean it can therefore be ignored.[82]

Either way, state consent, as is well known, creates difficulties of its own, and is often lamented as standing in the way of developing law in accordance with the needs of the international community.[83] It allows states not to be bound by putative obligations that many deem desirable, or even necessary; it allows for 'free riding'; it allows for 'holding out' or 'holding others hostage', all to the detriment of the global order and,

[78] Klabbers, Peters and Ulfstein, n. 9; likewise Krisch, n. 15.

[79] See the illuminating discussion of the Antarctic regime by Bruno Simma, suggesting that the regime's force on third parties is ultimately best explained by reference to their acquiescence, and acquiescence is best seen as a form of consent. Bruno Simma, 'The Antarctic Treaty as a Treaty Providing for an "Objective Regime"' 19 *Cornell International Law Journal* (1986) 189–209.

[80] Fassbender, n. 2.

[81] For brief critical discussion, see Kammerhofer, n. 35, at 77–78.

[82] There is a sense in which law cannot escape such circularities: think only of the *pacta sunt servanda* norm. See Gerald G. Fitzmaurice, 'Some Problems Regarding the Formal Sources of International Law' in F. M. van Asbeck *et al.* (eds), *Symbolae Verzijl* (Martinus Nijhoff 1958) 153–176.

[83] Emblematic is Jonathan Charney, 'Universal International Law' 87 *AJIL* (1993) 529–551.

more pragmatically, to the detriment of solving acute global crises. As a result, many would agree that in a globalising world, which demands something of a constitutional legal order,[84] the notion of state consent as the criterion for the validity of legal norms is no longer very fruitful – if it ever was.

Nonetheless, consent cannot easily be dismissed, precisely to preserve the very values at the heart of constitutionalism. The minimum of democracy required, as associated with any liberal conception of constitutionalism, suggests that peoples and their representatives, whether organised in states or in some other ways,[85] must have a say in the development of new legal norms, and some of the basic liberal rights of states and individuals would surely have to include the right to be free from unwanted intervention. This may not be of great concern to the positivist per se, but becomes a concern for liberal constitutionalists, including those of positivist persuasion.

This then results in something of a double dilemma. First, a constitutionalising legal order cannot do without a validity criterion, yet the traditional criterion is no longer deemed fit to use. Second, in order to protect the values of constitutionalism, something like the traditional criterion must be kept in place: if international law is to boast a minimum of democratic content and respect for the rights of the members of the global political community (which has to include states), then states must have the possibility to remain out of the reach of legal instruments they find unacceptable. And even if one would be inclined to disregard the rights of states and focus on the rights of individuals instead, nonetheless those individuals too ought not to be overpowered. Hence, a constitutionalising global legal order requires consent as the basis (although perhaps not the only basis, but that is a different discussion) for valid law, but without the requirement of consent being allowed to frustrate the achievement of fundamental global goods or meeting universal needs.

I have argued elsewhere that a possible answer may reside in the recognition of presumptive international law.[86] This is both normatively

[84] On the links between globalisation and constitutionalisation, see Klabbers, 'Setting the Scene', n. 9.

[85] Intriguingly, given that direct global democracy is not a realistic option, attempts to define statehood away tend to revert to entities which display an uncanny similarity to states. Among the more thoughtful attempts is Andrew Linklater, *The Transformation of Political Community* (Polity 1998).

[86] Jan Klabbers, 'Law-making and Constitutionalism' in Jan Klabbers, Anne Peters and Geir Ulfstein, *The Constitutionalization of International Law* (Oxford University Press 2009) n. 9, 81–125.

desirable, in light of the above, and eminently practicable, as international law already contains the basic elements of such an approach. A presumptive approach works on the idea that normative utterances by the relevant actors must be presumed to be 'law', unless there is evidence to rebut the presumption.[87] This is not nearly as eccentric as it may appear at first sight: it essentially amounts to reversing the burden of proof. Under the *Lotus* doctrine, international lawyers are socialised to presume that no law has been created unless there is evidence of state consent – the PCIJ even explicitly spoke of a presumption when it held that consent was necessary in a system of sovereign states because '[r]estrictions upon the independence of States cannot . . . be presumed'.[88] One can, of course, make light of *Lotus* given the absence of formal precedent in international law, but that is beside the point: the limited point, for present purposes, is that most international lawyers have been socialised into thinking in terms of a presumption about the non-existence of international law; a presumptive approach merely proposes to reverse that presumption. It does imply that 'normative utterances' must be distinguished from 'non-normative utterances', and such may on occasion prove difficult indeed, but such difficulties are not qualitatively different from the difficulties involved in interpreting law (or any other text or practice, for that matter) generally.[89]

If *Lotus* represented good and useful law for the inter-war years (which, certainly, has been widely contested by contemporary commentators),[90] today's world is rather different from that of eighty-five years ago – as is today's legal setting. If back then sovereignty and an emerging international judicial system demanded that restrictions on the independence of states could not be presumed, it may be time to reconsider that opinion, and start from the position that restrictions can actually be presumed, subject to rebuttal.

87 An important source of inspiration is the presumptive positivism of Schauer. Frederick Schauer, *Playing by the Rules: A Philosophical Examination of Rule-Based Decision-Making in Law and in Life* (Clarendon Press 1991).

88 *S.S. 'Lotus' (France v. Turkey)*, Judgment of 7 September 1927, PCIJ Series A No. 10 (1927) 18.

89 A recent and useful contribution is Ingo Venzke, *How Interpretation Makes International Law: On Semantic Change and Normative Twists* (Oxford University Press 2012).

90 E.g. James Leslie Brierly, 'The Basis of Obligation in International Law' in Hersch Lauterpacht, CHM Waldock (eds), *James Leslie Brierly: The Basis of Obligation in International Law and Other Papers* (Oxford University Press 1958) 1–67 (first published as: James Leslie Brierly, 'Le fondement du caractère obligatoire du droit international' 23 *Recueil des Cours* (1928) 463–592).

In fact, international law already recognises as much with regard to customary international law: in that setting, while consent still plays a role, the starting presumption once a customary rule is identified is that it applies across the board, also to those who have not actively participated in its formation. This may be most clearly visible when human rights or humanitarian law are involved, but would seem to apply in other branches of international law as well. Likewise, albeit of less practical urgency, general principles of law are often presumed to exist prior to positive affirmations by individual states or other actors. And the international law on state succession recognises the possibility for 'newly independent states' to opt out of regimes accepted by their predecessors: what is debated is whether this applies to all regimes (in particular, regimes for the protection of human rights),[91] but not the basic facility as such. Hence, it can confidently be claimed that large chunks of international law already operate on the basis of a presumptive approach.

In fact, the claim can even be extended. With written agreements too, there is a presumption that they bind their parties and thus constitute law (at least for those parties), unless the opposite is demonstrated. An attempt in the 1950s to hold that written agreements do not constitute law unless accompanied by an indication that they do not merely bind, but are also intended to create legal relations, has failed to convince.[92] At best (or worst), some claim that the position may be reversed when states conclude a Memorandum of Understanding: these would be presumed not to bind at law,[93] but with regular written agreements the starting point is that they bind their parties. And indeed, it could hardly be otherwise: no legal order can exist on the basis of a presumption that agreements reached are not legally binding,[94] a position also explicitly endorsed by the International Court of Justice.[95]

If it is accepted that presumptive international law is desirable and practicable in principle, then two issues need further reflection. The

[91] E.g. Menno T. Kamminga, 'State Succession in Respect of Human Rights Treaties' 7 *EJIL* (1996) 469–484.

[92] James E. S. Fawcett, 'The Legal Character of International Agreements' 30 *BYBIL* (1953) 381–400; for a critical discussion, see Klabbers, n. 27.

[93] Anthony Aust, *Modern Treaty Law and Practice* (2nd edn Cambridge University Press 2007).

[94] Frederick A. Mann, 'Reflections on a Commercial Law of Nations' 33 *BYBIL* (1957) 20–51.

[95] Most explicitly in *Maritime Delimitation and Territorial Questions between Qatar and Bahrain (Qatar v. Bahrain)*, Jurisdiction and Admissibility, Judgment of 1 July 1994, ICJ Reports (1994) 112.

first refers to the identity of those who can make presumptive international law; the second relates to the possible grounds for rebutting the presumption.

As for putative law-makers, operating on the basis of a presumptive approach allows for a rather broad spectrum. Adopting a criterion developed by Tamanaha, it might be sensible to hold that it is those who can make law who are habitually regarded as law-makers.[96] That does not render a presumptive approach to law akin to 'legal realism in disguise' or to a behaviourist approach,[97] as the argument is not that these entities invariably create law, but only that their normative utterances can be presumed to constitute law unless rebutted.

The broad group of possible law-makers thus identified comprises states, obviously, but may also encompass international organisations and more informal meetings of states or their representatives, either in networks of civil servants or at highly visible summit meetings. It may also encompass regulators operating within their sectors: bankers adopting Basel guidelines, securities oversight experts adopting securities regimes, etc. Standard-setters such as those at ISO or the Codex Alimentarius Commission need not a priori be excluded either: the results of their activities may be presumed to be law, unless the presumption is rebutted. A welcome side effect of the presumptive approach, therewith, is that it helps to relax the stranglehold that states have on the formal making of international law.

Rebutting the presumption may be possible on various grounds.[98] One ground may be that the entity concerned acts outside its jurisdiction, however vaguely circumscribed. Surely, there is little reason to treat instruments adopted by the Codex Alimentarius Commission as law if these aspire to regulate behaviour during armed conflict, or to treat as legal investment rules emanating from the International Council for the Exploration of the Seas.

The presumption of law may also be rebutted if the chosen form indicates a clear intention not to create law. This would help to safeguard the possibility of non-binding resolutions: states acting in the UN General Assembly vote for resolutions in the expectation that these do not become legally binding, and that is an expectation that needs to be respected.

[96] Brian Z. Tamanaha, *A General Jurisprudence of Law and Society* (Oxford University Press 2001).

[97] José E. Alvarez, *International Organizations as Law-Makers* (Oxford University Press 2005).

[98] For greater detail, see Klabbers, n. 86.

Likewise, context too can be of relevance. A unilateral promise made in jest during a press briefing or before a television audience will not be considered to give rise to binding obligations, whereas the same promise made in a formal setting, such as a General Assembly meeting, may well be presumed to be law.[99] Nonetheless, this cannot be taken to mean that it is only within the General Assembly that such statements can be made in order to acquire legally binding force; it only means that the context (any context) must suggest that the words were used with seriousness. Repetitions of the same promise may come to strengthen the presumption.

Rebuttal can also stem from the wording chosen. The formula that an agreement shall be applied 'on a voluntary basis' implies that no binding obligation has been created. Wording that leaves infinite discretion likewise suggests the absence of legal obligation or, at least, that the obligation may not go much beyond a duty to take it seriously in good faith. Surely, though, an obligation to 'accord high priority' to granting market access to developing nations is not entirely devoid of content, difficult as it may be to flesh out what constitutes the granting of high priority and how to enforce it.[100]

7 By way of conclusion

This chapter has discussed some of the connections between constitutionalism and positivism after the 'critical revolution', with positivism conceptualised by and large – and modestly – as legal thought that insists on international law being somehow man-made: traceable to the consent of the governed in one way or another, independent from moral considerations, and more or less objectively cognisable.

The point of the chapter has been to suggest that in a putatively constitutionalising global legal order, positivism is indispensable; anything else would be difficult to reconcile with the very idea of liberal constitutionalism (and the liberal version is the one in vogue). In this light, while it is no coincidence that a move towards accountability is taking place under the banner of constitutionalism, accountability alone cannot guarantee constitutionalism. In a liberal constitutional order, the subjects need to have a decent idea as to what is demanded from them; hence,

[99] The ICJ captured some of this in its argumentation in *Frontier Dispute (Burkina Faso/Republic of Mali)*, Judgment of 22 December 1986, ICJ Reports (1986) 554.

[100] Art. XXXVII General Agreement on Tariffs and Trade 1947.

some way must be found to incorporate law-making in a constitutionalist perspective. Some aim to do so by insisting on the relevance of linguistic indicators; some have sought to do so by invoking the legitimacy of rules. I have argued that such is unsatisfactory, and that presumptive law may be a better approach. Presumptive law has the great benefit – if that is what it is – of offering a pragmatic reconciliation between naturalist and positivist thought, and both are indispensable for a liberal constitutional order: constitutionalism is inspired by the former, and cannot do without the latter. Needless to say, all of this has remained rather sketchy: the picture painted above involves broad strokes. The main point should be clear though: any liberal conception of constitutionalism which foregoes positivism remains ultimately incoherent and, what is worse, runs the risk of becoming a fig leaf for hegemonic exercises of power cross-dressed in a mantle of universal values.

11

International legal positivism and new approaches to international law

SAHIB SINGH*

> A prominent scientist had just given a brilliant lecture on the foundations of the universe. During the question period an elderly lady suggested that there was a problem with the professor's analysis. 'What is that?' asked the professor cautiously. 'It's all wrong,' the woman replied, 'because the universe actually rests on the back of a giant turtle.' The professor, taken aback, forced a smile and then countered: 'If that's the case there is still the question, what is that turtle standing on?' The audience tittered, but the woman, undaunted, replied: 'Another, much larger turtle.' 'But . . . ' objected the professor. 'I'm sorry, Professor, it's turtles all the way down.'[1]

1 Introduction

Theory is an unrelenting and inescapable act of manipulation. It is an act perpetrated by both the form and substance of a theory, by its rhetorical economy and its substantive claims. My task, here, is to unravel these acts. But in unmasking the manoeuvres of particular theories, this chapter and these very words contrive to perpetuate a different form of control, no less violent than those used by what it seeks to dethrone. Manipulation is inescapable and this chapter is, therefore, culpable. To understand theory as a politically violent and power-based aesthetic is to remove it from

* An extended version of this chapter, with an application to Kelsen and Hart, will be published as: Sahib Singh, 'The Politics of Theory: Form' (forthcoming). Observations concerning the way in which this project has been presented are premised on an introduction written by the editors in October 2011 and comments/observations made in a workshop held in Amsterdam in November 2011. The former has since been significantly amended, but not viewed by this author.

[1] Roger Cramton, 'Demystifying Legal Scholarship' 75 *Georgetown Law Journal* (1986–1987) 1 at 1–2.

the realm of innocence and abstraction.[2] It is upon this foundation that this chapter will examine the relationship between neo-international legal positivism (neo-ILP)[3] and new approaches to international law (NAIL). Specifically, it will examine the politics that structure this *relationship* and the complicity of form in the politics of theory.

Neo-ILP and NAIL cannot solely be understood as a collection of substantive claims, of turtles, of ideas. They must be understood as projects.[4] They must be understood as deliberate social constructs whose ideological postures occur within a specific historical context, buttressed by material bases that ground their socio-political dimensions. There is insufficient space in this chapter to do justice to each of these angles as regards the stated projects, but they will not be entirely neglected in the analysis that follows. The power of an idea does not lie in its intrinsic merit. To receive, process and become self-conscious of an idea is insufficient for this idea to become consequential. It must be deployed according to accepted *forms* of knowledge-transmission[5] and it must affect one's socio-cognitive practices. The reduction of theory, as a collection of ideas, concepts and relationships, to the ideational – is corrosive (see also Section 2.3).[6] It elevates the power of a theory's substantive claims above its form, the ideational over the material, and the rational over the non-rational.

[2] Michel Foucault, *Discipline and Punish: The Birth of the Prison* (Alan Sheridan (tr.), 2nd edn Vintage 1995) 170; Michel Foucault, 'Two Lectures' in Colin Gordon (ed.), *Michel Foucault Power/Knowledge: Selected Interviews and Other Writings 1972–1977* (Pantheon 1980) 78–108 at 81–85.

[3] All references to neo-ILP in this chapter only seek to refer to the present project and the works of Kammerhofer, d'Aspremont and early Beckett. There is undoubtedly other contemporary positivist work being produced, but these are not subject to the critique presented here – even if such critique may be applicable.

[4] This term is deliberate and intended to take on the meaning provided by Duncan Kennedy: '[a] project is a continuous goal-orientated practical activity based on an analysis of some kind (with a textual or oral tradition), but the goals and the analysis are not necessarily internally coherent or consistent over time. It is a collective effort, but all the players can change over time, and people at any given moment can be part of it without subscribing to or even being interested in anything like all the precepts and practical activities.' Duncan Kennedy, *A Critique of Adjudication (fin de siècle)* (Harvard University Press 1997) 6.

[5] Michel Foucault, 'What is Critique?' in Sylvère Lotringer (ed.), *The Politics of Truth: Michel Foucault* (Lysa Hochroch (tr.), Semiotexte 1997) 23–82 at 52; Harry Johnson, 'The Keynesian Revolution and the Monetarist Counter-Revolution' 61 *American Economic Review* (1971) 1–14 (identifying how both revolutionary and counter-revolutionary ideas in economics had to obey a certain form).

[6] See generally David Harvey, 'Revolutionary and Counter Revolutionary Theory in Geography and the Problem of Ghetto Formation' in Harald Bauder, Salvatore Engel-Di Mauro (eds), *Critical Geographies: A Collection of Readings* (Praxis 2008) 110–125; Robert Gordon, 'Historicism in Legal Scholarship' 90 *Yale Law Journal* (1981) 1017–1056.

These biases pervade philosophy and normative jurisprudence. Both fields are pathologically obsessed with talking *around* turtles, i.e. substantive claims.[7] Neo-ILP and NAIL are not exceptions. But I have little interest in turtles. Of greater interest to me is *form*. To speak of form is to speak of how theories manipulate, manoeuvre and control. To speak of form is to speak of the language, grammar and aesthetics[8] of a theory – each of which frames our debates. It is to speak of a hidden, subtle exercise of power that enables ideas to flourish with the image of innocence. To expose form is to begin exposing the politics of theory. It is an attempt to reveal the concealed forces that shape our legal unconscious. This is the task I undertake in relation to the present project.

But turtles cannot be avoided.[9] Nor can the inevitable slippage and feelings of crises that follow. Of course, NAIL and neo-ILP are sets of substantive theoretical claims (i.e. turtles). Their respective positions may sometimes conflict, sit in uncomfortable agreement or simply look past each other. In organising the relationship between theories, a theorist is often defined by an underlying structure of feeling. It is a feeling of rupture, fracture and instability that arises from the realisation that no theory can sustain itself solely on its own terms. Epistemic crises emerge because rival theories make equally justifiable claims upon the theorist. This is both a modern and post-modern condition.[10]

7 Friedrich Nietzsche, *Beyond Good and Evil: Prelude to a Philosophy of the Future* (Marion Faber (tr., ed.), Oxford University Press 1998) 5–15. Normative jurisprudence is obsessed with talking around turtles in several senses: some theories seek to prove the old lady's point (critical legal studies), others reject the latter for being *too* anti-foundationalist while claiming that they are not being foundationalist – making claims on the type of turtle on which law rests, even if it is not the ultimate turtle, while discarding all other types of turtle as irrelevant (Kelsen's *Grundnorm*, Hart's Rule of Recognition, Rawls' justice, Dworkin's self-image, etc.).

8 This term is meant specifically as defined and circumscribed by Pierre Schlag: 'the aesthetic pertains to the forms, images, tropes, perceptions, and sensibilities that help shape the creation, apprehension, and even identity of human endeavors . . . [it is] those recurrent forms that shape the creation, apprehension, and identity of law . . . [it is] something that a legal professional both undergoes and enacts, most often automatically, without thinking . . . [and] aesthetics help shape the cognitive, emotive, ethical, and political preoccupations, goals, values, and anxieties of legal professionals.' Pierre Schlag, 'The Aesthetics of American Law' 115 *Harvard Law Review* (2002) 1047–1118 at 1050–1053.

9 Form always collapses into substance and vice versa: Sahib Singh, 'Narrative and Theory: Formalism's Eternal Return' 84 *BYBIL* (forthcoming, 2013) at Section 1.

10 Alasdair MacIntyre, 'Epistemological Crises, Dramatic Narrative, and the Philosophy of Science' 60 *The Monist* (1977) 453–472 at 453–455; David Harvey, *The Condition of Postmodernity: An Enquiry into the Origins of Cultural Change* (Basil Blackwell 1990) 9, 39; Richard Bernstein, 'Incommensurability and Otherness Revisited' in Richard Bernstein

To do theory is then to realise two things. First, that any sense of identity (of the self and of law) is displaced by rationality itself: one is always shifting to a position of disagreement with the position that one has already settled on. Second, that because there is no position outside theory where one may adjudge a theory, progress or change in theoretical thought is not so much the result of the progressive evolution of ideas, but rather the product of particular socio-political conditions or the structure from which they emerge.[11] These structuring feelings impact on how we can address the substantive positions that are integral to neo-ILP and NAIL. As lawyers, we should be concerned with delineating the boundaries and particularities of law. But theoretical positions precede our capability to engage with and cognise it, for they define what we perceive it to be. And yet any rational being will realise that no theory can sustain itself, given both internal (a 'hidden awareness of the impossibility of its own project')[12] and external conditions (socio-political considerations). The issue that then emerges is our ability to delineate the boundaries of our discipline with any security. But what shields us from these concerns, and the existential angst that inevitably follows, is the form of theory. It insulates a theory from that which can destabilise it (and the theorist). The analysis that follows looks at the form of the relationship between neo-ILP and NAIL. This foundational examination is elsewhere complemented with a detailed look at the form of Kelsenian and Hartian approaches – the main strands within neo-ILP.[13]

2 The politics of theory: comments on the form of a relationship

The present project, neo-ILP, is premised on a discursive engagement between theories. It asks where neo-ILP stands as a scholarly approach, where its future potential lies and what it has learned from the NAIL

The New Constellation: The Ethical-Political Horizons of Modernity/Postmodernity (MIT Press 1992) 57–78 at 57–58.

11 Reinhart Koselleck, *Futures Past: On the Semantics of Historical Time* (Keith Tribe (tr.), Columbia University Press 2004) 107–112.

12 David Kennedy, 'A Rotation in Legal Scholarship' in Christian Joerges, David M. Trubek (eds), *Critical Legal Thought: An American–German Debate* (Nomos 1989) 353–396 at 359.

13 Sahib Singh, 'The Politics of Theory: Form' (forthcoming); Sahib Singh, 'International Law as a Technical Discipline: Critical Perspectives on the Narrative Structure of a Theory' in Jean d'Aspremont (ed.), *Formalism and the Sources of International Law: A Theory of the Ascertainment of Legal Rules* (2nd edn Oxford University Press 2013) 236–261; Singh, n. 9.

charge.[14] Certainly, engagement is a significant and welcome advance on the 'detached, disengaged affair'[15] or lack of 'meaningful debate'[16] that typified the relationship between new and mainstream legal scholarship in the 1990s and 2000s. But it also comes with its own politics: the subtleties of how the debate is framed, the positions ascribed to various theories (and how these positions are evaluated), as well as the manner in which confrontation is avoided and at other times embraced. It is the narrative structure,[17] or rhetorical economy, and aesthetics of a project that expose these politics.[18] An analysis of form reveals the strategies of persuasion, manipulation and control that often go unnoticed and delicately structure an enquiry. I hope to make these explicit as regards the present project by looking at three different choices that structure the way in which dialogue between neo-ILP and NAIL is cast by the former.

2.1 The politics of choice → the politics of definition

Theory is rife with political struggle. On an ideational level, this struggle is enacted on the very paraphernalia of which theories are comprised. Concepts, categories, labels and constructed relationships are all primed

14 Jörg Kammerhofer, Jean d'Aspremont, 'Introduction: Mapping 21st Century International Legal Positivism' (unpublished paper, 2010) at 2 [Editors' note: the author refers to the first version of the introductory chapter; in order to preserve the references, that version has been made available at: http://ssrn.com/abstract=2372778]; Jörg Kammerhofer, 'International Legal Positivism in a Post-Modern World: A Proposal for Greater Focus in Scholarship' 3 *AjV Newsletter* (2013) 2–4 at 2–3.

15 Deborah Cass, 'Navigating the Newstream: Recent Critical Scholarship in International Law' 65 *Nordic Journal of International Law* (1996) 341–383 at 342.

16 Thomas Skouteris, Outi Korhonen, 'Under Rhodes' Eyes: The "Old" and "New" International Law at Looking Distance' 11 *LJIL* (1998) 429–440 at 430; see also Thomas Skouteris, 'Bridging the Gap? The 1999 Annual Meeting of the American Society of International Law' 12 *LJIL* (1999) 505–509.

17 For an introduction to critical narrative analysis as method in international law, see Singh, 'Discipline', n. 13; Singh, n. 9.

18 A brief comment on method: the relationship between narrative/rhetoric and aesthetics is an uneasy one. On the one hand, aesthetics may be but a subset of the rhetorical economy of a text; on the other hand, it structures that very rhetorical economy. Both are treated as interlinked but fundamentally distinct methods of analysis in the context of this chapter. But as methods, they can *only* perform a critical endeavour. An aesthetic or narrative understanding of theory and law precludes a claim to correctness: it only opens up an ontologically different position from that under examination and it cannot preclude that another narrative interpretation is any less 'correct'. Furthermore, this chapter is an aesthetic and narrative construct that cannot claim any further claim to being right – it does not seek to do so. By being reflexive, it can, however, be transparent in its motives. Both methods are forms of ideology critique.

for symbolic conflict. They do not have fixed meanings and contours, but cannot do without historical ones; they rather provide the surface upon which social and ideational conflict is waged and made visible.[19]

So, how the editors of this project frame the debate between neo-ILP and NAIL becomes increasingly important. What visions of these projects are foregrounded, which are marginalised and why? What is meant by the 'post-modern world' in which neo-ILP strives to exist? Is Critical Legal Studies (CLS) equated with the 'post-modern critique' in law? Why is there a felt need to reconstruct the theoretical foundations of neo-ILP in light of such critiques? What are the consequences of considering the works of Kennedy and Koskenniemi to be ones of deconstruction? Why are Kennedy and Koskenniemi engaged with and not Allott, Chimni, Anghie, Miéville or Marks?[20]

I contend that these rhetorical and symbolic manoeuvres, under the guise of description, legitimate, consciously or unconsciously, the prevailing legal ideology. The constructed narrative is one of neo-ILP as the underdog, the contemporary outsider so relegated in the battle of theories for discursive dominance. It is insulated from a range of critiques and elevated as a necessary and modern method. NAIL, on the other hand, suffers from reductionism, misapprehension and the consequences of negative connotations.

The first question-begging manoeuvre is the positioning of CLS (here, NAIL) alongside deconstruction.[21] Koskenniemi's and Kennedy's early works are often cast as ones of deconstruction, in my opinion incorrectly.[22] But neither *International Legal Structures* (*Structures*), nor *From Apology to Utopia* (*FATU*) are works of deconstruction, but rather, as stated by the

[19] Ernesto Laclau, *Emancipation(s)* (Verso 1996) 36–46, 84–104.

[20] Kammerhofer and d'Aspremont, n. 14 at 4, 6–7; Jean d'Aspremont, *Formalism and the Sources of International Law: A Theory of the Ascertainment of Legal Rules* (Oxford University Press 2011) 90–95, 110–117.

[21] Kammerhofer and d'Aspremont, n. 14 at 7. While the editors use CLS to indicate critical thought in international law, I will use this to refer to the American school of thought that flourished between the 1960s and 1990s. Instead, NAIL will refer to the strain of critical thought in international law that came into ascendance in the 1980s and continues today. There are considerable and important differences between the two schools.

[22] E.g. Iain Scobbie, 'Towards the Elimination of International Law: Some Radical Scepticism about Sceptical Radicalism' 61 *BYBIL* (1990) 339–362 at 339. Critical theorists also make this mistake: Anthony Carty, 'Critical International Law: Recent Trends in the Theory of International Law' 2 *EJIL* (1991) 66–96 at 69–70. Others get it right: Emmanuelle Jouannet, 'Koskenniemi: A Critical Introduction' in Martti Koskenniemi, *The Politics of International Law* (Hart 2011) 1–32.

authors themselves,[23] of structuralism. The differentiation is vital. It may be, as I contend, that these are works settled in modernity and are not 'post-modern critiques'.[24] If accepted, this has obvious consequences for the present project. Let me begin by first demonstrating my argument.

There are vital differences between structuralism and deconstruction.[25] Deconstruction undoes structuralism, while simultaneously making structuration unavoidable. Structuralism depends on a centre, 'that is, a set of constitutive norms and procedures through the totality of which the ideal model of a given activity is practically established, changed and enacted'.[26] This centre defines, imports and escapes, simultaneously, a totality (whether it be international law or some other structure). Deconstruction is the historical rupture that questioned the existence of the centre. It redefined how we think about the structurality of structure:

> Thus it has always been thought that the center, which is by definition unique, constituted that very thing within a structure, which while governing the structure, escapes structurality. This is why classical thought concerning structure could say that the center is, paradoxically, *within* the structure and *outside* it. The center is the center of the totality, and yet, since the center does not belong to the totality (is not part of the totality), the totality *has its center elsewhere*. The center is not the center.[27]

For the deconstructionist, the centre does not exist, but becomes 'a function, a sort of nonlocus in which an infinite number of sign-substitutions came into play . . . everything [becomes] discourse'.[28] Deconstruction would have potentially devastating consequences if applied to international law.[29] But in Koskenniemi's 1989 *FATU*, we find far more Saussure,

23 David Kennedy, 'Critical Theory, Structuralism and Contemporary Legal Scholarship' 21 *New England Law Review* (1986) 209–289 at 266 (fn. 137); Martti Koskenniemi, 'Letter to the Editors of the Symposium' 93 *AJIL* (1999) 351–361 at 355. Koskenniemi refers to his 1989 work as having deconstructionist elements: see Martti Koskenniemi, *From Apology to Utopia: The Structure of International Legal Argument* (Finnish Lawyers' Publishing Co. 1989, reissued Cambridge University Press 2005) 6–14, 536–537, 541. This perhaps elevates the potential for misapprehension, but see below.

24 Kammerhofer and d'Aspremont, n. 14 at 4.

25 See Derrida's famous deconstruction of structuralism: Jacques Derrida, 'Structure, Sign and Play in the Discourse of the Human Sciences' in Jacques Derrida, *Writing and Difference* (Alan Bass (tr.), University of Chicago Press 1978) 278–293.

26 Akbar Rasulov, 'International Law and the Poststructuralist Challenge' 19 *LJIL* (2006) 799–827 at 801.

27 Derrida, n. 25 at 279 (emphasis in original).

28 Derrida, n. 25 at 280.

29 For an overview, see Rasulov, n. 26 at 810–816.

Lévi-Strauss and the Frankfurt School's Critical Theory than we do Derrida. But there is plenty of room for ambivalence in his deployment of structuralism and Critical Theory.[30]

Koskenniemi, at points, refers to the method employed in *FATU* as deconstructionist.[31] But he is also perfectly aware that 'many' deconstructionists would not call, or accept, it as such.[32] The entire premise of *FATU* is to explicate the 'grammar', 'deep structure' or '*langue*' of international law. It attempts to describe the *structural* conditions that circumscribe what can be said in international legal argument. Apology and utopia, normativity and concreteness are opposites that *function as centres and structure the conditions of possibility* within and between which international legal argument operates.[33] A structuralist sustains the argumentative structure of law (however wide this may be), a deconstructionist throws them wide open, demonstrating the inevitable and continuous discursive slippage that follows from unavoidably proceeding outside of the structure.[34] Koskenniemi remains avowedly structuralist despite his

[30] I relegate my reading of Kennedy's *Structures* to a footnote because I consider it to be a clear-cut example of structuralist work. In contrast, Koskenniemi's *FATU* is somewhat more difficult to qualify; despite its methodological transparency. Kennedy looks at how international law is structured by a deep incoherence, between respecting sovereigns and governing them. It was an internal examination of international law that demonstrated the circular and recurring rhetorical structure. But the deep incoherence was precisely what structured the discipline. It is structuralist precisely because it sustained specific schema as stable and as constitutive of international law as a structure. See David Kennedy, *International Legal Structures* (Nomos 1987).

[31] See references in n. 23. [32] Koskenniemi, *FATU*, n. 23 at 10 and fn. 8.

[33] Koskenniemi, *FATU*, n. 23 at 11.

[34] For a great demonstration of this, see Pierre Schlag, 'Cannibal Moves: An Essay on the Metamorphoses of the Legal Distinction' 40 *Stanford Law Review* (1988) 929–972. Another way of viewing Koskenniemi's work is as artificially and prematurely arrested deconstruction. It has been terminated at precisely the point at which it could reconfigure and undermine international law as law. It has been terminated by Koskenniemi precisely so that he can sustain the functioning and identity of the international lawyer as social agent (Koskenniemi, *FATU*, n. 23 at 546–561). Chapter 8 of *FATU* tempers everything that came before it. Deconstruction is terminated in order to sustain a certain politics or normative agenda. The issue is not so much that one could want deconstruction to carry on forever, but that it has been terminated too soon. It has been terminated before it can shake the centres that determine the structure of international law. This position (the premature termination of deconstruction) is explained and critiqued in Pierre Schlag, '"Le Hors de Texte, C'est Moi": The Politics of Form and the Domestication of Deconstruction' 11 *Cardozo Law Review* (1989–1990) 1631–1674; Pierre Schlag, 'The Problem of the Subject' 69 *Texas Law Review* (1991) 1627–1743; Pierre Schlag, 'A Brief Survey of Deconstruction' 27 *Cardozo Law Review* (2005) 741–752; Peter Dews, *Logics of Disintegration: Post-Structuralist Thought and the Claims of Critical Theory* (Verso 1987)

contextualisation and historically contingent examination of the structure of international law. Koskenniemi's field of analysis is the international legal profession, not merely texts and doctrines – it proceeds, at its edges, to be an examination of a culture. Much as Lévi-Strauss did with myths,[35] Koskenniemi sought to take apart the assumptions and rules that governed the production of international legal arguments. This exposition made explicit the repeating patterns that transcend and order the content of individual arguments, exposing them to be part of a system of shifting internal references generated and sustained by various acts of abstraction. But Koskenniemi's structuralism was also complemented by Critical Theory. The former is not a theoretical straitjacket (given the contrasting approach to history taken in each of these).

Koskenniemi's structuralism sought to shake the normalcy and routine of objectified legal positions. In this endeavour he found an ally in the Frankfurt School and the works of Adorno, Habermas, Horkheimer and Marcuse.[36] But Critical Theory not only buttressed his critical endeavour. It also enabled Koskenniemi to sustain his politically idealistic belief in the agency of the international lawyer.[37] Koskenniemi sought to undo all 'objectifying knowledge [which] has seemed to work as an ideology, or a "false consciousness"'.[38] In this context, ideology is a form of consciousness that acts to change and limit the actions and ideas of the international lawyer, while simultaneously imposing itself on the world through the actions of said lawyer. In short, Critical Theory seeks to undo false consciousness. It does so by positing a theory that both exists in the

33–44, 200–219. For a similar reading of Koskenniemi to mine, see Outi Korhonen, 'New International Law: Silence, Defence or Deliverance?' 7 *EJIL* (1996) 1–28 at 19–21. A further point of note is that Koskenniemi relies a great deal on the work of Roberto Unger, perhaps one of the few forefathers of CLS to *never* come close to deconstructive analysis.

35 In particular, Claude Lévi-Strauss, *Structural Anthropology*, Vol. 1 (Claire Jacobson, Brooke Grundfest Schoepf (tr.), Penguin 1968); Claude Lévi-Strauss, *The Savage Mind* (University of Chicago Press 1966) (developing the concept of *bricolage* at 16–33).

36 Koskenniemi, *FATU*, n. 23 at 537–543. This reading of Koskenniemi finds certain agreement in Korhonen's cave metaphor – as a third reading of Koskenniemi, see Korhonen, n. 34 at 23–26.

37 Emancipation from objectifying knowledges must be through society (of international lawyers), through the actualising of theory in life. Critical Theory is heavily dependent on a mechanism for agency, just as Koskenniemi's reconstructive project and ethics of responsibility is. See, on Critical Theory, Max Horkheimer, 'Traditional and Critical Theory' in Max Horkheimer, *Critical Theory: Selected Essays* (Matthew J. O'Connell *et al.* (trs), Seabury Press 1972) 188–243 at 212–213. For Koskenniemi on critical normative practice and the international lawyer, see Koskenniemi, *FATU*, n. 23 at 545–563.

38 Koskenniemi, *FATU*, n. 23 at 538.

world and acts in the world to bring about changes in social behaviour. A critical theory avoids substituting its own false consciousness because its own claim to the social world is subject to its own critique: it is self-reflective.[39] By turning to the Frankfurt School, Koskenniemi was able to refine his critique of objectivity by developing his notion of critique, historically situate his structuralist analysis and open up the conceptual space to sustain his politico-moral stance on the reconstructed role of international lawyers and their agency. It was – in short – a deft, and necessary, methodological turn.[40]

If one accepts these arguments and their logic, *FATU* is not a work of deconstruction. The tragedy lies in the reading. Rhetorically, as a matter of form, neo-ILP first misapprehends nascent NAIL – not without the help of the latter. It then etches this misapprehension within Koskenniemi's text. And these moves are not without consequences. First, it invites the judgment and accusations of legal nihilism that inevitably accompany the label 'deconstruction'. James Crawford was almost certainly not alone when he commented that Koskenniemi had shown 'with overwhelming erudition the impossibility of our discipline'.[41] This is a common mainstream position. It reproaches early-NAIL for seeking to eliminate international law. And it is normally accompanied with other crude reductions (for example, reading 'international law is irreducibly political' as 'international law is politics').[42] The problem is that the narratives of liberalism and that of its critique have both inherited twin dichotomous reductions. Liberalism resorts to the reductionist allegation of nihilism in the face of a threat

[39] Koskenniemi, *FATU*, n. 23 at 540–543 (Koskenniemi avoids instituting his own false consciousness).

[40] The intellectual marriage of the two traditions (structuralism and Critical Theory) is highly problematic – but we do not see the inconsistencies emerge in Koskenniemi's anti-formalistic methodology. See, generally, Michel Foucault, 'Truth and Power' in James D. Faubion (ed.), *The Essential Works of Foucault 1954–1984*, Vol. 3: *Power* (Robert Hurley *et al.* (trs), Penguin 2002) 111–133 at 115–116.

[41] James Crawford, [Introductory Remarks to Martti Koskenniemi, 'The Wonderful Artificiality of States'] 88 *Proceedings of the American Society of International Law* (1994) 22 at 22; see also Rasulov, n. 26 at 807; Jason Beckett, 'Countering Uncertainty and Ending Up/Down Arguments: *Prolegomena* to a Response to NAIL' 16 *EJIL* (2005) 213–238 at 213; Nigel Purvis, 'Critical Legal Studies in Public International Law' 32 *Harvard International Law Journal* (1991) 81–127 at 121; Scobbie, n. 22.

[42] For a rebuttal, see Martti Koskenniemi, 'What Should International Lawyers Learn from Karl Marx?' in Susan Marks (ed.), *International Law on the Left: Re-Examining Marxist Legacies* (Cambridge University Press 2008) 30–52 at 43. Early NAIL circumvents nihilism through situationality and perspectivism; see Koskenniemi, *FATU*, n. 23; Korhonen, n. 34; Cass, n. 15.

to its form, and critical theories make similar reductionist allegations of objectivism. By giving Koskenniemi's and Kennedy's work the label of deconstruction, we are thrown into these beside-the-point rhetorical manoeuvres that are embedded within the ideologies of various positions. It is an inherited reality of the language: its myth. But this is not the real problem. Not only does neo-ILP inscribe a misapprehension into the theory of early-NAIL, but it exports this misapprehension. Its purported engagement with NAIL is premised on a falsity – on the exported misapprehension.[43] This not only nullifies the constructive potential of any such engagement, but more importantly, it stunts any transformative capacity that early-NAIL work may carry. The politics of choice are masked by the neutrality of definition. But definition is never neutral. It is the empty form on, and through, which social struggle is conducted. But it is an unjustified violence when it is wrong. Ideas are inhibited, subsumed and co-opted by precisely this manoeuvre. History has, however, taught us that none of these neutralising effects is new to dissident or revolutionary theories.[44]

2.2 *Insulating a theory: the politics of incommensurability*

Theorists make consistent and considered efforts to safeguard their ideas from competing theories. Theories must, after all, defend the conceptual space in which they wish to function. Part of doing so requires shielding the reader: she ought not to be torn in several different directions, between competing ideas and considerations. For epistemological rupture cannot aid in the socio-cognitive assimilation of an idea.[45] Different theories use different strategies – dependent on their intellectual heritage and determining aesthetics. Essentialist and incorrect delineations (with their

[43] It undermines the foundational questions on which the present project is based; see Kammerhofer and d'Aspremont, n. 14 at 4. Holistically, the project seems premised on a fallible house of cards: (a) CLS is founded upon the work of Kennedy's *Structures* and Koskenniemi's *FATU* and no other references are given to the school's diverse work; (b) these CLS works are deconstructionist and post-modern critiques; (c) neo-ILP is possible in this post-modern world if it can sustain its theoretical foundations given (a) and (b). Obviously, if either (a) or (b) are undermined, then the project – at least on its own terms – collapses, or at the very least, fails to deliver on its promises.

[44] See Section 2.3 below for further comments on the relationship between counter-revolutionary and revolutionary theories.

[45] On epistemological rupture, see text accompanying n. 10. Also see Singh, 'Discipline', n. 13 at 236.

inherited biases) regularly come to the fore. But perhaps most prominent in neo-ILP is the theory's approach to incommensurability.

A Kuhnian incommensurability thesis begins from the proposition that certain theories exist and 'practice their trades in different worlds'.[46] Incommensurable theories cannot make '*complete* contact with the other's viewpoints',[47] and may disagree on the definition of the problem, methods used to solve it and the standards imported into such methods. The thesis is one that posits an understanding of *how* theories can be compared and evaluated. Because there is no completely common language, translation between competing incommensurable theories is the site for political conflict.[48] The posited degree of incommensurability (or commensurability) between theories, as well as the nature of the translation that takes place between them, determines the extent, productivity and political economy of any discursive engagement between them.

Here, I argue that the incommensurability thesis – in various guises and forms – permeates the form and texture of the neo-ILP project. NAIL and neo-ILP have 'completely different points of origin', they disagree on the 'framework of academic enquiry', function with different linguistic theories, 'diverge [in regards the] constructive side in positivist epistemology' and take opposing views regarding the Enlightenment project.[49] The narrative established here, and elsewhere,[50] is that these theories occupy different ideational and conceptual worlds. They are, for the large part incommensurable, as regards the traditions they belong to, the intellectual

[46] Thomas S. Kuhn, *The Structure of Scientific Revolutions* (2nd edn University of Chicago Press 1970) 150; See also Thomas S. Kuhn, 'Theory Change as Structure Change: Comments on Sneed Formalism' in Robert E. Butts, Jaakko Hintikka (eds), *Historical and Philosophical Dimensions of Logic: Methodology and the Philosophy of Science* (Reidel 1977) 289–309; Paul Feyerabend, 'Explanation, Reduction and Empiricism' in Herbert Feigl, Grover Maxwell (eds), *Scientific Explanation, Space, and Time* (University of Minnesota Press 1962) 28–97; Bernstein, n. 10.

[47] Kuhn, *Structure*, n. 46 at 148 (emphasis added); see also Kuhn, 'Theory Change', n. 46 at 300–301.

[48] Incommensurable theories can still be compared because of the openness of our linguistic horizons. Translation occurs where there is no common language between incommensurable theories. Language enables communication. A given tradition is not *linguistically* rooted in its own world and rules. The 'myth of the framework' was rejected by Karl Popper, 'Normal Science and Its Dangers' in Imre Lakatos, Alan Musgrave (eds), *Criticism and the Growth of Knowledge* (Cambridge University Press 1970) 51–59 at 56.

[49] Kammerhofer and d'Aspremont, n. 14 at 6–7.

[50] See also d'Aspremont, n. 20 at 105–116; Jean d'Aspremont, 'Reductionist Legal Positivism in International Law' 106 *Proceedings of the American Society of International Law* (2012) 368–370 at 369.

frameworks they advance and the methods they use. But this must not be viewed as a self-evident categorisation, but a constructed one. Incommensurability is a methodological manoeuvre engineered to ensure a limited, but vital, immunity from the effects of critical positions. It may be manipulated to be both a shield and a sword, to insulate a theory from adversaries and to attack them.[51]

2.2.1 Insulation technique 1: false essentialism

If we accept, for the moment, that NAIL and neo-ILP are largely incommensurable theories, then in the very moment of acceptance we must acknowledge that neo-ILP is making a validity claim upon the premises of another theory – here, NAIL. In order to make statements and judgments on incommensurability, neo-ILP *must* assume and determine a set of characteristics for NAIL. I argue that these assumptions and determinations are not reasonable reductions, but fall under the rubric of what is often considered false essentialism. '[F]alse essentialism violently distorts the sheer complexity of overlapping traditions.'[52] It is a form of reductionism that disables communication between, and the comparability of, theories: one is disabled from *fully* discerning the points of overlap, conflict or incommensurability. False essentialism is perpetrated when NAIL theories are equated with deconstruction and post-modernism, when the early works of Kennedy and Koskenniemi are presumed to speak on behalf of the NAIL project. When considering NAIL why only consider Koskenniemi and Kennedy in early-NAIL and not Allott and Carty, who wrote equally influential work in the 1980s? Why only take up the NAIL critique of the 1980s and not of the late 1990s and 2000s: why not consider the work of China Miéville, Susan Marks, Anne Orford and the later work of Martti Koskenniemi? Why only consider the relationship of NAIL to deconstruction and not neo-Marxist theory, ideology critique, Critical Theory, Foucauldian genealogy or Polanyi's political economic thought?[53] The intellectual breadth and historical evolution of NAIL is all but nullified.

[51] Singh, 'Discipline', n. 13 at 240–243; Singh, n. 9 (critiquing how incommensurability is so used in d'Aspremont n. 20; d'Aspremont, n. 50).

[52] Bernstein, n. 10 at 66.

[53] The historical complexity of NAIL is explored in Akbar Rasulov, 'New Approach to International Law: Images of a Genealogy' in José María Beneyto, David Kennedy (eds), *New Approaches to International Law: The European and American Experiences* (T. M. C. Asser Press 2012) 151–192. See also generally Umut Özsu, 'The Question of Form: Methodological Notes on Dialectics and International Law' 23 *LJIL* (2010) 687–707.

False essentialism ensures that the various and complex points of interaction between neo-ILP and NAIL are not explored. Points of direct conflict are not seen, let alone addressed. Allott's evisceration of Hart would surely have some relevance for Jean d'Aspremont's reconstruction of the latter. Miéville's invocation of Pashukanis surely brings back images of the interaction between the latter and Kelsen. This conflict over theorising the legal form would surely go to the heart of Jörg Kammerhofer's project. Unger, Koskenniemi and Marks' reliance on ideology that perpetuates a false consciousness would surely have something to say about the ideological dominance of neo-ILP. NAIL has certainly not spared the social thesis or the formalised structure of Kelsen. Each of these threatens the foundations of the neo-ILP project, but they are cast aside. False essentialism insulates neo-ILP from those ideas that directly threaten it. Discourse, conflict and disagreement are all avoided as incommensurability is superficially and strategically deployed.

2.2.2 Insulation technique 2: specialisation and the post-modern form

The post-modern sensibility can be loosely defined by fragmentation, plurality and a 'resistance to all forms of *abstract* totality, universalism and rationalism'.[54] Incommensurability is itself a concept that emerges within this paradigm of thought. The concern to balance plurality/unity, commonality/difference, and the self/other is one that has emerged with vigour in our post-modern world. Intellectual and material fragmentation has been enabled by and is being perpetuated by specialisation. In the world of ideas, specialisation has become the norm, but it has also become representative of a distinctly post-modern form. Neo-ILP has adopted this particular aspect of the post-modern form: it has narrowed its claims and seeks to be 'modest'.[55] But the appropriation of the post-modern form is only a veneer under which the theory, yet again, insulates itself from critique.

The foundational tenet of neo-ILP is in fact one of a narrow formalism. The validity of a norm, its legal existence, is determined solely by its pedigree: its conformity with a system's sources.[56] Neo-ILP is *only*

[54] Bernstein, n. 10 at 57 (emphasis in original); see also Harvey, n. 10 at 9, 46–48; Terry Eagleton, 'Awakening from Modernity' *Times Literary Supplement*, 20 February 1987, 194.

[55] D'Aspremont, n. 50 at 370.

[56] Kammerhofer and d'Aspremont, n. 14 at 8; d'Aspremont, n. 50 at 368–369; Jörg Kammerhofer, 'The Pure Theory of Law and Its "Modern" Positivism: International Legal Uses

concerned with the cognition, identification and existence of legal rules. This claim to particularity allows for and necessitates other theories that can 'explain the whole phenomenon of law'.[57] This specialised claim is complemented by an effort to wrestle with unity and coexistence with other theories in the pluralised world of international legal theory. Neo-ILP has 'doctrinal conciliatory virtues . . . it helps reconcile some of the allegedly antonymic trends in international legal scholarship'.[58] Neo-ILP's formalism can 'underpin the continuously mutually enriching character of . . . multiple strands of contemporary legal scholarship', because it is 'non-exclusive, non-confrontational and conciliatory'.[59] Neo-ILP promotes 'ecumenism'[60] or unity within international legal scholarship. Neo-ILP's specialised claims underpin the potential for unity in legal scholarship.

To embrace specialisation is to take up post-modernism (and modernism) on its invitation to consider the world as irredeemably complex and as a consequence narrow any claimed conceptual ground. Adopting this post-modern form allows neo-ILP to achieve two things. First, it further insulates the theory from critical charges. Specialisation allows neo-ILP to carve up scholarly enquiry into a number of component parts each governed by different theories. Neo-ILP can govern the identification of rules; international legal realists, constructivists and NAIL can examine the international legal discipline as a social and material construct, as well as critiquing the *application* of legal rules; and so on.[61] This allows theoretical enquiry to be neatly pigeonholed. This process allows neo-ILP to cast aside competing theories as pertaining to different aspects of jurisprudential enquiry, even if these theories have plenty to say about how claims to the existence of rules are constructed, not to mention the pitfalls of neo-ILP's normative reconstruction of sources theory. Specialisation enables insulation.

for Scholarship' 106 *Proceedings of the American Society of International Law* (2012) 365–367 at 366; Jason Beckett, 'Behind Relative Normativity: Rules and Process as Prerequisites of Law' 12 *EJIL* (2001) 627–650 at 627.

57 D'Aspremont, n. 50 at 370.

58 D'Aspremont, n. 20 at 217, 218.

59 D'Aspremont, n. 20 at 218, 219.

60 D'Aspremont, n. 50 at 370.

61 This is also present within the neo-ILP project itself. Note the tension between Kammerhofer's Kelsenian project and d'Aspremont's Hartian project. 'Sure, Kelsen says, we can conduct sociological studies into whether the law is generally obeyed or not; this is a very valuable field of study. But sociologists or other empirical studies can only capture the periphery, not the norms themselves.' Kammerhofer, n. 56 at 366.

Second, specialisation allows neo-ILP to import a discourse of conciliation and harmony amongst plurality. But this is no more than a hegemonic manoeuvre garbed in conciliatory clothing. The discourse of conciliation and happy coexistence presumes the presence of incommensurability and elevates the image of a reasonable theorist: one that is aware of competing arguments and theoretical claims, but is capable of weaving himself between them. But a theory that lays claim to reality cannot be carved in terms of specialisations: its substantive claims may not be neatly categorised. The claims of totality cannot be so easily set aside. Matters are not so neat. Theory cannot be non-confrontational. It especially cannot be so when laying claim to international law's form. The sources of international law are the gateway to legality. Normative claims as to how formal they should be, or are, are not innocent and non-confrontational. When one considers that neo-ILP's specialisation (laying exclusive claim to being able to *identify* legal rules) alongside its importation of a series of normative projects, it is difficult to not conceive of neo-ILP's formalism as seeking a theoretical monopoly on international law's key: its sources. The 'responsibility assigned to [neo-ILP] remains, in my view, of primary importance'.[62] Conciliation and specialisation hides a certain exercise of power.

2.2.3 Privileging technique 1: post-modernism appropriated in the rationalist form

There is an incontestable incommensurability that implicitly structures the editors' project. In neo-ILP, we find the reconstruction of rationalist and partly modernist theories (Hartian and Kelsenian variants) that seeks to exist in a post-modern world.[63] '[P]ost-modern international legal

[62] D'Aspremont, n. 50 at 370.

[63] Kammerhofer and d'Aspremont, n. 14 at 1, 2, 7. For clarification, the argument here is not that Hart's or Kelsen's theories are in every way modernist and rationalist. Nor is this stated as regards d'Aspremont's reconstruction of Hart and Kammerhofer's of Kelsen. My argument is that both traditions are somewhat intellectually rooted in modernist and rationalist predispositions. These traditions are not controlling or total in their effect, but important enough to have a lasting effect on how the theories are deployed or function. They are modernist in their anti-foundationalism and rationalistic in their fidelity to the Enlightenment project. The incommensurability between rationalism and modernism (and between Hart and Kelsen) is set aside here, despite its importance. On the incommensurability between rationalism, modernity and post-modernity, see Pierre Schlag, 'Missing Pieces: A Cognitive Approach to Law' 67 *Texas Law Review* (1989) 1195–1250.

positivism'[64] seeks intellectual progress: to transcend its historical lineage in one paradigm and to subsist in another. And of course in rationalism/modernism and post-modernity, we find largely incommensurable intellectual and cognitive frameworks.[65] This incommensurability is just as true for those intellectual projects that embrace the Enlightenment project, such as neo-ILP, and those that reject its call to subservience to rationality, such as a variety of post-modern thinkers. How can ideas that draw upon and retain a limited fidelity to modernist and rationalist traditions *fully* sustain themselves in the incommensurable paradigm of post-modernity? Ideational progress and incommensurability sit in uncomfortable tension.

But neo-ILP's narrative prioritises its own lineage through the *rationalist* ideal of progress above the consideration of incommensurability. We do not need to shift frameworks – from modernism to post-modernism – and to abandon the rationalist/modernist elements of neo-ILP in order to exist in a post-modern world. In elevating this narrative, the extent of the incommensurability between post-modernism and modernist/rationalist frameworks is subsumed and relegated. Old ideas can exist in the new world, they just need to adjust or tinker their substantive claims and shed old skins. This incommensurability that structures this project is hidden from view and the narrative of *coherent* ideational evolution is implicitly elevated.[66] Neo-ILP as a theory seeks to function in a post-modern world, but sustain and promote an incommensurable rationalist form (aesthetic).[67]

64 Kammerhofer and d'Aspremont, n. 14 at 2.

65 There is perhaps one notable dissenter to this largely shared opinion: Jean-François Lyotard, *The Postmodern Condition: A Report on Knowledge* (Geoff Bennington, Brian Massumi (trs), Manchester University Press 1984) 79 ('A work can become modern only if it is first post-modern. Post-modernism thus understood is not modernism at its end but in the nascent state.') The majority of scholars, including Eagleton, Harvey, Jameson, Foucault, Habermas, etc. advance the contrary position – as advocated here.

66 The argument in this paragraph is also premised on the editors' own construction of what is post-modern (alongside Section 2.2.1). The post-modern seems to be equated to whatever work NAIL or CLS has produced in legal theory (this is a position taken by others; see Anne Peters, 'Realizing Utopia as a Scholarly Endeavour' 24 *EJIL* (2013) 533–552 at 548). More specifically it is equated to the works of Koskenniemi and Kennedy. On *their narrative of post-modernism*, there should be a greater understanding of incommensurability. But as Section 2.1 highlights, their understanding of Koskenniemi and Kennedy is incorrect. I posit later that both neo-ILP and early NAIL work is premised in the modernist tradition: the level of incommensurability between neo-ILP and NAIL is not as great as one would think. And certainly to overcome NAIL is not to make neo-ILP post-modern.

67 Schlag, n. 63 at 1212–1213 (discussing the aesthetics of rationalism).

2.3 Theory as theory: co-opted ideas

So far we have seen how neo-ILP employs specific rhetorical subtleties to defend, sustain and promote its positions. These have predominantly focused on the specificities of neo-ILP and NAIL: an exacting examination of the politics of definition and incommensurability that structure the relationship between the two theories. This section will take a step back: towards (and away from) epistemology and tradition. It argues that the reduction of theory to a set of ideas, concepts and relationships, to the ideational, is corrosive. To abstract knowledge from its materialistic basis, privileges certain theories and simultaneously sustains existing power inequalities (and claims to such).

Traditional (legal) theory is not about challenging the process, form and practice of our own thought. In such theory, the privileged reader is one who is fully informed and can make an autonomous choice between positions. The preservation of theory-independent (and therefore self-validating), rational and autonomous *choice* is key. Neo-ILP imports this liberal, plural rationalism.[68] Early-NAIL is arguably just as guilty.[69] It regards the choice of scholarly approach to be arbitrary and introduces a pluralist value-relativism regarding legal methodology.[70] According to this narrative, theories are a collection of ideas and one can make a choice between them in a non-political and neutral framework.[71] Neo-ILP reduces *all* legal theory down to a question of substance – *what* to think. But certain theories, like NAIL, question *how* we think. Such theories are subsumed by neo-ILP's rationalism as merely *another substantive* way to think, another theory: we can internalise this theory that questions how we think, if we so choose. Questioning how we think becomes merely another way to think about things: another idea, another theory that can be adopted. Rationalism is privileged as any challenge of form is reduced to another substantive idea. Rather than taking subject-decentring theory seriously on its own terms – as questioning the practice of theory – the impeding theory is co-opted. The point I wish to make is that neo-ILP

68 Singh, 'Discipline', n. 13 at 246–247.

69 See ns 36–40 and accompanying text. Also see Allott, who was so influential in early-NAIL: Philip Allott, *Eunomia: New Order for a New World* (2nd edn Oxford University Press 2001) 6–7, 39–52.

70 Kammerhofer and d'Aspremont, n. 14 at 8.

71 For a critique, see Koskenniemi, 'Letter', n. 23 at 352–353.

subsumes the NAIL challenge by distorting and degrading its nature. Let me explain.[72]

As we have seen, early-NAIL (as narrowly defined in this project) was intellectually rooted in the Frankfurt School and structuralism (Section 2.1). Both are schools of thought firmly embedded in totalising traditions.[73] This intellectual heritage is one of modernism, not post-modernism.[74] But even then, to be more specific, there is far more Habermas in Koskenniemi's writing than there is Adorno (and far more Horkheimer) – let alone Lyotard. Koskenniemi's project is both a part of modernity and a critique of it.[75] It aims to highlight the underside of reason, not abandon it.

> Applied in international law, the critical programme takes under scrutiny existing consciousness about international law and reality as this is expressed in conventional legal concepts and categories . . . Therefore, it tries to penetrate the naturalness of givenness (objectivity) of those concepts and reveal their context-bound character. Once conventional consciousness will thus appear as contingent and contestable, the actual will manifest itself in a new light . . . It seeks to undo the naturalness of conventional ways of thinking about law and proceeds to show that the way we conceptualise it binds us to certain, more fundamental commitments – commitments which may or may not be ones that we like to make.[76]

The modernist seeks to highlight and situate the limits of reason. She normally does so through some totalising, structuring construct. In the case of Koskenniemi, it is the discursive structure of international law. This is the crucial difference between the post-modern and the modern.[77] The latter does not seek to completely abandon the Enlightenment project

[72] A large part of what follows is influenced by the work of Pierre Schlag. See references in n. 34; Pierre Schlag, 'Normativity and the Politics of Form' 139 *University of Pennsylvania Law Review* (1991) 801–932; Pierre Schlag, 'Normative and Nowhere to Go' 43 *Stanford Law Review* (1990) 167–191.

[73] Kennedy, n. 23 at 271–276; Derrida, n. 25; Foucault, n. 40.

[74] See n. 54; Fredric Jameson, *The Political Unconscious: Narrative as a Socially Symbolic Act* (Cornell University Press 1981) 55.

[75] For a somewhat similar self-understanding, see Koskenniemi, n. 42 at 31–32. In many ways, Koskenniemi's fidelity to his descriptive or cognitive project requires that he so situate himself. This is the influence of the Critical Theory.

[76] Koskenniemi, *FATU*, n. 23 at 540–541.

[77] Jürgen Habermas, 'The Normative Content of Modernity' in Jürgen Habermas, *The Philosophical Discourse of Modernity: Twelve Lectures* (Frederick Lawrence (tr.), MIT Press 1987) 336–367 at 337–338; Frederic Jameson, 'The Politics of Theory: Ideological Positions in the Postmodernism Debate' 33 *New German Critique* (1984) 53–65 at 57–59.

and the rationality it imports. If anything, the modernist seeks to deepen the Enlightenment project.[78] Contrary to the narrative asserted by this project, early-NAIL, and in particular Koskenniemi, is neither deconstructionist nor post-modernist. Rather, it belongs within the best critical traditions of modernism. What emerges is a scathing critique of liberalism without the abandoning of its ideals. Again, this is just so much Habermas, with perhaps a splash of Horkheimer. Early-NAIL does *not* abandon the Enlightenment project, but takes it to its logical, contradictory and conflicting conclusions.[79] It forces us 'into seeing that commitment in a new light'.[80]

But modernism, and particularly this variant, challenges *how* one thinks about theory. Theory is both cognitive and emancipatory.[81] It can only be so if it is self-reflexive. For this, it must be both part of the world and a point of critique for it. An individual does theory as a historical subject.[82] Her relationship to the social is a matter of social production with a particular history. Any theory must apply this insight to itself: it must acknowledge that its cognitive vision of the world is subject to its own critique. Theory is both situated within and constitutive of the social. Theory is, then, among other things, about itself. In contrast, empiricist or rational theories, such as neo-ILP, are not self-reflexive and seem to presume the cognitive conclusions they posit.[83] For the critical theorist, theory no longer functions purely on the plane of epistemology or hermeneutics. 'Reason is simultaneously subject to the interest in reason. Reason, it can be said, pursues an emancipatory cognitive interest which aspires to the act of reflection as such.'[84]

[78] See David Kolb, *The Critique of Pure Modernity: Hegel, Heidegger and After* (University of Chicago Press 1986) 1–19.

[79] The attentive reader will note that the insulating incommensurability asserted by neo-ILP, between itself and NAIL, is now not so stark (see Section 2.2). That incommensurability is starting to crumble and along with it the insulation in which neo-ILP has clothed itself.

[80] Koskenniemi, *FATU*, n. 23 at 556.

[81] Koskenniemi, *FATU*, n. 23 at 537–538; Jameson, n. 74 at 281–299.

[82] Horkheimer, n. 37 at 200.

[83] Herbert Marcuse, *One Dimensional Man: Studies in the Ideologies of Advanced Industrial Society* (2nd edn Beacon Press 1991) 115–116. See Singh, 'Discipline', n. 13 at 249–260 (demonstrating how this takes place regarding neo-Hartian theories such as Jean d'Aspremont's).

[84] Jürgen Habermas, *Knowledge and Human Interests* (Jeremy J. Shapiro (tr.), Beacon Press 1971) 197–198.

This is apparent in early-NAIL writing,[85] but the challenge it represents is subsumed and co-opted by a single stroke. The critical position is reduced to just another idea, another theory. It is cast as another *ideational* position that can be adopted upon one's whimsy.[86] It presumes and sustains the image of the liberal autonomous individual who believes the privilege of his choice; to decide with complete autonomous rationality which idea may be used, which idea is useful and which is not.[87] This is the snare of liberal methodological pluralism. It privileges reason without recognising how it is thoroughly abused, and it assumes and sustains the very mechanism which enables this: 'the autonomous, coherent, integrated, rational, originary self'.[88] So when neo-ILP considers its relationship with NAIL, it assumes the very form or approach to theory that co-opts and subsumes the challenge of NAIL. It becomes a relationship determined by rational value-relativism, autonomy and the ideational.

This ideational co-option of NAIL has prevented the complete flowering of said thought. There is, then, some intuitive merit in considering neo-ILP as a counter-revolutionary theory.[89]

> A counter-revolutionary theory is one which is deliberately proposed to deal with a proposed revolutionary theory [here, NAIL] in such a manner

85 It is also found in a less totalising form in late-NAIL writings (post 2000). Notably, see Susan Marks, 'International Judicial Activism and the Commodity-Form Theory of International Law' 18 *EJIL* (2007) 199–211 at 208–209. This post-modernist approach to ideology critique can be contrasted with the modernist impulse we see in neo-Marxist strands of late-NAIL scholarship: China Miéville, *Between Equal Rights: A Marxist Theory of International Law* (Brill 2005).

86 '[I]t is to treat all these outlooks as if they were on the same footing, in the same philosophical competition – each waiting for you and me to buy its philosophical furniture for an already-created world.' Schlag, n. 63 at 1204–1205. See also Schlag, 'Normativity', n. 72 at 892–896.

87 Schlag, n. 63 at 1213–1217. Schlag also demonstrates how this takes place where one recognises one's choices are socially and rhetorically constructed. His notion of the 'relative autonomous self' concedes both autonomy and construction, but he demonstrates that autonomy always trumps. See Schlag, 'Normativity', n. 72 at 895; Pierre Schlag, 'Fish v. Zapp: The Case of the Relatively Autonomous Self' 76 *Georgetown Law Journal* (1987–1988) 37–58.

88 Schlag, 'Normativity', n. 72 at 175 (but talking about post-modernism, not high modernism: although the insight applies equally).

89 I draw upon the following insight of David Harvey: 'it seems intuitively plausible to think of the movement of ideas in the social sciences as a movement based on revolution and counter-revolution in contrast to the natural sciences to which such a notion does not appear to be so immediately applicable.' Harvey, n. 6 at 113.

> that the threatened social changes which general acceptance of the revolutionary theory would generate are, either by cooptation or subversion, prevented from being realized.[90]

But ideational co-optation still hides another level of privilege: arguably the driving level at which privilege is sustained. These are, of course, the material bases of neo-ILP and NAIL as well as the traditions they belong to. At the level of the academy, the institutional bases of NAIL are extremely limited (Harvard, LSE, SOAS, Helsinki, Toronto being the only sustained examples).[91] In contrast, to think of international law in terms of its social practice (judgments, ILC Reports, etc.), or even as a set of self-governing rules, is dominant in the university. These approaches govern education through supposing, and constantly buttressing the idea, that they alone speak about law. But neo-ILP will always assume a material and ideational dominance because the driving force behind paradigm formation in international law is its *practice*. Neo-ILP buttresses practice in a manner that NAIL cannot.

It may be essential to examine how the relationship between theories is cast. The rhetorical and discursive frameworks that are used to influence and manipulate the way in which we think about international law is key to accessing the discipline's operation. And it may be important to look at the politics of form between theories, to make transparent modes of manipulation. But it is perhaps more important to situate these forms, these politics, these theories in their material contexts. Ideas do not emerge, dominate or subjugate in a vacuum. This is a task which approaching theory as 'theory' sidelines. But only if one adopts a rationalist approach to theory. And one must resist being seduced by this dominantly solipsistic way of thinking.

3 Conclusion

This chapter is about the politics of theory. It has sought to briefly examine the structure and form of NAIL and neo-ILP, as well as their intellectual heritages. It has demonstrated how the form and structure of a theory is central to protecting and privileging it. Form will always be violent; it will always make a claim to an object outside of its own content. But to recognise how it constrains, structures and enables our choices is essential. This is all the more important when one considers international

[90] Harvey, n. 6 at 114. [91] See Rasulov, n. 53.

legal theory to be a competition between ideas that make demands on how we see the socio-legal world. Perspective is everything. And theory precedes perspective: 'society's theories are the atmosphere it breathes'.[92]

My task here has to been to highlight how form is complicit in structuring the way in which we think about both theory and the world. Confronting form allows us to confront the politics of theory and challenge our existing consciousness. To examine how, on an ideational level, theories reify certain visions of the world. Uncovering the creative and aesthetic aspects of our intellectual endeavours is but one way to take form seriously. With no sense of irony, neo-ILP seeks to transcend incommensurable frameworks of enquiry (modernism/rationalism and post-modernism) by utilising post-modern concepts and tactics (incommensurability, specialisation). To unmask these steps and contradictions is the modest step I have taken in this chapter.

[92] Allott, n. 69 at 31.

PART III

Using international legal positivism

12

Interpretation

GLEIDER I. HERNÁNDEZ

1 Sketching the *problématique*

Interpretation is a specific epistemological tool within the overall epistemological enterprise that is scholarship. A form of legal hermeneutics, to study the theory and practice of interpretation is to raise basic jurisprudential questions as to the nature of a legal order, the rules that it contains, and the actors vested with authority for the creation – and the interpretation – of such rules. For international legal scholarship in particular, these questions are key in identifying with any clarity the processes through which international law develops and evolves. Responding to such questions is challenging, and it is no surprise that scholars of international law approach questions of interpretation with some 'trepidation',[1] a doubt shared also in domestic legal scholarship.[2]

The process of interpretation, and the study thereof, is certainly a wider endeavour than can be systematised thoroughly in the present chapter alone. Hence, a few points merit mention from the outset, so as to situate and confine the contribution that I hope will be made here. First, the positivist concept of law in a post-modern world, as befits the title of this collection, can and does admit of the reality that the interpretative act has a constitutive – or, at the very least, a *normative* – effect on the development of international law: given that legal systems are essentially rooted in the power of linguistic constructions, the possibility of semantic indeterminacy remains a reality. In such contexts, the partially constitutive character of interpretative acts and practices ought to be uncontroversial, and has been readily conceded by both Hans Kelsen and Herbert Hart.[3]

[1] Arnold McNair, *The Law of Treaties* (2nd edn Clarendon Press 1961) 361.

[2] Lon L. Fuller, *The Morality of Law* (Yale University Press 1969) 224: 'Despite the basic significance of interpretation for every aspect of the legal enterprise, it has never been a subject with which analytical positivism has felt comfortable.'

[3] Both Hans Kelsen, *Pure Theory of Law* (Max Knight (tr.), University of California Press 1967) 348–356, and HLA Hart, *The Concept of Law* (2nd edn Oxford University Press

It is in partial reaction to this reality that concepts are put forward such as inter-temporal interpretation, the principle of 'effectiveness'[4] and the principle of 'systemic integration';[5] although these can only be touched upon in this chapter, they seek partially to restore the idea of determinacy within international law, a particularly indeterminate system by its very form.[6] Yet this indeterminacy occurs within the *frame* of international law, a point that will be briefly surveyed in the following section.

From this vantage point, the next section will proceed within the analytical framework of the interpretation of treaties, to challenge some of the presumptions of determinacy contained within this framework. This is so for two reasons. First, international treaties, as acts through which states consciously accept international legal obligations, allow us to consider the binding character of such obligations and rules while avoiding, to a degree, questions relating to the different forms of various international legal texts, such as the acts of international organisations or the judgments of international courts or tribunals. Second, the relatively well-specified rules on treaty interpretation contained in Articles 31 to 33 of the Vienna Convention on the Law of Treaties 1969 (VCLT) are frequently argued to be capable of wider abstraction to all international legal texts and acts, an assertion that will be challenged in the next section. Throughout, the analysis will be conducted with an eye on the *purpose* of interpretation according to positivism, that is, 'to specify the ambit and normative content of the relevant instrument'.[7] However, my analysis will be cautious as to the purpose of interpretation, bearing in mind Sir Humphrey Waldock's exhortation to the International Law Commission to this effect:

> [T]he process of interpretation, rightly conceived, cannot be regarded as a mere mechanical one of drawing inevitable meanings from the words in a text, or of search for and discovering some pre-existing specific intention

1994) 144–150, admit to the use of discretion by law-applying actors in resolving such indeterminacy.

4 As explored carefully in Hersch Lauterpacht, 'Restrictive Interpretation and the Principle of Effectiveness in the Interpretation of Treaties' 26 *BYBIL* (1949) 48–85.

5 Campbell McLachlan, 'The Principle of Systemic Integration and Article 31(3)(c) of the Vienna Convention' 54 *ICLQ* (2005) 279–319.

6 David Kennedy situates international law's structural indeterminacy in that it simultaneously purports to bind the subjects who are the source of the law itself: see generally David Kennedy, 'Theses about International Law Discourse' 23 *German Yearbook of International Law* (1980) 353–391.

7 Alexander Orakhelashvili, *The Interpretation of Acts and Rules in Public International Law* (Oxford University Press 2008) 285. He continues: interpretation 'is also denoted as the exercise that clarifies the sense of the treaty . . . and its effect; or ascertains the intention of the parties from the text, their common intention'.

> of the parties with respect to every situation arising under a treaty… In most cases interpretation involves *giving* a meaning to a text.[8]

The discerning of meaning is claimed to be the central purpose of the interpretative process; yet I submit that in fact, the interpretive process also involves a process of *constructing* meaning. The very character of interpretation cannot simply be assumed to have an objective character, given the difficulties raised by the so-called 'hermeneutic circle', or the claim that the meaning of a text as a whole can only be established by reference to its individual parts, and that one's understanding of each individual part is constructed only by reference to the whole.[9] This view holds that there is no neutral, external standpoint from which to measure objectively the meaning of a system of signs or actions; there is thus a need to remove what is arbitrary or extrinsic from the circle, and focus exclusively on the object of cognition.[10] The narrative of classical positivist theorising on interpretation (to the extent that there is such theorising) presumes the objectivity of the interpretative process, a process that aims purely to clarify, to develop a method to fill any ambiguities in the fabric of the legal system with the one correct response, based on reason.[11] So confined, the interpretative process can appear to be self-confirming, an unhappy conclusion if one considers that social constructions ought to have rational justification and empirical support. Accordingly, the last section of this chapter will consider some subjectivist theories of interpretation that have been presented, respectively, by leading figures in the New Haven School and the Critical Legal Studies (CLS) movements.

2 Semantic indeterminacy and the 'frame' of a legal system

2.1 A legal system as a 'frame' for interpretation

Kelsen's 'theory of legal science', as a project of cognising the law through the methods of striving for truth,[12] did contain certain categorical assertions relating to the nature of the interpretative process. Chief among

8 Humphrey Waldock, 'Third Report on the Law of Treaties', UN Doc. A.CN.4/167, A.CN.4/167/Add.1–3, 16 *Yearbook of the International Law Commission*, Vol. II (1964) 1–65 at 53 (Commentary to Arts 70–73, para. 1), citing: [Harvard Law School], 'Codification of International Law: Part III – Law of Treaties' 29 *AJIL Supplement* (1935) 653–1228 at 939 (emphasis in original).

9 See generally Martin Heidegger, *Sein und Zeit* (Niemeyer 1927).

10 Hans-Georg Gadamer, *Truth and Method* (Joel Weinsheimer, Donald Marshall (trs), 2nd edn Continuum 1989) especially at 266–267.

11 Kelsen, n. 3 at 351.

12 For further discussion see Kammerhofer, Chapter 4 at 85.

classical positivist claims is that participants in legal cognition, be they scholars, judges or practitioners, ought to be limited purely to cognising positive acts of law and measuring them according to their positive validity.[13] Yet to do so in international law is to conflate positivism with voluntarism;[14] and Kelsen and other 'modern' critics of classical legal positivism were sufficiently responsive to difficulties with indeterminacy in legal texts. Kelsen readily conceded the 'intentional indefiniteness' of certain law-applying acts and even the unintended indefiniteness inherent in the linguistic formulation of legal norms.[15] His vision of the legal system was that it formed a 'frame' that admitted of possible applications of norms in concrete cases,[16] as the act of individual application helped further to determine and constitute a general legal rule.[17] Kelsen's critique of classical legal positivism questioned the idea that the act of application was nothing but an act of understanding and clarification: he situated it as an act of will or cognition, a *choice*.[18] This characterisation renders untenable any categorical distinction, within a given frame, between law-creation and law-application by law-applying actors: to him, these were also law-making acts.[19] His solution was to admit of the constitutive nature of *discretion*, in the application of such rules, by law-applying authorities in a legal system. Similarly, Hart conceded a certain place for discretion in a legal system whose rules were sufficiently determinate to supply standards of correct judicial decision,[20] although he also foresaw that hard cases helped to prove a fundamental 'incompleteness' in law, where the law could provide *no* answer.[21] This is in part because Hart's theory was essentially reductionist[22] insofar as it tried to confine itself to describing how law and a legal system could arrive at the validity of rules, and not on the determinacy of the legal order itself.

It is well known that Ronald Dworkin rejected the idea that the law could be incomplete and contain gaps, choosing instead a view that law

13 Kammerhofer, Chapter 4 at 85.

14 Kammerhofer, Chapter 4 at 90; d'Aspremont, Chapter 5 at 146, suggests that reductionism is indifferent as to the material source of the law, concerning itself only with its *formal validity*.

15 Kelsen, n. 3 at 350.

16 Kelsen, n. 3 at 351.

17 Kelsen, n. 3 at 349.

18 Kelsen, n. 3 at 82–83.

19 Kelsen, n. 3 at 85. See also Ingo Venzke, *How Interpretation Makes International Law: On Semantic Change and Normative Twists* (Oxford University Press 2012) 31.

20 Hart, n. 3 at 145. Hart's reliance on specifically *judicial* discretion was premised on his view that judges are law-applying officials within a given legal system; and thus specifically entrusted with safeguarding that system.

21 Hart, n. 3 at 252 (in his 'Postscript').

22 D'Aspremont's term: d'Aspremont, Chapter 5 e.g. at 116.

is not incomplete and indeterminate, being supplemented by *principles*, principles that can themselves be derived from moral justifications if necessary.[23] This would have been inadmissible to Kelsen:

> It is, from a scientific and hence objective point of view, inadmissible to proclaim as solely correct an interpretation that from a subjectively political viewpoint is more desirable than another, logically equally possible, interpretation. For in that case, a purely political value judgment is falsely presented as scientific truth.[24]

In any event, what is interesting about Dworkin is that the discretion exercised in the interpretative act requires the construction and balancing of the principles underlying legal rules, a 'weak' form of discretion exercised within the 'open texture'[25] of a legal system. Legal interpretation would then become an act of cognising the possibilities available *within* the frame of the system;[26] in this respect at least, it is reconcilable with Kelsen and Hart, in that it also situates the interpretative process within the frame of a legal system. With respect to international law, such limits are part of its inner logic, and of inherent structural biases that are deeply embedded within the international legal system itself.[27]

2.2 Limits to indeterminacy

Although the indeterminacy of legal language is in many respects presumed, it does not allow for unlimited choice in how interpretation shapes and constructs the meaning of a text. Within that indeterminacy comes a measure of determinacy; the 'canonical terms' within a legal text provide a limit to the political choices available to the interpreter. He or she cannot arrive at interpretations that clearly offend the actual words

[23] Cf. Hart, n. 3 at 204–205, denying the legality of recourse to moral justification.

[24] Kelsen, n. 3 at 356.

[25] Ronald Dworkin, *Taking Rights Seriously* (Harvard University Press 1978) 31–32. He distinguished his form of 'weak' discretion from the 'strong' discretion that he purported Kelsen and Hart attributed to judges, which allowed them to reach for principles *outside* a legal system. Dworkin's point is fair. If one examines Kelsen, n. 3 at 352, his refusal to privilege any acceptable meaning within the frame is evident: '[f]rom the point of view of positive law, one method is exactly as good as the other'. Similarly, Hart, n. 3 at 204–205, admits that the interpretation of legal texts and precedents by judges leaves open a 'vast field' for judicial law-creation, yet gives few indicia as to what standards should guide judges should the legal rules in question be ambiguous.

[26] Kelsen, n. 3 at 351.

[27] Martti Koskenniemi, *From Apology to Utopia: The Structure of International Legal Argument* (Finnish Lawyers' Publishing Co. 1989, reissued Cambridge University Press 2005) 568.

used, or that are justified by policies and principles wholly absent from the canonical terms.[28] Certainly, the text is the 'first authoritative reference point'[29] through which the interpretation of a norm is constructed; but the text is not reducible to a fixed, immutable expression of the rule. What is more, the engagement of actors with a legal text is historically contingent: it is structured by the frame in which it is situated, and measured against rules contained within that frame, not to mention past practices of other actors or disputants.[30]

Therefore, the outer limits that mark the field of possible interpretations may be recognised in an act of scientific legal cognition by capable legal scholars;[31] but true to the Kantian inspiration of Kelsen's legal theory, the concrete meaning of a norm in the individually disputed case cannot be *discovered*, but only *created*. This is broadly consonant with Hart's social thesis, where the claim to authority of an interpretative act is to adhere to the standards of legal argument and interpretation that are *accepted* by officials within that system.[32] Understood thus, interpretation is a relatively open exercise taking place within a confined setting, a setting defined by the four corners of the text itself.[33] Even in classical legal positivism, there is a certain openness based in the *language* used in constructing a text: '[b]y virtue of linguistic openness, legal positivism in its purest form is never immune to such changes in meaning and to the consequent informal development of law'.[34] As such, the theoretical possibilities of reasonable meaning – and thus, the contestability of meaning – are limited by these practical limits, which would confirm the binding force of international law.[35]

3 The 'sources of sources' and the rules of interpretation

3.1 Articles 31 to 33 VCLT as abstract rules of interpretation?

The natural tendency of the international lawyer is to seek comfort in certainty,[36] and to seek authoritative rules that lend order to what

[28] Venzke, n. 19 at 5. [29] Venzke, n. 19 at 5. [30] Venzke, n. 19 at 49.

[31] Hans Kelsen, *General Theory of Norms* (Michael Hartney (tr.), Clarendon Press 1991) 44.

[32] Ronald Dworkin, *Law's Empire* (Hart 1986) 67. [33] Dworkin, n. 25 at 108–109.

[34] Ulrich Fastenrath, 'Relative Normativity in International Law' 4 *EJIL* (2003) 305–340 at 316.

[35] Venzke, n. 19 at 49.

[36] As was recalled by Special Rapporteur Ago during the first reading of the Draft Articles on the Law of Treaties (International Law Commission, 'Summary Records of the Sixteenth Session: Held at Geneva, from 11 May to 24 July 1964', UN Doc. A/CN.4/SER.A/1964, 16

otherwise could be excessively subjective: an express 'basic assumption that [a] legal regime can only be described in terms of a more or less coherent system of rules'.[37] However valid the criticism that the rules of interpretation are 'not the determining cause of judicial decisions, but the *form* in which the judge cloaks a result arrived at by other means',[38] Articles 31 to 33 VCLT carry with them that allure, with one view suggesting their transcendent nature as abstract rules of interpretation, extending beyond the remit of treaties.[39] That these articles settle the scope of the interpretative process is often taken as a matter of faith in establishing the 'objective' character of interpretation as a means to attaining legal certainty:

> [T]he rules of interpretation laid down in international law contain a description of the way an applier shall be proceeding to determine the *correct* meaning of a treaty provision considered *from the point of view of international law.*[40]

The appeal of recourse to Articles 31 to 33 VCLT goes further than mere coherence, especially given their now-accepted customary status in international law.[41] Classical legal positivism maintains that treaty

Yearbook of the International Law Commission, Vol. I (1964) 23 (726th meeting, 19 May 1964, para. 34)).

[37] Ulf Linderfalk, *On the Interpretation of Treaties: The Modern International Law as Expressed in the 1969 Vienna Convention on the Law of Treaties* (Springer 2007) 19.

[38] Lauterpacht, n. 4 at 53.

[39] Orakhelashvili, n. 7 at 294, again suggesting that the Vienna Convention has *posited* rules that *supersede* the objective and subjective approaches to interpretation delineated in Koskenniemi, n. 27. See also Alexander Orakhelashvili, 'Unilateral Interpretation of Security Council Resolutions: UK Practice' 2 *Göttingen Journal of International Law* (2010) 823–842 at 824, arguing for the applicability of the rules of treaty interpretation to resolutions passed by the Security Council.

[40] Linderfalk, n. 37 at 29 (emphasis added).

[41] Permanent Court of Arbitration, *Arbitration regarding the Iron Rhine ('IJzeren Rijn') Railway (Belgium/Netherlands)*, Award of 24 May 2005 at 23 (para. 45): 'it is now well established that the provisions on interpretation of treaties contained in Arts 31 and 32 of the Convention reflect pre-existing customary international law'. The Court even applies the VCLT between states not parties to it: see e.g. France in *Certain Questions of Mutual Assistance in Criminal Matters (Djibouti v. France)*, Judgment of 4 June 2008, ICJ Reports (2008) 177 at 219 (para. 112); Indonesia in *Sovereignty over Pulau Ligitan and Pulau Sipadan (Indonesia/Malaysia)*, Judgment of 17 December 2002, ICJ Reports (2002) 625 at 645–646 (para. 37); Botswana and Namibia in *Kasikili/Sedudu Island (Botswana v. Namibia)*, Judgment of 13 December 1999, ICJ Reports (1999) 1045 at 1059 (para. 18). Orakhelashvili, n. 7 at 313–315, cites substantial arbitral practice and a number of WTO Appellate Body decisions which take the same position.

interpretation represents the interpretation of an act essentially *posited* by states, and thus a source of obligation as much as a source of law.

A modern example of this position is Alexander Orakhelashvili, who suggests categorically that '[t]he Vienna Convention methods of interpretation, as the practice consistently demonstrates, are not only treaty-based methods but also constitute the generally accepted legal framework of constitutional significance'.[42] To him, therefore, interpretation as a cognitive process has been supplanted by the treaty-based Vienna Convention methods that have been posited. He continues:

> [T]he view that the rules of the Vienna Convention are merely working assumptions is misguided, being a mere assertion unsupported by any evidence. The text of the Vienna Convention, the process of its drafting and the practice of its application are all unanimous in affirming that the rules of treaty interpretation are fixed rules and do not permit the interpreter a free choice among interpretative methods.[43]

Similarly, Linderfalk claims that, with the entry-into-force of Articles 31 to 33 VCLT, many of the major controversies relating to interpretation writ large 'must be considered as finally resolved'.[44] His justification is practical, not doctrinal:

> Not only will such investigations contribute to reducing disagreement among appliers with regard to the contents of international law. They will also provide the foundation for a constructive and more rational discussion concerning how the freedom of action left to the appliers under international law should be used.[45]

[42] Orakhelashvili, n. 7 at 317. But see criticism of this point by Jörg Kammerhofer, '[Book Review:] Alexander Orakhelashvili, The Interpretation of Acts and Rules in Public International Law (2008)' 20 *EJIL* (2009) 1282–1286 at 1283–1284; Michael Waibel, '[Review Essay]: Demystifying the Art of Interpretation' 22 *EJIL* (2011) 571–588 at 583–584.

[43] Orakhelashvili, n. 7 at 309. Relying on the ILC (International Law Commission, 'Draft Articles on the Law of Treaties with Commentaries' in International Law Commission, Reports of the International Law Commission on the Second part of its Seventeenth Session and on its Eighteenth Session, UN Doc. A/6309/Rev.l, 18 *Yearbook of the International Law Commission*, Vol. II (1966) 187–274 at 219–220 (Commentary to Arts 27–28, para. 8)), Orakhelashvili, n. 7 at 310, concludes that 'the Vienna Convention conclusively and definitively replaced the relevance of various "schools" of interpretation by formulating a single regime of interpretation based on rules'. But what this suggests is that the Vienna Convention proposed a *single, coherent, general approach* (Orakhelashvili calls it 'holistic') and that the approach was designed to be totalising, to impose a standard of interpretation of all acts in all circumstances.

[44] Linderfalk, n. 37 at 3, although he tempers this with the discussion of radical legal scepticism versus the 'one-right-answer' thesis.

[45] Linderfalk, n. 37 at 6.

For all this, it seems to the present author that the rules on treaty interpretation of the VCLT do not lend themselves automatically, nor easily, to abstraction. First, the idea that posited rules of interpretation supersede the nature of the interpretative process as a cognitive faculty goes a step too far, reducing the nature of the international legal system to an unreflexive dogmatism. To adopt the VCLT's approach uncritically (which even the International Court of Justice itself was rather hesitant to do for some time, even when it was relying on the articles *sub silentio*), would even do violence to the Commission's own modesty when drafting what became Articles 31 to 33:

> [T]he question raised by jurists is rather as to the non-obligatory character of many of these principles and maxims. They are, for the most part, principles of logic and good sense valuable as guides to assist in appreciating the meaning which the parties may have intended . . . recourse to many of these principles is discretionary rather than obligatory . . . [46]

Even within a purely voluntarist concept of international law, the VCLT itself is nothing more than a multilateral treaty, and was not conceived as being hierarchically superior to other forms of treaties. Even if its substantive provisions on the rules of interpretation and other matters (*pacta sunt servanda, rebus sic stantibus*) are regarded as codifications of customary international law, they were never intended to be the 'source-law' for all treaties to which they apply.[47] As such, although they are a useful heuristic device through which to filter the debates within international legal scholarship, they cannot substitute for the reality of interpretation as both a cognitive and law-creative process.

In any event, the Vienna Convention rules are very much specific to the particular *form* of a treaty within international law. Certainly, there may be some principles that can be distilled from the VCLT rules that may be relevant for other legal texts insofar as they are paralleled by treaties, but only insofar as the intention *behind* such legal texts is similar.[48]

A particularly good illustration is to be found in the case law of the ICJ when interpreting resolutions of the Security Council, which are

[46] International Law Commission, n. 43 at 218–219 (Commentary Arts 27–28, paras 4–5), also cited in Ian Brownlie, *Principles of Public International Law* (6th edn Oxford University Press 2003) 602; Richard Gardiner, *Treaty Interpretation* (Oxford University Press 2007) 37; Humphrey Waldock, 'Sixth Report on the Law of Treaties', UN Doc. A/CN.4/186, A/CN.4/186/Add.1–7, 18 *Yearbook of the International Law Commission*, Vol. II (1966) 51–103 at 94.

[47] Jörg Kammerhofer, 'Systemic Integration, Legal Theory and the ILC' 13 *Finnish Yearbook of International Law 2008* (2010) 343–366 at 354–355.

[48] Lauterpacht, n. 4 at 78.

themselves written instruments, concluded by representatives of states, and capable of generating legal obligations. Faced with the opportunity to rely on the VCLT rules when interpreting Security Council resolution 1244 in the *Kosovo* advisory opinion of 2010, the Court drafted a cryptic paragraph concluding that the rules contained in the VCLT 'could provide guidance' for the interpretation of Security Council resolutions, but that other factors were to be taken into account.[49] Accordingly, it behoves the interpreter to consider the nature and form of a legal text, and recall Waldock's distinction between principles ('guides to assist in appreciating the meaning')[50] and methods (textual, subjective and teleological)[51] of interpretation: that distinction outlines the descriptive, and not consciously prescriptive, spirit which has always permeated the VCLT's approach.[52]

Even if the VCLT approach to treaty interpretation cannot be taken as gospel, the treaty has been the quintessential legal instrument upon which most scholarly theorising on interpretation has been aimed, and in order to engage with classical positivist theories of international legal interpretation on their own terms, the rules on treaty interpretation constitute a self-contained, complete analytical *frame* that has attempted to systematise and to structure the various possible methods for discerning the meaning of a legal text. As a frame, they are worthy of careful examination.

3.2 The 'crucible' approach of the VCLT

At its core, the object of treaty interpretation is '[t]o determine the meaning of a treaty provision'.[53] The act of interpretation, in this respect,

49 *Accordance with International Law of the Unilateral Declaration of Independence in Respect of Kosovo*, Advisory Opinion of 22 July 2010, ICJ Reports (2010) 403 at 442 (para. 94). This has been the Court's position for some time: see *Legal Consequences for States of the Continued Presence of South Africa in Namibia (South West Africa) notwithstanding Security Council Resolution 276 (1970)*, Advisory Opinion of 21 June 1971, ICJ Reports (1971) 16 at 53 (para. 114).

50 Waldock, n. 8 at 54 (Commentary to Arts 70–73, para. 6).

51 Waldock, n. 8 at 54 (Commentary to Arts 70–73, para. 7).

52 Waldock, n. 8 at 54 (Commentary to Arts 70–73, para. 8): the Commission's aspiration was to 'seek to isolate and to codify the comparatively few rules which appear to constitute the strictly legal basis of the interpretation of treaties'. See also Gardiner, n. 46 at 27: 'the Vienna rules ... [combine] a clear indication of *what* should be taken into account with some rather less prescriptive pointers as to *how* to use the indicated material, and in the final analysis leaving a margin of appreciation for the interpreter to produce an outcome.'

53 *Conditions of Admission of a State to Membership in the United Nations (Article 4 of the Charter)*, Advisory Opinion of 28 May 1948, ICJ Reports (1947–1948) 57 at 61.

suggests that meaning is not self-evident, or else the converse, that meaning *needs* to be determined, because several possibilities are left open by the legal order. As Kelsen has suggested, the system of norms in question thus leaves open a degree of *choice*: it 'leaves this decision to an act of norm creation to be performed'.[54] It also entails a condition of ambiguity: 'it is not permissible to interpret what has no need of interpretation'.[55] Yet perhaps this condition of ambiguity for the interpretative act is overstated: in order to discern whether ambiguity or lack of clarity exists, one must *first* interpret the relevant text, using the means of interpretation laid out in Articles 31 to 33 VCLT. In keeping with this point, one must turn to the Commission's view that Article 31, as a whole, sets out a single 'general rule of interpretation' consisting of four distinct, non-hierarchical modes of interpretation, all of which are technically primary rules of interpretation.[56] This is known as the ILC's 'crucible' metaphor: 'all the various elements, as they were present in any given case, would be thrown into the *crucible*,[57] and their interaction would give the legally relevant interpretation'.[58]

The 'crucible' metaphor is apposite in describing the array of approaches embodied in Article 31(1), which encompass good faith, ordinary meaning of the terms of the treaty, *in their context*, and in the light of the treaty's object and purpose. Already here, one begins to see contradictions and limitations in the terms of Article 31 itself in respect of elucidating the purpose of interpretation. The 'ordinary meaning' term

[54] Kelsen, n. 3 at 352.

[55] Emer de Vattel, *The Law of Nations*, Vol. 3 (Charles G. Fenwick (tr.), Carnegie Institution of Washington 1916) 199 (para. 263), cited in Lauterpacht, n. 4 at 48.

[56] Gardiner, n. 46 at 8.

[57] The 'crucible' approach also avoids hierarchy of application and in some respects reflects the reality that no one formal maxim objectively dominates the process of interpretation by a judicial institution: see Charles Fairman, 'The Interpretation of Treaties' 20 *Transactions of the Grotius Society* (1935) 123–139 at 134–135.

[58] International Law Commission, n. 43 at 219–220 (Commentary to Arts 27–28, para. 8), reprinted in: *United Nations Conference on the Law of Treaties: First and Second Sessions: Vienna, 26 March–24 May 1968 and 9 April–22 May 1969: Official Records: Documents of the Conference*, A/CONF.39/11/Add.2 (1971) 7–93 at 39 (emphasis added). See also Santiago Torres Bernárdez, 'Interpretation of Treaties by the International Court of Justice following the Adoption of the 1969 Vienna Convention on the Law of Treaties' in Gerhard Hafner *et al.* (eds), *Liber Amicorum Professor Ignaz Seidl-Hohenveldern* (Kluwer Law International 1998) 726 (para. 11): 'one of the most distinctive features of the Vienna Convention system . . . [is] that interpretation of a treaty, or a provision of a treaty, is a legal operation which should combine the various permitted elements and means of interpretation as they may be present in the case, while keeping *open* the interpretation until the very conclusion of the interpretative process' (emphasis added).

used therein presupposes the possibility of natural logic, or an objectivity of meaning in the text itself;[59] yet equally, and without hierarchy between the approaches, one must also interpret the terms of the treaty 'in their context and in the light of [the treaty's] object and purpose'.[60] Accordingly, it is not unreasonable to arrive at the peculiar conclusion that the ordinary meaning of a text can only be determined through its context[61] and with regard to the treaty's object and purpose, a conclusion that, if well founded, seems to dismiss outright the possibility of textual interpretation being conducted purely through reference to the immediate terms of a treaty, as 'it ultimately cannot help to see but many other words which again need interpretation'.[62]

To add to this complexity, Article 31(3) VCLT is relevant when we consider subsequent agreements, subsequent practice and 'other relevant rules of international law',[63] all of which are added to the crucible as *simultaneous primary sources for interpretation.*[64] As such, treaty interpretation cannot be seen as a quest merely to distil the original meaning of a statement or text, based on taking its words at their face value at the time they were drafted.[65] This cannot be so given the immediate link which Article 31 makes with context and with the requirement of consideration of the object and purpose of a treaty, *even before* further elements of the general rule, including subsequent practice and other 'relevant rules' of general international law, are taken into account.[66]

[59] As Venzke, n. 19 at 50, puts it, 'the *word* is in the beginning of interpretation'.

[60] Art. 31(1) VCLT.

[61] Art. 31(2) VCLT in fact defines 'context' broadly. 'Context' in interpretation may be found both internally, within the treaty and its terms, preamble and annexes, and externally, as comprising agreements or instruments 'relating' to the treaty.

[62] See generally Venzke, n. 19 at 3.

[63] For further discussion on the effects of Art. 31(3)(c) VCLT as a principle of 'systemic integration', see generally McLachlan, n. 5 especially at 280–282; Duncan French, 'Treaty Interpretation and the Incorporation of Extraneous Legal Rules' 55 *ICLQ* (2006) 281–314.

[64] It should be noted that subsequent practice is not conceptualised as a *modification* to a treaty: see McNair, n. 1 at 424; and as the Permanent Court of International Justice concluded in *Article 3, Paragraph 2, of the Treaty of Lausanne (Frontier between Turkey and Iraq)*, Advisory Opinion of 21 November 1925, PCIJ Series B No. 12 (1925) 24.

[65] As some would claim: see Jörg Kammerhofer, *Uncertainty in International Law: A Kelsenian Perspective* (Routledge 2011) 127–128, maintaining that a text is static: '[I]nternational treaty law is the text which remains; therefore, its meanings remain. The correct temporal reference point is *ex tunc*; anything else constitutes a change.'

[66] Gardiner, n. 46 at 26.

Even so, if the 'crucible' approach to the process of interpretation is essentially simultaneous, this exhortation cannot be taken too literally, as pragmatism dictates that elements are only taken up one at a time.[67] Accordingly, the various elements are cumulative, and must be evaluated as a whole.[68] As such, the process of interpretation may require elements to be considered more than once, as the different priorities enumerated in Article 31 in turn arise.[69] It is not for naught that critics of the 'crucible' approach have taken to task the immense complexity of this process, suggesting that Articles 31 and 32 VCLT are so contradictory to the point of being meaningless,[70] leaving more questions open than settled.[71] Moreover, whether ironic, or merely symptomatic[72] of the inherent difficulties in the Convention's provisions on interpretation, there exists considerable disagreement on the 'interpretation of the rules of interpretation', all of which seek to establish objectively the intention of the authors of a legal text. It is to these various approaches that the next section turns.

[67] As the ICJ has done since its early days: see *Competence of the General Assembly for the Admission of a State to the United Nations*, Advisory Opinion of 3 March 1950, ICJ Reports (1950) 4 at 8: 'the first duty of a tribunal which is called upon to interpret and apply provisions of a treaty, is to endeavour to give effect to them in their natural and ordinary meaning in the context in which they occur.' The ordinary meaning of the text thus takes precedence over the object and purpose of a treaty and other available means of interpretation.

[68] As the ILC noted in its Commentaries to the Draft Articles on the Law of Treaties (International Law Commission, n. 43 at 220 (Commentary to Arts 27–28, para. 8)). See also Waldock's comments in the Commission's debates: International Law Commission, 'Summary Records of the Eighteenth Session: Held at Geneva, from 4 May to 19 July 1964', UN Doc. A/CN.4/SER.A/1966, 18 *Yearbook of the International Law Commission*, Vol. I.2 (1966) 206 (873rd meeting, 20 June 1966, para. 36). See also the intervention by Yasseen, suggesting that the Commission's proposal prescribed 'a general method for achieving that purpose . . . The means enumerated were . . . arranged, not in any order of precedence, but in a practical order, which was self-evident in view of the circumstances.' International Law Commission (1966), n. 68 at 197 (871st meeting, 16 June 1966, para. 48).

[69] Gardiner, n. 46 at 30.

[70] Koskenniemi, n. 27 at 334 (fn. 89), wryly noted that Art. 31 refers to 'virtually all thinkable interpretative methods', blending textualism with intentionalism, context and object and purpose.

[71] As Philip Allott, 'The Concept of International Law' in Philip Allott, *The Health of Nations: Society and Law beyond the State* (Cambridge University Press 2002) 289–315 at 305 suggests, the VCLT 'merely reduced these disagreements to writing'.

[72] As observed by Antonios Tzanakopoulos, 'Review of Richard Gardiner's "Treaty Interpretation" and Ulf Linderfalk's "On the Interpretation of Treaties"' 53 *German Yearbook of International Law* (2009) 721–724 at 722.

4 The traditional theories on 'objective' interpretation

4.1 *The notion of 'plain meaning' and the faith in textualism*

Even though neither Article 31 nor Article 32 VCLT actually employs the term 'intention' in elucidating the rules of interpretation,[73] among classical positivist international lawyers at least, 'no one seriously denies that the *aim* of treaty interpretation is to give effect to the intentions of the parties'.[74] That faith that the text itself holds the key to identifying party intention is repeated to the present day.[75]

Yet even in the VCLT itself, there are a number of means by which the intention of the parties can be reconstructed. Chief among these methods is to uphold the ordinary meaning of the words of a text above all other means of interpretation, what will be termed here a *textualist* approach. It is characterised by two presumptions: first, the Vattelian faith that clear written language renders nugatory the need for interpretation or for an interpreter,[76] or at least minimises his role (to that of an applier); and second, a distrust of extra-textualism as encouraging the 'arbitrary introduction of unreliable and biased considerations in the guise of interpretation'.[77] According to the textualist position, whatever the psychological or internalised intentions of the parties, once these have intermingled and balanced, to then be abstracted into a written text, 'only its terms are agreed upon and only its terms the parties promise to abide

[73] Yet see Orakhelashvili, n. 7 at 312 (fn. 47): the term 'intention' is used some fifteen times throughout the VCLT.

[74] This would be the 'juridically natural view': see Gerald G. Fitzmaurice, 'The Law and Procedure of the International Court of Justice: Treaty Interpretation' 28 *BYBIL* (1951) 1–28 at 3–4; Gerald G. Fitzmaurice, 'The Law and Procedure of the International Court of Justice, 1951–1954: Treaty Interpretation and Other Treaty Points' 33 *BYBIL* (1957) 203–293 at 204. See also Lauterpacht, n. 4 at 52, 55, 75–76. But cf. Kammerhofer, n. 65 at 89, who emphasises the cognitive aspects of the process: 'The will of the parties is on this view not only a logical moment. The will has content; therefore, that juncture of wills is an intent or intention . . . Assuming all that, should not our cognition then aim for the "true" treaty, i.e. party intent?'

[75] Orakhelashvili, n. 7 at 286; Gardiner, n. 46 at 87; Jean-Marc Sorel, Valérie Boré-Eveno, 'Article 31' in Olivier Corten, Pierre Klein (eds), *The Vienna Conventions on the Law of Treaties: A Commentary* (Oxford University Press 2011) 804–837 at 806.

[76] Myres S. McDougal, Harold D. Lasswell, James C. Miller, *The Interpretation of Agreements and World Public Order: Principles of Content and Procedure* (Yale University Press 1967) 90, suggest that the position taken by the Commission in the Draft Articles 'comes perilously close to Vattel's assumption that there are plain and natural meanings that do not admit of interpretation'.

[77] Richard A. Falk, 'On Treaty Interpretation and the New Haven Approach: Achievements and Prospects' 8 *Virginia Journal of International Law* (1967–1968) 323–355 at 333.

by. The treaty text is specifically designed to express the intentions of the parties.'[78] Adherence to textualism thus creates a rebuttable presumption that the text, which is the *outcome* of the meeting of the minds, is presumed to embody the intentions of the drafters, which the International Law Commission's own Commentary to the Draft Articles on the Law of Treaties would seem to confirm:

> [T]he text must be presumed to be an authentic expression of the intention of the parties . . . in consequence, the starting point of interpretation is the elucidation of the meaning of the text, not an investigation *ab initio* into the intention of the parties.[79]

But the textualist approach goes further than merely suggesting that the text is a starting point: its principal claim is that if the text is clear, recourse to extra-textual means of interpretation should not be necessary.[80] The claim that 'declared will' takes priority over internal volition[81] is both methodological and conceptual,[82] and is underpinned by a faith in the determinacy of legal language: by reducing, confining and otherwise minimising the third-party interpreter's grounds for discretion,[83] his function is simply to illuminate the intention of the parties as expressed in the language of an agreement. Following the formula exactly is intended to yield the same, predictable result: it is a process of cognition. The over-abundance of caution inherent in legal drafting also belies a sense of complacency, as parties tend to lift, uncritically, text from other treaties and from judgments. This repetitive incantation of text 'that already works' has doubtless led to the recondite form that many contemporary treaties now take.

78 Kammerhofer, n. 65 at 89, reporting the position.

79 International Law Commission, n. 43 at 220 (Commentary to Arts 27–28, para. 11), reprinted in: UNCLT, n. 58 at 40.

80 For a concrete example of a textualist argument, see Frank Berman, 'Treaty "Interpretation" in a Judicial Context' 29 *Yale Journal of International Law* (2004) 315–322 at 320–321.

81 Charles de Visscher, *Problèmes d'interprétation judiciaire en droit international public* (Pedone 1963) 17; Fitzmaurice, 'ICJ' (1951), n. 74 at 3; Fitzmaurice, 'ICJ' (1957), n. 74 at 205–206.

82 Falk, n. 77 at 324: '[T]here is disclosed the wavering between the autonomy and objectivity of the interpretative process, on the one side, and its normative, instrumental function on the other. This wavering, and the obscurity of meaning that results from it, makes interpretation at once fascinating and mysterious as an object of inquiry.'

83 A view similar to that expressed by Jean d'Aspremont, *Formalism and the Sources of International Law: A Theory of the Ascertainment of Legal Rules* (Oxford University Press 2011) 157.

4.2 Beyond the text: constructing, objectively, the intention of the parties

The faith in the determinacy of legal language also leads to extravagant claims; according to Sir Gerald Fitzmaurice, the textualist approach presumes to have found '*where* those intentions are to be found, [and] where they are (primarily) to be looked for'.[84] It is myopic: the supposed simplicity and hermetic nature of 'plain' meaning does not exclude questionable or 'illusory' elements; in fact, the question of whether a particular meaning of the word 'plain' obtains is at 'the very heart of the task of interpretation'.[85] It also bears recalling that according to Article 31, 'plain' or ordinary meaning is always read in the context of the treaty and its object and purpose. As such, the canon upholding 'the context' not only complements or confirms the plain meaning, but can also correct the erroneous versions of it. Otherwise, context is irrelevant in the face of 'plain' meaning.[86] There is also confusion as to whether 'ordinary meaning' is a purely linguistic term; or whether it refers to the possibility of ordinary meaning *in international law*, an issue which raises wider questions beyond the scope of this chapter. In this respect, any canon of 'ordinary meaning' arguably withstands closer scrutiny if redefined as 'the ordinary meaning in the context'.[87]

Ultimately, the claim by textualism, that it is the one true method through which the intention of the parties can be divined,[88] 'puts the

[84] Fitzmaurice, 'ICJ' (1951), n. 74 at 90.

[85] Julius Stone, 'Fictional Elements in Treaty Interpretation: A Study in the International Judicial Process' 1 *Sydney Law Review* (1954) 344–368 at 355; at 356 he continues: 'the "plain" . . . or "ordinary" . . . meaning has no other claim to primacy other than that . . . words are ordinarily used in the sense in which they are ordinarily used . . . the generally used standard of meaning is the standard of meaning generally used' (emphasis removed). This circularity also has a strongly objective element: if the intention of the parties cannot be discerned, the 'plain' meaning given to terms seems to be that general or 'ordinary' meaning that non-parties, or in fact the third-party interpreter, would affix to the text.

[86] Stone, n. 85 at 357.

[87] *Interpretation of the Convention of 1919 Concerning Employment of Women during the Night*, Advisory Opinion of 15 November 1932, PCIJ Series A/B No. 50 (1932) 365 at 383 (Diss. Op. Anzilotti).

[88] Fitzmaurice, 'ICJ' (1957), n. 74 at 205; Ian M. Sinclair, *The Vienna Convention on the Law of Treaties* (2nd edn Manchester University Press 1984) 115, 141. As claims McNair, n. 1 at 365–366, the entirety of the maxims and canons of interpretation 'which have crystallised out . . . are merely *prima facie* guides to the intentions of the parties'. Or as Orakhelashvili, n. 7 at 286 would simplify it, '[a]ll international acts embody State consent and agreement, expressed in one or another form. Therefore, interpretation methods must be those which deduce the meaning exactly of what has been consented to and agreed.'

cart before the horse'.[89] As McDougal, Lasswell and Miller have claimed: '[r]eliance on declared instead of actual intent is non-consensual: its point is not to give effect to real will but to the legitimate expectations of other States. It is a standard of justice.'[90] Pure textualism, in this respect, falls short; and it is for this reason that the VCLT includes such a range of methods, both in its primary means of interpretation and in the supplementary means of interpretation contained in Article 32. Before turning to the other means of interpretation embodied in Article 31, a brief segue into the relationship between Articles 31 (primary means of interpretation) and 32 (supplementary means of interpretation) is relevant here, as recourse to preparatory work reflects most clearly the purpose of interpretation in attempting to construct the meaning of a treaty text.

4.3 Preparatory work as a supplementary means of interpretation

A proxy for the debate on intentionalism versus textualism is embodied in the 'supplementary' means of interpretation referred to in Article 32 VCLT. The interpretative elements of each paragraph of Article 31 are to be employed in determining the meaning of any treaty, while recourse to the sources and materials available under Article 32 is never obligatory, and may be used generally only to confirm an interpretation already arrived at.[91] The other justification for using the sources of interpretation enumerated in Article 32 is corrective: we are allowed to consider the *travaux préparatoires* as well as the factual circumstances obtaining at the time of a treaty's conclusion if, *and only if*, the interpretative rules under Article 31 leave the meaning ambiguous or obscure, or would lead to a result that is 'manifestly absurd or unreasonable',[92] one may consider the

89 Hersch Lauterpacht, 'The Doctrine of Plain Meaning' in Elihu Lauterpacht (ed.), *International Law: Being the Collected Papers of Hersch Lauterpacht*, Vol. 4 (Cambridge University Press 1978) 393–403 at 396.

90 Koskenniemi, n. 27 at 343.

91 In *Conditions of Admission*, n. 53 at 63, the Court considered that if a text is 'sufficiently clear', 'consequently it does not feel that it should deviate from the consistent practice of the Permanent Court of International Justice, according to which there is no occasion to resort to preparatory work if the text of a convention is sufficiently clear in itself'. Cf. Hersch Lauterpacht, 'De l'interprétation des traités: Rapport et projet de résolutions présentés à l'Institut de Droit International' 43 *Annuaire de l'Institut de Droit International* (1950) 366–460 at 433–434, which supported full recourse, as a primary means of interpretation, to 'duly authenticated and published' *travaux préparatoires*, suggesting their utility in establishing the intention of the parties.

92 Art. 32 VCLT.

travaux préparatoires and factual circumstances obtaining at the time of a treaty's conclusion. These *means* 'can be read as allied to, but contrasted with',[93] the *rules* in Article 31.

Whatever this secondary nature, in practice recourse to preparatory work is more widespread than its 'supplementary nature' would suggest: even if declining somewhat in recent years, 'most international lawyers will almost automatically include a discussion of preparatory works in legal argument, and will consider it vital to do so'.[94]

This surely makes logical sense: in seeking to identify the intention of the drafters of a legal text, it would seem not only impractical, but counter-intuitive, to postpone all consideration of the circumstances behind its conclusion until *after* subsequent practice and customary international law rules have been examined.[95] Preparatory work, in the widest sense, constitutes part of the context behind the final treaty text.[96] Moreover, international courts and tribunals do refer expressly to the drafting history of treaty provisions; even if they formally rely upon a treaty's drafting history only after applying the general rule, the impact it might have played in a court's reasoning and decision-making process should not be underestimated.[97] The real question is therefore the legitimacy of recourse to such methods. Given that the overriding intention of interpretation through the VCLT methods is to determine the intention of the parties, to dismiss outright recourse to preparatory work, even for the textualist, would be justifiable only:

> If one accepts that it is the goal or aim of treaty interpretation to find something beyond the text of the treaty and if one argues that that goal can only be validly reached by reference to the text, rather than extra-textual references.[98]

[93] Gardiner, n. 46 at 37. During the Commission's deliberations on the matter, Tunkin suggested that they are 'secondary sources of interpretation . . . which might have to be taken into account . . . [but] did not have the same legal force'. International Law Commission, n. 68 at 190 (870th meeting, 15 June 1966, para. 62).

[94] Jan Klabbers, 'International Legal Histories: The Declining Importance of *Travaux Préparatoires* in Treaty Interpretation?' 50 *Netherlands International Law Review* (2003) 267–288 at 268.

[95] Gardiner, n. 46 at 10.

[96] Klabbers, n. 94 at 285.

[97] The immediate example that comes to mind is *Application of the International Convention on the Elimination of All Forms of Racial Discrimination (Georgia v. Russian Federation)*, Preliminary Objections, Judgment of 1 April 2011, ICJ Reports (2011) 70. But it is not isolated: the history of a given treaty provision is often reviewed by courts and tribunals as part of the relevant law (i.e. the context), and arguably therefore plays an important role in a court's reasoning, even if it is usually only formally relied upon after applying the general rule. See, for further examples, Gardiner, n. 46 at 38–45.

[98] Kammerhofer, n. 65 at 90.

Quite simply, recourse to preparatory work, as an extra-textual source of interpretation, underscores the basic purpose of interpretation in discerning the intention of the authors to a legal text.[99] It constitutes recognition that the meaning of norms does not simply lie behind words, but is the product of interpretation. Yet looking through a text for the 'force behind it'[100] also brings with it certain problems, not least the difficulty in constructing a uniform collective intention of its authors,[101] or in situating how practice contributes to the interpretation of a text.[102]

4.4 *'Objective', 'dynamic', and 'evolutive' interpretation*

It is perhaps true that the VCLT's approach to interpretation strives to outline the means of identifying the intention of the parties in arriving at the legal text they have produced. Yet there are two important notes of caution to be raised, as one cannot adhere strictly to the belief that interpretation will always yield an objective conclusion as to the parties' intentions. First, parties' intentions cannot be assumed to be so transparent, for a number of reasons. Parties may, in good faith, have attached different meanings as to the language agreed between them.[103] Parties may be unable to reach agreement on certain details, and thus have deployed 'ambiguous or non-committal expressions';[104] this might even be in order 'to leave the divergence of views to be solved in the future by agreement or in some other way'.[105] Parties may not have envisaged that a given subject matter would be applied at the time of drafting; or drafters may have, whether by carelessness or design, included treaty provisions which contradict each other in application to a given subject matter.[106] This is also the case when the treaty 'actually registers the absence of any common intention . . . or contains provisions which are mutually inconsistent and which the creative work of interpretation must reduce to some coherent meaning'.[107] The linguistic basis of law and legal texts thus can and does admit of evolution in meaning.[108] Put differently:

99 McNair, n. 1 at 411. 100 Linderfalk, n. 37 at 43. 101 Venzke, n. 19 at 3.

102 Venzke, n. 19 at 4. 103 Lauterpacht, n. 4 at 77–78. 104 Lauterpacht, n. 4 at 77.

105 Lauterpacht, n. 4 at 77–78. Stone, n. 85 at 347 makes the same point less charitably.

106 What is particularly interesting is that resolving the contradiction is in fact 'imputing rather than discovering a common intention underlying the treaty as a whole': Lauterpacht, n. 4 at 81.

107 Lauterpacht, n. 4 at 52; see also Gardiner, n. 46 at 27. Orakhelashvili, n. 7 at 339, reduces ambiguity to a problem to be clarified, and concludes essentially that ambiguity is 'only a factor that opens the door for other factors of interpretation that are available within the framework of the relevant treaty'.

108 Venzke, n. 19 at 39–40, cites a number of judicial institutions giving sanction to this principle: the International Court of Justice, in *Aegean Sea Continental Shelf (Greece v.*

> If the *text* of a treaty is recognised as the object of interpretation [*Auslegung*], then nothing stands in the way of assuming that the text can experience a change of meaning in the course of its development even without any tacit modification of the treaty.[109]

Second, undue faith in intentionalism also underplays the possibility that the drafters intend to bestow expressly upon the interpreter the power to give meaning to the text, either to allow for the divergence to be resolved by agreement or otherwise,[110] to allow the text to evolve 'dynamically'.[111] This can be achieved through the use of generic terms whose meaning is susceptible to evolution over time.[112] That parties may choose to conclude texts of this sort makes it difficult to arrive at an objective interpretation based on their intentions at the time of the conclusion of a treaty, and requires one to give the treaty terms meaning at the time that an interpretation of its terms is required.[113]

Take the example of standard-setting instruments such as human rights conventions. Although formally structured like all other multilateral conventions,[114] these are framed so that the rights and obligations embodied in them are *integral*,[115] as obligations to all other

Turkey), Judgment of 19 December 1978, ICJ Reports (1978) 3 at 32 (para. 77); *Dispute Regarding Navigational and Related Rights (Costa Rica v. Nicaragua)*, Judgment of 13 July 2009, ICJ Reports (2009) 213 at 242–243 (para. 65); the European Court of Human Rights, in ECtHR, *Bayatyan v. Armenia*, Application No. 23459/03, Judgment of 27 October 2009, para. 63; ECtHR, *Scoppola v. Italy (No. 2)*, Application No. 10249/03, Judgment of 17 September 2009, ECHR Reports (2009) 1297 [42 *EHRR* (2010) 41] at para. 104; and the WTO Appellate Body, in WTO, *United States–Import Prohibition of Certain Shrimp and Shrimp-like Products*, WT/DS58/AB/R, adopted 6 November 1998, paras 127–131; WTO, *China–Publications and Audiovisual Products*, WT/DS363/AB/R, adopted 21 December 2009, para. 47.

109 Rudolf Bernhardt, *Die Auslegung völkerrechtlicher Verträge insbesondere in der neueren Rechtsprechung internationaler Gerichte* (Heymanns 1963) 132, translated by Venzke, n. 19 at 4.

110 Stone, n. 85 at 348.

111 See Hans Kelsen, *The Law of the United Nations: A Critical Analysis of Its Fundamental Problems* (Stevens & Sons 1950) xiv–xv.

112 The ICJ used this approach in *Navigational Rights*, n. 108 at 242–243 (paras 63–66).

113 Catherine Brölmann, 'Law-Making Treaties: Form and Function in International Law' (2005) 74 *Nordic Journal of International Law* 383–404; Gardiner, n. 46 at 27.

114 Bruno Simma, 'From Bilateralism to Community Interest in International Law' 250 *Recueil des Cours* (1994) 217–384 at 335. A more cautious, 'dynamic' interpretation of the UN Charter was previously advanced by Alfred Verdross and Bruno Simma, *Universelles Völkerrecht: Theorie und Praxis* (3rd edn Duncker & Humblot 1984) 496–497.

115 The concept of 'law-making treaties' ('*traités-lois*') was made prominent by Gerald Fitzmaurice in the ILC (Gerald G. Fitzmaurice, 'Law of Treaties: Second Report', UN

contracting parties, or in other words, as obligations *erga omnes partes*.[116] The very structure of such agreements, therefore, requires that legal provisions be interpreted with a view to the overall object and purpose of the convention, and where appropriate, a teleological, systematic interpretation which recalls the convention's place in the legal system as a whole.[117] Another example of such a treaty would be the UN Charter, the quintessential instrument on which it seems to be agreed that the teleological method of interpretation has 'pride of place'.[118] As Kammerhofer explains, besides the entire structure and framework of the Charter itself, to discern properly its *telos* it is both advisable and common to look extra-textually, both into its *travaux préparatoires*,[119] but also into the subsequent practice of its principal organs and its member states.[120]

Doc. A.CN.4/107, 9 *Yearbook of the International Law Commission*, Vol. II (1957) 16–70 at 31). Such treaties were said to establish 'inherent', 'non-reciprocal' obligations that required 'an absolute and integral obligation and performance under all conditions'.

116 Bruno Simma, Gleider Hernández, 'Legal Consequences of an Impermissible Reservation to a Human Rights Treaty: Where do we Stand?' in Enzo Cannizzaro (ed.), *The Law of Treaties beyond the Vienna Convention: Essays in Honour of Professor Giorgio Gaja* (Oxford University Press 2011) 60–85 at 67.

117 The mode of interpretation is thus partly contingent on the intention of the drafters themselves: see e.g. the 'living instrument' principle guiding the interpretation of the European Convention of Human Rights 'in the light of present day conditions': ECtHR, *Tyrer v. United Kingdom*, Application No. 5856/72, Judgment of 25 April 1978, ECHR Series A No. 26 (1978) 15–16 (para. 31); ECtHR, *Loizidou v. Turkey (Preliminary Objections)*, Application No. 15318/89, Judgment of 23 March 1995, ECHR Series A No. 310 (1995) [20 *EHRR* (1995) 99], para. 71. It is also endorsed by the UN Human Rights Committee, which tried to shoehorn its teleological interpretation within Art. 31 VCLT: see UNHRC, *Roger Judge v. Canada*, Communication No. 829/1995, UN Doc. CCPR/C/78/D/829/1998 (2003), Views of 5 August 2003, paras 10.3–10.4.

118 Kammerhofer, n. 65 at 99.

119 Kammerhofer, n. 65 at 99. See also Stephen M. Schwebel, 'May Preparatory Work be Used to Correct Rather than to Confirm the "Clear" Meaning of a Treaty Provision?' in Jerzy Makarcyzk (ed.), *Theory of International Law at the Threshold of the 21st Century: Essays in Honour of Krzysztof Skubiszewski* (Kluwer Law International 1996) 541–547 at 543: 'there is simply too much State practice and judicial precedent that accords preparatory work a greater place'. But cf. *Certain Expenses of the United Nations (Article 17, Paragraph 2, of the Charter)*, Advisory Opinion of 20 July 1962, ICJ Reports (1962) 151 at 185 (Sep. Op. Spender): 'The stated purposes of the Charter should be the prime consideration in interpreting its text.'

120 The trite, but most effective, example of this practice is the manner in which abstaining votes by the permanent members of the Security Council have come to fall within the expression 'concurring votes of the permanent members' contained in Art. 27(3) UN Charter. Through practice, it has come to be 'deemed as a constitutionally valid interpretation of the notion of "concurrence"', and acknowledged as such by the ICJ in *Namibia*, n. 49 at 22 (para. 22).

It is difficult to understand how preparatory works can hold a diminished place in teleological interpretation, as while their use to buttress the intentions of the parties might be 'tautologically limited', they seem eminently suited as a means to discover the object and purpose of the treaty. In short, in such circumstances, parties must be regarded as having consented to a dynamic, 'evolutive' approach to the interpretation of their respective obligations.[121]

The concerns expressed above aim to demonstrate that the intention of the parties simply cannot always be the prime consideration, even if it is highly relevant. Parties must be regarded as having assented to a treaty being situated within an intellectual framework that underpins the international legal order, with its terms being susceptible to interpretation according to the canons and processes of that frame. Their very consent, and not merely the legal text concluded between them, can be 'objectivised' rather than merely be seen as objective: the *process of interpretation* is removed from the parties. Had they intended otherwise, they would have subjected their treaty to another legal structure altogether. Moreover, although parties can reasonably expect disagreement over the meaning of terms, they do not expect every disagreement to signify a desire on the part of one or the other to terminate the relationship embodied in the treaty.[122] In short, parties to a treaty consent to obligations with the implicit understanding that there may be disagreements as to the tenor and scope of those obligations, and they consent to a system of rules to resolve those disagreements. In this respect, even if the sources and methods of interpretation are different, and the materials and references to be examined may vary somewhat, the teleological mode of interpretation can be distilled into seeking to discern what precisely the parties have agreed to be bound by, an essentially *objective* exercise.

As a matter of practice, parties are of course free to formulate rules strictly or expansively; and whatever their unilateral wish, as a general rule, it can be said that the common intention of parties should be distilled so that the rights and duties created in a treaty obligation can be equitably interpreted, in a spirit of good faith, common sense and reasonableness.[123]

121 A point taken up by Kammerhofer, n. 65 at 98.

122 Ian Johnstone, 'Treaty Interpretation: The Authority of Interpretive Communities' 12 *Michigan Journal of International Law* (1990–1991) 371–419 at 382.

123 Georg Schwarzenberger, 'Myths and Realities of Treaty Interpretation: Articles 27–29 of the Vienna Draft Convention on the Law of Treaties' 9 *Virginia Journal of International Law* (1968) 1–19 at 9. But cf. Kammerhofer, n. 65 at 91, who calls into question whether the intention one seeks to discern is the joint intention of parties, or even the unilateral intention of one party.

Even setting aside these platitudes, which provide little guidance to an impartial third party that seeks to reconcile the competing interpretations of parties and to identify the commonalities between their views, the various means of interpretation deployed in the VCLT demonstrate the difficulties of objective interpretation and the continued allure of more subjectivist approaches, to which this chapter now turns.

5 Subjectivity and interpretation

5.1 Beyond objectivism

The various theories described above all strive to delineate and describe a process of *objective* interpretation, one whose object is to distil *true* meaning *from* legal texts: even if one moves away from textualist assumptions about interpretation, one cannot supplement the text with anything that it does not already contain.[124] For all the rigour that the VCLT rules purport to establish in matters of interpretation, there is a serious theoretical problem with uncritical acceptance of these rules, which, after all, are based on the positivist aspiration to *identify* legal norms, and on the belief that such identification can be objective to the neutral, expert interpreter. Yet by its very nature, the process of interpreting a text requires cognition of that text, and a judgment as to how its meaning should be understood. As explained above, the interpretative act is a choice between the alternatives made simultaneously available and limited by that text. Such a claim defies the claim that meaning lays hidden behind a text, ready to be discerned objectively; it is the product of the cognitive process of interpretation. Moreover, because interpretation remains an epistemological tool and cannot be reduced to a set of posited rules, the process of interpretation must necessarily exist prior to the substantive or procedural rules or norms to be interpreted. In a sense, therefore, the rules of interpretation exist *outside* the realm of rules of law, as they are partially connected to the subjectivity of the interpreter and not to the purported objectivity of a text.

It is claimed that there is an ironic circularity in the VCLT rules in that Articles 31 to 33 must, in 'infinite regression', be interpreted.[125] More

[124] Robert Kolb, *Interprétation et création du droit international: Esquisse d'une herméneutique juridique moderne pour le droit international public* (Bruylant 2006) 412–413.

[125] Gardiner, n. 46 at 9; Klabbers, n. 94 at 270. That circularity has also been noted in the domestic law context: see Stanley Fish, 'Fish v. Fiss' 36 *Stanford Law Review* (1984) 1325–1347 at 1326.

generally, Hart suggests that rules of interpretation are themselves nothing but rules and subject to the same fate of interpretation.[126] This is an over-simplification, confusing the hermeneutic process of interpretation with such rules of interpretation as might be posited. As Kammerhofer explains, rules are 'acts of will purporting to modify the frame of the possible meanings of norms'.[127] The hermeneutic process of interpretation is anterior to such norms, and external to the frame. Yet, whatever views exist as to whether interpretation exists outside the frame or is part of the frame itself, the quasi-scientific approach to law has its weaknesses. As Koskenniemi notes, the one thing that unites Kelsen and McDougal is:

> [T]heir insistence on the indeterminate, subjective, political character of interpretation. They... criticize disguising the arbitrariness of interpretation under the fictions of textual clarity or juristic method. They propose that interpretation be conducted openly by reference to important values.[128]

As such, to anchor a positivist approach to interpretation too closely to objectivism constitutes an incomplete understanding of the positivist approach to interpretation. The idea that international law must merely be applied 'correctly' to yield a consistent answer each time to any given question suggests a certain objectivity in the rules of application that does not seem to be borne out in practice. The indeterminacy that is yielded through this undue faith in the VCLT rules of interpretation opens the door to Beckett's criticism that these rules privilege desirability through their sheer contradiction: 'one can add or remove words to realise the *telos* imposed... as in the end, Art. 31 mandates "decontextualised and arbitrary reasoning"'.[129]

5.2 *The policy-oriented jurisprudence of the New Haven school*

Accordingly, a few tentative steps outside what is generally understood as 'positivist' are necessary, and at this juncture, it is interesting to focus on the essence of the argument favoured by the founders of the New Haven School of policy-oriented jurisprudence. In *The Interpretation of*

[126] Hart, n. 3 at 126. [127] Kammerhofer, n. 65 at 112–113.

[128] Koskenniemi, n. 27 at 341.

[129] Jason Beckett, 'Fragmentation, Openness, and Hegemony: Adjudication and the WTO' in Meredith K. Lewis, Susy Frankel (eds), *International Economic Law and National Autonomy* (Cambridge University Press 2010) 44–70 at 57, citing Margaret Young, 'The WTO's Use of Relevant Rules of International Law: An Analysis of the *Biotech* Case' 56 *ICLQ* (2007) 907–930 at 922, 924.

Agreements and World Public Order, McDougal, Lasswell and Miller sought to elucidate a different *mode* of interpretation, one which set that process within their conceived framework of world public order.[130] Part of a consciously different 'intellectual strategy for restating a subject of basic importance',[131] the New Haven approach flowed from redefining the very concept of 'international agreement':

> The most comprehensive and realistic conception of an international agreement . . . is . . . not that of a mere collocation of words or signs on a parchment, but rather that of a continuing process of communication and collaboration between the parties in the shaping and sharing of demanded values.[132]

The divergence from the VCLT methods of interpretation is conscious and emphatic, as is exemplified by the scathing attack on textualism by McDougal, Lasswell and Miller:

> It is the grossest, least defensible exercise of arbitrary formalism to arrogate to one particular set of signs – the text of a document – the role of serving as the exclusive index of the parties' shared expectations.[133]

Instead, they argue that:

> [T]he primary aim of a process of interpretation by an authorized and controlling decision maker can be formulated in the following proposition: discover the *shared expectations* that the parties to the relevant communication succeeded in creating in each other.[134]

The approach favoured is contextual: to situate international agreements and the obligations they contain as part of a larger context, thus engaging in a 'systematic, comprehensive examination of all the relevant features of that context, with conscious and deliberate appraisal of their significance'.[135]

New Haven was thus the outline of a *method*, one entirely different from the positivism that permeated the VCLT approach, although both ostensibly sharing the primary aim of ascertaining the intention of parties

130 McDougal, Lasswell and Miller, n. 76 especially at 197–201.

131 Falk, n. 77 at 331; according to him, the 'chief value of the New Haven Approach is to provide a persuasive reorientation of inquiry into the interpretative process, not that the approach is so definitive as to put to rest the need for inquiry.'

132 McDougal, Lasswell and Miller, n. 76 at xxiii.

133 McDougal, Lasswell and Miller, n. 76 at xvii.

134 McDougal, Lasswell and Miller, n. 76 at xvi (emphasis added).

135 McDougal, Lasswell and Miller, n. 76 at 337.

to an agreement.[136] What is particular about the New Haven School is that it redefines the intentions of parties into their 'shared expectations', which are to fit into a distinctive view on the nature of the international legal system:

> This primary, distinctive goal [of interpretation] stipulates that decision-makers undertake a disciplined, responsible effort to ascertain the genuine shared expectations of the particular parties to an agreement. The link with fundamental policy is clear: to defend the dignity of man is to respect *his* choices and not, save for overriding common interest, to impose the choices of others upon him.[137]

The distinguishing feature, aiming to ascertain the 'shared subjectivities of communicators',[138] is wholly to remove the text as the principal object of the interpretative process. The consent-based, intentionalist elements of the VCLT approach remain alive, but the objective character of legal texts is subordinated, instead being replaced by an enquiry into the subjective, common agreement of the parties, which in turn is understood against a common (objective) 'standard of justice'. The formalism of the VCLT approach, which insisted on the importance of the text as a primary element to be considered in the interpretative process, is lost.

5.3 *Implications of interpretation according to the New Haven school*

The shortcomings in the purported objectivity of the VCLT approach to interpretation are one matter, but it is the totalising pretensions of the New Haven School, of interpreting all legal texts from a purported common standard of justice, that are genuinely problematic. The principal criticism to be levelled against the New Haven School is rooted in the indeterminacy of the international legal system, at the very least with regard to the values it means to embody. The New Haven School elides the possibility that there remain a multiplicity of values and objectives, all possibly mutually contradictory, embedded in supposedly objective, 'positivist' law. Instead, the New Haven School portrays the international legal frame as fully

[136] This is no creation of a paper tiger: at the same period McDougal, Lasswell and Miller were writing, mainstream scholarship sought to uphold the intentions of the parties as the ideal towards which treaty interpretation should aspire: see e.g. Francis G. Jacobs, 'Varieties of Approach to Treaty Interpretation: with Special Reference to the Draft Convention on the Law of Treaties before the Vienna Diplomatic Conference' 18 *ICLQ* (1969) 318–346.

[137] McDougal, Lasswell and Miller, n. 76 at 40–41, see also 367–368.

[138] McDougal, Lasswell and Miller, n. 76 at xix.

determinate, complete through its abiding quest to elucidate and advance 'the realization of a world public order of human dignity',[139] which in turn is based on its own conception of what such human dignity would entail. As such, it falls prey to the concern that interpreters will, more or less unquestioningly, conduct the interpretative process with reference to their individualised conception of these values: 'interpretation may . . . have recourse to values already embodied within the system to determine which interpretation best makes sense systemically'.[140]

Moreover, although it is true that the New Haven School has never purported to settle questions of interpretation by endowing a text with a clarity that it does not possess,[141] its emphasis on specific policy objectives in fact embodies an important characteristic shared with the objectivist schools of interpretation. Both approaches attempt to define the interpretative process by advancing a more or less objective claim as to the *nature* of the international legal system as a determinate, complete system. While classical positivist theory situates the VCLT rules, arrived at consensually, as part of the 'inner coding'[142] of the international legal system, the New Haven School merely situates that focus differently: international agreements are to be measured by some overriding, nebulous, 'common standard of justice',[143] or alternatively, a substantive overarching end of 'protecting human dignity'.[144] Both traditions create an expectation as to what constitutes a right and proper interpretation *within* the international legal system, and offer, therefore, a form of operational closure:[145] a set of rules and techniques not only defined by international lawyers *for* international lawyers, but also a systemic understanding that comes to define the international legal system. Interpretation, the epistemic exercise through which the system constructs its own realities and applies them to concrete cases, in this respect remains '*autopoeisis*' at its best, impacting and affecting the system as rapidly as it creates expectations for how the system is meant to function.[146] In short, interpretation theory remains

139 McDougal, Lasswell and Miller, n. 76 at 395.

140 Iain Scobbie, 'Towards the Elimination of International Law: Some Radical Scepticism about Sceptical Radicalism' 61 *BYBIL* (1990) 339–362 at 349.

141 Although one cannot take too far Falk's point that the very existence of a dispute presupposes equally valid adversary interpretations of a text: see Falk, n. 77 at 346.

142 Beckett, n. 129 at 51.

143 McDougal, Lasswell and Miller, n. 76 at 40, see also 367–368.

144 Myres S. McDougal, 'International Law, Power, and Policy: A Contemporary Conception' 82 *Recueil des Cours* (1954) 133–259 at 137, *passim*.

145 Beckett, n. 129 at 50–51.

146 Beckett, n. 129 at 50.

rooted in a faith that there is 'truth' to be found in the legal system, and that the system, even if imperfect, is perfectible through technique. It is that quest for truth that will be examined in the concluding arguments of this chapter.

5.4 The 'search for truth' immanent in interpretation theory

Perhaps it is to be left to the 'post-modernists' to salvage the thoughts of the 'modernists' in search for a fuller understanding of the interpretative process. In an early article,[147] David Kennedy challenged that very search for truth – 'the idea of an unknowable subject that demands understanding'[148] – inherent in interpretation theory. Part of his challenge is based in the difficulty in actually discerning objective truth: 'The view that things "really are" or really could be completely open ended is either nihilism or lunacy. But it is a lunacy that interpretation seems able to cure.'[149] According to Kennedy, 'truth' is not to be found in the text, the authors, nor the context, a claim that would obliterate the VCLT rules. Nor would truth be found in the interpreter. His claim focuses on the 'hermeneutic moment' in which the interpreter resolves the meaning of a legal text:

> This movement from truth to power is constructed so as to deny both the authority of any theory of truth and the exercise of any power. The hermeneutic moment is supplemental to the stable standoff of the interpretive process. As theorists, we achieve it, in part, by focusing upon what the interpreter must have been thinking given his admittedly socially constructed consciousness . . . we get out of the stalemate of conflicting and irresolvable truth claims.[150]

The unknowable 'hermeneutic moment' shifts the focus of discussion, suggesting that the purpose of hermeneutics within a discipline is not to dictate a method of interpretation for that discipline, but, rather, to assess empirically the 'self-understanding' of the interpreter and to scrutinise how the interpretative process works in practice.[151] David Hoy claims

[147] David Kennedy, 'The Turn to Interpretation' 58 *Southern California Law Review* (1985) 251–275.

[148] Kennedy, n. 147 at 255. [149] Kennedy, n. 147 at 252. [150] Kennedy, n. 147 at 255.

[151] Kammerhofer, n. 65 at 122, invokes Joachim Hruschka, *Das Verstehen von Rechtstexten: Zur hermeneutischen Transpositivität des positiven Rechts* (C. H. Beck 1972) 10 (translation by Kammerhofer): 'the question concerning the phenomenon of understanding legal texts . . . is not concerned with how the "interpreter" *ought to interpret*, but how the interpreter *has always been behaving* in the process of understanding a legal text. Which preconditions have to be fulfilled in order to be able to call it "understanding legal texts"?'

that the emphasis on empiricism allows us to suspend the assumption that law is 'miraculously rational' or merely ad hoc,[152] and that the emphasis on the hermeneutic moment is the sole outcome once a totalising moment can be reduced to a privileging of textual oppositions: without that hermeneutic moment, 'we cannot really contemplate an infinity of meanings and still claim to be understanding the text'.[153] This turn to empiricism, accordingly, also represents an emphasis on the manner in which actors entrusted with interpretative authority provide legitimation for their practices and methods.[154] Moreover, it allows the identification of larger struggles for semantic authority, in which 'actors craft legal interpretations in an attempt to implement meanings of legal expressions that are aligned with their convictions or interests'.[155]

Yet, such a turn to empiricism is problematic in that it transforms hermeneutics into meta-theorising about interpretation practice, a 'theory of theories', privileging interpreters' self-understanding, to the extent that this is even feasible. As Kennedy underlines, a turn to empiricism confines hermeneutics to:

> [C]onsumption by the analytic elite; those whose consciousness positions them above the judicial interpreters themselves, but who can escape responsibility for their own 'understanding and interpretation' by flaunting the infinite regress of their methodology and by calling it 'modesty' about 'practical' effects.[156]

Accordingly, it becomes impossible to engage in a critique of reason as the discussion becomes centred on sources and actors making claims to interpretative authority. To do so, even while demonstrating the fragility of privileging one source over another, or the intention of the interpreter over that of the author of a legal text, leads nowhere else than to the 'authority fetishism' rebuked by Kennedy,[157] which merely displaces speculation relating to the intentions and mindset of the authors of a legal text over to the interpreters of that text. Such emphasis on actors incorrectly situates the focus of analysis, ignoring how successful interpretations become 'expressions of power in the sense that they influence what the law means

152 David Couzens Hoy, 'Interpreting the Law: Hermeneutical and Poststructuralist Perspectives' 58 *Southern California Law Review* (1985) 135–176 at 172.

153 Kennedy, n. 147 at 261, in response to Hoy, n. 152 at 169.

154 Kennedy, n. 147 at 262.

155 Venzke, n. 19 at 58.

156 Kennedy, n. 147 at 258; at 275 he concludes: 'The turn to interpretation in legal theory, by accepting the inevitability of elite management, reconfirms the structured distinction between truth and power which in turn sustains the position of the manager.'

157 Kennedy, n. 147 at 260.

and thus shape others in the determination of their own circumstances and fate'.[158]

And what if this line of reasoning leads one to the conclusion that there is no such thing as the 'truth'; of a universal morality being impossible? Venzke makes an interesting claim to agnosticism, a minimal commitment through which a 'minimal residual element of subjectivity' is sufficient to admit of genuine agreement.[159] Without this, the analysis becomes exclusively structural, entirely ignoring the practice of relevant actors: it denies the constructive or constitutive power of actors, of the normativity or power of the law. The acceptance of international actors, which is a necessary condition for the development of international law, demands an understanding of interpretation as an *act of authority*, dependent on its ability to induce acceptance by way of argument or persuasion, rather than an *act of power*.[160]

Ultimately, the true value of hermeneutics in interpretation theory lies elsewhere, in leading us to consider and to theorise about the *structure* of interpretation, rather than interpretation itself. This would allow scholars of interpretation theory to continue to consider, or even 'recuperate', the text as part of their own project,[161] but without becoming slavishly dogmatic as to its centrality to interpretation.

6 Conclusion

There is something compelling in Martti Koskenniemi's claim in *The Gentle Civilizer of Nations* that the international legal profession's evolution through the early twentieth century consummated its maturity as a discipline by suppressing its link to describing the practice of nations (and thus describing relations of power).[162] International lawyers claimed authority for international law through a turn to what is now classical legal positivism, brought about by a claim about the 'truth' of the law and legal texts. Yet, the interpretative process remains a set of shared vocabularies and techniques which are to be mastered *by* international lawyers *for* international lawyers. The abdication of political responsibility that can result from this blind focus on technical prowess and objectivity risks the classical positivist international lawyer becoming rather far removed from

[158] Venzke, n. 19 at 62. [159] Venzke, n. 19 at 62.

[160] Venzke, n. 19 at 63. See also Lyndel V. Prott, 'Argumentation in International Law' 5 *Argumentation* (1991) 299–310.

[161] Beckett, n. 129 at 1046. [162] This is the leitmotif that permeates Koskenniemi, n. 27.

questions of ideology and power.[163] In this respect, an 'oecumenical'[164] rejuvenated legal positivism holds appeal; one can draw from the lessons on semantic indeterminacy of Kelsen and Hart, as well as both the subjectivist, ideological critiques of interpretation expressed by more critical voices. For all its flaws, even the value-laden approach of the New Haven School may be helpful: it has the virtue of seeking to engage with the law (albeit instrumentally), breaking at least partially with the truth-seeking of classical legal positivism and transparently acknowledging the interpenetration of law and policy.[165]

For better or for worse, one's views on the interpretative process will necessarily remain coloured by one's views as to what is the object of interpretation: is it a search for objective truth? A reconciliation of 'shared subjectivities'? An 'infinite regress' of methodology? All of these highlight the basic tension as to the (possibly radical?)[166] (in)determinacy of law for positivists, and whether rules of interpretation can actually aspire to entrench and enhance the effectiveness of international legal rules. In the final analysis, the real question is not whether rules of interpretation yield fruit in a quixotic quest for legal certainty. Instead, equally relevant remain the rich milieu of sources and materials surrounding the legal text itself: methods and forms of interpretation (for example, the limits of grammatical interpretation when faced with the inevitable indeterminacy of language), the actors who are involved in the act of interpretation and the authority they claim to wield, and the sources of law which fall to be interpreted. And as Kennedy reminds us, if the analysis that drives us through this enquiry is complete, this panoply of sources will – and should – yield conflicting signals.[167] Such ambiguity is not meant to be a failure of interpretation, but a reflection of ambiguities within the legal system itself. As such, in a sense, any study of the rules of interpretation, which indeed is but a secondary topic in the light of the role of interpretation as a hermeneutic tool, necessarily extends further than the rules

[163] In the domestic context, Kennedy, n. 147 at 252, suggests that this removal from the political scene has been 'achieved through a continued repetition of the difference between truth and power, each time subtly privileging one over the other.'

[164] A term borrowed from Jean d'Aspremont, 'Reductionist Legal Positivism in International Law' *106 Proceedings of the American Society of International Law* (2012) 368–370 at 368.

[165] China Miéville, *Between Equal Rights: A Marxist Theory of International Law* (Brill 2005) 43 has made this point.

[166] Koskenniemi, n. 27 at 591; Jason Beckett, 'Rebel without a Cause: Martti Koskenniemi and the Critical Legal Project' 7 *German Law Journal* (2006) 1045–1088 at 1046, *passim*.

[167] Kennedy, n. 147 at 271.

themselves, and must also study the *practice* of relevant law-applying actors as an equally important locus for the construction of meaning. For it is the claim of law-applying actors to 'semantic authority', or the 'capacity to influence and shape meanings . . . as authoritative reference points in legal discourse',[168] that is equally important. The focus on interpretative authority opens a discussion on legal normativity, going beyond obligation and very much into the practice of international actors. Any such study might even address the conceptual disagreement as to the *form* of international law itself, a much wider project for all international lawyers.

The possibility remains that a fetishisation of the interpretative process gives the international lawyer a false sense of safety, reassuring him or her of the objectivity of the rules of interpretation. By burying interpretation theory in technical or theoretical rationalisations, the curious divorce between what interpretation 'is' and what interpretation 'means' suggests two conclusions: by seeking refuge in the *form* of interpretation, the lawyer can evade responsibility for the outcome of an interpretative process. Yet more than that, by reducing the study of interpretation and interpretation theory to exclude all that one does not wish to consider simply by dismissing it as being 'improperly legal', one loses sight of how interpretation permeates all of legal life.[169]

[168] Venzke, n. 19 at 63.

[169] Although Kammerhofer, n. 65 at 122–123, accepts the transcendental aspect of the question.

13

Teaching general public international law

FLORIAN HOFFMANN

1 Introduction

Teaching 'public international law' (PIL) is a tricky if fulfilling business. It tends to be slated either at the very beginning of a typical law curriculum when students have little idea yet of how law as such 'works', or at its very end, when the majority of students who do not wish to become international lawyers see little point in studying what to them appears a marginal and softish subject. In either case, the job is not made easier by having to introduce a type of normativity that is both archaic and ephemerous by the canonical standards of 'the Law'. Inevitably, questions about the legality and relevance of the body of rules referred to as international law feature prominently in introductory discussions, accompanied, sometimes, by discrete musings on the part of students about what international lawyers 'really' do in life and for a living. Yet, the comparatively high entry threshold that characterises PIL teaching is also what, arguably, makes it so rewarding and fascinating a subject to teach. For it is (only) because of lingering questions such as 'is international law really law?' that the PIL teacher is forced to continuously retell its story, to argue its point, to justify its existence.[1] There is, of course, a considerable amount of literature on international law teaching and an even greater one on the historical roots of modern, or, to go by this volume's editors' preference, post-modern international law as a distinct discipline and field of study.[2] It would probably take a multi-volume treatise to review this literature and provide a systematic account of the specific predicament faced by teachers of international law. However, the task set by the editors was

[1] For an excellent summing up of the predicament of teaching PIL, see Gerry Simpson, 'On the Magic Mountain: Teaching International Law' 10 *EJIL* (1999) 70–92.

[2] An overview of the considerable specialist literature on international law teaching has usefully been compiled by the Thomas Jefferson School of Law, available at www.tjsl.edu/slomansonb/6th_Teach_Bib.pdf.

'only' to engage with the legacy of legal positivism in the international law classroom, not with legal positivism in and of itself, or with teaching law in and of itself. Yet, as those engaged in international legal theory well know, it is, in this multi-faceted field, nearly impossible to do such a thing without also looking at the broader picture, at the defining debates and streams in contemporary international legal discourse. However, as that, too, would require a multi-volume dissertation, the thoughts presented below are, by necessity, somewhat mosaic and epigrammatic, perhaps occasionally even a bit short-circuited. This is meant to serve the purpose of cutting through, within limited space, to what are here taken to be some of the central points of the debate about the positivist legacy and the specific challenges of teaching it, though at the cost of nuance and comprehensiveness.

The story of international law is, of course, the story of a paradox, namely of what Martti Koskenniemi has notoriously described as the dichotomy between apology and utopia, that is, between a reality shaped by power and an ideal represented by legal norms.[3] Hence, as a language game conceived to give voice to the paradigm of the 'modern state system' –territorially based nation-states defined by sovereignty – international law has always at once had to represent and to constitute the world of states and their dealings with each other. As such, it has been seen both as a function of the powers that constitute – sovereign will,[4] cosmopolitan values,[5] colonialism,[6] capitalism,[7] etc. – and as governing these powers from the vantage point of an independent and, from its own perspective, politically progressive purpose. This paradoxical 'structural coupling' makes international law a methodologically unique field of jurisprudence. It articulates a horizontal, rather than vertical, normativity in which there is neither a clear-cut international *pouvoir constituant*

[3] Martti Koskenniemi, *From Apology to Utopia: The Structure of International Legal Argument* (Finnish Lawyers' Publishing Co. 1989, reissued Cambridge University Press 2005).

[4] See exemplarily Ian Brownlie, *Principles of Public International Law* (7th edn Cambridge University Press 2008).

[5] For instance, Mortimer Sellers, 'Parochialism, Cosmopolitanism, and Justice' in Mortimer Sellers (ed.), *Parochialism, Cosmopolitanism, and the Foundations of International Law* (Cambridge University Press 2011) 250–276.

[6] Anthony Angie, *Imperialism, Sovereignty and the Making of International Law* (Cambridge University Press 2007).

[7] See, generally, Susan Marks, *International Law on the Left: Re-Examining Marxist Legacies* (Cambridge University Press 2008); and, in particular, China Miéville, *Between Equal Rights: A Marxist Theory of International Law* (Brill 2005).

nor a universal sovereign.[8] Its traditional sources bind it to the facticity of inter-state relations, yet it is also meant to constrain and regulate these relations. Unlike domestic law, its practice is not merely about applying norms to facts, but also always about (re-)establishing the particular normativity that is to apply. As a discipline, international law is, therefore, inherently argumentative, and its practice is deeply theoretical, yet, it has struggled with a self-reflexive and self-conscious engagement with its own methodological identity.

In part, this difficulty stems from the underlying theoretical assumptions that inform international law's practice, including its teaching, which, arguably, tend to be informed by a sort of *positivisme diminué*. Rather than being appreciated as a substantive (theoretical) position on the autonomy of (international) legal norms, positivism is held to be a didactic programme through which international law is made to emulate the structure of the positivised law of the constitutional state.[9] Its horizontal fluidity is replaced by a simulacrum of verticality through the canonisation of its sources and subjects, so that its student encounters a law much like all other (state) laws with which she has become acquainted. This programme, manifest in the textbook tradition, engenders, in turn, the expectation on the part of students that international law be taught as if it was just like any other legal subject.[10] The challenge faced by teachers of international law, then, is to reach through the pseudo-positivist textbook tradition and to reconstruct positivism as a distinct perspective. To that end, the specific challenges of teaching international law need to be considered, as well as the strategies available to deal with them. This, in turn, will throw light on how and why such pseudo-positivism emerges in the classroom, and it will allow the reconstruction of positivism proper as both a methodological stance and as a historically influential legal theory. It will also enable a reassessment of the role of positivism in contemporary international law and its teaching.

8 For an approximation, see Philipp Dann and Zaid Al-Ali, 'The Institutionalized *Pouvoir Constituant* – Constitution-Making under External Influence in Iraq, Sudan and East Timor' 10 *Max Planck Yearbook of United Nations Law* (2006) 423–463.

9 Armin von Bogdandy, 'Constitutionalism in International Law: Comment on a Proposal from Germany' 47 *Harvard International Law Journal* (2006) 223–242.

10 David Sugarman, 'Legal Theory, the Common Law Mind and the Making of the Textbook Tradition' in William Twining (ed.), *Legal Theory and Common Law* (Blackwell 1986) 26–62; Anthony Carty, 'A Colloquium on International Law Textbooks in England, France and Germany: Introduction' 11 *EJIL* (2000) 615–619.

2 Doctrine v. practice v. theory: the predicament of teaching public international law

It is a well-known experience shared by teachers across diverse legal systems that to many law (school) students, international law is at first a confusing subject.[11] They tend to be taught 'the law' through a set of strictly prescribed methods by which to identify and apply clearly delimited rules to facts. What is worse, these methods vary across national legal systems and are largely incommensurable, thus locking their practitioners into the professional horizon of a particular country or region. Hence, from the vantage point of the domestic lawyer, and law student, international law represents not just a different subject matter, but an entirely different episteme. As a consequence, students tend to initially either reject it in broadly Austinian terms as not really law, but a positive international morality;[12] or they confuse it with diplomatic history or 'international affairs' generally. Not that students would a priori lack interest in such issues as recognition, jurisdiction, responsibility or, indeed, territorial title or even maritime zoning, but few would initially approach these as purely legal, rather than primarily political or moral issues. The legality of international law remains, thus, not only the defining theme of the discipline's self-reflection, but also the core challenge to teaching it. This begins with international law's horizontality, that is, the absence of a clearly identifiable international source of legal authority beyond the hypostatised collective will of states. Whereas this poses no great problem for either 'pure' practitioners, who tend not to waste their time with conceptual intricacies, nor for professional scholars, who have learned to countenance the indeterminacy of international law's foundations, it does represent a major entry barrier to law students who are being trained to decipher legal rules by identifying their precise place within a preordained and largely static hierarchy.

The idea that the legal authority of a norm has to be ascertained in each case from among several sources of equal status before it can be applied to any factual situation at first appears strange to many students.[13] The

[11] 'Teaching of International Law', Material from an ASIL Teaching Initiative and ILA Committee on Teaching International Law Joint Workshop held in Washington, DC, on 3 April 2004; available at www.ila-hq.org.

[12] John Austin, *Lectures on Jurisprudence or the Philosophy of Positive Law*, Vol. 1 (Robert Campbell (ed.), 5th edn John Murray 1885) 61.

[13] For an excellent discussion of this, see the first part of Jean d'Aspremont, *Formalism and the Sources of International Law: A Theory of the Ascertainment of Legal Rules* (Oxford

sources themselves then add to this sense of strangeness, with their centrepiece, custom, meant to be ascertained through the counter-intuitive linking of what states seem to be doing and what they 'think' they are doing.[14] Add to this an indeterminate set of general principles the main distinguishing mark of which – from many a student's perspective – is that they are spelled out in Latin, as well as the (apparent) possibility to simply bypass all of these sources altogether by resorting to an equitable, i.e. judge-made, solution, and students are likely to give up on trying to comprehend international law as a coherent normative system. As if this was not enough, the lack of a comprehensive scheme to enforce these norms is taken in many classrooms to further undermine their legal character. Without a credible story about the power behind the norms, international law may easily appear as mere 'lawyer's law', made to sustain the profession's utopia in the face of impotence vis-à-vis almighty sovereigns. Related to this, at least in students' minds, is the question of the separability of legality from legitimacy.[15] While this is one of the core features of legal positivism, it is by no means self-evident to the student. From her vantage point, submission to international rules can initially only be made plausible if these rules are shown to either advance a however defined collective interest or if they serve some higher moral purpose;[16] conversely, international law is deemed illegitimate if it is seen as preventing the pursuit of either.[17] This attitude expresses, of course, an often inadvertent scepticism about the autonomy of norms in inter-state relations, which contrasts with the equally inadvertent acceptance of the facticity of that autonomy in domestic law. Here, too, international law is held to be fundamentally different from domestic law. The predicament

University Press 2011); see also David Kennedy, 'The Sources of International Law' 2 *American University Journal of International Law and Policy* (1987) 1–96.

14 Koskenniemi, n. 3 at 389–396.

15 Originally so formulated by HLA Hart, *The Concept of Law* (3rd edn Oxford University Press 2012) 185–212 and, arguably, reinforced in his article: HLA Hart, 'Positivism and the Separation of Law and Morals' 71 *Harvard Law Review* (1957–1958) 593–629; also John Gardner, 'Legal Positivism: 5½ Myths' 46 *American Journal of Jurisprudence* (2001) 199–227.

16 A good way to exemplify this sentiment is the current discussion on the 'responsibility to protect'; see, inter alia, Jutta Brunnée, 'International Law and Collective Concerns: Reflections on the Responsibility to Protect' in Tafsir Malick Ndiaye, Rüdiger Wolfrum (eds), *Law of the Sea, Environmental Law and Settlement of Disputes: Liber Amicorum Judge Thomas A. Mensah* (Brill 2007) 35–52; Anne Orford, *International Authority and the Responsibility to Protect* (Cambridge University Press 2011).

17 For a contemporary articulation of this critique, see Jack Goldsmith, Eric Posner, *The Limits of International Law* (Oxford University Press 2006).

in which many teachers of international law, therefore, see themselves is one in which they continuously run up against a wall of doubt, not least about the place of international law in the general law curriculum, its professional aura, and its relevance to the political issues it means to address.

There are, in essence, three strategies available to teachers of international law to approach the subject and scale this wall of doubt. Positivism as a term of art and a mindset plays a key role in each of these, although, as shall be seen later on, these roles differ starkly in terms of the meaning they attribute to positivism. They can, in shorthand, be named, respectively, as 'doctrine', 'practice' and 'theory'. The first emanates from the medieval and Renaissance natural law tradition and refers to interpretation and systematisation of the law.[18] It has always been the legal scholar's, and, therefore, by implication, also the teacher's 'natural' approach as it presents students with a rationalised and coherent system of rules that, as such, is the construct of reflection rather than operation. Yet, unlike what is here labelled as the – distinct – theory-oriented approach, doctrine does not purport to provide understanding of the law from some external vantage point, but it merely seeks to explain it from within. It does so by attempting to unite an otherwise disparate set of norms, principles, administrative acts, court cases and procedural habits into a logically structured system. In this it follows the scholastic form out of which the legal doctrinal approach grew, notably by organising the 'real' world of legal concepts hierarchically, making each identifiable through its particular place on a vertical scale. Insofar as the doctrinal approach grew out of the medieval reception of Roman law, this ordering was largely representational and not practical, its primary purpose was knowledge and not the settlement of disputes.[19] Doctrine is, thus, quintessentially academic law geared to be taught in the privileged forum of the university through prescribed methods. There was, hence, initially, a professional gap between the doctrinalist and the practitioner, which went along with different conceptions of the law and of legal education. This lies, of course, at the root of the differentiation at least of Euro-American legal systems and the agglomeration of national legal systems alongside the

[18] Anthony Carty, 'Convergences and Divergences in European International Law Traditions' 11 *EJIL* (2000) 713–732; Anthony Carty, *Philosophy of International Law* (Edinburgh University Press 2007) 1–25 (ch. 1).

[19] Raoul Charles van Caenegem, *Judges, Legislators and Professors: Chapters in European Legal History* (Cambridge University Press 1992).

fundamental divide between the civil and the common law tradition.[20] Hence, today, doctrine in this wider sense forms a core aspect of legal education across the systemic divide. It has also transcended the categorisation as being a purely scholarly exercise and has, instead, acquired one of being a foundation for practice. Colloquially, the term is now used to denote the systematisation of the rule clusters that form the distinct sub-areas of the law. It thus comprises, from a common law perspective, the authoritative interpretation of case law as much as principles and secondary rules.[21]

The second strategy used to approach the predicament of international law teaching is to focus on practice. Certainly, contemporary international law doctrine is also deeply infused with practice, but what is often referred to as the practitioners' approach seeks deliberately to dispense with the sort of internal rationalisation characteristic of doctrine.[22] Here, the starting point – and for traditional practitioners, natural boundary – is state practice, taken to be the constitutive element of international law. Rather than to deduct, as in the doctrinal approach, such practice from the interplay between the different components of an international legal system, however defined, the practitioner's approach simply reconstructs international law inductively, as the sum of individual instances of norm-application. However, the objective here is not to represent international law as a system, but to explain how it works in 'reality'. The practice-oriented approach does not, therefore, generally engage in the questions that lie at the heart of doctrine, such as the nature of legal obligations, but presumes the existence of valid international norms on the basis of the apparent facticity of normativity as a basis for inter-state relations. However, unlike the doctrinal approach, the practitioner's perspective is fundamentally elastic with regard to observed and observable (state) practice and is, as such, empiricist, as opposed to idealist, in its epistemology. Teaching-wise, the practice approach implies a strong emphasis on jurisprudence which makes international law appear, in students' eyes, like a web of cases connected by a set of overarching principles. Here, knowing the law means knowing how the law works rather

20 Thomas Lundmark, *Charting the Divide between Common and Civil Law* (Oxford University Press 2012).

21 See, for instance, the presentation in a typical textbook such as Malcolm Shaw, *International Law* (6th edn Cambridge University Press 2008).

22 The quintessential example of this is, of course, Brownlie, n. 4; for a critical discussion of Brownlie's approach, see Colin Warbrick, 'Brownlie's Principles of Public International Law: An Assessment' 11 *EJIL* (2000) 621–636.

than what it means. As such, the practitioner's approach is also inherently pragmatic, based on (legal) fact and geared towards (successful) action.

Third, there is the strategy of theorising (about) international law. As a field of practice, international law is, of course, inherently argumentative and, therefore, deeply, if often inadvertently, theoretical. During the foundation period of the discipline up to the nineteenth century, this was unproblematic, as international lawyers tended to be general scholars in the humanist tradition who combined a wide array of vocabularies and methods to deduce the law of nations and offer it to the prince's ear.[23] Theory was then seen to be at the heart of practice. It was only from the latter part of the nineteenth century that a gap began to open up between the attempt to understand the normative quality of international relations and the practice of applying an increasingly canonical body of well-established 'objective' rules to the conduct of states and other international actors. Initially (and arguably), that gap was still seen as a development rather than a divide, for the practice of positivised international law was closely associated with theoretically inspired concerns with world peace and social justice.[24] Yet, especially as of the inter-war and then post-war periods, and helped by the seeming breakdown of the theoretical constructs on which the older law of nations had been built, the 'practitioner's approach' came to dominate the discipline.[25] This meant a shift away from scholarly argument to judge-made law, with the emphasis on formal legal process reducing the reflective space for theorising. As a result, theory has tended to be confused with doctrinal analysis reduced to the systematisation of a canonical body of rules, with (theoretical) questions about their historical pedigree or their political connotation being considered outside the remit of the international lawyer. Theorisation in order to understand rather than to merely explain international law has, thus, been pushed to the fringe of the discipline or beyond it. This has, as will be discussed below, led to an outcasting of explicit theorising from the canon and, consequently, to a severing of its ties with doctrine and practice. This, as will be seen, makes employing it as an alternative teaching strategy difficult.

[23] Martti Koskenniemi, 'Miserable Comforters: International Relations as New Natural Law' 15 *European Journal of International Relations* (2009) 395–422.

[24] Martti Koskenniemi, *The Gentle Civilizer of Nations: The Rise and Fall of International Law 1870–1960* (Cambridge University Press 2002).

[25] Carty, *Philosophy*, n. 18 at 9.

3 Emperor without clothes? Positivism in the classroom

Where, in these strategic (teaching) choices, is legal positivism? Indeed, what is legal positivism (in the classroom)? The answer to both questions is complicated by both terminology and tradition. In terms of the former, legal positivism is initially just a particular way of understanding law. Its central concern is the autonomy of law as a discrete field of threat-backed or acculturated ought propositions.[26] From within these premises, there is no wall of doubt, and no need to engage in pragmatic argument to scale it, but simply the objective fact of a(n international) law. It is an objectivity posited upon an empirical reality, not upon an ideal moral universe, as in the earlier natural law tradition. However, following legal positivism's script, the empirical reality on which international law's objectivity is premised is not itself taken to belong to the realm of law and the teaching thereof. Instead, law's reality is represented, notably through such concepts as state consent,[27] international legal process[28] or *pacta sunt servanda*,[29] that is, through common substantiations of a basic norm, a Rule of Recognition, or a 'first constitution'.[30] Being an offspring of the neo-Kantian attempt to salvage philosophy in an age of scientific positivism, it is fundamentally about defining a specifically legal category of cognition, and differentiating it against other categories.[31] Its central purpose is to bestow upon law an unmistakable identity that is autonomous of an empirical (social) reality that could only be described in extra-legal terms. Legal positivism aims both to explain that autonomy,

[26] Definitions of legal positivism abound, but among the most comprehensive and yet concise is Jörg Kammerhofer, 'Positivism' in Anthony Carty (ed.), *Oxford Bibliographies Online: International Law* (Oxford University Press 2012), available at www.oxfordbibliographies.com.

[27] See Brownlie's notorious statement that there is the 'principle that the general consent of States creates rules of general application' (Brownlie, n. 4 at 3).

[28] The classic here is Abram Chayes, Thomas Ehrlich, Andreas Lowenfeld, *International Legal Process: Materials for an Introductory Course* (Little Brown 1973).

[29] Hans Kelsen, *Das Problem der Souveränität und die Theorie des Völkerrechts: Beitrag zu einer reinen Rechtslehre* (J. C. B. Mohr 1920); later modified, by Kelsen, to mean 'states ought to behave as they have customarily behaved'. Hans Kelsen, *Principles of International Law* (Rinehart & Co. 1952).

[30] See, respectively, Hans Kelsen, *The Pure Theory of Law* (Max Knight (tr.), University of California Press 1967) and Hart, *Concept*, n. 15; also the discussion by Kammerhofer, Chapter 4 at 94–105.

[31] Stefan Hammer, 'A Neo-Kantian Theory of Legal Knowledge in Kelsen's Pure Theory of Law' in Stanley L. Paulson, Bonnie Litschewski Paulson (eds), *Normativity and Norms: Critical Perspectives on Kelsenian Themes* (Oxford University Press 1998) 177–194.

and to outline the conditions for understanding law as law.[32] As such, it is, arguably, both a theory of law – i.e. a legal theory – and part of a more general theory of knowledge – i.e. an epistemology. Yet, this dual character of legal positivism betrays its complicated pedigree in the history of ideas and reveals why it has become at once an imperial and absent force – not least in the classroom.

As part of a wider intellectual movement, legal positivism is deeply entangled with the rise of both empiricism and rationalism. Some trace its earliest antecedents – beyond ubiquitous if diffuse Greek roots – to Thomas Aquinas, Marsilius of Padua and William of Ockham,[33] although by most encyclopaedic counts, its direct philosophical undercurrents are Hobbes and Hume, while its trajectory as a distinct theory of law is generally begun with Jeremy Bentham, followed, in rather large historical steps, by John Austin, Hans Kelsen and HLA Hart, with, perhaps, Joseph Raz commonly cited as the most prominent contemporary theorist of legal positivism.[34] Yet, while especially Austin, Kelsen and Hart have acquired the label of quintessential legal positivists, their commonality is really a retrospective reconstruction of the characteristics taken to define legal positivism. Behind the label lurks a complex historical entanglement of positions on general epistemology, the philosophy of science and legal philosophy. Kant and Hegel enter the story through a (continental) backdoor, as does the scientific positivism of the second half of the nineteenth century. Specifically in legal thought, a continental and an Anglo-Saxon brand of positivism emerge. The former is connected to the evolution of the German school of historical jurisprudence into both the *Begriffsjurisprudenz* ('conceptual jurisprudence') of the late nineteenth century and the *Interessenjurisprudenz* ('jurisprudence of interests') of the early twentieth century, and culminating in their (neo-Kantian) transcendence by Kelsen.[35] The latter, in the form of the tradition of analytical

[32] This refers, of course, to the so-called *Methodenstreit* (quarrel over methods) that emerged when, in the early twentieth century, the social sciences began to emerge as a distinct discipline, claiming interpretive 'understanding' as the methodological base of its science, as opposed to the causality-oriented 'explanation' method of the natural sciences. See, inter alia, Toby E. Huff, *Max Weber and the Methodology of the Social Sciences* (Transaction Publishers 1984).

[33] Gerald Postema, 'Legal Positivism: Early Foundations', UNC Legal Studies Research Paper No. 1975470, available at http://ssrn.com/abstract=1975470.

[34] Joseph Raz, *The Authority of Law: Essays on Law and Morality* (2nd edn Oxford University Press 2009).

[35] Arthur Kaufmann, Winfried Hassemer, Ulfried Neumann, *Einführung in die Rechtsphilosophie und Rechtstheorie der Gegenwart* (7th edn C. F. Müller 2004); see also Gabriel

jurisprudence, led by its twentieth-century *doyen*, HLA Hart, eventually reconnected the two lines in his explicit critique of Kelsen.[36] In terms of intellectual history, the Anglo-Saxon line is, unsurprisingly, the more purely empiricist and utilitarian, or, by today's nomenclature, functionalist, one, whereas the continental trajectory intermixes empiricist motives such as historicism and scientific positivism with rationalist ones coming, in part, from the neo-Kantian programme of salvaging a distinct space for rational reflection within the positivist paradigm.[37]

Both lines converge in their historical practice with their emphasis on the *lex lata* and the strong espousal of the legality derived thereof, that is, of rule by law rather than merely with law.[38] Hence, objectivism is not merely legal positivism's epistemological position with regard to legal cognition, but it may also be seen as implying a stance as to the precedence of law over other fields or functional logics, most notably over politics. Although the latter position does not derive from the premises of legal positivism itself, it has come to be seen as its hallmark: legal positivists are generally seen to believe in and actively defend the rule of law over other paradigms of governance, a legacy for which not least Kelsen, for all his 'purity' but to his honour, is co-responsible.[39] This, then, is part of the reason why legal positivism has, arguably, become a dominant influence in the international law classroom, while being almost entirely absent from it. It is commonly seen as the default position for a formalist approach to law and legal teaching, that is, one which focuses on law as an objective reality, a particular language game, the grammar and syntax of which must be learned more than understood, a particular professional idiom,

Nogueira Dias, *Rechtspositivismus und Rechtstheorie: Das Verhältnis Beider im Werke Hans Kelsens* (Mohr Siebeck 2005) 74–88.

36 Gerald Postema, *Legal Philosophy in the Twentieth Century: The Common Law World* (Springer 2011).

37 Jörg Kammerhofer, *Uncertainty in International Law: A Kelsenian Perspective* (Routledge 2011) 250–251.

38 Jörg Kammerhofer, Jean d'Aspremont, 'Introduction: Mapping 21st Century International Legal Positivism' (unpublished paper, 2010). [Editors' note: the author refers to the first version of the introductory chapter; in order to preserve the references, that version has been made available at http://ssrn.com/abstract=2372778.]

39 This alludes, of course, to the notorious opposition between Hans Kelsen and Carl Schmitt during the so-called *Weimarer Staatsrechtslehrerstreit*, the dispute over the Weimar constitution, in which Kelsen fronted positivism, understood as the articulation of the rule of (positive) law, against Schmitt's decisionism; see David Dyzenhaus, *Legality and Legitimacy: Carl Schmitt, Hans Kelsen and Hermann Heller in Weimar* (Clarendon Press 1999); however, some would argue that, during that debate, Kelsen was arguing from the methodologically distinct perspective of politics rather than law.

fluency of which is the distinguishing mark of the lawyer as opposed to the non-lawyer.[40] And the former is what, arguably, a large majority of law students, including international law students, wish to become. For this group, legal positivism is not so much a theory as a label attached to the formalist style in which law tends to be taught and which is associated with the typical self-differentiating slogans of the professional lawyer, notably that she or he does 'hard law' as opposed to 'soft theory' or 'dirty politics', that she or he is an operator of a ruling discourse, and, as such, a wielder of real power, and that the discourse can be operated without any knowledge of its grounding (or not) in morality or political legitimacy. From this perspective, all 'real' lawyers are legal positivists.

What exacerbates this phenomenon further is, of course, the reality of teaching (international) law. In that reality, the three teaching strategies discussed above are not co-equal alternatives in the international law classroom, for embeddedness in a particular legal tradition is still the primary determinant for the way in which teachers think about their subject. Although today's global knowledge exchange makes it increasingly possible to reach intellectual horizons beyond the methodological traditions of one's respective locality, language and (legal) culture, it is the deeply vested expectations of colleagues and students within a specific curricular tradition as much as the teacher's own cognitive horizon that limit the actual choice of teaching method.[41] From this vantage point, it is, of course, only the doctrinal and the practice-oriented approach that are seen to be rooted in a legal tradition, whereas explicit theorising has, as already hinted, always been seen, by lawyers and law students, as an artificial and contrived way of approaching law, one coming from and fundamentally remaining outside of what, to them, law is all about. Theory does not, therefore, tend to be part of the introductory international law curriculum, and, this being so, legal positivism, too, is by and large not dealt with as what it is, namely a legal theory. Yet, for all this deliberate omission of theory in the classroom, traces of legal positivism are all about it, not through explicit reference to the autonomy of law or legal cognition, but in the way in which law is represented as a coherent and canonical system of rules derived from a fixed set of sources and manifest

[40] See the *German Law Journal* Special Issue on Martti Koskenniemi's *From Apology to Utopia*: Alexandra Kemmerer, Morag Goodwin (eds), 'From Apology to Utopia: A Symposium' 7 *German Law Journal* (2006) 977–1108), especially Florian Hoffmann, 'An Epilogue on an Epilogue' 7 *German Law Journal* (2006) 1095–1102.

[41] Carty, n. 10.

(mostly) in the jurisprudence of authoritative judicial bodies. It is these traces of positivism that provide the cognitive framework for the textbook synthesis of international law encountered by students in the classroom.

This textbook framework is meant to provide a simulacrum of objectivity by alluding to, while not openly articulating, a pseudo-positivism that runs like a red line through both the doctrinal and the practice-oriented approach. Despite all their difference, both of these strategies are deeply entangled with each other, forming, as it were, the methodological amalgam known as the 'mainstream approach'.[42] Hence, with few exceptions, the case-based framework of the common law-inspired Anglo-American style, once converted into the textbook, does not resist the temptation of systematisation, hinting, thereby, at a meta-theoretical standpoint on international law as a body of rules unified by a set of structural elements.[43] Conversely, the doctrinal constructs of the continental approach are inherently challenged by both the fluidity and the fragmentation of international case law.[44] Thus, in the 'mainstream' teaching style, the continental system is effectively coupled with the Anglo-American case-orientated approach to produce a narrative apt to breach the wall of doubt. The representation of this narrative may still moderately differ across traditional divides, from a relatively loose system of overarching principles and a canonical delimitation of the elements of general international law to a fully blown scholastic hierarchy, but both versions share an essential commitment to the discrete identity and objectivity of international law.[45] This 'mainstream position' of doctrinalised practice is the manifestation of a pseudo-positivism which lingers as the hidden elephant in the (class)room. It provides the hoped-for outcome of

[42] The term 'mainstream' is, of course, the coinage of scholars generally critical of it, 'mainstreamers' themselves hardly use the term for self-description; although, in these critical circles it is used with frequency, its precise pedigree is difficult to ascertain and it should probably be seen more as a somewhat diffuse 'fighting term' than as a precise term of art. It is here used to denote the pseudo-positivist self-understanding of that majority of international lawyers who tend not to be theoretically self-reflective. For illustrations of use of the term, see, inter alia, Benedict Kingsbury, 'Positivism as Normative Politics: International Society, Balance of Power and Lassa Oppenheim's Positive International Law' 13 *EJIL* (2002) 401–436 or James Gathii, 'International Law and Eurocentricity' 9 *EJIL* (1998) 184–211.

[43] If one looks at international law textbooks used in the United Kingdom, Brownlie, n. 4, is clearly the most resistant to this; Shaw, n. 21 is already much more systematising, with, for instance, the structure of Malcolm D. Evans (ed.), *International Law* (3rd edn Oxford University Press 2010) being outright doctrinal.

[44] Carty, n. 10; Carty, 'Convergences', n. 18; Carty, *Philosophy*, n. 18.

[45] See, again, Koskenniemi, n. 3 at 16–17.

mainstream legal teaching, notably the gradual substitution, in students' minds, of the question of why there is international law for the question of how it works. Their mind is then rendered amenable to being trained, rather than reconstructed, which is the typical teaching style of domestic law in both the civil and the common law traditions. Yet, this only works if, indeed, the positivist elephant remains hidden, that is, if it is not revealed as just a legal theory among other legal theories, or, put more broadly, as a theory-based perspective of reality, but if, instead, it shows international law as both the discipline and normative field dealing with the facticity and the validity of law in international affairs.

However, hiding the discipline's positivist premises serves not only to mainstream it into the (domestic) law curriculum, but also allows for it to be 'enriched' with desired substances well beyond the ambit of legal positivism. Indeed, invisibly, the elephant is transformed into a conceptual chimera that incorporates both naturalist and realist elements under the veil of its pseudo-positivist appearance.[46] Any of the resulting paradoxes cannot be queried for as long as pseudo-positivism provides an invisible authority for the mainstream programme. That authority rests on canonisation which, in turn, rests on the cumulative *opinio iuris* of the epistemic community of international lawyers, as articulated in relevant international legal institutions – tribunals, the ILC, the IDI, etc. – and systematised and archived in international law textbooks. This way, the wall of doubt is countered by a wall of certainty upheld through the mechanism of professional self-identification; an international lawyer 'proper' is one who operates within that wall and who will not seriously question or challenge the canon. After all, being canonical is seen by most adherents of this mainstream not as something either methodologically problematic or politically one-sided. Indeed, as Koskenniemi has argued with his 'culture of formalism', mainstream international law is a language game amenable to being used for many ends, including those defined – by extra-legal criteria – as politically progressive.[47] And no matter where (mainstream) international lawyers would position themselves on the political spectrum, the vast majority would, arguably, claim that certain values are inherent in law, in general, and in international law, in

[46] Kammerhofer, Chapter 4. See also the insightful piece, William George, 'Grotius, Theology, and International Law: Overcoming Textbook Bias' 14 *Journal of Law and Religion* (1999–2000) 605–631.

[47] Koskenniemi, n. 24. For a critical-constructive treatment, see d'Aspremont, n. 13.

particular, such as justice, non-violence and equality.[48] From this perspective, the legalisation of international politics has in and of itself a positive connotation, and all those involved in this project are ultimately 'doing good'. This, then, is a major selling point for mainstream international law in classrooms increasingly occupied by students immersed in media-fed images of heroic lawyers and activist lawyering. Once doubt has been substituted by (pseudo-positivist) certainty, international law turns out to be, to many a student, an elegant way to 'improve the world' through professional commitment. Here, international law as a whole is seen as an inherently reasonable discourse that aims to introduce just and equitable standards into a political realm seen to be marked by dishonesty, hypocrisy, intrigue and always the potential for violence.[49] To its adherents, mainstream international law is, therefore, much more than just the pseudo-positivist textbook approach: it is a programme and a mission.[50]

The values that make it so and that transform the positivist elephant into a pseudo-positivist chimera come, of course, from elsewhere, namely from positivism's nemeses: naturalism and realism. And they, arguably, creep in on account of a deep-seated resistance to one of positivism's central tenets, notably its relativism. As was seen, legal positivism is fundamentally about giving law its conceptual due; it asks what law is and how it works, not why it is, what it is, nor what it does beyond itself. Certainly, if the law happens to enshrine values judged to be right in a particular situation – such as fundamental rights vis-à-vis fascist encroachments – then defending legality is itself a value-based action.[51] However, from the positivist perspective, there are no criteria within the law to make this judgment, nor is law capable of incorporating the relevant values on its own behest. Under positivist premises, law must be conceived as value free, and, thus, in strictly relativist terms; an autonomous conceptual identity comes with this self-limitation.[52] An odd corollary of this is, of course, that

[48] Koskenniemi, n. 3; Hoffmann, n. 40.

[49] The value-basis of this view may be particularly pronounced in the British tradition of (formalist) international law teaching which informs the present author's own teaching (and learning) experience; however, it is, arguably, also implicit in many strands of the continental tradition with their priorisation of rule-conformity and lawfulness.

[50] Well exposed in Kingsbury, n. 42; highly critical of this are, of course, Goldsmith and Posner, n. 17.

[51] Peter Caldwell, *Popular Sovereignty and the Crisis of German Constitutional Law: The Theory and Practice of Weimar Constitutionalism* (Duke University Press 1997).

[52] Raz, n. 34.

explicit legal positivism has less difficulty with recognising the distinct role and importance of moral and political discourse than mainstream pseudo-positivism. The latter incorporates both behind the veil of formalism, while nominally denouncing them as 'a-legal'.[53] The underlying reason for this duplicity is, arguably, that hard-edged relativism is fundamentally unattractive to most adherents of the mainstream perspective, running counter to their professional self-perception. Most (mainstream) international lawyers, arguably, wish to 'do good' and have a more or less progressive agenda – be it to uphold world peace by seconding the state system or to fight for human dignity through international human rights. They are decidedly not indifferent, relativist or even nihilist in their outlook, but they wish not to appear to hold any of these positions themselves, or to be associated with personal politics or bias. Instead, the politics of international lawyering is represented as being inherent to the law, a law which is 'merely' applied by the legal practitioner. Political responsibility is not attributed to her, but rather to 'the law'. The international lawyer's politics is, thus, concealed beneath a veil of (political) ignorance and not amenable to be openly debated. Instead, for the mainstream, the law itself does the job, simply on account of being law and, as such, of expressing not personal politics but 'objective' values.

Hans Kelsen discerned this well when he deconstructed the continental jurisprudential schools of the late nineteenth century, not least the long-dominant conceptual jurisprudence (*Begriffsjurisprudenz*) and its naturalist presumption of the coherence of and causality within a legal system conceived as deriving from historically grown fundamental principles.[54] The formalism he set out against was one in which the categories of validity and effectiveness were still merged and where the historical nation-state and the normative concept of statehood were still thought together and as manifestations of a super-historical meaning. Neo-Kantianism, through which Kelsen laboured, sought to simultaneously philosophise the positivist spirit of the times and to counter its inherent materialism by purporting to purge all Hegelian and post-Hegelian remnants from conceptual thought and by concentrating, instead, on the category of validity. By insisting on an autonomous realm of 'ought-'relations, legal positivism brought the naturalist presumptions of earlier formalisms out into the

[53] An anecdotal account of this is given in an ASIL President's Column: José Alvarez, 'International Law 101: A Post-Mortem', ILpost, American Society of International Law, 12 February 2007.

[54] Dias, n. 35 at 105–111.

open. Yet, in doing so, it ironically ended up providing a format through which pseudo-positivism could survive the loss of Hegelian substance. For such a 'pure', apparently value-neutral, normative objectivism was more attuned to the sensitivities of the post-war twentieth-century world than the bombastic state-centrism of the nineteenth, provided it still fundamentally expressed much of the same values underneath. Kelsen's name would, contrary to his intentions, eventually become one of the authorities used to underwrite this pseudo-positivism, while his actual theory, having been self-consciously styled as precisely that, a *theory*, was shelved into a far corner of the international law library, deemed largely irrelevant to teaching and practice.[55]

However, if the trajectory of continental doctrine provides the format for mainstream pseudo-positivism, the Anglo-American practice-oriented approach provides its substance. Two versions of this approach can be distinguished, one centred around traditional state practice, the other around de facto legal process. The first is closely associated with the British pragmatic approach to international law after the Second World War, the second with a specific interpretation of the American realist tradition.[56] Both view law as the better politics and see it as a privileged language to articulate the values that should prevail in international affairs. In case of the former, this programme results from the conclusion by many among the war-generation international lawyers that legalisation was the lesson to be learned from the preceding catastrophe.[57] Although this position conceived itself in opposition to the strict consensualism then associated with positivism, it retained the primary vestige of positivism in its positing the objectivity of international law independent of state volition. And it engaged in a textbook and teaching programme which expounded that law in its practical operation, most notably before international tribunals. The judge, thus, came to incorporate the quintessential international lawyer, her perspective defined and limited by the practical demands of adjudication based on an objectively ascertainable body of

[55] Martti Koskenniemi, 'The Wonderful Artificiality of States' 88 *ASIL Proceedings* (1994) 22–29; Anthony Carty, 'Interwar German Theories of International Law: The Psychoanalytical and Phenomenological Perspectives of Hans Kelsen and Carl Schmitt' 16 *Cardozo Law Review* (1995) 1235–1292.

[56] For an overview of some of the repercussions of this, see Gerry Simpson, 'The Situation on the International Legal Theory Front: The Power of Rules and the Rule of Power' 11 *EJIL* (2000) 439–464.

[57] On this, see Martti Koskenniemi, 'Lauterpacht: The Victorian Tradition in International Law' 2 *EJIL* (1997) 215–263.

rules.[58] The motivation behind this 'practitioners' approach' is, however, not the concretisation of a theoretical demand (of positivism), but the conviction that a judicially enforced international rule of law represents in itself a desirable value that ought to be propagated. In parallel, certain strands or outgrowths of American legal realism have also fed into the contemporary mainstream, most notably those concerned with international legal process and 'law as policy'.[59] In both versions, the objectivity of a – procedurally conceived – international law is presupposed, as are certain values embodied by international legal process. Neither perspective is overtly positivist or formalist, but they, arguably, make up part of the imagery of mainstream formalism. Legal positivism, then, is present through its absence in the international law classroom. It is like the emperor without clothes, or rather, an emperor adorned with clothes which are at once too large and too small. He,[60] at any rate, appears as something quite different from his (classroom) subjects, a Hercules rather than a Hermes. Perhaps, that is what most students want to see.

4 Clothes without an emperor: piecing together global normativity

Yet, what else could they see? Is there a viable alternative strategy to the mainstream of doctrinalised practice for international law teaching? Or, indeed, to legal positivism proper, that is, to the 'science of law' as Kelsen imagined it? What does the theory front have on offer? A central problem for contemporary international legal theory remains its methodological haziness. The discipline's theory-aversion has meant that the common jurisprudential approaches have only been partially or imperfectly present in international legal theorising, while explicitly theoretical endeavours have favoured methodological *bricolage*, drawing on a range of 'external' disciplines and vocabularies in order to construct specific arguments rather than to build *grand theory*.[61] Although

[58] Anthony Carty, 'Why Theory? The Implications for International Law Teaching' in Philip Allot *et al.* (eds), *Theory and International Law: An Introduction* (British Institute of International and Comparative Law 1991) 73–104.

[59] Mark Weston Janis, *America and the Law of Nations 1776–1939* (Oxford University Press 2010); Harold Hongju Koh, 'Why Do Nations Obey International Law?' 106 *Yale Law Journal* (1997) 2599–2659.

[60] The male form is used here merely on account of the title of the tale by Hans Christian Andersen, 'The Emperor's New Clothes' (1837).

[61] See exemplarily Anthony Carty, 'Critical International Law: Recent Trends in the Theory of International Law' 2 *EJIL* (1991) 1–27; see also, again, Simpson, n. 56.

the meta-theoretical divide between rationalism and empiricism cuts through the theorising of international normativity in the same way as it does in any other social science discipline, there is little engagement with epistemological foundations and scientific method. Many of the (meta-)theoretical moves that have shaped other disciplines have been received into international law, if at all, with delay and in outdated or simplified form. The belated 'discovery' of the concept of culture,[62] the (earlier) turn to language[63] and the (later) turn to history,[64] or the idea of legal pluralism in the international sphere[65] are but a few examples. Generally, international law as a discipline continues to struggle with a self-reflexive and self-conscious engagement with its own methodological identity. Some of those who aim to provide its theoretical undercurrents have taken a rationalist turn (to philosophy and related humanities) or an empiricist one (to sociology and related social sciences). The theoretically interested majority has, arguably, tried to budge that choice by turning to history and hermeneutics.

A number of theoretical currents have come out of these choices and frame the contemporary debate: the most common of these is, arguably, neo-formalism, which seeks to encapsulate the 'practitioner's approach' by building on the positivist tradition; in so doing, it has appealed to many theory-friendly practitioner-scholars, but also to a number of critical thinkers who have seen in the 'culture of formalism' a progressive contribution to international politics.[66] The self-conceived counterpart

62 See exemplarily Paul Meerts (ed.), *Culture and International Law* (T. M. C. Asser Press 2008); Sally Engle Merry, 'Constructing a Global Law – Violence against Women and the Human Rights System' 28 *Law and Social Inquiry* (2003) 941–974.

63 This was, of course, the general move within critical legal studies. See, for instance, Costas Douzinas, Adam Geary, *Critical Jurisprudence: The Political Philosophy of Justice* (Hart 2005).

64 George Galindo, 'Martti Koskenniemi and the Historiographical Turn in International Law' 16 *EJIL* (2005) 539–559; the continuing trend towards historisation in international law is also impressively articulated through this recent book: Bardo Fassbender, Anne Peters (eds), *Oxford Handbook of the History of International Law* (Oxford University Press 2013).

65 Peer Zumbansen, 'Transnational Legal Pluralism' 1 *Transnational Legal Theory* (2005) 141–189.

66 An illustration is provided by the various reviews of *The Gentle Civilizer* (Koskenniemi, n. 24) such as Marius Emberland, '[Book Review:] Martti Koskenniemi, The Gentle Civilizer of Nations: The Rise and Fall of International Law 1870–1960' 52 *ICLQ* (2003) 272–274; Robert Cryer, '*Déjà vu* in International Law' 65 *Modern Law Review* (2002) 931–949; Brian Simpson, '[Book Review:] Martti Koskenniemi, The Gentle Civilizer of Nations: The Rise and Fall of International Law 1870–1960' 96 *AJIL* (2002) 995–1000. See also the insightful reflection by Jason Beckett, 'The Politics of International Law –

to formalism and formalists is, in turn, played by the highly disparate set of approaches commonly grouped under the label of critical (legal) thought. They, broadly, fall into three methodological streams, notably: postmodern perspectives inspired, inter alia, by French post-structuralism, linguistics, and psychoanalysis and interested mainly in the indeterminacy of legal language and the politics behind the law;[67] Marxist perspectives drawing on a historical-materialist framework of analysis and mainly interested in international law's implication in imperialism, colonialism and global capitalism;[68] and pragmatic/legal realist perspectives focusing on the techniques and strategies of international legal governance.[69] In combination, they have provided the theoretical undercurrents for a number of critical movements such as 'new approaches to international law' (NAIL) or 'third world approaches to international law' (TWAIL).[70] At the opposite end of the critical spectrum and clearly outside the bounds of 'critical legal theory', yet critical nonetheless, lies the currently foremost jurisprudential trend in North America, namely the economic analysis of law (EAL). Building on the legal realist tradition and methodologically premised on rational choice theory, its foray into international law has been largely deconstructive of the mainstream position and its inherent legalism.[71]

Much of the theoretical debate within international law has been shaped by these two master perspectives, although a number of other approaches have emerged in their shadow. Most methodologically distinct are the sociological approaches to international law that focus on the taxonomy and systematisation of international legal phenomena; among them

Twenty Years Later: A Reply' *EJIL: Talk!* 19 May 2009, available at www.ejiltalk.org/the-politics-of-international-law-twenty-years-later-a-reply/.

67 Peter Fitzpatrick, Patricia Tuitt (eds), *Critical Beings: Law, Nation and the Global Subject* (Ashgate 2004) and the insightful review by Akbar Rasulov, 'International Law and the Poststructural Challenge' 19 *LJIL* (2006) 799–827.

68 See, again, Marks, n. 7.

69 See exemplarily David Kennedy, *The Dark Side of Virtue: Reassessing International Humanitarianism* (Princeton University Press 2005).

70 Akbar Rasulov, 'New Approaches to International Law: Images of a Genealogy' in José María Beneyto, David Kennedy (eds), *New Approaches to International Law: The European and the American Experiences* (Springer 2013) 151–192; James Thuo Gathii, 'TWAIL: A Brief History of its Origins, its Decentralized Network and a Tentative Bibliography' 3 *Trade, Law and Development* (2011) 26–48.

71 See, again, Goldsmith and Posner, n. 17, as well as Eric Posner, *The Perils of Global Legalism* (University of Chicago Press 2009).

are such projects as global administrative law (GAL),[72] the Policy Science approach (New Haven School),[73] international legal process[74] and, indeed, the theory of autopoietic law.[75] Perhaps furthest out on the margins today is the predominant school of the past, namely natural law, the concern of which with the deeper rationality of rules lives on in the reception of analytical naturalism in international law and, of late, in a more continental-humanist project seeking to reframe the language of international legal discourse.[76]

These theoretical divides and thematic concerns are cross-cut by geographical dimensions, with certain approaches to international law being associated, often stereotypically, with scholarship from particular places. In this scheme, Europe tends to be seen as formalist and the United States as realist, and within Europe the United Kingdom as most purely formalist, France as formalist-sociological and Germany as formalist-constitutional. Lastly, the theorisation of international law from within the discipline has to be seen in the broader context of its theorisation from outside and, most notably, from the perspective of 'international relations' (IR). Having emerged as a methodologically distinct discipline in the post-war period, theory has always played a self-consciously constitutive role in IR, with its methodological foundations and theoretical vocabularies far more systematically developed than those of international law.[77] Curiously, the latter has not tended to be among the primary subjects of IR research, with there even being a degree of residual scepticism about the currency of international normativity especially among realist schools.

[72] Benedict Kingsbury, Nico Krisch, Richard B. Stewart, 'The Emergence of Global Administrative Law' 68 *Law & Contemporary Problems* (2005) 15–61; critically, Ming-Sung Kuo, 'Taming Governance with Legality? Critical Reflections upon Global Administrative Law as Small-C Global Constitutionalism' 44 *New York University Journal International Law and Politics* (2011) 55–102.

[73] Harold Hongju Koh, 'Is There a "New" New Haven School of International Law?' 32 *Yale Journal of International Law* (2007) 559–574.

[74] See, again, Chayes, Ehrlich and Lowenfeld, n. 28 and for a more recent elaboration, arguably, Anne-Marie Slaughter, 'International Law in a World of Liberal States' 6 *EJIL* (1995) 503–538.

[75] Gunther Teubner, Andreas Fischer-Lescano, 'Regime-Collisions: The Vain Search for Legal Unity in the Fragmentation of Global Law' 25 *Michigan Journal of International Law* (2004) 999–1046.

[76] For the former, see Stephen Hall, 'The Persistent Spectre: Natural Law, International Order and the Limits of Legal Positivism' 12 *EJIL* (2001) 269–307; for the latter, see Carty, n. 18.

[77] Jeffrey L. Dunoff, Mark A. Pollack (eds), *Interdisciplinary Perspectives on International Law and International Relations: The State of the Art* (Cambridge University Press 2012).

However, with the rise of constructivism as a theoretical endeavour in IR, international law and, generally, the role of norms in international affairs has become an important research concern. Here, the question of compliance has been a particular interest, shared by and partially examined in conjunction with the sociological currents in international legal theory.

However, while an aversion to 'theory as theory' continues to be a strong undercurrent in the discipline, a number of issues have emerged over the past decade or so which have brought overtly theoretical concerns into the 'mainstream'. The alleged fragmentation of the canonical corpus of international law into distinct legal regimes, operating in an increasingly autonomous and partially incompatible fashion, has triggered a new interest in the (theoretical) reflection on the systematicity of international law. The most coherent and school-like of the theoretical endeavours that have come out of this concern has been constitutionalist thought which seeks to identify emerging standards of global (legal) governance in different regimes such as international trade law, human rights, humanitarian law or international criminal law.[78] In parallel, the proliferation of non-state actors has fostered a new theoretical engagement with the quality of sovereignty and the sources recognised to identify it.[79] Lastly, the perennial problem of compliance has continued to inspire theoretical reflection on the nature of statehood, normativity and legal governance.[80]

Yet, which of these theoretical alternatives to positivism would do as a viable alternative in the introductory international law classroom? Which of these have similar systemic aspirations as legal positivism, which set out a coherent enough alternative language game to work in and for a professional epistemic community, which might be amenable to a new form of practice? The answer to this is neither facile nor would it be properly covered in a piece on international law teaching. Indeed, whether there is an alternative to (pseudo-)positivism is, perhaps, the cutting-edge question of contemporary international legal theory. Part of the difficulty of identifying any particular theoretical position in this respect lies in

[78] Bogdandy, n. 9; Jeffrey L. Dunoff, Joel P. Trachtman (eds), *Ruling the World? Constitutionalism, International Law, and Global Governance* (Cambridge University Press 2009).

[79] E.g. Anthea Elizabeth Roberts, Sandesh Sivakumaran, 'Lawmaking by Nonstate Actors: Engaging Armed Groups in the Creation of International Humanitarian Law' 37 *Yale Journal of International Law* (2012) 107–152.

[80] Kal Raustiala, Anne-Marie Slaughter, 'International Law, International Relations and Compliance' in Walter Carlnaes, Thomas Risse, Beth A. Simmons (eds), *Handbook of International Relations* (Sage Publications 2002) 538–558.

the fact that few if any current theorising of international law engages in self-conscious grand theory with systematic aspirations. Most of the positions mentioned above do not purport to substitute international law as a positivised system of rules with anything else, but they merely aim to either complement the current canon – such as by proposing a more pluralist sources doctrine – or to critique it by uncovering its structural bias and its inherent indeterminacy. None of them purports to substitute the idea of legality, and with it, the legalisation of international affairs, with anything else – such as their re-politicisation.[81] Virtually all of their proponents identify themselves as international lawyers – with the obvious exception of international relations scholars – and appear weary to sacrifice the professional benefits of belonging to this caste by fundamentally stepping outside of the mainstream.

Of the approaches mentioned above, the overtly critical lines of thought (CLS and EAL) are, by and large, premised on the existing mainstream and its shortcomings. They either focus on the micro-level (post-modern and realist CLS as well as EAL) and, thus, on the rationality and ethics of the agents of international law, or on the macro-level (Marxist CLS) and on its structural determinants. The sociological frameworks, in turn, fulfil the prerequisites for being systematic alternatives to the mainstream narrative to a much greater degree, but, in terms of their significance for the international law classroom, they suffer from either a lack of comprehensiveness or of professional relevance, or both. While the original New Haven approach certainly represented a self-conscious attempt to put in place an alternative logic as well as language for international normativity, and while it aspired to comprehensiveness, it never managed to gain any wider adherence in professional legal or political circles. Although it was conceived as the legal international arm of a general concept of scientific policy-making, it was marred by its explicit bias towards so-called 'Western values' and a language that, contrary to its aspirations, did not reflect the 'real' language of international policy-making.[82] By contrast, the global administrative law project aims to go back to the original purpose behind international law as a jurisprudential discipline, namely

[81] For an as yet very tentative hint towards how such a re-politicisation could be conceived, see Florian Hoffmann, 'Facing the Abyss: International Law before the Political' in Marco Goldoni, Christopher McCorkindale (eds), *Hannah Arendt and the Law* (Hart 2012) 173–190.

[82] Hengameh Saberi, 'Love it or Hate it, but for the Right Reasons: Pragmatism and the New Haven School's International Law of Human Dignity' 35 *Boston College International and Comparative Law Review* (2012) 59–144.

that of identifying, collecting and systematising the rules that govern international affairs. As such, it is essentially an attempt to modernise the canon by opening up the box and creating a clean slate in terms of the ways in which global norms are identified today. What it finds is not merely a multiplicity of sources that breach the traditional divides between public and private, international and transnational, hard and soft, but a more or less comprehensive system of administrative principles that configure the way in which norms are created and applied in any setting. This global administrative law as they see it is a sort of meta-law that pervades and ultimately controls all legal fields.[83] Although the GAL project is still somewhat incipient and has not yet drawn a comprehensive map of administrative meta-legality, it clearly aims to eventually be a powerful alternative to the canon, with its power coming from its rootedness in factual normative phenomena as opposed to idealist norm constructions. Yet, it, too, has been critiqued for being inherently biased towards Western principles of good governance and, thus, for shrouding an idealist conception of global governance under a cloak of purported empirical fact. In a sense, global administrative law sets out to be the new positivism, but, having done away with either state consent or a universally accepted basic norm as a foundation for the legitimacy of global (legal) governance, it, as yet, floats in the air. That said, many of its precepts are creeping into professional legal discourse and the growing de facto currency global administrative principles carry in legal proceedings ought not to be underestimated. But is it ready, yet, to take over in positivism's stead and be taught?

The same question has to be put to the third of the sociological approaches, the theory of autopoietic systems as applied to international law. For some time now, Luhmannian legal thought has transcended the analytical bounds of (so-called) domestic law and has reached out to transnational and global normativity. In fact, it has provided the most comprehensive and coherent, if not uncontested, analytical vocabulary through which transnational legal governance and global law can be theoretically captured.[84] Yet, the empirical focus of this analysis has mostly

[83] Benedict Kingsbury, 'The Concept of "Law" in Global Administrative Law' 20 *EJIL* (2009) 23–57 and Alexander Somek's engaging reply: Alexander Somek, 'The Concept of "Law" in Global Administrative Law: A Reply to Benedict Kingsbury' 20 *EJIL* (2009) 985–995.

[84] See exemplarily Gunther Teubner (ed.), *Global Law without a State* (Dartmouth 1997).

been on (so-called) private legal processes, such as on the notorious *lex mercatoria*,[85] not least as it is in the complex unfolding of transnational private rule-making that a global legal process emancipated from the state is in clearest evidence. More recently, however, an attempt has been made to broaden the (legal) systems theoretical perspective and (re-)describe the internal functioning of and interaction among public legal and, in particular, constitutionalised legal fields. Here, autopoiesis and regime theory have been merged in order to reframe what, from the perspective of more traditional legal analysis, has appeared as the intractable problem of fragmentation.[86] In their ground-breaking work on regime collision, Gunther Teubner and Andreas Fischer-Lescano have put what amounts to an 'autopoietic regime theory' to work on some of the most deadlocked debates in international law, such as intellectual property (in relation to medicines), transnational criminal law or cybercrime, among others.[87] What makes this approach so innovative is that it radically breaks with the logic of unity and hierarchical organisation which underlies the conventional model of international law. For the latter is bound to consider the de facto legal polycentricity that characterises international normativity as an undesirable fragmentation in need to be overcome through a complex system of secondary and tertiary rules that re-unify everything in a hard normative centre.[88] Instead, they postulate the inevitability of legal polycentricity on the basis of Luhmann's early observation that world society is (inherently) without a head or a centre,[89] and re-describe international law as a transnational network of differentiated norm systems that dynamically interact.[90] Indeed, interaction is the core feature

85 See, inter alia, Gunther Teubner, 'Breaking Frames: Economic Globalization and the Emergence of Lex Mercatoria' 5 *European Journal of Social Theory* (2002) 199–217.

86 See, generally, Gunther Teubner, Andreas Fischer-Lescano, *Regime-Kollisionen: Zur Fragmentierung des globalen Rechts* (Suhrkamp 2006).

87 Teubner and Fischer-Lescano, n. 86.

88 See, for instance, the report by the International Law Commission (Martti Koskenniemi, 'Fragmentation of International Law: Difficulties Arising from the Diversification and Expansion of International Law: Report of the Study Group of the International Law Commission', UN Doc. A/CN.4/L.682 (13 April 2006)).

89 Niklas Luhmann, 'Die Weltgesellschat' 57 *Archiv für Rechts- und Sozialphilosophie* (1971) 1–35.

90 Teubner and Fischer-Lescano, n. 75 at 999; Teubner and Fischer-Lescano, n. 86 at 7; Gunther Teubner, '"Global Bukowina": Pluralism in the World Society' in Gunther Teubner (ed.), *Global Law without a State* (Aldershot 1997) 3–28; Gralf-Peter Calliess, 'Systemtheorie: Luhmann/Teubner' in Sonja Buckel, Ralph Christensen, Andreas Fischer-Lescano (eds), *Neue Theorien des Rechts* (Lucius & Lucius 2006) 57–71.

of this network, with mutual irritation and adaptation being the forces that hold it together. From this perspective, global law essentially emerges from and through regime collision, which is, hence, at the core of this type of legal analysis. This collision is taken to have two causes: first, each such regime has an inherent tendency to maximise its own particular rationality (*Eigenrationalität*) against other regimes, thereby increasing fragmentation and creating a relation of antagonism between different regimes.[91] And second, functional differentiation means that norms and institutions increasingly fulfil only one, rather than several, functions in a highly specialised and, hence, efficient way. This, in turn, means that the specific risks associated with that function are minimised or 'absorbed' in ways that may be incompatible with the risk absorption strategy of other functional systems.[92] As a consequence, a regime's optimised risk absorption strategy may represent increased risk or danger for another regime; regime conflict is, hence, a 'natural' result. Perhaps even more so than global administrative law, autopoietic legal theory provides a powerful analytical framework with which to explain many of the international legal phenomena that remain unexplained, and, thus, ignored, by (traditional) legal positivism. Yet, unlike global administrative law, it is a purely extra-legal perspective that reconstructs global law through the logic of systems theory. As such, it is most closely related to the Marxist framework of macroscopic analysis, focusing on the forces behind or, rather, underneath the law seen as a mere epiphenomenon. It consequently serves critical insight but not professional training, or, put differently, it explains how law functions and why the operators of the law do what they do, but it does not provide an understanding of that operation from the perspective of the operator.

There remains, then, paradoxically, this very perspective as an alternative to the pseudo-positivist mainstream, notably neo-formalism. The most coherent contemporary articulation by far has been provided by Martti Koskenniemi's 'culture of formalism', which seeks to reframe international legal discourse from within formalist premises, notably by showing it to contain all the elements necessary to move it back from the current apologism to a politically progressive utopia. Thus, to Koskenniemi, the vocabulary of formal (legal) norms and the judicial and quasi-judicial institutions within which it is performed provides the most

[91] Teubner and Fischer-Lescano, n. 75 at 1005.
[92] Teubner and Fischer-Lescano, n. 75 at 25.

hopeful platform for transformative politics under current global conditions, provided such strategic legal interventionism is aware of its own contingency and refrains from essentialising its lacking centre through reified concepts such as governance, human rights, constitutionalisation, etc.[93] Indeed, the emphasis is all on strategic processes that avoid crystallisation into firm institutions or structures and thereby stay clear of the legal managerialism which has, for Koskenniemi, taken over the profession.[94] Even though the theoretical underpinnings of the 'culture of formalism' clearly betray its critical pedigree, it has nonetheless left the door open for interested members of 'the profession' – since their professional practice would appear to be quite compatible with Koskenniemi's 'strategic formalism' – provided their political intentions are progressive, as would, arguably, be the case with many contemporary practitioners of 'lawfare',[95] especially in such legal fields as human rights, humanitarian law, environmental law or labour law. The 'culture of formalism' has, in other words, also and, perhaps, especially appealed to 'practitioners' in search of a theory. More importantly, perhaps, it deals out a new hand for international legal theorising, for it confronts any quest for alternatives with the facticity and functionality of 'traditional' formal legal language and the 'real existing' interpretative community of international lawyers. This, then, is both a critical and an affirmative move, based, in essence, on the idea that exposing pseudo-positivism to deconstructive critique and, thereby, showing that the nakedness of the emperor does not, in fact, do away with him, but brings out his real powers. These powers, to Koskenniemi, consist of the relative universality which an aesthetically well-crafted language game can provide. As such, the 'culture of formalism' can be seen as a post-modern development of the idea of legal positivism, away from epistemology and towards action. Would this then open up a new way of teaching old international law, with less pretence and the courage to see its relativism in the eye? As yet, the 'culture of formalism' is only a sketch, with its drafter having, meanwhile, performed a *Kehre* towards history, leaving grand theorising behind. Is the proposition of a post-modern

[93] See, however, for a more nuanced examination of the relationship between acknowledged contingency and 'false' necessity, Susan Marks, 'False Contingency' 62 *Current Legal Problems* (2009) 1–21.

[94] Martti Koskenniemi, 'The Politics of International Law – 20 Years Later' 29 *EJIL* (2009) 7–19.

[95] Iain Scobbie, 'On the Road to Avila? A Response to Koskenniemi' *EJIL: Talk!*, 20 May 2009, available at www.ejiltalk.org/on-the-road-to-avila-a-response-to-koskenniemi/.

positivism, perhaps, a next step towards converting this sketch into a full picture?

5 From positivist teaching to teaching positivism

What could that picture look like in the international law classroom, which teaching strategy could follow from it? Surely not 'doctrine' and 'practice', as both are, as was seen, the pillars of the pseudo-positivist mainstream. Nor, however, merely 'theory', as that only aims at external explanation rather than internal understanding, even if any neo-formalist/post-modern positivist teaching strategy would have to include a heavy dose of 'theory' so as to generate distancing and self-reflection. A first positive step in the construction of such a strategy would probably have to be a refocusing of the teaching experience, away from logical game-playing (doctrine) or training (practice) and towards critical knowledge construction. This would imply that students were equipped with the tools to simultaneously learn the vocabulary, grammar and syntax of the language game of international law and to reflect on their doing so from a meta-perspective. The aim would be for students to be able to speak the language at the same time as they understand its linguistic deep structure, and to become sensitive to the tension between these two perspectives as well as to make that tension productive. This flows from the precepts of the concept of relativist practice which underlies neo-formalism and, arguably, post-modern legal positivism. It would, ultimately, be all about learning to tolerate the fact that the emperor is naked and to grasp the full force that his nakedness represents. A precondition for this learning experience would, of course, be that the aura of objectivity that pseudo-positivism creates is dissolved, and with it, the halo of professional authority that surrounds it. Teaching positivism stripped of its metaphysical cloak means to teach students to withstand the terrifying spectacle of the pure relativity of (positive) law, to countenance its closedness, to affirm its solipsism. This would imply teaching without the cosmetics of institutional gravitas or activist lawfaring; instead, it would require a refocusing, from 'within', on the critical reflection of doctrine and on the self-distancing from practice.[96] Such naked positivism would, perhaps ironically, free international law students to discern the 'other' of (international) law, namely politics, more

[96] This is not identical to, but is resonant of, Martti Koskenniemi's ideas on legal education, as expounded in Martti Koskenniemi, 'International Law: Constitutionalism, Managerialism and the Ethos of Legal Education' 1 *European Journal of Legal Studies* (2007) 1–21.

succinctly, thereby putting them in a better position to judge what is law's and what is politics' domain, and to act accordingly. Thus, the wall of doubt would not need to be artificially dispelled, but would, instead, be the basis for the critical consciousness necessary to distinguish law from politics. This, in turn, would be the precondition for rendering the tension between the two productive in and for the 'international'.

14

International law in domestic and supranational settings

BEATRICE I. BONAFÉ

1 Introduction

Generally neglected by recent international law scholars, the relationship between legal orders is one of the crucial issues of legal theory lying at the heart of legal positivism. The way in which legal orders relate to each other is essential to understanding their foundational and most characteristic features. A few recent examples would suffice to recall the enduring importance of the conceptualisation of the relationship between international and municipal law in the framework of a general appraisal of the paradigms of international legal positivism. In the case concerning *Jurisdictional Immunities of the State*, the ICJ decided that Italy:

> [M]ust, by enacting appropriate legislation, or by resorting to other methods of its choosing, ensure that the decisions of its courts and those of other judicial authorities infringing the immunity which the Federal Republic of Germany enjoys under international law cease to have effect.[1]

In other words, an *international* judgment dictates the unenforceability of *domestic* decisions, imposing on the state the obligation to deprive them of any legal effect. Thus, once it is established that Italian decisions are in conflict with international law, it is necessary to consider the way in which Italy must proceed in order to ensure that its international obligation is implemented internally.

In 2011, the Special Tribunal for Lebanon held that, 'as a general rule, international norms criminalizing conduct are non-self-executing, for their implementation requires national legislation defining the crime and

[1] *Jurisdictional Immunities of the State (Germany v. Italy: Greece intervening)*, Judgment of 3 February 2012, ICJ Reports (2012) 99 at 155 (para. 139(4)). It must be noted that international decisions explicitly aimed at depriving domestic judgments of any legal effect are quite uncommon.

the relevant penalty'.[2] Accordingly, domestic judges would not be able to apply provisions having an international origin if this proves contrary to the domestic principle of legality. Again, what is at issue is a potential conflict between international and municipal law.

These are just two examples among many similar cases. Every day, municipal courts deal with cases involving, directly or indirectly, the need to ensure compliance with international obligations. International law is routinely interpreted and applied by domestic courts. Generally, the domestic application of international law does not raise particular problems. However, there are difficult cases in which domestic courts are confronted with a conflict between international and municipal law. In order to solve such conflicts, domestic courts must inevitably address the question of the legal foundations of the application of international law in domestic legal orders. This issue is crucial not only because of its practical consequences, but also because it raises a number of key theoretical questions about the nature of international law itself.[3]

Admittedly, the relationship between international and municipal law can be examined from two different perspectives. From the standpoint of international law, it concerns the possibility to apply municipal law internationally and the primacy, in case of conflict between international and municipal norms, to be accorded to one of these norms. Likewise, from the standpoint of municipal law, it concerns the possibility to apply international law internally and the primacy, in case of conflict, of one of these norms. However, only the latter aspect will be taken into account and the following analysis will be limited to the relationship between international and municipal law seen from the perspective of the domestic application of international law.[4] The domestic application of international law is generally considered to be the more problematic of these two perspectives, with different commentators holding diverging opinions.

One of the most problematic issues entailed by the relationship between international and municipal law regards the uncertainties surrounding the

[2] STL, *Prosecutor v. Salim Jamil Ayyash et al.*, Case No. STL-11–01/I/AC/R176bis, Appeals Chamber, Interlocutory Decision on the Applicable Law: Terrorism, Conspiracy, Homicide, Perpetration, Cumulative Charging of 16 February 2011, para. 76. This is a particularly interesting example because it is difficult to find such a broad statement concerning the non-self-executing character of an entire set of international rules.

[3] Dionisio Anzilotti, *Il diritto internazionale nei giudizi interni* (Zanichelli 1905).

[4] With regard to the international application of municipal law, see Carlo Santulli, *Le statut international de l'ordre juridique étatique: Étude du traitement du droit interne par le droit international* (Pedone 2001).

theoretical foundation of the domestic application of international law. Whereas the doctrines traditionally elaborated to explain the relationship between international and municipal law, namely, monism and dualism, have always been an object of debate, the more recent critique of monism and dualism raises a particular concern because it challenges the common positivist foundation of international law. The current state of affairs is usually described as a mixture of continuity and 'self-containedness' of legal orders; a mixture that defeats any theoretical construction of the relationship between international and municipal law.[5]

The purpose of this chapter is to show the enduring importance of the positivist methodology[6] and its traditional doctrines of monism and dualism. Without denying the fact that different legal orders interact with each other, and increasingly so, a positivist approach remains an essential starting point in explaining such interactions. Of particular relevance is the openness domestic courts exhibit with regard to international law.

The chapter will first describe the common positivist foundation of monism and dualism. Then the main objections raised against monism and dualism will be spelled out, and the uncertainties concerning the theoretical appraisal of the relationship between international and municipal law that characterise recent international practice will be taken into account. In order to determine whether the positivist approach maintains its cogency, international practice will be examined with particular reference to cases where domestic courts rely on the doctrines of direct effect and consistent interpretation because these doctrines, at least in part, escape the traditional monist/dualist logic. Finally, the role that positivism actually plays in solving the apparent inconsistencies between continuity and exclusivity of legal orders will be highlighted.

2 The common positivist foundation of monism and dualism: the exclusivity principle

The relationship between international and municipal law has long been the field of confrontation of two theories, monism and dualism.[7] But

[5] See Section 3.

[6] See the distinction made by Norberto Bobbio between positivism as a methodology, a theory and an ideology in Norberto Bobbio, *Giusnaturalismo e positivismo giuridico* (Edizioni di Comunità 1965).

[7] For an overview of the issues entailed by the relationship between legal orders, see Beatrice I. Bonafé, 'Adattamento del diritto interno al diritto internazionale' in Sabino Cassese (ed.), *Dizionario di diritto pubblico* (Giuffré 2006) 98–111. For the notion of monism, see

while these two theories once dominated international law discourses, they are now seen as rather outdated by today's 'pragmatic, inductive, largely anti-theoretical scholarship'.[8]

Monism and dualism are quite opposite doctrines, but they have, among others, a common element: they both provide a positivist account of the relationship between international and municipal law. It is not my intention to describe the complex historical origins of monism and dualism. However, both doctrines display a similar rejection of the natural law approach. With some oversimplification, dualism was elaborated in opposition to natural law doctrines considered to be 'basically flawed' and 'anti-scientific' because they were regarded as the expression of 'anti-positive' thinking,[9] and monism was elaborated in opposition to dualism because in the end dualism would have transformed international law into a sort of 'moral or natural law' depriving international law of its character of 'real law', i.e. of 'positive law'.[10] As has been pointed out, both doctrines share a common conception of the legal order:

> Selon cette conception, l'unité des normes multiples qui composent un même ordre juridique leur est conférée par leur identité d'origine, par le fait qu'elles proviennent toutes, en dernière analyse, des mêmes sources et, par conséquent, finissent par se rattacher aux mêmes normes originaires, d'où ces sources procèdent.[11]

Thus, the common positivist foundation of monism and dualism lies in what has been called the *principe d'exhaustivité* of legal orders.[12] According to both monist and dualist doctrines, each legal order is 'self-contained'[13]

in particular Hans Kelsen, *Pure Theory of Law* (Max Knight (tr.), University of California Press 1967) and Hans Kelsen, *Principles of International Law* (Rinehart & Co. 1952) 401–447. For the notion of dualism, see in particular Anzilotti, n. 3; Heinrich Triepel, 'Les rapports entre le droit interne et le droit international' 1 *Recueil des Cours* (1923) 77–121; Gaetano Arangio-Ruiz, 'Dualism Revisited: International Law and Interindividual Law' 86 *Rivista di diritto internazionale* (2003) 909–999.

8 Janne E. Nijman, André Nollkaemper, 'Introduction' in Janne E. Nijman, André Nollkaemper (eds), *New Perspectives on the Divide between National and International Law* (Oxford University Press 2007) 1–14 at 2.

9 Anzilotti, n. 3 at 5.

10 Hans Kelsen, 'Les rapports de système entre le droit interne et le droit international public' 14 *Recueil des Cours* (1926) 231–332 at 276.

11 Michel Virally, 'Sur un pont aux ânes: les rapports entre droit international et droits internes' in *Mélanges offerts à Henri Rolin: Problèmes de droits de gens* (Pedone 1964) 488–505 at 492.

12 Christophe Grzegorczyk, 'Introduction' in Christophe Grzegorczyk, Françoise Michaut, Michel Troper (eds), *Le positivisme juridique* (LGDJ 1992) 33–67 at 34.

13 Giorgio Gaja, 'Dualism – A Review' in Janne E. Nijman, Andre Nollkaemper (eds), *New Perspectives on the Divide between National and International Law* (Oxford University Press 2007) n. 8, 52.

in the sense that it rejects 'external' sources of obligations, such as natural law. According to positivist thinking, each legal system should provide for criteria making it possible to identify the legal rules that belong to the system, and to determine the validity of such rules. Monism has a wider scope because the legal order has its legal foundation in international law and includes domestic legal systems. Dualism has a much narrower scope because the legal order has its legal foundation in either national law or international law. But both monism and dualism erect 'barriers' in order to separate what is to be included and what is to be excluded from the system.

Cognition of legal order is central in legal positivism. The purpose of positivism is to avoid, at least in principle, any uncertainty. To this end, it formalises criteria for the objective identification of the norms that belong to a legal system.[14] On the one hand, this cognitive move purports to determine whether or not a certain norm is part of the legal system. According to the principle of exclusivity, international law can be applied by the domestic judge either because the domestic legal order has adopted a monist approach to the relationship between international and municipal law, and international law is part of the unique legal system that includes domestic law, or because a dualist approach is preferred, and international law has been somehow incorporated into domestic law. On the other hand, legal cognition seeks to ensure the unity of the legal system and to avoid conflicts of norms belonging to different systems of norms.[15] According to both monism and dualism, such conflicts are simply inconceivable as they are transformed into 'internal' conflicts between norms belonging to the same legal system.[16]

3 Monism and dualism under attack

Both monism and dualism have been criticised, their major flaws have been pointed out, and even the possibility of 'third ways' has been

[14] Kammerhofer, Chapter 4 at 84–85 (fn. 10 and accompanying text). See also d'Aspremont, Chapter 5 at 120–127, and more generally on the formal criteria of law-ascertainment in the theory of international law sources, Jean d'Aspremont, *Formalism and the Sources of International Law* (Oxford University Press 2011).

[15] On the 'internal' unity of the legal system, see Jörg Kammerhofer, 'Kelsen – Which Kelsen? A Reapplication of the Pure Theory to International Law' 22 *LJIL* (2009) 233–236, 240–244; Jochen von Bernstorff, *The Public International Law of Hans Kelsen: Believing in Universal Law* (Oxford University Press 2010) 78–84.

[16] See Section 3.

explored.[17] But generally the aim of the early critique was to improve either the monist or the dualist scheme (or a mix of them). Arguments were put forward along the lines of the basic assumptions of the monist or dualist doctrine with the purpose of defining a better general scheme capable of explaining international practice. In other words, this 'traditional' critique of monism and dualism did not put into question the positivist framework in which a general understanding of the relationship between international and municipal law had to be elaborated, but tried to adapt it to the developments of international practice.

Modern critique is different. It seems that the idea is gaining ground that we should simply get rid of monism and dualism. According to Brownlie:

> [A]n increasing number of jurists wish to escape from the dichotomy of monism and dualism, holding that the logical consequences of both theories conflict with the way in which international and national organs and courts behave.[18]

Today, the recurring leitmotif to be found in most textbooks of international law is that monism and dualism have no explanatory power, and that they are totally useless in providing solutions to the concrete problems concerning the relationship between international and municipal law.[19] It is commonly observed that domestic courts need to apply international rules, and that sometimes they refuse to do so; that there is inevitably a mixture of continuity and separation between the international and municipal legal orders. What seems most disturbing to modern scholars is that, in the end, it is not possible to say whether either monism or dualism is to be preferred, and that international law is *neutral* in that regard.[20]

The described reasoning seems to presuppose that the question of whether these doctrines are acceptable (or better yet, whether just one of them is acceptable) depends on the possibility to choose between a monist and a dualist approach. But the question here is not one of

[17] E.g. Gerald G. Fitzmaurice, 'The General Principles of International Law Considered from the Standpoint of the Rule of Law' 92 *Recueil des Cours* (1957) 5–227 at 70–85; Enzo Cannizzaro, 'The Neo-Monism of the European Legal Order' in Ramses Alexander Wessel, Enzo Cannizzaro, Paolo Palchetti (eds), *International Law as the Law of the European Union* (Martinus Nijhoff 2012) 35–58.

[18] Ian Brownlie, *Principles of Public International Law* (Oxford University Press 2008) 33.

[19] E.g. Benedetto Conforti, *Diritto internazionale* (8th edn Editoriale scientifica 2010) 308.

[20] E.g. André Nollkaemper, *National Courts and the International Rule of Law* (Oxford University Press 2011) 299–300.

choice; it is to determine whether their common foundation in positivist thinking is still capable of explaining present-day practice. In addition, modern scholars generally, and most of the time implicitly, seem to expect international law to provide the answer to the question concerning the 'right' theoretical approach to the relationship between international and municipal law. In other words, they ask whether international law imposes a certain theoretical scheme and, if it does not, then it is concluded that both monism and dualism are to be set aside. But again the fact that international law does not impose either monism or dualism on every state does not defeat the common positive foundation of these doctrines, i.e. the principle of exclusivity of legal orders. At least the alleged neutrality of international law with regard to the relationship between international and domestic law defeats monism, since for certain domestic legal orders international law would not provide the legal foundation justifying the application of international rules at the municipal level, and the inclusion of such rules in the domestic legal system can only be dictated by the domestic legal system itself.

Yet the critique of monism and dualism recently elaborated by international scholars is generally framed in very broad terms. It is merely maintained that dogmatism is to be avoided and that monism and dualism are to be set aside. Stated more bluntly:

> Monism and dualism should cease to exist as doctrinal and theoretical notions for discussing the relationship between international law and internal law. Perhaps they can continue to be useful in depicting a more open or more hesitant political disposition toward international law. But from a scholarly perspective, they are intellectual zombies of another time and should be laid to rest, or 'deconstructed'.[21]

We might concede that, in the end, monism and dualism say very little about the way in which legal orders actually interact and the way in which possible conflicts between rules belonging to different legal orders are solved in specific cases. According to dualism, no relationship seems possible because legal orders are conceived of as autonomous and self-contained. The same is true for monism since the abstract possibility of a relationship dissolves in the unity of all legal systems. In the former case, no conflict is conceivable between rules belonging to separate and independent legal systems. In the latter case, the conflict is internalised

[21] Armin von Bogdandy, 'Pluralism, Direct Effect, and the Ultimate Say: On the Relationship between International and Domestic Constitutional Law' 6 *International Journal of Constitutional Law* (2008) 397–413 at 400.

and solved as a normal conflict between internal rules according to the internally established hierarchy of norms. However, this does not mean that the exclusivity principle underlying both positivist doctrines is to be set aside and can in no way explain the interactions between legal orders that emerge from current international practice.

A more specific critique of the positivist approach underlying monist and dualist doctrines is to be found among the advocates of global legal pluralism, although this fast-growing but disparate critique does not directly address the relationship between international and municipal law and hardly mentions monism and dualism.[22] Both social scientists[23] and legal theorists[24] increasingly advance the idea that today, global, inter-, supra- or transnational law are no longer state-centred, but rather consist of a plurality of 'inchoate forms of law'.[25]

Part of this critique is pertinent to the present enquiry provided it explicitly challenges some basic tenets of positivism, in particular the exclusivity principle. On the one hand, global legal pluralism indirectly challenges monism because it opposes the 'unity of the law', which is viewed as a threat to the diversity of legal culture,[26] and it rejects the existence of unified formal criteria allowing the determination of the validity of law rules.[27] Global law should include spontaneous, private forms of law 'produced hetero-referentially by an independent "public" legal order' without a Rule of Recognition;[28] legal pluralism should be built on a pluralistic theory of norm production.[29] On the other hand, dualism is not considered to be a viable alternative. Legal pluralism equally rejects 'sovereigntist territorialism' or some positivists' exclusive focus on state law because the state no longer has a monopoly on norm production;[30] other 'entities', 'communities', 'networks', 'peripheries' or 'jurisdictions' are said to exercise autonomous law-making and law-enforcement.[31] Legal pluralism is no longer synonymous with separation and self-containedness. And at the end of the day, neither is it

[22] For an overview, see Ralf Michaels, 'Global Legal Pluralism' 5 *Annual Review of Law and Social Science* (2009) 243–262.

[23] In particular, Gunther Teubner, '"Global Bukowina": Legal Pluralism in the World Society' in Gunther Teubner (ed.), *Global Law without a State* (Dartmouth 1997) 3–28.

[24] In particular, Paul Schiff Berman, 'Global Legal Pluralism' 80 *Southern California Law Review* (2007) 1155–1238.

[25] Teubner, n. 23 at 4. [26] Teubner, n. 23 at 7. [27] Berman, n. 24 at 1166.

[28] 'Contracting' is regarded as the 'primary source of law' and a 'self-legitimating' process is considered to be a sufficient basis for global legal pluralism by Teubner, n. 23 at 14.

[29] Teubner, n. 23 at 9. [30] Berman, n. 24 at 1180–1189. [31] Teubner, n. 23 at 6–7.

synonymous with dualism, as it was in the beginning,[32] and still is from a certain perspective.[33] A plurality of state, private, international, transnational (and so on) legal orders are said to interact, and by definition they are not self-contained. This clearly has nothing to do with the position defended by Anzilotti at the beginning of the twentieth century.

More generally, global legal pluralism intends to broaden the scope of what constitutes 'law', and therefore puts into question the positivist principle of exclusivity, essentially because it includes in the legal system rules that cannot be traced back to a unified criterion of validity. Together with the disappearance of the self-contained character of the legal order (monism) or of all legal orders (dualism), one wonders whether it is possible to speak of a relationship, dialogue or interactions between normative systems that remain indeterminate.

Indeterminacy is undoubtedly the central feature of this modern critique of positivist thinking.[34] In particular, legal pluralism seems to accept that the content of primary international rules remains indeterminate and that the normative power is fragmented among a number of undefined entities. Despite its focus on the interactions between different legal systems, their relationship vanishes together with the absence of a definition of substantive rules, of what a legal system is, and of the entities that have the power to perform a normative function.[35] Legal pluralism undoubtedly enlarges the notion of legal system in order to include inchoate forms of normativity, but it seems that the price to be paid in terms of normative indeterminacy is particularly high.

4 Indeterminacy v. exclusivity

The various critiques of monism and dualism described above should be taken into account as long as they draw attention to the need to address seriously the question of the interactions between legal orders. It is undeniable that legal orders do interact in a number of different ways. But is that fact enough to justify the outright rejection of the positivist

[32] Anzilotti, n. 3.

[33] Gaetano Arangio-Ruiz, 'International Law and Interindividual Law' in Janne E. Nijman, Andre Nollkaemper (eds), *New Perspectives on the Divide between National and International Law* (Oxford University Press 2007) n. 8, 15–51.

[34] D'Aspremont, n. 14 at 94–95.

[35] E.g. according to Berman, the existence of normative systems is to be presupposed and their definition is regarded as superfluous: 'pluralism frees scholars from needing an essentialist definition of "law" . . . the whole debate about law versus non-law is largely irrelevant'. See Berman, n. 24 at 1177.

account of the relationship between legal orders, that is, the exclusivity principle?

In order to answer that question, we should turn to an analysis of how domestic courts actually behave. In the following text, we examine whether there are criteria that guide domestic courts in the solution of the possible conflicts between international and municipal law and whether such criteria are consistently relied upon. Put in very concrete terms, the question raised by the domestic application of international law is whether we can pass judgment on the way in which states enforce international obligations in their domestic legal orders.

To give an example, the German Federal Constitutional Court held that, '*for states that are not involved in a proceeding before the International Court of Justice*, the judgments of the Court shall have a normative directing function'[36] (*Orientierungswirkung*), and they should be taken into account by German courts. Can we say that the way in which the German Constitutional Court secures a certain interaction between international obligations and municipal law is correct or not?

Monism and dualism have been elaborated in order to provide a general theoretical scheme as well as specific criteria allowing us to answer that question. And in both cases a positivist account of the relationship between international and municipal law provides an affirmative answer. According to monism, the answer is yes, we can decide whether domestic courts have correctly applied international law, and this evaluation is to be made against international law.[37] As international and municipal law belong to the same legal system, international rules should be applied domestically and should even be accorded primacy over municipal law. According to dualism, the answer is again yes, but the judgment is to be formulated according to municipal law alone. International law and municipal law are strictly separate legal orders, as they have a different

36 'Für Staaten, die nicht an einem Verfahren beteiligt sind, haben die Urteile des Internationalen Gerichtshofs Orientierungswirkung', German Federal Constitutional Court, '*WÜK*', 2 BvR 2115/01, 2 BvR 2132/01, 2 BvR 348/03, joined cases, Order of 19 September 2006, paras 59–61 (citation at para. 61, emphasis added).

37 Monism is used here to refer to that variant of the monist conception which places international law above national law. Of course, a different answer would ensue if the relationship were to be conceived of upside down with national law above international law, the latter being the expression of 'external state law'. According to Kelsen, the choice between the two approaches is merely dictated by ideological-political reasons (see Bernstorff, n. 15 at 104–107; Kammerhofer, n. 15 at 243). In any case, this would not change the foregoing conclusion: once a choice is made between the two approaches, the answer on the primacy of international or national law would ensue.

legal foundation and different legal addressees. International law should be applied domestically as long as it is incorporated and does not conflict with municipal law. From the viewpoint of international law, states enjoy complete freedom in ensuring domestic compliance with international obligations and the absence of compliance can only entail the international responsibility of the state.

On the other hand, if the modern critique is taken to its extreme consequences, the answer to the question would be no. Leaving aside those versions of legal pluralism that can be assimilated to dualism as they rely on similar assumptions and reach similar results, the modern critique seems to lead to and even accepts the indeterminacy of the relationship between international and municipal law. Thus, the way in which states ensure domestic compliance with their international obligations would be largely unpredictable. The status of international law under municipal law would vary from one country to another and even from one court to another inside the same municipal system. Thus, the way in which domestic courts apply international law would be, in the end, exempt from scrutiny.

Therefore, we are confronted with two alternatives. We can surrender to at least a certain degree of 'chaos' (on the ground that this degree of chaos is necessary for adapting the legal system to a changing reality);[38] we can admit that states are in part at liberty to give domestic execution to international obligations and in part 'influenced' by international law in that regard (those parts being largely unknown);[39] and we can even accept that 'what we cannot speak about we must pass over in silence' since legal systems and substantive rules remain largely indeterminate.[40] Or we can agree that certain legal expectations deserve to be taken into account, and that, to a certain extent, the predictability and certainty of the law must be ensured, and that present-day international practice, confusing as it may often be, can indeed be explained according to some general positive account of the relationship between international and municipal law.

Going back to the key question concerning the possibility to evaluate the way in which domestic courts enforce international obligations, it is possible to argue – contrary to some of the modern discourse that I have

[38] Christine Chinkin, 'Monism and Dualism: The Impact of Private Authority on the Dichotomy between National and International Law' in Janne E. Nijman, Andre Nollkaemper (eds), *New Perspectives on the Divide between National and International Law* (Oxford University Press 2007) n. 8, 134–162 at 161.

[39] Nollkaemper, n. 20 at 301–304.

[40] See ns 34 and 35 and accompanying text.

already mentioned – that monism and dualism are in fact quite useful in answering that question and defining the relationship between legal orders.

5 The oscillations of international practice

Undeniably, the current practice of domestic courts is characterised by a certain degree of confusion. Domestic courts seem to use monist and dualist arguments interchangeably, either to accept or to deny domestic enforceability of international obligations. On the one hand, monist arguments have been invoked to avoid the domestic application of international obligations: in *Medellin*, the US Supreme Court held that ICJ decisions are not automatically enforceable in domestic courts, primarily because they are not directly enforceable *under international law*.[41] In particular, Article 94 of the UN Charter provides only for a political, diplomatic, non-judicial remedy.[42] As Article 94(2) includes a non-compliance option, direct enforceability of ICJ decisions is not dictated by international law.[43]

Less surprisingly, recourse to dualist arguments is made in order to achieve the same result: in *Kadi*, the European Court of Justice rejected the direct applicability of Security Council resolutions basically on the ground of the *separation* between international and EU law.[44] The reasoning of the Court started with a major assumption:

> [T]he lawfulness of any legislation adopted by the Community institutions, including an act intended to give effect to a resolution of the Security Council remains subject, by virtue of Community law, to full review by the Court, *regardless of its origin*.[45]

Accordingly, 'the review of lawfulness thus to be ensured by the Community judicature applies to the Community act intended to give effect to the international agreement at issue, and *not to the latter as such*'.[46] In any event:

[41] US Supreme Court, *Medellin v. Texas*, Judgment of 25 March 2008, 552 US 491 (2008).

[42] *Medellin v. Texas*, n. 41 at 509.

[43] *Medellin v. Texas*, n. 41 at 511.

[44] ECJ, *Yassin Abdullah Kadi and Al-Barakaat International Foundation v. Council of the European Union and Commission of the European Communities*, Joined Cases C-402/05 P and C-415/05 P, Judgment (Grand Chamber) of 3 September 2008, [2008] ECR I-6351.

[45] *Kadi*, n. 44 at para. 278 (emphasis added).

[46] *Kadi*, n. 44 at para. 286 (emphasis added).

> [A]ny judgment given by the Community judicature deciding that a Community measure intended to give effect to such a resolution is contrary to a higher rule of law in the Community legal order would *not* entail any challenge to the primacy of that resolution *in international law*.[47]

On the other hand, a monist line of reasoning has also been adopted in order to secure the domestic application of international obligations: in *Dorigo*, the Italian Corte di Cassazione examined the legal effects of the judgments rendered by the ECtHR and held that they can 'directly produce rights and obligations for the parties to the dispute that is both States and individuals'. In particular, the Italian Court considered that 'it is undeniable that the influence of the effects of the judgment of the Court is not restricted to the supranational sphere, but constitute rights and obligations which also operate within the domestic legal order'.[48] Accordingly, the Court recognised that the applicant was entitled to invoke, before domestic courts, the right to the review of his criminal proceedings established by the decision of the ECtHR even if that right puts into question the domestic principle of *res iudicata*.

At the same time, the 'openness' of the domestic legal order with regard to international law has been justified according to a traditional dualist line of reasoning: in *Görgülü*, the German Constitutional Court held:

> [T]he binding effect of [municipal] law also includes a duty to take into account the guarantees of the Convention and the decisions of the ECtHR as part of a methodologically justifiable interpretation of the law. Both a failure to consider a decision of the ECtHR and the 'enforcement' of such a decision in a mechanical way, in violation of prior-ranking law, may therefore violate fundamental rights in conjunction with the principle of the rule of law . . . The obligation created by the *enabling legislation* to take into account the guarantees of the ECHR and the decisions of the ECtHR at least demands that notice is taken of the relevant texts and case-law and that they are part of the process of developing an informed opinion of the court appointed to make a decision, of the competent authority or of the legislature.[49]

47 *Kadi*, n. 44 at para. 288 (emphasis added).

48 Italian Corte di Cassazione, '*Dorigo*', Decision No. 2800, Judgment of 25 January 2007, ILDC 1096 (IT 2007), reprinted in 90 *Rivista di diritto internazionale* (2007) 601–610 at 607 ('è innegabile che gli effetti della sentenza della Corte hanno una incidenza non limitata alla sfera sovranazionale, ma sono costitutivi di diritti e di obblighi operanti anche all'interno dell'ordinamento nazionale').

49 German Federal Constitutional Court, '*Görgülü*', 2 BvR 1481/04, BVerfGE 111, 307–322, Judgment of 14 October 2004, paras 47–48 (emphasis added) ('Zur Bindung an Gesetz und Recht gehört aber auch die Berücksichtigung der Gewährleistungen der

Despite appearances, a positivist account of the relationship between international and municipal law can shed light on the way in which municipal courts justify the application of international law at the national level. In this regard, I would propose two points. First, monism and dualism remain essential points of reference for domestic courts that need to identify a legal ground for their application of international law. Second, a positive account can explain why the most problematic cases are those in which it is uncertain whether a legal order has adopted either a monist or dualist approach.

6 Interactions between legal orders before domestic courts

When asked to apply or take international law into account, domestic courts can either accept or refuse. In any case, they have to provide reasons for their decision and identify legal grounds for applying international law or giving precedence to municipal law over international obligations. Case law shows that domestic courts feel the need to rely on a positivist approach, because they have to justify the fact that they apply a certain legal norm according to the legal order in which they operate. They have to justify both the validity and the rank of the legal norms they rely upon, and this in the end amounts to adopting a monist or dualist approach.

Among the most diverse forms that the interaction between legal orders can take, two examples can show the enduring importance of a positivist approach with regard to the relationship between international and municipal law, namely: the doctrines of direct effect and consistent interpretation. These two examples are particularly interesting because they are commonly cited as doctrines that challenge the traditional monist–dualist divide and point to a certain continuity between legal orders.

Europäischen Menschenrechtskonvention und der Entscheidungen des Gerichtshofs im Rahmen methodisch vertretbarer Gesetzesauslegung. Sowohl die fehlende Auseinandersetzung mit einer Entscheidung des Gerichtshofs als auch deren gegen vorrangiges Recht verstoßende schematische "Vollstreckung" können deshalb gegen Grundrechte in Verbindung mit dem Rechtsstaatsprinzip verstoßen . . . Die über das *Zustimmungsgesetz* ausgelöste Pflicht zur Berücksichtigung der Gewährleistungen der Europäischen Menschenrechtskonvention und der Entscheidungen des Gerichtshofs erfordert zumindest, dass die entsprechenden Texte und Judikate zur Kenntnis genommen werden und in den Willensbildungsprozess des zu einer Entscheidung berufenen Gerichts, der zuständigen Behörde oder des Gesetzgebers einfließen.')

6.1 Direct effect

When accepting or denying the direct effect of international norms, domestic courts ground the domestic enforceability of international law either on international law or on municipal law. Thus, private persons are able to invoke international law before domestic courts either because this is expressly provided for under international law, or because municipal law has incorporated the relevant international norm and the corresponding municipal norm creates rights or obligations that individuals are entitled to rely upon before domestic courts. It would not be possible here to give an exhaustive account of the case law of domestic courts in that regard; the following are just a few examples of a much broader phenomenon.

In 1828, the US Supreme Court looked at international law to find the legal justifications for considering that the decisions of an international commission should be regarded as directly enforceable in the domestic legal order. In particular, it held:

> The object of the treaty was to invest the commissioners with full power and authority to receive, examine, and decide upon the *amount* and *validity* of the asserted claims upon Spain for damages and injuries. Their decision, within the scope of this authority, is conclusive and final. If they pronounce the claim valid or invalid, if they ascertain the amount, their award in the premises is not reexaminable. The parties must abide by it as the decree of a competent tribunal of exclusive jurisdiction. A rejected claim cannot be brought again under review in any judicial tribunal; an amount once fixed is a final ascertainment of the damages or injury.[50]

A well-known example of a similar monist foundation for recognising the direct effect of treaty obligations is found in *Van Gend en Loos*. In 1963, the ECJ held that Article 12 of the EEC Treaty (i.e. a norm prohibiting new customs duties and increases of existing duties) was directly enforceable 'according to the spirit, the general scheme and the wording'[51] of the provisions of the Treaty itself, and consequently nationals of member states could, on the basis of Article 12, claim rights that the national courts had to protect.

More commonly, the legal foundation of direct effect of international norms has been grounded on the constitutional provisions of the legal

[50] US Supreme Court, *Comegys and Pettit v. Vasse*, Judgment of 7 March 1828, 26 US 193 (1828).

[51] ECJ, *NV Algemene Transport- en Expeditie Onderneming Van Gend & Loos v. Nederlandse Administratie der Belastingen*, C-26/62, Judgment of 5 February 1963, [1963] ECR 1 at 13.

order of the forum state. This is the attitude, for example, of a number of countries regarding the ECHR. In 2003, the Supreme Administrative Court of Bulgaria held that Article 6(1) of the ECHR was domestically enforceable because, under Article 5(4) of the Constitution, the ECHR was incorporated into domestic law and was accorded priority over conflicting domestic legislation.[52]

In 2004, the German Federal Constitutional Court justified the domestic recognition of the legal effects of the decisions of the ECtHR in the following terms:

> The law of international agreements applies on the domestic level only when it has been incorporated into the domestic legal system in the proper form and in conformity with substantive constitutional law... On this basis, the legal effect of the decisions of an international court that was brought into existence under an international agreement is determined according to the content of the incorporated international agreement and the relevant provisions of the Basic Law as to its applicability. If the Convention law of the ECHR, and with it the federal legislature on the basis of Article 59(2) of the Basic Law, has provided that the legal decisions are directly applicable, then they have this effect below the level of constitutional law.[53]

On similar grounds, in 1992, the Argentine Supreme Court of Justice accepted that Article 14(1) of the American Convention on Human Rights had direct effect.[54] First, the validity and supremacy of the relevant international obligation was grounded on the Argentine Constitution. Second, Article 14(1) was considered to be directly enforceable because it did not require implementing legislation.

The recognition of the direct effect of international rules in domestic legal orders has a very broad scope. It includes treaty and general

[52] Bulgarian Supreme Administrative Court, *Al-Nashif v. National Police Directorate at the Ministry of the Interior*, judicial review, No. 4332; ILDC 608 (BG 2003), Judgment of 8 May 2003, para. 11.

[53] 'Völkervertragsrecht gilt innerstaatlich nur dann, wenn es in die nationale Rechtsordnung formgerecht, und in Übereinstimmung mit materiellem Verfassungsrecht inkorporiert worden ist... Die Rechtswirkung der Entscheidungen eines völkervertraglich ins Leben gerufenen internationalen Gerichts bemisst sich auf dieser Grundlage nach dem Inhalt des inkorporierten völkerrechtlichen Vertrages und den entsprechenden Geltungsanordnungen des Grundgesetzes. Wenn das Konventionsrecht der Europäischen Menschenrechtskonvention und mit ihm der Bundesgesetzgeber auf der Grundlage von Art. 59 Abs. 2 GG eine unmittelbare Geltung der Rechtsentscheide angeordnet haben, so entfalten sie unterhalb des Verfassungsrechts diese Wirkung.' *Görgülü*, n. 49 at paras 36–37.

[54] Argentine Supreme Court, *Ekmekdjian v. Sofovich*, No. E 64 XXIII, Judgment of 7 July 1992.

international law rules, and ranges from commercial law to human rights law. Direct effect allows specific international rules to operate directly at the municipal level, where they can be relied upon to decide private claims. Therefore, it entails a remarkable interaction between international and national law.

The problematic aspect of direct effect is that it is generally unclear whether a norm has direct effect by virtue of international law itself (as the international obligation is intended to operate directly at the municipal level) or whether direct effect is freely determined at the domestic level according to purely internal parameters (such as the sufficiently precise character of the relevant provisions, the existence of domestic rights of action, or more generally the internal separation of powers).[55] In any case, what is relevant to the present discussion is the fact that domestic courts systematically have recourse to a monist or dualist foundation in order to justify the recognition of direct effect for certain international rules.

6.2 Consistent interpretation

A duty of consistent interpretation, according to which national law is to be construed in conformity with international law, has been widely recognised by domestic courts. This is a powerful instrument at the disposal of domestic courts to secure compliance with international obligations, since it is commonly used as a mechanism to prevent normative conflicts.[56] In most cases, consistent interpretation results in according priority to the international interpretation of a certain rule and hence in setting aside applicable domestic legislation or domestic precedents. This is a further reason why domestic courts feel the need to identify precise legal grounds for relying on the duty of consistent interpretation. Sometimes the legal justification for having recourse to consistent interpretation is found in a

[55] See, in general, Joe Verhoeven, 'La notion d' "applicabilité directe" du droit international' 15 *Revue belge de droit international* (1980) 243–264. For the need to distinguish between 'compulsory' direct effect under international law and direct effect 'freely' determined at the domestic level in the specific context of the EU legal order, see Beatrice I. Bonafé, 'Direct Effect of International Agreements in the EU Legal Order: Does It Depend on the Existence of an International Dispute Settlement Mechanism?' in Ramses Alexander Wessel, Enzo Cannizzaro, Paolo Palchetti (eds), *International Law as the Law of the European Union* (Martinus Nijhoff 2012) 229–248.

[56] This does not mean that consistent interpretation actually solves normative conflicts. It is a technique merely aimed at avoiding them. See in this respect Jörg Kammerhofer, *Uncertainty in International Law: A Kelsenian Perspective* (Routledge 2010) 174–175 and Jörg Kammerhofer, 'Systemic Integration, Legal Theory and the ILC' 19 *Finnish Yearbook of International Law 2008* (2010) 167–168.

general presumption, other times more detailed domestic provisions are invoked.[57] In any event, domestic courts in their case law regularly provide the justifications for relying on the duty of consistent interpretation.

In 2005, the Supreme Court of Canada held that certain domestic criminal provisions had to be interpreted in accordance with the relevant decisions of international criminal tribunals notwithstanding the fact that 'the decisions of the ICTY and the ICTR are not binding upon this Court' and that this implied the reconsideration of a precedent of the Supreme Court itself.[58] A number of arguments were put forward in order to substantiate the duty of consistent interpretation: these included, in particular, the authority of these tribunals in interpreting customary international law, the fact that the relevant provisions of the Criminal Code expressly incorporated customary international law, the fact that Canada is bound by the Genocide Convention, the fact that the principles underlying the Genocide Convention are recognised as part of customary international law, and the fact that the Supreme Court itself had already had the occasion to emphasise the importance of interpreting domestic law in a manner that accords with the principles of customary international law.

As mentioned above, in 2006 the German Federal Constitutional Court recognised that the duty of consistent interpretation also extended to decisions of the ICJ to which Germany was not a party. In order to justify such a broad understanding of the principle of consistent interpretation, the German Court relied on the general acceptance of the ICJ jurisdiction by Germany and on a general principle of 'openness' towards international law to be deduced from a number of provisions of the German Constitution.[59]

Exceptionally, certain constitutions explicitly provide for the duty of consistent interpretation. This is, for example, the case in Article 10(2) of the Spanish Constitution (1978). Other constitutional provisions are drafted in very broad terms, but have been interpreted as providing for such a duty. For example, in 2005, the Supreme Court

57 On the uncertain foundation of consistent interpretation, see Jean d'Aspremont, 'The Systemic Integration of International Law by Domestic Courts: Domestic Judges as Architects of the Consistency of the International Legal Order' in Ole Kristian Fauchald, André Nollkaemper (eds), *The Practice of International and National Courts and the (De-) Fragmentation of International Law* (Hart 2012) 144.

58 Canadian Supreme Court, *Mugesera v. Canada (Minister of Citizenship and Immigration)*, Judgment of 28 June 2005, [2005] 2 SCR 100, para. 126.

59 *WÜK*, n. 36 at para. 61.

of Argentina declared contrary to the constitution two amnesty laws enacted in Argentina at the end of the 1980s relying on previous decisions of the Inter-American Court and Commission on Human Rights in cases to which Argentina was not a party. The Supreme Court inferred a principle of consistent interpretation from Article 75(22) of the Argentine Constitution (1994) that gave constitutional rank to certain human rights treaties 'en las condiciones de su vigencia', that is, according to the Supreme Court, as interpreted by the relevant international monitoring bodies.[60]

Finally, there are even cases in which domestic courts have accorded a certain role to international obligations that are not binding on the state. In 1995, the Supreme Court of South Africa interpreted section 35(1) of the Constitution of 1996 – according to which certain provisions of the Constitution have to be interpreted in conformity with public international law – as referring both to non-binding as well as binding law.[61]

Undoubtedly, consistent interpretation represents a form of interaction between municipal law and international law. In contrast to direct effect, it does not lead to the application of specific international rules, but allows entire parts of the international legal order to operate at the domestic level and to shape the application of municipal law. Accordingly, consistent interpretation entails a particular form of interaction between international and municipal law.

The problematic aspect of consistent interpretation is the special nature of this mechanism of interaction between legal orders. Consistent interpretation does not consist in a *renvoi* to a specific international rule, but it implies the acceptance that the international legal order as such should permeate the application of municipal law. In certain areas of law in which there are clear international standards, the 'common' understanding of a rule should be preferred to a purely unilateral interpretation. In particular, when international courts and tribunals perform an

[60] Treaties referred to in Art. 75(22) of the Constitution 'deben ser aplicados en la Argentina tal como funcionan en el ordenamiento internacional incluyendo, en su caso, la jurisprudencia internacional relativa a esos tratados y las normas de derecho internacional consuetudinario reconocidas como complementarias por la práctica internacional pertinente' (Argentine Supreme Court, *Sentencia declarando la nulidad de las leyes de impunidad y ratificando condena por crímenes contra la humanidad*, Judgment of 14 June 2005, available at www.derechos.org).

[61] South African Constitutional Court, *State v. Makwanyane and Another*, Case CCT/3/94, Judgment of 6 June 1995.

interpretative function, consistent interpretation reveals the recognition that such competence should be accorded priority over domestic interpretation. Notwithstanding the difficulty of framing consistent interpretation in terms of a monist or dualist doctrine, the practice of domestic courts shows that the degree of openness to international law is regularly justified by reference to a positivist account of the relationship between international and municipal law.

7 Exclusivity and the 'internal' consistency problem

The judicial practice of domestic courts shows that when they have to take international rules into account – in the framework of either consistent interpretation or the recognition of direct effect – they systematically adopt a positivist approach. They feel the need to justify the inclusion of international rules in the legal system in which they operate, and to identify a legal ground for relying on international law. No matter if they adopt a monist rather than a dualist approach, the practice of domestic courts shows that, inevitably, each domestic legal order has to make a choice and identify the legal ground justifying the domestic application of international law. For example, in a dualist country, courts would be expected to apply international rules incorporated into municipal law. Thus, the certainty and predictability of the law are ensured by the uniform application of the chosen approach inside each legal order.

It is according to that choice (monism, dualism, maybe a third way) that it is possible to say whether or not the way in which states enforce international obligations in their domestic legal order is correct. The judgment can be formulated according to the 'internal' consistency of the decisions of domestic courts with regard to the specific approach adopted by their legal order. The positive account of the relationship between international and municipal law proves to be essential to evaluate the way in which international law is applied domestically. Indeed, the confusion of recent practice concerning the relationship between international and municipal law can be largely explained as a problem of 'internal' consistency. And the most problematic decisions are those in which there is no clear identification of legal grounds allowing for the domestic application of international law.

First, decisions of domestic courts in legal orders adopting a monist (or a dualist) approach can be misleading when they rely on arguments that can be criticised from the same monist (or dualist) perspective. For example, this partly explains the uncertainty entailed by the *Medellin* decision. One may well wonder whether it is correct, from a monist perspective, to conclude that domestic enforceability is to be denied to every international norm whose enforceability is not secured by a judicial remedy at the international level.[62] Not to mention the fact that, as a consequence, the vast majority of international norms will lack direct effect. Thus, in monist (or dualist) countries, it is possible to criticise the decisions of domestic courts that do not apply that approach properly.

Second, decisions of domestic courts in legal orders adopting a dualist (or a monist) approach can be problematic when they rely on monist (or dualist) arguments to decide a particular case. It is true that, generally speaking, the existence of supreme courts secures the internal consistency of each domestic legal order. For example, in Italy – a well-known dualist country – the Corte di Cassazione has widely relied on monist arguments in order to recognise the direct enforceability of decisions of the ECtHR notwithstanding the applicability of conflicting national legislation.[63] The reaction of the Italian Constitutional Court has been a strong reaffirmation of the dualist paradigm and the impossibility of setting aside domestic legislation or final domestic judgments in the absence of enabling legislation.[64] Therefore, once a choice is made on the approach determining the relationship between international and municipal law, domestic courts are expected to apply it consistently.

Finally, the described positivist account explains why a more radical type of uncertainty may arise from cases, decided by different courts belonging to the same legal order, which cast doubts on the general approach adopted by the legal order itself. The *Kadi* judgments of the Court of First Instance and the European Court of Justice provide a good example. Whereas the ECJ had traditionally adopted a monist approach in respect of the relationship between EU law and member states' legal orders, and whereas the CFI seemed to confirm the presumption that the same (monist) approach would be applicable to the (different) relationship between international and EU law,[65] most commentators considered that the ECJ changed course dramatically in that case and adopted a clear

[62] If international and municipal law belong to the same legal order, the domestic judge should ensure compliance with both municipal law and international obligations.

[63] E.g. *Dorigo*, n. 48.

[64] Italian Constitutional Court, Decision Nos 348/2007 and 349/2007, Judgment of 24 October 2007.

[65] CFI, *Yassin Abdullah Kadi v. Council of the European Union and Commission of the European Communities*, T-315/01, Judgment of 21 September 2005, [2005] ECR II-3649.

dualist approach.[66] In other words, the decision was problematic because it cast doubts on the internal consistency of the case law of the ECJ concerning the relationship between legal orders. What seems crucial is not that the ECJ adopted a different approach with regard to the relationship between EU law and member states' legal orders, on the one hand, and with regard to the relationship between international and EU law, on the other. In the end, nothing prevents a court from relying on different approaches with regard to different relationships between legal orders. The key issue is that the monist or dualist approach to the relationship between international and EU law should be relied upon consistently.

8 Reconciling exclusivity and interaction

The foregoing analysis shows that legal orders can interact. Certainly, interaction takes different forms and occurs in varying degrees. There are more traditional forms of interaction, such as direct effect, which can largely be explained in terms of a positivist account of the relationship between international and municipal law. A specific international rule is applied at the municipal level because it is conceived of either as an 'internal' rule (monism) or as an 'external' rule incorporated into municipal law. But there are also particular forms of interaction, such as consistent interpretation, in which a legal order accepts to take into account an 'external' legal order as such. This mixture of separation and openness is clearly more difficult to reconcile with either a monist or a dualist approach.

However, both forms of interaction are commonly justified in the practice of domestic courts through reliance on the traditional positivist doctrines of monism and dualism. The principle of exclusivity of legal orders is generally upheld, and the domestic application of international law is explained in terms of its being part of the 'internal' legal order or the fact that municipal law accepts the application of 'external' law.

It might be a pure fiction, but national judges need to know where to find the law,[67] and how to identify the different applicable law. They also need precise criteria to govern the application of international law,

[66] See in general Gráinne De Búrca, 'The European Court of Justice and the International Legal Order after Kadi', Jean Monnet Working Paper 01/09, esp. 2–3.

[67] Mireille Delmas-Marty, *Towards a Truly Common Law: Europe as a Laboratory for Legal Pluralism* (Cambridge University Press 2002) 7.

in particular where applying international rules entails the setting aside of municipal law.

But the exclusivity principle is not only essential to provide a solid ground for the validity of domestic courts' decisions. It is also indispensable to define the legal systems whose relationship is the object of the present enquiry. In the absence of a positivist approach, the legal orders that are supposed to interact would simply be unidentifiable. There would be no difference between 'internal' and 'external' normativity. Practice shows that each legal order decides whether, or at least to what extent, it interacts with 'external' forms of normativity. In other words, interactions between legal orders are possible first of all because 'external' normativity is recognised and accepted.

15

Transnational governance regimes

DENNIS PATTERSON*

1 Introduction

This chapter takes up 'post-modern positivism' in the context of transnational law. The basic theme I shall develop is that transnational legal phenomena pose a strong challenge to post-modern positivism in that these phenomena problematise the notion of 'validity' that is central to positivism and post-modern positivism. I begin by explicating the notion of 'positivism'. Here I sketch the basic features of the two leading positivist accounts of law, those of HLA Hart and Hans Kelsen. As I explain, despite the differences in their views, both Hart and Kelsen advance the same 'model' of a legal order, that is, one that is built from the bottom up. For each, the 'bottom' represents a norm that provides the foundation for a legal order.

For Kelsen, the Basic Norm (*Grundnorm*) provides the criteria for legal validity. For Hart, validity is a function of the Rule of Recognition. The Rule of Recognition (Hart) or the *Grundnorm* (Kelsen) provides the tools necessary to identify legal norms as such. Transnational legal phenomena pose a challenge to this picture insofar as transnational legal phenomena arguably cannot be explained or accounted for within this conception of a legal order.

Before taking up the question of the status of transnational legal phenomena, I detail Kelsen's and Hart's respective views on the nature of international law as 'law'. Transnational law arises against the background of the traditional contrast between municipal and international law. To make that discussion more salient, it is necessary, or at least helpful, to provide detail on Hart's and Kelsen's views on the status of international law.[1]

* I thank my research assistant, Anna Södersten, for her assistance with this chapter.

[1] Some might view an explication of the 'basics' of Kelsen and Hart on international law as an unnecessary exercise in pedantry. I run the risk of this criticism because I believe that there is widespread disagreement and misunderstanding of the central views of both of

With regard to transnational legal phenomena, two questions may be asked. The first is 'causal' in that it asks the question of 'how' or 'why' transnational legal phenomena are making their appearance. While there are surely several reasons why this might be so, the causal explanation is a prelude to the main discussion, which is the question of whether transnational legal phenomena are genuinely new phenomena or simply variants of existing forms of legality. To answer this question, I adduce three examples of transnational legal phenomena. With regard to each, the question is the same: do these phenomena fall outside the positivist or post-modern positivist account of a legal order?

To answer the question of the status of transnational legal phenomena, I turn to the work of Jean d'Aspremont. As a post-modern positivist, d'Aspremont argues that transnational phenomena do not pose a genuine threat to the positivist account of law. D'Aspremont makes a strong case for the proposition that positivism's tools of 'law recognition' can accommodate transnational legal phenomena. I raise some questions in this regard and indicate what issues remain on the table.

2 'Positivism'

Although there are some basic features upon which most scholars converge in their judgments about the fundamentals of positivism, prudence dictates that one's conception of this central notion be given at least some depth and detail. One reason for this is that there are different constituencies for competing conceptions of 'positivism'. I shall mention two. The first is general jurisprudence, specifically analytic jurisprudence. The legacy of HLA Hart has devolved into an intramural dispute between two conceptions of how to carry on the positivist project. Whether inclusive or exclusive positivism[2] wins the day in the forum of analytic jurisprudence, the victory will be narrow in scope. In the international law context, 'positivism' denotes an approach to the art of interpretation, that is, deciding what the law is. While positivism has a long and distinguished history in the international law context, it is today largely a matter of conventional doctrinal practice.

The two most important historical figures in the development of positivist legal theory are Hans Kelsen and HLA Hart. I want to talk about

these seminal jurisprudes. Thus, I want to get my views on the table, as it were, so that there is no misunderstanding about my point of departure.

2 Inclusive positivists (e.g. Jules Coleman) argue that morality can be part of law and exclusive positivists (e.g. Joseph Raz) reject this claim.

transnational legal phenomena from the point of view of two of their central ideas, those being the *Grundnorm* (Kelsen)[3] and the Rule of Recognition (Hart).[4] Each of these notions was developed to solve the same problem, that of the validity of law. For a norm to be a valid norm of a legal system or legal order, it must derive its validity from another norm. Legal orders are comprised of hierarchies of norms, all of which are grounded in a basic norm. As mentioned, for Hart this basic norm is identified as the Rule of Recognition, the most important of what Hart termed 'secondary rules'. By contrast, Kelsen's *Grundnorm* is 'hypothetical' in nature in that its existence is presupposed in order to provide the needed basic norm from which unity arises.

Simply from the point of view of 'form', there is little substantive difference between Kelsen's[5] and Hart's approaches to the ultimate ground of a legal order. The difference between the *Grundnorm* and the Rule of Recognition is largely metaphysical. Kelsen's *Grundnorm* is a neo-Kantian, transcendental product. By contrast, Hart's Rule of Recognition is a sociological phenomenon: it exists as a social practice among officials. Apart from these differences, there is a great deal of overlap between the two theorists' accounts of the structure of a legal system.

What is the function of the Rule of Recognition[6] in a legal order? Hart saw the Rule of Recognition as providing criteria of legality. A rule is a valid legal norm if it passes all of the tests of validity found in the Rule of Recognition. Importantly, the validity tests – the criteria of legality – are grounded solely in an inter-subjective practice of officials. Nothing grounds the Rule of Recognition in the same way as do other legal rules. As a social practice, the Rule of Recognition provides the 'grounds' of law, but is itself neither valid nor invalid.[7] Its validity is a matter of ongoing practice among officials. The only 'ground' of the Rule of Recognition is the inter-subjective agreement among officials on the criteria of legality.

[3] Hans Kelsen, *Pure Theory of Law* (Max Knight (tr.), University of California Press 1967).

[4] HLA Hart, *The Concept of Law* (Clarendon Press 1961).

[5] Kaarlo Tuori nicely summarises the Kelsenian perspective thus: 'Kelsen's hierarchical legal order, *Stufenbau*, is, above all, the legal order of a nation state: the basic norm crowning the hierarchy commands obedience to the (historically first) constitution of the nation state, while the norms on the lower echelons are issued by state organs empowered by this constitution.' Kaarlo Tuori, 'Towards a Theory of Transnational Law' (unpublished paper, 26 August 2010). For a different approach to Kelsen, see Kammerhofer, Chapter 4.

[6] From this point forward, I shall refer only to the Rule of Recognition and not to Kelsen's *Grundnorm*. Of course, there are differences between the two notions. But for my purpose, which is a discussion of the ultimate validity of a legal system, the differences are not important.

[7] See d'Aspremont, Chapter 5 at 121–123.

Whether expressed in Kelsenian or Hartian terms, the notion of a Rule of Recognition is not without its critics. Dworkinians, for example, dispute the very existence of a Rule of Recognition. In other words, they think it is sociologically or factually incorrect to claim that there is a Rule of Recognition. The Dworkinian thesis of 'theoretical disagreement' is an attempt to put the lie to the idea that judges do, in fact, agree on criteria of legality.[8] As evidence of this fact, one need look no further than disputes among judges. If there is a Rule of Recognition, Dworkinians ask, what are judges fighting about when they dismiss one another's claims about the grounds of law?

One need not be a Dworkinian to have doubts about the explanatory power of the Rule of Recognition. Of course, it is entirely plausible that judges can both share criteria of validity and sometimes dispute whether or not those criteria have been satisfied. In other words, dispute is not always evidence of the lack of agreement. In the view of some, agreement is a necessary presupposition of healthy dispute.[9] But what if a disagreement is so basic that it might be the case that a Rule of Recognition is not even shared by disputants? Can there be multiple Rules of Recognition? If there are, what does this do to the idea of legal validity?

I want to suggest that the context of transnational law may be a place where a new challenge to the explanatory power of the Rule of Recognition could be seen to arise. To set the stage for making this point, I will address three questions regarding transnational legal phenomena. First, what are transnational legal phenomena? Second, what are the jurisprudential problems posed by transnational legal phenomena? Finally, what happens to the core positivist idea of a *Grundnorm* or Rule of Recognition in the context of transnational law?

For Hart, Kelsen and their jurisprudential contemporaries, cross-border law was largely international law. The sovereign state controlled the domestic municipal sphere, while the state, by virtue of its sovereignty, created treaty relations with other sovereign states. The form of bilateral joinder is the treaty which, as critics of international law never tire of pointing out, can only sometimes be enforced against an uncooperative sovereign. As the conventional wisdom dictates, sovereignty – specifically state sovereignty – lies at the bottom of both the domestic (i.e. municipal) and the international legal order.

[8] Ronald Dworkin, *Law's Empire* (Harvard University Press 1986).

[9] I develop this point in Dennis Patterson, 'Interpretation in Law' 42 *University of San Diego Law Review* (2005) 685–709.

Before discussing transnational law, I shall spell out the contrasting views of Kelsen and Hart on the status of international law as 'law'. This will provide the necessary background for assessment of the impact of transnational legal phenomena on the concept of law, specifically the question of whether the positivist accounts of Kelsen and Hart can accommodate transnational legal phenomena.

3 Kelsen and Hart on 'international law'

For Kelsen, the requisite of a legal order is that it is a 'coercive order',[10] i.e. 'a set of norms regulating human behaviour by attaching certain coercive acts (sanctions) as consequences to certain facts, as delicts, determined by this order as conditions'.[11] The possibility of sanctions is thus the requisite of a coercive order.[12] In Kelsen's view, such sanctions are available in international law. He identifies them as reprisals and war. These sanctions allow international law to qualify as a legal order, and international law is thus 'law' in the same sense as national law.

Why are reprisals and war sanctions? Kelsen explains that a state, which considers its interests violated by another state, is authorised to resort to reprisals or war. They take place against the will of the state that has violated the other state's interests. Under normal circumstances, reprisals and war are prohibited under international law: they are only permissible as reactions against violations of international norms. If they are not such reactions, they are themselves international delicts. This is the principle of *bellum iustum*, or 'just war'. Kelsen finds this assumption well founded, as this doctrine is enshrined in the UN Charter, which is accepted by most states.[13] In Kelsen's view, reprisals and war are thus the appropriate sanctions for violations of international norms. Kelsen explains that the sanctions in international law are no different in content

[10] Kelsen, n. 3 at 30–58. For discussion, see Jörg Kammerhofer, 'Kelsen – Which Kelsen? A Reapplication of the Pure Theory to International Law' 22 *LJIL* (2009) 225–249 at 227–233, 236–240, 244–245. See generally Jörg Kammerhofer, 'Robert Walter, die Normkonflikte und der zweite Stufenbau des Rechts' in Clemens Jabloner *et al.* (eds), *Gedenkschrift Robert Walter* (Manz 2013) 237–256 at 244–248.

[11] Kelsen, n. 3 at 320.

[12] In Kelsen's view, international law regulates the behaviour of human beings even where it regulates the behaviour of states. Kelsen, n. 3 at 320–347.

[13] Kelsen, n. 3 at 322. Kelsen explains that the difference between reprisal and war is one of degree.

from sanctions of national law.[14] In that sense, international law shows the same characteristics as national law.

However, for Kelsen, international law is a primitive legal order.[15] He explains that international law is 'in a state of decentralization', which is 'only at the beginning of a development which national law has already completed'.[16] International law is a primitive legal order because it does not have special organs for the creation and application of its norms. The norms are created by the members of the legal community themselves, and not by a legislative organ. When it comes to the application of norms, it is the state itself that has to decide whether the fact of a delict exists, and there exists no authority to decide the conflict: '[t]he technique of self-help, characteristic of primitive law, prevails'.[17] But Kelsen foresees an evolution of international law from this primitive condition. The development is directed towards 'centralisation', and the ultimate goal is 'the emergence of a world state'.

Despite these shortcomings, even a decentralised order is a legal order in Kelsen's view. Unlike Austin's view, the lack of specialised organs for implementing the law – the lack of a sovereign above the state – does not preclude the conception of international law as a legal order. For Kelsen, the central element is the existence of rules regarding the exercise of force, codified as the *bellum iustum* doctrine. Therefore, according to Kelsen, rejecting the *bellum iustum* doctrine is equivalent to denying the very legal nature of international law.

Having defined the nature of international law, Kelsen then explicates the relationship between international law and national (municipal) law. In Kelsen's general theory of law, he sees a legal order as a system with hierarchically organised norms. In this hierarchical system, lower-order norms derive their validity from higher-order norms, until the *Grundnorm* is reached. Kelsen advocates a monistic approach, that is, he sees international law and national law as a unity. This means that international law and national law are subject to the same basic norm, which must be found either in international law or in the national legal order.[18]

[14] 'These sanctions, like the sanctions of national law consist in the forcible deprivation of life, liberty, and other goods, notably economic values. In a war, human beings are killed maimed, imprisoned, and national or private property is destroyed; by way of reprisals national or private property is confiscated and other legal rights are infringed. These sanctions of international law are not different in content from those of national law. But they are "directed against the state" as the saying goes.' Kelsen, n. 3 at 322.

[15] Kelsen, n. 3 at 323. [16] Kelsen, n. 3 at 323. [17] Kelsen, n. 3 at 323.

[18] For Kelsen, this monistic construction is 'inevitable'. He says that 'international law must be conceived either as a legal order delegated by, and therefore included in, the national

Kelsen rejects a dualistic construction where international law is regarded as a system of binding norms, valid but standing beside national law norms. According to Kelsen, the dualistic construction fails in explaining how the norms of international law obligate individuals.[19]

In establishing his monistic construction, Kelsen first addresses the question of whether there can be an irresolvable conflict between the international legal order and the national legal order.[20] If such conflicts exist, only a dualistic or pluralistic construction would be possible, and a monistic approach would then be excluded. Kelsen explains that insofar as international law is regarded as a system of valid norms (independent of each other in their validity), 'the relations could be interpreted only either from the viewpoint of the national legal order or from that of the international legal order'.[21]

For Kelsen, national legal norms cannot be in contradiction with international norms. Such conflicts do not exist. Kelsen writes: '[t]he situation is exactly analogous to a situation within the state's legal order, without, on that account, causing any doubts as to its unity'.[22] He explains that a statutory norm in contradiction with the constitution remains valid because the legal order may not provide a special procedure to abolish it. In the same vein, a norm of the national order in contradiction with international law remains valid, because international law provides no procedure in which the norm can be abolished. Kelsen points out that the creation of norms with 'opposite content' may activate the condition to which international law attaches its sanctions (reprisals or war).

Kelsen presents two different approaches to his monistic construction. In establishing the unity of international law and national law, one can start either from international law or national law as a valid legal order. He explains:

> International law must be conceived either as a legal order delegated by, and therefore included in, the national legal order; or as a total legal order comprising all legal orders as partial legal orders, and superior to all of them.[23]

legal order; or as a total legal order comprising all national legal orders as partial orders, and superior to all of them' Kelsen, n. 3 at 333.

19 Kelsen, n. 3 at 325 (individuals are obligated under international law 'indirectly' through the national legal order).

20 Kelsen, n. 3 at 329.

21 'The view that national and international law are two different legal orders, independent from each other in their validity, is usually justified by the existence of insoluble conflicts between them.' Kelsen, n. 3 at 330.

22 Kelsen, n. 3 at 330. 23 Kelsen, n. 3 at 333.

If one starts from the validity of a national legal order, the reason for the validity of international law is found in the national legal order. According to this view, general international law is valid for a state only if it is recognised by an individual state as binding.[24] International law is then regarded as part of national law, or as a legal order delegated by the national legal order. The representatives of this approach start from the validity of their own national order, which they consider self-evident.

Kelsen is equally open to taking international law as the starting point for validity, thus placing it at the apex of the pyramid in Kelsen's hierarchical system. From this point of view, the international legal system is characterised as a universal legal order. The international legal system is the 'total system', which encompasses all national legal orders, which are merely 'partial legal orders'. The state is an order delegated by international law in its validity. Kelsen rejects the objection that historically the states preceded the creation of general international law and that the individual state therefore cannot be conceived as an order delegated by international law. He argues that historical and normative-logical relations should not be confounded.[25]

In Kelsen's monistic construction, the content in international law is the same whether the validity of national law or international law takes precedence. The function of international law is thus the same: through the principle of effectiveness, it determines the reason and sphere of validity of national legal orders. The difference between the two is only the reason for the validity for international law.

The concept of sovereignty is the heart of Kelsen's monistic construction. Kelsen explains state sovereignty as the decisive factor for assuming the primacy of the national legal order. He writes:

> For a state to be 'sovereign' merely means that the establishment of the historically first constitution is presupposed as a law-creating fact without a positive norm of international law taken into account which institutes this fact as a law-creating fact.[26]

In his view, sovereignty is a presupposition of a normative order as the highest order whose validity is not derivable from any other higher order. But the idea of international law as a 'universal legal order' is incompatible with this idea of state sovereignty. If one takes international law as the

[24] The recognition can be express recognition (by an act of the legislature or of the government) or by tacit recognition (by application of the norms, e.g. by the conclusion of treaties).

[25] Kelsen, n. 3 at 339.

[26] Kelsen, n. 3 at 335.

starting point, the concept of sovereignty has to be a different one. Kelsen explains: '[o]nly the international legal order, not the national legal order, is sovereign',[27] and if states are denominated 'sovereign', this means only that they are subject to the international legal order. The concept of 'state' cannot be defined without reference to international law.

From a logical point of view, Kelsen sees these two systems, these two different monistic constructions, as 'equally correct and equally justified'. He explains: '[i]t is impossible to decide between them on the basis of the science of law'. Kelsen claims that the decision can only be made on non-scientific, political considerations. He writes:

> He who treasures the idea of sovereignty of his state... will prefer the primacy of the national legal order. He who values the idea of legal organization of the world, will prefer the primacy of international law.[28]

Turning now to Hart, he develops his approach to international law in the final chapter of *The Concept of Law*.[29] In Hart's view, international law is 'law', but it lacks the main characteristics of a legal system (i.e. secondary rules): Rules of Recognition, change and adjudication. Without these characteristics, international law is not a legal system, merely a set of primary rules. He comes to this conclusion by comparing international law and municipal law, finding that they are analogous in content and function, but different in form.

Hart identifies the two main objections (or 'sources of doubt') as to why international law is not regarded as law. Both of these objections start from municipal law as the standard example of what 'law' is. The first objection is that international law is not binding because it lacks sanctions. As Hart points out, the question 'is international law binding?' expresses a doubt about the general legal status of international law. It is

[27] Kelsen, n. 3 at 338.

[28] Kelsen, n. 3 at 346. Kelsen stresses that the theory of the primacy of national law is no less favourable to the idea of a legal organisation of the world than the theory of the primacy of international law. But it seems to supply the justification for a policy that rejects far-reaching restrictions of the state's freedom of action. He explains that this justification is based on a fallacy caused by the ambiguity of the concept of sovereignty as either highest legal authority or unlimited freedom of action. He writes, 'this fallacy has to be accepted as an essential element of the political ideology of imperialism, which operates with the dogma of state sovereignty'. And likewise, the theory of the primacy of international law seems to justify more a far-reaching 'limitation of a state's freedom of action than the primacy of the national legal order'. This justification is based on a fallacy, which 'plays a decisive part in the political ideology of pacifism' (Kelsen, n. 3 at 346–347).

[29] Hart, n. 4 at 208–231.

not a doubt about its applicability. The second objection is the claim that states are fundamentally incapable of being subject to legal obligations. States cannot both be sovereign and at the same time have obligations under international law. Hart repudiates both of these objections.

Hart first addresses the objection that international law cannot be law because it lacks sanctions. He points out that Chapter VII of the UN Charter cannot remedy this objection. As Hart sees it, those international sanctions cannot be equated with the sanctions of municipal law, because they are largely inefficient. Whenever their use is of importance, the law-enforcement provisions of the UN Charter are likely to be paralysed by a veto in the Security Council. Thus, for Hart, international law lacks 'real' sanctions. But he rejects the notion that this absence disqualifies international law from being law. Hart explains that the view that international law is not law because it lacks sanctions tacitly accepts the conception of law as a matter of orders backed by threats. This is Austin's command theory, which Hart repudiates in his general theory of law. As Hart shows, the command theory is untenable even in municipal law, so this theory cannot possibly disqualify international law from being law.

Hart also provides an additional argument in the same context. While the existence of sanctions might be a necessary condition in municipal law, sanctions might play a different role in international law. He writes: '[i]n societies of individuals, approximately equal in strength and vulnerability, physical sanctions are both necessary and possible'.[30] In municipal law, sanctions may be used successfully with small risk, and the threat of them would add much to the natural deterrent. But the situation is different in the international context. Hart claims that the organisation of international sanctions involves risks, and the threat of them adds little to natural deterrence. The use of violence on the international level is public, which means that there is a risk that third parties will get involved: '[t]o initiate a war is, even for the strongest power, to risk much for an outcome which is rarely predictable with reasonable confidence'.[31] On the international level, there is an unequal distribution of power and strength among states, and sanctions do not guarantee that powerful states obey the rules. Hart argues that although sanctions might have different functions in international law than in municipal law, this is not a reason for depriving international law of its character as law.

The second objection Hart considers is that states are incapable of being subjects of legal obligation, i.e. states cannot both be sovereign

[30] Hart, n. 4 at 213. [31] Hart, n. 4 at 214.

and at the same time have obligations under international law. Hart sees this as a 'radical inconsistency'. He repudiates the assumption that sovereignty would mean being above the law, a notion associated with voluntarist theories or theories of auto-limitation. These theories claim that international obligations arise from the consent of the party bound. Hart argues that auto-limitation theories fail to explain not only how it is known that states can be bound by self-imposed obligations, but also why their absolutist view of sovereignty should be accepted. Hart further argues that not all international obligations are self-imposed. He provides two examples showing that the voluntarist doctrine cannot be correct. The first example is the case of a new state. A new state is bound by the general obligations of international law, including the rules that give binding force to treaties. The second example is the case of a state acquiring territory or undergoing some other change. He writes: this 'brings with it . . . the incidence of obligations under rules which previously it had no opportunity to observe or break, and . . . no occasion to give or withhold consent'.[32]

For Hart, sovereignty means independence. He shows that there are many possible forms and degrees of dependence and independence.[33] For Hart, it is instead the international rules that define the scope of sovereignty: 'we can only know which states are sovereign, and what the extent of their sovereignty is, when we know what the rules are'.[34]

After having answered two objections to the statute of international law as law, Hart turns to the claim that international law is best understood as morality. This insistence, he argues, is sometimes inspired by the dogmatism that any form of social structure that is not reducible to orders backed by threats can only be a form of 'morality'. Hart offers some reasons why this is untenable. First, states often reproach one another for immoral conduct or praise themselves or others for living up to a standard of international morality. Hart points out that such appraisals are recognisably different from legal assessments under the rules of international law. When states address one another over disputed matters of international law, they refer to precedents, treaties and juristic writings, but often no mention is made of morality. Thus, states differentiate between moral and legal assessments.

[32] Hart, n. 4 at 221.

[33] 'Dependence of one territorial unit on another . . . is not . . . the only form in which its independence may be limited.' Hart, n. 4 at 217.

[34] Hart, n. 4 at 218.

The second reason why international law cannot be reduced to morality is that the rules of international law (like rules of municipal law) are morally indifferent. Hart explains that unlike morality, legal rules contain much specific detail, and draw arbitrary distinctions. He writes: 'Regard for forms and detail carried to excess, has earned for law the reproaches of "formalism" and "legalism".'[35] Hart explains that some rules exist only because it is convenient to have some clear fixed rule about the subjects with which it is concerned, but not because any moral importance is attached to the particular rule.

The third reason is that, unlike morality, the rules of international law are subject to deliberate change. Morality is conceived as the ultimate standards by which human actions are evaluated. The notion of a legislature making moral rules is therefore absurd. Hart contrasts this with the situation in international law, where the lack of a legislature is just a defect that might one day be repaired. Hart finally points out that there can be many reasons why states obey international obligations, and moral obligations may be one of them. But it is not a necessary feature of international law.

In the final part of his chapter on international law, Hart explains why international law is not a 'legal system'. The absence of an international legislature, courts with compulsory jurisdiction and centrally organised sanctions make international law resemble a simple form of social structure. In Hart's view, international law resembles a simple regime of primary rules in form, but not in content. International law resembles a municipal system, but only in function and content, not in form.

Hart explains that in minimising the formal differences between international law and municipal law, some theorists have exaggerated the analogies. The fact that the parties generally follow judgments of the International Court of Justice could not compensate for the lack of a compulsory and comprehensive jurisdiction of any international court. He also considers analogies between the use of force, as a sanction in municipal law, and the 'decentralised sanctions' in international law (for example, for Kelsen, the sanctions of international law are war and reprisal). Hart reminds us that there is no international court with a jurisdiction similar to courts in municipal law, and that the law enforcement provisions under the UN Charter have been paralysed by veto.

Hart then considers Kelsen's insistence that international law must contain a basic norm, which represents the ground of the validity of all

[35] Hart, n. 4 at 224.

norms, and which constitutes the unity in the international legal system. According to Hart, the opposite view is that international law merely consists of a set of primary rules of obligations. Hart reminds us that there have only been fruitless attempts to formulate a unifying basic norm in international law. Thus, the suggestion that the basic norm could be the principle *pacta sunt servanda* is 'incompatible with the fact that not all obligations under international law arise from "*pacta*"'.[36] Equally untenable is the rule that 'states should behave as they customarily behave'. Hart sees this as a 'useless reduplication'[37] of the fact that the international society observes certain standards of conduct as obligatory rules.

In Hart's view, there is no Rule of Recognition in international law. Since there is no Rule of Recognition, international law cannot be a legal system. It is instead a 'set' of rules. But a Rule of Recognition is not a necessity for international rules to be binding.[38] The existence of international rules depends instead on whether they are accepted. International law is thus a set of social rules. In his view, no other social rules are so close to municipal law as those of international law.

Hart argues that the differences between international law and municipal law might eventually be overcome. International law might be in a stage of transition, which would bring it nearer in structure to a municipal system. This would be the case if it were generally recognised that multilateral treaties could bind states that are not parties. Such treaties would be legislative enactments. A Rule of Recognition could then be formulated in international law, and international law would then resemble municipal law not only in content and function, but also in form.

4 Transnational legal phenomena

Against the background of the two most important positivist accounts of international law, we come to the phenomenon of 'transnational law'. Globalisation (or denationalisation)[39] has produced transnational legal phenomena that challenge the boundaries of traditional legal theory such as positivism. In *Legality's Borders*, Keith Culver and Michael Giudice identify four novel forms of legal order that challenge the conventional

[36] Hart, n. 4 at 228. [37] Hart, n. 4 at 230.

[38] Hart writes: 'It is . . . a mistake to suppose that a basic rule or a rule of recognition is a generally necessary condition of the existence of rules of obligations or "binding" rules. This is not a necessity, but a luxury, found in advanced social systems.' Hart, n. 4 at 229.

[39] Saskia Sassen, 'Globalization or Denationalization?' 10 *Review of International Political Economy* (2003) 1–33.

'law-state'[40] understanding of a legal order. They are: intra-state legality (for example, distributed or shared governance); trans-state legality (i.e. legality produced by non-state agents that is somehow 'binding' upon the law-state); supra-state legality (for example, the European Union) and super-state legality (for example, *ius cogens*).[41] Each form of legal order presents its own explanatory challenges to the traditional law-state conception of a legal order. As mentioned at the outset, I shall discuss just one of these, that of trans-state or transnational law.

The concept of transnational law starts with Philip Jessup who, in 1956, described it as 'all law which regulates actions or events that transcend national frontiers. Both public and private international law are included, as are other rules which do not wholly fit into such standard categories'.[42] Transnational legal challenges are now often referred to as issues of 'global governance', which, according to Peer Zumbansen, exhibit 'frustration with and problematisation of the absence of stable institutions of norm-creation and enforcement outside of the nation state'.[43] 'Global governance' identifies a need, that is, a need for regulation. The mode of regulation under law is norms. Even assuming stable institutions, norm-creation outside the nation-state poses a problem of 'validity' or 'legitimacy'. By what authority are norms created by non-state actors? In virtue of what are those norms valid? Can those norms be challenged, altered or extinguished, and by whom? These are just a few of the challenges posed by normativity outside the bounds of the nation-state.

4.1 Causal and normative questions

There are two different types of questions one might ask about transnational legal phenomena. These questions usually appear in the form of

[40] According to Giudice and Culver, the theories of Hart and Raz are good examples of theories of the 'law-state'. The nation-state is the source of law, the state is jurisdictionally limited, and nothing can be 'law' that is not produced or at least sanctioned by the state. '[S]tate law exists where there are primary rules of obligation and secondary rules of recognition, change and adjudication which in combination and in the hands of central law-applying officials claim with a certain degree of success to govern comprehensively, supremely and openly.' Keith C. Culver, Michael Giudice, *Legality's Borders: An Essay in General Jurisprudence* (Oxford University Press 2010) xxiv.

[41] Giudice and Culver, n. 40 at xi.

[42] Philip C. Jessup, *Transnational Law* (Yale University Press 1956) 2.

[43] Peer Zumbansen, 'Transnational Legal Pluralism' 10 *Transnational Legal Theory* (2010) 141–189 at 142.

two different types of explanation. I have in mind the distinction between causal and normative explanation. I shall explain each of these.

Causal explanation answers a 'why' question, for example why have private legal orders appeared now?[44] Consider Lisa Bernstein's work on private legal orders:[45] why have the merchants she describes opted out of the legal system and promulgated and functioned with their own set of norms? What explains this? Why has this development occurred?

All of these questions seek a causal explanation: we want to know the forces behind the appearance of this phenomenon. No position need be taken on the merits of a phenomenon. All that is asked is some explanation of 'Why this, why now?' There can be several explanations for the appearance of a private order. Dissatisfaction with some aspect of the state system is the most obvious explanation. Whether it be time delays, costs or lack of expertise on the part of the regulator (for example, an administrative agency), a causal explanation seeks to identify why some development has come to pass.

Causal explanations can serve as background to legal discussions, but lawyers are interested in normative or conceptual questions. Typical jurisprudential questions include border disputes between law and morality and the grounds of legal validity. In the transnational sphere, our interest lies in the 'ontology' of norms. We want to know whether transnational legal phenomena are of a different kind or order than what we normally find in the municipal sphere. If these phenomena are different, by virtue of what are they different? These may sound like empirical questions, but they are not. The reason for this is that the answers are driven by concepts of law, concepts that are largely normative in character.

4.2 Transnational law: examples

I now turn to three examples of transnational law. With each example, I endeavour to sustain the claim that normativity arises outside a municipal legal order only to reach inside that legal order with an effect no less efficacious than domestic legal norms. Obviously, my claim is both empirical

[44] E.g. Robert C. Ellickson, *Order without Law: How Neighbors Settle Disputes* (Harvard University Press 1991) 126–132; Eric A. Posner, *Law and Social Norms* (Harvard University Press 2000); Barak D. Richman, 'Firms, Courts, and Reputation Mechanisms: Towards a Positive Theory of Private Ordering' 104 *Columbia Law Review* (2004) 2328–2367 at 2338–2348.

[45] E.g. Lisa Bernstein, 'Opting Out of the Legal System: Extralegal Contractual Relations in the Diamond Industry' 21 *Journal of Legal Studies* (1992) 115–157.

and conceptual. The empirical dimension is a matter of adducing facts in support of my contention that these phenomena now exist. The conceptual claim is the more difficult one to sustain, that is, my contention that these phenomena cannot be accounted for by positivist or post-modern positivist models of law.

My first example is the North American Free Trade Agreement 1994 (NAFTA). Under NAFTA, a 'foreign' (vis-à-vis domestic court) tribunal may pass judgment on the degree to which domestic courts (for example, US courts) have provided 'fair process'. The NAFTA treaty does not permit NAFTA tribunals to overturn or alter domestic judgments. However, the treaty does enable the tribunals to impose financial sanctions against the federal governments of domestic states.

Thus, in the *Loewen* case,[46] a Mississippi State Supreme Court decision was found to violate due process norms. As mentioned, the tribunal enjoys only the power of financial sanction (against the federal government, not the state of Mississippi). Is this decision part of the law of Mississippi? Will it serve as a precedent? If it does serve as a precedent, under what account of precedent would such a decision be made part of Mississippi law? I submit that there are no easy answers to these questions.

I now turn to EU law, in which there is an important distinction between so-called primary and secondary law. The EU treaties, which are adopted by the Member States, constitute primary law.[47] In contrast, secondary law, for example, directives and regulations, are derived from the EU Treaties, and adopted by the EU institutions.[48] While primary law can be labelled 'acts of the Member States', secondary law can be described as 'Union acts'.[49] It is sometimes argued that the ability to adopt secondary norms, which are binding and directly applicable, is a feature that distinguishes the European Union from international organisations.[50] Indeed,

46 ICSID, *Loewen Group, Inc. and Raymond L. Loewen v. United States of America*, ARB(AF)/98/3, Award of 26 June 2003, para. 137.

47 In addition to the EU Treaties, primary law consists of protocols and annexes (which according to Art. 51 TEU form an integral part of the treaties) and the acts of accession.

48 The EU Treaties provide a set of legal acts: regulations, directives and decisions, recommendations and opinions, Art. 288 TFEU.

49 Trevor Hartley makes this distinction in Trevor Hartley, *The Foundations of European Union Law* (7th edn Oxford University Press 2010). In EU law, general principles and international agreements are often described as separate sources of law. In the hierarchy between primary law and secondary law, they are placed somewhere in between.

50 As Bruno de Witte notes, there are different views on what kind of 'creature' the EU is. Some scholars argue that the EU has evolved and moved beyond the status of an international organisation. In their view, the EU is a *sui generis* order, which does not fit

the Court of Justice of the European Union characterises the EU legal order as an 'autonomous legal system', distinct from both international law and national (municipal) law.[51] But as Kaarlo Tuori points out, not only is EU law intertwined with the legal systems of Member States, 'when national courts apply EU norms, they act simultaneously as institutions of both the municipal and the EU legal system'.[52]

My third and final example is similar to that of EU law. It is the law of the World Trade Organization (WTO). Like the European Union, WTO law is treaty-based. The institutional structure of the WTO is such that disputes are settled by panels (dispute settlement panels), whose decisions may be appealed to the Appellate Body. Again, quoting Tuori, '[t]hese organs also produce normative material specifying and complementing treaty provisions'.[53] It is these decisions, and their normative content, which are both produced in a manner 'beyond' the international treaty and binding within the municipal orders of all signatory states.

I have advanced these three examples to support the claim that there are legal phenomena not cognisable under the rubric 'law' as understood by positivism. With regard to the key concept(s) of Rule of Recognition or *Grundnorm*, these three phenomena fall outside the scope of this central analytical precept of positivism. If this central claim is false, then positivism survives as a jurisprudential account of 'law'. Can these phenomena be accommodated by the Rule of Recognition?

into the dichotomy between international organisations and the traditional notion of a state. They emphasise the EU's 'supranational' decision-making procedures, its extensive scope of competence, its effective judicial enforcement, and its direct effect and primacy in the national legal orders of member states. Other scholars, mainly in the field of public international law, prefer to describe the EU as a highly developed international organisation. See Bruno de Witte, 'The European Union as an International Legal Experiment' in Gráinne de Búrca, Joseph Weiler (eds), *The Worlds of European Constitutionalism* (Cambridge University Press 2011) 19–56.

51 Already in 1964, in the landmark case *Costa v. ENEL*, the Court held that Community law was autonomous in relation to the law of its member states: 'the law stemming from the Treaty, an independent source of law'. ECJ, *Flaminio Costa v. ENEL*, C-6/64, Judgment of 15 July 1964, [1964] ECR 585 at 594. A similar formulation is found in ECJ, *Internationale Handelsgesellschaft mbH v. Einfuhr- und Vorratsstelle für Getreide und Futtermittel*, C-11/70, Judgment of 17 December 1970, [1970] ECR 1125 at 1134 (para. 3). See also the *Kadi* judgment, where the Court referred to the autonomy in relation to international law: ECJ, *Yassin Abdullah Kadi and Al-Barakaat International Foundation v. Council of the European Union and Commission of the European Communities*, Joined Cases C-402/05 P and C-415/05 P, Judgment (Grand Chamber) of 3 September 2008, [2008] ECR I-6351, paras 282, 316.

52 Tuori, n. 5 at 6.

53 Tuori, n. 5 at 6.

4.3 A post-modern positivist conceptualisation of transnational law?

In his finely wrought *Formalism and the Sources of International Law*,[54] Jean d'Aspremont directly takes up the question of law-ascertainment by non-state actors. Believing that the products of such non-state actors can be incorporated into 'law', d'Aspremont is sceptical of the notion that the phenomena described above are 'new' in the sense that they are produced by non-state actors (he concedes this, as he must), but, importantly, are binding within the municipal legal order in ways not explicable by a concept of law with the Rule of Recognition as the centerpiece of validity claims.

To make his case, d'Aspremont relies upon Brian Tamanaha's reconstruction/enhancement of Hart's understanding of who is a 'legal official' vis-à-vis the Rule of Recognition. As d'Aspremont explains, '[t]he refinement advocated by Tamanaha boils down to considering that a "legal official" is whomever, as a matter of social practice, members of the group (including legal officials themselves) identify and treat as "legal officials"'.[55] The key to Tamanaha's position and, thus, d'Aspremont's, is in the capacious account they provide of who is a 'legal official' for purposes of law production. It is by thus revamping Hart's Social Theory of Rules that d'Aspremont is able to say '[t]he social practice on which the rule of recognition is based must accordingly not be restricted to strictly-defined law applying officials but must include all social actors'.[56]

An uncharitable reading of this move is that it is question-begging. The very matter in dispute – i.e. who counts as a 'legal official' – cannot be waved away with the platitude 'anyone is a legal official who is recognized as a "legal official"'.[57] This is the same problem with Tamanaha's account of the nature of law.[58] Law is whatever is called 'law'. D'Aspremont seems to sense that more needs to be said, for, indeed, he has more to say.

[54] Jean d'Aspremont, *Formalism and the Sources of International Law: A Theory of the Ascertainment of Legal Rules* (Oxford University Press 2011).

[55] D'Aspremont, n. 54 at 60. [56] D'Aspremont, n. 54 at 203–204.

[57] D'Aspremont, n. 54 at 203–204.

[58] Tamanaha writes: 'What law is and what law does cannot be captured in any single concept, or by any single definition. Law is whatever we attach the label law to, and we have attached it to a variety of multifaceted, multifunctional phenomena: natural law, international law, state law, religious law, and customary law on the general level, and an almost infinite variety on the specific level . . . Despite the shared label "law", these are diverse phenomena, not variations of a single phenomenon, and each one of these does many different things and/or is used to do many things . . . No wonder, then, that the multitude of concepts of law circulating in the literature have failed to capture the essence

Instead of focusing on who counts as a legal official, d'Aspremont looks at what domestic judges do. His central contention is even if 'international law is not the "law of the land" because it has not been incorporated, it may still yield effects in the domestic legal order if judges interpret national law in accordance with international law'.[59] As long as the practice of officials is such that there is inter-subjective agreement on sources of law, then fatal indeterminacy is avoided. D'Aspremont describes this as a system of 'mutual confirmation'[60] of law-ascertainment criteria.[61]

What is one to say if Mississippi courts start to make decisions that pay sufficient attention to the demands of fair process? Will the social rules thesis of Hart, duly enhanced by Tamanaha and d'Aspremont, be vindicated? One way to look at the matter is through the lens of power. By signing on to the NAFTA, the United States forced every state in the United States to comply with a certain level of due process. This was akin to the imposition of Federal Law on states; hardly a new phenomenon.

But the point is that without the acquiescence of the federal government, no norms would have gained entry into the legal sphere of the United States. The power point is that the federal government possesses the power to force states to comply with increased standards of due process. In other words, the federal government has the power to coerce compliance with the due process standards of the NAFTA and anything else it deems appropriate and within the limits of its constitutional powers. When the story is told this way, it seems to have the effect of deflating the ontological claims for 'new legal phenomena'. In fact, one has the impression that the state has found new ways of accommodating the need for regional economic agreements and uses the treaty powers of the federal government to further those ends. In short, nothing new.

5 Conclusion

We are in a time of increasing growth in transnational legal phenomena. It is all but impossible to deny the growth in courts and similar institutions,

of law – it has no essence.' Brian Z. Tamanaha, *A General Jurisprudence of Law and Society* (Oxford University Press 2001) 193.

59 D'Aspremont, n. 54 at 206. D'Aspremont makes the same point about non-state actors and the norms they produce: '[i]t cannot be denied that some non-State actors also provide interesting insights as to the meaning of law-ascertainment criteria' (at 207).

60 D'Aspremont, n. 54 at 202.

61 D'Aspremont, n. 54 at 207: 'It has thus become undeniable that domestic courts count as actors participating in the generation of the communitarian semantics of law-ascertainment as well.'

all of which are producing normativity that seemingly arises outside the jurisdictional boundaries of the state. And yet, it does seem that each example of transnational phenomena has a state somewhere near the centre of the story. It is, perhaps, too early to tell if non-state normativity is indeed a genuine phenomenon or whether it is the state doing what states do, but in a manner more indirect and less obvious. Finally, it is still unclear whether or not these phenomena pose a serious challenge to the theoretical foundations of positivism. It may simply be too early to tell.

16

Human rights from a neo-voluntarist perspective

THÉODORE CHRISTAKIS

1 Introduction

Legal positivism has been the object of systematic criticism and condemnation in international legal scholarship and has often been presented as the 'big bad wolf' of legal philosophy.[1] It is especially in the field of human rights, considered by many scholars as 'natural' and 'inalienable' rights,[2] that the criticism against positivism has been particularly harsh.[3] My objective here will not be to examine to what extent the international human rights 'posited' and proclaimed by states in regional or universal treaties have a natural law foundation, nor to establish what could be the consequences in case of an affirmative answer.[4] My goal will be instead to examine the particularly complicated relations between the organs who apply international human rights law every day, the various human rights treaty bodies (HRTBs), and the creators of these organs, the sovereign states which drafted the different human rights treaties.

The French scholar Michel Virally observed in 1960, when legal positivism was still very much in vogue, that 'the success of legal positivism has had as a counterpart that nobody knows anymore what exactly this term designates'.[5] In a remarkable study published in the same period

1 Matthew Kramer, 'The Big Bad Wolf: Legal Positivism and Its Detractors' 49 *American Journal of Jurisprudence* (2004) 1–10.

2 E.g. Martial Mathieu (ed.), *Droit naturel et droits de l'homme* (Presses Universitaires de Grenoble 2011).

3 E.g. Stephen Hall, 'The Persistent Spectre: Natural Law, International Order and the Limits of Legal Positivism' 12 *EJIL* (2001) 269–307 at 301–302.

4 The Universal Islamic Declaration of Human Rights 1981 considers that 'God, and God alone, is the Law Giver and the Source of all human rights'. (See also Cairo Declaration on Human Rights in Islam 1990.) For me, the proclamation of human rights was, instead, a great achievement of humanity. And the enormous disparities in international human rights protection among the different regions of the world demonstrates that what the sovereign states 'did', 'proclaimed' and 'posed' really counts, notwithstanding the 'naturalistic' arguments about the pre-existing universality of human rights.

5 Michel Virally, *La pensée juridique* (LGDJ 1960) v (author's translation).

in the *American Journal of International Law*, Roberto Ago explained the different meanings of this term in international law.[6] I will of course not revisit this problem here nor try to present all possible definitions of positivism. I need nonetheless to make some preliminary remarks on the meaning that I will give to positivism in the present chapter and to explain how this chapter relates to the overall project of this book.

For the purpose of my analysis, I will focus here on the link between *ius positivum* and *ius voluntarium* and on the perception of international law as a unified system of rules that emanates from states' own free will. The 'old', 'classical' approach to legal positivism considered that international law is a law created by states as opposed to natural law theories. It has been expressed, for example, in Anzilotti's main idea that states are bound because, and so far only as, they wish to be bound,[7] or in the PCIJ's famous dictum in *Lotus*: 'The rules of law binding upon States . . . emanate from their own free will . . . Restrictions upon the independence of States cannot therefore be presumed.'[8]

Since then, 'classical' international legal positivism has often been criticised on several grounds, including for being overly deferential to state sovereignty. This has led both to important historical efforts to revise legal positivism[9] and to various calls to abandon it altogether. Indeed, taking into consideration the frontal attacks on positivism during the last twenty years by the Critical Legal Studies (CLS) movement, the editors of this book write in their description of the project that: '[e]specially in Anglo-Saxon international legal scholarship, the *ancien régime* of positivism is dead'.[10] Their project is thus presented as an attempt to 'reanimate international legal posivitism'.[11] In their project, international legal positivism

[6] Roberto Ago, 'Positive Law and International Law' 51 *AJIL* (1957) 691–733.

[7] Among many studies discussing the positivist approach of Anzilotti, see Denis Alland, *Anzilotti et le droit international public: Un essai* (Pedone 2012). See also the texts published in the symposium: 'The European Tradition in International Law: Dionisio Anzilotti' 3 *EJIL* (1992) 92–172.

[8] *S.S. 'Lotus' (France v. Turkey)*, Judgment of 7 September 1927, PCIJ Series A No. 10 (1927) 18.

[9] For a history of these efforts, see Ago, n. 6; Roberto Ago, 'Positivism' in Rudolf Bernhardt (ed.), *Encyclopedia of Public International Law*, Vol. 3 (North Holland 1997) 388–392. See also Collins, Chapter 2.

[10] Jörg Kammerhofer, Jean d'Aspremont, 'Introduction: Mapping 21st Century International Legal Positivism' (unpublished paper, 2010) at 4. [Editors' note: the author refers to the first version of the introductory chapter; in order to preserve the references, that version has been made available at http://ssrn.com/abstract=2372778.]

[11] Jean d'Aspremont, 'The Politics of Deformalization in International Law' 3 *Göttingen Journal of International Law* (2011) 503–550 at 546. See also generally: Jörg Kammerhofer, *Uncertainty in International Law: A Kelsenian Perspective* (Routledge 2010); Jean

is 'loosely defined' and includes several premises, but also the conviction that we must do away with state-centrism and consensualism.[12] Indeed, their project is premised on the idea that there is a new stream of positivism which does not have 'state will' as the necessary source of international law.

While the author of this chapter agrees with some of the editors' ideas and premises, he cannot join this effort to eliminate the will of states and the voluntarist paradigm altogether from the equation of international law. In all his writings and teachings until today, this author has constantly maintained that, although international legal positivism has evolved significantly since the nineteenth century and has been greatly informed by its critics,[13] the will of states still remains an important (although of course not exclusive) explanatory factor in the process of international law-making and a major methodological tool in order to identify the existing rules (the *lex lata* as opposed to *lex ferenda*) and to make convincing legal arguments.[14] Of course, the *Lotus* dictum must be read correctly today. It should not be considered as implying the 'absolute power' of the will of states or the idea that they are the only subjects of international law.[15] It should not lead either to the extremist view that states are bound only to what they have *explicitly* consented to.[16] Instead, the *Lotus* dictum should be read in a negative way: states should not be bound *against* their will, by what they have not *explicitly* or *implicitly* consented to.[17] Indeed, I believe that there is nothing incoherent in the continuing relevance of the will of states in the process of creating and accepting international legal obligations in the face of the frequent absence of formal law-making in international law (for example, the different mechanisms of acquiescence and tacit consent) – especially taking into consideration the fact that other mechanisms (such as protest or objections) permit to avoid

d'Aspremont, *Formalism and the Sources of International Law: A Theory of the Ascertainment of Legal Rules* (Oxford University Press 2011).

12 See Kammerhofer and d'Aspremont, n. 10.

13 Bruno Simma, Andreas L. Paulus, 'The Responsibility of Individuals for Human Rights Abuses in Internal Conflicts: A Positivist View' 93 *AJIL* (1999) 302–316 at 306–307.

14 Olivier Corten, *Méthodologie du droit international public* (Editions de l'Université de Bruxelles 2009) 135–262.

15 Indeed, states decided voluntarily to recognise the international legal personality of other actors such as of international organisations or, to a certain extent, of individuals.

16 See my analysis in Théodore Christakis, Marie-Pierre Lanfranchi, *La licéité de l'emploi d'armes nucléaires devant la Cour internationale de Justice: Analyse et documents* (Économica 1997) 48–125.

17 The interest of this positivist approach preserving the voluntarist paradigm is to provide valuable tools and methods in order to establish if a state is thus bound or not by an international legal obligation.

undesired opposability of new norms. Instead of adhering to a theory of 'post-modern international legal positivism' which tries to reinstate formalism while excluding voluntarism, I prefer a vision of positivism which preserves the sovereignty of states in relation with the *opposability* of new international legal obligations, while considering that the variations between formal requirements and degrees of deformalisation within the existing system of sources are merely the result of the will of states. There is also no contradiction between this voluntarist paradigm and the power of states to use their present freedom to limit (substantially sometimes) their future freedom[18] which is, precisely, 'an attribute of State sovereignty'.[19] It goes without saying that this 'moderately voluntarist' approach is just one of many ways to cognise international law in general and positive international law in particular.[20] 'Old fashioned' or '*ancien régime*' as this theory might appear to some, reports of its death have probably been greatly exaggerated.[21]

Having said this, I will acknowledge immediately that there are probably few other areas of international law where the 'voluntarist paradigm' of legal positivism, even in the 'informed' and 'moderate' version I defend, is challenged as much as in the area of human rights. The bustling activity of HRTBs in all regional systems and (even though to a lesser extent) at the universal level gives the impression of a complete departure from voluntarist values and often confirms the anti-consensualist approach of post-modern legal positivism (Section 2). It is nonetheless still possible to undertake an effort of 'reconciliation' between human rights and the informed voluntarist paradigm insisting on the particular nature of human rights treaties and the tolerant attitude of state parties (Section 3).

18 Théodore Christakis, 'Article 56' in Olivier Corten, Pierre Klein (eds), *The Vienna Conventions on the Law of Treaties: A Commentary* (Oxford University Press 2011) 1251–1276 at 1261–1266.

19 See the well-known dictum of the PCIJ in its judgment in *S.S. 'Wimbledon' (Great Britain, France, Italy, Japan, Poland (intervening) v. Germany)*, Judgment of 17 August 1923, PCIJ Series A No. 1 (1923) 25; *Customs Régime between Germany and Austria (Protocol of March 19th, 1931)*, Advisory Opinion of 5 September 1931, PCIJ Series A/B No. 41 (1931) 37 at 57–58 (Sep. Op. Anzilotti).

20 Indeed, both the classical normativist school and the 'post-modern' approach to positivism advanced by the editors and many of the contributors in this book exclude voluntarism. This does not mean nonetheless that 'post-modernists' can decide in an arbitrary way that voluntarist approaches to international law can no longer be called 'positivism', as Kammerhofer suggests. See Jörg Kammerhofer, 'International Legal Positivism in a Post-Modern World: A Proposal for Greater Focus in Scholarship' *AjV Newsletter* (2013) 2–4 at 2, available at http://ssrn.com/abstract=2282529.

21 See in general Prosper Weil, 'Le droit international en quête de son identité: Cours général de droit international public' 237 *Recueil des Cours* (1992) 9–370.

2 The fall of voluntarism and the rise of a new model?

Following the innovative and bold model of the European Court of Human Rights (ECtHR), many other HRTBs have engaged, during the last two decades, in an impressive enterprise of 'rewriting' human rights treaties through dynamic interpretation of the original provisions. I will limit myself here to nine observations which seem to leave little room for the voluntarist paradigm while confirming nonetheless in some cases the premises of post-modern legal positivism.

2.1 *The neglect of* travaux préparatoires

Recourse to the preparatory work of a treaty is sometimes considered to be one of the most voluntarist techniques in order to elucidate the states' original intent.[22] It is well known that the Vienna Convention on the Law of Treaties 1969 (VCLT) 'downgraded' the importance of preparatory works to 'supplementary means of interpretation'.[23] This was not because the Vienna Convention's drafters wanted to avoid taking into consideration the original intent of states (as it appears in the *travaux préparatoires*), but, on the contrary, because preparatory works were often inconclusive about this will.[24] Indeed, the proclaimed intent of one of the participating states in the negotiations does not necessarily reflect the intention of the others and several similar factors could also 'diminish the relevance of preparatory works'.[25] Notwithstanding these considerations, the preparatory works could be, when available and clear, a privileged way of identifying the 'subjective' or 'real' intent of state parties. But following the attitude of the European Commission on Human Rights and the ECtHR,[26] the HRTBs have almost entirely (with few exceptions) dismissed this technique.

[22] Olivier Corten, 'Les techniques reproduites aux articles 31 à 33 des Conventions de Vienne: Approche objectiviste ou approche volontariste de l'interprétation?' 115 *Revue Générale de Droit International Public* (2011) 351–366 at 353.

[23] Art. 32 VCLT.

[24] Yves Le Bouthillier, 'Article 32' in Olivier Corten, Pierre Klein (eds), *The Vienna Conventions on the Law of Treaties: A Commentary* (Oxford University Press 2011) 841–865 at 856.

[25] Le Bouthillier, n. 24 at 857–858.

[26] Starting with the *Golder* case where the Court dismissed the need to resort to 'supplementary means of interpretation' as envisaged in Art. 32 VCLT in order to ascertain the existence of an un-enumerated right of access to a court under Art. 6 ECHR. ECtHR, *Golder v. United Kingdom*, Application No. 4451/70, Judgment of 21 February 1975, ECHR Series A No. 18 (1975) [1 EHRR (1975) 524], para. 36.

Indeed, although two well-known judges of the ECtHR and the Inter-American Court of Human Rights (IACtHR) insisted on the fact that these two courts 'have never set aside the principle of consultation of preparatory works',[27] HRTBs have often emphasised that preparatory work is an unreliable method of interpreting human rights treaties. As one scholar observed, reference to the *travaux préparatoires* 'has arisen more frequently in dissenting opinions than in the judgments'[28] of these courts and bodies.

Even more interesting is that in some cases these treaty bodies did not hesitate to adopt solutions which seemed *contrary* to the position of states as appearing in the preparatory works. Thus, in *Young, James and Webster v. United Kingdom* before the ECtHR in 1981, the responding government quoted the *travaux préparatoires* in order to demonstrate that the drafters voluntarily excluded from the Convention and Article 11 a 'right not to be compelled to join an association', but the court dismissed the argument.[29]

More recently, the United States has relied heavily on the *travaux préparatoires* of the International Covenant on Civil and Political Rights 1966 (ICCPR) in order to demonstrate that the Covenant has a strictly territorial sphere of application and does not have any extraterritorial reach. But both the Human Rights Committee (HRC)[30] and the ICJ[31] have recognised the extraterritorial effect of the ICCPR. Both the ICJ[32] and several scholars have questioned the United States' reading of the preparatory works.[33] This is probably just further proof of the inconclusive character of the preparatory works and justifies the choices made by the drafters of the VCLT in 1969.

[27] Lucius Caflisch, Antônio Cançado Trindade, 'Les conventions américaine et européenne des droits de l'homme et le droit international général' 108 *Revue Générale de Droit International Public* (2004) 5–62 at 20.

[28] Robin C. A. White, Clare Ovey, *The European Convention on Human Rights* (5th edn Oxford University Press 2010) 67.

[29] ECtHR, *Young, James and Webster v. United Kingdom*, Application No. 7601/76, 7806/77, Judgment of 13 August 1981, ECHR Series A No. 44 (1981) [4 EHRR (1981) 38], para. 51.

[30] Starting with UNHRC, *Sergio Ruben Lopez Burgos v. Uruguay*, Communication No. 52/1979, UN Doc. CCPR/C/13/D/52/1979 (1981), Views of 29 July 1981.

[31] *Legal Consequences of the Construction of a Wall in the Occupied Palestinian Territory*, Advisory Opinion of 9 July 2004, ICJ Reports (2004) 136 at 180 (para. 111).

[32] *Wall*, n. 31 at 179 (para. 109).

[33] E.g. Marko Milanovic, *Extraterritorial Application of Human Rights Treaties: Law, Principles, and Policy* (Oxford University Press 2011) 224–225; Nigel Rodley, 'The Extraterritorial Reach and Applicability in Armed Conflict of the International Covenant on Civil and Political Rights: A Rejoinder to Dennis and Surena' 9 *European Human Rights Law Review* (2009) 628–636.

2.2 Constant recourse to evolutive interpretation

The treaty bodies all too often use evolutionary interpretation as a tool in order to 'adapt' and specify concepts and notions contained in the human rights conventions in a rapidly evolving world. As the President of the ECtHR summed it up in a recent seminar organised on this topic in Strasbourg:

> The fact is that, more or less since the beginning, the Convention organs... have taken the view that the text should be interpreted, and applied, by adapting it to the changes that have taken place over time – to changes in society, in morals, in mentalities, in laws, but also to technological innovations and scientific progress. The Convention is sixty years old: history has moved inexorably onward during that period and this contextual evolution has been highly significant. The Convention's interpreters expressly rejected a static or finite analysis. I am convinced they were right.[34]

This use (and sometimes abuse?) of 'teleological' or 'evolutive' or 'creative' interpretation, and the constant recourse to the idea that human rights treaties are 'living instruments', the interpretation of which inevitably requires a dynamic process, sometimes gives the impression that HRTBs transform the original conventions in some kind of 'magical hat-trick', pulling out an endless number of white rabbits, i.e. new obligations for states. Specific examples in the case law of European,[35]

[34] Jean-Paul Costa, '[Untitled Speech]' in European Court of Human Rights, Council of Europe (eds), *Dialogue between Judges 2011: What are the Limits to the Evolutive Interpretation of the Convention?* (European Court of Human Rights 2011) 5 at 5.

[35] The ECtHR first used the expression that 'the Convention is a living instrument which must be interpreted in the light of present-day conditions' in *Tyrer*, which concerned the outlawing of the punishment of 'caning' in a secondary school. ECtHR, *Tyrer v. United Kingdom*, Application No. 5856/72, Judgment of 25 April 1978, ECHR Series A No. 26 (1978) [2 EHRR (1978) 1]. Since then, the expression has been used constantly in order to justify innovative solutions and readings of the convention and even, sometimes, some spectacular reversals of the ECtHR's own previous judgments. One well-known example is *Goodwin*, where the Court, taking into consideration societal evolution, abandoned its previously settled case law which refused to extend to post-operative transsexuals the right under Art. 8 ECHR to regularise their new gender by asking the government to alter the initial official registers of births. ECtHR, *Christine Goodwin v. United Kingdom*, Application No. 28957/95, Judgment of 11 July 2002, ECHR Reports (2002-VI) 588 [35 EHRR (2002) 18]. As Michael Goldhaber wrote in his book on landmark and historic judgments: 'for better or for worse, the ECHR has shown a willingness to get ahead of local public opinion on certain issues'. Michael D. Goldhaber, *A People's History of the European Court of Human Rights* (Rutgers University Press 2007) 102.

American[36] and African treaty bodies,[37] but also, to a lesser extent, in the practice of universal bodies such as the HRC,[38] indicate not only a trend towards stretching the treaty provisions to their outer limits, but also, occasionally, various efforts to 'rewrite' the original texts.

2.3 *The invention of 'positive obligations'*

The introduction of the whole chapter of 'positive obligations', requiring public authorities to take affirmative steps to ensure that rights holders can effectively exercise their rights, is another major and bold achievement of HRTBs. This was not guaranteed on the basis of textualism and was in sharp contrast with interpretation of human rights by some domestic legal orders and jurisdictions.[39] Since *Marckx v. Belgium* and *Airey v. Ireland* in 1979,[40] the ECtHR has accepted the concept of positive obligations and the idea that a violation of the Convention committed by a private individual may engage the responsibility of the state when the state has made it possible or probable, either through negligence or through tolerance. In such a case, it is the state's wrongful omission, not its wrongful action, which triggers its responsibility under international law.[41]

36 E.g. IACtHR, *Mayagna (Sumo) Awas Tingni Community v. Nicaragua*, Merits, Judgment of 31 August 2001, IACtHR Series C No. 79 (2001), para. 146.

37 For an analysis and cases, see Kofi Oteng Kufuor, *The African Human Rights System: Origin and Evolution* (Palgrave Macmillan 2010) 37–60. He explains that the African Commission on Human and Peoples' Rights undertook, under the cover of 'dynamic interpretation', a major effort to 'rewrite the African Chapter' and uses evolutive interpretation in order to 'practically nullify' the 'clawback clauses' initially introduced by states in the African Charter'.

38 E.g. UNHRC, *Roger Judge v. Canada*, Communication No. 829/1995, UN Doc. CCPR/C/78/D/829/1998 (2003), Views of 5 August 2003, para. 10.3.

39 The comparison has often been made with the US Constitution, which has been described by some authors as 'exclusively a document of authorization and limitation'; Paul McKaskle, 'The European Court of Human Rights: What It Is, How It Works, and Its Future' 40 *University of San Francisco Law Review* (2005) 1–84 at 55–56.

40 ECtHR, *Marckx v. Belgium*, Application No. 6833/74, Judgment of 13 June 1979, ECHR Series A No. 31 (1979) [2 EHRR (1979) 330]; ECtHR, *Airey v. Ireland*, Application No. 6289/73, Judgment of 9 October 1979, ECHR Series A No. 32 (1979) [2 EHRR (1979) 305].

41 Among many publications on this topic, see Dimitris Xenos, *The Positive Obligations of the State under the European Convention of Human Rights* (Routledge 2012); Riccardo Pisillo Mazzeschi, 'Responsabilité de l'état pour violation des obligations positives relatives aux droits de l'homme' 333 *Recueil des Cours* (2008) 175–506; Alastair Mowbray, *The Development of Positive Obligations under the European Convention on Human Rights by the European Court of Human Rights* (Hart 2004).

It is thus interesting to note that while the US Supreme Court in *DeShaney v. Winnebago County* in 1989 made reference to the 'original intent' of the drafters in order to reject an 'expansive reading of the constitutional text' and the idea of positive obligations,[42] the ECtHR had no difficulty recognising exactly the contrary without feeling the need to refer to the 'original intent' of the drafters. In sharp contrast to *DeShaney*, the ECtHR recognised in several cases that a member state had violated Article 3 of the Convention when it failed to act to protect children who were living in an abusive situation.[43] The concept of positive obligations has also been recognised in relation to many other important articles of the Convention, such as Articles 2, 8 or 11. Other regional human rights bodies such as the IACtHR,[44] or even universal bodies, such as the HRC,[45] have also adopted the open-ended scope of positive obligations early on, which, undoubtedly, enlarges in a spectacular way the obligations of states under human rights treaties.

2.4 Distrust of domestic law? The theory of 'autonomous concepts'

Relying, for the purposes of interpreting the terms appearing in different human rights treaties, on the meaning given to them by the national authorities in the relevant domestic legal systems, would have been a solution friendly to the classical 'voluntaristic' and 'state friendly' paradigm. As George Letsas notes:

> We can see why a textualist approach to interpretation would encourage such a view: textualists insist that the meaning of legal provisions tracks common usage at the time of enactment and that interpretations which transcend common usage of terms be ruled out. Given that many terms of the Convention are legal *fictions*, textualism would require placing great

42 The US Supreme Court held that the state had no constitutional duty to protect the child from his father even after receiving complaints of possible abuse: US Supreme Court, *DeShaney v. Winnebago County Department of Social Services*, Judgment of 22 February 1989, 489 US 189 (1989).

43 ECtHR, *Z and Others v. United Kingdom*, Application No. 29392/95, Judgment of 10 May 2001, ECHR Reports (2001-V) 333 [34 EHRR (2002) 3] at para. 73.

44 Several judgments of the IACtHR use the concept of positive obligations, according to Laurence Burgorgue-Larsen and Amaya Úbeda de Torres, *The Inter-American Court of Human Rights: Case-Law and Commentary* (Rosalind Greenstein (tr.), Oxford University Press 2011) 880.

45 UNHRC, General Comment No. 31 (80): The Nature of the General Legal Obligation Imposed on States Parties to the Covenant, UN Doc. CCPR/C/21/Rev.1/Add.13, 21 March 2004, paras 6–8.

> emphasis on the ordinary meaning assigned to those terms within the legal tradition of member states.[46]

Instead, however, all human rights bodies have followed the ECtHR[47] along the path of 'autonomous concepts' which indicates that these terms do not necessarily have the same meaning as in domestic legal orders.[48]

2.5 'New' obligations by transposition of external elements

More and more of the HRTBs permit the 'transposition' of solutions given in other systems and regimes after a comparative analysis. The interaction and cross-fertilisation among regional and (to a lesser extent) universal human rights treaties is a classical and old phenomenon of international human rights law. Indeed, as Antônio Cançado Trindade wrote in 1987:

> Given the multiplicity of co-existing human rights instruments in our days, it comes as little or no surprise that the interpretation and application of certain provisions of one human rights treaty have at times been resorted to as orientation for the interpretation of corresponding provisions of another (usually newer) human rights treaty.[49]

The influence of the jurisprudence of the ECtHR in the case law of other HRTBs has often been highlighted,[50] but the ECtHR itself has also often

[46] George Letsas, 'Strasbourg's Interpretive Ethic: Lessons for the International Lawyer' 21 *EJIL* (2010) 509–541 at 523.

[47] The ECtHR started using the theory of 'autonomous concepts' as early as 1976. See ECtHR, *Engel and Others v. Netherlands*, Application No. 5100/71, 5101/71, 5102/71, 5354/72, 5370/72, Judgment of 8 June 1976, ECHR Series A No. 22 [1 EHRR (1976) 647]. For a detailed discussion, see Elias Kastanas, *Unité et diversité: Notions autonomes et marge d'appréciation des Etats dans la jurisprudence de la Cour europeénne des droits de l'homme* (Bruylant 1996); Frédéric Sudre, 'Le recours aux "notions autonomes"' in Frédéric Sudre (ed.), *L'interprétation de la Convention europeénne des droits de l'homme* (Bruylant 1998) 93–131; George Letsas, 'The Truth in Autonomous Concepts: How to Interpret the ECHR' 15 *EJIL* (2004) 279–305.

[48] Following the path of the ECtHR, the HRC had, by 1979, emphasised that the interpretation of the Covenant must be 'based on the principle that the terms and concepts of the Covenant are independent of any particular national system of law and of all dictionary definitions. Although the terms of the Covenant are derived from long traditions within many nations, the Committee must now regard them as having an autonomous meaning'. UNHRC, *Gordon C Van Duzen v. Canada*, Communication No. 50/1979, UN Doc. CCPR/C/15/D/50/1979 (1982), Views of 7 April 1982, para. 10.2.

[49] Antônio Cançado Trindade, 'Co-existence and Co-ordination of Mechanisms of International Protection of Human Rights (at Global and Regional Levels)' 202 *Recueil des Cours* (1987) 9–435 at 101.

[50] Jean-François Flauss, Gérard Cohen-Jonathan, *Le rayonnement international de la jurisprudence de la CEDH* (Bruylant 2005).

received major inspiration from external regimes.[51] This has sometimes led to spectacular decisions which not only were unsupported by the text and the drafting history of the ECHR, but which also often departed from the previous established case law of the Court itself.[52] Similarly, the African Commission of Human Rights has often transposed the solutions given by the ECtHR and other HRTBs in order to interpret the provisions of the African Charter.[53]

This attitude does not really create major problems when the analogy used refers to treaty regimes binding upon the state parties to a specific human rights treaty.[54] But it becomes much more disturbing, from a voluntarist point of view, when a specific HRTB gets inspiration or transposes solutions given in entirely different treaty systems and regimes where the state parties to the human rights convention *cannot* or – worse – *do not* wish to participate. In his recent study concerning the transposition of external elements in the jurisprudence of the IACtHR in order to expand the content of rights in the American Convention of Human Rights 1969 (ACHR), Lucas Lixinski gives as an example the 2005 case of *The Yean and Bosico Girls v. Dominican Republic.*[55] In that case, the IACtHR invoked the UN Convention on the Reduction of Statelessness 1961 as a relevant instrument for ascertaining the Dominican Republic's obligations with regard to the right to a nationality protected by the ACHR (Article 20), even though the Dominican Republic was not a party to the instrument.[56]

[51] For a recent and complete account on this phenomenon, see Magdalena Forowicz, *The Reception of International Law in the European Court of Human Rights* (Oxford University Press 2010).

[52] Among other examples, in *Mamatkulov and Askarov* the Court carried out a comparative study of the positions of the ICJ and several HRTBs (such as the HRC, the UN Committee against Torture and the IACtHR) in order to reverse its previous jurisprudence according to which state parties to the Convention were not obliged to comply with the interim measures indicated by the ECtHR under Rule 39 of the Rules of Court. ECtHR, *Mamatkulov and Askarov v. Turkey*, Application No. 46827/99, 46951/99, Judgment of 4 February 2005, ECHR Reports (2005-I) 64 [41 EHRR (2005) 25] at paras 40–53.

[53] Kufuor, n. 37 at 47, for a discussion of some cases.

[54] E.g. it is logical that the ECtHR refers to the ICCPR or follows HRC case law when the respondent state is party to both treaties.

[55] IACtHR, *The Girls Yean and Bosico v. Dominican Republic*, Judgment of 8 September 2005, IACtHR Series C No. 130 (2005).

[56] Lucas Lixinski, 'Treaty Interpretation by the Inter-American Court of Human Rights: Expansionism at the Service of the Unity of International Law' 21 *EJIL* (2010) 585–604 at 598.

2.6 *Taking into consideration soft-law and non-binding instruments*

The recent trend of getting inspiration from soft-law and non-binding instruments seems like a real 'anathema' to the voluntarist lawyer to the extent that it could lead to confer a binding character to what states only accepted as 'hortatory' or 'programmatory' law.[57] Letsas observed that, since 2000, the ECtHR:

> [H]as taken into account an impressive number of materials – most of which were non-binding on the respondent state – such as: recommendations and resolutions of the Committee of Ministers and the Parliamentary Assembly, reports of the 'Venice Commission', reports of the European Commission Against Racism . . . [58]

Similarly, Shiyan Sun has noted that the HRC does not hesitate to take into account 'soft-law' instruments in order to interpret the provisions of the ICCPR.[59] The Inter-American Court of Human Rights and the Inter-American Commission on Human Rights (IAComHR) not only refer to soft-law instruments in their case law,[60] but also (notoriously) apply a soft-law text – namely, the American Declaration of the Rights and Duties of Man, in their contentious (Commission) or advisory (Court) functions.[61]

2.7 *Ius cogens status as a tool to crush state resistance*

The Inter-American Commission and Court of Human Rights have been pioneers here. The ability of the Inter-American organs to refer, directly

[57] See e.g. Weil, n. 21 at 215–219; Prosper Weil, 'Towards Relative Normativity in International Law?' 77 *AJIL* (1983) 413–442 at 414–417.

[58] Letsas, n. 46 at 522.

[59] Shiyan Sun, 'The Understanding and Interpretation of the ICCPR in the Context of China's Possible Ratification' 6 *Chinese Journal of International Law* (2007) 17–42 at 34.

[60] In *Vargas-Areco v. Paraguay*, the Court referred to many international law instruments, including several reports, recommendations and other soft law instruments, in order to demonstrate that there was an 'international tendency' to avoid the recruitment of child soldiers. IACtHR, *Vargas-Areco v. Paraguay*, Judgment of 26 September 2006, IACtHR Series C No. 155 (2006), paras 111–134. See Lixinski, n. 56 at 593.

[61] IACtHR, *Interpretation of the American Declaration of the Rights and Duties of Man within the Framework of Article 64 of the American Convention on Human Rights*, Advisory Opinion OC-10/89, Opinion of 14 July 1989, IACtHR Series A No. 10 (1989). The Court explained nonetheless that this conclusion is justified by the will of the American states within the OAS.

or indirectly, to new rules of *ius cogens* is so impressive that the old maxim comes immediately to mind: *uti, non abuti*.[62]

One of the best examples in using the concept of *ius cogens* in order to annihilate states' resistance to the evolution of human rights norms is undoubtedly the 2002 decision of the IAComHR in *Michael Domingues v. United States*.[63] In this case, the United States argued that it was not bound by any international norm prohibiting the execution of juvenile offenders. Specifically, the United States contended that it had consistently asserted its right to execute juvenile offenders, by making reservations to treaties, filing briefs before national and international tribunals, and making public statements and correspondingly that even if a norm of customary international law establishing 18 years to be the minimum age for the imposition of the death penalty had emerged, the United States should be considered as a 'persistent objector' and thus considered as not bound by such a customary rule.[64] The IAComHR made a big concession to the sovereignty of states by conceding that 'as customary international law rests on the consent of nations, a state that persistently objects to a norm of customary international law is not bound by that norm'.[65] But immediately afterwards, the IAComHR explained that prohibition of the death penalty for juvenile offenders below the age of 18 years is now an international *ius cogens* norm and, as such, it 'binds the community of States, including the US. The norm cannot be validly derogated from, whether by treaty or by the objection of a state, persistent or otherwise'.[66]

2.8 Invalidating reservations and applying the 'severability' doctrine

Another field where HRTBs have often been accused of completely disregarding the sovereign will of states is the field of reservations to human rights treaties. The reaction of some states and most prominently the United States to the application of the doctrine of severability by the HRC is well known. In General Comment No. 24 of 1994, the HRC followed

[62] Catherine Maïa, 'Le *jus cogens* dans la jurisprudence de la Cour interaméricaine des droits de l'homme' in Ludovic Hennebel, Hélène Tigroudja (eds), *Le particularisme interaméricain des droits de l'homme: En l'honneur du 40e anniversaire de la Convention américaine des droits de l'homme* (Pedone 2009) 271–311. See also more generally Andrea Bianchi, 'Human Rights and the Magic of *Jus Cogens*' 19 *EJIL* (2008) 491–508.

[63] IAComHR, *Michael Domingues v. United States*, Case 12.285, Merits, Report of 22 October 2002, Report No. 62/02.

[64] *Domingues*, n. 63 at para. 101.

[65] *Domingues*, n. 63 at para. 49.

[66] *Domingues*, n. 63 at para. 85.

the path traced by the ECtHR in *Belilos v. Switzerland*[67] and took the position that '[i]t necessarily falls to the Committee to determine whether a specific reservation is compatible with the object and purpose of the Covenant' and that:

> The normal consequence of an unacceptable reservation is not that the Covenant will not be in effect at all for a reserving party. Rather, such a reservation will generally be severable, in the sense that the Covenant will be operative for the reserving party without benefit of the reservation.[68]

France, the United Kingdom and the United States reacted to this. In its letter to the HRC, the US Government stated that General Comment No. 24 'appears to go much too far'. Its conclusion about severability is 'completely at odds with established legal practice . . . and the fundamental principle of the law of treaties: obligation is based on consent'.[69] We do know nonetheless that, despite these reactions, both the HRC and other HRTBs applied the severability approach.[70]

2.9 Judicial activism and the government of judges

The different phenomena discussed in Section 2 raise the question of the limits of judicial activism and also raise the fear of a 'Government of the Judges' which, under cover of interpretation, might take over the legislative power of states.[71] Of course, this is a classical and more general problem of law, well known also in domestic legal orders, and concerns

[67] ECtHR, *Belilos v. Switzerland*, Application No. 10328/83, Judgment of 29 April 1988, ECHR Series A No. 132 [10 EHRR (1988) 466].

[68] UNHRC, General Comment No. 24 (52): Issues Relating to Reservations Made upon Ratification or Accession to the Covenant or the Optional Protocols thereto, or in Relation to Declarations under Article 41 of the Covenant, UN Doc. CCPR/C/21/Rev.1/Add.6, 2 November 1994, para. 18.

[69] Observations on General Comment No. 24 (52), on Issues Relating to Reservations made upon Ratification or Accession to the Covenant or the Optional Protocols thereto, or in Relation to Declarations under Article 41 of the Covenant: A. United States of America [Letter of 28 March 1995], in 19 *Report of the Human Rights Committee*, Vol. 1, UN Doc. A/50/40 (1996) 126–130 at 126, 129.

[70] In its *Guide to Practice on Reservations to Treaties*, the ILC tried to reconcile this practice with the sovereign will of states by opening the possibility of opting out (International Law Commission, 'Guide to Practice on Reservations to Treaties', in *Report of the International Law Commission: Sixty-Third Session (26 April–3 June and 4 July–12 August 2011)*, UN Doc. A/66/10 (2011) 19–49 at Section 4.5.3 (Status of the author of an invalid reservation in relation to the treaty)).

[71] As two scholars wrote in relation to the ECtHR, some human rights judges 'sont disposés à faire fi des principles les mieux établis du droit international des traités pour verser, au nom de la "bonne cause", dans le gouvernement des Juges'. Gérard Cohen-Jonathan,

the essence and the limits of judicial function. In his *Spirit of Laws*, Montesquieu was already insisting that judges 'are no more than the mouth that pronounces the words of the law, mere passive beings, incapable of moderating either its force or rigour'.[72] As Robert Kolb explains in his thorough analysis on interpretation and creation of international law, positions like the one of Montesquieu should be assimilated to a complete 'negation of the interpretative function' of the judge.[73] Lord Reid, a Scottish judge, responded to this with humour in 1972:

> There was a time when it was thought almost indecent to suggest that judges make law – they only declare it. Those with a taste for fairy tales seem to have thought that in some Aladdin's cave there is hidden the Common Law in all its splendour and that on a judge's appointment there descends on him knowledge of the magic words Open Sesame. Bad decisions are given when the judge has muddled the pass word and the wrong door opens. But we do not believe in fairy tales any more.[74]

In the field of international human rights protection, it is clear that nobody believes anymore in the dogma of 'original sovereign intent', but the exact limits of judicial activism remain controversial. In 1990, Paul Mahoney tried to appease the fears of rampant judicial activism within the ECtHR, concluding that judicial activism and judicial self-restraint were 'two sides of the same coin' as they were complementary components of the methodology of judicial review that was inherent in the nature of the Convention.[75]

Nonetheless, taking into consideration the often audacious and impressive case law of the ECtHR, some commentators have concluded that the

Jean-François Flauss, 'La Cour européenne des droits de l'homme et le droit international général' 51 *Annuaire Français de Droit International* (2005) 675–698 at 682.

72 Charles de Montesquieu, *The Spirit of Laws* (J. V. Prichard (ed.), Thomas Nugent (tr.), George Bell & Sons 1914) 229 (Book IX, ch. 6).

73 Robert Kolb, *Interprétation et création du droit international: Esquisses d'une herméneutique juridique moderne pour le droit international public* (Bruylant 2006) 17. Taking a more flexible view, Francis Bacon wrote that '[j]udges ought to remember that their Office is *ius dicere* and not *ius dare*, to interpret Law, and not to make Law or give Law'. Francis Bacon, 'Of Judicature' in Francis Bacon, *The Essaies of Sr Francis Bacon* (1613) 121–130 at 121.

74 Lord Reid, 'The Judge as Law Maker' 12 *Journal of the Society of Public Teachers of Law* (1972) 22–29 at 22, quoted by Brenda Hale, 'Common Law and Convention Law: The Limits to Interpretation' 5 *European Human Rights Law Review* (2011) 534–543 at 535. See also Alexander Orakhelashvili, *The Interpretation of Acts and Rules in Public International Law* (Oxford University Press 2008) 287.

75 Paul Mahoney, 'Judicial Activism and Judicial Self-Restraint in the European Court of Human Rights: Two Sides of the Same Coin' 11 *Human Rights Law Journal* (1990) 57–88.

two methods of the Court's judicial approach discussed by Paul Mahoney should no longer be considered as equal, because judicial activism has clearly prevailed in the Court's jurisprudence.[76] The extent to which judicial activism can take the judge 'into the realm of the policy maker',[77] or can extend states' obligations under human rights treaties in an almost 'unlimited' way,[78] has often been discussed in human rights scholarship raising the question of the legitimacy of the mandate of judges of the Strasbourg court or members of other HRTBs to engage in dynamic reinterpretation and even 'rewriting'[79] of human rights treaties as to important matters of policy that might well be viewed differently by states and democratically elected parliaments. Shotaro Hamamoto spoke about 'undemocratic guardians of democracy' in order to depict the activism of some universal HRTBs,[80] while Bernard Edelman went as far as to ask if the ECtHR was 'tyrannical'.[81] Judicial activism has also been criticised very often in the separate or dissenting opinions of several judges of the ECtHR. If the separate opinions of Sir Gerald Fitzmaurice in cases such as *Golder* and *Tyrer* are now part of the anthology of reactions to the rapid evolution of international human rights law,[82] other judges have often considered that some positions of the ECtHR overstepped the permissible limits,[83]

[76] Dragoljub Popovic, 'Prevailing of Judicial Activism over Self-Restraint in the Jurisprudence of the European Court of Human Rights' 42 *Creighton Law Review* (2009) 361–396 at 361.

[77] White and Ovey, n. 28 at 75.

[78] Sébastien Touzé, 'Les techniques interprétatives des organes de protection des droits de l'homme' 115 *Revue Générale de Droit International Public* (2011) 517–532 at 523.

[79] Kufuor, n. 37.

[80] Shotaro Hamamoto, 'An Undemocratic Guardian of Democracy: International Human Rights Complaint Procedures' 38 *Victoria University of Wellington Law Review* (2007) 199–216.

[81] Bernard Edelman, 'La Cour européenne des droits de l'homme: Une juridiction tyrannique?' 28 *Recueil Dalloz* (2008) 1946–1953 at 1948. See also one of the responses to this article: Stéphanie Hennette-Vauchez, 'Droits de l'homme et tyrannie: De l'importance de la distinction entre esprit critique et esprit de critique' 4 *Recueil Dalloz* (2009) 238–243.

[82] In all these and other cases, Sir Gerald Fitzmaurice tried to defend the original intent of states against any attempt of evolutive or dynamic interpretation made by judges; see *Golder*, n. 26, Sep. Op. Fitzmaurice, para. 37; *Tyrer*, n. 35, Sep. Op. Fitzmaurice, para. 12. Against: Letsas, n. 46 at 518; Edouard Dubout, 'Interprétation téléologique et politique jurisprudentielle de la Cour européenne des droits de l'homme' 74 *Revue Trimestrielle des Droits de l'Homme* (2008) 383–418 at 396–397; Alastair Mowbray, 'The Creativity of the ECHR' 5 *Human Rights Law Review* (2005) 57–79 at 58, 61–62.

[83] ECtHR, *Scoppola v. Italy (No. 2)*, Application No. 10249/03, Judgment of 17 September 2009, ECHR Reports (2009) 1297 [42 EHRR (2010) 41] at Partly Diss. Op. Nicolaou, joined by Bratza, Lorenzen, Jočiené, Villiger and Sajó.

or highlighted that the Court should use great care in reinterpreting the provisions of the Convention.[84]

3 Preserving the relevance of voluntarism in human rights law

We will make here seven quick observations in defence of the continuing relevance of the moderated and 'informed' version of voluntarism presented in Section 1 in the field of human rights.

3.1 Human rights treaty bodies often refer to the VCLT

As a former President of the ECtHR recently wrote:

> Operating under an international treaty, the Court is guided mainly by the rules in the Vienna Convention on the Law of Treaties, 1969, which it first invoked in 1975 [in the *Golder* v. *United Kingdom* case].[85]

Indeed, the case law not only of the ECtHR[86] or the IACtHR,[87] but of almost all the HRTBs also,[88] shows that all of these bodies refer to the VCLT during their respective interpretative process while of course using at the same time the specific provisions on interpretation incorporated in the relevant human rights instruments.[89] This could be considered as a 'path' towards reconciliation with the positivist foundations of international law and the will of states as codified by the VCLT.

In reality, the situation is more complex. Indeed, it could easily be argued that Articles 31 and 32 of the VCLT not only reflect a voluntarist view, but also an objectivist approach. The 'object and purpose' clause of

84 ECtHR, *Kroon and Others v. Netherlands*, Application No. 18535/91, Judgment of 27 October 1994, ECHR Series A No. 297 C (1994) [19 EHRR (1995) 263] (Diss. Op. Morenilla).

85 Jean-Paul Costa, 'On the Legitimacy of the European Court of Human Rights' Judgments' 7 *European Constitutional Law Review* (2011) 173–182 at 176–177.

86 For a detailed analysis of the use of the VCLT by the ECtHR, see Forowicz, n. 51 at 23–71.

87 E.g. IACtHR, *'Other Treaties' Subject to the Consultative Jurisdiction of the Court (Art. 64 of the American Convention on Human Rights)*, Advisory Opinion OC-1/82, Opinion of 24 September 1982, IACtHR Series A No. 1 (1982), para. 33.

88 The HRC had already made it clear in 1986, in its decision *JB et al. v. Canada*, that it interpreted Art. 22 of the Covenant in accordance with Arts 31 and 32 of the VCLT. UNHRC, *JB et al. v. Canada*, Communication No. 118/1982, UN Doc. CCPR/C/28/D/118/1982 (1986), Decision of 18 July 1986, para. 6.3.

89 See e.g. Lixinski, n. 56 at 588, explaining that 'Article 29 of the American Convention leads to rules very similar to those in Article 31 of the VCLT'.

Article 31, so much used by HRTBs, could lead, following different ideological standpoints, to completely different results: an objectivist could argue that this is an open invitation to the HRTBs to focus on realising social needs and objective 'ends' using teleological interpretation and neglecting, if needed, both the text and the preparatory works; the voluntarist will, on the contrary, argue that the only aim of the interpreter must be to realise the original intent of states.[90]

3.2 Human rights treaties require dynamic and evolutive interpretation

As Olivier Corten points out, different kinds of treaties might require different approaches to interpretation.[91] It is only logical that a multilateral human rights treaty will not be interpreted in the same way as a bilateral treaty concerning the delimitation of borders. Human rights treaties have, indeed, a unique character. As the ECtHR affirmed as long ago as 1978 in *Ireland v. United Kingdom*:

> [U]nlike international treaties of the classic kind, the Convention comprises more than mere reciprocal engagements between contracting States. It creates, over and above a network of mutual, bilateral undertakings, objective obligations which, in the words of the Preamble, benefit from a 'collective enforcement'.[92]

The same idea has often been expressed by the IACtHR:

> [M]odern human rights treaties in general . . . are not multilateral treaties of the traditional type concluded to accomplish the reciprocal exchange of rights for the mutual benefit of the contracting States. Their object and purpose is the protection of the basic rights of individual human beings irrespective of their nationality, both against the State of their nationality and all other contracting States. In concluding these human rights treaties, the States can be deemed to submit themselves to a legal order within which they, for the common good, assume various obligations, not in relation to other States, but towards all individuals within their jurisdiction.[93]

90 For a very good analysis on this point, see Corten, n. 22 at 351–366. For interpretation and post-modern positivism, see Hernández, Chapter 12; Kammerhofer, n. 11 at 88–96.

91 Corten, n. 22 at 360.

92 ECtHR, *Ireland v. United Kingdom*, Application No. 5310/71, Judgment of 18 January 1978, ECHR Series A No. 18 (1978) [2 EHRR (1978) 25] 90, para. 239.

93 IACtHR, *The Effect of Reservations on the Entry Into Force of the American Convention on Human Rights (Arts. 74 and 75)*, Advisory Opinion OC-2/82, Opinion of 24 September 1982, IACtHR Series A No. 2 (1982), para. 29.

This 'objective character' of human rights treaties, also highlighted by various universal HRTBs,[94] has many consequences including in the field of interpretation. Indeed, it would be completely absurd to argue that drafting states had 'intentions' regarding 'the almost infinite number of cases which may arise under the different Convention rights'.[95] It is easier to presume that their general intention was to put in place an effective regime of protection of human rights which necessarily must evolve in time in order to adapt to new realities. States have a complete discretion in matters of interpretation. In the field of human rights, they have decided, for obvious reasons, to entrust this everyday mission to the human rights monitoring bodies. From this point of view, the domain of human rights is necessarily the 'kingdom' of evolutionary interpretation. This is exactly what states 'wanted'. The voluntarist paradigm is safe!

3.3 Human rights treaty bodies exercise self-control and self-restraint

The HRTBs understand that there are limits to the dynamic interpretation of human rights treaties,[96] especially taking into consideration the important effects of their decisions on domestic legal orders. This ranges from 'testing the water' and the reaction of states before proceeding to a new 'dynamic interpretation',[97] to a refusal to proceed to such a 'dynamic

[94] See e.g. General Comment No. 31, n. 45.

[95] Letsas, n. 46 at 523. In reality, this also happens in other fields of international law. This is why states often use very 'generic' and polysemic terms in some treaties in order to leave open the window of interpretation. See Jean Salmon, 'Les notions à contenu variable en droit international public' in Chaim Perelman, Raymond Vender Elst (eds), *Les notions à contenu variable en droit* (Bruylant 1984) 251–268. From this point of view, pretending to research the 'real intention' of state parties in order to give the 'good' interpretation of a treaty is often just a 'fiction', as explained by Robert Kolb. For him, the 'will' of states is like a 'divinity subject to the Metamorphoses of Ovid'. The effort of the interpreter to justify his choices by reference to the 'intention' of states is often nothing more than a deferral to the sovereignty of states and an attempt to demonstrate that he remains 'inside the circle of positivist methods', in order to avoid being accused of exceeding his powers or, worse, of legislating (Kolb, n. 73 at 622).

[96] Simma and Paulus, n. 13 at 305: 'The power-conferring capacity of norms is not alien to positivists. But positive law also sets substantive limits on any delegation of powers. If tribunals exceed the discretion inherent in the delegation, they act *ultra vires* and are prone to lose not only their legal authority but also their political influence'.

[97] One of the most interesting recent examples is the case *Schalk and Kopf*. 'Testing' the reaction of states in relation to the important question of same-sex marriage, the Court said that it 'would no longer consider that the right to marry enshrined in Article 12 must in all circumstances be limited to marriage between two persons of the opposite sex', but declined nonetheless to find a violation of this Article by the responding government by

interpretation' if the HRTB considers that states are not ready for this[98] or that this could be at odds with some important rules of international law that states have adopted outside the context of human rights regimes.[99] The quest for judicial security is also an important factor. As Judge Françoise Tulkens recently wrote: 'The time of wild reversal of precedent in human rights jurisprudence is definitively over.'[100]

3.4 *Evolutive interpretation balanced by 'consensual interpretation'*

HRTBs refer increasingly to states and the 'common denominator' among them in order to 'legitimate' the evolutive interpretation of human rights treaties. From this point of view, the attitude of HRTBs seems to be respectful of the will of states and their understanding of the evolution of the rights proclaimed by the different human rights treaties. Indeed, as President Costa recently wrote in relation to the attitude of the ECtHR:

> Evolutive interpretation, where it occurs, is rooted in and shaped by sufficient indicators of a developing consensus within European states, often accompanied by the development of new or higher international standards (Council of Europe, European Union, different bodies within the United Nations system).[101]

saying that 'as matters stand, the question whether or not to allow same-sex marriage is left to regulation by the national law of the Contracting State'. ECtHR, *Schalk and Kopf v. Austria*, Application No. 30141/04, Judgment of 24 June 2010, ECHR Reports (2010) 996 at para. 61. For a critical approach of this judgment, see Théodore Christakis, 'Interprétation évolutive ou confusion jurisprudentielle? Le risque de dilution de la notion de "droit" par le recours à la "marge nationale d'appréciation" dans l'arrêt Schalk and Kopf c. Autriche du 24 juin 2010 de la CEDH', available at: http://cesice.upmf-grenoble.fr/groupe-de-recherche-droits-humains.

98 The case of *Pretty v. United Kingdom* is one of the best examples of this. The Court declined to recognise the existence of a 'right to die' under Article 2 or a positive obligation upon states under Article 3 to authorise assisted suicide of a terminally ill person. ECtHR, *Pretty v. United Kingdom*, Application No. 2346/02, Judgment of 29 April 2002, ECHR Reports (2002-III) 427 [35 *EHRR* (2002) 1] at para. 54; cf. Mowbray, n. 82 at 68.

99 A good example of this is ECtHR, *Al-Adsani v. United Kingdom*, Application No. 35763/97, Judgment of 21 November 2001, ECHR Reports (2001-XI) 79 [34 EHRR (2002) 273] at para. 55.

100 Françoise Tulkens, 'Discutant' 115 *Revue Générale de Droit International Public* (2011) 533–540 at 540 (author's translation). Another judge of the court stated: 'The Court does not act every day as a legislator constantly changing its case law and inventing new approaches to the European protection of human rights. Judicial restraint is usually the name of the game.' Christos Rozakis, 'The European Judge as Comparatist' 80 *Tulane Law Review* (2005) 257–280 at 262 (fn. 9).

101 Costa, n. 85 at 178.

The existence of a European consensus can then facilitate the dynamic interpretation of the Convention, like in the landmark *Dudgeon* or *Sunday Times* cases,[102] while lack of consensus may prevent a dynamic 'new' reading of the Convention, like in the *Pretty* case. The quest for consensus acquires sometimes such an importance that Howard Charles Yourow observed that '[t]he law of the Convention sometimes seems neither more nor less than consensus, or lack thereof, in the law and practice of the constituent State's parties'.[103] According to the conclusions of a more recent study: 'European consensus provides a sufficient response to the legitimacy challenges made against evolutive interpretation.'[104]

In a similar way, other HRTBs rely on 'international consensus' in order to legitimate a dynamic interpretation of their respective human rights treaties. In *Roger Judge v. Canada* in 2003, the HRC relied heavily on the 'broadening international consensus in favour of abolition of the death penalty' in order to overturn its own previous jurisprudence and conclude that, for countries that have abolished the death penalty, there is now an obligation not to expose a person to the real risk of its application by extradition or expulsion.[105]

In its 2002 decision in *Michael Domingues v. United States*, the Inter-American Commission based its whole reasoning on the existence of 'a broad consensus on the part of the international community repudiating the execution of offenders under 18 years of age', which led, according to the Commission, to the emergence of not only a custom, but also

[102] ECtHR, *Dudgeon v. United Kingdom*, Application No. 7525/76, Judgment of 22 October 1981, ECHR Series A No. 45 (1981) [4 EHRR (1981) 149]; ECtHR, *Sunday Times v. United Kingdom*, Application No. 6538/74, Judgment of 26 April 1979, ECHR Series A No. 30 (1979) [2 EHRR (1979) 245].

[103] Howard Charles Yourow, *The Margin of Appreciation Doctrine in the Dynamics of European Human Rights Jurisprudence* (Martinus Nijhoff 1996) 195. This observation remains topical today as the Court's referrals to the existence of a consensus (or lack of it) become increasingly frequent, with some notable exceptions nonetheless, like in the recent *A, B and C v. Ireland* case, where the Court declined to follow the European consensus of authorising abortion in order to accommodate the cultural and religious sensibilities of Ireland. ECtHR, *A, B and C v. Ireland*, Application No. 25579/05, Judgment of 16 December 2010, ECHR Reports (2010) 2032 at para. 236. For a commentary, see Mihaela Ailincai, 'Quand l'existence d'un consensus européen ne suffit pas pour restreindre la marge d'appréciation d'un Etat au sujet de l'avortement', available at http://cesice.upmf-grenoble.fr/groupe-de-recherche-droits-humains.

[104] Kanstantsin Dzehtsiarou, 'European Consensus and the Evolutive Interpretation of the European Convention on Human Rights' 12 *German Law Journal* (2011) 1730–1745 at 1730.

[105] *Roger Judge*, n. 38 at para. 10.3.

of a *ius cogens* rule annihilating the 'persistent objection' of the United States.[106] It is very interesting to note that even the US Supreme Court acknowledged in its *Roper v. Simmons* judgment of 2005 that international consensus in this field has some importance for the interpretation of the US Constitution and the decision to overturn its previous well-established jurisprudence and to prohibit from now on the execution of offenders under 18 years of age.[107]

This effort of HRTBs to justify the dynamic interpretation of human rights treaties by making reference to the 'consensus' of state parties[108] has caused some important reactions by scholars who criticised both the absence of a 'comprehensive and rigorous methodology for applying the European consensus inquiry'[109] and the important risks of 'conditioning the enjoyment of the ECHR rights on the currently held moralistic preference of the majority, and hence offending one of the most fundamental moral values which human rights serve'.[110] These and other views, which constitute the counterpart to the reactions to judicial activism and the recourse to the 'living instrument' doctrine, demonstrate probably that HRTBs try to strike a balance between the need for change and the will of states.

3.5 The 'national margin of appreciation' and 'subsidiarity' doctrines

When a 'consensus' among state parties is absent, the ECtHR (and other HRTBs) often use another technique of deference to the sovereignty of

106 *Domingues*, n. 63 at paras 57, 85.

107 Justice Kennedy, writing for the majority, cited the ICCPR and other human rights treaties as evidence of an international consensus prohibiting the juvenile death penalty and asserted that such a consensus, 'while not controlling our outcome, does provide respected and significant confirmation for our own conclusions'. US Supreme Court, *Roper v. Simmons*, Judgment of 1 March 2005, 543 US 551 (2005) at 24.

108 The term 'consensus' implies a general agreement or position reached by the whole group of states and can thus perfectly accommodate the positivist-voluntaristic approach. In reality, the ECtHR and other HRTBs sometimes use other expressions such as the agreement of a 'great majority' or a 'great number' of states or the existence of a 'general' or 'modern trend'. These terms refer to a majority rule (mindful of the process of emergence of new custom in international law) and cannot automatically explain why a 'new' interpretation should be binding to a state which is not part of this majority.

109 Laurence Helfer, 'Consensus, Coherence and the European Court of Human Rights' 26 *Cornell International Law Journal* (1993) 133–165 at 135.

110 See especially George Letsas, *A Theory of Interpretation of the European Convention on Human Rights* (Oxford University Press 2009) 120–130.

contracting states: the doctrine of 'national margin of appreciation'.[111] This doctrine was first recognised by the ECtHR in 1961 in the *Lawless v. Ireland*[112] case, in relation to the problem of derogations under Article 15, and has constantly been used since then in a great variety of cases. The basic idea behind this doctrine is that a human rights treaty like the ECHR does not aspire to strict uniformity among states in the protection of human rights and can, on the contrary, accommodate the great diversity of national traditions and practices in different areas. As the ECtHR said in the *Handyside v. United Kingdom*[113] judgment of 1976 in relation to the permissibility of restrictions under Article 10:

> By reason of their direct and continuous contact with the vital forces of their countries, State authorities are in principle in a better position than the international judge to give an opinion on the exact content of these requirements as well as on the 'necessity' of a 'restriction' or 'penalty' intended to meet them.[114]

The phrase has been used dozens of times since then, not only in relation to derogations and restrictions, but also, more generally, in order to authorise states to give their own solutions concerning some important societal issues such as the beginning of life, abortion, reproductive rights, same-sex marriage, assisted suicide and euthanasia, among others. Even though the Court always explains that this national discretion goes hand in hand with European supervision and control, there is no doubt about the fact that this doctrine tries to strike a balance between the 'judicial activism' of the Court and the sovereignty of the member states.[115]

111 See among others: Jan Kratochvíl, 'The Inflation of the Margin of Appreciation by the European Court of Human Rights' 29 *Netherlands Quarterly of Human Rights* (2011) 324–357; Yutaka Arai-Takahashi, *The Margin of Appreciation Doctrine and the Principle of Proportionality in the Jurisprudence of the ECHR* (Intersentia 2002); Steven Greer, *The Margin of Appreciation: Interpretation and Discretion under the European Convention on Human Rights* (Council of Europe 2000).

112 ECtHR, *Lawless v. Ireland (No. 3)*, Application No. 332/57, Judgment of 1 July 1961, ECHR Series A No. 3 (1961) [1 EHRR (1961) 15].

113 ECtHR, *Handyside v. United Kingdom*, Application No. 5493/72, Judgment of 7 December 1976, ECHR Series A No. 24 (1976) [1 EHRR (1976) 737].

114 *Handyside*, n. 113 at para. 48.

115 As one author writes: 'Thankfully the use of the doctrine appears to have been in retreat in recent years following criticisms by academics and judges alike.' Letsas, n. 46 at 531–532. It does seem, however, that the Court has recently renewed the margin of appreciation doctrine in some high profile and important cases such as *Schalk and Kopf*, n. 97; *A, B and C*, n. 103; ECtHR, *Lautsi and Others v. Italy*, Application No. 30814/06, Judgment of 18 March 2011, ECHR Reports (2011) 2412 [54 EHRR (2012) 3]. This is probably a sign of the effort of the Court to 'appease' the increasing reactions of some states.

The margin of appreciation doctrine, described by the Court itself as a 'tool to define relations between the domestic authorities and the Court'[116] is, with some other devices,[117] part of the principle of subsidiarity which reflects the idea that the states have the first responsibility to protect Convention rights domestically. These two principles of subsidiarity and margin of appreciation are great contributors to the idea of 'vital space' reclaimed by sovereign states and it comes as no surprise that states are extremely attached to them, as will be shown in Section 3.7.

3.6 Other 'bold' techniques and the will of states

Many of the 'bold' techniques discussed in Section 2 are closer to the voluntarist paradigm than we might initially think. The 'referral to external elements' discussed in Section 2.5 is thus not only authorised, but, sometimes, required by some human rights treaty provisions such as Articles 60 and 61 of the African Chapter or Article 29 of the ACHR. This is, of course, in harmony with consensualism.

The same applies to other techniques which finally tend to realise Article 31 of the VCLT by proposing methods of interpretation of human rights treaties consistent with the 'context' and the 'subsequent practice' of states. Innovations such as the 'positive obligations' doctrine have been introduced smoothly and followed by numerous conditions so as not to impose an undue burden on states. Indeed, the ECtHR insists especially on the fact that positive obligations to protect individuals from other individuals are 'obligations of means', not 'obligations of results'. In several cases, it has declined to engage the responsibility of a state party in such situations considering that the restrictive conditions have not been met.

We must also notice that the 'evolutive interpretation' technique is used not only in favour of an extensive reading of human rights, but also, sometimes, in favour of the capacity of state parties to adopt derogations or restrictions to human rights.[118] This means that this method also

[116] ECtHR, *A and Others v. United Kingdom*, Application No. 3455/05, Judgment of 19 February 2009, ECHR Reports (2009) 301 [49 EHRR (2009) 29] at para. 184.

[117] Such as exhaustion of local remedies or the principle that, in the first place, it is the national courts that interpret and apply the Convention, under the 'final European supervision' of the Court.

[118] See e.g. Tulkens, n. 100 at 537; Alexander Orakhelashvili, 'Restrictive Interpretation of Human Rights Treaties in the Recent Jurisprudence of the European Court of Human Rights' 14 *EJIL* (2003) 529–568 at 529.

benefits states and contributes to explain why they are willing to accept it. As for the theory of 'autonomous concepts' (discussed in Section 2.4), is not that revolutionary or against the 'state friendly paradigm'. Indeed, as Alexander Orakhelashvili has noted:

> It is accepted in jurisprudence that the plain meaning of treaty provisions has to be considered as their autonomous meaning, that is their meaning as part of the relevant treaty arrangement and not, for instance, the same meaning as the relevant word would possess under the national law of the State-party.[119]

Other positions of HRTBs, which prima facie seem hostile to the sovereign will of states, are in reality much more in conformity with legal positivism. For example, the assertion by the HRC in 1997[120] regarding the 'continuous' character of the obligations subscribed pursuant to the ICCPR and the impossibility of withdrawing from the Covenant, could be viewed as a position extremely hostile to the sovereign will of states. As Emil Giraud wrote, international conventions, which, by definition are 'fundamentally voluntary and free', cannot 'be transformed into prisons from which it is impossible to escape once they have been entered into'.[121] But, in reality, the HRC only applied the rule codified in Article 56 of the VCLT, which, as we have shown elsewhere,[122] is not incompatible with positivism or state sovereignty.

3.7 Reactions of states to judicial activism

Strong reactions of states to the methods used by HRTBs could be seen as an indication of the fact that judicial activism has crossed the Rubicon. It is nonetheless interesting to notice that states have reacted (at least until now) in a rather limited way to judicial activism. Of course, states sometimes react strongly to *specific* decisions concerning them.[123] But

[119] Orakhelashvili, n. 74 at 335; cf. Jörg Kammerhofer, '[Book Review:] Alexander Orakhelashvili, The Interpretation of Acts and Rules in Public International Law (2008)' *20 EJIL* (2009) 1282–1286 at 1284–1285 (arguing that there is no such thing as 'plain meaning' and that such arguments are no longer used by a theoretically sophisticated positivism).

[120] UNHRC, General Comment No. 26 (61): Continuity of Obligations, UN Doc. CCPR/C/21/Rev.1/Add.8/Rev.1, 19 October 1997.

[121] Emil Giraud, 'Modification et terminaison des traités collectifs: Exposé preliminaire' 49(1) *Annuaire de l'Institut de Droit International* (1961) 5–156 at 75.

[122] Christakis, n. 18 at 1261–1266.

[123] ECtHR, *Lautsi v. Italy*, Application No. 30814/06, Judgment of 3 November 2009, ECHR Reports (2009) 1901.

they only rarely take up arms against the *methods* used by HRTBs and the general trends of 'dynamic interpretation' mobilised by them. States could, as a matter of fact, do at least three things in order to oppose the methods used by HRTBs.

They could first of all withdraw, either alone or en masse, from human rights treaties. The weapon of denunciation of human rights treaties, very often available,[124] is nonetheless rarely used.[125] Indeed, some states like Switzerland, after the *Belilos* judgment of 1988,[126] or the United Kingdom after the *Hirst* judgment of 2005,[127] considered the possibility of withdrawing from the ECHR, only to change their minds later. In the history of the ECHR, the only precedent of withdrawal is (at least for the time being)[128] the decision of the military regime in Greece to denounce the Convention in 1969 in anticipation of the pending condemnation of this regime by the organs of the Council of Europe. In the Americas, nonetheless, denunciation has been used more frequently. Trinidad and Tobago withdrew from the ACHR in 1998; Peru tried unsuccessfully to withdraw from the IACtHR's jurisdiction in 1999;[129] and more recently, on 10 September 2012, Venezuela gave notice of its intention to withdraw in a year's time from the American Convention on Human Rights.[130] To my knowledge, there has been no withdrawal from the *substantive* UN human rights treaties[131] – although some states have withdrawn from

[124] Most human rights treaties contain a denunciation clause. Among the few that remain silent, we have seen that the HRC took the position that, in conformity with Art. 56 of the VCLT, a state cannot withdraw from the ICCPR.

[125] For a general view, see Yogesh Tyagi, 'The Denunciation of Human Rights Treaties' 79 *BYBIL* (2009) 86–193; Ed Bates, 'Avoiding Legal Obligations Created by Human Rights Treaties' 57 *International and Comparative Law Quarterly* (2008) 751–788.

[126] The Swiss Council of States rejected a call to denounce the convention by one single vote. See Iain Cameron and Frank Horn, 'Reservations to the ECHR: The Belilos Case' 33 *German Yearbook of International Law* (1990) 69–129.

[127] ECtHR, *Hirst v. United Kingdom (No. 2)*, Application No. 74025/01, Judgment of 6 October 2005, ECHR Reports (2005-IX) 681 [42 EHRR (2006) 41].

[128] An increasing number of conservative voices in the United Kingdom are currently asking for a withdrawal of the United Kingdom from the ECHR. See e.g. Michael Pinto-Duschinsky, *Bringing Rights Back Home: Making Human Rights Compatible with Parliamentary Democracy in the UK* (Policy Exchange 2011) 49–53.

[129] See www.cidh.oas.org/countryrep/Peru2000en/chapter3.htm.

[130] See www.oas.org/en/media_center/press_release.asp?sCodigo=E-307/12.

[131] On 25 August 1997, the UN Secretary-General received from the Democratic People's Republic of Korea a notification of withdrawal from the ICCPR. He responded that, as the Covenant does not contain a withdrawal provision and on the basis of Art. 56 VCLT, a withdrawal from the Covenant would not appear possible unless all state parties to the Covenant agree with such a withdrawal. The withdrawal remained ineffective and the DPRK submitted its second periodic report in May 2000.

Optional Protocols such as the first Optional Protocol to the ICCPR either definitely[132] or temporally in order to re-ratify them later with a purportedly new reservation.[133]

The second thing that states unhappy with the judicial activism of HRTBs could do is to enter into a 'systematic non-compliance' posture with the decisions of these bodies. But this does not really seem to be the case either, at least not for the regional human rights courts which can adopt binding judgments.[134] A recent study has thus concluded that the judgments of the IACtHR 'could be seen as effective regarding the modification of the Member States [sic] conduct in some areas'.[135] The effectiveness of the judgments of the ECtHR is also well known, and this is in spite of a few recent contrary examples concerning (especially) non-compliance with (binding) interim measures under Rule 39.[136] It is also important to highlight that the major paradigm of the ECtHR demonstrates that a real 'dialogue' emerges often between the HRTBs and domestic judges and national authorities. Initial hostility gives way to (generally smooth) cooperation and even, sometimes, anticipation: domestic jurisdictions (i.e. the states) sometimes get inspired by the dynamic methods of interpretation of human rights used by the international bodies. This is just another confirmation of the fact that the current human rights system is not in open conflict with the will of states.[137]

The third, and probably most important, technique that states unhappy with the judicial activism of HRTBs could use is to employ their treaty-making power to amend constitutive treaties in order to restrict the

132 On 23 October 1997, Jamaica became the first state to denounce the first ICCPR Protocol, followed by Trinidad and Tobago on 27 March 2000.

133 E.g. Guyana withdrew on 5 January 1999 from the first ICCPR Protocol, but re-acceded to the Protocol five months later with a death penalty-related reservation.

134 For compliance with the HRC views under the Optional Protocol to the ICCPR, see Hamamoto, n. 80 at 210–211.

135 Damián González-Salzberg, 'The Effectiveness of the Inter-American Human Rights System: A Study of the American States' Compliance with the Judgments of the Inter-American Court of Human Rights' 16 *Revista Colombiana de Derecho Internacional* (2010) 115–142 at 118.

136 See e.g. ECtHR, *Ben Khemais v. Italy*, Application No. 246/07, Judgment of 24 February 2009, ECHR Reports (2010) 859 or ECtHR, *Mannai v. Italy*, Application No. 9961/10, Judgment of 27 March 2012 (not yet reported).

137 See Costa, n. 85 at 182. For a general overview, see François Lichère, Laurence Potvin-Solis, Arnaud Raynouard (eds), *Le dialogue entre les juges europeéns et nationaux: incantation ou réalité?* (Bruylant 2004); Helen Keller, Alec Stone Sweet, *A Europe of Rights: The Impact of the ECHR on National Legal Systems* (Oxford University Press 2008).

powers of HRTBs and to impose a more 'state friendly' and less dynamic interpretation of human rights. One example concerns the current negotiations within the Organization of American States (OAS) to 'strengthen the Inter-American Human Rights system', a euphemism, according to some commentators,[138] used in order to weaken the region's human rights structures. Another example is the recent campaign against the ECtHR orchestrated by the United Kingdom and followed by some other states.[139] During the Brighton Conference of April 2012, the United Kingdom advanced some suggestions of amendments which could substantially limit the powers of the ECtHR. These suggestions met with resistance from many other state parties and have not been adopted.[140] The Brighton Declaration reflects nonetheless the existing tensions between the Court and some states. It put a high emphasis on the margin of appreciation doctrine and the principle of subsidiarity,[141] and it concluded that a reference to the principle of subsidiarity and the doctrine of the margin of appreciation as developed in the Court's case law should be included in the Preamble to the Convention – despite the scepticism of the President of the Court Sir Nicolas Bratza in this respect.[142] While the ECtHR was able to 'cross the Brighton storm without sinking',[143] the sea is not calm yet. It remains to be seen to which extent some states will strengthen their resilience to the ECtHR and it will also be interesting to observe to what extent the Court will try to appease this resistance by using (excessive?) self-restraint.

[138] Eliot Engel, 'Strengthening the Inter-American Human Rights System', available at http://thehill.com/blogs/congress-blog/foreign-policy/289811-strengthening-the-inter-american-human-rights-system.

[139] See e.g. Martine Jacot, 'La Cour européenne des droits de l'homme menacée' *Le Monde*, 30 October 2011, No. 20769, 3; Marie Boëton, 'Droits de l'homme: la Cour de Strasbourg sur la sellette' *La Croix*, 5 March 2012, available at www.la-croix.com; Marc Semo, Sonia Delesalle-Stolper, 'La Cour des droits de l'homme en accusation' *Libération*, 18 April 2012, No. 9672, 8–9.

[140] For a detailed analysis, see Nicolas Hervieu, 'Préparatifs et discussions préliminaires à la Conférence de Brighton sur l'avenir de la Cour européenne des droits de l'homme', *Lettre Actualités Droits-Libertés du CREDOF*, 4 March 2012; Nicolas Hervieu, 'Bilan contrasté pour la périlleuse conférence de Brighton sur l'avenir de la Cour européenne des droits de l'homme', *Lettre Actualités Droits-Libertés du CREDOF*, 23 April 2012, both available at http://combatsdroitshomme.blog.lemonde.fr/.

[141] High Level Conference on the Future of the European Court of Human Rights: Brighton Declaration, available at http://hub.coe.int/20120419-brighton-declaration.

[142] High Level Conference, Brighton, 18–20 April 2012, Sir Nicolas Bratza, President of the European Court of Human Rights, Draft speaking notes, available at http://hub.coe.int/20120419-nicolas-bratza.

[143] Hervieu, 'Bilan', n. 140.

4 Conclusion

This chapter shares the editors' hypothesis of the continuous need for international legal positivism as a tool permitting to focus on the law in force and ensure its systematic cognition. It confirms the view that the law-making process in the field of human rights is complex and includes several actors other than states. Indeed, the evolution of human rights law is a process implicating international courts, non-judicial monitoring bodies, international organisations, NGOs and the civil society, not to mention the real beneficiaries of this branch of international law: individuals.

At the same time, I strongly disagree with the effort to eliminate state will and consensualism from the equation of international legal positivism.[144] There are probably few fields of international law where the voluntarist paradigm, even in its 'moderated' and 'informed' version I defend (Section 1), is challenged as much as in the area of international human rights law. The several elements discussed in Section 2 could indeed give the impression that states are absent from the law-making and law-applying process. Nonetheless, this is just an illusion created by the various techniques of deformalisation used in a branch of international law where states voluntarily created monitoring bodies and entrusted them with the mission to interpret and apply day after day to an almost infinite number of cases some ageing treaties, which initially said few things. There is no doubt that by opting for *independent* monitoring bodies and by conferring important powers to them, states limited significantly their initial freedom, but they did so *voluntarily.* Without discussing here the risks of the omnipotence paradox[145] or opening the debate about the limits to the power of auto-limitation, I can say that, as demonstrated in Section 3, the will of states still counts from several points of view in the field of human rights.

This is reassuring for both theoretical and practical reasons. From a theoretical point of view, it supports the idea that human rights are proclaimed and 'posited' by human beings themselves in international instruments adopted voluntarily by their *states* – as opposed to the theological or natural law visions of the origin of human rights. Human

[144] See Section 1, esp. n. 20.

[145] Often expressed in the question: 'Can an omnipotent being create a stone so heavy that it cannot lift it?' In the voluntarist paradigm, the question becomes: 'Can the omnipotent will of states lead them to voluntarily relinquish this will?'

rights are thus not the result of divine intervention nor a fairy tale, but a great achievement of *some* states (human societies) which decided to put in place an effective international protection of individuals in their territories and created powerful monitoring organs – even if they knew that the price to pay would be to limit their initial freedom. A comparison between the effectiveness of international protection of human rights in Europe and the almost complete absence of such a protection in places like the Asia/Pacific region (where states have *decided not to* put in place a regional protection and have often not accepted all universal treaties or their monitoring mechanisms) is enough to confirm the central role of the will of states for the creation and the evolution of human rights regimes. From a practical point of view, this paradigm is also reassuring because it offers the guarantee that if things go wrong with international human rights law – let us, for example, conjure up the disturbing notion of a future world where the majority of states share in a treaty or a custom the idea that women should have limited rights and get stoned for adultery – some states will still be able to avoid opposability of such new rules and defend their freedom.[146]

[146] This chapter covers events up to May 2013.

17

International criminal law

DOV JACOBS*

> Whoever commits an action which the law declares to be punishable or which is deserving of punishment according to the fundamental idea of a penal law and the sound perception of the people, shall be punished. If no determinable penal law is directly applicable to the action, it shall be punished according to the law, the basic idea of which fits it best.[1]

1 Introduction

Criminal law features prominently in the traditional debate surrounding legal positivism and its limits. There is no better testimony to this than the seminal Hart–Fuller discussion which explored the question of the legality of post-Second World War prosecutions in Germany and was a core point of contention between them.[2] It is therefore of particular interest to address the question of positivism in international criminal law (ICL). The main argument put forward in this chapter is that the principle of legality, as positivised in ICL, is more than just a substantive rule of this field of international law. It has theoretical and methodological implications, notably in the relation between law and morals and on the

* The author would like to thank Jean d'Aspremont, Axelle Reiter, Oles Andriychuk and Yannick Radi for their companionship in the discovery of legal theory over the years. The author also thanks Joe Powderly for his insights. And the authors of this volume for the food for thought they provided at the workshop organised in Amsterdam in the autumn of 2011, and of course the editors of this book, Jean d'Aspremont and Jörg Kammerhofer for their patience and support.

1 Amendment to § 2 of the German Penal Code, enacted by the National Socialist regime in 1935 (§ 2 Strafgesetzbuch für das Deutsche Reich 1871 i.d.F. Gesetz zur Änderung des Strafgesetzbuchs vom 18. Juni 1935, RGBl. I, S. 839). (Translation by Lawrence Preuss: Lawrence Preuss, 'Punishment by Analogy in National Socialist Penal Law' 26 *Journal of the American Institute of Criminal Law and Criminology* (1935–1936) 847–856 at 847.)

2 HLA Hart, 'Positivism and the Separation of Law and Morals' 71 *Harvard Law Review* (1958) 593–629; Lon L. Fuller, 'Positivism and Fidelity to Law – A Reply to Professor Hart' 71 *Harvard Law Review* (1958) 630–672. See also Gustav Radbruch, 'Statutory Lawlessness and Supra-Statutory Law' (Bonnie Litschewski Paulson and Stanley L. Paulson (trs)) 26 *Oxford Journal of Legal Studies* (2006) 1–11.

debates that are at the heart of this volume in the intellectual project of post-modern international legal positivism. More particularly, this chapter will address two specific issues: how the principle of legality affects the theory of sources of ICL and how it affects the rules of interpretation of ICL.

As a preliminary point, it is, however, necessary to briefly explain what the principle of legality entails in ICL. This chapter is not the place to propose a general discussion on the principle of legality in criminal law in general,[3] nor will I elaborate on the emergence of this principle in ICL, from its relative ignorance in the trials that followed the Second World War, to its consecration in more recent experiences of international justice, such as the International Criminal Court (ICC). Suffice it to say that today this principle is well recognised, notably in the Statute of the ICC, and has even been held to be a norm of *ius cogens* by the Special Tribunal for Lebanon (STL).[4] It is useful from the outset to summarise the four most important dimensions of this principle that are relevant for the developments of this chapter.[5]

The first dimension is that of *nullum crimen sine lege.* This means that a person cannot be criminally responsible if the conduct did not constitute a crime at the time it took place.[6] Concern for this led the UN Secretary-General to claim that 'the application of the principle *nullum crimen sine lege* requires that the international tribunal [ICTY] should apply rules of international humanitarian law which are beyond any doubt part of customary law'.[7] The second dimension is that of specificity. This means that the provision providing for the criminalisation of certain conduct must be sufficiently specific for individuals to understand what is prohibited and what is permissible.[8] The third dimension is that of foreseeability

[3] Kenneth S. Gallant, *The Principle of Legality in International and Comparative Law* (Cambridge University Press 2009).

[4] STL, *Prosecutor v. Salim Jamil Ayyash et al.*, Case No. STL-11–01/I/AC/R176bis, Appeals Chamber, Interlocutory Decision on the Applicable Law: Terrorism, Conspiracy, Homicide, Perpetration, Cumulative Charging of 16 February 2011, para. 76.

[5] For a comprehensive discussion on the various dimensions of the principle of legality, see Gallant, n. 3.

[6] Art. 22 ICC Statute.

[7] Report of the UN Secretary-General Pursuant to Paragraph 2 of Security Council Resolution 808 (1993), UN Doc. S/25704 (3 May 1993) 9, para. 34.

[8] Mohamed Shahabuddeen, 'Does the Principle of Legality Stand in the Way of Progressive Development of Law?' 2 *Journal of International Criminal Justice* (2004) 1007–1017 at 1008; ICTY, *Prosecutor v. Vasiljević*, Case No. IT-98–32-T, Trial Chamber, Judgment of 29 November 2002, para. 193.

or accessibility. This criterion requires that the norm criminalising a certain conduct be accessible to the alleged perpetrator, and that therefore prosecution for that conduct would be foreseeable.[9] The fourth dimension is that of strict interpretation. This implies that the definition of a crime shall be strictly construed, without any extension by analogy,[10] and that in case of ambiguity, the *in dubio pro reo* rule should apply, i.e. that the interpretation most favourable to the defendant be adopted.[11]

With this in mind, the chapter will first set out the relationship between the principle of legality and post-modern international legal positivism (Section 2), before addressing two distinct issues: the role of customary international law in ICL (Section 3) and the applicable rules of interpretation (Section 4). The conclusion (Section 5) will offer some broader considerations on the field of ICL and its approach to the principle of legality.

2 The principle of legality and post-modern international legal positivism

How does this chapter, through its invitation to understand international criminal law through the lens of the principle of legality, fit in the intellectual project that underlies the current volume, i.e. the promotion of a post-modern international positivism? It is difficult to answer this question, given the diversity of views on positivism, let alone post-modern positivism. As aptly put by Jörg Kammerhofer, 'the differences between positivists are so considerable that it would be moot to try to impose a lowest common denominator or a definition of positivism'.[12] This most certainly applies to post-modern positivism. As a testimony to that, it suffices to read Jean d'Aspremont's Hartian position in this volume, and more particularly his portrayal of the social thesis, and Jörg Kammerhofer's thorough rebuttal of it through a Kelsenian perspective.[13]

9 Shahabuddeen, n. 8 at 1008; *Vasiljević*, n. 8 at para. 193; ICTY, *Prosecutor v. Hadžihasanović, Alagić, Kubura*, Case No. IT-01–47-AR72, Appeals Chamber, Decision on Interlocutory Appeal Challenging Jurisdiction in Relation to Command Responsibility of 16 July 2003, para. 34.

10 Art. 22 ICC Statute.

11 ICTY, *Prosecutor v. Limaj, Bala, Musliu*, Case No. IT-03–66-A, Appeals Chamber, Judgment of 27 September 2007, para. 21; Art. 22 ICC Statute.

12 Jörg Kammerhofer, 'Positivism' in Anthony Carty (ed.), *Oxford Bibliographies Online: International Law* (2012), available at www.oxfordbibliographiesonline.com.

13 D'Aspremont, Chapter 5 at 120–127; Kammerhofer, Chapter 4 at 97–105.

The current chapter, which deals with the particular field of ICL, is not the place to engage in systematic debates with these and other authors on such fundamental issues as the theory of sources, the source of validity of a legal order or the norms it produces. What is certain, and what suffices to say, is that the approach adopted in the following developments is resolutely positivist in a number of ways, which will be sketched out briefly in this section.

2.1 The principle as a rule of conflict of theories

One of the main claims of this chapter is that, with the recognition of the principle of legality, criminal law has acquired a thoroughly positivist touch, by excluding recourse to any other source of punishment than positive law (however flexible this notion might be). In other words, criminal law, by integrating the rules of the principle of legality *within* itself, has actually explicitly integrated some of the basic tenets of positivism in its daily functioning, to the point that one could claim, rather provocatively, that criminal law is one field of law where the classic debate between positivists and natural lawyers has in fact been resolved in favour of positivism and that therefore a jurist must necessarily be a positivist if he wants to study criminal law.

Of course, things are not this simple. The profoundly moral dimension of criminal law and the demands for substantial justice in the absence of formal norms means that the tension between morality and legality is unlikely to ever disappear. This is especially so in the field of ICL, as will be seen in the following section, which deals with mass atrocities on a scale that far exceeds the common criminality that most national systems routinely handle. Moreover, despite its recognition in the domestic setting and in international human rights law, it is still in theory possible to critique the principle of legality itself from other angles besides the positivist one, which would qualify its ambit in relation to other requirements, whether those of utility or morality.[14]

The claim of this chapter, however, is that, at a minimum, by putting the principle of legality at its heart, criminal law has rather originally internalised and formalised the legal theory debate opposing positivists

[14] For a discussion of the various theoretical ways in which the principle of legality can be argued, see Bostjan M. Zupancic, 'On Legal Formalism: The Principle of Legality in Criminal Law' 27 *Loyola Law Review* (1981) 369–456; specifically in the context of Nuremberg, see M. Cherif Bassiouni, *Crimes against Humanity: Historical Evolution and Contemporary Application* (Cambridge University Press 2011) 307.

and natural lawyers. More specifically, in the same way that legal mechanisms often contain 'rules of conflict of laws' to determine the applicable law to a given solution, the principle of legality operates in the field of criminal law as a rule of conflict of theories, whereby, to put it rather schematically, depending on the content given to the principle of legality, it will determine whether any given case can be resolved either through natural law or a more positivist methodology.

Similarly, while this chapter focuses on the natural law/positivism dichotomy, it should be pointed out that this also applies to alternative theories of law. For example, the New Haven School sees international law as a 'whole process of authoritative decisions in the world arena'.[15] However, while this might, on principle, be an acceptable theory to explain the long-term and ever-ongoing law-making process, it cannot be seen to be a direct challenge to positivism in criminal law, given the requirement that one be able to identify the actual 'frozen' content of the law at a specific point in time in order to conform with the principle of legality.[16] Applying this idea of the principle of legality as a rule of conflict of theories, it can certainly be said, on balance, that in the domestic context, the current approach to the principle of legality tips the balance towards positivism. It remains to be seen if that is also true of ICL.

2.2 The principle in relation to post-modern international legal positivism

While it might be difficult to determine the exact contours of post-modern international legal positivism, there seem to be some minimal 'tenets' of it that can be referred to.[17] The first way in which the approach adopted in this chapter relates to the overall framework of this book is through its value-neutral bias.[18] This applies on two levels. First, there is no normative attachment here to the principle of legality as a 'better' solution. The starting point of the chapter is that, once the principle is adopted and

15 Myres S. McDougal, *Studies in World Public Order* (Yale University Press 1960) 169.

16 Equally, the novel concept of 'standardization' proposed by Yannick Radi is not a 'solution' to the requirements of the principle of legality in criminal law. See Yannick Radi, 'Standardization: A Dynamic and Procedural Conceptualization of International Law-Making' 25 *LJIL* (2012) 283–307.

17 Jörg Kammerhofer, Jean d'Aspremont, 'Introduction: Mapping 21st Century International Legal Positivism' (unpublished paper, 2010) at 7–8. [Editors' note: the author refers to the first version of the introductory chapter; in order to preserve the references, that version has been made available at http://ssrn.com/abstract=2372778.]

18 Kammerhofer and d'Aspremont, n. 17 at 8.

framed as it is, for whatever reason, it has certain consequences, more particularly on the sources of ICL and the rules of interpretation. This is why the reasons of morality or justice that led to the adoption of the principle of legality in the first place will not be addressed.[19] Second, the adoption of the principle of legality in ICL leads inevitably, as explained in the previous sub-section, to the exclusion of moral considerations in the application of ICL.

The second tenet is the move away from a state-centric and voluntarist approach usually associated with traditional international legal positivism.[20] While this chapter, given its narrow focus on ICL, does not propose a general theory of sources, this distancing from the voluntarist doctrine is exemplified in both the rejection of customary international law as a source of ICL[21] and the diminished importance given to the intention of states in the rules of interpretation of ICL.[22] In other words, specifically in ICL, the principle of legality, while not rejecting the importance of states in the creation of international law, makes their consent a more relative factor to take into account. More generally, given its functioning, ICL by definition implies a more flexible take on the role of the state. Indeed, ICL provides for obligations under international law that rest on individuals, rather than on states. In addition, there is an increased recognition of the role of victims in international criminal proceedings[23] that also leads to their recognition as subjects of international law.

The third tenet that is adhered to here is that international legal positivism presupposes a theory of sources.[24] To the extent that one can identify sources of international law more generally, it is argued more specifically in the context of ICL that the principle of legality arguably excludes some of these sources due to the specific requirements of this principle, being those of specificity or foreseeability.[25] In relation to this, Jean d'Aspremont has argued that the principle of legality should not in fact be linked to the sources of international law at all.[26] Rather than

[19] On such a discussion, see Larry May, 'International Criminal Law and the Inner Morality of Law' in Peter Crane (ed.), *The Hart–Fuller Debate in the Twenty-First Century* (Hart 2010) 79–96; and the response: Christopher Kutz, 'On Visibility and Secrecy in International Criminal Law' in Peter Crane (ed.), *The Hart–Fuller Debate in the Twenty-First Century* (Hart 2010) 97–106.

[20] Kammerhofer and d'Aspremont, n. 17 at 8. See also Collins, Chapter 2 for a discussion of the voluntarist doctrine in traditional international legal scholarship.

[21] See Section 3. [22] See Section 4. [23] See Art. 68(3) ICC Statute.

[24] Kammerhofer and d'Aspremont, n. 17 at 8. [25] See Section 3.

[26] Jean d'Aspremont, 'Théorie des Sources [An Autonomous Regime of Identification of Customary International Humanitarian Law: Do Not Say What You Do or Do Not Do

linking respect of the principle of legality to the source of the incrimination, the focus should be on whether the alleged perpetrators were aware of the criminal character of their acts.[27] I disagree with this proposal for a number of reasons. First, the solution advocated simply resituates the problem at another level. Based on what does the person know that his act was criminal? There has to be a source of the incrimination somewhere, which needs to be identified. According to Jean d'Aspremont, reference could be made to the intrinsic gravity of the acts, their criminalisation in the national criminal code of the accused or in a number of international and national legal documents.[28] However, this does not solve the problem. The intrinsic gravity of the acts cannot be a valid criterion, because it removes the border between law and morality and essentially empties the principle of legality of its purpose. Moreover, referring to national law or international instruments is still referring to sources of law, albeit of a more diverse kind than just customary international law, which, as discussed below, has indeed been the preferred source of reference of international tribunals, at least until now.

Finally, I argue[29] that while the source of incrimination must be *somewhere*, it cannot be *anywhere*. The respect of the principle of legality is context-specific and institution-specific, i.e. it should not only be foreseeable that the acts are criminal, but also that the prosecution for those acts is foreseeable. As a consequence, I believe on the contrary that the principle of legality not only requires that sources of the incrimination be specifically identified, but that they should be identified in relation to the jurisdiction of a given institution. The principle of legality is therefore clearly linked for me to a theory of sources in ICL.

A consequence of the positivisation of the principle of legality in ICL is that it affects any possible theories of interpretation that one might develop more generally in international legal positivism. Indeed, while this is once again not the place to engage in a general discussion on theories of interpretation and positivism, in the specific field of ICL, the positivisation of the principle of legality means that there is less room for importing discussions on the indeterminacy of language and the linguistic turn. While there are of course problems of indeterminacy in international criminal law provisions, as elsewhere, the principle of legality, and the application of the *in dubio pro reo* rule, make the issue less important

What You Say?]' in Raphaël van Steenberghe (ed.), *Droit international humanitaire: Un régime spécial de droit international?* (Bruylant 2013) 67–95 at 82.

[27] D'Aspremont, n. 26 at 84. [28] D'Aspremont, n. 26 at 84. [29] See Section 3.

in ICL. Indeed, while there certainly can be a number of context-specific interpretations of a given legal provision, as the endless debates in scholarship on Hart's 'vehicle in the park' scenario show,[30] there are considerably fewer interpretations that are more favourable to the person. This does not make all problems of interpretation in ICL disappear, but it certainly puts them in a different perspective compared to more general discussions on interpretation in international legal scholarship.

3 The principle of legality and customary international law

There is no doubt that customary international law constitutes a recognised source of international law for most international legal scholars. It is therefore not surprising that it will be referred to as a source of international criminal law.[31] This raises a certain number of difficulties, specifically in the context of ICL.

3.1 Customary law and specificity

Customary law can be seen to be in contradiction with the rule of specificity in a number of ways. The most obvious reason is that customary international law norms are not written down, making it difficult to imagine that they would be specific enough to satisfy the requirement of specificity.

A related problem is the variety of sources of evidence that are taken into account to determine the existence and content of a customary norm. International criminal tribunals have in the past relied on a combination of practices from a number of sources, such as treaty practices, resolutions of international organisations, national documents, such as army manuals and decisions from domestic courts and tribunals.[32] Moreover, there is no consistency in the relative weight given to these elements of evidence, nor is there consistency, more generally, on the relative weight that needs

[30] Hart, n. 2 at 607. For an entertaining take on these debates, see Pierre Schlag, 'No Vehicles in the Park' 23 *Seattle University Law Review* (1999) 381–389.

[31] UNSG, n. 7 at 9 (para. 34).

[32] Lorenzo Gradoni, '*Nullum crimen sine consuetudine*: A Few Observations on How the International Criminal Tribunal for the Former Yugoslavia Has Been Identifying Custom', paper at the Inaugural Conference of the European Society of International Law, Florence, 13–15 May 2004 (2004) 8, available at www.esil-sedi.eu/sites/default/files/Gradoni_0.PDF.

to be given to the two constituent elements of custom, *opinio iuris* and state practice.[33]

It is interesting to point out that this lack of specificity, while particularly noticeable in the case of customary international law, is certainly a feature of international law as a whole, even treaty law. In fact, this has often been put forward as one of the reasons to limit the application of the principle of legality. What a number of scholars have said is that, given that international law is the result of a political negotiation[34] that needs to produce a compromise by drafters who are moreover not professionals in the drafting of international law,[35] the principle of legality cannot apply in the same way as in national systems. This argument can nonetheless be contested on two grounds. First of all, this comparison seems to implicitly suggest that such problems do not exist in the national setting, which is obviously not the case. Law-makers in the domestic context are rarely lawyers and the production of laws is most often the result of political compromise. More fundamentally, it poses the problem upside down. The starting point should be the principle of legality, not the nature of international law. If an international norm does not conform to that principle, it is not applicable, irrespective of the reasons for this lack of conformity. Ultimately, the underlying rationale behind all proposed limitations to the principle of legality will be in reference to the teleological function of criminal law, as will be discussed briefly in the conclusion.[36]

3.2 Customary law and foreseeability

A second dimension of the principle of legality that is difficult to reconcile with customary law is the question of foreseeability. By definition, the process of formation of customary law is an ambiguous process in which the border between law and non-law is difficult to determine and where, in effect, such rules are condemned 'to being dangerously indeterminate, at least as long as they have not been certified by a law-applying authority'.[37] This need not be, in itself, a problem in general international law and allows legal theorists to theorise the particular nature of this type of

[33] On this issue, see Section 3.3. [34] Bassiouni, n. 14 at 182–200.

[35] Beth Van Schaak, '*Crimen Sine Lege*: Judicial Lawmaking at the Intersection of Law and Morals' 97 *Georgetown Law Journal* (2008) 119–192 at 135.

[36] See Section 5.

[37] Jean d'Aspremont, *Formalism and the Sources of International Law* (Oxford University Press 2011) 164.

norm. However, in the specific field of ICL, it raises a particular challenge. Indeed, how can a person foresee that his conduct is criminal, in the absence of the issue having already been settled by a judge? It is only once the content of the norm has been formally defined by the international criminal tribunal before which he faces charges, that the person will know, but only in hindsight that there existed a norm criminalising such acts, therefore constituting de facto retroactive punishment. This has not, however, proved to be an obstacle in international case law.

The effect of the customary law process on foreseeability is compounded by the rather liberal use by international tribunals of evidence that post-dates the actual conduct under investigation. For example, the ICTY has extensively relied on the ICC Statute to determine the existence of an *opinio iuris* or practice relating to certain crimes.[38] The same holds true for the Special Court for Sierra Leone (SCSL) in determining the customary criminalisation of the use of child soldiers.[39]

A related problem is the foreseeability not only of the criminalisation of the conduct, but also of the foreseeability of the prosecution of the individual. However, the idea that the principle of legality might also require the pre-existence of a court having jurisdiction over the offence, which is debated in the national context,[40] has been completely ignored at the international level. International criminal tribunals have entertained challenges to the legality of their creation, but neither the defendants nor the judges seem to have approached this specifically from the perspective of the principle of legality, or when they have done so, only incidentally. For example, in the case of the ICTY, its legality was challenged in respect of the Security Council's power to create such a tribunal and the lack of respect for state sovereignty.[41] The Special Tribunal for Lebanon and the Special Court for Sierra Leone faced a similar challenge, which included the violation of the national constitution.[42]

The closest that one came to the principle of legality is when the ICTY was challenged as a court not 'established by law', as required by international human rights law. Interpreting Article 14(1) of the ICCPR,

[38] Gradoni, n. 32 at 5. [39] Van Schaak, n. 35 at 162. [40] Gallant, n. 3 at 39.

[41] ICTY, *Prosecutor v. Duško Tadić*, Case No. IT-94–1, Appeals Chamber, Decision on the Defence Motion for Interlocutory Appeal on Jurisdiction of 2 October 1995.

[42] STL, *Prosecutor v. Salim Jamil Ayyash et al., Decision on the Defence Challenge to the Jurisdiction and Legality of the Tribunal*, Case No. 11–01/PT/TC, Trial Chamber, Decision of 27 July 2012; SCSL, *Prosecutor v. Kallon, Norman, Kamara*, Case No. SCSL-2004–15-AR72(E), SCSL-2004-14-AR72(E), SCSL-2004–16-AR72(E), Appeals Chamber, Decision on Constitutionality and Lack of Jurisdiction of 13 March 2004.

the Appeals Chamber found that this expression did not mean 'pre-established by law', but rather that it meant that fair trial rights were respected within the tribunal.[43] However, relying exclusively on the drafting history of the ICCPR, the Appeals Chamber did not discuss the issue in relation to the principle of legality.

In effect, it is considered that 'retroactive substantive criminalization is not the same as the procedural legislative retrospective assumption of jurisdiction by a court over conduct that was criminal at the time that it was committed'.[44] However, the claim here is that the exercise of jurisdiction is not merely a procedural issue, that there is over-reliance on the substantive criminalisation of conduct to justify prosecution and that, as a result, more consideration should be given to the pre-existence of an international criminal tribunal as a requirement of the principle of legality.

However, this is one occasion when the actual reality of the functioning of ICL should have been used in favour of a wider, rather than narrower, application of the principle of legality, to include the obligation that a court must exist before the set of events which form the basis for a prosecution have taken place. Indeed, in a structured national context, where the enactment of laws takes place in a context where there are established enforcement mechanisms, there is some logic to the presumption that violation of a norm will lead to prosecution, and that there is therefore foreseeability of such prosecution. This makes the requirement of the existence of a pre-established court less necessary. On the contrary, in international law, the standard situation is usually the absence of enforcement mechanisms and, therefore, the absence of prosecution for the commission of international crimes is foreseeable. As a consequence, the international prosecution of international crimes can only be foreseeable if there is already a tribunal with jurisdiction over the facts in existence. This applies even given the recent increase in the creation of international tribunals. Indeed, while there has certainly been an explosion in the setting up of international tribunals since the beginning of the 1990s, compared to the total impunity in the Cold War years, the fact remains

43 *Tadić*, n. 41 at para. 45. This can in itself be contested because, if 'established by law' meant 'respect for fair trial rights', what would be the point of including separately in all international human rights instruments fair trial requirements?

44 Sharon A. Williams, 'Article 11: Jurisdiction Ratione Temporis' in Otto Triffterer (ed.), *Commentary on the Rome Statute of the International Criminal Court* (Hart 2008) 539–545 at 539.

that, statistically, a majority of international crimes do not lead to the creation of an international tribunal *ex post facto*.

It should be noted that the question is moot at the ICC, which explicitly excludes the exercise of its jurisdiction for crimes that occurred prior to the entry-into-force of the Statute.[45] While the inclusion of this provision can arguably be analysed as a pragmatic concession to states to obtain wider support for the Statute, it remains that it is the first statute to explicitly contain such a limitation and it is an indication that such a rule could be generalised in international prosecutions. In support of this view, it can be noted that the drafting history of this provision shows that it was for a long time combined with the discussions on the *nullum crimen sine lege* articles of the Statute.[46]

On a final note, it should be pointed out that some decisions have solved the problem of foreseeability and customary law by delinking the former from any specific source of international law. In *Hadžihasanović*, for example, the Appeals Chamber of the ICTY, in response to a challenge based on the lack of foreseeability of a prosecution under the doctrine of command responsibility due to the lack of clarity of customary law on the issue, responded that 'as to foreseeability, the conduct in question is the concrete conduct of the accused; he must be able to appreciate that the conduct is criminal in the sense generally understood, without reference to any specific provision'.[47] As discussed above,[48] this decoupling of foreseeability of criminalisation from 'any specific provision' empties the meaning of the principle of legality and destroys the separation between law and morals, because the discussion moves away from ascertaining the content of a norm, in this case the criminal norm, to discussing what 'criminal in the sense generally understood' means, which arguably has no place in a criminal court.

3.3 *Customary law,* opinio iuris *and natural law*

As mentioned previously, one of the difficulties in determining the existence and the exact content of a customary norm is the fluctuating weight given to state practice and *opinio iuris*.[49] This is not a new problem. The fact that international tribunals vary in their consideration of the importance of state practice and *opinio iuris* has been widely discussed in the literature and explanations put forward to shed light on it. One popular explanation is that there is a moral sliding scale according to which the

[45] Art. 11(1) ICC Statute. [46] Williams, n. 44 at 542.
[47] *Hadžihasanović*, n. 9 at para. 34. [48] See Section 2.2. [49] See Section 3.1.

more morally charged the issue is, the more likely courts are to rely on *opinio iuris* and ignore state practice to the contrary.[50] A more subjective, and in my view more accurate, way of presenting this sliding scale is that it depends not on an objective moral dimension of the issue, but on the judge's own subjective evaluation of its morality. In any case, this model finds an application in a number of fields of international law, such as human rights and ICL.

The difficulties that arise from this approach are numerous, especially in relation to specificity and foreseeability. One particular issue that needs to be highlighted is how this approach ultimately leads to the confusion between *opinio iuris* and moral condemnation, and therefore to a conflation of moral condemnation and criminalisation, to the point where it can hardly be spoken of as a *process* of customary law formation and we find ourselves confronting a traditional natural law argument. Indeed, while it might be perfectly legitimate that moral considerations be considered when determining the coming-into-existence of a customary norm,[51] it is not legitimate for judges to use this as a pretext to put forward their own moral agenda. Examples of this abound in the case law of international tribunals.

In *Tadić*, the Appeals Chamber, when considering the application of prohibitions of certain means and methods of warfare to non-international armed conflicts, adopted the following reasoning:

> Indeed, elementary considerations of humanity and common sense make it preposterous that the use by States of weapons prohibited in armed conflicts between themselves be allowed when States try to put down rebellion by their own nationals on their own territory. What is inhumane, and consequently proscribed, in international wars, cannot but be inhumane and inadmissible in civil strife.[52]

This claim, as a basis for prohibition, is hardly reconcilable with any of the requirements of the customary law process. To be fair to the Appeals Chamber, it then goes on to list an extensive list of practices by states in respect of the point under consideration. But this has not always been the case.

50 Frederic L. Kirgis, 'Custom on a Sliding Scale' 81 *AJIL* (1987) 146–151; and for a more recent conceptualisation, see Anthea Elizabeth Roberts, 'Traditional and Modern Approaches to Customary International Law: A Reconciliation' 95 *AJIL* (2001) 757–791.

51 Noora Arajärvi, 'Between Lex Lata and Lex Ferenda? Customary International (Criminal) Law and the Principle of Legality' 15 *Tilburg Law Review* (2010) 163–182 at 168.

52 *Tadić*, n. 41 at para. 119.

Indeed, in *Kupreškić*, the Trial Chamber found that the Martens Clause[53] illustrated the fact that 'principles of humanitarian law may emerge through a customary process under the pressure of the demands of humanity or the dictates of public conscience, even where State practice is scant or inconsistent'[54] and then applied it to the question of reprisals against civilians. It should be noted that the Trial Chamber had earlier rejected the direct application of the Martens Clause as a source of ICL.[55] This illustrates the fact that international tribunals, while adopting a natural law perspective, usually veil it in positivist reasoning.[56]

This veil, however, does not remove the tension that arises between this approach and the principle of legality. Whatever the inherent ambiguities of the customary law formation process and its judicial ascertainment, it does not seem difficult to affirm that this natural law conclusion does not fit in any of the possible boxes of customary law, if it is to retain any element of positive law. In relation to this, it is interesting to recall the strong US opposition to the prosecution of violations of the 'principles of humanity' after the First World War, on the premise that:

> The laws and customs of war are a standard certain, to be found in books of authority and in the practice of nations. The laws and principles of humanity vary with the individual, which, if for no other reason, should exclude them from consideration in a court of justice, especially one charged with the administration of criminal law.[57]

One could argue that this position still holds true today, despite the apparent consensus on what the 'demands of humanity' require, especially in light of the principle of legality.

[53] This clause was introduced in the Hague Convention on the Customs of War on Land 1899, Preamble, para. 9 and states that: 'Until a more complete code of the laws of war is issued, the High Contracting Parties think it right to declare that in cases not included in the Regulations adopted by them, populations and belligerents remain under the protection and empire of the principles of international law, as they result from the usages established between civilised nations, from the laws of humanity and the requirements of the public conscience.'

[54] ICTY, *Prosecutor v. Kupreškić et al.*, Case No. IT-95–16-T, Trial Chamber, Judgment of 14 January 2000, para. 527.

[55] *Kupreškić*, n. 54 at para. 525.

[56] Robert Cryer, 'The Philosophy of International Criminal Law' in Alexander Orakhelashvili (ed.), *Research Handbook on the Theory and History of International Law* (Edward Elgar 2011) 232–267 at 250.

[57] 'Commission on the Responsibility of the Authors of the War and on Enforcement of Penalties: Report Presented to the Preliminary Peace Conference' 14 *AJIL* (1920) 95–154 at 134.

3.4 The future of customary law in ICL

This section has identified how the inherent workings of the customary law process can lead to tensions with the principle of legality. In addition, these difficulties are not just conceptual or theoretical. In practice, it usually takes judges dozens of pages, through consideration of dozens of national laws and decisions as well as treaties, to determine that a rule has reached customary status. Moreover, this is often followed by strong dissenting opinions from some of the judges sitting on the same bench,[58] other tribunals,[59] as well as numerous conflicting views from experts in the fields, both practitioners and academics.[60]

In light of all this, it is hard to take seriously the claim that an alleged perpetrator is expected to know that his conduct was criminal at the time it occurred when faced with a customary rule. In this sense, it is unlikely that reference to customary international law in the field of ICL will ever meet even a minimum standard of foreseeability. In other words:

> [H]ow could a private person be satisfactorily informed of the existence or exact content of a customary international rule . . . which the states themselves remain largely ignorant of and which are far from constituting for the individuals 'clear' and 'accessible' norms?[61]

In essence, this means that customary law should be avoided as far as possible as a source of ICL. While judges might lament the extreme precision of the Rome Statute,[62] it is probably to be welcomed that the

58 ICTY, *Prosecutor v. Galić*, Case No. IT-98–29-A, Appeals Chamber, Judgment of 30 November 2006, 219 (Sep. and Partially Diss. Op. Schomburg, para. 21), where the judge, rejecting the finding that 'terror as a war crime' existed under customary law, made the following statement: 'It would be detrimental not only to the Tribunal but also to the future development of international criminal law and international criminal jurisdiction if our jurisprudence gave the appearance of inventing crimes – thus highly politicizing its function – where the conduct in question was not without any doubt penalised at the time when it took place.'

59 ECCC, *Prosecutor v. Ieng Sary, Ieng Thirith and Khieu Samphan*, Case No. 002, Pre-Trial Chamber, Decision on the Appeals against the Co-Investigating Judges Order on Joint Criminal Enterprise (JCE) of 20 May 2010, Doc. No. D97/15/9 (rejecting the *Tadić* finding that JCE III was customarily established as a mode of liability).

60 E.g. the definition of terrorism identified by the STL was strongly criticised. See Ben Saul, 'Legislating from a Radical Hague: The United Nations Special Tribunal for Lebanon Invents an International Crime of Transnational Terrorism' 24 *LJIL* (2011) 677–700.

61 Joe Verhoeven, 'Article 21 of the Rome Statute and the Ambiguities of Applicable Law' 33 *Netherlands Yearbook of International Law* (2002) 3–22 at 22.

62 See e.g. David Hunt, 'The International Criminal Court: High Hopes, "Creative Ambiguity" and an Unfortunate Mistrust in International Judges' 2 *Journal of International Criminal Justice* (2004) 56–70; Shahabuddeen, n. 8.

ICC has not chosen to ground its jurisdiction on customary international law, as was the case in the ad hoc tribunals. Indeed, a number of combined factors make the possible role of customary international law in the ICC framework quite limited.[63] First of all, the definition of crimes themselves is far more precise, especially given the adoption of a comprehensive document on the Elements of Crimes by the Assembly of States Parties. This will reduce the need to resort to customary international law to identify the exact content of these norms. In addition, it should be noted that, while the statutes of the ad hoc tribunals explicitly referred back to other treaties, most notably the Geneva Conventions, with open-ended definitions of specific crimes, the ICC Statute either avoids this altogether, or follows any outside reference with what seems to be closed lists of prohibited acts.[64]

Moreover, the ICC Statute is the first international criminal tribunal to include a provision on the 'Applicable Law',[65] which clearly defines a hierarchy between the Statute and sources of international law, which might only be referred to 'where appropriate',[66] thus reducing the possible scope of reference to customary international law. One can note that the expression does not even appear in Article 21, reinforcing the conclusion that it has become a marginal source of law, at least for the ICC. While some have argued that 'there is little doubt'[67] that the provision refers to customary law, one cannot help but recognise the drafters' caution towards it, given that it is such a traditional source of international criminal law and when so many other categories are mentioned explicitly.

4 The principle of legality and the tools of interpretation in ICL

The traditional way adopted by judges of approaching the question of interpretation of criminal statutes is twofold. They first refer to the general principles of interpretation of international law, essentially drawn from

[63] Leena Grover, 'A Call to Arms: Fundamental Dilemmas Confronting the Interpretation of Crimes in the Rome Statute of the International Criminal Court' 21 *EJIL* (2010) 543–583 at 563; Dapo Akande, 'Sources of International Criminal Law' in Antonio Cassese (ed.), *The Oxford Companion to International Criminal Justice* (Oxford University Press 2009) 41–53.

[64] Art. 8(2)(a) and (c) ICC Statute.

[65] Art. 21 ICC Statute.

[66] Art. 21(1)(b) ICC Statute.

[67] Alain Pellet, 'Applicable Law' in Antonio Cassese, Paola Gaeta, John Jones (eds), *The Rome Statute of the International Criminal Court* (Oxford University Press 2002) 1051–1084 at 1071.

the Vienna Convention on the Law of Treaties (VCLT), and then eventually include the specific rules of interpretation that flow from the criminal law nature of the tribunal, and from the principle of legality.[68] Despite this widespread acceptance of the recourse to the VCLT rules of interpretation, whether implicitly or through direct application of the Convention, I would argue that the existence of the principle of legality justifies the non-application of the VCLT.

This non-application could be justified substantially. Indeed, discussions on the rules of interpretation of ICL statutes often ignore the 'elephant in the room',[69] i.e. the requirements of the principle of legality. In fact, there is often a contradiction between the rules laid down in the VCLT and the principle of legality. It would be cumbersome to systematically analyse the ways in which the application of these rules may contravene the principle of legality. For example, the reference to subsequent practice in Article 31(3) could very well conflict with the rules on non-retroactivity. Equally, whereas ambiguity of a term is to be resolved through the supplementary means of interpretation according to Article 32, the principle of legality would require that any ambiguity be resolved in favour of the accused.[70] However, while a number of explanations can be put forward for privileging more flexible rules of interpretation (Section 4.1), there are a number of reasons that favour, beyond the contradiction with the principle of legality, the non-applicability of the VCLT to international criminal law statutes (Section 4.2).

4.1 Explanations for the adoption of flexible tools of interpretation

In addition to the reasons that had already justified the creative approaches to the sources of law, notably in relation to the nature of international law making,[71] two additional explanations can be put forward specifically in relation to rules of interpretation.

[68] For examples, see Joseph Powderly, 'Judicial Interpretation at the *Ad Hoc* Tribunals: Method From Chaos' in Shane Darcy, Joseph Powderly (eds), *Judicial Creativity at the International Criminal Tribunals* (Oxford University Press 2010) 17–44; William A. Schabas, 'Interpreting the Statutes of the *ad hoc* tribunals' in Lal Chand Vohrah *et al.* (eds), *Man's Inhumanity to Man: Essays on International Law in Honour of Antonio Cassese* (Kluwer Law International 2003) 847–888 at 847. For a typical example of this approach, see Interlocutory Decision, n. 4 at para. 27–32. For the ICC, see ICC, *Prosecutor v. Lubanga*, Case No. ICC-01/04-168, Appeals Chamber, Judgment on the Prosecutor's Application for Extraordinary Review of Pre-Trial Chamber I's 31 March 2006 Decision Denying Leave to Appeal of 13 July 2006, para. 33.

[69] Powderly, n. 68 at 40. [70] Akande, n. 63 at 45. [71] See Section 3.1.

First, as seen before, a notable reason for referring to the VCLT seems to be the international character of the statutes. While this justification will be contested below, it is interesting here to acknowledge another reason why the VCLT was used, namely the reference in the statutes to external sources, such as the Geneva Conventions. Indeed, by making the interpretation of the provisions of the statute dependent on the content of the provisions of international humanitarian law (IHL), the judges were prompted to consider the interpretation of the IHL treaties themselves. This 'secondary' practice of interpretation therefore can be seen as 'severing' the link momentarily with the criminal proceedings, and therefore the requirements of the principle of legality.

A second reason that has been put forward is the idea that not adopting flexible rules of interpretation could lead to a situation of *non liquet*. For example, according to the Appeals Chamber of the STL:

> Judges are not permitted to resort to a *non liquet* (that is, to declare that it is impossible for them to reach a decision because the point at issue 'is not clear' in default of any rule applicable to the case).[72]

The reference was also picked up by some scholars.[73] However, this is a most puzzling argument. Indeed, a criminal trial has no room for a *non liquet* situation, which applies when two parties come before a court to obtain the resolution of their dispute and are faced with a refusal by the judges to decide the case in the absence of the clarity of the law. In criminal proceedings, the situation is simple: if the law is silent or unclear, then the accused goes free. There is no lack of clarity in that solution and therefore no *non liquet.*[74]

4.2 The case for excluding the Vienna Convention as a method of interpretation

There is nothing particularly original in identifying the difficulties in applying the rules of interpretation of the VCLT to the particular circumstances of the criminal trial and the requirements of the principle of legality. A vast majority of authors who address this issue have

[72] Interlocutory Decision, n. 4 at para. 24.

[73] Van Schaak, n. 35 at 137; Powderly, n. 68 at 24; Vladimir-Djuro Degan, 'On the Sources of International Criminal Law' 4 *Chinese Journal of International Law* (2005) 45–83 at 51.

[74] On the underlying rationale of this argument, see Section 5.3.

identified these difficulties.[75] However, given the uneasy relationship between the rules of the VCLT and the principle of legality, one cannot be satisfied by the general claim that both should apply and that somehow the result will be harmonious. A more acceptable solution, if a little radical, would therefore be that international criminal courts only apply rules of interpretation that are in conformity with the principle of legality and therefore exclude *ab initio* any formal reference to the VCLT. There are two ways of arguing this position.

A traditional international legal way of approaching this problem would be to consider that the rules of interpretation contained in the Vienna Convention only come into play in the absence of specific rules of interpretation contained in a specific treaty. In other words, because the principle of legality lays down particular requirements for the interpretation of criminal provisions, it acts as a *lex specialis* to the general rules of interpretation under international law. This statement is fairly uncontroversial, as the idea of the primacy of *lex specialis* is well recognised in international law in the context of secondary norms of state responsibility.[76] While this argument might certainly be difficult to apply to the ad hoc tribunals, the statutes of which do not in fact ever contain any explicit provisions on interpretation, it works perfectly in the case of the ICC. Indeed, as recalled previously,[77] the ICC contains explicit rules of interpretation that flow from the principle of legality, such as the rules of strict interpretation, the prohibition of analogy and the *in dubio pro reo* principle. In light of this, there would seem to be room to exclude the VCLT as a source for applicable rules of interpretation.

A more innovative way of approaching the problem is through the functional duality of the statutes of international criminal tribunals. The idea behind this is that the nature of an instrument is not solely dependent on its mode of creation, but also on the institutional context in which it is applied. An example of this is the dual nature of the rules of an international organisation. It can indeed be argued that they are both rules of international law, as the result of a negotiation between states enshrined most of the time in a treaty, and internal rules when applied in the vertical relationship between the organisation and its member states.[78]

75 Schabas, n. 68 at 847; Akande, n. 63 at 41–53; Powderly, n. 68, generally; Van Schaak, n. 35 at 135; Grover, n. 63.

76 See e.g. Art. 55 Articles on State Responsibility.

77 See Section 2.

78 Christiane Ahlborn, 'The Rules of International Organizations and the Law of International Responsibility' 8 *International Organizations Law Review* (2011) 397–482.

Applied to the statutes under consideration, this means that their mode of creation is in fact secondary. The fact that they are the legislative outcome of a treaty[79] or a Security Council resolution[80] does not mean that they are international instruments in the specific context of the criminal proceedings that they allow. On the contrary, it is argued here that when a judge applies the ICC Statute in criminal proceedings, for example, he is not applying it *qua* treaty, but applying it as the internal instrument for the functioning of the Court, which therefore does not automatically warrant, as usually claimed, the reference to the VCLT as providing the rules of interpretation. If, on the other hand, two states were to disagree on the interpretation of a particular provision of the Statute, relating to heads of state immunities, for example,[81] this would justify the application of the VCLT because the ICC Statute would be considered as a treaty as between the two states.

5 Conclusion

This chapter has explored how the positivisation of the principle of legality in ICL affects both the theory of sources of ICL and the applicable rules of interpretation. In relation to sources, the principle of legality should lead to the exclusion of customary international law as a source of ICL. In relation to interpretation, the principle of legality should supersede the VCLT as providing the appropriate rules of interpretation for ICL. More fundamentally: once positivised, the principle of legality rather originally acts as a rule of conflict of theories in the field of ICL, mostly in favour of a more or less strict legal positivism. In this concluding section, I would like to put forward three final considerations that move slightly away from the discussions on international legal positivism, to focus on the different perspectives that one can take to ICL in general, and how they can inform debates relating to the role of the principle of legality in this field more generally.

5.1 The international–criminal divide

In addition to the traditional positivism–natural law dichotomy that shapes discussions on international criminal law, another, sometimes overlapping, dichotomy comes into play when trying to understand the

[79] As in the case of the SCSL or the ICC.

[80] As in the case of the ICTY, ICTR or, arguably, the STL.

[81] Art. 98 ICC Statute.

specificities of positivism in the concept of this field of law: that between international lawyers and criminal lawyers. This international–criminal distinction brings in another layer of complexity, between an international law version of positivism and a criminal law version of positivism. In a nutshell, international lawyers will tend to see international criminal law in the general context of public international law, whereas for criminal lawyers, the specificity and differentiation of ICL is the starting point. These different vantage points have a number of consequences in the way of approaching certain issues.

The first major consequence is that the international lawyer will consider *ab initio* that ICL can be analysed through the lens of general rules and principles of public international law. This applies particularly to the sources of international criminal law and the rules of interpretation. On the contrary, the criminal lawyer will tend to develop specific rules in these areas, based on the particular nature of the criminal process.

The second related major consequence is that the international lawyer will be tempted to systematically look at the interrelations between ICL and other bodies of international law, notably human rights law and international humanitarian law. Moreover, linked to this, the international lawyer will more easily have in mind questions of unity and coherence of the international legal order as a whole and the progressive development of international law. As a result, from a normative point of view, an international lawyer will be more inclined to advocate a dynamic interaction between these bodies of law and, in the context of international criminal proceedings, will be more sympathetic to the application and interpretation of a number of relevant sources by the international criminal judge. The criminal lawyer, on the other hand, will, here again, tend to be less amenable to such porosity between ICL and other fields of international law, given the perceived specific requirements and objectives of criminal law in general.

While both approaches have valid justifications, in light of the obvious fact that ICL is both international and criminal, and even if it would be a caricature to proclaim in a rigid way that one approach should be adopted at the expense of the other, it is obvious that this chapter tended to privilege the criminal vis-à-vis the international law dimension, as a natural consequence of the positivisation of the principle of legality within ICL, which calls for adapting the general international law approach to the specificities of ICL. Indeed, it should be pointed out that such preference for the criminal law approach of course does not exclude all considerations of the international law dimensions of ICL. Even if they do have a certain number of particularities, the sources of this field of law must be viewed in light of their relations to the sources of public international law. Moreover, despite the distinct function of the international criminal judge, any considerations of his role should be seen within the context of discussions of the role of international courts in general. Finally, adopting a criminal law approach does not mean that we refuse to consider the specific history of this field of law developing in the international context, as compared with how criminal law developed in the national context.[82]

5.2 Why ICL might be different

This chapter took as a given the existence of a field of ICL, functioning as a criminal law system. It is within this assumption that I developed my understanding of the principle of legality and criticism of current practice relating to it. However, an entirely different question is whether the concept itself of ICL is sound in the international context, given the various dynamics that explain the commission of international crimes. The most notable distinguishing feature between national crimes and international crimes is the collective dimension of the latter. This raises the question of whether it actually makes sense to transpose the philosophy of criminal law and its focus on individual responsibility to the international level.[83] But the fact remains that, as long as there is an ambition of the international community to apply a criminal law model to such events, it is not possible to do so without respect for the principle of legality.[84]

5.3 Why ICL might not be so different

Finally, once the criminal law logic has indeed been exported to the international level, it becomes quite apparent that there is a tendency to exaggerate the particularities of the international context to justify limitations to the principle of legality. As suggested previously,[85] national law-makers, for example, are no less prone to political compromise and

[82] Whether this actually has or should have a bearing on the nature and functioning of ICL is a different matter.

[83] Mark Drumbl, *Atrocity, Punishment and International Law* (Cambridge University Press 2007).

[84] For a recent attempt at reconciling the alleged particularities of ICL and the principle of legality, see Darryl Robinson, 'A Cosmopolitan Liberal Account of International Criminal Law' 26 *LJIL* (2013) 127–153.

[85] See Section 3.1.

poor drafting than their international counterparts. This does not prevent national courts from respecting the principle of legality to a much higher degree. A national example can serve as a case in point. In May 2012, the French Constitutional Council found the law on sexual harassment to be too imprecise and declared that all prosecutions on its basis should be stopped immediately. As a result, a new law had to be adopted, which respected the rule of specificity.[86] This illustrates that, despite the public outcry, the French courts upheld the principle of legality in light of their constitutional duty to do so.

There is no reason why ICL should in principle be any different, especially when it comes to the role of judges. Their role is not to develop 'progressively' international criminal law,[87] nor to 'fill interstices and lacuna'.[88] Their role is to ensure that the procedure by which the guilt or innocence of an individual is determined is fair and impartial, which requires the respect for the principle of legality.

Ultimately, when one strips away the unconvincing arguments for limiting the application of the principle of legality, one is left with a simple, and somewhat unoriginal, moral claim to knowing who should be punished, irrespective of the prescriptions of the law. A typical example, identified earlier,[89] is that of *non liquet*. Behind the fallacy of this falsely procedural argument lies a presumption that the correct solution is that the accused should be found guilty, his release, because morally acceptable, being labelled as a *non liquet*.

The moral claim that now remains before us is certainly not illegitimate per se. While this chapter certainly takes a position in favour of the principle of legality as a mediator to the direct imposition of moral values, I acknowledge that this does not put an end to the traditional debate over the question. What is less legitimate is the idea advocated by proponents of international justice that this moral claim should be viewed differently in the case of ICL than it is in any criminal law system. That is not true. The tension between moral condemnation and criminal law is at the heart of all legal systems. By inviting us to think about these problems purely in the international context, we are asked to ignore the centuries of evolution of national systems where safeguards were put in place to prevent judges, and institutions of authority in general, from imposing their moral views. There are those who affirm that 'international judges . . . are better able

[86] Loi n° 2012–954 du 6 août 2012 relative au harcèlement sexuel, JORF n° 0182 du 7 août 2012, p. 12921.

[87] Shahabuddeen, n. 8.

[88] Van Schaak, n. 35 at 137.

[89] See Section 4.1.

to represent the moral condemnation of the international community'[90] and claim that:

> Unfortunately, men's criminal imagination appears unlimited and, by enclosing the definition of the crimes in narrow, punctilious formulations, [the drafters of the Rome Statute] have forbidden the judges in advance to suppress future malevolent inventions of the human spirit . . . [91]

It could be said of these claims that they in fact illustrate the fundamental immaturity of the international legal order.[92] This immaturity should be a matter of concern, rather than being glorified. Indeed, it puts ICL in a family of systems that accept the statement cited at the beginning of this chapter, an amendment to § 2 of the German Penal Code, enacted by the National Socialist regime in 1935, which provided that:

> Whoever commits an action which the law declares to be punishable or which is deserving of punishment according to the fundamental idea of a penal law and the sound perception of the people, shall be punished. If no determinable penal law is directly applicable to the action, it shall be punished according to the law, the basic idea of which fits it best.[93]

While there is, of course, no attempt here to create a moral equivalence between the National Socialist regime and the supporters of ICL, it should at least give them pause in their 'march to progress' that such a statement could have been inserted without notice in most judgments of the international criminal tribunals. If the international criminal justice system is ever going to reach its maturity, it will necessarily have to acknowledge these difficulties at some point.

[90] Van Schaak, n. 35 at 192. [91] Pellet, n. 67 at 1059.
[92] On this see Collins, Chapter 2 at 48. [93] § 2 RStGB, n. 1.

18

International humanitarian law

YAËL RONEN

1 Introduction

This chapter considers the evolution of international legal positivism in the context of international humanitarian law (IHL). It espouses an understanding of 'legal positivism' as unity of sources, recognising as law only those norms which are generated by a pre-set legal procedure, independent of any inherent value.[1] It is thus closely connected to, although not identical to, the notion of formalism, understood here as the identification of norms through formal criteria.[2]

Modern-day laws of armed conflict present an important critique to the traditional positivist sources doctrine. It is often contended that if state practice on the battlefield is the yardstick to be used to identify rules of IHL, then IHL is in a precarious state, given the prevalence of practice contrary to alleged prohibitions, which puts into doubt the existence of law in the first place, or, where the law had been established, suggests that it has been modified.[3] In addition, it is said that positivist approaches to the sources of IHL hamper its ability to address contemporary realities and challenges, such as the massive involvement of non-state actors in armed conflicts. Classical doctrines on sources of law, as described below, thus encounter difficulties in conceptualising IHL in a manner which retains the latter's legitimacy. This chapter evaluates these claims in light

[1] Frauke Lachenmann, 'Legal Positivism' in Rüdiger Wolfrum (ed.), *Max Planck Encyclopedia of Public International Law*, Vol. 6 (Oxford University Press 2012) 785–797 at 786 (MN 3).

[2] Jean d'Aspremont, *Formalism and the Sources of International Law: A Theory of the Ascertainment of Legal Rules* (Oxford University Press 2011) 24.

[3] Josef L. Kunz, 'The Nature of Customary International Law' (1953) 47 *AJIL* 662–669 at 668. For a different formulation of this problem, see Jean d'Aspremont, 'Théorie des Sources [An Autonomous Regime of Identification of Customary International Humanitarian Law: Do Not Say What You Do or Do Not Do What You Say?]' in Raphaël van Steenberghe (ed.), *Droit international humanitaire: Un régime spécial de droit international?* (Bruylant 2013) 67–95 at 77–78.

of developments in the theory of sources and in its application specifically to IHL.

Following some preliminary remarks on the role of positivism in IHL, Sections 2, 3 and 4 examine the challenges to a positivist account of IHL in the context of the specific sources of international law – treaties, custom and general principles. It is not the purpose of this chapter to account for every norm of IHL through each of the sources or to provide an exhaustive account of each source of law. Rather, it is to highlight some of the strengths and weaknesses of each of the sources as they are manifested in present-day IHL, and the manner in which sources doctrine has been modified to preserve its authority in the face of these challenges.

Before embarking on an investigation of positivism's present-day persistence with regard to IHL, one implied proposition merits scrutiny, namely that a positivist approach *is capable* of accounting for IHL. If this proposition is questionable, it is because international law in general is difficult to account for in value-neutral terms. Even the identification of the ostensibly objective element of customary international law, namely state practice, is not value-neutral. The choice to regard certain conduct or inaction, but not other, as relevant to the formation of custom, and the relative weight given to the practice of different states at different times, are all value-laden decisions. The interpretation of state conduct is not an automatic operation, but involves the choice and use of conceptual matrices that are controversial and that usually allow one to argue either way.[4] Indeed, positivism is merely an attempt at taming the complexity of cognition politics.

At the same time, a positivist approach is crucial to the authority of IHL. Implementation of IHL is ultimately in the hands of military persons on the battlefield, in situations of life-threatening urgency. Under such circumstances, the law cannot be effective if it is perceived as morally negotiable. More generally, a positivist approach is an important tool in pursuing a policy of greater compliance.[5] In this IHL differs, for example, from areas of international law which are regarded as facilitative and in which reciprocal obligations provide an incentive for compliance. Although compliance with the laws of armed conflict may be promoted by the expectation of reciprocation by adversaries, failure of the latter does

[4] Martti Koskenniemi, 'Review: The Pull of the Mainstream' 88 *Michigan Law Review* (1990) 1946–1962 at 1951.

[5] Thus explaining the liberal interpretation of state practice adopted by the ICRC; see d'Aspremont, n. 3 at 90.

not exempt from obligation. IHL also differs from areas of international law where there are extra-legal incentives for compliance, such as economic advantages. The laws of armed conflict are rarely accompanied by corresponding benefits, at least not in the immediate term. It is therefore particularly important to establish the force of the law, and consequently the commitment of the state, through a mechanism that is undisputed in form or content. Indeed, governments charged with violations constantly invoke the difference between what the law is and what it should be.[6] The inherent political and moral enmity which characterises the situations in which IHL is invoked makes the appeal to the morality of governments an unlikely vehicle for furthering humanitarian goals. In addition, a positivist approach is indispensable in international criminal law, an aspect of IHL which has acquired particular prominence in scholarship and practice since the 1990s. The principle of legality dictates that only a positivist approach to law can support a criminal process.[7] The positivist doctrine has therefore not lost its appeal, despite the value-laden agenda of IHL. Yet, the tension between the naturalist agenda and the source doctrine is an undeniable challenge. The following sections consider various attempts to attenuate this tension.

2 Treaties as a source of IHL

The written form provides a strong practical foundation, notwithstanding the fact that the content of written norms is often contested. For military personnel, the availability of the rules in black and white holds a promise of being readily applicable without requiring extensive research on practice.[8] IHL is not only one of the earliest[9] and most codified branches of international law, but its numerous instruments are also well coordinated.[10] Despite the lamentation of its paucity,[11] conventional IHL is continuously

6 Bruno Simma, Andreas Paulus, 'The Responsibility of Individuals for Human Rights Abuses in Internal Conflicts: A Positivist View' 93 *AJIL* (1999) 302–316 at 303.

7 Simma and Paulus, n. 6 at 303.

8 Marco Sassòli, Antoine Bouvier, Anne Quintin (eds), *How Does Law Protect in War? Cases, Documents and Teaching Materials on Contemporary Practice in International Humanitarian Law*, Vol. 1 (3rd edn ICRC 2011) 149–150.

9 Stephen C. Neff, 'A Short History of International Law' in Malcolm Evans (ed.), *International Law* (3rd edn Oxford University Press 2010) 3–31 at 20.

10 Sassòli, Bouvier and Quintin, n. 8 at 149.

11 Theodor Meron, *Human Rights and Humanitarian Norms as Customary Law* (Clarendon Press 1989); Theodor Meron, 'The Continuing Role of Custom in the Formation of International Humanitarian Law' 90 *AJIL* (1996) 238–249 at 247.

expanding, primarily in the areas of prohibitions and restrictions on weapons and participation of particular groups in armed conflict. Numerous treaties have been adopted in recent years that deal specifically with situations of armed conflict,[12] in addition to treaties of a more general application that might be applicable also in situations of armed conflict. As late as 1983, Meron, later one of the strongest proponents of basing IHL in customary international law, advocated the development of a new conventional instrument to fill a gap in the then-sparse law of non-international armed conflict.[13]

Yet, treaty law has its limitations. The main difficulty often cited in relying on it to substantiate any area of law is that treaties per se only bind states which are party to them. Importantly, however, while this is a strong proposition against the efficacy of treaty law as source of law in general, as a matter of practice, the four Geneva Conventions, which contain the bulk of IHL, have been accepted by all states in the world. These are in fact the only international treaties which enjoy universal membership.[14] The importance of the latter cannot be overstated, as will be discussed below.

[12] International Convention against the Recruitment, Use, Financing and Training of Mercenaries 1989, 2163 UNTS 75 (Mercenaries Convention 1989); Convention on the Prohibition of the Development, Production, Stockpiling and Use of Chemical Weapons and on their Destruction 1993, 1974 UNTS 45 (CWC 1993); Additional Protocol to the Convention on Prohibitions or Restrictions on the Use of Certain Conventional Weapons which may be deemed to be Excessively Injurious or to have Indiscriminate Effects (Protocol IV, entitled Protocol on Blinding Laser Weapons) 1995, 1380 UNTS 370; Protocol on Prohibitions or Restrictions on the Use of Mines, Booby-Traps and Other Devices as amended on 3 May 1996 (Protocol II to the 1980 Convention, as amended on 3 May 1996) 2048 UNTS 93; Convention on the Prohibition of the Use, Stockpiling, Production and Transfer of Anti-Personnel Mines and on their Destruction 1997, 2056 UNTS 211 (Ottawa Convention 1997); Rome Statute of the International Criminal Court 1998; Second Protocol to the Hague Convention of 1954 for the Protection of Cultural Property in the Event of Armed Conflict 1999 (P II Cultural Property Convention 1999); Optional Protocol to the Convention on the Rights of the Child on the Involvement of Children in Armed Conflict 2000, 2173 UNTS 222; Protocol on Explosive Remnants of War to the Convention on Prohibitions or Restrictions on the Use of Certain Conventional Weapons which may be deemed to be Excessively Injurious or to have Indiscriminate Effects 1980 (Protocol V) 2003, 2399 UNTS 100; Protocol additional to the Geneva Conventions of 12 August 1949, relating to the Adoption of an Additional Distinctive Emblem (Protocol III) 2005; Convention on Cluster Munitions 2008 (Cluster Munitions 2008).

[13] Theodor Meron, 'On the Inadequate Reach of Humanitarian and Human Rights Law and the Need for a New Instrument' 77 *AJIL* (1983) 589–606.

[14] With regard to other IHL treaties, the number of state parties ranges from 60 parties and 15 signatories to the Second Protocol 1999 to 188 parties and two signatories to the CWC 1993.

A more significant drawback to the reliance on treaty law in IHL is the fact that treaties, including the Geneva Conventions, are often subject to reservation and denunciation. IHL treaties are no exception. The post-1980 IHL treaties, dealing with weapons and prohibited classes of participants, all contain provisions on denunciation. Most of them are silent on reservations, thereby implicitly permitting them,[15] provided that they are not incompatible with the object and purpose of the treaty.[16] However, in the absence of an authorised monitoring body, the assessment of whether a reservation is lawful remains a matter of state parties' judgment. The practice of states to date has been to remain silent on the matter.

Perhaps the strongest critique of treaty law as a source of IHL has been that it does not adequately cover important areas of armed conflict, most crucially non-international conflicts, which constitute the bulk of contemporary armed conflicts.[17] Although most IHL treaties concluded since the 1990s apply also in non-international armed conflicts,[18] it is true that the majority of IHL, as embodied in The Hague and Geneva instruments, applies to non-international armed conflict only to the limited extent of Common Article 3 and of Additional Protocol II, which has not been widely accepted by states.

The limited content of conventional IHL, particularly on non-international armed conflict, is cited as one of the major stimuli for turning to customary international law as a source of IHL rather than

15 Arts XVI, XXII CWC 1992; Arts 20, 19 Ottawa Convention 1997; Arts 20, 19 Cluster Munitions Convention 2008 permit withdrawal but no reservations; Art. 20 Mercenaries Convention 1989 permits denunciation and allows reservation only to the dispute settlement mechanism; Art. 9 Convention on Prohibitions or Restrictions on the Use of Certain Conventional Weapons Which May be Deemed to be Excessively Injurious or to Have Indiscriminate Effects 1980 (CCW Convention 1980); Art. 45 Second Protocol 1999; Art. 11 Optional Protocol to the Convention on the Rights of the Child on the Involvement of Children in Armed Conflict 2000 permit denunciation and are silent on reservations.

16 Art. 19 Vienna Convention on the Law of Treaties 1969; *Reservations to the Convention on the Prevention and Punishment of the Crime of Genocide*, Advisory Opinion of 28 May 1951, ICJ Reports (1951) 15 at 29.

17 Jean-Marie Henckaerts, 'International Humanitarian Law as Customary International Law' 21 *Refugee Survey Quarterly* (2002) 186–193 at 187.

18 Treaties that apply also in non-international armed conflict are: the ICC Statute 1998; the 1996 Amended Mines Protocol; the CWC 1992; the Convention for the Protection of Cultural Property in the Event of Armed Conflict 1954 and its Second Protocol 1999; Protocol Additional to the Geneva Conventions of 12 August 1949, and relating to the Protection of Victims of Non-International Armed Conflicts (Protocol II) 1977; Art. 3 Geneva Conventions I–IV 1949 ('Common Article 3'); the Ottawa Convention 1997; the Convention on Cluster Munitions 2008.

treaty law.[19] At the same time, treaty interpretation has also undergone a process of emancipation from traditional forms, making increasing reference to the practice of relevant international bodies. It is argued that state parties to the Geneva Conventions, having in good faith undertaken treaty obligations, are subsequently bound to accept the amplification of their treaty obligations as elaborated through virtually unanimous international practice.[20] One set of norms and standards (particularly attractive candidates for this paradigm, although not without some qualifications) is the jurisprudence of the International Criminal Tribunal for the former Yugoslavia (ICTY) and other tribunals, which is of particular importance since it deals extensively with non-international armed conflict. Often, this jurisprudence is put forward as an element in the formation of customary international law or of general principles of international law.[21] However, while it is questionable whether tribunals can be regarded as participants in the creation of law, in which case the role of jurisprudence in the formation of custom is at least doubtful, there is no doubt that tribunals have a role in shedding light on existing law. Their jurisprudence may therefore be regarded as an interpretation of Common Article 3. Given the widespread acceptance of this jurisprudence, it may also be regarded as authoritative.[22] Such characterisation avoids the difficulties associated with establishing customary international law, discussed below. It is also more appropriate than characterisation as general principles of international law, since much of the ICTY's jurisprudence is nuanced and cannot be claimed to reflect general principles.[23]

A further critique of the limited value of treaty law as a source of IHL is that treaties do not bind key participants in armed conflict, namely non-state armed groups. This argument rests on the principle of *pacta tertiis nec nocent nec prosunt.* However, while this principle applies in the relations among states, it does not necessarily preclude the binding effect

[19] John Murphy, *The Evolving Dimensions of International Law: Hard Choices for the World Community* (Cambridge University Press 2010) 164–165.

[20] For implementation of this approach with regard to human rights law, see Bruno Simma and Philip Alston, 'The Sources of Human Rights Law: Custom, Jus Cogens, and General Principles' 12 *Australian Year Book of International Law* (1988) 82–107 at 100–102.

[21] Simma and Paulus, n. 6 at 313. See subsequent parts for discussion of tribunal jurisprudence under these categories.

[22] On impact-based conceptions of international law-ascertainment, see d'Aspremont, n. 2 at 122–127.

[23] Nonetheless, the jurisprudence of the Tribunals as interpretation of Common Art. 3 requires acceptance of this Article as the basis for individual criminal responsibility in non-international armed conflict. This, itself, is less than obvious. Simma and Paulus, n. 6 at 311–312.

of treaties on sub-state entities. States, as the fundamental units of the global order, by definition exist to exercise authority over individuals and sub-state groups, and thus can bind the latter on the basis of their own sovereignty and independence.[24] When a state accepts a treaty, it does so not only on behalf of itself, but, insofar as this is relevant, also on behalf of all individuals within its territory.[25] This understanding of the role of treaties is evident in Common Article 3, which was clearly intended to serve as a means of imposing international obligations on non-state armed groups. The same is true today for various treaties which purport to bind non-state parties to armed conflicts.[26] There is no reason to distinguish, in this respect, between treaty law and customary international law.[27]

Moreover, non-state armed groups need not be only 'third parties'. There are occasional treaty mechanisms that expressly invite non-state actors to adhere to them. Even in IHL, such a possibility exists (Article 96(3) Additional Protocol I). In specific instances, bilateral agreements between a state and an armed group, or between an armed group and an international organisation, could be considered a treaty or akin to a treaty.[28]

Finally, whatever the flaws of treaty law as a means of binding non-state actors, it would be erroneous to assume that they can be rectified by resort to customary international law.[29] Customary international law does not apply to non-state actors any more automatically than treaty law. Such application depends on the subject matter, namely on whether the norm was intended to apply to non-state actors. If the norm itself is not substantively directed at non-state actors, it makes little difference whether it is classified as conventional or customary.

24 Marko Milanović, 'Is the Rome Statute Binding on Individuals? (And Why We Should Care)' 9 *Journal of International Criminal Justice* (2011) 25–52 at 39.

25 Sandesh Sivakumaran, 'Binding Armed Opposition Groups' 55 *ICLQ* (2006) 369–394 at 381.

26 Art. 19 Hague Convention 1954; Amended Art. 1(3) CCW Convention 1980/2001; Art. 1(3) Amended Protocol II to the Convention on CCW, all provide that 'each party to the conflict shall be bound to apply' certain rules. Sandesh Sivakumaran, 'Re-envisaging the International Law of Internal Armed Conflict' 22 *EJIL* (2011) 219–264 at 248. See criticism by Alexander Zahar, 'Civilizing Civil War: Writing Morality as Law at the ICTY' in Bert Swart, Alexander Zahar, Göran Sluiter (eds), *The Legacy of the International Criminal Tribunal for the Former Yugoslavia* (Oxford University Press 2011) 469–506.

27 Admittedly, this does leave open the question of transnational groups over which states do not claim legal or physical authority, such as the Palestinian Authority. However, such exceptional instances hardly detract from the validity or utility of the general proposition.

28 Sandesh Sivakumaran, 'The International Law of Internal Armed Conflict' 9 *Journal of International Criminal Justice* (2011) 281–295 at 294; Sivakumaran, n. 25.

29 For potential explanations, see Sivakumaran, n. 25.

In conclusion, notwithstanding certain limitations to the efficacy of treaty law as a source of IHL, treaties continue to play a vital role in substantiating IHL. This should be borne in mind when evaluating the critique that has been voiced against reliance on treaty law at the turn of the twenty-first century, particularly in support of turning to customary international law as a panacea. The difficulties in this approach are discussed in the following section.

3 Customary international law as a source of IHL

Customary international law is binding upon all states, and it cannot be denounced or qualified by reservation, although states can contract out of it when it does not reflect *ius cogens* or object to it persistently. These qualities are counterbalanced by the more complex process by which custom emerges. In other words, theoretically at least, there is a trade-off between the creation of customary law, which sets more rigorous conditions than the creation of treaty law, and the stability of custom as a source of law once it is found to exist. Yet, the authority of customary international law as a source of IHL runs into a serious obstacle, namely the fact that state practice during armed conflict often runs directly counter to the alleged norms. In the wake of both world wars, acknowledgement of the limitlessness of war had in fact led some to declare the demise of IHL;[30] others questioned the tenability of according to state conduct absolute primacy in the creation of international law.[31] Yet, customary international law has not lost its appeal. Instead, it has undergone a modification intended to preserve its validity, a modification labelled by d'Aspremont as 'emancipation'. This process has not been openly acknowledged by its authors, but its pervasiveness cannot be disputed.[32] Indeed, with time, the perception of customary international law has evolved considerably to compensate for the shortfall in state conduct.

3.1 New customary international law

A major shift in the perception of customary international law as a source of law, apparently from within the positivist approach, appeared in the

[30] For an account and critique of views to the effect that there were no longer laws of armed conflict, see Josef L. Kunz, 'The Chaotic Status of the Laws of War and the Urgent Necessity for Their Revision' 45 *AJIL* (1951) 37–61.

[31] Josef L. Kunz, 'The Laws of War' 50 *AJIL* (1956) 313–337 at 337.

[32] D'Aspremont, n. 3 at 90.

judgment of the ICJ in the *Nicaragua* case, which concerned not so much IHL as general international law. Nicaragua brought a claim against the United States for unlawful use of force. The United States' consent to the ICJ's jurisdiction, as interpreted by the Court, was limited to the extent that the dispute concerned customary international law. Consequently, the Court had to consider the rules of customary international law relating to the use of force.[33]

Rather than examine instances of state practice, in which case it would have faced the difficulty that state practice with regard to non-use of force was at best inconsistent if not outright contrary, the Court reasoned that 'practice' for the purpose of establishing a customary norm need not be in absolutely rigorous conformity with the rule, provided it is consistent 'in general' with such rules, and provided contrary conduct is generally treated as a breach rather than as an indication of a new rule.[34] The Court thus set the stage for dispensing with the need to establish uniform and consistent state practice where *opinio iuris* is well established.

The Court's reasoning was hailed by some as a means of salvaging certain legal norms from annihilation, when the gap between states' commitments and their actual practice cannot be denied. Various theories have been put forward for reconciling the Court's reasoning with the traditional formulation of custom, revealing differences on the relationship between state practice and *opinio iuris*, which are inextricably linked to the debates on what state practice consists of beyond physical acts.[35] Kirgis, for example, pursues the traditional perception of state practice as comprising physical acts, but proposes that state practice and *opinio iuris* may be balanced against each other given appropriate circumstances.[36] Similarly, Simma and Alston note that in areas of law where the obligation is to refrain from action, such as the rules on the use of force and

33 *Military and Paramilitary Activities in and against Nicaragua* (*Nicaragua v. United States of America*), Merits, Judgment of 27 June 1986, ICJ Reports (1986) 14 at 98 (para. 186).

34 *Nicaragua*, n. 33 at 98 (para. 186): 'In order to deduce the existence of customary rules, the Court deems it sufficient that the conduct of States should, in general, be consistent with such rules, and that instances of State conduct inconsistent with a given rule should generally have been treated as breaches of that rule, not as indications of the recognition of a new rule. If a State acts in a way prima facie incompatible with a recognized rule, but defends its conduct by appealing to exceptions or justifications contained within the rule itself, then whether or not the State's conduct is in fact justifiable on that basis, the significance of that attitude is to confirm rather than to weaken the rule.'

35 Jörg Kammerhofer, 'Uncertainty in the Formal Sources of International Law: Customary International Law and Some of Its Problems' 15 *EJIL* (2004) 523–553 at 525–529, 552.

36 Frederic L. Kirgis, 'Custom on a Sliding Scale' 81 *AJIL* (1987) 146–151 at 149.

IHL prohibitions, *opinio iuris* carries a particularly heavy weight.[37] Other commentators expand the scope of state practice to encompass verbal statements and adherence to treaties: this enables them not only to find evidence of state practice,[38] but also to demonstrate that practice is not inconsistent with *opinio iuris* (as physical acts might be). D'Amato relies on verbal statements to such a large degree as to argue that not only can statements replace practice, but the absence of statements can imply an absence of practice.[39]

Redefining state practice as extending beyond actual conduct permits the use of another doctrine to establish the existence of custom, namely the inference of practice from *opinio iuris*. Specifically with regard to IHL, the trend to replace state practice by *opinio iuris* or abandon the former entirely for the latter was accompanied by a converse doctrine, of inferring *opinio iuris* from practice that conforms with an alleged norm.[40] Thus, the International Committee of the Red Cross (ICRC) Study concluded that '[w]hen there is sufficiently dense practice, an *opinio juris* is generally contained within that practice and, as a result, it is not usually necessary to demonstrate separately the existence of an *opinio juris*'.[41]

A different approach from the rampant conduct contrary to alleged norms is that which openly advocates custom-ascertainment based on substantive criteria.[42] Tasioulas and Meron propose that the weight of such considerations should depend on the nature of the subject matter,[43]

37 Simma and Alston, n. 20 at 99–100.

38 Theodor Meron, 'The Geneva Conventions as Customary Law' 81 *AJIL* (1987) 348–370 at 361; Simma and Paulus, n. 6 at 306–307, describing with approval the reasoning in *Tadić* (ICTY, *Prosecutor v. Duško Tadić*, Case No. IT-94–1, Appeals Chamber, Decision on the Defence Motion for Interlocutory Appeal on Jurisdiction of 2 October 1995).

39 '[T]orture does not count as practice if no state cites it as practice', Anthony D'Amato, 'New Approaches to Customary International Law' 105 *AJIL* (2011) 163–167 at 164.

40 Meron, n. 38 at 368: 'observance of the provisions of the Conventions, especially if accompanied by verbal affirmations supporting the binding, even *erga omnes*, character of the humanitarian principles stated in the Conventions, may constitute *opinio juris*'.

41 Jean-Marie Henckaerts, Louise Doswald-Beck, *Customary International Humanitarian Law*, Vol. 1 (Cambridge University Press 2005) xl.

42 D'Aspremont, n. 2 at 119–120.

43 Meron, n. 38 at 368–369: 'Perhaps because of the strong moral claim for the application and observance of the norms in instruments relating to international human rights and humanitarian law (to which these comments are confined), and because of the different kinds of evidence of state practice involved, both scholarly and judicial sources have shown reluctance to reject as candidates for customary law status, because of contrary practice, conventional norms whose content merits such status' (footnotes omitted); John Tasioulas, 'In Defence of Relative Normativity: Communitarian Values and the Nicaragua Case' 16 *Oxford Journal of Legal Studies* (1996) 85–128.

while Roberts offers a complex matrix, according to which, where practice (defined widely) *combined* with *opinio iuris* is inconclusive, and where normative subject matters are at issue (such as peremptory norms), rather than facilitative ones (such as regulating maritime traffic), normative considerations would come into play.[44] Needless to say, in view of the differences over the various components of custom, the spectrum of possible interpretations of what constitutes custom is extremely broad.[45]

Common to the divergent understandings of the precise contours of state practice, *opinio iuris* and their interrelationship, is an acknowledgment that modification of the traditional custom-creating process is appropriate for bodies of law which contain a strong moral element.[46] Not surprisingly, the modern claim how to ascertain the existence of custom has found particular favour with international human rights lawyers, where the gap between the norms stated and actual practice tends to be especially wide.[47] Other bodies of law suggested as candidates for applying the new approach to creating custom are the rules on the use of force and environmental issues.[48] Interestingly, however, there has been little mention of the relevance of the doctrine to IHL. In *Nicaragua*, the ICJ's engagement with IHL was confined to a laconic statement *ex cathedra* that common Articles 1 and 3 of the Geneva Conventions constituted customary law.[49] The Court avoided making a direct statement as to whether the modern methodology for identifying custom applied also within IHL.

Meron anticipated that the Court's characterisation of Common Articles 1 and 3 of the Geneva Conventions as customary international law would, because of their humanitarian content, be invoked to support the customary character of the Geneva Conventions.[50] Indeed, he himself did so at a later stage.[51] Otherwise, academic scholarship had not invested

44 Anthea Elizabeth Roberts, 'Traditional and Modern Approaches to Customary International Law: A Reconciliation' 95 *AJIL* (2001) 757–791 at 764.

45 For an exposition of the uncertainties as to custom, see Kammerhofer, n. 35.

46 Kirgis, n. 36 at 147–148; Tasioulas, n. 43; Roberts, n. 44 at 762–764; Simma and Paulus, n. 6 at 308.

47 Meron, n. 38 at 363.

48 Roberts, n. 44 at 764; Jan Wouters, Cedric Ryngaert, 'Impact on the Process of the Formation of Customary International Law' in Menno T. Kamminga, Martin Scheinin (eds), *The Impact of Human Rights Law on General International Law* (Oxford University Press 2009) 111–131 at 128.

49 *Nicaragua*, n. 33 at 113 (para. 218).

50 Meron, *Human Rights*, n. 11 at 37.

51 Theodor Meron, 'International Criminalization of Internal Atrocities' 89 *AJIL* (1995) 554–577 at 561; Theodor Meron, 'The Humanization of Humanitarian Law' 94 *AJIL* (2000) 239–278 at 248.

heavily in the application of the new approach to ascertaining customary law specifically to IHL. This changed with the advent of two projects. One was the ICRC study on customary international law. The very engagement of the ICRC in the mapping of international customary law arose from its conviction that customary law can fulfil an important role in covering gaps in the application of treaty law.[52] The ICRC Study relied on both physical and verbal acts of states as state practice. Physical acts include, for example, battlefield behaviour, the use of certain weapons and the treatment afforded to different categories of persons. Verbal acts include military manuals, national legislation, national case law, instructions to armed and security forces, military communiqués during war, diplomatic protests, executive decisions and regulations, pleadings before international tribunals, statements in international fora, and government positions on resolutions adopted by international organisations. The study also took into account resolutions adopted by states in the framework of international organisations, in particular the United Nations and regional organisations.[53] The Study's justification for this choice echoed the reasoning of the ICJ in *Nicaragua*: 'Where violations have been accompanied by excuses or justifications by the party concerned and/or condemnation by other States, they are not of a nature to challenge the existence of the rule in question.'[54]

The other project which advanced the new approach to ascertainment of custom was the development of international criminal law. IHL scholarship of the twenty-first century tends to focus on post-1993 jurisprudence and particularly the practice of the ICTY as the watershed moment in the revival of customary international law as a source of IHL. However, reliance on customary IHL in international criminal law actually goes further back to post-Second World War jurisprudence with regard both to individual criminal responsibility (in international armed conflict), and determining the content of international crimes.

In 1946, the International Military Tribunal in Nuremberg was at pains to establish the crimes enumerated in its Charter as law applicable to the conduct of the defendants at the time of the commission of the alleged offences. It laconically stated that the 1907 Hague Convention IV had been, and at any rate had become, declaratory of the laws and customs of

52 Henckaerts, n. 17 at 186–188.

53 Jean-Marie Henckaerts, 'Customary International Humanitarian Law: Taking Stock of the ICRC Study' 78 *Nordic Journal of International Law* (2010) 435–468 at 444–445.

54 Jean-Marie Henckaerts, 'Study on Customary International Humanitarian Law: A Contribution to the Understanding and Respect for the Rule of Law in Armed Conflict' 87 *International Review of the Red Cross* (2005) 175–212 at 180.

war.[55] Similar lack of concern for rigorous proof of the existence of practice or *opinio iuris* was evident in the International Military Tribunal for the Far East's characterisation of the Hague Convention IV as 'good evidence of the customary law of nations';[56] and in the US military tribunal in *US v. von Leeb* ('German High Command Trial') in which the Tribunal extrapolated from The Hague Regulations to the 1929 Geneva Convention on Prisoners of War.[57] Clearly, the most fundamental context in which the criminal tribunals' disinterest in a rigorous examination of the fulfilment of the requisites of custom is the very notion of individual criminal responsibility under international law. Oddly enough, it is in the area of criminal law that the flexibility in defining customary international law has reached its peak, with the tribunals abandoning all pretence of relying on state practice, resorting instead exclusively and expressly to extra-legal normative considerations.

In the *Eichmann* case, which for many years served as the authority for the existence of universal jurisdiction under international law, the Israeli Supreme Court noted the doctrinal controversy over the existence of a right to exercise universal jurisdiction, and then proceeded to state that the rationale for employing universal jurisdiction with regard to piracy 'justifies its exercise in regard also to the crimes which are the subject of the present case'.[58] In other words, the Court did not shy away from

[55] IMT Nuremberg, Judgment of 1 October 1946, in *Trial of the Major War Criminals before the International Military Tribunal, Nuremberg 14 November 1945–1 October 1946*, Vol. 1 (1947) 171–341 at 220–221, 228: 'The Hague Convention of 1907 prohibited resort to certain methods of waging war . . . Many of these prohibitions had been enforced long before the date of the Convention; but since 1907 they have certainly been crimes, punishable as offences against the laws of war; yet the Hague Convention nowhere designates such practices as criminal, nor is any sentence prescribed, nor any mention made of a court to try and punish offenders. For many years past, however, military tribunals have tried and punished individuals guilty of violating the rules of land warfare laid down by this Convention . . . Article 6(b) of the Charter provides that "ill-treatment . . . of civilian population of or in occupied territory . . . killing of hostages . . . wanton destruction of cities, towns or villages" shall be a war crime. In the main these provisions are merely declaratory of the existing laws of war as expressed by the Article 46 of the Hague Convention, which stated: "Family honour and rights, the lives of persons and private property, as well as religious convictions and practices must be respected."'

[56] IMT Far East, [*Hirota and Others*], Judgment of 4 November 1948, 15 ILR (1948) 356–376 at 366.

[57] IMT Nuremberg, [*The High Command Case*], Judgment of 27–28 November 1948, in *Trials of War Criminals before the Nuremberg Military Tribunals under Control Council Law No. 10 Nuernberg October 1946–April 1949*, Vol. 10 (US Government Printing Office 1951) 462–694.

[58] Supreme Court of Israel, *Attorney General v. Eichmann*, Judgment of 29 May 1962, 36 ILR (1968) 277–344 at 300 (emphasis added).

confirming its jurisdiction on normative rather than positive grounds, notwithstanding the fact that at issue was a criminal process.

In *Tadić*, the first case heard by the ICTY, the defendant challenged the Tribunal's competence inter alia on the ground that the subject matter jurisdiction under the ICTY Statute did not extend to crimes committed in the context of a non-international armed conflict. The Tribunal rejected this argument, concluding that its jurisdiction under the Statute extended also over violations of IHL committed in an internal conflict.[59] It then proceeded to examine what these criminal acts included. If one expected the Tribunal to examine state practice and *opinio iuris*, and then possibly confront any shortcomings that those would reveal, such expectation was thwarted. The Tribunal explained why state practice – whether physical or verbal – can be dispensed with when ascertaining the existence of a customary rule or general principle:

> It is difficult, if not impossible, to pinpoint the actual behaviour of the troops in the field, because access to the theatre of military operations is normally refused to independent observers, information on the actual conduct of hostilities is withheld by the parties to the conflict, and, what is worse, often recourse is had to misinformation with a view to misleading the enemy as well as public opinion and foreign Governments. Consequently, in appraising the formation of customary rules, on account of the inherent nature of this subject matter, reliance must primarily be placed on such elements as official pronouncements of States, military manuals and judicial decisions.[60]

In this statement, the Tribunal went far beyond the pre-existing propensity to rely on verbal acts to replace physical ones:[61] it abandoned altogether the 'state practice' element in the identification of custom, opting for the ultra-modern method of reliance only on abstract, principled *opinio iuris* (leaving aside the question[62] of whether manuals reflect *opinio iuris* or policy considerations).[63] This reasoning of the Tribunal is open to

59 *Tadić*, n. 38, paras 65–95. 60 *Tadić*, n. 38, para. 99.

61 Dealing with the same practical difficulty of ascertaining significant state practice in periods of hostilities, Meron had earlier advocated consideration of verbal statements (through manuals of military and internal law) 'as among the best types of evidence of such practice and, sometimes perhaps, as a statement of *opinio juris* as well' (Meron, n. 38 at 361).

62 E.g. John Bellinger III, William Haynes II, 'A US Government Response to the International Committee of the Red Cross Study *Customary International Humanitarian Law*' 89 *International Review of the Red Cross* (2007) 443–471 at 445.

63 The notion that even verbal statements in the context of specific conflicts must be regarded with suspicion was taken up by the ICRC, which also notes the difficulty of ascertaining

criticism, to say the least. Active battlefields are growing more, rather than less, transparent with time. If considerations of convenience had not led to the abandonment of state conduct as an element in creating IHL until now, there is hardly reason to go this way today. Furthermore, the Tribunal openly admitted its ideological project, stating, for example, that the distinction between international and internal armed conflict '*should* gradually lose its weight';[64] that 'elementary considerations of humanity and common sense *make it* preposterous' that use of weapons that are prohibited in international conflicts be permitted in internal conflicts, because 'what is inhumane, and consequently proscribed, in international wars, cannot but be inhumane and inadmissible in civil strife';[65] with regard to individual criminal responsibility the ICTY said that 'the notion that serious violations of international humanitarian law governing internal armed conflicts entail individual criminal responsibility *is* also fully warranted from the point of view of substantive justice and equity'.[66]

This trend of dispensing with the requirement of practice of any kind was taken up by later ICTY judgments. In *Kupreškić*, the Trial Chamber noted with respect to reprisals against civilians that it is 'an area where *opinio juris sive necessitatis* may play a much greater role than *usus*'. Accordingly, *opinio iuris* may turn out to be the decisive element heralding the emergence of a general rule of humanitarian law.[67] The Tribunal then concluded that 'principles of international humanitarian law may emerge through a customary process under the pressure of the demands of humanity or the dictates of public conscience, even where State practice is scant or inconsistent'.[68] In *Stakić*, Judge Shahabuddeen's dissent went so far as to suggest that 'the question is not whether the law, as it stands, was ever applied concretely to a particular set of circumstances, but whether the law, as it stands, was reasonably capable of applying to those circumstances'.[69]

state practice when individual soldiers' conduct may be in violation of military orders. At the same time, statements of third states on the behaviour of belligerents are included as relevant practice. Sassòli, Bouvier and Quintin, n. 8 at 152–153.

64 *Tadić*, n. 38 at para. 95. 65 *Tadić*, n. 38 at para. 119 (emphasis added).

66 *Tadić*, n. 38 at para. 135 (emphasis added).

67 ICTY, *Prosecutor v. Kupreškić et al.*, Case No. IT-95–16-T, Trial Chamber, Judgment of 14 January 2000, para. 527.

68 *Kupreškić*, n. 67 at para. 531 (emphasis added).

69 ICTY, *Prosecutor v. Stakić*, Case No. IT-97–24-A, Appeals Chamber, Judgment of 22 March 2006, Partly Diss. Op. Shahabuddeen, paras 23–32.

3.2 Critique of the new approach to customary international law with regard to IHL

IHL is thus increasingly shaped by extra-legal normative considerations even if those fly in the face of state practice. This new approach has been criticised for subjecting positive law to personal political goals.[70] The present contribution proposes to add to this critique, by engaging with the new approach on its own terms, noting that the strong extra-legal normative influence on customary international law is informed by the context in which it developed, namely the *Nicaragua* judgment and international criminal judgments. Application of this new approach to customary international law to IHL more generally is consequently not without difficulty.

First, in both *Nicaragua* and the definition of crimes (but not of individual responsibility) in the criminal tribunals, the norms in question were prohibitions. With regard to such norms, it is difficult to point to state conduct, rendering the replacement of actual conduct by verbal acts unavoidable. IHL, however, does not consist of prohibitions alone, but also imposes positive obligations. Applying the same methodology to ascertain its content as custom is therefore not in all cases appropriate.

The replacement of physical acts by verbal statements as constitutive of state practice rests on another premise that may not be wholly valid with regard to IHL. In *Nicaragua*, the ICJ relied on *opinio iuris* to establish a customary prohibition on the use of force despite contrary practice on the ground that:

> If a State acts in a way prima facie incompatible with a recognized rule, but defends its conduct by appealing to exceptions or justifications contained within the rule itself, then whether or not the State's conduct is in fact justifiable on that basis, the significance of that attitude is to confirm rather than to weaken the rule.[71]

This proposition assumes that while state practice is divergent, *opinio iuris* is preponderantly consistent. As Simma and Alston note, this proposition is suitable when the law is already settled.[72] It is suitable primarily with regard to peremptory norms such as the prohibitions on the use of force and on torture, with which it is most often associated, because the validity

[70] Jörg Kammerhofer, 'Orthodox Generalists and Political Activists in International Legal Scholarship' in Matthew Happold (ed.), *International Law in a Multipolar World* (Routledge 2010) 138–157.

[71] *Nicaragua*, n. 33 at 98 (para. 186).

[72] Simma and Alston, n. 20 at 97.

of such norms is not affected by contrary practice. It is in this light that one should read Cassese's statement in 1984 applying the *Nicaragua* formula with regard to Common Article 3 when he wrote that it has:

> [G]radually turned into a set of rules that all States regarded as fundamental, regardless of their being parties to the Geneva Conventions . . . it has become legally impossible for any State to deny the applicability of those fundamental safeguards in cases of civil strife.[73]

This statement builds on a proposition noted by the ICJ, that certain IHL norms are peremptory.[74] However, while certain IHL norms may be clear and even of peremptory character, such as the prohibition on intentional targeting of non-combatants or the protections to which protected groups are entitled, other fundamental terms of IHL are still under debate, such as the meaning of proportionality (for example, how does force protection factor into the calculation of excessive incidental injury) or the permissibility of reprisals. The *Nicaragua* formula is much less suitable for such issues, where the norms are in the process of formation. Nonetheless, it has permeated into IHL, with the ICRC noting that in identifying state practice, the corollary of an acting state's stance was the response of other states:

[73] Antonio Cassese, 'The Geneva Protocols of 1977 on the Humanitarian Law of Armed Conflict and Customary International Law' 3 *UCLA Pacific Basin Law Journal* (1984) 55–118 at 108.

[74] In *Legality of the Threat or Use of Nuclear Weapons*, Advisory Opinion of 8 July 1996, ICJ Reports (1996) 226 at 257 (para. 79), the ICJ refrained from deciding whether the pertinent principles and rules were in fact peremptory on the ground that this question went to the legal character of the norm, a matter which the Court did not need to pronounce on (at 258 (para. 83)). Other than in *Nicaragua*, the Court has avoided using the term 'peremptory norms' or *ius cogens*, but has used other terms which seemed to bear, in its view, a similar effect. Alexander Orakhelashvili, *Peremptory Norms in International Law* (Oxford University Press 2006) 41–43. For example, in *Wall*, it stated that some international humanitarian law norms have an *erga omnes* character: *Legal Consequences of the Construction of a Wall in the Occupied Palestinian Territory*, Advisory Opinion of 9 July 2004, ICJ Reports (2004) 136 at 199 (paras 155, 157). See also International Law Commission, 'Draft Articles on Responsibility of States for Internationally Wrongful Acts' in International Law Commission, Report of the International Law Commission on the Work of its Fifty-Third Session 23 April to 1 June and 2 July to 10 August 2001, UN Doc. A/56/10, 53 *Yearbook of the International Law Commission*, Vol. II.2 (2001) 26–143 at 112–113 (Commentary to Art. 40, paras 4, 5); but see *Wall*, n. 74 at 217 (Sep. Op. Higgins, para. 39). Stefan Kadelbach, '*Jus Cogens*, Obligations *Erga Omnes* and other Rules – The Identification of Fundamental Norms' in Christian Tomuschat, Jean-Marc Thouvenin (eds), *The Fundamental Rules of the International Legal Order: Jus Cogens and Obligations Erga Omnes* (Martinus Nijhoff 2006) 21–40 at 30–31.

> When an operational practice is generally considered to be a violation of existing rules – e.g., the targeting of civilian installations – that is all it is, a violation not of a nature to modify existing rules. This explains why acts such as attacks against civilians, pillage and sexual violence remain prohibited notwithstanding numerous reports of their commission. The conclusion that these acts are considered to be violations of existing rules can be derived only from the way they are received by the international community through verbal acts . . . These verbal acts provide the lens through which to look at operational practice.[75]

Identifying norms according to normative considerations and then declaring any contrary practice to be in violation of the norm runs the risk of creating law where it did not exist previously.[76] This is particularly apparent in the work of the international criminal tribunals. When the ICTY was established, the UN Secretary-General explained the confinement of the Tribunal's subject matter jurisdiction to customary law as a means of circumventing questions of adherence by some but not all states to specific instruments.[77] In practice, however, the reliance on new custom enabled the ICTY to overcome a fundamental obstacle to its operation, namely the fact that individual criminal responsibility had barely been established in international law, and certainly not with regard to crimes committed in a non-international armed conflict. Had the Tribunal attempted to rely on treaty law, this obstacle would have been amply visible, and prosecution would have been in violation of the principle of legality. Reliance on customary law allowed the obfuscation of the obstacle. Ironically, in proving the existence of customary norms, tribunals have often relied on treaty provisions, both accepted by relevant states and others. But the treatment of treaty provisions as reflective of customary law rather than as treaty law provides an immediate escape from two constrictions of the latter. One is the date on which the norm has come to

[75] Henckaerts, n. 53 at 444.

[76] For the question of whether (and what level of) compliance with a norm is required for its validity, see Jörg Kammerhofer, *Uncertainty in International Law: A Kelsenian Perspective* (Routledge 2010) 85–86.

[77] Report of the UN Secretary-General Pursuant to Paragraph 2 of Security Council Resolution 808 (1993), UN Doc. S/25704 (3 May 1993) 9 (para. 34) (one might question the implied premise of these statements, namely that customary international law was directly binding upon the alleged offenders). Thus, the ICTY itself later commented that if a treaty had been available that was binding at the time of the commission of the alleged offence and that established individual criminal responsibility, it would have provided a good basis for prosecution. Milanović, n. 24 at 44; ICTY, *Prosecutor v. Kordić and Čerkez*, IT-95–14/2-A, Appeals Chamber, Judgment of 17 December 2004, paras 40–46.

exist,[78] which is clear in treaties but less so in custom. The other is the rules of interpretation of treaties, which, for example, require reliance on the wording of the treaty unless it is ambiguous.[79] By regarding treaty text as an expression of state practice or *opinio iuris*, tribunals have been able to advance teleological interpretations even when the language of the treaty was clear. The development of individual criminal responsibility in non-international armed conflict is a clear example of such engineering: the general absence of treaty law on non-international armed conflict and of individual criminal responsibility in such conflicts is the result of a deliberate choice by states to exclude such commitment and responsibility.[80] A rigorous application of the requirements of custom in the traditional manner would have revealed this. Yet, by dispensing with the requirement of state practice on the one hand, and by including under *opinio iuris* an unlimited range of sources, tribunals have been able to conceive new law when none existed before.

The development of new custom in the context of international criminal law is particularly worrying in view of the requirement under the principle of legality of strict interpretation of norms. The international tribunals' jurisprudence has not only adopted the modern method of ascertaining custom which modified the intractable element of state practice, but has taken it to the extreme of eliminating the requirement of state practice altogether. While the moral imperative guiding the various tribunals' vigorous policy, each in its own turn, is evident, it is precisely against the potential for misuse and abuse of the latitude of new customary international law that Judge Robertson warned in the *Child Recruitment* case in the Special Court for Sierra Leone, arguing forcefully against resort to substantive justice based on normative considerations. He wrote that it is precisely when the acts are abhorrent and deeply shocking that the principle of legality must be most stringently applied, to ensure that a defendant is not convicted out of disgust or of a non-existent crime.[81]

Although the need to renew customary international law has been forcefully advocated since the 1990s, its relevance to IHL arose in very

78 SCSL, *Prosecutor v. Norman*, SCSL-2004–14-AR72(E), Appeals Chamber, Decision on Preliminary Motion Based on Lack of Jurisdiction (Child Recruitment) of 31 May 2004, Diss. Op. Robertson, para. 13.

79 For a discussion of treaty interpretation, see Hernández, Chapter 12.

80 David Forsythe, 'Legal Management of Internal War: The 1977 Protocol on Non-International Armed Conflicts' 72 *AJIL* (1978) 272–295; Sivakumaran, n. 26 at 222; Zahar, n. 26.

81 *Norman*, n. 78 at para. 2 (Diss. Op. Robertson).

specific circumstances. In *Nicaragua*, at issue was the enforcement of state responsibility, which was hindered by a particular reservation to the ICJ Statute's optional clause granting the ICJ jurisdiction in contentious cases. That this involved a determination on the formation of customary international law was a particular consequence of the idiosyncrasies of the specific case. To illustrate this particularity, suffice it to note that had there not been a matter of potential impact of the judgment on El Salvador, the ICJ would have been able to adjudicate the case on the basis of the UN Charter, and the existence of customary law might have continued to depend, as a matter of doctrine, on evidence of state practice. Similarly, if the dispute had not been about the prohibition on the use of force but about a different peremptory norm, such as the prohibition on slavery, the Court might still not have had the opportunity to develop its new doctrine, because state practice would have been sufficiently consistent to fulfil the requisites for the existence of custom.

Thus, Kirgis rightly noted that 'the alternative [to finding customary international law] would be an international legal order containing ominous silences – where treaty commitments cannot be found – concerning the ways in which states impose their wills on other states or on individuals'.[82]

The fact is, however, that there *were* treaty commitments reflecting the norms in question, and this was no coincidence; it is the very uniformity of *opinio iuris* that the Court relied on to establish the existence of custom that had also enabled the conclusion of the treaty commitment (in the UN Charter). It is because of this that state practice is so important: if *opinio iuris* is perceived as sufficient for the creation of custom, the latter becomes indistinguishable from an un-adopted treaty text – but unlike such text, it is binding.[83] Other than in the context of peremptory norms, this outcome is unacceptable. Accordingly, irrespective of the merits of the modern version of custom more generally, the circumstances of *Nicaragua* were sufficiently unique so as to preclude or at least militate against any general inferences from it.

Moreover, in both the ICJ and the criminal frameworks, the modification of customary international law took place in the context of establishing the formal or substantive jurisdiction of a legal means of enforcement, the Achilles heel of international law. Neither concerned state responsibility – the classic context in which IHL is invoked.

[82] Kirgis, n. 36 at 148.

[83] Against this background, Simma and Alston suggest differentiating customary international law from general principles of law (Simma and Alston, n. 20).

The developments discussed here demonstrate how sources theories have been liberally applied to IHL to serve various political agendas, such as maintenance of peace and security, and confirmation of the importance of the principle of legality. D'Aspremont queries whether this emancipation from traditional doctrines constitutes fragmentation of source theory in the field of IHL, concluding that it is too early to declare that a new doctrine has been established.[84] It appears pertinent to add that the process was not triggered from within the context of IHL, although it has had a profound impact on the field. This is not to say that customary law is superfluous or that the new method of identifying it is generally inappropriate, but merely to point out that the idiosyncrasies of the landmark instances where the modern custom developed should be taken into account before the doctrine is extended elsewhere. Whether new customary international law is an appropriate vehicle for classic IHL thus remains an open question.

4 General principles of international law

The notion of general principles of humanitarian law appears in the practice of the ICJ,[85] but has not received much scholarly attention.[86] In the late 1990s, dissatisfied with the direction in which custom was developed in order to account for international human rights law, Simma and Alston proposed that international human rights law may be classified as general principles of international law. According to Simma and Alston, what is required for the establishment of norms as general principles is essentially the same kind of convincing evidence of general acceptance and recognition that are necessary in order to arrive at customary law; unlike state practice, general principles of law are a more direct and spontaneous expression in legal form of moral and humanitarian considerations.[87]

The main difference between customary international law and general principles according to these authors is thus precisely in the weight attached to articulation of generalised *opinio iuris* as against state practice. To maintain the distinction between the two sources, Simma and

[84] D'Aspremont, n. 3 at 85–94.

[85] *Nuclear Weapons*, n. 74 at 266; *Corfu Channel (United Kingdom v. Albania)*, Merits, Judgment of 9 April 1949, ICJ Reports (1949) 4 at 22. See also *Nicaragua*, n. 33 at 113 (para. 218).

[86] For a discussion of existing literature on general principles see Kammerhofer, Chapter 4 at 105–122.

[87] Simma and Alston, n. 20 at 105.

Alston's proposal effectively distinguishes between *opinio iuris* of individual states as a requisite component in the creation of customary law, and generalised *opinio iuris* as expressed, for example, in the work of international organisations.[88] Conceived in this manner, general principles of law provide a suitable means of expanding positive IHL in terms of both participants and content. Simma and Alston note, for example, that widespread acceptance of the jurisprudence of the international tribunals on individual criminal responsibility for violations of IHL in internal conflicts can be taken as evidence that such enforcement is nowadays permitted by a general principle of law.[89] The same can be said for other elements in the jurisprudence of the tribunals.

One might consider that it is a matter of semantics – Simma and Alston reclassify as general principles of law what other scholars have entitled customary international law. However, general principles of law differ from custom in that they remain in the more abstract level. On the one hand, this allows incorporation of a more substantial extra-legal normative component in the law, because of the open-endedness of principles as opposed to rules. On the other hand, the same open-endedness may also undermine the usefulness of principles because they stop short of establishing rules. For example, the two fundamental principles of IHL, humanity[90] and military necessity, are both established beyond doubt, but constitute standards, not practicable rules. It is the balance between them that informs specific rules of IHL, and this balance can hardly be regarded as 'principled'. Thus, general principles of law provide a useful point of departure, but they do not account for particular rules that derive from principles. In this respect, their utility for international human rights law might be greater than for IHL, and not easily transposed to it.[91]

5 Conclusion

Despite the crisis of credibility that positivism has been undergoing, it remains the *lingua franca* of international lawyers,[92] evidencing its enduring utility. At the same time, traditional source doctrines present

88 Simma and Alston, n. 20 at 102–103. 89 Simma and Paulus, n. 6 at 312–313.

90 The ICJ in the *Corfu Channel* case referred to 'certain general and well-recognized principles, namely: elementary considerations of humanity' (*Corfu Channel*, n. 85 at 22).

91 On the role of standards and rules in IHL, see Amichai Cohen, 'Rules and Standards in the Application of International Humanitarian Law' 40 *Israel Law Review* (2008) 41–67.

92 Steven Ratner, Anne-Marie Slaughter, 'Appraising the Methods of International Law: A Prospectus for Readers' 93 *AJIL* (1999) 291–302 at 293.

challenges to substantiation of IHL, indeed of international law.[93] This acknowledgement has led to a development of a modern, qualified form of positivism in the context of the sources of law, particularly the less stringent form of creating custom that has emerged with full force in the 1980s and 1990s.

The limits of this development should also be acknowledged. First, the dispensation with state practice – physical and even verbal – is grounded in a set of assumptions and aimed at goals that are not universally applicable, and their applicability to IHL is questionable. Second, in distinction from other areas of law, conventional law provides a surprisingly robust basis for IHL, due to the universal membership in the Geneva Conventions. Moreover, the difficulty in filling the gap in treaty law by recourse to customary international law is that the shortfall of treaty law is not a mere technicality, but a deliberate refusal of states to commit themselves to law in certain areas. The engagement of international tribunals in issues related to IHL has provided an opportunity for this shortfall to be obfuscated. States have not expressed much objection to the jurisprudence of the tribunals, thereby permitting the impression that the new customary international law is acceptable across the board. However, whether this holds true beyond criminal proceedings remains to be seen. It is not beyond the bounds of reason that once the responsibility of states under IHL is invoked, their willingness to discount the absence of practice will be much more limited. For this reason, it may be advantageous to invest in the development of more nuanced treaty law and interpretation than in an unbridled resort to customary international law as a catch-all concept.

[93] Martti Koskenniemi, 'International Legal Theory and Doctrine' in Rüdiger Wolfrum (ed.), *Max Planck Encyclopedia of Public International Law*, Vol. 5 (Oxford University Press 2012) 976–986.

19

Use of force

CHRISTIAN J. TAMS AND ANTONIOS TZANAKOPOULOS

1 Introduction

The legal regime governing recourse to force in international law, or what is called the *ius ad bellum*, needs little introduction. Its basic tenets, as established at the end of the Second World War, are well known.[1] Above all, it comprises a general prohibition on the threat or use of armed force by states, as per Article 2(4) of the UN Charter; this general prohibition admits of one exception – the use of force by states in individual or collective self-defence (Article 51 of the UN Charter) – and it does not apply to collective enforcement measures authorised by the UN Security Council (Article 42 of the UN Charter).[2]

The precise scope of these rules is highly contested, and has been so since their inception.[3] Notwithstanding this uncertainty, the legal regime regulating recourse to force is generally considered to be of crucial importance for international relations: the relevant UN Charter rules are referred to as the 'cornerstone' of the contemporary international legal order,[4] and

1 For detailed assessments, see Olivier Corten, *Le droit contre la guerre: L'interdiction du recours à la force en droit international contemporain* (Pedone 2008); Tarcisio Gazzini, *The Changing Rules on the Use of Force in International Law* (Manchester University Press 2006); Christine Gray, *International Law and the Use of Force* (3rd edn Oxford University Press 2008); Yoram Dinstein, *War, Aggression and Self-Defence* (5th edn Cambridge University Press 2012); Thomas M. Franck, *Recourse to Force: State Action against Threats and Armed Attacks* (Cambridge University Press 2002). Literature on the topic is abundant. The subsequent discussion, focused on the specific question of contemporary positivism, will provide no more than a handful of references to the most commonly available and authoritative treatments.

2 This summary ignores the Charter's now obsolete enemy clauses. It should also be noted that the current understanding of Art. 42 as permitting the authorisation of (mandated) military measures was initially controversial. See Gazzini, n. 1 at 35–36 for a summary of debates.

3 For an early example, see *Corfu Channel (United Kingdom v. Albania)*, Merits, Judgment of 9 April 1949, ICJ Reports (1949) 4 at 34–35.

4 *Armed Activities on the Territory of the Congo (Democratic Republic of the Congo v. Uganda)*, Judgment of 19 December 2005, ICJ Reports (2005) 168 at 223 (para. 148); James L. Brierly,

are considered to form part of the various categories of 'higher law' developed over the last decades – from *ius cogens* to *erga omnes.* Perhaps as a consequence, compliance with the rules governing the use of force has always been seen – for better or worse – as a test case for the success or failure of international law more generally: once the prohibition is allegedly violated, inevitably the soul-searching begins, and scholars engage in speculation about the death (or properly legal character) of international law.[5]

As a result of these factors, the use of force has been a key battleground in debates between those subscribing to a positivist analysis of the law and those openly or more covertly disavowing the positivist approach. Because of the high stakes, different methodological approaches have been applied to the *ius ad bellum*, and conversely, debates about the *ius ad bellum* have been influential in reshaping methodological approaches more generally. This chapter revisits, and comments upon, these debates. In so doing, it traces the evolution of positivist thinking and identifies the particular challenges facing a contemporary positivist approach to the legal regulation of military force. It does so by briefly introducing key features of positivism and the criticism levelled against it (Section 2); and then goes on to show how positivism as a doctrine has been readjusted in response to criticisms (Section 3). The last substantive section turns to the particular challenges facing positivist approaches to the *ius ad bellum* and suggests how they might be accommodated (Section 4).

2 Positivism: core claims, criticisms and lessons learned

The previous remarks presuppose a certain notion of positivism, and of the role of method in international law more generally. These themes have

The Law of Nations: An Introduction to the International Law of Peace (Humphrey Waldock (ed.), 6th edn Oxford University Press 1963) 414.

[5] For relevant comments (prompted by the 2003 invasion of Iraq), see Jochen Frowein, 'Ist das Völkerrecht tot?' *Frankfurter Allgemeine Zeitung* (23 July 2003) 6; Thomas M. Franck, 'What Happens Now? The United Nations after Iraq' 97 *AJIL* (2003) 607–620 at 610: 'Article 2(4) has died again, and, this time, perhaps for good'. For an earlier eulogy of the prohibition of the use of force, see Thomas M. Franck, 'Who Killed Article 2(4)? or: Changing Norms Governing the Use of Force by States' 64 *AJIL* (1970) 809–837 and the response by Louis Henkin, 'The Reports of the Death of Article 2(4) are Greatly Exaggerated' 65 *AJIL* (1971) 544–548. These and other debates are assessed and situated in Jean d'Aspremont, 'Mapping the Concepts Behind the Contemporary Liberalization of the Use of Force in International Law' 31 *University of Pennsylvania Journal of International Law* (2010) 101–159.

been developed elsewhere – notably in the introduction to this volume[6] – but a few essential points may be conveniently summarised in order to set the stage for the subsequent debate.

2.1 Core positivist claims

The first point concerns our understanding of positivism. Positivism is an ambiguous term. On the one hand, it represents (in the words of Nicholas Onuf) '[t]he unimpeachable doctrine for most of us',[7] yet on the other, it is often perceived as a mix of 'old-fashioned, conservative, continental European nineteenth-century views – naïve ideals of dead white males'.[8] Being a positivist can be a badge of pride just as much as a stigma, depending on the context. The underlying concept, positivism, has many meanings, in law and in other social sciences.[9] As a scientific approach, it rose to prominence in the nineteenth century when the 'positivist revolution'[10] modernised law as a discipline. It claimed exactness and sought to turn law into a 'proper science'; it promised a move towards objectivity, a technocratic, a-political approach with the lawyer-scholar as a neutral observer. In essence, positivism in law deals with law as hard facts – 'posited' rules. This implies a distinction between the existing, *posited* law and the law that might come into existence, often termed as *lex lata* versus *lex ferenda*. More specifically, international legal positivism is characterised by three core claims:[11]

First, the claim that posited law cannot simply be deduced from any extra-legal code (morals, religion, humanitarian concerns, political

[6] D'Aspremont and Kammerhofer, Chapter 1. See further the useful survey of methods in Steven R. Ratner, Anne-Marie Slaughter (eds), 'Symposium on Method in International Law' 93 *AJIL* (1999) 291–423 (with contributions by Bruno Simma and Andreas L. Paulus; Siegfried Wiessner and Andrew R. Willard; Mary Ellen O'Connell; Martti Koskenniemi; Kenneth W. Abbott; Hilary Charlesworth; Jeffrey L. Dunoff and Joel P. Trachtman).

[7] Nicholas Onuf, 'International Legal Theory: Where We Stand' 1 *International Legal Theory* (1995) 2–5 at 3. Onuf's own approach – which does not sit easily in the debates about international legal positivism – is set out e.g. in Nicholas Onuf, 'Global Law-Making and Legal Thought' in Nicholas Onuf (ed.), *Law-Making in the Global Community* (Carolina Academic Press 1982) 1–81 and more generally in Nicholas Onuf, *World of Our Making. Rules and Rule in Social Theory and International Relations* (Routledge 1989).

[8] Bruno Simma and Andreas L. Paulus, 'The Responsibility of Individuals for Human Rights Abuses in Internal Conflicts: A Positivist View' 93 *AJIL* (1999) 302–316.

[9] See generally Matthew H. Kramer, *In Defense of Legal Positivism: Law without Trimmings* (Oxford University Press 1999) 1–17; beyond the field of law, see Auguste Comte, *A General View of Positivism* (John H. Bridges (tr.), Trübner and Co. 1865).

[10] Stephen C. Neff, 'A Short History of International Law' in Malcolm D. Evans (ed.), *International Law* (3rd edn Oxford University Press 2010) 3–31 at 14.

[11] The points summarised in the following are explored in Simma and Paulus, n. 8, as well as in Ulrich Fastenrath, 'Relative Normativity in International Law' 4 *EJIL* (1993) 305–340.

necessities), but is created by the actors of international law and derives from their collective will.[12] The scholar's role then is to 'find' it by identifying the created rules. This has sometimes been taken to extremes, as for example evident in the claim that a particular norm either exists (is valid) according to a normative order or does not, an answer which the positivist scholar would try to trace scientifically.[13]

Second, as law is posited, positivism has emphasised the need to look at the rules on law-generation, i.e. the formal sources of international law. All legal norms must derive their pedigree from one of the accepted sources of international law.[14] The positivist era is characterised by a focus on questions of sources. The sources in turn are seen as vehicles of voluntarism: law is 'an emanation of state will'; 'states create law by reaching consent on the content of a rule'.[15] While there are different ways of construing such consent, this premise has on occasion been formulated rather strictly, prominently so in the famous *Lotus* dictum in which the PCIJ seemed to require a 'direct link' between expressions of state will and rules of law.[16]

Third, positivist international law does not claim to judge the morality, or quality, of existing law. Law as derived from one of the sources can be

[12] This was put particularly clearly in the ICJ's *South West Africa* cases, where the Court observed: 'Throughout this case, it has been suggested, directly or indirectly, that humanitarian considerations are sufficient in themselves to generate legal rights and obligations, and that the Court can and should proceed accordingly. The Court does not think so. It is a court of law, and can take account of moral principles only in so far as they are given a sufficient expression in legal form . . . Humanitarian considerations may constitute the inspirational basis for rules of law, just as, for instance, the preambular parts of the United Nations Charter constitute the moral and political basis for the specific legal provisions thereafter set out. Such interests do not in themselves amount to rules of law. All States are interested – have an interest – in such matters. But the existence of an "interest" does not of itself entail that this interest is specifically juridical in character . . . In order to generate legal rights and obligations, [the interest] must be given juridical expression and be clothed in legal form.' *South West Africa (Ethiopia v. South Africa, Liberia v. South Africa)*, Second Phase, Judgment of 8 July 1966, ICJ Reports (1966) 6 at 34 (paras 49–51).

[13] Hans Kelsen, *Pure Theory of Law* (Max Knight (tr.), University of California Press 1967) 205. This does not mean that there can be only one correct answer as to the *content* of the norm that has been asserted to exist: see Hans Kelsen, *The Law of the United Nations: A Critical Analysis of Its Fundamental Problems* (Stevens & Sons 1950) xiii–xvii. Divorcing the existence of a norm from its content, however, may be an impossible endeavour at times.

[14] As clearly put by Oppenheim in the first edition of Lassa Oppenheim, *International Law: A Treatise*, Vol. 1 (Longmans, Green and Co. 1905) 22.

[15] Simma and Paulus, n. 8 at 303 with further references.

[16] *S.S. 'Lotus' (France v. Turkey)*, Judgment of 7 September 1927, PCIJ Series A No. 10 (1927) 18: '[t]he rules of law binding upon States therefore emanate from their own free will as expressed in conventions or by usages generally accepted as expressing principles of law'.

'good law' or 'bad law'. Whether a certain proposition has the force of law is one question; whether it is just or not is another: the two enquiries are different exercises. In his first edition, Lassa Oppenheim proudly claimed that he had sought to present 'international law as it is, not as it ought to be'.[17]

2.2 Criticisms

What once was refreshingly modern can soon become established. Positivism is no exception. Having risen to prominence, it soon began to draw criticism. Just as legal positivism generally, positivist international law has been under attack for decades. The critique has come from many directions, but three prongs seem to be particularly relevant:

(i) Many have criticised the positivist focus on rules. 'Rules' seemed to suggest that the law was, if not immutable, then inimical to change, incapable of accommodating it easily. This drew fire in particular from the policy-oriented, process-based New Haven School. In *Problems and Process*, Rosalyn Higgins formulates the essence of this criticism: '[i]f international law was just "rules", then international law would indeed be unable to contribute to, and cope with, a changing political world.' And further:

> To rely merely on . . . rules when the context in which they were articulated has changed . . . is to ensure that international law will not be able to contribute to today's problems and, further, that it will be disobeyed for that reason.[18]

Instead of rules, many versions of 'anti-positivist' critique have advocated a focus on decisions, and (with many variations) have sought to emphasise the importance of values – whether or not embodied in rules under some interpretation or other – guiding decisions, especially where rules are unclear.

(ii) A second wave of critiques has taken issue with the perceived neutrality of the law – and of positivism itself. To view law as objective, neutral, simply waiting to be 'found' was attacked as naive. Legal rules were instruments of politics, and by pretending to scientifically 'find'

[17] Oppenheim, n. 14 at ix. Even in their exposition of an 'enlightened' positivism (on which more below), Simma and Paulus, n. 8 at 316 consider that the 'professional ethics of a lawyer requires the impartial mediation of attitudes, ideologies or conflict'.

[18] Rosalyn Higgins, *Problems and Process: International Law and How We Use It* (Oxford University Press 1995) 3.

them, or de-politicise them, positivists would simply perpetuate existing policy choices.[19] Accordingly, one common demand has been for positivist international lawyers to 'identify the politics they pursue through international law'; '[i]f politics were explicitly acknowledged, then doctrinal biases would be disclosed'.[20]

(iii) Finally, critics have attacked the positivist fixation on the *lex lata*, with the concomitant side-lining of the *lex ferenda*. The contention is that legal scholarship should adopt a reformist agenda, highlighting and embracing under-represented values with a view to mending the (neither objective nor neutral) law. The relevant values deserving support and serving as the basis for the agenda of reform vary, naturally, with the theorist articulating them. But in terms of the methodological agenda, Hilary Charlesworth, arguing from one particular reformist perspective, may have expressed a general critique when suggesting that the feminist approach to international law was 'challeng[ing] . . . scholarly traditions' precisely because it 'may clearly reflect a political agenda rather than striv[ing] to attain an objective truth on a neutral basis'.[21]

2.3 Lessons learned

These criticisms imply different understandings of what we mean by 'law' and 'legal scholarship': is law the *lex lata* – or also the law in waiting? Do legal scholars find or shape the law? On these questions, answers are probably not right or wrong, but depend on choices and assumptions (in terms of logic, 'premises'). In fact, looking at some of the key debates, one gets the impression that assumptions determine everything, but as they are usually not negotiated, and sometimes even presumed to be non-negotiable, commentators often speak past each other.[22] Against that background,

19 See generally Martti Koskenniemi, *From Apology to Utopia: The Structure of International Legal Argument* (Finnish Lawyers' Publishing Co. 1989, reissued Cambridge University Press 2005).

20 Deborah Z. Cass, 'Navigating the Newstream: Recent Critical Scholarship in International Law' 65 *Nordic Journal of International Law* (1996) 341–383 at 378, 377.

21 Hilary Charlesworth, 'Feminist Methods in International Law' 93 *AJIL* (1999) 379–394 at 380.

22 See the very different understandings of 'positivism' used by participants in the AJIL symposium on method (Ratner, Slaughter, n. 6). Cf. e.g. Ratner and Slaughter's summary of positivism, suggesting that '[p]ositivism . . . tends to view states as the only subjects of international law' (Steven R. Ratner, Anne-Marie Slaughter, 'Appraising the Methods of International Law: A Prospectus for Readers' 93 *AJIL* (1999) 291–302 at 293) with Simma

it is important to note that in the course of the last decades, positivist thinking has undergone important developments. Core positivist claims in their sometimes 'crude' incarnation (as characterised by some of the extreme positions quoted in the penultimate section) are today no longer en vogue; the approach to these core claims has largely become more 'enlightened',[23] reformed, and has arguably led to a 'post-modern' international legal positivism. This reformed, post-modern positivism would readily acknowledge a number of criticisms while still insisting on the need for a 'positivist' approach. Three points seem particularly important – and they can be illustrated with regard to the specific features of the *ius ad bellum.*

(i) First, very few contemporary positivists would claim that the legal regime regulating recourse to force does anything but to reflect the political choices of the authorised law-makers, i.e. states. It is obvious that to agree on a ban against inter-state military force – and to treat it as the cornerstone of the international legal order, a norm of *ius cogens*, and the foundational principle of the United Nations – is anything but a neutral decision. Rather, it reflects important political choices: the choice to distinguish between military force and other forms of coercion – such as economic or political coercion; the emphasis on inter- as opposed to intra-state conflict; the decision to outlaw military threats to global welfare while sidelining other significant threats such as poverty, hunger or inequality. Modern (or 'post-modern') positivism accepts this, in underlining that these are the choices reflected in the relevant provisions of the UN Charter, without this necessarily meaning that they are the right choices. Few scholars would question that the rules on the use of force, as embodied in the UN Charter, are a reflection of the political choices of the authorised law-makers of 1945. In fact, many have criticised them precisely on this basis for their inadequacy in safeguarding international peace and security in a much changed world – but, as positivists, have at the same time continued to treat them as the *lex lata.*

(ii) Second, few positivists today really argue that rules can be applied mechanically, and that there is always *one* correct answer. Again, this is

and Paulus' claim that '[o]ther actors than states are assuming growing importance' (Simma and Paulus, n. 8 at 306).

23 The term has been popularised by Simma and Paulus, n. 8 at 307, and aptly describes trends to which we refer in Section 3. Whether Simma and Paulus themselves went too far in 'bending' positivism is another matter.

particularly obvious with regard to the *ius ad bellum*, where every possible view seems to be held. And while this may be pathological (an issue to be taken up below),[24] it is clear that at least the text of the treaty-based *ius ad bellum* is quite open. If anything, the text allows much latitude of interpretation on account of the open-ended terms employed. There is no obviously correct or undoubtedly objective answer to any of the crucial questions surrounding the relevant provisions of the UN Charter: what is or should be the meaning of the term 'force' in Article 2(4)?[25] What does it mean that the right to self-defence in Article 51 is characterised as 'inherent'?[26] What is an 'armed attack' and when does it actually 'occur'?[27] And when can it be said that the Security Council has taken the measures 'necessary' to maintain or restore international peace and security?[28] Do Articles 2(4) and 51 deal with force by or against entities other than states?[29] Is there a gap between the use of force prohibited by Article 2(4) and the 'armed attack' that triggers the right to self-defence in Article 51 – and, if so, is it to be filled, and how?[30] Do the Charter rules regulating the use of force coincide with the customary rules on the matter?[31] And can

24 See Section 4.

25 E.g. the discussions in Ian Brownlie, *International Law and the Use of Force by States* (Clarendon Press 1963); Oscar Schachter, 'The Right of States to Use Armed Force' 82 *Michigan Law Review* (1984) 1620–1646 at 1624; Dinstein, n. 1 at 88 with further references.

26 E.g. the discussion in Jörg Kammerhofer, *Uncertainty in International Law: A Kelsenian Perspective* (Routledge 2011) 7–9 with further references; Dinstein, n. 1 at 191–193.

27 See generally Tom Ruys, *'Armed Attack' and Article 51 of the UN Charter: Evolutions in Customary Law and Practice* (Cambridge University Press 2010); Jan Wouters, Tom Ruys, 'The Legality of Anticipatory Military Action after 9/11: The Slippery Slope of Self-Defense' 59 *Studia Diplomatica* (2006) 45–67; Dominic Raab, '"Armed Attack" after the *Oil Platforms* Case' 17 *LJIL* (2004) 719–735.

28 See generally Malvina Halberstam, 'The Right to Self-Defense Once the Security Council Takes Action' 17 *Michigan Journal of International Law* (1996) 229–248 with further references.

29 See generally Noam Lubell, *Extraterritorial Use of Force against Non-State Actors* (Oxford University Press 2010); Christian J. Tams, 'The Use of Force against Terrorists' 20 *EJIL* (2009) 359–397; Nicholas Tsagourias, 'Non-State Actors in International Institutional Peace and Security: Non-State Actors and the Use of Force' in Jean d'Aspremont (ed.), *Participants in the International Legal System: Multiple Perspectives on Non-State Actors in International Law* (Routledge 2011) 326–341.

30 E.g. Dinstein, n. 1 at 207–212; Albrecht Randelzhofer, 'Article 51' in Bruno Simma (ed.), *The Charter of the United Nations: A Commentary* (2nd edn Oxford University Press 2002) 788–806 at 790–792 (MN 4–8), 796 (MN 20).

31 E.g. Kammerhofer, n. 26 at 7–9 and the discussion in the sources cited there; and the discussion in Dinstein, n. 1 at 99–100; Randelzhofer, n. 30 at 805–806 (MN 43–45).

there be exceptions to the prohibition on the use of force other than those written in the Charter, or can such further exceptions evolve without Charter amendment?[32]

Positivists – just as those subscribing to other legal methods – discuss all of these questions, and tend to disagree on them. Stepping back, it seems that there are different plausible answers to each of them, answers which have but 'varying degrees of legal merit'.[33] But this is something accepted by modern positivists, as they themselves give different answers to the questions above, all the while having adopted a positivist analytical framework: in short, the positivist aim is to find '*a* – not *the* – correct solution to a legal problem'.[34]

(iii) Finally, given claims about the 'immutability' of rules, it is important to note that while the text of the UN Charter (as far as the *ius ad bellum* is concerned) has remained unaltered for more than 65 years, the law on the use of force evolves over time on account of practice by actors accorded law-developing power under international law. This is a realisation that does not escape modern positivists; in fact, it is difficult to exclude in a system of sources that recognises the relevance of 'subsequent practice' and 'international practice' for the interpretation and determination of legal rules.[35] In the process of constant assessment and reassessment of the state of the *ius ad bellum*, the changing perceptions of the assessors and the evolving political, historical, economic and scientific circumstances have constituted the basis for arguments that the law has developed or evolved in this or that direction. These are, of course, just that: arguments with 'varying degrees of legal merit'.[36] But the shifting majorities in fora like the General Assembly or indeed in legal academia would seem to suggest that some development has taken place.[37] Plausible claims of normative change would include, for example, the expansion of the ban on direct military force by 1974 to include indirect aggression,[38] as well as force targeting stabilised territorial entities that are not

[32] See the discussion in Vaughan Lowe and Antonios Tzanakopoulos, 'Humanitarian Intervention' in Rüdiger Wolfrum (ed.), *Max Planck Encyclopedia of Public International Law*, Vol. 5 (Oxford University Press 2012) 47–59 at 53–55 (MN 26–35).

[33] Hersch Lauterpacht, *The Development of International Law by the International Court* (Stevens & Sons 1958) 398.

[34] Simma and Paulus, n. 8 at 316.

[35] For more on sources, see Sections 3.1 and 3.2.

[36] Lauterpacht, n. 33 at 398.

[37] For more on the underlying perception of the Charter as capable of – even in matters of military force – 'meeting the threat of obsolescence with adaptation', see Franck, n. 1 at 1–9.

[38] Art. 3(f)–(g) Definition of Aggression, UN Doc. A/RES/3314 (XXIX) (14 December 1974).

states.[39] The limited use of force to rescue nationals abroad has always been problematic, but there has been increasing acceptance of the justification in the last decades (even as – or perhaps precisely because – the practice of justifying the use of force on this basis has decreased).[40] Some developments have even taken place only to regress later: in the 1970s, for example, a plausible argument could have been (and was) made that the law on the use of force had evolved to allow forcible support of armed liberation movements,[41] but this claim has now largely been abandoned.

In the last couple of decades, debates have centred on the availability of self-defence against terrorist attacks not attributable to states under the traditional rules of state responsibility,[42] or on the temporal limits to or else the rejection of the requirement that an armed attack 'occur' before force can be used in self-defence.[43] Many believe that the law has changed on either or both of these points in the last years. Irrespective of the merits of such claims, the debate demonstrates that the law on the use of force may be anything but static: rather, it is constantly under pressure from practice, and thus the question of whether it has or has not developed in this or that direction is constantly a matter of debate, a subject of continuous argumentation and (re-)negotiation.

3 Shoring up positivism

If contemporary positivists have been able to accept these lessons, then this is because positivism itself has not been static, but has evolved. In response to these critiques, positivism has been 'shored up'[44] and some of its more

39 Principle I, para. 6 Declaration on Principles of International Law concerning Friendly Relations and Co-operation among States in Accordance with the Charter of the United Nations, UN Doc. A/RES/2625 (XXV) (24 October 1970).

40 Christian J. Tams, 'Prospects for Humanitarian Uses of Force' in Antonio Cassese (ed.), *Realizing Utopia: The Future of International Law* (Oxford University Press 2012) 359–374 at 367–372. For detailed discussions, see e.g. Kristen Eichensehr, 'Defending Nationals Abroad: Assessing the Lawfulness of Forcible Hostages Rescues' 28 *Virginia Journal of International Law* (2007) 451–484; Natalino Ronzitti, *Rescuing Nationals Abroad through Military Coercion and Intervention on Grounds of Humanity* (Martinus Nijhoff 1985).

41 For an account, see Antonio Cassese, *Self-Determination of Peoples: A Legal Reappraisal* (Cambridge University Press 1995) 150–158.

42 For an overview, see Tams, n. 29 at 359.

43 E.g. Hannes Hoffmeister, 'Pre-emptive Strikes: A new Normative Framework' 44 *Archiv des Völkerrechts* (2006) 187–200; Sean D. Murphy, 'The Doctrine of Pre-emptive Self-Defense' 50 *Villanova Law Review* (2005) 699–748; Michael Bothe, 'Terrorism and the Legality of Pre-emptive Force' 14 *EJIL* (2003) 227–240.

44 Onuf, 'Legal Theory', n. 7 at 4.

ambitious claims abandoned. The move towards this reformed (or perhaps, to use the terminology employed in this book, 'post-modern') positivism is a general development. However, some of the great debates surrounding the rules on the use of force – whether in the context of the *Nicaragua* case,[45] or regarding the intervention in Kosovo and the justifiability of forcible unilateral humanitarian intervention, or, particularly in the aftermath of the September 11 attacks, the availability of military responses against terrorism – would seem to have been catalysts of general developments.

The shoring up of positivism has been achieved largely by a liberalisation of the traditional sources doctrine. As noted above, sources – as the key to identifying the rest of the *lex lata*, i.e. the substantive norms regulating conduct – are of major importance to international legal positivism. This remains true even under a reformed/enlightened approach; but what has changed is the process by which legal rules are ascertained: in this respect, the general trend has been one of 'deformalization'.[46] With regard to the *ius ad bellum*, two aspects of such deformalisation – affecting custom and treaty as the two relevant sources respectively – would seem to be of particular importance.

3.1 Custom and diluted consent

The first form of deformalisation relates to the identification of custom. On the face of it, not that much has changed. Pursuant to the common understanding, customary rules are based on state practice and *opinio iuris*; these two components – referred to, albeit misleadingly, in Article 38(1)(b) of the ICJ Statute – remain lynchpins of the regime of customary international law-making.[47] Yet, 'below the surface', the application of the two components seems to have undergone change. Notably, it now seems agreed that a wide range of materials can be used to demonstrate the existence of state practice and *opinio iuris* required for the formation and modification or development of customary rules. 'State practice means' – as Michael Akehurst put it succinctly with regard to the former element – 'any act or statement by a State from which views about customary law

[45] *Military and Paramilitary Activities in and against Nicaragua* (*Nicaragua v. United States of America*), Merits, Judgment of 27 June 1986, ICJ Reports (1986) 14.

[46] The point is made, and explored in depth, in Jean d'Aspremont, *Formalism and the Sources of International Law: A Theory of the Ascertainment of Legal Rules* (Oxford University Press 2011) 118–136.

[47] For a detailed treatment, see Kammerhofer, n. 26 at 59–86.

can be inferred'.[48] Among other things, General Assembly resolutions and declarations have been taken as evidence of state consent to a particular rule.[49] These 'more liberalised' forms of state consent – evident, for example, in the *Nicaragua* judgment, where the Court discussed relevant General Assembly practice at length, and attached significant weight to it[50] – have enabled scholars and decision-makers alike to explain the existence of a particular rule regulating recourse to force and to ground it in the traditional sources of international law without abandoning the positivist framework demanding the demonstration of state consent for the positing of international law rules.

In line with this development, the role of 'actual' practice in the determination of customary international law – i.e. 'what states do' – seems to have gradually decreased.[51] Especially in areas such as the *ius ad bellum* or human rights, where the 'actual practice' (at least in its well-recorded form) often takes the form of wrongful conduct, weight has been given to acts such as protests and responses characterising the violative acts as precisely that, i.e. as breaches of the law rather than as accepted conduct under the rule.[52] Furthermore, 'actual' practice has come to be seen in the wider context of the justifications offered for the conduct in question, scholars according no weight to practice that is argued by those engaged in it to come within the purview of exceptions to the rule. This refined approach to the element of practice is informed by a more general understanding of the significance of the tripartite distinction between prescriptive, permissive and proscriptive (or prohibitive) rules. In reality, it is impossible to meaningfully demonstrate any actual practice for the latter category,

48 Michael Akehurst, 'Custom as a Source of International Law' 47 *BYBIL* (1974–1975) 1–53 at 53.

49 For references, see e.g. Tullio Treves, 'Customary International Law' in Rüdiger Wolfrum (ed.), *Max Planck Encyclopedia of Public International Law*, Vol. 2 (Oxford University Press 2012) 937–957 at 946–947 (MN 44–46). Inclusive approaches to practice and *opinio iuris* have notably been advanced by Akehurst, n. 48; Karl Zemanek, 'What is State Practice and Who Makes It?' in Ulrich Beyerlin *et al.* (eds), *Recht zwischen Umbruch und Bewahrung: Völkerrecht, Europarecht, Staatsrecht: Festschrift für Rudolf Bernhardt* (Springer 1995) 289–306. Kammerhofer provides a critical assessment: Kammerhofer, n. 26 at 62–70.

50 *Nicaragua*, n. 45 at 99–104 (paras 188–195).

51 Not without opposition: see notably Anthony A. D'Amato, *The Concept of Custom in International Law* (Cornell University Press 1971) 88, who argues that 'claims themselves, although they may articulate a legal norm, cannot constitute the material component of custom [i.e. practice]'; what mattered was 'what the state will actually do'. Subsequent debates have gone beyond this: see e.g. the account in d'Aspremont, n. 46 at 161–174.

52 Again, this is anchored in the ICJ decision in *Nicaragua*, n. 45 at 98 (para. 186).

as has become evident since *Lotus*.[53] 'States often do nothing, and for a wide range of reasons'[54] – hence practice for prohibitive rules (such as those relating to the *non-use* of force) has to be construed from responses to alleged breaches rather than be found through an examination of what states do not do.

Finally, the role of actual consent of states, as manifested through practice and *opinio iuris*, may have been affected by the judicial recognition of a special role for specially affected states.[55] This is best understood as qualifying the requirement of *generality* of practice, and it is a more controversial development than the ones previously addressed, as it seems to run counter to the principle of sovereign equality.[56] Yet, in its effects, it can be assimilated to the previous tendencies: just as these, it stretches the link between a state's consent and customary international law. And conversely, it introduces a further variable: just as arguments about custom can draw on a broad range of material sources, so they can be based on a differentiated weighing of evidence. This makes debates about custom even more flexible.

3.2 Liberalised treaty interpretation

Just as customary international law has been liberalised, so has treaty interpretation; this is the second aspect of the deformalisation of the sources doctrine. Treaties, of course, remain directly linked to state consent; and as a general matter, states not willing to accept a treaty are protected by the *pacta tertiis* rule.[57] However, the regime of treaty interpretation seems to have been opened up. The Vienna Convention on the Law of Treaties, reflecting, as it does, customary law on this point, marked a move away from historical interpretation, which focuses on the subjective intent of the drafters (thus emphasising the need to 'find' what states originally intended to consent on),[58] towards a method of interpretation (the ILC's

[53] *Lotus*, n. 16.

[54] Vaughan Lowe, *International Law* (Oxford University Press 2007) 41.

[55] *North Sea Continental Shelf (Federal Republic of Germany/Denmark, Federal Republic of Germany/Netherlands)*, Judgment of 20 February 1969, ICJ Reports (1969) 3 at 42 (para. 73).

[56] Hence there is considerable debate, see the useful summary in Ruys, n. 27 at 44–47.

[57] Art. 34 VCLT.

[58] Art. 32 VCLT (recourse to the *travaux* is allowed either only to confirm the meaning resulting from an interpretative exercise in accordance with the general rule of interpretation (Art. 31 VCLT) or to determine the meaning of a provision when the meaning yielded by interpretation in accordance with the general rule is ambiguous or obscure, or

'crucible' approach) that, from the perspective of individual states, is less predictable and more indeterminate. This is crucial when discussing the regulation of the use of force, as the basis for all discussion is the particularly open-textured text of the UN Charter and the liberties it allows through its alleged gaps.

Purposive treaty interpretation is the first notion that would seem to increase the room for argumentative manoeuvring. Enshrined in Article 31(1) of the Vienna Convention on the Law of Treaties, purposive interpretation is without doubt a key element of the contemporary regime of treaty interpretation,[59] and it is regularly employed in debates about the proper interpretation of the *ius ad bellum*. For present purposes, it is important to note that reliance on the object and purpose of a treaty increases the range of interpretative arguments, as agreement on the object and purpose of a treaty may not be easily reached. Debates about the proper understanding of the *ius ad bellum* illustrate this. According to some, restrictive readings are warranted precisely because they would best give effect to the Charter's overall purpose of 'sav[ing] succeeding generations from the scourge of war' and minimising unilateral recourse to force.[60] Others have taken a different view of the Charter's object and purpose,[61] stressing its embrace of human rights, in order to support their preferred interpretations of, for example, the prohibition of the use of force as it relates to forcible humanitarian intervention.[62] The point here is not to engage in the debate, but rather to emphasise that the rise of purposive treaty interpretation has increased the range of arguments that can be made within a positivist framework.

leads to a manifestly absurd result), e.g. *LaGrand* (*Germany v. United States of America*), Judgment of 27 June 2001, ICJ Reports (2001) 466 at 503–504 (para. 104).

59 See generally Richard Gardiner, *Treaty Interpretation* (Oxford University Press 2008); Jean-Marc Sorel, Valérie Boré Eveno, 'Article 31' in Olivier Corten, Pierre Klein (eds), *The Vienna Convention on the Law of Treaties – A Commentary* (Oxford University Press 2011) 804–837.

60 UN Charter, Preamble; see Stuart Ford, 'Legal Processes of Change: Article 2(4) and the Vienna Convention on the Law of Treaties' 4 *Journal of Conflict and Security Law* (1999) 75–116 at 80–81; Peter Malanczuck, *Akehurst's Modern Introduction to International Law* (7th edn Routledge 1997) 310–311.

61 See the considerations set out in Karl Zemanek, 'New Trends in the Enforcement of Obligations *Erga Omnes*' 4 *Max Planck Yearbook of United Nations Law* (2000) 1–52 at 37–38.

62 While humanitarian intervention has been a focus of debates, it is not the only question on which purposive readings of the Charter can make a difference. Other examples include expansive notions of 'threat to the peace' in Art. 39 UN Charter and foreign involvement in wars of national liberation.

That trend is corroborated by the broadening of actors involved in the process of treaty interpretation. In the Charter context, UN organs have been key players. As noted briefly above, their pronouncements have often had a decisive influence on the understanding of the *ius ad bellum*.[63] Court decisions as well as resolutions by the United Nations' two main political organs are treated – crucially by states, the law-makers in international law – as having given expression to, and thereby having shaped, the law. In terms of treaty interpretation, their status is not entirely clear: some see resolutions as forms of subsequent practice in the sense of Article 31(3) VCLT, others seem prepared to accord them a more authoritative role, perhaps even a status as an authentic (subsequent) interpretation.[64] But whichever approach is preferred, it is clear that in practice, interpretation of the Charter – including on questions of military force – has gone 'beyond the formal letter of the original instrument' and instead is informed by 'its operation in actual practice and in the light of the revealed tendencies in the life of the Organization'.[65] Just as with the move towards purposive readings, this has had the effect of restricting the 'control' of states over the process of treaty interpretation, and it has broadened the range of evidence on which interpreters can draw.

3.3 *The price of adaptation*

The two forms of deformalisation discussed in the preceding sections have changed positivism. By liberalising the sources doctrine – which, it bears reminding, is of crucial relevance as it defines how the law is 'posited' – positivism has reinvented itself. The resulting reformed/post-modern positivism 'is able to adapt to new developments in international affairs';[66] it can incorporate societal values; and it can accommodate change much more easily and treat processes of rule application as legally relevant. This adaptation has been – to quote Nicholas Onuf again – 'a great practical success'.[67] It has meant that positivism is no longer an easy target for critics (a development not always appreciated).[68] Yet, adaptation has come

[63] See text at ns 37–39.

[64] For details, see Georg Ress, 'Interpretation' in Bruno Simma (ed.), *The Charter of the United Nations: A Commentary* (2nd edn Oxford University Press 2002) 13–31 at 27–30.

[65] *Voting Procedure on Questions Relating to Reports and Petitions Concerning the Territory of South-West Africa*, Advisory Opinion of 7 June 1955, ICJ Reports (1955) 67 at 106 (Sep. Op. Lauterpacht).

[66] Simma and Paulus, n. 8 at 307.

[67] Onuf, 'Legal Theory', n. 7 at 4.

[68] Jörg Kammerhofer, Jean d'Aspremont, 'Introduction: Mapping 21st Century International Legal Positivism' (unpublished paper, 2010) at 6. [Editors' note: the authors refer

at a price. In the process of 'shoring up'[69] and of deformalisation, 'the beauty of the traditional theory – namely, its clarity and rigidity'[70] – has been affected, and 'as a theoretical system, positivism is considerably less tidy than it once was'.[71]

4 Current challenges

It is against this background that current challenges facing positivist approaches to the *ius ad bellum* need to be discussed. As a general rule, these profit from the shoring up of positivism and the more liberal approach to sources, developments which have enabled positivists to take account of UN practice and the Charter's purposes in interpreting the Charter regime, and to integrate a wide range of acts and statements into their construction of customary law on the use of force. At the same time, the *ius ad bellum* presents considerable challenges for contemporary positivism. Two of them seem particularly relevant and will be singled out: the increase of uncertainty about the substance of the law, and the blurring of lines between legal and '*quasi*-legal' arguments.

4.1 Increased uncertainty

Increased uncertainty is a direct consequence of the deformalisation of sources addressed above. Whereas positivism has traditionally been accused of narrowness and rigidity, the present positivist debates about the scope of the *ius ad bellum* would seem to be characterised by their lack of direction. In their quest for '*a* – not *the* – correct solution',[72] positivists come up with an increasingly broad range of answers to most of the pertinent legal problems. Some of the big debates have been referred to already, but it may be useful to pinpoint the problem by taking one particular example that keeps commentators busy at the moment, namely the use of force against terrorists. In this respect, it really seems that

to the first version of the introductory chapter; in order to preserve the references, that version has been made available at: http://ssrn.com/abstract=2372778.]

69 Onuf, 'Legal Theory', n. 7 at 4.

70 Simma and Paulus, n. 8 at 307.

71 Onuf, 'Legal Theory', n. 7 at 4. Both points made in the preceding paragraph are echoed in the following remark by Jean d'Aspremont: 'international lawyers have found a formidable instrument in deformalization . . . Yet, deformalization does not come without costs . . . [and e.g. affects] the normative character and authority of international law.' Jean d'Aspremont, 'The Politics of Deformalization in International Law' 3 *Göttingen Journal of International Law* (2011) 503–550 at 535.

72 Simma and Paulus, n. 8 at 316.

for positivists, anything goes. The following are just some of the more controversial questions:

- Does self-defence permit forcible responses against terrorism abroad? Some think so, others deny it.[73]
- Does anti-terrorist self-defence need to be justified within the parameters of inter-state self-defence? Does it presuppose a nexus between the terrorists targeted by responses and their host state? Some would say so, others view anti-terrorist self-defence as an autonomous version of self-defence.[74]
- If a link is required, then how can it be construed: as attribution; connivance; harbouring; passivity? Commentators have proposed all sorts of tests.[75]
- As regards the framework of argument, there is little agreement either: some confidently identify changes in the law on the basis of a handful of reactions by states considered specially affected; others insist on generality of practice and on sovereign equality in law-making and legal development.[76]
- As regards the justification invoked, while most argue from within the Charter regime, some commentators rely on pre-Charter self-defence construed in the light of the *Caroline* formula or else resurrect

[73] The whole spectrum of views is presented in the following contributions: Antonio Cassese, 'Terrorism is Also Disrupting Some Crucial Legal Categories of International Law' 12 *EJIL* (2001) 993–1001; Jörg Kammerhofer, 'The *Armed Activities* Case and Non-State Actors in Self-Defence Law' 20 *LJIL* (2007) 89–113; Christian Tomuschat, 'Der 11. September und seine rechtlichen Konsequenzen' 28 *Europäische Grundrechte-Zeitschrift* (2001) 535–546; Sean D. Murphy, 'Terrorism and the Concept of "Armed Attack" in Article 51 of the UN Charter' 43 *Harvard International Law Journal* (2002) 41–51; Markus Krajewski, 'Selbstverteidigung gegen bewaffnete Angriffe nicht-staatlicher Organisationen' 40 *Archiv des Völkerrechts* (2002) 183–214; Olivier Corten, 'Self-Defence against Non-State Entities: What can be Learned from Recent Practice?' 109 *Kokusaiho Gaiko Zassi* (2010) 129–152; Pierre Klein, 'Le droit international face à l'épreuve du terrorisme' 311 *Recueil des Cours* (2006) 203–484 at 386–415; Tams, n. 29 at 359.

[74] Cf., e.g. Kimberley N. Trapp, 'The Use of Force against Terrorists: A Reply to Christian J. Tams' 20 *EJIL* (2009) 1049–1055; Christian J. Tams, 'The Use of Force against Terrorists: A Rejoinder to Federico Sperotto and Kimberley N. Trapp' 20 *EJIL* (2009) 1057–1062.

[75] Ruys and Verhoeven provide a very useful summary: Tom Ruys, Sten Verhoeven, 'Attacks by Private Actors and the Right of Self-Defence' 10 *Journal of Conflict and Security Law* (2005) 289–320.

[76] See notably Corten, n. 73 at 129.

doctrines of 'armed reprisals' or 'necessity' as separate grounds for forcible conduct.[77]

The point in raising all of these questions is not to say that each of the answers to them is equally convincing. Of course, they have 'varying degrees of legal merit'[78] – and in fact, we might add that there is considerable variation of merit. However, it is important to note that the differing views are advanced from within a positivist framework; by and large writers referred to claim to state 'international as it is, not as it ought to be'.[79] This suggests that while the traditional critique had accused positivism of producing false certainties – the allegedly *one correct solution* resulting from an objective and impartial interpretation and application of the *lex lata* – the real problem for positivists assessing the *ius ad bellum* today is one of *uncertainty* about the basic premises. This to some extent reflects the sensitivity of the specific subject matter in which disagreement is likely, and perhaps also the varying quality of legal scholarship (which can be solid or not). However, for present purposes, it is crucial to note that the liberalisation of sources has increased the room for argument and has made it more difficult to dismiss certain claims *a limine*. On the basis of a liberalised sources doctrine, many arguments can claim some level of plausibility.

If looked at from a different angle, perhaps the matter can be explained by the absence of processes of authoritative norm interpretation. Unlike in other areas of law, there are few accepted mechanisms deciding between different plausible interpretations of 'varying legal merit'. International courts have addressed the *ius ad bellum*, but have done so in individual cases only, and their jurisprudence has not been able to shape the law.[80]

[77] E.g. Nicholas Tsagourias, 'Necessity and the Use of Force: A Special Regime' 41 *Netherlands Yearbook of International Law* (2010) 11–44; William V. O'Brien, 'Reprisals, Deterrence and Self-Defense in Counterterror Operations' 30 *Virginia Journal of International Law* (1990) 421–478; and already Oscar Schachter, 'The Lawful Use of Force by a State against Terrorists in Another Country' 19 *Israel Yearbook on Human Rights* (1989) 209–231.

[78] Lauterpacht, n. 33 at 398. [79] Oppenheim, n. 14 at ix.

[80] Certainly, ICJ pronouncements – notably those in *Corfu Channel*, n. 3 and *Nicaragua*, n. 45 – have been crucial in establishing the 'robust' understanding of the *ius ad bellum* dominant until the 1990s. However, since then, the 'orthodox view' they represented has come under pressure, and more the recent jurisprudence – notably the brief comment on self-defence in the *Legal Consequences of the Construction of a Wall in the Occupied Palestinian Territory*, Advisory Opinion of 9 July 2004, ICJ Reports (2004) 136 – has drawn much criticism. For a summarised assessment of these developments (each of which would deserve a fuller treatment), see Tams, n. 29 esp. at 373–374 and 384; as

The two UN organs have often pronounced on questions relating to the use of force, and some of their resolutions have been extremely influential. However, the General Assembly in particular seems less willing today to take a proactive role in 'norm management' than it was in the 1970s. Instead, we see 'each principal organ [of the UN] and the [UN] members... continuously interpret[ing] the Charter [regime] and do[ing] so in accordance with the requisites of ever-changing circumstances'.[81] As a result, deformalised positivism, adapted and shored up as it may be, has not been checked and balanced, and it seems to have lost its power to shape the argumentative process.

4.2 The rise of quasi*-law*

The second problem is more fundamental, and it is more specific to the *ius ad bellum*. In some of the 'hard cases', it seems that even shored-up positivism is not flexible enough and a surprising number of (self-proclaimed or purported) positivists – problematically – advance arguments that can no longer be brought within the remit of, even a liberated, sources doctrine.[82] For the sake of convenience, we refer to this as '*quasi*-law'.

Quasi-law comes in different forms, but in essence it can be seen as an attempt to overcome the binary distinctions between law and non-law or legality and illegality. Exploring the middle ground seems an attractive option for positivists willing to engage with the *lex lata*, but unhappy (for whatever reason) with the outcome of their interpretation. Nowhere has this been more clearly at play than in debates about 'humanitarian

well as Jörg Kammerhofer, 'Orthodox Generalists and Political Activists in International Legal Scholarship' in Matthew Happold (ed.), *International Law in a Multipolar World* (Routledge 2011) 138–157 at 139–140. For details on the ICJ's contribution (and a more positive assessment), see Christine D. Gray, 'The ICJ and the Use of Force' in James Sloan, Christian J. Tams (eds), *The ICJ and the Development of International Law* (Oxford University Press 2013) 237–262.

81 Franck, n. 1 at 7; *Documents of the United Nations Conference on International Organization*, Vol. 13 (UNIO 1945) 709–710 more generally on decentralised interpretation of the UN Charter.

82 Of course, international law generally has had to grapple with the challenge of '*quasi*-law', most prominently with regard to the 'soft law challenge'. However, in no other area are '*quasi*-law' arguments as prevalent as in the *ius ad bellum*. For early views on soft law, see René-Jean Dupuy, 'Droit déclaratoire et droit programmatoire: de la coutume sauvage à la "soft law"' in Société française pour le droit international (ed.), *L'élaboration du droit international public: Colloque de Toulouse* (Pedone 1975) 132–148 at 132; for more recent clarifications, see Jean d'Aspremont, 'Softness in International Law: A Self-Serving Quest for New Legal Materials' 18 *EJIL* (2008) 1075–1093.

uses of force', most notably during the Kosovo campaign. Faced with the not insignificant problems of accepting a right to use force unilaterally to avert a humanitarian catastrophe under positive law on the one hand, and their perception that the plight of a population in grave danger would need to be taken into account on the other, legal scholars have relied on all sorts of *quasi*-legal arguments. Many have rediscovered 'legitimacy',[83] or have described conduct that could not be justified to be excusable.[84] Others have argued for the acceptance of 'a plea in mitigation', arguing that certain uses of force may be 'justifiable, even if illegal',[85] while others have maintained that only a 'thin red line' would separate humanitarian intervention from international legality in certain cases.[86]

Reliance on such *quasi*-legal language enables positivist scholars to avoid the law/non-law dichotomy; it thus clearly serves a function and it may be entirely understandable, or – if the term is permitted – even 'legitimate'. One should be aware of the cost, though. Commentators relying on *quasi*-legal categories argue within a different reference system whose parameters do not depend on the (diluted) formal law-generation processes. This risks confirming clichés about the allegedly neutral nature

[83] E.g. Antonio Cassese, '*Ex iniuria ius oritur*: Are We Moving towards International Legitimation of Forcible Humanitarian Countermeasures in the World Community?' 10 *EJIL* (1999) 23–30 at 25 (considering the Kosovo campaign to have been not legal but legitimate).

[84] Jost Delbrück, 'Die Effektivität des Gewaltverbots' 74 *Friedens-Warte* (1999) 139–158.

[85] Franck, n. 1 at 134, 174.

[86] Bruno Simma, 'NATO, the UN, and the Use of Force: Legal Aspects' 10 *EJIL* (1999) 1–22. Perhaps one can see the rise of *quasi*-law as an affirmation of positivism's potential to shape debates, notwithstanding concerns about a loss of predictability: arguments about legitimacy and the like, after all, are made by those who feel that *within the regular positivist framework*, they could not justify a result that to them seemed mandated. Yet this only seems to work for individual commentators, not for the debate as such. And in fact, others have had far fewer qualms to consider the Kosovo campaign to be perfectly legal according to their own positivist interpretation of the law: e.g. Christopher Greenwood, 'Humanitarian Intervention: The Case of Kosovo' 10 *Finnish Yearbook of International Law* (1999) 141–175; Karl Doehring, *Völkerrecht* (2nd edn Müller 2004) 446–449 (MN 1012–1015). For attempts to 'open up' the Charter's *ius ad bellum* regime to integrate humanitarian considerations, see Knut Ipsen, 'Der Kosovo-Einsatz – Illegal? Gerechtfertigt? Entschuldbar?' 24 *Friedens-Warte* (1999) 19–23 at 21; Christian Tomuschat, 'International Law: Ensuring the Survival of Mankind on the Eve of a New Century' 281 *Recueil des Cours* (1999) 9–438 at 218–226. For more on the relationship between law and legitimacy as regards the *ius ad bellum*, see Alain Pellet, 'Le recours à la force, le droit et la legitimité' in Andreas Fischer-Lescano *et al.* (eds), *Frieden in Freiheit – Peace in Liberty – Paix en liberté: Festschrift für Michael Bothe zum 70. Geburtstag* (Nomos 2008) 249–268 at 249; Ian Brownlie, 'Thoughts on Kind-Hearted Gunmen' in Richard B. Lillich (ed.), *Humanitarian Intervention and the United Nations* (University Press of Virginia 1973) 139–148.

of positivism: when push comes to shove, the positivist framework needs to be abandoned for sense to be made (or for one to be able to sleep at night). But perhaps more importantly, the rise of *quasi*-law would seem to run counter to features that remain essential even to contemporary positivism of the deformalised variant: namely, the insistence on the *lex lata*, and the understanding of interpretation as a cognitive process.[87]

5 Conclusion

To sum up, it seems plain that the *ius ad bellum* presents real challenges for contemporary positivists. A quick glance at the literature suggests that positivist commentators make maximum use of the liberalised sources doctrine, which results in increased uncertainty. And in sensitive, 'hard' cases, even the deformalised positivism does not seem flexible enough, and many positivists feel the need to seek refuge in *quasi*-law.

The two challenges raise different issues, and they need to be addressed at different levels. The latter – the rise of *quasi*-law – is fundamental, but can be remedied fairly easily. It is, strictly speaking, not a problem of positivism, but of (certain) positivists. It arises from the merger of roles: that of the law-interpreter and that of the individual assessing a legal rule against a different reference system (legitimacy, morality, etc.); and it might be addressed by separating the two roles. This should not be read as a plea against non-legal arguments. No doubt often these are determinative: for winning over public opinion, for securing parliamentary approval, for being able to sleep at night. Nobody disputes that uses of force need to be assessed and justified within a range of value systems; in fact, international law may at times even be a negligible component of the overall assessment. All we suggest is that the different roles be kept separate, and that the move from the *lex lata* to a different system of reference be made express. If nothing else, this may be a question of argumentative fairness: because it is by no means obvious that positivist scholars whose expertise relates to legal matters should be claiming an *expert* voice when the argument moves to a different level. In this case indeed, as put by Vaughan Lowe, sometimes 'it is much better to call upon a politician, or a priest, or a doctor, or a plumber'.[88]

The challenge of 'anything goes' calls for a different response. As noted above, it is a consequence of the high political stakes as well as two more

[87] Kammerhofer and d'Aspremont, n. 68 at 7–8. [88] Lowe, n. 54 at 290.

specific factors: the absence of authoritative mechanisms of norm clarification and the deformalisation of sources. Neither of these is easily remedied. As regards authoritative mechanisms, one can of course hope that influential agents of legal development – notably the General Assembly, perhaps the ICJ – will provide clarification about the scope of the *ius ad bellum* in the future and thus restrict the room for reasonable disagreement, yet that remains a hope more than anything else.

As regards doctrine, there have, no doubt, been various attempts to 'tidy up' the positivist approach to the sources of law, notably with regard to customary international law. As regards recent variations of this long-standing quest for order, scholars like Olivier Corten have argued for a more rigorous approach to the identification of relevant practice and emphasised the requirement of a widespread and general body practice of equal sovereigns.[89] This is probably unlikely to set off the 'pull of flexibility', and it does need to address the fact that some degree of differentiation between regular and specially affected states is built into the system.[90] Yet, the approach would seem to point in the right direction and might help to refocus the deformalised sources doctrine. Perhaps one may hold out some cautious hope that in the mid-term, more methodologically principled approaches will gain the upper hand in what remains a fairly heterogeneous body of scholarship. In the meantime, positivist scholars are probably best advised to approach legal issues relating to the use of force in the way described by Hans Kelsen in the 'Preface: On Interpretation' to his Charter Commentary:[91] by analysing and seeking to understand the law in force, and by setting out different plausible interpretations of the norms on the use of force, thus both exposing the inherent indeterminacy in language and the law and weighing the legal merits of plausible interpretations. Where positivists can make the difference is by demonstrating the relative merits of each plausible interpretation and rejecting the implausible ones. As is clear from the arguments presented above, notwithstanding the abundance of (positivist and other) scholarship on

89 E.g. Corten, n. 1; Olivier Corten, *Le discours du droit international: Pour un positivisme critique* (Pedone 2009).

90 See Section 3.1.

91 See the preface in Kelsen, *United Nations*, n. 13 at xiii–xvii. Compare the development of this argument with regard to application (rather than just interpretation) of the law by Vaughan Lowe, 'The Politics of Law-Making: Are the Method and Character of Norm Creation Changing?' in Michael Byers (ed.), *The Role of Law in International Politics: Essays in International Relations and International Law* (Oxford University Press 2000) 207–226 at 213–214.

the use of force, the spectrum of views presented in the literature remains immense. The present cacophony is unlikely to yield to unison any time soon. Admittedly, this is in large part due to the decentralised nature of the international legal system, which is painfully evident in the case of the *ius ad bellum.*

INDEX

For EU product safety concerns, contact us at Calle de José Abascal, 56–1°,
28003 Madrid, Spain or eugpsr@cambridge.org.

www.ingramcontent.com/pod-product-compliance
Lightning Source LLC
LaVergne TN
LVHW011533200926
848484LV00001B/252
* 9 7 8 1 1 0 7 0 1 9 2 6 3 *